Lecture Notes in Computer Science 3193

Commenced Publication in 1973
Founding and Former Series Editors:
Gerhard Goos, Juris Hartmanis, and Jan van Leeuwen

Pierangela Samarati   Peter Ryan
Dieter Gollmann   Refik Molva (Eds.)

Computer Security – ESORICS 2004

9th European Symposium on Research in Computer Security
Sophia Antipolis, France, September 13 - 15, 2004
Proceedings

 Springer

Volume Editors

Pierangela Samarati
Università degli Studi di Milano, Dipartimento di Tecnologie dell'Informazione
Via Bramante 65 - 26013 Crema, Italy
E-mail: samarati@dti.unimi.it

Peter Ryan
University of Newcastle upon Tyne, School of Computing Science
Newcastle upon Tyne, NE1 7RU, UK
E-mail: peter.ryan@ncl.ac.uk

Dieter Gollmann
Technische Universität Hamburg-Harburg
Harburger Schloßstraße 20, 21079 Hamburg, Germany
E-mail: diego@tu-harburg.de

Refik Molva
Institut Eurécom Corporate Communications Department
2229 Route des Crêtes, BP 193, 06904 Sophia Antipolis Cédex, France
E-mail: molva@eurecom.fr

Library of Congress Control Number: 2004111116

CR Subject Classification (1998): E.3, D.4.5, C.2.0, H.2.0, K.6.5, K.4.4

ISSN 0302-9743
ISBN 3-540-22987-6 Springer Berlin Heidelberg New York

Springer is a part of Springer Science+Business Media

springeronline.com

© Springer-Verlag Berlin Heidelberg 2004
Printed in Germany

Typesetting: Camera-ready by author, data conversion by Olgun Computergrafik
Printed on acid-free paper   SPIN: 11315414   06/3142   5 4 3 2 1 0

Preface

Foreword from the Program Chairs

These proceedings contain the papers selected for presentation at the 9th European Symposium on Research in Computer Security (ESORICS), held during September 13–15, 2004 in Sophia Antipolis, France.

In response to the call for papers 159 papers were submitted to the conference. These papers were evaluated on the basis of their significance, novelty, and technical quality. Each paper was reviewed by at least three members of the program committee. The program committee meeting was held electronically; there was an intensive discussion over a period of two weeks. Of the papers submitted, 27 were selected for presentation at the conference, giving an acceptance rate lower than 17%. The conference program also included an invited talk.

A workshop like this does not just happen; it depends on the volunteer efforts of a host of individuals. There is a long list of people who volunteered their time and energy to put together the workshop and who deserve special thanks. Thanks to all the members of the program committee, and the external reviewers, for all their hard work in the paper evaluation. Due to the large number of submissions the program committee members were really required to work hard in a short time frame, and we are very thankful to them for the commitment they showed with their active participation in the electronic discussion. We are also very grateful to all those people whose work ensured a smooth organization process: Refik Molva, who served as the General Chair, Marc Dacier, the Sponsoring Chair, Yves Roudier, who served as the Publicity Chair and maintained the Web pages, Sabrina de Capitani di Vimercati, who helped in the review process, Dieter Gollmann, who served as the Publication Chair and collated this volume, and Anne Duflos and Laurence Grammare for helping with the local arrangements.

Last, but certainly not least, our thanks go to all the authors who submitted papers and all the attendees. We hope you find the program stimulating.

Peter Ryan and Pierangela Samarati
(Program Co-chairs)

Foreword from the General Chair

Initially established as the European conference in research on computer security, ESORICS has reached the status of a main international event gathering researchers from all over the world. Taking place in a different European country every other year during its first seven occurrences, it has been a yearly conference since 2003.

ESORICS 2004 was organized by the Institut EURECOM and took place in Sophia Antipolis, France, September 13–15, 2004.

The organization of such an important event required a major effort and we wish to express our sincere appreciation to the organization committee members for their excellent work.

We would like to express our special appreciation to the Program Chairs Pierangela Samarati and Peter Ryan for coming up with a high-quality technical program that was the result of a complex evaluation process they handled very smoothly.

We are also indebted to the Institut EURECOM who not only allowed us and other organization committee members to dedicate considerable time and energy to the organization of this event, but also provided logistic and financial support to host it.

Sophia Antipolis, September 2004   Refik Molva

Program Committee

Vijay Atluri	Rutgers University, USA
Giampaolo Bella	Università di Catania, Italy
Joachim Biskup	Universität Dortmund, Germany
Jan Camenisch	IBM Research, Switzerland
Germano Caronni	Sun Microsystems Laboratories, USA
David Chadwick	University of Salford, UK
Ernesto Damiani	University of Milan, Italy
Sabrina De Capitani di Vimercati	University of Milan, Italy
Yves Deswarte	LAAS-CNRS, France
Alberto Escudero-Pascual	Royal Institute of Technology, Sweden
Csilla Farkas	University of South Carolina, USA
Simon Foley	University College Cork, Ireland
Dieter Gollmann	TU Hamburg-Harburg, Germany
Joshua D. Guttman	MITRE, USA
Sushil Jajodia	George Mason University, USA
Sokratis K. Katsikas	University of the Aegean, Greece
Maciej Koutny	University of Newcastle upon Tyne, UK
Peng Liu	Pennsylvania State University, USA
Javier Lopez	University of Malaga, Spain
Roy Maxion	Carnegie Mellon University, USA
Patrick McDaniel	AT&T Labs-Research, USA
John McHugh	CERT/CC, USA
Catherine A. Meadows	Naval Research Lab, USA
Refik Molva	Institut Eurécom, France
Peng Ning	NC State University, USA
LouAnna Notargiacomo	The MITRE Corporation, USA
Eiji Okamoto	University of Tsukuba, Japan
Stefano Paraboschi	University of Bergamo, Italy
Andreas Pfitzmann	TU Dresden, Germany
Bart Preneel	Katholieke Universiteit Leuven, Belgium
Jean-Jacques Quisquater	Microelectronic Laboratory, Belgium
Peter Ryan (co-chair)	University of Newcastle, UK
Pierangela Samarati (co-chair)	University of Milan, I
Steve Schneider	University of London, UK
Christoph Schuba	Sun Microsystems Inc., USA
Michael Steiner	IBM T.J. Watson Research Lab., USA
Paul Syverson	Naval Research Laboratory, USA
Kymie M. C. Tan	Carnegie Mellon University, USA
Dan Thomsen	Tresys Technology, USA
Moti Yung	Columbia University, USA

Additional Reviewers

Carlos Aguilar, Farid Ahmed, Ben Aziz, Walid Bagga, Endre Bangerter, Lejla Batina, Alex Biryukov, Rainer Böhme, R. Bouroulet, Laurent Bussard, David Byers, Alex Bystrov, Shiping Chen, Ioan Chisalita, Mathieu Ciet, Sebastian Clauß, Stefano Crosta, Roberto Delicata, Alex Dent, Thomas Dübendorfer, Claudiu Duma, Neil Evans, Ulrich Flegel, Elke Franz, Qijun Gu, James Heather, Almut Herzog, Manuel Hilty, John Iliadis, Ryszard Janicki, Mohamed Kaâniche, Ioanna Kantzavelou, Kevin Killourhy, Herbert Klimant, Stefan Köpsell, Spyros Kokolakis, Thomas Kriegelstein, Klaus Kursawe, Costas Lambrinoudakis, Thomas Leineweber, Benoît Libert, Donggang Liu, Pietro Michiardi, Jose A. Montenegro, Fabrice Mourlin, Vincent Nicomette, Melek Onen, Sassa Otenko, Giuseppe Pappalardo, Jörg Parthe, E. Pelz, Olivier Pereira, Thomas Quillinan, Josyula R. Rao, Douglas S. Reeves, Marc Rennhard, Pankaj Rohatgi, Rodrigo Roman, Yves Roudier, Dagmar Schönfeld, Diana Senn, Stefaan Seys, Barbara Sprick, Sandra Steinbrecher, Reto Strobl, Linying Su, Kun Sun, Eduard Turcan, Torben Weibert, Duminda Wijesekera, Sandra Wortmann, Dingbang Xu, Jun Xu, Meng Yu, Wanyu Zang, Christophe Zanon, Homgbin Zhou

Organisation Committee

Refik Molva (General Chair), Yves Roudier (Publicity Chair), Marc Dacier (Sponsoring Chair), Dieter Gollmann (Publication Chair), Anne Duflos (Conference Secretary), and Laurence Grammare (Communications)

ESORICS 2004 was supported by SAP, @sec, and Conseil Régional Provence Alpes Côte d'Azur.

Steering Committee

Elisa Bertino (University of Milan, I), Joachim Biskup (Universität Dortmund, D), Frédéric Cuppens (ENST-Bretagne, F), Marc Dacier (Eurecom, F), Yves Deswarte (LAAS-CNRS, F), Gérard Eizenberg (ONERA, F), Simon Foley (University College Cork, IE), Dieter Gollmann (TU Hamburg-Harburg, D), Franz-Peter Heider (debis IT Security Services, D), Jeremy Jacob (University of York, UK), Sokratis Katsikas (University of the Aegean, GR), Helmut Kurth (atsec, D), Peter Landrock (Cryptomathic, UK), Jean-Jacques Quisquater (UCL, B), Peter Ryan (University of Newcastle, UK: Steering Committee Chair), Pierangela Samarati (University of Milan, I: Steering Committee Vice-Chair), Einar Snekkenes (Gjøvik University College, N), Michael Waidner (IBM Research, CH).

Table of Contents

Incorporating Dynamic Constraints
in the Flexible Authorization Framework

Shiping Chen, Duminda Wijesekera, and Sushil Jajodia

Center for Secure Information Systems, George Mason University,
Fairfax, VA 22030-4444, USA
{schen3,dwijesek,jajodia}@gmu.edu

Abstract. Constraints are an integral part of access control policies. Depending upon their time of enforcement, they are categorized as static
or dynamic; static constraints are enforced during the policy compilation
time, and the dynamic constraints are enforced during run time. While
there are several logic-based access control policy frameworks, they have
a limited power in expressing and enforcing constraints (especially the
dynamic constraints). We propose dynFAF, a constraint logic programming based approach for expressing and enforcing constraints. To make
it more concrete, we present our approach as an extension to the *flexible authorization framework (FAF)* of Jajodia et al. [17]. We show that
dynFAF satisfies standard safety and liveliness properties of a safety
conscious software system.

1   Introduction

Constraints are a powerful mechanism for specifying high-level organizational
policies [21]. Accordingly, most access control policies contain constraints, usually categorized as static or dynamic, referring to their time of enforcement by
the access controller. As examples, consider the following two constraints: *an
undergraduate student should not be permitted to grade qualifying examinations
at the PhD level*, and *an author should not be allowed to review his/her own
manuscript*. The first constraint can be enforced by prohibiting *grading* permissions on PhD examinations for every undergraduate student, thereby making
it statically enforceable. The second constraint requires an access controller to
evaluate if the requesting subject is also an author of the document to be reviewed when the request is made. This constraint cannot be evaluated prior to
the request, making the constraint dynamically, but not statically, enforceable.
Enforcing the latter kind of constraints over access permissions expressed as
Horn clauses is the subject matter of this paper.

The past decade has seen several logic based *flexible* access control policy
specification frameworks. Woo and Lam [25] propose the use of *default logic* for
representing access control policies. To overcome the problems of undecidability
and non-implementability that arise in Woo and Lam's approach, Jajodia et
al. [17] propose an access control policy specification framework (FAF) based
on a restricted class of logic programs, viz., those that are *locally stratifiable*.

P. Samarati et al. (Eds.): ESORICS 2004, LNCS 3193, pp. 1–16, 2004.

Bertino et al.'s framework [6] uses *C-Datalog* to express various access control policies [6]. Barker and Stuckey use *constraint logic programming* for multi-policy specification and implementation [4].

Although they are powerful in expressing access control policies, these frameworks have a limited power in specifying and enforcing constraints. For instance, Jajodia et al. [17] use an integrity rule (a logic rule with an error() head) to specify constraints. Barker and Stuckey [4] define some special consistency checking rules (with head of predicates *inconsistent_ssd, inconsistent_dsd*) to encode the separation of duty constraints. However, the enforcement of the constraints is left outside the framework; as a result, dynamic constraints cannot be enforced in the access control engine properly.

To overcome these drawbacks, we propose a constraint logic programming based approach to express and enforce dynamic constraints. To make it more concrete, we present our approach as an extension to *Flexible Authorization Framework (FAF)* proposed by Jajodia et al. [17]. Our approach is applicable to other logic based access control frameworks because our constraint specification and enforcement modules are built on top of the existing framework modules. The proposed extension, called *dynFAF*, has two extra modules. First module, the *integrity constraint specification and derivation module (ISM)*, is responsible for specifying the atomic conflicts and deriving all possible complex conflicts in the system that represent the constraints. The second module, the *dynamic access grant module (DAM)*, is responsible for enforcing the constraints specified by ISM dynamically. In addition, DAM allows subjects to *relinquish* permissions that were granted to them. In our design, FAF composes the *static* component, and ISM and DAM compose the *dynamic* component of dynFAF.

We show that dynFAF satisfies safety and liveliness properties granting any access that does not violate derivable constraint, and denying those that do. Because FAF policies are stratified logic programs, they have a stable model semantics [14]. Our constraint specification policies taken together with FAF policies also have a local stratification, thereby admitting a stable model that extends the former. In addition, proposed dynamic access grant module enriches the syntax of the former by having yet another layer of constrained logic programs, that taken as a whole extends the former local stratification. Therefore, a dynFAF specification admits a well-founded model in which some predicate may result in an *undefined* truth in addition to the usual *true* or *false* values; however, our design ensures that any access requested of dynFAF returns only *true* or *false*.

The remainder of the paper is structured as follows. Section 2 contains a brief overview of FAF, followed by a description of its limitations. Section 3 presents the architecture of dynFAF, including the descriptions of ISM and DAM modules. Section 4 presents the semantics of dynFAF syntax. Section 5 shows that dynFAF satisfies the traditional safety and liveliness properties, and that the semantics of the granting and relinquishing access rights are enforced properly. Section 6 compares our work to those of others. Section 7 concludes the paper.

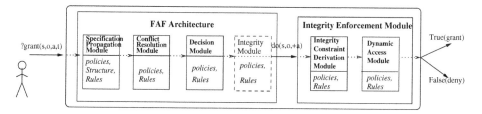

Fig. 1. dynFAF Architecture

2 Overview of FAF

FAF [17] is a logic-based framework to specify authorizations in the form of rules, based on four stages (each stage corresponds to a module) that are applied in a sequence, as shown in FAF Architecture part of Figure 1. In the first stage of the sequence, some basic facts such as authorization subject and object hierarchies (for example directory structures) and a set of authorizations along with rules to derive additional authorizations are given. The intent of this stage is to specify basic authorizations and use structural properties to derive new authorizations. Hence, they are called *specification and propagation policies*. Although propagation policies are flexible and expressive, they may result in *over-specification* resulting in conflicting authorizations. FAF uses *conflict resolution policies* to weed out these in the second stage. At the third stage, *decision policies* are applied in order to ensure the completeness of authorizations. The last stage consists of checking for integrity constraints, where all authorizations that violate integrity constraints will be denied. In addition, FAF ensures that every access request is either granted or rejected, thereby providing a built-in completeness property.

FAF syntax consists of terms that are built from constants and variables (no function symbols) and they belong to four sorts, viz., subjects, objects, actions, and roles. We use the capital letters with subscripts such as X_s, Y_o, X_a, and X_r to denote the respective variables belonging to them, and lower case letters such as s, a, o, and r for constants. FAF has the following predicates:

1. A ternary predicate cando(s, o, a), representing grantable or deniable requests (depending on the sign associated with the action) where s, o, and a are subject, object, and signed action terms, respectively.
2. A ternary predicate dercando(s, o, a), with the same arguments as cando. The predicate dercando represents authorizations derived by the system using inference rules modus ponens plus rule of stratified negation [2].
3. A ternary predicate do, with the same arguments as cando, representing the access control decisions made by FAF.
4. A 4-ary predicate done(s, o, a, t), meaning subject s has executed action a on object o at time t, t is a natural number.
5. Two binary predicate symbols over$_{AS}$ and over$_{AO}$, each taking two subject and object terms as arguments two object terms respectively.

6. A predicate symbol without argument, `error`, symbolizing violation of an integrity constraint, where a rule with an `error` head must not have a satisfiable body.
7. Other terms and predicates necessary to model specific applications. For example, constants AOH, ASH denote object and subject hierarchies with in, where in(x,y,H) denotes that x $\leq$ y in hierarchy H. For example, we denote the fact that usr\local is below usr in the object hierarchy AOH by in(usr\local, usr, AOH).

Because any FAF specification is a locally stratified logic program, it has a unique stable model [14], and a well-founded model (as in Gelfond and Lifshitz). In addition, the well-founded model coincides with the unique stable model [3, 17]. Furthermore, the unique stable model can be computed in quadratic time data complexity [24]. See [17] for details.

2.1   Limitations of FAF

In its current design, FAF has these limitations. First, FAF expresses constraints using integrity rules of the kind `error()` $\leftarrow L_i, \ldots, L_n$ where `error`   is an argument-less predicate that should not be valid in any model and $L_i, \ldots, L_n$ are other literals. Ensuring that granted permissions do not imply `error` is enforced outside of the logical machinery of FAF. Accordingly, it is not within the logical inference engine of FAF to avoid constraint violations. To elaborate further, FAF evaluates an access request as a query ?do(s, o, a), and ensures the completeness and consistency of the specification, consisting of the rules from the first three modules, by ensuring that one and only one of do$(s, o, +a)$ or do$(s, o, -a)$ evaluates to *true*. However, it is possible that both $(s, o, +a)$ and $(s, o, -a)$ could be rejected by the integrity enforcement module making the eventual outcomes incomplete, as the inference rules are unaware of rejections by the integrity enforcement module. Thus, the integrity enforcement needs to be brought inside the reasoning engine, as done in dynFAF.

Second, FAF does not allow constraint derivation, although this occurs in practice. For example, role based access control (RBAC) models have conflicting roles (say, r_1 and r_2) where a single subject assuming them simultaneously violate the policy. In addition, an application may want to declare junior roles of conflicting roles to be conflicting. That is, if roles r_3, r_4 are junior to roles r_1 and r_2, respectively, by satisfying the constrains $r_3 \leq r_1$ and $r_4 \leq r_2$, then no subject should be allowed to assume r_3 and r_4 simultaneously. Our extension facilitates constraint derivation.

Third, in FAF each access request is either granted or denied on its own merit. But some applications may want *controlled (don't care) nondeterminism.* For example, a subject is allowed to assume role r_1 or role r_2, but not both, with no preference for either. If we are to accept a unique stable model, then either r_1 or r_2, but not both can be assumed by the subject. dynFAF facilitates controlled nondeterminism in granting permissions.

Finally, and importantly, FAF does not consider an evolving access control system. That is, if $do(o, s, +a)$ is in the stable model of an authorization specification, the access request (o, s, a) is always permitted. In practice, an authorization may be relinquished by the user or the administrator some time after it is authorized (e.g., in workflow management systems). Consequently, some authorization that is not allowed at a point of time because of constraints restriction may be allowed later if the conflicting authorizations are relinquished. Notice that inserting a negative authorization $cando(o, s, -a)$ does not model this situation. The soon to be described *dynamic access grant module* of dynFAF provides this functionality.

3   dynFAF: A Constraint Logic Programming Based Extension to FAF

To address the problems described in the previous section, FAF is enhanced by adding an *integrity constraint specification and derivation module* (ISM) and a *dynamic access grant module* (DAM), grants accesses that avoid those conflicts. FAF enhanced with these two modules are referred to as *dynFAF*, shown in Figure 1. An access request for (s, o, a) is modeled in dynFAF as a predicate instance $request(s, o, \pm a, t)$, where $(s, o, +a, t)$ is a request to obtain permission for (s, o, a) at time t (equals to a query ?grant(s,o,a,t)) and $(s, o, -a, t)$ is a request to relinquish already existing permission for (s, o, a) at time t (equals to a query ?relinquish(s,o,a,t)). dynFAF ensures that any request for permission is statically granted by FAF, and granting it does not violate any constraints specified by ISM.

3.1   Integrity Constraint Specification and Derivation Module (ISM)

ISM uses two predicates:

- A binary predicate symbol, conflict, where conflict(x,y) is an atomic conflict where x and y can be either (subject,object,action) triples or object, action, or subject terms.
- A binary predicate symbol derConflict. derConflict has the same arguments as conflict. derConflict(x,y) is true iff x,y constitute a derivable conflict.

We use Horn clause rules to specify atomic conflicts and derivable conflicts based on already defined atomic conflicts. The corresponding rules are called *conflict rules* and *conflict derivation rules*, respectively. Each conflict rule has a conflict predicate as its head and some cando, dercando, done or rel-literals as its body.

Example 1 (Conflict Rules)

$$\texttt{conflict}(r_1, r_2) \leftarrow \tag{1}$$

$$\texttt{conflict}(org_A, org_B) \leftarrow \tag{2}$$

$$\texttt{conflict}((o, a), (o', a')) \leftarrow \texttt{isPerm}(o, a), \texttt{isPerm}(o', a'). \tag{3}$$

$$\texttt{conflict}((X_s, X_o, X_a), (X'_s, X_o, X_a)) \leftarrow (X_s \neq X'_s), \texttt{in}(X_s, G, \mathsf{ASH}),$$
$$\texttt{in}(X'_s, G, \mathsf{ASH}). \tag{4}$$

Rule 1 says that r_1 and r_2 are conflicting roles. Rule 2 says that org_A and org_B are conflicting organizations. Rule 3 says that (o, a) and (o', a') are conflicting permissions. Here the predicate isPerm(x,y) is true if x is an object and y is an action. Rule 4 says that any two users in group G trying to execute the same operation on the same object is a conflict (i.e., only one subject can have the permission at any one time such as a semaphore).

Each conflict derivation rule has a `derConflict` predicate as its head and some `conflict`, `derConflict`, `cando`, `dercando`, `done`, or `rel`-literals as its body. As it is used recursively, all appearances of `derConflict` literals in the body of conflict derivation rules must be positive. Example 2 shows some conflict derivation rules.

Example 2 (Conflict Derivation Rules)

$$\texttt{derConflict}(X, Y) \leftarrow \texttt{conflict}(X, Y). \tag{5}$$

$$\texttt{derConflict}(X_r, Y_r) \leftarrow \texttt{derConflict}(X_{r'}, Y_{r'}),$$
$$\texttt{in}(Y_r, Y_{r'}, ASH), \texttt{in}(X_r, X_{r'}, ASH). \tag{6}$$

$$\texttt{derConflict}((X_s, X_o, X_a), (X_s, X'_o, X'_a)) \leftarrow$$
$$\texttt{conflict}((X_o, X_a), (X'_o, X'_a)). \tag{7}$$

$$\texttt{derConflict}(X_o, Y_o) \leftarrow \texttt{derConflict}(org_A, org_B),$$
$$\texttt{in}(Y_o, org_B), \texttt{in}(X_o, org_A). \tag{8}$$

$$\texttt{derConflict}((X_s, X_o, read), (X_s, X'_o, read)) \leftarrow \texttt{derConflict}(X_o, X'_o). \tag{9}$$

$$\texttt{derConflict}((X_s, X_r, \texttt{activate}), (X_s, Y_r, \texttt{activate})) \leftarrow \texttt{conflict}(X_r, Y_r). \tag{10}$$

Rule 5 says that every conflict is a derivable conflict. Rule 6 says roles junior to conflicting roles are also conflicting. Rule 7 says that obtaining conflicting permissions leads to a conflict. Rule 8 and rule 9 say that any pair of objects that belong to two conflicting organizations are conflicting objects, and each subject can read only one of them. Rule 10 says activating conflicting roles leads to conflicts.

Note that the conflicts specified in FAF and ISM are different. The former, refers to static compile time conflict, arises out of over specification of permissions, and the latter arises due to application specified conflicts that have to be resolved dynamically by the run time constraint enforcement module DAM. We have chosen to represent only binary conflicts as integrity constraints, inspired by the work such as [16, 5, 20, 15, 19, 20], where most constraints are binary conflicts.

3.2 The Dynamic Access Grant Module (DAM)

As stated earlier, the dynamic access grant module first checks if a requested permission $(s, o, +a, t)$ is permissible under static FAF policies (by checking if $\mathsf{do}(s, o, +a)$ is true). If so, then it will further check if granting (s, o, a) at time t would violate any integrity constraints specified in ISM. If the answer is negative, the requested granted and denied otherwise. DAM is based on some assumptions and design choices outlined below.

First, DAM allows requesters to relinquish already granted access rights. Suppose dynFAF granted access request (s, o, a), and after some time the requester s is willing to relinquish the access right (s, o, a). This kind of actions is widely seen in practical systems. (e.g., in workflow management systems) dynFAF allows this kind of actions by modeling it as a query of $?\mathsf{relinquish}(s, o, a, t)$ with an insertion of $\mathsf{request}(s, o, -a, t)$ into the authorization specification program. Similarly, $\mathsf{relinquish}(s, o, a, t)$ has no effect on $\mathsf{do}(s, o, \pm a)$ and, therefore, does not alter the unique stable model of the static FAF policy (sans the error rules).

Second, we assume that access requests are considered in sequence, *one at a time*, at *discrete time intervals*, referred to as the *synchrony* hypothesis, under which dynFAF accepts only two kinds of requests: to obtain a new permission or to relinquish a permission obtained earlier. They are modelled as inserting instances of $\mathsf{request}(s, o, +a, t)$ and $\mathsf{request}(s, o, -a, t)$ into the logic program, respectively. dynFAF's answer to requests are computed as an evaluation of $\mathsf{grant}(s, o, a, t)$ or $\mathsf{relinquish}(s, o, a, t)$, depending upon the chosen sign $\pm$ for the action a in $\mathsf{request}(s, o, \pm a, t)$.

Third, we assume that neither $\mathsf{grant}(s, o, a, t)$ nor $\mathsf{relinquish}(s, o, a, t)$ implies or is implied by $\mathsf{done}(s, o, a, t)$ for some time term t. We only assume that whenever an (o, a) is executed by s at a time t, $\mathsf{done}(s, o, a, t)$ will be inserted into FAF, satisfying the following conditions: 1) there is a time t' exists such that $\mathsf{grant}(s, o, a, t')$ and $t' < t$ hold, 2) there is no t'' exists such that $t'' \in (t', t)$ and $\mathsf{relinquish}(s, o, a, t'')$ hold. We call this the *system integrity hypothesis*.

3.3 DAM Syntax

The dynamic access grant module uses five 4-ary predicates grant, $\mathsf{relinquish}$, $\mathsf{validity}$, holds, and $\mathsf{request}$ with arguments subject, object, action and time terms, and a 3-ary predicate $\mathsf{conflictingHold}$. The time parameter t here has no relation with the clock time, but serves as a counter of the sequence of requests made to the dynFAF since its inception.

1. $\mathsf{grant}(s, o, a, t)$ means that access (s, o, a) is granted at time t.
2. $\mathsf{relinquish}(s, o, a, t)$ means that access (s, o, a) is relinquished at time t.
3. $\mathsf{validity}(s, o, +a, t)$ means that granting permission (s, o, a) at t does not violate any constraints, while $\mathsf{validity}(s, o, -a, t)$ means that granting permission (s, o, a) at time t does violate some constraints.
4. $\mathsf{holds}(s, o, a, t)$ means that s holds a access to o at time t.

5. $\texttt{request}(s, o, +a, t)$ means that at time t subject s requests permission (o, a), while $\texttt{request}(s, o, -a, t)$ means that at time t subject s requests to relinquish permission (o, a). Whenever a request (grant or relinquish) is made, the corresponding predicate is inserted into dynFAF as fact.

6. $\texttt{conflictingHold}((s, o, a), (s', o', a'), t)$ means the authorization (s', o', a') is conflicting with (s, o, a) and is holding at time t.

We now specify the rules of DAM that recursively define predicates $\texttt{grant}$, $\texttt{relinquish}$, $\texttt{holds}$, $\texttt{conflictingHold}$, and $\texttt{validity}$ as follows:

$$\texttt{grant}(x_s, x_o, x_a, 0) \leftarrow \texttt{request}(x_s, x_o, +x_a, 0), \texttt{do}(x_s, x_o, +x_a). \tag{11}$$

$$\texttt{grant}(x_s, x_o, x_a, x_t + 1) \leftarrow \texttt{validity}(x_s, x_o, +x_a, x_t), \neg\texttt{holds}(x_s, x_o, x_a, x_t),$$
$$\texttt{request}(x_s, x_o, +x_a, x_t + 1). \tag{12}$$

$$\texttt{relinquish}(x_s, x_o, x_a, x_t + 1) \leftarrow \texttt{holds}(x_s, x_o, x_a, x_t),$$
$$\texttt{request}(x_s, x_o, -x_a, x_t + 1). \tag{13}$$

Rule 11 says that the first permission that is granted by the dynamic access grant module must be statically permissible and requested. Rule 12 says that any permission that is not already being held, requested and valid (i.e. would not violate any constraints) at time x_t can be granted at time $x_t + 1$. The next set of rules recursively update the $\texttt{holds}$ predicate that capture permissions already being held by a subject.

$$\texttt{holds}(x_s, x_o, x_a, x_t) \leftarrow \texttt{grant}(x_s, x_o, x_a, x_t). \tag{14}$$

$$\texttt{holds}(x_s, x_o, x_a, x_t + 1) \leftarrow \texttt{holds}(x_s, x_o, x_a, x_t), \neg\texttt{relinquish}(x_s, x_o, x_a, x_t + 1). \tag{15}$$

Rule 14 says that a permission $(x_o, +x_a)$ granted to x_s at time x_t is held by x_s at time x_t. Rule 15 says that any action other than relinquishing the same permission by itself does not change the holding state of a subject. The following rule defines the predicate $\texttt{conflictingHold}$.

$$\texttt{conflictingHold}((x_s, x_o, x_a), (x'_s, x'_o, x'_a), x_t)$$
$$\leftarrow \texttt{derConflict}((x_s, x_o, x_a), (x'_s, x'_o, x'_a)), \texttt{holds}(x'_s, x'_o, x'_a, x_t). \tag{16}$$

The rest of the rules recursively define $\texttt{validity}$ that computes if granting a permission to a subject will conflict with the outstanding ones at time x_t.

$$\texttt{validity}(x_s, x_o, +x_a, 0) \leftarrow \neg\texttt{derConflict}((x'_s, x'_o, x'_a), (x_s, x_o, x_a)),$$
$$\texttt{do}(x_s, x_o, +x_a), . \tag{17}$$

$$\texttt{validity}(x_s, x_o, +x_a, x_t) \leftarrow \texttt{grant}(x_s, x_o, x_a, x_t). \tag{18}$$

$$\texttt{validity}(x_s, x_o, +x_a, x_t) \leftarrow \texttt{relinquish}(x_s, x_o, x_a, x_t). \tag{19}$$

$$\texttt{validity}(x_s, x_o, \pm x_a, x_t + 1) \leftarrow \texttt{grant}(x'_s, x'_o, x'_a, x_t + 1), \texttt{validity}(x_s, x_o, \pm x_a, x_t),$$
$$\neg\texttt{derConflict}((x_s, x_o, x_a), (x'_s, x'_o, x'_a)),$$
$$(x_s, x_o, x_a) \neq (x'_s, x'_o, x'_a). \tag{20}$$

$$\texttt{validity}(x_s, x_o, -x_a, x_t + 1) \leftarrow \texttt{grant}(x'_s, x'_o, x'_a, x_t + 1), (x_s, x_o, x_a) \neq (x'_s, x'_o, x'_a),$$
$$\texttt{derConflict}((x_s, x_o, x_a), (x'_s, x'_o, x'_a)). \tag{21}$$

$$\text{validity}(x_s, x_o, \pm x_a, x_t + 1) \leftarrow \text{relinquish}(x'_s, x'_o, x'_a, x_t + 1),$$
$$\text{validity}(x_s, x_o, \pm x_a, x_t),$$
$$\neg \text{derConflict}((x_s, x_o, x_a), (x'_s, x'_o, x'_a)),$$
$$(x_s, x_o, x_a) \neq (x'_s, x'_o, x'_a). \tag{22}$$

$$\text{validity}(x_s, x_o, -x_a, x_t + 1) \leftarrow \text{validity}(x_s, x_o, -x_a, x_t),$$
$$\text{relinquish}(x'_s, x'_o, x'_a, x_t + 1),$$
$$\text{derConflict}((x_s, x_o, x_a), (x'_s, x'_o, x'_a)),$$
$$(x_s, x_o, x_a) \neq (x'_s, x'_o, x'_a), \text{holds}(x''_s, x''_o, x''_a, x_t),$$
$$(x_s, x_o, x_a) \neq (x''_s, x''_o, x''_a), (x'_s, x'_o, x'_a) \neq (x''_s, x''_o, x''_a),$$
$$\text{derConflict}((x_s, x_o, x_a), (x''_s, x''_o, x''_a)). \tag{23}$$

$$\text{validity}(x_s, x_o, +x_a, x_t + 1) \leftarrow \text{relinquish}(x'_s, x'_o, x'_a, x_t + 1),$$
$$\text{validity}(x_s, x_o, -x_a, x_t), (x_s, x_o, x_a) \neq (x''_s, x''_o, x''_a),$$
$$\text{derConflict}((x_s, x_o, x_a), (x'_s, x'_o, x'_a)),$$
$$(x_s, x_o, x_a) \neq (x'_s, x'_o, x'_a), (x'_s, x'_o, x'_a) \neq (x''_s, x''_o, x''_a),$$
$$\neg \text{derConflict}((x_s, x_o, x_a), (x''_s, x''_o, x''_a)). \tag{24}$$

$$\text{validity}(x_s, x_o, +x_a, x_t + 1) \leftarrow \text{relinquish}(x'_s, x'_o, x'_a, x_t + 1),$$
$$\text{validity}(x_s, x_o, -x_a, x_t), (x_s, x_o, x_a) \neq (x'_s, x'_o, x'_a),$$
$$\text{derConflict}((x_s, x_o, x_a), (x'_s, x'_o, x'_a)),$$
$$(x_s, x_o, x_a) \neq (x''_s, x''_o, x''_a), (x'_s, x'_o, x'_a) \neq (x''_s, x''_o, x''_a),$$
$$\neg \text{conflictingHold}((x_s, x_o, x_a), (x''_s, x''_o, x''_a), x_t). \tag{25}$$

$$\text{validity}(x_s, x_o, -x_a, x_t) \leftarrow \neg \text{validity}(x_s, x_o, +x_a, x_t). \tag{26}$$

Rule 17 is the base step of the recursion saying that every permission that is allowed by the static component FAF and there is no conflicting permissions existing is valid when the dynamic grant module begins. The next two rules 18 and 19 state that an authorization (s, o, a) is valid at time t if it is granted or relinquished at time t. Rules 20 and 21 consider how some other (subject,object,action) pair being granted affects the validity of a permission. Rule 20 leaves the validity if a non-conflicting permission was granted at time x_t. Rule 21 invalidates it if another conflicting permission was granted at x_t.

The next four rules address what happens to the state of validity of a permission if some other permissions were relinquished. Rule 22 says that if the relinquished permission is not conflicting with the considered one, then the validity remains the same. Rule 23 says that if there are other conflicting authorizations held in the system, then the validity states of the considered one remains invalid. Rule 24 says that if the relinquished permission is the only conflicting permission with the considered one in the system, the validity state of the considered one will be changed to valid. Rule 25 says that although there are still other conflicting permissions with the considered one, if they are all not holding, then the validity state of the considered one will be valid. The last rule, rule 26 says that $\text{validity}(x_s, x_o, -x_a, x_t)$ succeeds, when $\text{validity}(x_s, x_o, +x_a, x_t)$ fails. This rule is necessary because of the following reason. In rules 20, 22, 23 and 24, $\text{validity}(x_s, x_o, \pm x_a, x_t + 1)$ depends upon $\text{validity}(x_s, x_o, \pm x_a, x_t)$.

Thus, in order for the inductive computation of other steps to proceed from x_t to $x_t + 1$ it is necessary to have $\texttt{validity}(x_s, x_o, -x_a, x_t)$ which is not given by rule 21. Therefore, the rule 26 allows us to infer $\texttt{validity}(x_s, x_o, -x_a, x_t)$ from the failure of $\texttt{validity}(x_s, x_o, +x_a, x_t)$.

In section 5 we show that in view of the synchrony hypothesis, $\texttt{grant}$, $\texttt{relinquish}$, $\texttt{validity}$ and $\texttt{holds}$ are correctly specified. That is $\texttt{grant}$ and $\texttt{relinquish}$ satisfy both safety and liveliness properties and have the required anti-idempotency properties. In other words, no subject can relinquish permissions that it does not hold and a subject cannot obtain permissions that it already holds.

Example 3 (Interacting with DAM) *Consider the separation of duty example which states that two processes p_1 and p_2 may not get write locks on a file "foo" at the same time, but otherwise both processes have static permissions to write to "foo". These requirements are captured by dynFAF as follows.*

$$\texttt{do}(p_1, \text{``}foo\text{''}, +write) \leftarrow . \tag{27}$$

$$\texttt{do}(p_2, \text{``}foo\text{''}, +write) \leftarrow . \tag{28}$$

$$\texttt{derConflict}((p_1, \text{``}foo\text{''}, write), (p_2, \text{``}foo\text{''}, write)) \leftarrow . \tag{29}$$

Rules 27 and 28 state static write permissions to "foo" is given to p_1 and p_2 respectively. Rule 29 says that, although p_1 and p_2 have static write permissions, they may not use them simultaneously.

Now consider a request to obtain write permission to "foo" by p_1 at time 0. That means, $\texttt{request}(p_1, \text{``}foo\text{''}, +write, 0)$ now becomes a part of the DAM rules. Therefore, $\texttt{grant}(p_1, \text{``}foo\text{''}, write, 0)$ now is evaluated to be true as, by rule 11, $\texttt{grant}(p_1, \text{``}foo\text{''}, write, 0)$ holds if $\texttt{request}(p_1, \text{``}foo\text{''}, +write, 0)$ and $\texttt{do}(p_1, \text{``}foo\text{''}, +write)$ are valid. As a result, p_1 is granted write permission on "foo".

Now consider a request to write "foo" issued by p_2 at time 1. This request is modeled by entering $\texttt{request}(p_2, \text{``}foo\text{''}, +write, 1)$ into dynFAF's rule set. Because $\texttt{derConflict}((p_1, \text{``}foo\text{''}, write), (p_2, \text{``}foo\text{''}, write))$ holds, by rule 17 we can not get $\texttt{validity}(p_2, \text{``}foo\text{''}, +write, 0)$. Therefore $\texttt{grant}(p_2, \text{``}foo\text{''}, write, 1)$ cannot become valid as the only applicable rule 12 results in finite failure. Similarly, $\texttt{grant}(p_1, \text{``}foo\text{''}, write, 1)$ also fails in the alternate addition of $\texttt{request}(p_1, \text{``}foo\text{''}, +write, 1)$ instead of $\texttt{request}(p_2, \text{``}foo\text{''}, +write, 1)$ because $\texttt{holds}(p_1, \text{``}foo\text{''}, write, 1)$ is valid by rule 14 and 15.

Now suppose that p_1 wishes to relinquish its "write" permission to "foo" at time 2. This is done by entering $\texttt{request}(p_1, \text{``}foo\text{''}, -write, 2)$ into dynFAF's rule set. Then by rule 13, $\texttt{relinquish}(p_1, \text{``}foo\text{''}, write, 2)$ evaluates to true because of $\texttt{holds}(p_1, \text{``}foo\text{''}, write, 1)$ and $\texttt{request}(p_1, \text{``}foo\text{''}, -write, 2)$. Now suppose p_2 requests write permission to "foo" again by inserting $\texttt{request}(p_1, \text{``}foo\text{''}, write, 3)$. At this time $\texttt{grant}(p_2, \text{``}foo\text{''}, write, 3)$ succeeds by rule 12 as $\texttt{validity}(p_2, \text{``}foo\text{''}, +write, 2)$ holds by rule 24. As a result, $\texttt{request}(p_2, \text{``}foo\text{''}, write)$ is granted at time 3.

4   Semantics of dynFAF

This section describes models of dynFAF syntax. All lemmas and theorems in this section are given without proof. We refer the reader to [9] for the formal proofs. We consider a dynFAF specification to consist of FAF rules (without the `error` predicates), conflict rules, conflict derivation rules, a collection of appropriately constructed (soon to be described) `request` predicates, and rules from 11 to 26. As argued in [17], FAF policies are locally stratified logic programs. We now show that dynFAF specifications form locally stratified logic programs.

Lemma 1 (Local stratification and stable models of dynFAF).
Any dynFAF specification constitutes a local stratification on its Herbrand base. Consequently, dynFAF rules restricted to FAF and ISM have a unique stable model that coincides with its well-founded model.

At any time n, a dynFAF specification consists of the following four kinds of rules: FAF rules, ISM rules, a set of n instances of `request` predicates $\{$`request`$(\_,\_,\_,i) : i \leq n\}$, and DAM rules consisting of rules 11 through 26, that we refer to as F, C, Tr_n, D, respectively. Lemma 1 says that $F \cup C$ has a unique stable model, denoted by $\mathcal{M}(F \cup C)$. Now we build a model, notated as $\mathcal{M}(F \cup C \cup Tr_n \cup D)$, for $F \cup C \cup Tr_n \cup D$ for each n and another model $\mathcal{M}(F \cup C \cup (\cup_{i \in \omega} Tr_i) \cup D)$ for $F \cup C \cup (\cup_{i \in \omega} Tr_i) \cup D$ as three-valued Kripke-Kleene (also known as Fitting-Kunen)models [18, 11] over $\mathcal{M}(F \cup C)$. We show that every `grant` or `relinquish` query instance over either of these models evaluate to either true or false, and therefore the three-valued model takes only two truth values. In doing so, we have to choose a constraint domain and interpretation for negation. We choose the finite integer domain, $CLP(\mathcal{R})$, as our constraint domain and interpret negation as *constructive* negation [7, 8] as have been used for negation by Fages [13, 10]. The latter choice is due to the almost universally accepted stance on using constructive negation instead of its classical counterpart or negation as failure [22, 23, 13, 10]. The former choice is due to the fact that constructive negation proposed by Stuckey [22, 23] requires that the constraint domain be *admissible closed*, whereas that proposed by Fages [13, 10] does not (at the cost of requiring some uniformity in computing negated subgoals of a goal). We now give formal details. As a notational convention hereafter we denote $\mathcal{M}(F \cup C \cup Tr_n \cup D)$ by $\mathcal{M}(F, C, Tr_n, D)$ and $\mathcal{M}(F \cup C \cup (\cup_{i \in \omega} Tr_i) \cup D)$ by $\mathcal{M}(F, C, Tr_*, D)$.

Definition 1 (n-traces, *-traces and models) *For every numeral n, any set of predicate instances of the form $\{$`request`$(\_,\_,\_,i) : i \leq n\}$, $\{$`request`$(\_,\_,\_,i) : i \in \omega\}$ are said to be an n-trace and a *-trace respectively, where every `request`$(\_, \_, \_, i)$ term is variable free.*
*Let F, C, Tr_n, Tr_*, and D be respectively FAF, ISM, n-trace, *-trace, and DAM rules. Let Φ be the three-valued Kripke-Kleene immediate consequence operator. Then we say that $\bigcup_{i \in \omega} \Phi^i_{R \cup D}(F \cup C)$ are the models $\mathcal{M}(F, C, R, D)$ where R is either an n-trace Tr_n or an *-trace Tr_*.*

As stated in definition 1, a model of $\mathcal{M}(F, C, R, D)$ is obtained by evaluating the Φ operator over a FAF+ISM model $\mathcal{M}(F, C)$ ω many times. The reasoning behind our choice for the semantics is that FAF already has a (two-valued) stable model. In [12], Fitting shows that $\bigcup_{i \subset \omega} \Phi^i_{Tr_n \cup D}(F \cup C) = \bigcup_{i \in \omega} \Phi^i_{Tr_n \cup D, F \cup C}(\emptyset)$. The dynamic grant policy then extends this stable model. Following two claims clarify this statement.

Theorem 1 (Finite termination of dynFAF queries).
For every numeral n, every grant$(\_, \_, \_, n)$, relinquish$(\_, \_, \_, n)$, holds$(\_, \_, \_, n)$, *and* validity$(\_, \_, \_, n)$ *query either succeeds or fails finitely, given that query over $\mathcal{M}(F, C)$ has the same property.*

Consequently, for every numeral n, the three valued model $\mathcal{M}(F, C, R, D)$ evaluates every instance of grant$(\_, \_, \_, n)$ *or* relinquish$(\_, \_, \_, n)$ *query to be either true or false.*

Theorem 1 shows that dynFAF acts like FAF in the sense that every request is either honored or rejected. But theoretically there is a remarkable difference between a FAF model and a dynFAF model. While every FAF model is a (least) fixed point of a monotonic operator (conventionally referred to as the classical immediate consequence operator **T**), a dynFAF model is not a fixed point of the so called *Fitting-Kunen* Φ operator [12, 10], as it is well known that the closure ordinal of the Fitting-Kunen Φ operator is not ω. ([12] gives a simple counterexample) In contrast, a dynFAF model $\mathcal{M}(F, C, R, D)$ is an ω-closure of the Φ operator of $\mathcal{M}(F, C)$ under rules 11 through 26.

The other pertinent point is that nothing in the logical machinery guarantees that the synchrony hypothesis is valid, but conversely the correctness of the dynamic access grant module depends upon this externally enforced assumption. The next set of results show the connections between different traces.

Definition 2 (Trace chains) *We say that a set of n-traces $\{Tr_n : n \geq 0\}$ is a trace chain iff each Tr_n is an n-trace and $Tr_n \subset Tr_{n+1}$. Then we say that $Tr_* = \bigcup_{i \in \omega} Tr_i$ is the limit of the trace set $\{Tr_n : n \geq 0\}$.*

Following results are valid for any trace chain.

Lemma 2 (Compactness of Traces).
Suppose $\{Tr_n : n \geq 0\}$ is a trace chain. Then the following holds:

1. $\mathcal{M}(F, C, Tr_n, D) \models \phi$ *iff* $\mathcal{M}(F, C) \models \phi$ *for every FAF or ISM predicate instance ϕ.*
2. $\mathcal{M}(F, C, Tr_n, D) \models \phi$ *iff* $\mathcal{M}(F, C, Tr_{n+1}, D) \models \phi$ *for every DAM predicate instance where the last variable of ϕ is instantiated to m for any $m \leq n$.*
3. $\mathcal{M}(F, C, Tr_*, D) \models \phi$ *iff* $\mathcal{M}(F, C, Tr_n, D) \models \phi$ *where ϕ is a variable free DAM predicate where the numeral instance is n.*

Lemma 2 says that any model $\mathcal{M}(F, C, Tr_n, D)$ of $F \cup C \cup Tr_n \cup D$ only validates the history of dynamic changes taking place over the static model $\mathcal{M}(F, C)$

up to and including time n. It also says that evaluating the Fitting-Kunen Φ closure operator ω many times does not add any more *truth* to $\mathcal{M}(F, C, Tr_n, D)$ than n many times. In that respect, our semantics is finite over finite lifetimes of dynFAF evolutions.

5   Correctness of DAM

This section shows that dynFAF functions correctly. All lemmas and theorems in this section are given without proof. We refer the reader to [9] for the formal proofs. Our notion of correctness consists of two parts: (1) dynFAF satisfies traditional safety and liveliness properties. (2) `grant` and `relinquish` function as expected. By *safety* we mean that any granted permission does not violate any constraint. By *liveliness*, we mean that any requested permission that does not conflict with any other outstanding permissions is granted. By the expected functionality of `grant` we mean that any request for already granted permission fails. Similarly, the expected functionality of `relinquish` is that only granted permissions are relinquishable. In order to prove these results, we prove Lemma 3, that guarantees the correctness of `holds` and `validity`, the two other predicates that are for *internal* use in DAM.

Lemma 3 (Correctness of `holds` and `validity`).
The following statements hold for every numeral n and every permission triple (s, o, a):

1. $\mathcal{M}(F, C, Tr_n, D) \models \text{holds}(s, o, a, n)$ *iff* $\mathcal{M}(F, C, Tr_n, D) \models \text{grant}(s, o, a, n')$ *for some* $n' \leq n$ *and* $\mathcal{M}(F, C, Tr_n, D) \not\models \text{relinquish}(s, o, a, m)$ *for all* m *satisfying* $n' < m \leq n$.
2. $\mathcal{M}(F, C, Tr_n, D) \models \text{validity}(s, o, +a, n)$ *iff there is no permission* (s', o', a') *satisfying* $\mathcal{M}(F, C, Tr_n, D) \models \text{holds}(s', o', a', n) \wedge \text{derConflict}((s, o, a), (s', o', a')) \wedge \text{do}(s', o', +a')$.

Now we use this result to prove the safety and the liveliness as promised.

Theorem 2 (Safety and liveliness of dynFAF).
The following holds for all permissions (s,o,a) and all times n:

Safety: *Suppose* $\mathcal{M}(F, C, Tr_n, D) \models \text{holds}(s, o, a, n)$. *Then there is no other permission* (s', o', a') *satisfying* $\mathcal{M}(F, C, Tr_n, D) \models \text{holds}(s', o', a', n) \wedge \text{derConflict}((s, o, a), (s', o', a'))$.

Liveliness: *Suppose* $\mathcal{M}(F, C, Tr_n, D) \models \text{validity}(s, o, a, n) \wedge \neg \text{holds}(s, o, a, n)$. *Then there is a trace* Tr_{n+1} *satisfying* $\mathcal{M}(F, C, Tr_{n+1}, D) \models \text{grant}(s, o, a, n + 1) \wedge \text{holds}(s, o, a, n + 1)$.

Now we show that `grant` and `relinquish` has the required prerequisites. That is, $\text{request}(\_, \_, (+)\_, n)$ succeeds and results in $\text{grant}(\_, \_, \_, n)$ evaluating to *true* only if this permission has not already outstanding. Similarly, $\text{request}(\_, \_, (-)\_, n)$ succeeds and results in $\text{relinquish}(\_, \_, \_, n)$ evaluating to *true* only if this permission is already outstanding.

Theorem 3 (Prerequisites of grant and relinquish).
The following holds for all (s,o,a) and all n:

grant: $\mathcal{M}(F, C, Tr_{n+1}, D) \models$ grant$(s, o, a, n + 1)$ *only if* $\mathcal{M}(F, C, Tr_n, D) \not\models$
    holds(s, o, a, n).
relinquish: $\mathcal{M}(F, C, Tr_{n+1}, D) \models$ relinquish$(s, o, a, n + 1)$ *only if* $\mathcal{M}(F, C,$
    $Tr_n, D) \models$ holds(s, o, a, n).

6   Related Work

Ahn and Sandhu introduce a logical language for specifying role-based authorization constraints named *RCL2000* [1]. They identify conflicts as originating from conflicting permissions, users and roles, and constraints are stated using cardinalities of sets of access or their intersections where most cardinalities are restricted to one. They specify several kinds of *dynamic separation of duty*, without showing enforcement mechanisms.

Bertino et al. propose a framework for specification and enforcement of authorization constraints in workflow management systems [5]. They present a language to express authorization constraints as clauses in a logic program and propose algorithms to check for the consistency of the constraints and to assign roles and users to the workflow tasks in such a way that no constraints are violated. The consistency checking algorithms is executed by the security officer in role or user planning.

Similar to FAF, Barker and Stuckey [4] define some special consistency checking rules (with head of predicates *inconsistent_ssd, inconsistent_dsd*) to encode the separation of duty constraints. The constraints are checked by the security officer whenever new user-role or new role-permission assignments are inserted.

In comparison, dynFAF has the following advantages in expressing and enforcing constraints. First, we add the ability to derive all binary constraints from atomic constraints specified by the SSO using predefined derivation rules. Second, derived constraints are enforced dynamically in the model itself. That is, all those and only those access requests that do not violate any constraint will be granted – referred to as liveliness and safety, respectively.

7   Conclusions

In this paper, we described a constraint logic programming-based approach, dynFAF, for expressing and enforcing dynamic constraints as an extension to the framework FAF proposed by Jajodia et al. [17]. We limited FAF to rules without **error** predicates; then we enriched FAF with the ability to specify atomic binary conflicts and derive complex conflicts using user specified rules. This extension constitutes the ISM module. We showed how to extend this syntax with an appropriate dynamic access grant module DAM. DAM grants requests that do not violate any conflicts. In return, DAM expects the user of the system to relinquish granted permissions once they are no longer in need. dynFAF works under the assumptions that access requests are submitted in sequence, one at a time and that the permissions obtained are relinquished by giving them up to the access controller. The current design of dynFAF requires that these are enforced external to the system.

We have shown that dynFAF models have a unique three-valued model used in (constraint) logic programming. We have further shown that any stable model (correspondingly well-founded) FAF model is extendible to a three-valued dyn-FAF model. In addition, we showed that every instance of a request to grant or relinquish permissions made to dynFAF always terminates without floundering as a constraint logic program.

Acknowledgments

This work was partially supported by the National Science Foundation under grant CCR-0113515 and IIS-0242237. We thank the anonymous reviewers for their valuable comments.

References

1. G. Ahn and R. Sandhu. Role-based authorization constraints specification. *ACM Transactions on Information and Systems Security*, 3(4):207–226, November 2000.
2. K. R. Apt, H. Blair, and A. Walker. Towards a theory of declarative knowledge. In *Foundations of Deductive Databases and Logic Programming*, pages 89–148. Morgan Kaufmann, 1988.
3. C. Baral and V. S. Subrahmanian. Stable and extension class theory for logic programs and default theories. *Journal of Automated Reasoning*, 8(3):345–366, June 1992.
4. S. Barker and P. Stuckey. Flexible access control policy specification with constraint logic programming. *ACM Transactions on Information and System Security*, 6(4):501–546, 2004.
5. E. Bertino and V. Atluri. The specification and enforcement of authorization constraints in workflow management. *ACM Transactions on Information Systems Security*, 2(1):65–104, February 1999.
6. E. Bertino, B. Catania, E. Ferrari, and P. Perlasca. A logical framework for reasoning about access control models. *ACM Transactions on Information and System Security*, 6(1):71–127, February 2003.
7. D. Chan. Constructive negation based on the completed databases. In R. A. Kowalski and K. A. Bowen, editors, *Proc. International Conference on Logic Programming (ICLP)*, pages 111–125. The MIT Press, 1988.
8. D. Chan. An extension of constructive negation and its application in coroutining. In E. Lusk and R. Overbeek, editors, *Proc. North-American Conference on Logic Programming*, pages 477–489. The MIT Press, 1989.
9. S. Chen, D. Wijesekera, and S. Jajodia. Incorporating dynamic constraints in the flexible authorization framework. Technical Report CSIS-TR-04-01, Center for Secure Information Systems, George Mason University, June 2004.
10. F. Fages. Constructive negation by pruning. *Journal of Logic Programming*, 32(2):85–118, 1997.

11. M. Fitting. A kripke-kleene semantics for logic programs. *Journal of Logic Programming*, 2(4):295–312, 1985.
12. M. Fitting and M. Ben-Jacob. Stratified, weak stratified, and three-valued semantics. *Fundamenta Informaticae, Special issue on LOGIC PROGRAMMING*, 13(1):19–33, March 1990.
13. F. Francois and G. Roberta. A hierarchy of semantics for normal constraint logic programs. In *Algebraic and Logic Programming*, pages 77–91, 1996.
14. M. Gelfond and L. Lifschitz. The stable model semantics for logic programming. In *Proc. Fifth International Conference and Symposium on Logic Programming*, pages 1070–1080, 1988.
15. T. Jaeger. On the increasing importance of constraints. In *Proc. of the Fourth Role Based Access Control*, pages 33–42, Fairfax, VA, 1999.
16. T. Jaeger, A. Prakash, J. Liedtke, and N. Islam. Flexible control of downloaded executable content. *ACM Transactions on Information Systems Security*, 2(2):177–228, May 1999.
17. S. Jajodia, P. Samarati, M. L. Sapino, and V. S. Subrahmanian. Flexible support for multiple access control policies. *ACM Transactions on Database Systems*, 26(2):214–260, June 2001.
18. K. J. Kunen. Negation in logic programming. *Journal of Logic Programming*, 4(4):298–308, December 1987.
19. M. Nayanchama and S. Osborn. The role graph model and conflict of interest. *ACM Transactions on Information and Systems Security*, 2(1):3–33, February 1999.
20. S. Osborn, R. Sandhu, and Q. Munawer. Configuring role-based access control to enforce mandatory and discretionary access control policies. *ACM Transactions on Information and Systems*, 3(2):85–106, May 2000.
21. R. Sandhu, E. Coyne, H. Feinstein, and C. Youman. Role-based access control models. *IEEE Computer*, 29(2):38–47, Febraury 1996.
22. P. Stuckey. Constructive negation for constraint logic programming. In *Logic in Computer Science*, pages 328–339, 1991.
23. P. Stuckey. Negation and constraint logic programming. *Information and Computation*, 118(1):12–33, 1995.
24. A. van Gelder. The alternating fixpoint of logic programs with negation. In *Proc. 8th ACM Symposium on Principles of Database Systems*, pages 1–10, 1989.
25. T. Y. C. Woo and S. S. Lam. Authorizations in distributed systems: A new approach. *Journal of Computer Security*, 2(2-3):107–136, 1993.

Access-Condition-Table-Driven Access Control for XML Databases

Naizhen Qi (Naishin Seki) and Michiharu Kudo

IBM Research, Tokyo Research Laboratory,
1623-14, Shimo-tsuruma, Yamato-shi,
Kanagawa 242-8502, Japan
{naishin,kudo}@jp.ibm.com

Abstract. Access control represented by XPath expressions allows for access restrictions on elements, attributes, and text nodes according to their locations and values in an XML document. Many XML database applications call for such node-level access control on concerned nodes at any depth. To perform such node-level access control, current approaches create heavy loads on XML database applications since these approaches incur massive costs either at runtime or for data optimization. In order to solve these problems, we introduce an access condition table (ACT), a table equivalent to an access control policy, where Boolean access conditions for accessibility checks are stored. The ACT is generated as a means of shifting the extra runtime computations to a pre-processing step. Experimental results show that the proposed ACT can handle accesses to arbitrary paths at a nearly constant speed.

1 Introduction

The Extensible Markup Language (XML [6]) is widely used for data presentation, integration, and management because of its rich data structure. Since data with different security levels may be intermingled in a single XML document, such as business transactions and medical records, access control is required on both the element- and attribute-level to ensure that sensitive data will be accessible only to the authorized users. In most of the current research, such node-level access control is specified with XPath [10] to identify the sensitive portion.

Since the utilization of global elements and global attributes may scatter data throughout an XML document, the node-level access control specification is required to cover affected nodes at any depth. For instance, in XML-formatted medical records, doctors' comments may appear anywhere as the occasion demands. Therefore, to hide comments from unauthorized users, it is required to select all of the comments regardless of their locations.

Many approaches (e.g. [3, 11, 21, 24]) fulfill access control on arbitrary nodes with the `descendant-or-self` axis of XPath (//) and the propagation mechanism. Since // selects a specific descendant in the subtree and propagation mechanism brings access down to the subtree, both of them require node traversal of

P. Samarati et al. (Eds.): ESORICS 2004, LNCS 3193, pp. 17–32, 2004.
© Springer-Verlag Berlin Heidelberg 2004

the entire subtree. Especially for deeply layered XML documents, the enforcement of // and propagation imposes heavy computational costs. Therefore, some of the approaches(e.g. [3, 11, 17, 21]) trade efficiency off against *expressiveness*[1].

Ideas to efficiently perform an arbitrary XML node selection are also proposed by [16, 19, 20, 22, 28], in which the result of access control is cached for each affected node. Since such optimization is generally on a per-document basis, the databases with few document updates and document insertions may profit from these approaches. However, in real XML database applications, new XML documents may frequently be inserted into the database. For instance, as E. Cecchet[7] shows, the interaction of EJB-based business applications may happen 10 to 200 times per second. If each interaction is recorded into an XML document, document-based optimization will be performed frequently and potentially lead to unacceptable performance. Therefore, we think efficiency should be achieved independent of the data in the XML documents. We call this requirement *document-independency*.

In this paper, we introduce a novel access-condition-table-driven mechanism which achieves high *expressiveness* with good *document-independent* efficiency. The access condition table (ACT) is a table storing the paths and the two types of access conditions, which are Boolean expressions. Given a path, the ACT can provide a proper access condition according to the path location. Then the provided access condition is evaluated to decide the accessibility. As far as we know, our ACT-driven approach is the first one capable of processing the access to an arbitrary path at a nearly constant speed irrespective of the XML document. The ACT is free from re-computation as long as the access control policy is not updated. In addition, the ACT can provide applicable access control for various query languages including XQuery, SQL XML, and XPath.

1.1   Related Work

Many approaches to enforcing XML access control have been proposed. Some of them support full XPath expressions but perform with naive implementations which may incur massive computations. For instance, when the access control policy is large or the XML document is deep layered, Kudo et al. [21] and Gabillon [17] may suffer from high runtime costs, since they create the projection of the access control policy on a DOM [18] tree and then evaluate the accessibility at each node. The mechanisms proposed in [2, 3, 11, 12] also encounter the same problem at runtime since the node-level access control on a DOM-based view can be expensive especially for a large XML document.

Substantial performance costs can be a fatal weakness for a secure XML database, access control with a pre-processing optimization to improve runtime efficiency has been explored in many research projects [1, 8, 14, 24, 28]. For example, the static access optimization algorithm in Murata et al. [24] minimizes the runtime checks by determining the accessibility of nodes in a query with pre-computed automata which is *document-* and *schema-independent*. However,

---

[1] We use *expressiveness* to describe the support to //, predicates, and propagation.

more than access control policy, the queries, which can be complicatedly expressed in XQuery, are required by the system. Our approach is complement to their method that we supports node-level access control for more query languages but also with more limitations on policy specifications. Yu et al. [28] enforces access control by obtaining accessibility from an accessibility map which is optimized on the basis of the XML document and therefore document updates and insertions may trigger re-computations. In addition, there are XPath-based documents filtering systems [1, 8, 14] satisfying the requirements of *expressiveness* and *document-independency* through pre-computed special data structures. However, these approaches do not support to eliminate a denial node from a grant tree or sub-tree; therefore, they may be unable to afford appropriate access control for some XML database applications.

Optimization is also done in a number of research efforts on XML query languages (e.g., XPath and XQuery [5]). The methods include query optimization based on (i) the tree pattern of queries [9, 13, 23, 25–27], (ii) XML data and XML schema [16, 19, 20, 22] and (iii) the consistency between integrity constraints and schemas [15]. However, these data selection mechanisms are not applicable to other query languages and primitive APIs such as DOM.

Outline. The rest of this paper is organized as follows. After reviewing some preliminaries in Section 2, we introduce the features of the ACT in Section 3 and the construction of the ACT in Section 4. Experimental results are reported in Section 5 and the conclusions and future work are summarized in Section 6.

2   Preliminaries

XPath. An XPath expression can select nodes based on the document structure and the data values in an XML document. A structure-based selection relies on the structural relationships, which is expressed by / and //. For example, /record//name selects all name in the subtree of record. In addition, value-based selection is done by attaching a value-based condition on a specific node: if the condition is satisfied, the node is selected. For instance, the XPath expression /disclosure[@status='published'] selects disclosure whose status attribute equals 'published'. In this XPath expression, @status='published' is a value-based condition which is called a *predicate*.

Access Condition Policy. Various access control policy models have been proposed, but we use the one proposed by Murata et al. [24] in which an access control policy contains a set of 3-tuples rules with the syntax: *(Subject, Permission Action, Object)* as shown in Table 1. The subject has a prefix indicating the type such as *uid* and *group*. '+' stands for a grant rule while '−' for a denial one. The action value can be either *read, update, create,* or *delete*. Due to the lack of space, we focus on the read action in this paper though the others can be implemented with the same mechanisms. The rule with +R or −R is propagation permitted that the access can be propagated downward on the entire subtree, while +r is propagation denied. As an example, (uid:Seki, +r, /a) specifies

Table 1. Access Control Rule Syntax

Field	Description
Subject	A human user or a user process with a *uid* or *role* prefix
Permission	Grant access (+) or denial access(-)
Action	r: without propagation; R: with propagation
Object	An XPath expression selects affected nodes

user Seki's access to /a is allowed but to /a/b is implicit specified since *grant* is not propagated down to the descending paths of /a owing to r. Moreover, according to the *denial downward consistency* in [24] that the descendants of an inaccessible node are either inaccessible, there is an accessibility dependency between the ancestors and the descendants. Therefore, it is obvious that -r is equivalent to -R; and thus, we specify denial rules only with -R in this paper. In addition, in order to maximize the security of the data items, we (i) resolve access conflicts with the *denial-takes-precedence* [4], and (ii) apply the default denial permission on the paths if no explicit access control is specified.

3   Features of the Access Condition Table (ACT)

Before entering the details, we list up some requirements considered to be important to an access control system for XML databases.

- *Document-independency* and *schema-independency* should be satisfied.
- Document updates and document insertions should not trigger any re-computation.
- Access control should be applicable to query languages including XQuery, SQL XML, and XPath.

However, we consider these requirements in a system where the frequency of the policy updating is far lower than the frequencies of the actions performed.

3.1   Structure of the ACT

The ACT is directly generated from an access control policy. Different from the access control policy, the ACT separates the affected paths and the related conditions from the object. We call the affected paths the *target paths*. The values of each target path are two types of access conditions: *access condition* and *subtree access condition*. The access conditions are for the accessibility checks on the target paths, and the subtree access conditions are for the descending paths. Featured with two types of access conditions, the ACT enables access control on a path of any length. The key idea of this structure is based on the following two observations.

- Each // in an XPath expression can be regarded as a divider. The part on the right of // is the condition that should be satisfied by the descending paths in the subtree of the part on the left of //. For instance, granting access on /a//c specifies *if the node is c in the subtree of a, the access to the node is granted*. As a result, the accesses to /a/c, /a/b/c, and /a/b/c/d are granted since they are cs in the subtree of a. Therefore, an subtree access condition can be prepared at /a, which is responsible for the access to any path in the subtree of /a.
- Propagation is the mechanism controlling the access of the entire subtree. For instance, granting access to /a with propagation specifies *the accesses to a itself and its descendants are granted*. However, granting access to /a without propagation specifies *the access to a is granted but to the descendant is denied*. Since the access conditions to /a and to its subtree can be separately specified, we can prepare the access conditions separately as well.

As a result, we generate two types of access conditions: one is the access condition for a path itself like a in the above two examples, and the other is the access condition for the entire subtree such as the subtree of a in the examples. Example 1 shows a simple access control policy and its equivalent ACT.

Example 1. Given an access control policy P consisting of rules R1, R2, R3, and R4 as follows, the equivalent ACT is as Table 2 shows.

R1: (uid:Seki, +r, /a),   R2: (uid:Seki, +R, /a/b)

R3: (uid:Seki, +r, /a/c[g>1]), R4: (uid:Seki, -R, /a/b//e)

Table 2. Structure of the ACT

Target Path	Access Condition	Subtree Access Condition
/a	true	false
/a/b	true	not (ancestor-or-self::e)
/a/c	g>1	false

We use an accessibility marked tree, the abstract representation of an XML document, to reflect the access control result of P with accessible and inaccessible nodes individually distinguished. It also reflects the ACT shown in Table 2 since the ACT leads to the same accessibility marked tree. In Fig. 1, grant access is propagated from b to e, i, j, f, k and l owing to R2 while denial access is propagated from e to i and j owing to R4. Therefore, access conflicts occur on e, i and j. Finally, e, i and j are inaccessible based on the *denial-takes-precedence* principle. On the other hand, the nodes without access specification, d, g, h, and m are ultimately inaccessible owing to the default denial permission. In addition, the accessibility of c is decided by the value of g : if g>1 then accessible, otherwise inaccessible.

3.2   Pre-computation

The ACT generation can be considered as a pre-computation stage in which some extra computations are shifted from the runtime. Generally, the extra

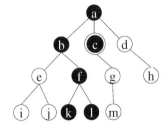

- Black nodes: accessible nodes
- Circled black nodes: value-based accessible nodes
- White nodes: inaccessible nodes

Fig. 1. The accessibility marked tree of P

computations are caused by the processes of propagation and conflict resolution. Conflict arises when a node is granted access and denied access at the same time. For instance, (i) (Sbj, +R, /a), and (ii) (Sbj, -R, /a/b) cause conflict on b since b is granted owing to the propagation from a and at the same time denied because of the denial specification. Moreover, if multiple bs are subordinate to the same a, the propagation and the conflict identically occur on each b. Obviously, such repeated processes should be optimized to conserve resources. The ACT-driven mechanism moves the processes of propagation and conflict resolution into the ACT generation to achieve high runtime performance.

3.3   Access Conditions and Subtree Access Conditions

Access conditions and subtree access conditions are Boolean expressions evaluated for accessibility. They are *true* or *false* when the objects do not contain either a // or a predicate. Only for the objects containing a // or a predicate, is the XPath expression representing the structure-based or value-based condition involved in the condition expressions.

For instance, for R2 in Example 1, the access condition on /a/b is *true* and the subtree access condition of /a/b is *true* too since 'true' is permitted to spread down to the entire subtree of /a/b owing to 'R'.

3.4   ACT-Driven Access Control Enforcement

Since access conditions are path-specific, each node in an XML document can obtain a proper access condition through its path expression on the basis of its location: one of the target paths or the descending path in someone's subtree.

Access control is enforced via an ACT handler that, upon receiving a user request, returns accessible data to the user. The user request contains the user information and the access target, which can be either a path or an XML document. For a path, the accessibility is decided by evaluating the access condition according to its location: if the path is a target path in the ACT, the access condition is evaluated; otherwise, the closest ancestor is searched for and its subtree access condition is evaluated. For an XML document, the ACT handler traverses the document to check the accessibility of each path: if the path is found to be accessible, it is added to the user view. In order to improve the performance in processing XML documents, the ACT handler adopts a *check-skip* mechanism to skip accessibility checks on the nodes with an inaccessible ancestor. According to the denial downward consistency, the nodes with an inaccessible ancestor are definitely inaccessible, so the checks on them can be skipped.

Table 3. Accessibility checks for Seki

Requested Path	Target	Access Condition	Accessibility Result
/a	/a	true	Accessible.
/a/c	/a/c	g>1	Accessible when g is bigger than 1, otherwise inaccessible.
/a/b/h	/a	false	Inaccessible.
/a/b/e/i	/a/b	not(ancestor-or-self::e)	Inaccessible.

Using the ACT in Table 2, we show four examples in Table 3. For instance, Seki requests to access a, the ACT handler finds /a in the ACT and therefore the access condition, *true*, is evaluated. Consequently, the access to a is allowed. When Seki accesses i whose path is /a/b/e/i, the ACT handler finds it absent from the ACT. However, the closest ancestor target path, /a/b, is found and the subtree access condition, not(ancestor-or-self::e), is provided. Since not(ancestor-or-self::e) is evaluated *false* for /a/b/e/i, the access is denied.

3.5 Limitations on the ACT

In order to keep the ACT simple, the following four limitations on XPath expressions are specified.

- // is limited to appear only once. (i.e. /a//c//e is not allowed.)
- A wildcard * should always be accompanied with a // in the form of //*. (i.e. /a//b/*/@d is not allowed.)
- // and * never appear in predicates. (i.e. /a[*>1]/b is not allowed.)
- Only one node can be identified after //. (i.e. /a//c/d is not allowed.)

The limitations restrict the expressiveness of the access control policies. Nonetheless, the specification of a node at any depth, e.g. //*[@level='classified'] and //comment, are supported. In addition, some of these limitations can be resolved by XPath extension functions.

4   Construction of the ACT

The ACT is generated from the access control policy by fowllowing 5 steps:

- Step 1: Generate the target paths
- Step 2: Generate the local access conditions

– Step 3: Generate the local subtree access conditions
– Step 4: Perform propagation
– Step 5: Perform conflict resolution and expression combination

Note that the access conditions and the subtree access conditions generated in Step 2 and Step 3 are local since propagation has not yet occurred. In Step 4, local subtree access control with propagation permission is spread down to the descending target paths in the ACT. In Step 5, access conditions and subtree access conditions residing on each target path are individually combined. At the same time, conflicts are also resolved with the conflict resolution mechanism.

4.1 Generating the Target Paths

The target path is generated from the object by removing the additional access conditions. If the object contains //, the prefix to // is the target path. If the object contains predicates, then the path after removing predicates is the target path. However, if the object contains both // and predicates, the path after removing the predicates in the prefix is the target path.

For instance, since R3's object in Sect. 3.1 contains a predicate, the target path is /a/c after removing the predicate from /a/c[g>1]. Moreover, for R4's object /a/b//e, the prefix to //, which is /a/b, is the target path.

4.2 Generating the Local Access Conditions

Local access conditions on each target path are generated from the action and the object. If the object contains predicates or //, the additional access conditions should be included.

When the object does not contain either a // or a predicate, the action decides the local access condition: true for + and false for -. When the object contains a predicate, the predicate relative to the target path is generated as the local access condition. If the object contains multiple predicates, the local access condition is generated by connecting the predicates relative to the target path with 'and'. However, for the object containing //, the local access condition is not available since it specifies access for the descendants rather than for the target path itself.

In the example in Sect. 3.1, the access conditions of /a and /a/b are 'true' since the actions of R1 and R2 are both r. However, the access condition of /a/c is the predicate g>1 which is the value-based condition imposed on c.

4.3 Generating the Local Subtree Access Conditions

The intuition for subtree access conditions is to combine both information on (i) the accessibility dependency from the root to the target path, and (ii) the ancestor-descendant relationship from the target path to an arbitrary descending path. Only when both (i) and (ii) are satisfied can the nodes in the subtree be accessible. We use ancestor-or-self axis and descendant-or-self axis to describe the structural relationship between ancestors and descendants. Algorithm 1 shows the subtree access condition generation when given the action A and the object T. In addition, in this section we address the case that predicates and // do not appear in the same T.

Algorithm 1. Subtree access condition generation.
If T contains //, then T can be represented as $/e_1//e_n$.

```
   if (T contains '//') then
if (A is '+R') then
subtree access condition ← ancestor-or-self::en or
descendant-or-self::en
else if (A is '+r') then
subtree access condition ← descendant-or-self::en
else if (A is '-R') then
subtree access condition ← not(ancestor-or-self::en)
end if
else
if (A is '+R') then
subtree access condition ← true
else if (A is '-R') then
subtree access condition ← false
else
return          // local subtree access condition is N/A
end if
end if
```

According to the above algorithm, R4: (uid:Seki, -R, /a/b//e) in Sect. 3.1 leads to a local subtree access condition not(ancestor-or-self::e) stating that *if the requested node is* e *below* /a/b *or has such an ancestor* e, *it is inaccessible.* Therefore, subtree access conditions enable access control on a path of any depth.

4.4   Performing Propagation

The propagation mechanism brings the local subtree access conditions to a wide descendant area. In our approach, propagation is performed by adding the local subtree access condition to both the access conditions and the subtree access conditions of the descending target paths. To reduce the runtime computation costs, at this step the propagated subtree access conditions are evaluated as to whether or not they are satisfied by the current descending target path. If so, the access conditions are rewritten as true or false based on the propagated access.

4.5   Performing Expression Combination and Conflict Resolution

Since the propagation mechanism transmits ancestral access to the descending target paths, multiple access conditions and subtree access conditions may apply to each target path. Rather than simply connect all of the conditions with the Boolean operators *and* or *or*, we logically combine the access conditions into a Boolean expression. In addition, when access conflict happens, it is resolved with the *denial-takes-precedence* policy.

In Example 1 of Sect. 3.1, after performing the four steps, two different subtree access conditions are imposed on /a/b. One is *true* specified by R2, the other is `ancestor-or-self::e` specified by R4. According to the expression combination, the subtree access condition is `true and not(ancestor-or-self::e)`, which can be rewritten to `not(ancestor-or-self::e)`.

4.6   Enhanced Subtree Access Conditions

In this section, we introduce a mechanism to handle the case where a predicate and the permitted propagation appear at the same time, which is not handled by the algorithm in Sect. 4.3.

Suppose there is a P' containing a propagation permitted third rule that R3':`(uid:Seki, +R, /a/c[g>1])`. Owing to propagation, R3' implies the access to g and m should be decided by evaluating the predicate relative to c. Therefore, it is required to convert the predicate relative to c into the ones relative to c from the accessed descendants, such as `..[g>1]` from g and `../..[g>1]` from m. It is obvious that the descendant at a different depth leads to a different relative predicate, and it is necessary to describe this non-deterministic relative relationship in a static way.

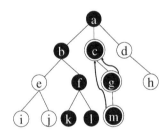

- Black nodes: accessible nodes
- Circled black nodes: value-based accessible nodes
- White nodes: inaccessible nodes

Fig. 2. The accessibility marked tree of P'

However, according to the denial downward consistency, we can say when c is accessible its descendants are all accessible if no other denial access is imposed. Therefore, the non-deterministic relative relationship can be regarded as a value-based accessibility dependency on c in this example. Moreover, regardless of the locations, all descendants below c can share the same value-based accessibility dependency. A system variable `ref(target path)` is used to represent this dependency: if the value-based `target path` is evaluated accessible, then the descendant is accessible.

Fig. 2 shows the accessibility marked tree for P' in which arrows starting with g and m ending with ancestor c represent the accessibility dependency. The local subtree access condition of R3' can be simply notated as `ref(/a/c)`. Furthermore, the accessibility reference is also required when the object contains // with a predicate before, like (`uid:Seki, +r, /a/b[f>1]//e`). Using the same mechanism, the local subtree access condition is therefore `ref(/a/b)` and `descendant-or-self::e`.

5   Experiments

To validate the efficiency of the ACT, we ran a variety of experiments to see how our techniques perform. We measured *view generation time*, the time cost to generate the view of an XML document based on the policy, to compare the performance between our ACT-driven enforcement and a simple implementation without pre-computing access conditions. The purposes of the experiments are to see (i) how the policy size works on the view generation time, (ii) how the ACT performs comparing with the simple implementation, and (iii) how ACT performs when // appears.

5.1   Experimental Data

Experimental Environment. All experiments were run on a 3.06 GHz Xeon processor with 2.50 GB RAM. In this paper, we report on an XML document obtained from http://www.w3c.org, which was generated on the basis of xmlspec-v20.dtd, with a data size of almost 200 KB, 768 types of paths, and 4,727 nodes when represented as an XML tree.

For simplicity in the experiments, we created policies for a single user. Nonetheless, we can use multiple ACTs for multi-user scenario. Moreover, we ran comparison experiments for structure-based access control, but did not for value-based since the performance partly depends on the efficiency of the predicate evaluation. However, we can infer the performance from the results of our experiments.

Access Control Policy Patterns: *pattern-a* **and** *pattern-b*. The access control policies were not randomly generated. In particular, we guaranteed that no duplicated access was imposed on the inaccessible descendants, since 'denial' is already contained in the inaccessible ancestor according to the denial downward consistency.

We generated the policy with accessible nodes as the object and +r as the action, and named it *pattern-a* access control policy. We also generated a corresponding reverse version, *pattern-b*, that contained denial rules on the most ancestral node of each denial subtree. In addition, *pattern-b* also contains a grant rule specified on the root node with +R. Conceptually, *pattern-a* selects the accessible nodes from the inaccessible region while *pattern-b* selects the inaccessible nodes from an accessible region. Fig. 3 shows an example for the accessibility marked tree *Tree*, with the corresponding access control policies in *pattern-a* and *pattern-b* as shown in the figure.

Access control policy in *pattern-a*:
(uid:Seki, +r, /a)
(uid:Seki, +r, /a/b)
(uid:Seki, +r, /a/c)

Access control policy in *pattern-b*:
(uid:Seki, +R, /a)
(uid:Seki, -r, /a/d)

Tree

Fig. 3. Access control policies for *Tree*

Access Control Policies. We generated 11 paired sets of the access control policies in *pattern-a* and *pattern-b* with an access ratio varying from 0.03 to 0.95, where the access ratio is the fraction of the accessible nodes in the XML structure tree. The XML structure tree is the one built by the set of the paths appearing in the XML document. *Policy size* is the number of rules in an access control policy. The policy sizes of these access control policies are different, as Fig. 4 shows. Since in *pattern-a* the greater the access ratio is, the more nodes are explicitly

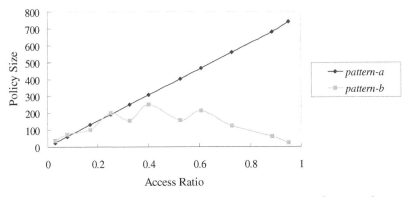

Fig. 4. Policy Size versus Access Ratio in *pattern-a* and *pattern-b*

specified, the size of the policy increases proportionally. On the other hand, in *pattern-b* rather than listing up each inaccessible node, only those inaccessible ones with an accessible parent are specified denial access. Consequently, the size of *pattern-b* is much smaller than *pattern-a* and without a regular form.

For the access control policies in both patterns, the size of the corresponding ACT is almost the same for each policy size, and thus Fig. 4 can be regarded as the chart for the ACT size.

5.2   Experimental Results

We show the advantages of the ACT through performance comparisons between the ACT-driven and a simple enforcement, which has a hash table structure storing the *Subject*, *Object*, and *Permission Action* introduced in Table 1. In the simple enforcement, each requested path is checked by evaluating the access control policies with *Objects* matched by the requested path. The check-skip mechanism introduced in Sect. 3.4 is also used by the simple enforcement.

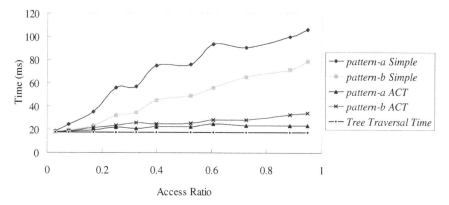

Fig. 5. View Generation Time versus Access Ratio

Relationship Between the Policy Size and the View Generation Time. Fig. 5 respectively shows the view generation times of the simple enforcement (Simple) and the ACT-driven enforcement (ACT) for both *pattern-a* and *pattern-b*, when the access ratio is varied from 0.03 to 0.95. In addition, in the figure we also show the *tree traversal time*, which is the time required by traversing the entire DOM structure. Time costs on accessibility checks for both Simple and ACT are the results by subtracting the *tree traversal times* from the *view generation times*.

From the figure, we can see that the chart of *pattern-b* is very similar to that of *pattern-a* in the trend: the larger the access ratio, the more time is required by Simple but ACT is almost constant. In particular, for *pattern-a*, when the access ratio is higher than 60%, ACT performs more than 4 times faster than Simple and when the access ratio is 95%, it reaches 5 times; while for *pattern-b*, Simple takes more than 2 times as long compared to ACT, while ACT shows quite slow growth. Furthermore, for the time costs on accessibility checks, which ignores the time of a DOM-based traversal, ACT performs much better than Simple that ACT is 11 ∼ 15 times faster than Simple for *pattern-a* when the access ratio is higher than 60%, and approximately 4 times faster for *pattern-b*.

In our experiments, a DOM-based traversal is used to retrieve paths from the XML document. However, other means of path retrievals may lead to less view generation times. Nonetheless, time costs on accessibility checks will not change for both ACT and Simple, which we have shown above.

How ACT Performs for //. To illustrate the advantages of the ACT-driven access control specified with //, we also ran experiments on the third set of access control policy data. We converted 20%, 25%, and 33% percentage of access control rules in *pattern-b* into rules with objects containing a //. The results are quite similar to each other, and therefore we show only the 20% case in Fig. 6.

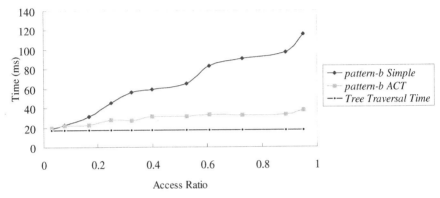

Fig. 6. Simple versus ACT on //

From the figure, we can see that ACT takes less time on view generation and the time increases slightly as the access ratio grows. In particular, ACT is faster than Simple by more than 3 times when the access ratio is 60% and by 5 times when 95%. Moreover, for the time costs on accessibility checks, ACT performs 6 times faster than Simple at most.

Our comparison experiment results show the ACT can perform almost constantly no matter with the policy size. And it is clear that the ACT-driven access control enforcement also shows advantages for //. The efficiency of the ACT is achieved with minimum computation costs by eliminating the processing of propagation and conflict resolution from the runtime.

6   Conclusion and Future Work

In this paper, we proposed an ACT-driven access control mechanism to provide efficient node-level access control. Using document- and schema-independent optimization features, the ACT is capable of handling various XML database applications without re-computation triggered by data and schema updates. In addition, our approach shifts most of the extra computations to the pre-processing stage to save on the runtime costs, which yields efficient performance that it can provide structure-based access control nearly in constant time.

On the other hand, some further research work is required. We have placed four limitations on access control policy, some of them can be resolved by XPath extension functions. Another important effort is to integrate the ACT approach with the static analysis method [24] in a well-balanced manner to improve expressiveness and performance.

Acknowledgments

We would like to thank Makoto Murata for discussions and comments on this work.

References

1. M. Altinel and M. Franklin: Efficient filtering of XML documents for selective dissemination of information. VLDB (2000) pp.53-64.
2. E. Bertino, S. Castano, E. Ferrari, and M. Mesiti: Controlled access and dissemination of XML documents. ACM WIDM (1999) pp.22-27.
3. E. Bertino and E. Ferrari: Secure and selective dissemination of XML documents. ACM TISSEC (2002) pp.290-331.
4. E. Bertino, P. Samarati, and S. Jajodia: An extended authorization model for relational database. IEEE trans. on Knowledge and Data Engineering (1997).
5. S. Boag, D. Chamberlin, M. F. Fernandez, D. Florescu, J. Robie, and J. Simeon: XQuery 1.0: An XML query language, W3C Working Draft 12 November 2003. Available at http://www.w3.org/TR/xquery/.
6. T. Bray, J. Paoli, and C. M. Sperberg-McQueen: Extensible Markup Language (XML) 1.0. W3C Recommendation. Available at http://www.w3g.org/TR/REC-xml (Feb. 1998).
7. E. Cecchet, J. Marguerite, and W. Zwaenepoel: Performance and scalability of EJB applications. OOPSLA (2002) pp.246-261.
8. C. -Y. Chan, P. Felber, M. Garofalakis, and R. Rastogi: Efficient filtering of XML documents with XPath expressions. ICDE (2002) pp.235-244.
9. S. Cho, S. Amer-Yahia, L. V. S. Lakshmanan, and D. Srivastava: Optimizing the secure evaluation of twig queries. VLDB (2000) pp.490-501.
10. J. Clarkand S. DeRose: XML Path Language (XPath) version 1.0. W3C Recommendation. Available at http://www.w3g.org/TR/xpath (1999).
11. E. Damiani, S. De Capitani di Vimercati, S. Paraboschi, and P. Samarati: Design and Implementation of an Access Control Processor for XML documents. WWW9 (2000).
12. E. Damiani, S. De Capitani di Vimercati, S. Paraboschi, and P. Samarati: A Fine-Grained Access Control System for XML Documents. ACM TISSEC (2002) pp.169-202.
13. A. Deutsch and V. Tannen: Containment of regular path expressions under integrity constraints. KRDB (2001).
14. Y. Diao, P. Fischer, M. Franklin, and R. To.: YFilter: Efficient and scalable filtering of XML documents. Demo at ICDE (2002) pp.341.
15. W. Fan and L. Libkin: On XML integrity constraints in the presence of DTDs. Symposium on Principles of Database Systems (2001) pp.114-125.
16. M. F. Fernandez and D. Suciu: Optimizing regular path expressions using graph schemas. ICDE (1998) pp.14-23.
17. A. Gabillon and E. Bruno: Regulating Access to XML Documents. Working Conference on Database and Application Security (2001) pp.219-314.
18. A. L. Hors, P. L. Hegaret, L. Wood, G. Nicol, J. Robie, M. Champion, and S. Byrne: Document Object Model (DOM) Level 3 Core Specification. Available at http://www.w3.org/TR/2004/PR-DOM-Level-3-Core-20040205 (2004).

19. R. Kaushik, P. Bohannon, J. F. Naughton, and H. F. Korth: Covering indexes for branching path queries. ACM SIGMOD (2002) pp.133-144.
20. D. D. Kha, M. Yoshikawa, and S. Uemura: An XML Indexing Structure with Relative Region Coordinate. ICDE (2001) pp.313-320.
21. M. Kudo and S. Hada: XML Document Security based on Provisional Authorization. ACM CCS (2000) pp.87-96.
22. Q. Li and B. Moon: Indexing and Querying XML Data for Regular Path Expressions. VLDB (2001) pp.361-370.
23. G. Miklau and D. Suciu: Containment and equivalence for an XPath fragment. ACM PODS (2002) pp.65-76.
24. M. Murata, A. Tozawa, M. Kudo and S. Hada: XML Access Control Using Static Analysis. ACM CCS (2003) pp.73-84.
25. F. Neven and T. Schwentick: XPath containment in the presence of disjunction, DTDs, and variables. ICDT (2003) pp.315-329.
26. Y. Papakonstantinou and V. Vassalos: Query rewriting for semistructured data. ACM SIGMOD (1999) pp.455-466.
27. P. T. Wood: Containment for XPath fragments under DTD constraints. ICDT (2003) pp.300-314.
28. T. Yu, D. Srivastava, L. V. S. Lakshmanan, and H. V. Jagadish: Compressed Accessibility Map: Efficient Access Control for XML. VLDB (2002) pp.478-489.

An Algebra for Composing Enterprise Privacy Policies

Michael Backes[1], Markus Dürmuth[2], and Rainer Steinwandt[2]

[1] IBM Zurich Research Laboratory, Switzerland
mbc@zurich.ibm.com
[2] IAKS, Arbeitsgruppe Systemsicherheit, Prof. Dr. Th. Beth,
Universität Karlsruhe, Germany
markus.duermuth@web.de, steinwan@ira.uka.de

Abstract. Enterprise privacy enforcement allows enterprises to internally enforce a privacy policy that the enterprise has decided to comply to. To facilitate the compliance with different privacy policies when several parts of an organization or different enterprises cooperate, it is crucial to have tools at hand that allow for a practical management of varying privacy requirements.

We propose an algebra providing various types of operators for composing and restricting enterprise privacy policies like conjunction, disjunction, and scoping, together with its formal semantics. We base our work on a superset of the syntax and semantics of IBM's Enterprise Privacy Authorization Language (EPAL), which recently has been submitted to W3C for standardization. However, a detailed analysis of the expressiveness of EPAL reveals that, somewhat surprisingly, EPAL is not closed under conjunction and disjunction. To circumvent this problem, we identified the subset of well-founded privacy policies which enjoy the property that the result of our algebraic operations can be turned into a coherent privacy policy again. This enables existing privacy policy enforcement mechanisms to deal with our algebraic expressions. We further show that our algebra fits together with the existing notions of privacy policy refinement and sequential composition of privacy policies in a natural way.

1 Introduction

Not only due to the increasing privacy awareness of costumers, the proper incorporation of privacy considerations into business processes is gaining importance. Also regulatory measures like the Children's Online Privacy Protection Act (COPPA) or the Health Insurance Portability and Accountability Act (HIPAA) illustrate that avoiding violations of privacy regulations is becoming a crucial issue. While the Platform for Privacy Preferences Project (P3P) [21] is a valuable tool for dealing with privacy concerns of web site users, the fine-grained treatment of privacy policies in business-to-business matters is still not settled satisfyingly. E.g., a language for the internal privacy practices of enterprises and for technical privacy enforcement must offer more possibilities for fine-grained distinction of data users, purposes, etc., as well as a clearer semantics. To live up to these requirements, enterprise privacy technologies are emerging [9]. One approach for capturing the privacy requirements of an enterprise – which however does not specify the implementation of these requirements – is the use of formalized enterprise privacy policies [11, 17, 16].

P. Samarati et al. (Eds.): ESORICS 2004, LNCS 3193, pp. 33–52, 2004.
© Springer-Verlag Berlin Heidelberg 2004

Although the primary purpose of enterprise privacy policies is enterprise-internal use, many factors speak for standardization of such policies. E.g., it would allow certain technical parts of regulations to be encoded into such a standardized language once and for all, and a large enterprise with heterogeneous repositories of personal data could then hope that enforcement tools for all these repositories become available that allow the enterprise to consistently enforce at least the internal privacy practices chosen by the CPO (chief privacy officer). For these reasons, IBM has proposed an Enterprise Privacy Authorization Language (EPAL) as an XML specification, which has been submitted to W3C for standardization. EPAL allows for a fine-grained description of privacy requirements in enterprises and could become a valuable tool for (business) processes that span several enterprises or different parts of a larger organization.

An enterprise privacy policy often reflects different legal regulations, promises made to customers, as well as more restrictive internal practices of the enterprise. Further, it may allow customer preferences. Hence it may be authored, maintained, replaced, and audited in a distributed fashion. In other words, one will need a life-cycle management system for the collection of enterprise privacy policies. However, despite considerable advancement in this area, current approaches are based on monolithic and complete specifications, which is very restrictive given that several policies might have to be enforced at once while being under control of different authorities. Having in mind actual use cases where sensitive data obeying different privacy regulations has to be merged or exchanged, this situation calls for a composition framework that allows for integrating different privacy policies while retaining their independence. While such thoughts occur as motivation in most prior work on enterprise privacy policies, the few tools provided so far are not very expressive, and even intuitively simple operations have not been formalized yet.

Motivated by successful applications of algebraic tools in access control [7, 24, 8, 25], our goal is to provide an expressive algebra over enterprise privacy policies together with its formal semantics, offering operators for combining and restricting policies, along with suitable algebraic laws that allow for a convenient policy management. We do this concretely for the IBM EPAL proposal. However, for a scientific paper it is desirable to avoid the lengthy XML syntax and use a corresponding abstract syntax presented in [2, 4] and known as E-P3P (which, like EPAL, is based on [17]).

To employ existing privacy policy enforcement mechanisms to our algebraic expressions, it is necessary to represent the results of the operators as a syntactically correct privacy policy again. While achieving this representation has been identified as a core property in previous work on algebras for access control policies [7], and also explored there in detail, achieving the same result for enterprise privacy policies as in EPAL seems rather involved because of the treatment of obligations, different policy scopes, default values as well as a sophisticated treatment of deny-rules. In fact, our analysis of the expressiveness of EPAL shows that EPAL is not closed under operations like conjunction and disjunction, hence the aforementioned representation can often not be achieved. To circumvent this problem, we identify the set of well-founded policies, which constitutes a subset of all EPAL policies, for which we can give a constructive algorithm that represents the results of our algebraic operations as a well-founded EPAL policy again.

The first operators we define are policy conjunction and disjunction, which serve as the basic building blocks for constructing larger policies. For instance, an enterprise might first take all applicable regulations and combine them into a minimum policy by means of the conjunction operator. A general promise made to the customers, e.g., an existing P3P translated into the more general language, may be a further input. As one expects, these operators are not a simple logical AND respectively OR for expressive enterprise privacy policies for the reasons depicted above. We show that these operators enjoy the expected algebraic laws like associativity or distributivity. Our third operator – scoping – allows for confining the scope of a policy to sub-hierarchies of a policy. This is of major use in practice as it enables managing respectively reasoning about privacy requirements that involve only certain parts of an organization.

We further sketch some extensions of our algebra; in particular, we incorporate the sequential composition of privacy policies, which has been introduced in [4], and we explore its relationship to our remaining operators.

Further related literature. Policy composition has been treated before, in particular for access control [7, 8, 10, 19, 15, 26], systems management [20], separation-of-duty [23, 13], or IPSEC [12]. The algebra discussed below is clearly motivated by existing work on algebras for access control polices [7, 24, 8, 25]. We are not aware of a similar proposal for privacy policies although certain aspects have been addressed before, e.g., [18] points out possible conflicts if EPAL policies from different origins have to be dealt with. The publication closest to our algebra of privacy policies is [4], which introduces a notion of sequential composition of privacy policies as well as the notion of policy refinement. The present paper tries to extend this pool of algebraic tools. Compared with existing access-control languages, the core contribution of new privacy-policy languages [11, 17, 16] is the notion of purpose and purpose-bound collection of data, which is essential to privacy legislation. Other necessary features that prevent enterprises from simply using their existing access-control systems and the corresponding algebras are obligations and conditions on context information. Individually, these features were also considered in literature on access control, e.g., purpose hierarchies in [6], obligations in [5, 14, 22], and conditions on context information in [26].

2   Syntax and Semantics of E-P3P Enterprise Privacy Policies

Informally speaking, the aim of a privacy policy is to define by whom, for which purposes, and in which way collected data can be accessed. Further on, a privacy policy may impose obligations onto the organization using the data. Privacy policies formalize privacy statements like "we use data of a minor for marketing purposes only if the parent has given consent" or "medical data can only be read by the patient's primary care physician". This section mainly recalls the abstract syntax and semantics E-P3P [2, 4] of IBM's EPAL privacy policy language [1] up to some augmentations needed to achieve the desired algebraic properties, e.g., that obligations are already structured in a suitable way. Motivated by recent changes in EPAL, our specification of E-P3P deviates from the one in [4] in the handling of so-called "don't care" rulings: In analogy to EPAL 1.2, we only allow the default ruling to return a "don't care", and we demand that no obligations may be imposed in this case.

2.1 Hierarchies, Obligations, and Conditions

First, we recall the basic notions of hierarchies, obligations, and conditions used in E-P3P, and operations on them as needed in later refinements and operators of our algebra. For conveniently specifying rules, the data, users, etc. are categorized in E-P3P as in many access-control languages. The same applies to the purposes. To allow for structured rules with exceptions, categories are ordered in hierarchies; mathematically they are forests, i.e., multiple trees. For example, a user "company" may group several "departments", each containing several "employees". The enterprise can then write rules for the whole "company" with exceptions for some "departments".

Definition 1 (Hierarchy). *A hierarchy is pair $(H, >_H)$ of a finite set H and a transitive, non-reflexive relation $>_H \subseteq H \times H$, where every $h \in H$ has at most one immediate predecessor (parent). As usual we write $\geq_H$ for the reflexive closure.*
For two hierarchies $(H, >_H)$ and $(G, >_G)$, we define

$$(H, >_H) \subseteq (G, >_G) :\Leftrightarrow (H \subseteq G) \wedge (>_H \subseteq >_G);$$
$$(H, >_H) \cup (G, >_G) := (H \cup G, (>_H \cup >_G)^*);$$

where $*$ denotes the transitive closure. Note that a hierarchy union is not always a hierarchy again.   ◇

As mentioned above already, E-P3P policies can impose obligations, i.e., duties for an organization/enterprise. Typical examples are to send a notification to the data subject after each emergency access to medical data, or to delete data within a certain time limit. Obligations are not structured in hierarchies, but by an implication relation. E.g., an obligation to delete data within 30 days implies that the data is deleted within 2 months. The overall obligations of a rule in E-P3P are expressed as sets of individual obligations which must have an interpretation in the application domain. As multiple obligations may imply more than each one individually, the implication relation (which must also be realized in the application domain) is specified on these sets of obligations. We also define how this relation interacts with vocabulary extensions.

Definition 2 (Obligation Model). *An obligation model is a pair $(O, \rightarrow_O)$ of a set O and a transitive relation $\rightarrow_O \subseteq \mathfrak{P}(O) \times \mathfrak{P}(O)$, spoken implies, on the powerset of O, where $\bar{o}_1 \rightarrow_O \bar{o}_2$ for all $\bar{o}_2 \subseteq \bar{o}_1$, i.e., fulfilling a set of obligations implies fulfilling all subsets. For $O' \supset \mathfrak{P}(O)$, we extend the implication to $O' \times \mathfrak{P}(O)$ by $((\bar{o}_1 \rightarrow_O \bar{o}_2) :\Leftrightarrow (\bar{o}_1 \cap O \rightarrow_O \bar{o}_2))$.*
For defining the AND and OR-composition of privacy policies in a meaningful way, we moreover assume that $\mathfrak{P}(O)$ is equipped with an additional operation $\vee$, such that $(\mathfrak{P}(O), \vee, \cup)$ is a distributive lattice; the operator $\vee$ reflects the intuitive notion of OR (in analogy to the set-theoretical union $\cup$ which corresponds to AND). In particular, we require the following:

- *for all $\bar{o}_1, \bar{o}_2 \subseteq O$ we have $\bar{o}_1 \rightarrow_O (\bar{o}_1 \vee \bar{o}_2)$*
- *for all $\bar{o}_1, \bar{o}_2, \bar{o}'_1, \bar{o}'_2 \subseteq O$ we have $(\bar{o}_1 \rightarrow_O \bar{o}_2) \wedge (\bar{o}'_1 \rightarrow_O \bar{o}'_2)$ implies both $(\bar{o}_1 \vee \bar{o}'_1) \rightarrow_O (\bar{o}_2 \vee \bar{o}'_2)$ and $(\bar{o}_1 \cup \bar{o}'_1) \rightarrow_O (\bar{o}_2 \cup \bar{o}'_2)$.*

Finally, we assume that all occurring obligation models $(O, \rightarrow_O)$ *are subsets of a fixed (super) obligation model* $OM_0 = (O_0, \rightarrow_{O_0})$ *such that* $\rightarrow_O$ *is the restriction of* $\rightarrow_{O_0}$ *to* $\mathfrak{P}(O) \times \mathfrak{P}(O)$. $\diamond$

The decision formalized by a privacy policy can depend on context data like the age of a person. In EPAL this is represented by conditions over data in so-called containers [1]. The XML representation of the formulas is taken from [26], which corresponds to a predicate logic without quantifiers. In the abstract syntax in [2], conditions are abstracted into propositional logic, which is too coarse for our purposes. Hence, as in in [4] we use an extension of E-P3P formalizing the containers as a set of variables with domains and the conditions as formulas over these variables.

Definition 3 (Condition Vocabulary). *A* condition vocabulary *is a pair* $Var = (V, Scope)$ *of a finite set* V *and a function assigning every* $x \in V$, *called a* variable, *a set* $Scope(x)$, *called its* scope.

Two condition vocabularies $Var_1 = (V_1, Scope_1)$, $Var_2 = (V_2, Scope_2)$ *are compatible if* $Scope_1(x) = Scope_2(x)$ *for all* $x \in V_1 \cap V_2$. *For that case, we define their* union *by* $Var_1 \cup Var_2 := (V_1 \cup V_2, Scope_1 \cup Scope_2)$. $\diamond$

One may think of extending this to a full signature in the sense of logic, i.e., including predicate and function symbols – in EPAL, this is hidden in user-defined functions that may occur in the XACML conditions. For the moment, we assume a given universe of predicates and functions with fixed domains and semantics.

Definition 4 (Condition Language). *Let a condition vocabulary* $Var = (V, Scope)$ *be given.*

- *The* condition language $C(Var)$ *is the set of correctly typed formulas over* V *using the assumed universe of predicates and functions, and in the given syntax of predicate logic without quantifiers.*
- *An* assignment *of the variables is a function* $\chi: V \rightarrow \bigcup_{x \in V} Scope(x)$ *with* $\chi(x) \in Scope(x)$ *for all* $x \in V$. *The set of all assignments for the set* Var *is written* $\mathfrak{Ass}(Var)$.
- *For* $\chi \in \mathfrak{Ass}(Var)$, *let* $eval_\chi: C(Var) \rightarrow \{true, false\}$ *denote the evaluation function for conditions given this variable assignment. This is defined by the underlying logic and the assumption that all predicate and function symbols come with a fixed semantics.*
- *For* $\chi \in \mathfrak{Ass}(Var)$, *we denote by* $c_\chi \in C(Var)$ *some fixed formula such that* $eval_\chi(c_\chi) = true$ *and* $eval_{\chi'}(c_\chi) = false$ *for all* $\chi' \in \mathfrak{Ass}(Var) \setminus \{\chi\}$. $\diamond$

We do not consider partial assignments as is done in [4] since they do not occur in EPAL 1.2 any more.

2.2 Syntax of E-P3P Policies

An E-P3P policy is a triple of a vocabulary, a set of authorization rules, and a default ruling. The vocabulary defines element hierarchies for data, purposes, users, and actions, as well as the obligation model and the condition vocabulary. Data, users, and actions are as in most access-control policies (except that users are typically called "subjects" there, which in privacy would lead to confusion with data subjects), and purposes are an important additional hierarchy for the purpose binding of collected data.

Definition 5 (Vocabulary). *A* vocabulary *is a tuple* $Voc = (UH, DH, PH, AH, Var, OM)$ *where* UH, DH, PH, *and* AH *are hierarchies called user, data, purpose, and action hierarchy, respectively, and* Var *is a condition vocabulary and* OM *an obligation model.* $\diamond$

As a naming convention, we assume that the components of a vocabulary Voc are always called as in Definition 5 with $UH = (U, >_U)$, $DH = (D, >_D)$, $PH = (P, >_P)$, $AH = (A, >_A)$, $Var = (V, Scope)$, and $OM = (O, \rightarrow_O)$, except if explicitly stated otherwise. In a vocabulary Voc_i all components also get a subscript i, and similarly for superscripts. Differing from [4] we require that a set of authorization rules (short *ruleset*) only contains authorization rules that allow or deny an operation, i.e., we do not allow rules which yield a "don't care" ruling. This reflects the latest version of EPAL. Further on, motivated by EPAL's implicit handling of precedences through the textual order of the rules, we call a privacy policy *well-formed* if rules which allow for contradicting rulings do not have identical precedences (actually, in EPAL two rules can *never* have identical precedences).

Definition 6 (Ruleset and Privacy Policy). *A* ruleset *for a vocabulary* Voc *is a subset of* $\mathbb{Z} \times U \times D \times P \times A \times C(Var) \times \mathfrak{P}(O) \times \{+, -\}$.

A privacy policy *or* E-P3P *policy is a triple* (Voc, R, dr) *of a vocabulary* Voc, *a rule-set* R *for* Voc, *and a* default ruling $dr \in \{+, \circ, -\}$. *The set of these policies is called* EP3P, *and the subset for a given vocabulary* $EP3P(Voc)$. *Moreover, we call* $(Voc, R, dr) \in EP3P$ *well-formed, if for all rules* $(i, u, d, p, a, c, \bar{o}, r), (i, u', d', p', a', c', \bar{o}', r') \in R$ *with identical precedences and for all assignments* $\chi \in \mathfrak{Ass}(Var)$ *the implication* $(eval_\chi(c) = true = eval_\chi(c')) \Rightarrow (r = r')$ *holds.* $\diamond$

The rulings $+$, $\circ$, and $-$ mean "allow", "don't care", and "deny"; the value $\circ$ is special in the sense, that it can only be assigned to the default ruling of a policy. As a naming convention, we assume that the components of a privacy policy called Pol are always called as in Definition 6, and if Pol has a sub- or superscript, then so do the components.

2.3 Semantics of E-P3P Policies

An E-P3P request is a tuple (u, d, p, a) which should belong to the set $U \times D \times P \times A$ for the given vocabulary. Note that E-P3P and EPAL requests are not restricted to "ground terms" as in some other languages, i.e., minimal elements in the hierarchies. This is useful if one starts with coarse policies and refines them because elements that are initially minimal may later get children. For instance, the individual users in a "department" of an "enterprise" may not be mentioned in the CPO's privacy policy, but in the department's privacy policy. For similar reasons, we also define the semantics for requests outside the given vocabulary. We assume a superset S in which all hierarchy sets are embedded; in practice it is typically a set of strings or valid XML expressions.

Definition 7 (Request). *For a vocabulary Voc, we define the set of* valid requests *as* $Req(Voc) := U \times D \times P \times A$. *Given a superset $\mathcal{S}$ of the sets U, D, P, A of all considered vocabularies, the set of* all requests *is $Req := \mathcal{S}^4$.*

For valid requests $(u, d, p, a), (u', d', p', a') \in Req(Voc)$ we set

$$(u, d, p, a) \leq (u', d', p', a') :\Leftrightarrow u \leq_U u' \text{ and } d \leq_D d' \text{ and } p \leq_P p' \text{ and } a \leq_A a'.$$

Moreover, we set $(u, d, p, a) <_1 (u', d', p', a')$ if and only if there is exactly one $x \in \{u, d, p, a\}$ such that x' is the parent of x and for all $y \in \{u, d, p, a\} \setminus \{x\}$ we have $y = y'$. Finally, we refer to a valid request $(u, d, p, a) \in Req(Voc)$ as leaf or leaf node *if u, d, p, and a are leaves in the respective hierarchy. We denote the set of all leaves of $Req(Voc)$ by $L(Voc)$ and for $q \in Req(Voc)$, we set $L(q, Voc) := \{q' \in L(Voc) \mid q' \leq q\} \setminus \{q\}$.* ◇

The semantics of a privacy policy Pol is a function $eval_{Pol}$ that processes a request based on a given assignment. The evaluation result is a pair $(r, \bar{o})$ of a ruling (also called *decision*) and associated obligations; in the case of a "don't care"-ruling ($r = \circ$) we necessarily have $\bar{o} = \emptyset$, i.e., no obligations are imposed in this case. Our semantics follows the E-P3P semantics in [4], but we restrict our definition to the (from the practical point of view most relevant) case of well-formed policies, which simply avoids a separate treatment of conflicts among rules. We further permit the exceptional ruling *scope_error* which indicates that a request was out of the scope of the policy.

The semantics is defined by a virtual pre-processing that unfolds the hierarchies followed by a request processing stage. We stress that this is only a compact definition of the semantics and not an efficient real evaluation algorithm.

Definition 8 (Unfolded Rules). *For a privacy policy $Pol = (Voc, R, dr)$, the* unfolded rule set $UR(Pol)$ *is defined as follows:*

$$URD(Pol) := \{(i, u', d', p', a', c, \bar{o}, r) \in R \mid \exists (i, u, d, p, a, c, \bar{o}, r) \in R$$
$$\text{with } u \geq_U u' \wedge d \geq_D d' \wedge p \geq_P p' \wedge a \geq_A a'\};$$
$$UR(Pol) := URD(Pol)$$
$$\cup \{(i, u', d', p', a', c, \bar{o}, -) \in R \mid \exists (i, u, d, p, a, c, \bar{o}, -) \in URD(Pol)$$
$$\text{with } u' \geq_U u \wedge d' \geq_D d \wedge p' \geq_P p \wedge a' \geq_A a\}. \quad ◇$$

A crucial point in this definition is the fact that "deny"-rules are inherited both downwards and upwards along the four hierarchies while "allow"-rules are inherited downwards only. The reason is that the hierarchies are considered groupings: If access is forbidden for some element of a group, it is also forbidden for the group as a whole.

Next, we define which rules are applicable for a request given an assignment of the condition variables. These (unfolded) rules have the user, data, purpose, and action as in the request, and we make

Definition 9 (Applicable Rules). *Let a privacy policy $Pol = (Voc, R, dr)$, a request $q = (u, d, p, a) \in Req(Voc)$, and an assignment $\chi \in \mathfrak{Ass}(Var)$ be given. Then the set of* applicable rules *is*

$$AR(Pol, q, \chi) := \{(i, u, d, p, a, c, \bar{o}, r) \in UR(Pol) \mid eval_\chi(c) = true\}. \quad ◇$$

To formulate the semantics, it is convenient to define the maximum and minimum precedence of a policy.

Definition 10 (Precedence Range). *For a privacy policy* $Pol = (Voc, R, dr)$, *let* $max(Pol) := \max\{i \mid \exists(i, u, d, p, a, c, \bar{o}, r) \in R\}$ *and* $min(Pol) := \min\{i \mid \exists(i, u, d, p, a, c, \bar{o}, r) \in R\}$. $\diamond$

We can now define the actual semantics, i.e., the result of a request given an assignment:

Definition 11 (Semantics). *Let a well-formed privacy policy* $Pol = (Voc, R, dr)$, *a request* $q = (u, d, p, a) \in Req$, *and an assignment* $\chi \in \mathfrak{Ass}(Var)$ *be given. Then the evaluation result* $(r, \bar{o}) := eval_{Pol}(q, \chi)$ *of policy* Pol *for* q *and* χ *is defined by the following algorithm, where every "return" is understood to abort the processing of the algorithm.*

1. Out-of-scope testing. *If* $q \notin Req(Voc)$, *return* $(r, \bar{o}) := (scope\_error, \emptyset)$.
2. Processing by precedence. *For each precedence level* $i := max(Pol)$ *down to* $min(Pol)$:
   - Accumulate obligations. $\bar{o}_{acc} := \bigcup_{(i, u, d, p, a, c, \bar{o}, r) \in AR(Pol, q, \chi)} \bar{o}$
   - Normal ruling. *If some rule* $(i, u, d, p, a, c, \bar{o}, r) \in AR(Pol, q, \chi)$ *exists, return* $(r, \bar{o}_{acc})$.
3. Default ruling. *If this step is reached, return* $(r, \bar{o}) := (dr, \emptyset)$.

We also say that policy Pol *rules* $(r, \bar{o})$ *for* q *and* χ, *omitting* q *and* χ *if they are clear from the context.* $\diamond$

2.4   Refinement and Equivalence of Well-Formed Privacy Policies

Basically, refining a policy Pol means adding more details to it, i.e., enriching the vocabulary and/or the set of rules without changing the meaning of the policy with respect to its original vocabulary. To be useful for actual use cases, it is essential that operators defined on privacy policies behave in a well-specified and an "intuitive" manner with respect to refinement relations. Thus, before we can make concrete statements about the refinement properties of the operators introduced in the next section, we need some additional terminology, and end this section with recalling some definitions from [4].

Definition 12 (Compatible Vocabulary). *Two vocabularies* Voc_1 *and* Voc_2 *are compatible if their condition vocabularies are compatible and* $UH_1 \cup UH_2, DH_1 \cup DH_2, PH_1 \cup PH_2, AH_1 \cup AH_2$ *are hierarchies again.* $\diamond$

The notion of compatible vocabularies is a technicality that turns out to be necessary to specify operations that combine different policies which are not necessarily formulated in terms of identical vocabularies, and this leads to

Definition 13 (Union of Vocabularies). *The* union *of two compatible vocabularies* Voc_1 *and* Voc_2 *is defined as* $Voc_1 \cup Voc_2 := (UH_1 \cup UH_2, DH_1 \cup DH_2, PH_1 \cup PH_2, AH_1 \cup AH_2, Var_1 \cup Var_2, OM)$, *where* $OM = (O, \rightarrow_O)$ *is the obligation model with the lattice* $(\mathfrak{P}(O), \vee, \cup)$ *being generated by* $\mathfrak{P}(O_1)$ *and* $\mathfrak{P}(O_2)$, *and* $\rightarrow_O$ *being the restriction of* $\rightarrow_{O_0}$ *to* $\mathfrak{P}(O) \times \mathfrak{P}(O)$. $\diamond$

Next, we need the refinement of obligations whose definition requires some care, as a refined policy may well contain additional obligations, whereas at the same time some others have been omitted. As consequence of this observation, the definition of refinement of obligations makes use of both obligation models, that of the original (coarser) policy and that of the refined policy:

Definition 14 (Refinement and Equivalence of Obligations). *Let two obligation models* $(O_i, \rightarrow_{O_i})$ *and* $\bar{o}_i \subseteq O_i$ *for* $i = 1, 2$ *be given. Then* $\bar{o}_2$ *is a* refinement *of* $\bar{o}_1$*, written* $\bar{o}_2 \prec \bar{o}_1$ *if and only if the following holds:*

$$\exists \bar{o} \subseteq O_1 \cap O_2 : \bar{o}_2 \rightarrow_{O_2} \bar{o} \rightarrow_{O_1} \bar{o}_1.$$

We call $\bar{o}_1$ *and* $\bar{o}_2$ equivalent, *written* $\bar{o}_1 \equiv \bar{o}_2$, *if and only if* $\bar{o}_1 \prec \bar{o}_2$ *and* $\bar{o}_2 \prec \bar{o}_1$. *For* $r_1, r_2 \in \{+, -, \circ, scope\_error\}$, *we further define* $(r_1, \bar{o}_1) \equiv (r_2, \bar{o}_2)$ *if and only if* $r_1 = r_2$ *and* $\bar{o}_1 \equiv \bar{o}_2$. ◇

We can now formalize the notion of (weak) refinement of well-formed policies. Our definition of refinement closely resembles the one presented in [4], but it excludes partial assignments and conflict errors, which are not supported by the latest EPAL version. The notion of weak refinement has not been introduced before.

Definition 15 (Policy Refinement). *Let two well-formed privacy policies* $Pol_i = (Voc_i, R_i, dr_i)$ *for* $i = 1, 2$ *with compatible vocabularies be given, and set* $Pol_i^* = (Voc_i^*, R_i, dr_i)$ *for* $i = 1, 2$ *where* $Voc_i^* := (UH_1 \cup UH_2, DH_1 \cup DH_2, PH_1 \cup PH_2, AH_1 \cup AH_2, Var_i, OM_i)$.
  Let $r_1, r_2 \in \{+, -, \circ, scope\_error\}$ *and* $\bar{o}_i \subseteq O_i$ *for* $i = 1, 2$ *be arbitrary. We say that* $(r_2, \bar{o}_2)$ refines $(r_1, \bar{o}_1)$ *(in* OM_1 *and* OM_2*), written* $(r_2, \bar{o}_2) \prec (r_1, \bar{o}_1)$, *if and only if one of the following two conditions holds*

  (1) $(r_1, \bar{o}_1) \in \{(scope\_error, \emptyset), (\circ, \emptyset)\}$ (2) $r_1 \in \{+, -\}, r_2 = r_1, \bar{o}_2 \prec \bar{o}_1$.

We say that $(r_2, \bar{o}_2)$ weakly refines $(r_1, \bar{o}_1)$ *(in* OM_1 *and* OM_2*), written* $(r_2, \bar{o}_2) \tilde{\prec} (r_1, \bar{o}_1)$, *if and only if one of the following three conditions holds:*

  (1) $(r_2, \bar{o}_2) \prec (r_1, \bar{o}_1)$ (2) $r_1 = +, r_2 = -$ (3) $(r_1, \bar{o}_1) = (+, \emptyset), r_2 = \circ$.

We call Pol_2 *a* refinement *of* Pol_1*, written* $Pol_2 \prec Pol_1$ *if and only if for every assignment* $\chi \in \mathfrak{Ass}(Var_1 \cup Var_2)$ *and every authorization request* $q \in Req$, *we have* $eval_{Pol_2^*}(q, \chi) \prec eval_{Pol_1^*}(q, \chi)$. *We call* Pol_2 *a* weak refinement *of* Pol_1 *if the same holds with* $\prec$ *replaced by* $\tilde{\prec}$. ◇

Intuitively, a privacy policy that weakly refines another policy is at least as restrictive as the coarser one: Even if the original policy rules "allow" for a certain request, after a weak refinement the same request may be denied, or – provided that no obligations get lost – an "allow" can be transformed into a "don't care".
  Finally, the equivalence of two well-formed privacy policies is defined in the obvious manner:

Definition 16 (Policy Equivalence). *Two well-formed privacy policies Pol_1 and Pol_2 are called* equivalent, *written $Pol_1 \equiv Pol_2$, if and only if they are mutual refinements, i.e., $Pol_1 \equiv Pol_2 :\Leftrightarrow (Pol_1 \prec Pol_2 \wedge Pol_2 \prec Pol_1)$.* $\diamond$

While this notion of policy equivalence is rather intuitive, it turns out that in some situations only a weaker form of equivalence can be achieved, and we therefore conclude this section with the definition of weak policy equivalence.

Definition 17 (Weak Policy Equivalence). *Two well-formed privacy policies Pol_1 and Pol_2 are called* weakly equivalent, *written $Pol_1 \approx Pol_2$, if and only if they are equivalent on their joint vocabulary, i.e., if and only if $(Voc_1 \cup Voc_2, R_1, dr_1) \equiv (Voc_1 \cup Voc_2, R_2, dr_2)$.* $\diamond$

3   Defining Operators

Basically, defining symmetric operations on privacy policies reflecting the intuitive notions of conjunction (AND) and disjunction (OR) looks rather simple. Unfortunately, with a straightforward yet intuitive approach it happens that the conjunction or disjunction of two privacy policies might no longer constitute a syntactically correct privacy policy. From a practical point of view such a behavior is not desirable: First, available tools to enforce a(n EPAL) privacy policy are designed to handle privacy policies only. Thus, to handle compositions of privacy policies these tools had to be modified or new tools had to be developed. The obvious solution to this problem – making use of a wrapper program that queries several policies by means of existing tools and combines their results appropriately – is not always acceptable. In particular such a workaround might violate conditions that were necessary to pass some (expensive) certification process. Secondly, the combined privacy policies can originate in rather different sources which are separated though significant geographical distances. Consequently, in larger, say multinational, projects, where policies of many different organizations have to be combined, it can be infeasible or at least very inconvenient to store all (component) policies that contribute to the ruling of the composition.

To circumvent these problems, it is desirable to work in a subset of *EP3P* that is on the one hand closed under conjunction and disjunction as well as other suitable algebraic operations, and on the other hand is still expressive enough to capture typically used privacy policies. The following lemma, whose proof we omit due to lack of space, characterizes the expressiveness (and therewith also limits) of E-P3P policies.

Lemma 1 (Expressiveness of E-P3P). *Let Voc be a vocabulary and $\varphi \colon Req(Voc) \times \mathfrak{Ass}(Var) \to \{+, \circ, -\} \times \mathfrak{P}\{O\}$ be an arbitrary function. Then there exists a well-formed privacy policy $Pol = (Voc, R, dr)$ with $eval_{Pol}(q, \chi) = \varphi(q, \chi)$ for all $(q, \chi) \in Req(Voc) \times \mathfrak{Ass}(Var)$ if and only if for all valid requests $q \in Req(Voc)$ and all assignments $\chi \in \mathfrak{Ass}(Var)$, the following four conditions are satisfied:*

1. $\varphi(q, \chi) = (+, \bar{o}) \Rightarrow \forall q' \leq q : \varphi(q', \chi) = (+, \bar{o}')$ (possibly with $\bar{o}' \neq \bar{o}$).
2. $\varphi(q, \chi) = (-, \bar{o}) \Rightarrow \forall q' \geq q : \varphi(q', \chi) = (-, \bar{o}')$ (possibly with $\bar{o}' \neq \bar{o}$).

3. $\varphi(q, \chi) = (-, \bar{o})$ *implies that one of the following conditions holds:*
   (a) $q \in L(Voc)$,
   (b) $\exists q' <_1 q : \varphi(q', \chi) = (+, \bar{o}')$ *(possibly with $\bar{o}' \neq \bar{o}$)*,
   (c) $\exists C \subseteq \{q' <_1 q, \varphi(q', \chi) = (-, \bar{o}_{q'})\} : C \neq \emptyset \wedge \bar{o}' = \bigcup_{q' \in C} \bar{o}_{q'}$.
4. *If $\varphi(q, \chi) = (\circ, \bar{o})$, then $\bar{o} = \emptyset$.*   □

3.1   Conjunction, Disjunction and the Non-closedness of EPAL

Unlike in typical access control settings, for defining the conjunction and disjunction of privacy policies, we have to take care of the "don't care" ruling $\circ$, whose semantics is different from both "allow" and "deny". Motivated by the intuition behind the ruling $\circ$, we decided for definitions that are in analogy to the conjunction and disjunction in a three-valued Łukasiewicz logic Ł$_3$. To handle the obligations, we use the operator $\vee$ provided by the obligation model.

AND	$(+, \bar{o}')$	$(-, \bar{o}')$	$(\circ, \emptyset)$
$(+, \bar{o})$	$(+, \bar{o} \cup \bar{o}')$	$(-, \bar{o}')$	$(\circ, \emptyset)$
$(-, \bar{o})$	$(-, \bar{o})$	$(-, \bar{o} \cup \bar{o}')$	$(-, \bar{o})$
$(\circ, \emptyset)$	$(\circ, \emptyset)$	$(-, \bar{o}')$	$(\circ, \emptyset)$

OR	$(+, \bar{o}')$	$(-, \bar{o}')$	$(\circ, \emptyset)$
$(+, \bar{o})$	$(+, \bar{o} \vee \bar{o}')$	$(+, \bar{o})$	$(+, \bar{o})$
$(-, \bar{o})$	$(+, \bar{o}')$	$(-, \bar{o} \vee \bar{o}')$	$(\circ, \emptyset)$
$(\circ, \emptyset)$	$(+, \bar{o}')$	$(\circ, \emptyset)$	$(\circ, \emptyset)$

Intuitively, we do not want to give a positive answer to a request if one of the two policies that are to be combined by AND denies the access. Further on, if one policy allows the access, and the other one "does not care", then returning a "don't care" seems plausible and is indeed needed to ensure the distributivity of the operators AND and OR. Similarly, for OR we allow an access, if at least one of the two involved policies allows the request. Moreover, we "do not care", if one of the operands "does not care" – except if the other operand explicitly "allows" the request.

Lemma 2. *Fix some obligation model and denote by $(\mathfrak{P}(O), \vee, \cup)$ the corresponding lattice of obligations. Then $((\{+, -\} \times \mathfrak{P}(O)) \cup \{(\circ, \emptyset)\}, OR, AND)$ is a distributive lattice.*   □

We omit the proof of this and most of the subsequent lemmas due to space limitations and refer the reader to the long version of this paper [3].

The natural definition of conjunction of two privacy policies Pol_1 and Pol_2 would be that whenever Pol_i rules $(r_i, \bar{o}_i)$ for a given assignment and request, then the conjunction of Pol_1 and Pol_2 should yield $(r_1, \bar{o}_1)$ AND $(r_2, \bar{o}_2)$, and similar for disjunction. However, an easy corollary of Lemma 1 yields that such a policy is not necessarily a valid EPAL policy anymore, i.e., EPAL is neither closed under conjunction nor under disjunction given the above definitions.

Corollary 1 (Non-closedness of EPAL). *There exist policies Pol_1, Pol_2 such that for any policy Pol, we have that there exists an assignment $\chi \in \mathfrak{Ass}(Var_1 \cup Var_2)$ and a request $q \in Req(Voc_1 \cup Voc_2)$ such that $eval_{Pol}(q, \chi) \not\equiv eval_{Pol_1}(q, \chi)$ op $eval_{Pol_2}(q, \chi)$ where op $\in \{AND, OR\}$.*   □

Proof. For showing the statement for conjunction, we consider the policies depicted at the left-hand side of Figure 1. Let Pol_i for $i = 1, 2$ such that each of DH_i, PH_i, AH_i

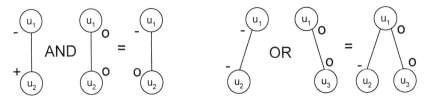

Fig. 1. Examples that EPAL is not closed under conjunction or disjunction.

consists of a single element, and let UH_i contain two elements u_1, u_2 such that u_1 is a parent of u_2. Further assume that the condition vocabulary and the obligation model are empty. The rules in Pol_1 allow user u_2 to access the data whereas u_1 is forbidden to do so. The rules in Pol_2 don't care for both users. The conjunction would then yield a policy in which u_1 is not allowed to access the data whereas the policy does not care for u_2. This immediately yields a contradiction to Lemma 1. The claim can be shown similarly for disjunction and the policies depicted at the right-hand side of Figure 1. ∎

It is is easy to see that adapting the definition of AND and OR in obvious ways (like redefining the occurrences of ○) does not solve this problem without violating other essential conditions, e.g., the distributivity of the operators. As a remedy we identify the subset of *well-founded* privacy policies in the next section, which allows for a very intuitive handling in terms of defining conjunction and disjunction of privacy policies. Actually, for practical cases, the restriction to those privacy policies is not really an obstacle, and in the next section we take a closer look at such policies.

3.2   Well-Founded Privacy Policies

The intuition underlying the notion of well-founded policies can be described as follows:

- Suppose the ruling specified for some group is "deny", but none of the group members is denied from accessing the respective data. Then this contradicts the idea that in EPAL the group ruling is to reflect ("to group") the rulings of the individual group members.
- If each member of a group is permitted to perform some action, then intuitively the group as a whole is permitted to perform this action, too.
- Assume that both the ruling specified for a group and for a member of this group is "allow", and assume further that the obligations of the group are not a superset of the obligations of the group member. Then the group member may be able to avoid certain obligations by submitting a query where the user is specified to be the group as a whole. Typically, the availability of such a "workaround" is not desirable. On the other hand, if the obligations of the group are stricter than the union of the obligations of the group members and we (re)define the group obligations to be the union of the individual obligations then no harm (in the sense that a group member can gain additional privileges) is caused by querying the group.

Formally, well-founded policies are captured as follows:

Definition 18 (Well-Founded Policy). *Let Pol be a well-formed policy. Then we call Pol well-founded if and only if for all $(q, \chi) \in Req(Voc) \times \mathfrak{Ass}(Var)$ the following conditions are fulfilled:*

- *If q is no leaf node and $eval_{Pol}(q, \chi) = (-, \bar{o})$, then there exists $q' <_1 q$ such that $eval_{Pol}(q', \chi) = (-, \bar{o}')$ for some $\bar{o}'$.*
- *If $eval_{Pol}(q', \chi) = (+, \bar{o}_{q'})$ for each $q' <_1 q$ and arbitrary $\bar{o}_{q'}$, then $eval_{Pol}(q, \chi) = (+, \bar{o})$ for some $\bar{o}$.*
- *If $eval_{Pol}(q, \chi) = (r, \bar{o})$, then $\bar{o} = \bigcup_{q' <_1 q, eval_{Pol}(q', \chi) = (r, \bar{o}')} \bar{o}'$.*   ◇

Up to equivalence, well-founded policies are already uniquely determined by the rulings of the leaf nodes:

Lemma 3. *Let Pol_1, Pol_2 be well-founded privacy policies with $Voc_1 = Voc_2$ and let $eval_{Pol_1}(q, \chi) = eval_{Pol_2}(q, \chi)$ for every $q \in L(Voc_1)$ and every $\chi \in \mathfrak{Ass}(Var_1)$. Then $Pol_1 \equiv Pol_2$.*   □

Actually, the predetermined allow and deny rulings for the set of leaf nodes can be chosen arbitrarily. The subsequent algorithm demonstrates how in principle a well-founded policy can explicitly be written down that is consistent with any predetermined set of rulings for all leaf nodes. Note however that the algorithm does not aim at generating small policies; optimizing it for practical purposes is considered as future work.

Input: • a vocabulary Voc and
  • a ruling $(r_{q,\chi}, \bar{o}_{q,\chi}) \in (\{+, -\} \times \mathfrak{P}(O)) \cup \{(\circ, \emptyset)\}$
    for all $q \in L(Voc), \chi \in \mathfrak{Ass}(Var)$.
Output: a well-founded privacy policy $Pol = (Voc, R, dr)$ such that for all
  $q \in L(Voc), \chi \in \mathfrak{Ass}(Var)$ the equality $eval_{Pol}(q, \chi) = (r_{q,\chi}, \bar{o}_{q,\chi})$ holds.

```
/* Assign identical precedences to leaf rulings different from (○, ∅) */
R := ∅
for each q := (u, d, p, a) ∈ L(Voc)
    if (r_{q,χ}, ō_{q,χ}) ≠ (○, ∅)
        then R := R ∪ {(0, u, d, p, a, c_χ, ō_{q,χ}, r_{q,χ})}              (1)
    end if
end for


/* Insert missing positive rulings with low precedence */
for each χ ∈ 𝔄ss(Var) and each q := (u, d, p, a) ∈ Req(Voc) do
    if r_{q',χ} = + for all q' ∈ L(q, Voc)
        then R := R ∪ {(i, u, d, p, a, c_χ, ⋃_{q'∈L(q,Voc)} ō_{q',χ})}      (2)
            such that i < i'
            for all (i', u', d', p', a', c', +, ō') ∈ R : q > (u', d', p', a')
    end if
end for


return (Voc, R, ○)
```

Lemma 4. *The above algorithm is totally correct, i.e., it terminates and for inputs as specified in the algorithm, it computes a policy as specified in the output description.* □

3.3   Conjunction and Disjunction of Privacy Policies

We now define the conjunction and disjunction of two well-founded privacy policies. From Lemma 3 we know that it is sufficient to define the operations for those requests that are leaves of the considered hierarchies since once the evaluations on the leaves are fixed, the corresponding privacy policy is, up to equivalence, uniquely determined. With the algorithm in Section 3.2 we can then explicitly compute a policy that is consistent with the given evaluations of the leaf nodes. However, to make definitions of the operators independent of an algorithmic specification, we will formulate the actual definitions in such a way that the result of a conjunction/disjunction of two privacy policies constitutes an equivalence class of policies – not a specific privacy policy. For practical purposes this is not really a problem as we can, e.g., use the algorithm from Section 3.2 to derive a concrete policy from the equivalence class.

The motivation for defining an AND operation on privacy policies is rather straightforward: Assume that an enterprise takes part in some project for which data has to be accessed and processed that is controlled by some external project partner. Then the access to and processing of such data shall only be allowed, if none of the individual privacy policies of the participating enterprises is violated.

Definition 19 (Policy Conjunction). *Let Pol_1, Pol_2 be two well-founded privacy policies such that $Pol_i^* = (Voc_i^*, R_i, dr_i)$ for $i = 1, 2$ with $Voc_i^* := (UH_1 \cup UH_2, DH_1 \cup DH_2, PH_1 \cup PH_2, AH_1 \cup AH_2, Var_i, OM_i)$ are also well-founded privacy policies.*

Then the conjunction of Pol_1 and Pol_2, is the equivalence class (w.r.t. $\equiv$) of all well-founded privacy policies Pol on the joint vocabulary $Voc := Voc_1 \cup Voc_2$ such that for all leaf nodes $q \in L(Voc)$ and for all assignments $\chi \in \mathfrak{Ass}(Var)$ we have $(r_1, \bar{o}_1) \equiv (r_2, \bar{o}_2)$, where

$$(r_1, \bar{o}_1) := eval_{Pol}(q, \chi) \text{ and}$$
$$(r_2, \bar{o}_2) := eval_{Pol_1^*}(q, \chi) \text{ AND } eval_{Pol_2^*}(q, \chi).$$

By $Pol_1 \& Pol_2$ we denote any representative of this equivalence class (which can, e.g., be computed by means of the algorithm in Section 3.2).   ◇

Note that this definition only imposes conditions on the leaf nodes, hence the question arises to what extent "inner" queries obey the defining table for AND, too. Indeed, the desired relations are fulfilled for arbitrary queries:

Lemma 5. *Let Pol_1, Pol_2 be well-founded privacy policies that satisfy the requirements of Definition 19 and let $Pol = Pol_1 \& Pol_2$. Then for all requests $q \in Req(Voc)$ and for all assignments $\chi \in \mathfrak{Ass}(Var)$ we have the equivalence $eval_{Pol}(q, \chi) \equiv eval_{Pol_1^*}(q, \chi) \text{ AND } eval_{Pol_2^*}(q, \chi)$ with Pol_i^* as in Definition 19.*   □

Similar to conjunction, the disjunction of privacy policies is essential for a variety of use cases. For example, consider two departments of an enterprise that cooperate in some project. For carrying out this project, it should then be possible to access data items whenever one of the individual privacy policies of the two departments grants such an access. This idea of "joining forces" is captured by the following definition.

Definition 20 (Policy Disjunction). *Let Pol_1, Pol_2 be two well-founded privacy policies such that $Pol_i^* = (Voc_i^*, R_i, dr_i)$ for $i = 1, 2$ with $Voc_i^* := (UH_1 \cup UH_2, DH_1 \cup DH_2, PH_1 \cup PH_2, AH_1 \cup AH_2, Var_i, OM_i)$ are also well-founded privacy policies.*

Then the disjunction *of Pol_1 and Pol_2 is the equivalence class (w. r. t. $\equiv$) of all well-founded privacy policies Pol on the joint vocabulary $Voc := Voc_1 \cup Voc_2$ such that for all leaf nodes $q \in L(Voc)$ and for all assignments $\chi \in \mathfrak{Ass}(Var)$ we have $(r_1, \bar{o}_1) \equiv (r_2, \bar{o}_2)$ where*

$$(r_1, \bar{o}_1) := eval_{Pol}(q, \chi) \text{ and}$$
$$(r_2, \bar{o}_2) := eval_{Pol_1^*}(q, \chi) \text{ OR } eval_{Pol_2^*}(q, \chi).$$

By $Pol_1 + Pol_2$ we denote any representative of this equivalence class (which can, e.g., be computed by means of the algorithm in Section 3.2). ◇

Unfortunately, for the disjunction of privacy policies, we have no analogue to Lemma 5, i.e., in general we cannot achieve an equivalence of the form $eval_{Pol}(q, \chi) \equiv eval_{Pol_1^*}(q, \chi) \text{ OR } eval_{Pol_2^*}(q, \chi)$ for arbitrary requests q and assignments χ. In fact, it is not difficult to construct examples where imposing such a "node-wise equivalence" yields a contradiction to well-foundedness. Fortunately, also for the "inner nodes" the policy obtained by disjunction is still rather close to what one would expect intuitively:

Lemma 6. *Let Pol_1, Pol_2 be well-founded privacy policies that satisfy the requirements of Definition 19 and let $Pol = Pol_1 + Pol_2$. Then for all $q \in Req(Voc)$ such that $eval_{Pol}(q, \chi) = (-, \bar{o})$ or $eval_{Pol_1^*}(q, \chi) \text{ OR } eval_{Pol_2^*}(q, \chi) = (+, \bar{o})$ holds for some $\bar{o}$, we have $eval_{Pol_1^*}(q, \chi) \text{ OR } eval_{Pol_2^*}(q, \chi) \prec eval_{Pol}(q, \chi)$.* □

3.4 Scoping of a Privacy Policy

One of the most desirable operations in practice is to restrict the scope of a policy, i.e., to restrict large policies to smaller parts. Examples for this so-called *scoping* are omnipresent in practical policy management, e.g., deriving a department's privacy policy from the enterprise's global privacy policy, or considering only those rules that specifically deal with marketing purposes. Formally, we define the following scoping operator:

Definition 21 (Scoping). *Let Pol be a well-founded privacy policy and let $V := (UH', DH', PH', AH')$ where $UH', DH', PH',$ and AH' are arbitrary subhierarchies of UH, DH, PH, AH, respectively.*

Then the scoping *of Pol with respect to V is the equivalence class (with respect to $\equiv$) of all well-founded privacy policies Pol' on the vocabulary $Voc' := (UH', DH', PH', AH', Var, OM)$ such that for all leaves $q \in L(Voc')$ and for all assignments $\chi \in \mathfrak{Ass}(Var)$ we have*

$$eval_{Pol'}(q, \chi) \equiv eval_{Pol}(q, \chi).$$

By $Pol|_V$ we denote any representative of this equivalence class (which can, e.g., be computed by means of the algorithm specified in Section 3.2). ◇

Ideally, scoping would yield a privacy policy such that not only for the leaf nodes, but also for the "inner" requests we always obtain equivalent rulings from Pol and $Pol|_V$. However, in general this contradicts the well-foundedness of the privacy policy derived via scoping unless additional assumptions on the considered hierarchies are imposed:

Example 1. Consider a well-founded privacy policy Pol such that each of DH, PH, AH consists of a single element. For the sake of simplicity assume that the condition vocabulary is empty, and let UH contain three users u_0, u_1, u_2. The rules in Pol allow user u_1 to access the data with obligations $\bar{o}_1$, and user u_2 can access the data with obligations $\bar{o}_2$. Finally the "superuser" u_0 – the parent of u_1 and u_2 in the user hierarchy UH – can access the data with obligations $\bar{o}_1 \cup \bar{o}_2$ to ensure the well-foundedness of Pol. If we scope this policy w. r. t., $(\{u_0, u_1\}, DH, PH, AH)$, then user u_1 can still access the data with obligations $\bar{o}_1$, but due to the well-foundedness of $Pol|_{(\{u_0,u_1\}, DH,PH,AH)}$, now the superuser u_0 can also access the data with obligations $\bar{o}_1$, in other words the obligations $\bar{o}_2$ are "lost".

However, even without imposing additional constraints on the considered hierarchies, we can exploit the well-foundedness of the policies to establish the following lemma:

Lemma 7. *Let Pol be a well-founded privacy policy with vocabulary Voc and $V :=$ (UH', DH', PH', AH') a tuple of subhierarchies of UH, DH, PH, AH, respectively. Then $Pol \tilde{\prec} Pol|_V$.* $\qquad\square$

In dependence on the precise kind of scoping considered, even stronger preservation properties can be proven, e.g., if the scoped policy is well-founded again then we obtain equivalent rulings also for inner requests. This is the case if we for instance apply a scoping operation under which the leaf requests are invariant, i.e., if the considered vocabularies are non-appending. Albeit this looks rather restrictive from a theoretical point of view, for the kind of scoping needed in practice – say extracting a department's privacy policy from an enterprise's privacy policy – this requirement is often met.

Lemma 8. *Let Pol be a well-founded privacy policy, and $V := (UH', DH', PH', AH')$ a tuple of subhierarchies of UH, DH, PH, AH, respectively, such that for $Voc' := (UH', DH', PH', AH', Var, OM)$ and all $q \in Req(Voc')$, we have $L(q, Voc) = L(q, Voc')$. Then for all $q \in Req(Voc')$ and for all assignments $\chi \in \mathfrak{Ass}(Var)$ we have $eval_{Pol}(q, \chi) \equiv eval_{Pol|_V}(q, \chi)$.* $\qquad\square$

3.5   Further Extensions of the Algebra

There are certainly further operators one would like to add to the set of available tools. From a practical point of view, it is in particular desirable that the operators discussed in this paper can be combined with the sequential form of composition of E-P3P policies proposed in [4]. Since we try to stay close to the latest version of EPAL that has been submitted to W3C for standardization, the E-P3P variant underlying [4] is slightly different from the variant that we consider here, hence some care has to be taken in combining operations/results from [4] and the ones presented above. Fortunately, carrying over the operator for sequentially composing privacy policies from [4] – there called *ordered composition* – to the situation considered here is straightforward.

As a technical tool, [4] introduces *policies with removed default rulings*, which means that an E-P3P policy is transformed into an equivalent one with default ruling "don't care". However, from Lemma 3 we know how to represent any well-founded privacy policy in this way, and so we can do without this technical trick here. As in [4] we make use of the concept of *precedence shift*, which adds a fixed number to the precedences of all rules in a policy. This can be used, for instance, to shift a department policy downwards, so that it has lower precedences than the CPO's privacy policy.

Definition 22 (Precedence Shift). *Let* $Pol = (Voc, R, dr)$ *be a privacy policy and* $j \in \mathbb{Z}$. *Then* $Pol + j := (Voc, R + j, dr)$ *with* $R + j := \{(i + j, u, d, p, a, c, \bar{o}, r) \mid (i, u, d, p, a, c, \bar{o}, r) \in R\}$ *is called the* precedence shift *of Pol by* j. *We define* $Pol - j := Pol + (-j)$. ◇

To formalize the sequential composition of two well-founded policies Pol_1, Pol_2 with compatible vocabularies, we assume that both of them have a "don't care" default ruling. If this is not the case, we first apply an algorithm like the one in Section 3.2 to derive equivalent privacy policies which have a "don't care" default ruling. After that, we shift the two policies accordingly, and then join their vocabularies and rulesets:

Definition 23 (Sequential Composition). *Let* Pol_1, Pol_2 *be well-founded privacy policies with compatible vocabularies, where w. l. o. g.* $dr_1 = \circ = dr_2$. *Let* $(Voc_1, R''_1, \circ) := Pol_1 - max(Pol_1) - 1$ *and* $(Voc_2, R'_2, \circ) := Pol_2 - min(Pol_1) + 1$. *Then*

$$Pol_1 \,\underline{\cup}\, Pol_2 := (Voc_1 \cup Voc_2, R''_1 \cup R'_2, \circ)$$

is called the sequential composition *of* Pol_1 *under* Pol_2. ◇

Intuitively, a sequential composition of Pol_1 under Pol_2 should serve as a refinement of Pol_2 which is formally captured in the following lemma.

Lemma 9. *For all well-founded privacy policies* Pol_1 *and* Pol_2 *with compatible vocabularies and* $dr_1 = \circ = dr_2$, *we have* $Pol_1 \,\underline{\cup}\, Pol_2 \prec Pol_2$. □

Obviously, the sequential composition of two well-founded privacy policies is in general no longer well-founded. So when combining $\underline{\cup}$ with the operators $+$ and $\&$ to form more complex privacy policies, some care has to be taken. In general, the sequential composition of policies should always be the last operation applied, as it is the only one which does not preserve well-foundedness.

4   Algebraic Properties of the Operators

Since the operator definitions proposed in the previous section are quite intuitive, one would not expect "unpleasant surprises" when using these operators to form more complex privacy policies involving three, four, or more operands. As actual use cases often involve more than only one or two different privacy policies, we have to ensure that our operators do not yield non-intuitive behaviors in such scenarios. Fortunately, this is not the case, and the usual algebraic laws apply:

Lemma 10. *Let* Pol_1, Pol_2, Pol_3 *be well-founded E-P3P policies such that the following expressions are well-defined, i.e., the respective requirements in Definition 19 respectively Definition 20 are met. Then the following holds:*

$$Idempotency: Pol_1 \& Pol_1 \equiv Pol_1, \tag{1}$$
$$Pol_1 + Pol_1 \equiv Pol_1,$$
$$Commutativity: Pol_1 \& Pol_2 \equiv Pol_2 \& Pol_1, \tag{2}$$
$$Pol_1 + Pol_2 \equiv Pol_2 + Pol_1,$$
$$Associativity: Pol_1 \& (Pol_2 \& Pol_3) \equiv (Pol_1 \& Pol_2) \& Pol_3, \tag{3}$$
$$Pol_1 + (Pol_2 + Pol_3) \equiv (Pol_1 + Pol_2) + Pol_3,$$
$$Distributivity: Pol_1 + (Pol_2 \& Pol_3) \equiv (Pol_1 + Pol_2) \& (Pol_1 + Pol_3), \tag{4}$$
$$Pol_1 \& (Pol_2 + Pol_3) \equiv (Pol_1 \& Pol_2) + (Pol_1 \& Pol_3),$$
$$Strong\ Absorption: Pol_1 + (Pol_1 \& Pol_2) \prec Pol_1. \tag{5}$$

$\square$

It is worth noting that our proof of the strong absorption property relies on both Lemma 5 and Lemma 6, and although it may look tempting, one cannot simply switch the roles of conjunction and disjunction in the proof to derive a "dual" strong absorption law with the roles of $\&$ and $+$ being exchanged.

In addition to purely algebraic properties of the operators, one can also establish several refinement results. In particular we can prove the following relations, which from the intuitive point of view are highly desirable:

Lemma 11. *Let* Pol_1, Pol_2 *be well-founded privacy policies such that the respective requirements of Definition 19 and Definition 20 are met. Then we have*

$$Weak\ Multiplicative\ Refinement: Pol_1 \& Pol_2 \tilde{\prec} Pol_i \quad (i = 1, 2), \tag{6}$$
$$Weak\ Additive\ Refinement: Pol_i \tilde{\prec} Pol_1 + Pol_2 \quad (i = 1, 2). \tag{7}$$

$\square$

Finally, we state a refinement result which relates the sequential composition operator to the operators for conjunction and disjunction:

Lemma 12. *Let* Pol_1, Pol_2 *be well-founded policies such that the respective requirements of Definition 19, Definition 20, and Definition 23 are met. Then we have*

$$Weak\ Operator\ Refinement: Pol_1 \& Pol_2 \tilde{\prec} Pol_1 \underset{<}{\bigcup} Pol_2 \tilde{\prec} Pol_1 + Pol_2. \tag{8}$$

$\square$

5   Conclusion

Motivated by the need for practical life-cycle management systems for the collection of enterprise privacy policies, we have introduced several algebraic operators for combining enterprise privacy policies, and we have shown that they enjoy the expected algebraic laws. Our operators allow for a convenient, modular use of existing EPAL policies as building blocks for new ones, and they hence avoid the difficulties that naturally arise for the usually very complex monolithic privacy specifications.

An analysis of the expressiveness of EPAL further revealed that, somewhat surprisingly, EPAL policies are not closed under intuitive notions of policy conjunction and policy disjunction; however, such operations are crucial for actual use cases. We have circumvented this problem by identifying a suitable subclass of EPAL policies that is closed under desired algebraic operations. Further on, the introduced tools for combining privacy policies satisfy natural requirements like associativity, commutativity, and distributivity, as well as appropriate refinement relations. In addition to conjunction and disjunction operators, our algebra provides a scoping operation which allows for managing and reasoning about privacy requirements that involve only certain parts of an organization. Finally, we have shown that the already existing notion of sequential composition of privacy policies fits naturally into our setting. As future work we consider it a worthwhile goal to add further operations to our algebra in order to further facilitate a convenient handling of privacy policies.

References

1. P. Ashley, S. Hada, G. Karjoth, C. Powers, and M. Schunter. Enterprise Privacy Authorization Language (EPAL). Research Report 3485, IBM Research, 2003.
2. P. Ashley, S. Hada, G. Karjoth, and M. Schunter. E-P3P privacy policies and privacy authorization. In *Proc. 1st ACM Workshop on Privacy in the Electronic Society (WPES)*, pages 103–109, 2002.
3. M. Backes, M. Dürmuth, and R. Steinwandt. An algebra for composing enterprise privacy policies. Research Report 3557, IBM Research, 2004.
4. M. Backes, B. Pfitzmann, and M. Schunter. A toolkit for managing enterprise privacy policies. In *Proc. 8th European Symposium on Research in Computer Security (ESORICS)*, volume 2808 of *LNCS*, pages 162–180. Springer, 2003.
5. C. Bettini, S. Jajodia, X. S. Wang, and D. Wijesekerat. Obligation monitoring in policy management. In *Proc. 3rd IEEE International Workshop on Policies for Distributed Systems and Networks (POLICY)*, pages 2–12, 2002.
6. P. A. Bonatti, E. Damiani, S. De Capitani di Vimercati, and P. Samarati. A component-based architecture for secure data publication. In *Proc. 17th Annual Computer Security Applications Conference*, pages 309–318, 2001.
7. P. A. Bonatti, S. De Capitani di Vimercati, and P. Samarati. A modular approach to composing access control policies. In *Proc. 7th ACM Conference on Computer and Communications Security*, pages 164–173, 2000.
8. P. A. Bonatti, S. de Capitani di Vimercati, and P. Samarati. An algebra for composing access comtrol policies. *ACM Transactions on Information and System Security*, 5(1):1–35, 2002.
9. A. Cavoukian and T. J. Hamilton. *The Privacy Payoff: How successful businesses build customer trust*. McGraw-Hill/Ryerson, 2002.
10. S. De Capitani di Vimercati and P. Samarati. An authorization model for federated systems. In *Proc. 4th European Symposium on Research in Computer Security (ESORICS)*, volume 1146 of *LNCS*, pages 99–117. Springer, 1996.
11. S. Fischer-Hübner. *IT-security and privacy: Design and use of privacy-enhancing security mechanisms*, volume 1958 of *LNCS*. Springer, 2002.

12. Z. Fu, S. F. Wu, H. Huang, K. Loh, F. Gong, I. Baldine, and C. Xu. IPSec/VPN security policy: Correctness, conflict detection and resolution. In *Proc. 2nd IEEE International Workshop on Policies for Distributed Systems and Networks (POLICY)*, volume 1995 of *LNCS*, pages 39–56. Springer, 2001.

13. V. D. Gligor, S. I. Gavrila, and D. Ferraiolo. On the formal definition of separation-of-duty policies and their composition. In *Proc. 19th IEEE Symposium on Security & Privacy*, pages 172–183, 1998.

14. S. Jajodia, M. Kudo, and V. S. Subrahmanian. Provisional authorization. In *Proc. E-commerce Security and Privacy*, pages 133–159. Kluwer Academic Publishers, 2001.

15. S. Jajodia, P. Samarati, M. L. Sapino, and V. Subrahmanian. Flexible support for multiple access control policies. *ACM Transactions on Database Systems*, 26(4):216–260, 2001.

16. G. Karjoth and M. Schunter. A privacy policy model for enterprises. In *Proc. 15th IEEE Computer Security Foundations Workshop (CSFW)*, pages 271–281, 2002.

17. G. Karjoth, M. Schunter, and M. Waidner. The platform for enterprise privacy practices – privacy-enabled management of customer data. In *Proc. Privacy Enhancing Technologies Conference*, volume 2482 of *LNCS*, pages 69–84. Springer, 2002.

18. S. Lakshminarayanan, R. Ramamoorthy, and P. C. K. Hung. Conflicts in inter-prise epal policies. In *W3C Workshop on the long term Future of P3P and Enterprise Privacy Langugate; Position Papers*. World Wide Web Consortium, 2003.

19. J. McLean. The algebra of security. In *Proc. 9th IEEE Symposium on Security & Privacy*, pages 2–7, 1988.

20. J. D. Moffett and M. S. Sloman. Policy hierarchies for distributed systems management. *IEEE JSAC Special Issue on Network Management*, 11(9):1404–31414, 1993.

21. Platform for Privacy Preferences (P3P). W3C Recommendation, Apr. 2002.

22. C. Ribeiro, A. Zuquete, P. Ferreira, and P. Guedes. SPL: An access control language for security policies with complex constraints. In *Proc. Network and Distributed System Security Symposium (NDSS)*, 2001.

23. R. T. Simon and M. E. Zurko. Separation of duty in role-based environments. In *Proc. 10th IEEE Computer Security Foundations Workshop (CSFW)*, pages 183–194, 1997.

24. D. Wijesekera and S. Jajodia. Policy algebras for access control – the propositional case. In *Proc. 8th ACM Conference on Computer and Communications Security*, pages 38–47, 2001.

25. D. Wijesekera and S. Jajodia. A propositional policy algebra for access control. *ACM Transactions on Information and System Security*, 6(2):286–325, 2003.

26. eXtensible Access Control Markup Language (XACML). OASIS Committee Specification 1.0, Dec. 2002. www.oasis-open.org/committees/xacml.

Deriving, Attacking
and Defending the GDOI Protocol

Catherine Meadows[1] and Dusko Pavlovic[2,*]

[1] Naval Research Laboratory, Washington, DC 20375
meadows@itd.nrl.navy.mil
[2] Kestrel Institute, Palo Alto, CA 94304
dusko@kestrel.edu

Abstract. As a part of a continued effort towards a logical framework for incremental reasoning about security, we attempted a derivational reconstruction of GDOI, the protocol proposed in IETF RFC 3547 for authenticated key agreement in group communication over IPsec. The difficulties encountered in deriving one of its authentication properties led us to derive an attack that had not surfaced in the previous extensive analyses of this protocol. The derivational techniques turned out to be helpful not only for constructing, analyzing and modifying protocols, but also attacks on them. We believe that the presented results demonstrate the point the derivational approach, which tracks and formalizes the way protocols are designed informally: by refining and composing basic protocol components.

After a brief overview of the simple authentication logic, we outline a derivation of GDOI, which displays its valid security properties, and the derivations of two attacks on it, which display its undesired properties. We also discuss some modifications that eliminate these vulnerabilities. Their derivations suggest proofs of the desired authentication. At the time of writing, we are working together with the Msec Working Group to develop a solution to this problem.

1 Introduction

A key feature needed to support the integration of formal methods into cryptographic protocol design is composability. Most of the design of a working cryptographic protocol is incremental in nature. One starts with a simple pattern that gives the basic skeleton of the protocol. One then adds the particular functionality needed for the particular application in mind. Some of the added functions may be optional, leading to different versions of the protocol. Finally, if some of the added features require interaction between the principals, it may be necessary to compose the protocol with some other protocol or protocols. For example, if one wants a key distribution protocol to enforce perfect forward secrecy, one may want to compose it with the Diffie-Hellman protocol by using Diffie-Hellman generated keying material as input into the key.

* Supported by ONR N00014-03-C-0237 and by NSF CCR-0345397.

In a situation like this it would be ideal if one could verify as well as design incrementally. It should be possible to identify situations in which properties that have been proven to be true remained true even after the protocol was modified in certain constrained ways. Unfortunately, this is in general a very hard problem in formal methods. In the general case, even minor changes can fail to preserve properties that had previously held.

A solution, of course, is to restrict oneself to properties and transformations that *can* be reasoned about incrementally; and more generally, to develop techniques to recognize conditions under which the security properties of interest are preserved under refinement, composition, or transformations at large. One such technique, in the framework of protocol derivations, has been studied in [8]. In the context of general theory of protocols, the issue of compositionality has been widely investigated, in various abstract process models. Some of the recent references are [6, 2, 15]. While the general problem of compositionality and monotonicity of security properties remains open, particular applications do allow useful deployment of incremental methods, informally used in many protocol development efforts and publications. We believe that such practices can and should be formalized.

With this in mind, we have been developing a monotone epistemic logic that provides a straightforward way of composing derivations of properties. In this logic, all statements express agents' knowledge about concrete situations and events such as the possession of keys and the sending and receipt of messages. These statements can then be composed to prove the desired conclusions about the sequences of events that must occur in a protocol. The current version, addressing only authenticity, however, does not involve composition of knowledge modalities, so that the epistemic nature of this logic remains on a rather rudimentary level. While it resembles BAN logic [5] in this restriction to authentication, the present logic is much simpler, with the order of actions as its only non-logical primitive.

Most importantly, the logic proceeds in much the same way as a protocol is designed. One starts with some simple patterns, for which some basic properties are established in advance. These patterns are then composed into the basic protocol. The properties add up in so far as they preserve each other's assumptions [8]. The next step is to add specific features that the protocol must provide: these would include, for example, the actual data that the protocol is intended to distribute securely. At this step, the protocol can also be composed with other, auxiliary, patterns.

An interesting and useful feature of the logic is that the same approach can be used to derive attacks on insecure protocols as to prove security properties of sound ones. This is often done by lifting a simple attack on a simple protocol component to a more subtle attack on a more complex protocol. The attack on a component C is expressed as a process on its own, say $\widetilde{C}$, corresponding to a logical statement of an undesired property. If the protocol P has been derived by using C in a derivation Δ, then replacing C by $\widetilde{C}$ in Δ will yield a derivation $\widetilde{\Delta}$ of an attack $\widetilde{P}$ on P, whenever the relevant undesired property is preserved.

The result is that we are able to take advantage of our knowledge of $\widetilde{C}$ to derive the attack $\widetilde{P}$.

Other attacks on protocols, of course, may not arise from attacks on their components, but may emerge, e.g., from insecure composition of secure components. Such attacks can still be derived, just like counterexamples are derived in logic, by changing the derivation goals. Since attacks, like protocols, are often based on simple patterns, attack derivations have the potential to be a useful feature for parlaying knowledge about basic attacks, and about propagating insecurities, into understanding of the vulnerabilities of complex protocols, just like protocol derivations parlay knowledge about basic protocols and their of security properties.

The logic used in our derivations draws upon the ideas of earlier derivational formalisms, developed in [10, 7]. The crucial difference is again that the statements of the new logic are couched entirely in terms of partial orders (distributed traces) of actions, as observed by each agent, or derived from her observations and the common axioms. One consequence of this is that we are now less likely to encounter some of the problems that epistemic logics at large have had in the past, where it was sometimes difficult to determine from the conclusions of an analysis what actual behavior was expected of a protocol, e.g., what sequence of events was actually supposed to occur. Another consequence is that our derivation system has a smaller syntax and simpler semantics than its predecessors. Nevertheless, a logic capturing the *distributed* reasoning in *dynamic* protocol interactions remains a challenge, not only conceptual, but even notational: writing down the views of the principals in a sequence does not display the essence. Understanding protocols requires new semantics, deriving them also requires new interfaces, and very much depends on the available tools. The current system suggests some of the notational forms, supported by a tool developed at Kestrel Institute. The space permits only a broad overview of a fragment; the goal is to show it at work on GDOI.

The Group Domain of Interpretation (GDOI) [3] protocol, developed by the Internet Engineering Task Force (IETF), is not only of great practical interest, because of its wide applications in secure multicast, and in secure group communication at large [3, sec. 1.1], but also of particular conceptual interest, because of the previous detailed analyses using the NRL Protocol Analyzer (NPA) [16]. The NPA is a model checker that, like the logic described in this paper, can be used to both provide security proofs and discover attacks, but does not support incremental or compositional verification. Interestingly, a failed composition involving a portion of the protocol called the "Proof of Possession" pointed up a potential problem with an optional means for providing authorization, which, because of a misunderstanding of the requirement, had been missed in the NPA analysis. The attack presented in this paper has arisen from an attempt to derive the GDOI protocol with the Proof of Possession option: the analysis of the step composing the core GDOI with the subprotocol underlying Proof of Possession has shown that the insufficient binding between the two components allowed deriving attacks, rather than the desired security property.

The rest of the paper is organized as follows. In section 2 we describe the GDOI protocol. In sec. 3 we give a brief overview of the logic. In sec. 4 we describe the derivation of the Core GDOI protocol. In sec. 5 we describe the derivation of the Proof of Possession protocol and its composition with the core GDOI protocol. In sec. 6 we discuss the derivation of the attack and some suggestions for fixing the protocol. In sec. 7 we compare our results with the earlier NPA analysis and conclude the paper.

2   The GDOI Protocol

GDOI actually consists of two main protocols: the GROUPKEY-PULL protocol, which is used when a new member joins the group, and the GROUPKEY-PUSH datagram, which is used to distribute keys to current members. In this paper we are concerned with the GROUPKEY-PULL protocol.

The GROUPKEY-PULL protocol takes place between a Group Controller/ Key Server (GCKS) and a member who wants to join the group. Authentication and secrecy are provided by a key that was previously exchanged using the Internet Key Exchange (IKE) protocol [13]. The purpose of IKE is to provide secure key distribution between two principals. Keys are distributed by IKE in two phases: long term Phase 1 keys, which in turn are used to distribute shorter-term Phase 2 keys. GDOI makes use of IKE Phase 1 only; GDOI can be thought of as taking the place of IKE Phase 2 for groups.

The GROUPKEY-PULL protocol serves two purposes: one is to distribute the current group key to the member, the other to provide mutual authentication and authorization between the member and GCKS. Furthermore, the latter purpose can be realized in two ways:

(i) by using the Phase 1 key for authentication, and storing the authorization information with principal's Phase 1 identity, where it can be readily looked up,

(ii) by storing the authorization information in a certificate that contains principal's public key, allowing it to be authenticated by a signature with the corresponding private key.

In the latter case, known as the Proof of Possession (PoP), it is not the purpose of a certificate, as usual, to allow the verification of a signature, but rather it is the purpose of the signature to authenticate the certificate. A principal uses the PoP to prove that he possesses the key in the certificate by using it to sign the other principal's nonce.

An interesting feature of the above options, specified in the GDOI RFC [3] is that the identity, contained in the certificate in (ii), can be, and is expected to be, *different* from the Phase 1 identity, used in (i)[1]. Allowing multiple identities can be useful for security associations, has been used in the recent versions of IKE, envisioned for Phase 1 of GDOI, and is not insecure in itself. In this case, however, it does cause problems, as we shall soon see.

---

[1] This is explicit for the group member, and left open for the GCKS.

The GDOI message flows, relevant for our analysis, are given below. The messages are passed along a secure channel where authentication and secrecy are provided by the key passed in Phase 1 IKE, and which is identified by an IKE header and Message ID. Since in this paper we are considering authentication issues alone, we do not specify the encryption and identification functions explicitly. We also leave off an optional Diffie-Hellman exchange, since it is not relevant to our analysis of authentication properties of the protocol.

Let A be a group member and B a GCKS.

(i) $A \rightarrow B : H^{AB}(m, id), m, id$

Here, m is A's nonce, id is the ID of the group, and H^{BA} denotes computation of a hash using the Phase 1 key shared between A and B.

(ii) $B \rightarrow A : H^{BA}(n, m, sa), n, sa$

Here n is B's nonce and sa stands for the security association associated with the key. Note that the keyed hash here is denoted H^{BA} instead of H^{AB}. This is to reflect the requirement that the input to the hashes be formatted in such a way that a message from an initiator be distinguishable from a message from a responder. This is not an issue for this specification, but will become so later for various partial specifications of the protocol.

(iii) $A \rightarrow B : H^{AB}(n, m, C^{A'}, S^{A'}(n, m)), C^{A'}, S^{A'}(n, m).$

Here $C^{A'}$ denotes a certificate pertaining to A's new identity, A'. This certificate contains a public key, and $S^{A'}$ denotes a signature by the corresponding private key.

(iv) $B \rightarrow A : H^{BA}(n, m, C^{B'}, sq, k, S^{B'}(n, m)), sq, k, S^{B'}(n, m)$

Here k is the actual keying material, and sq is a sequence number indicating the current GROUPKEY-PUSH message.

Irrelevant information is omitted wherever the confusion seems unlikely. For example, responder's nonce will be left out of the final hash in GDOI, since it plays no role in the analysis. For similar reasons, keying material and sequence numbers passed to the group member will also be omitted.

3   Brief Overview of Challenge Response Logic

The logic describes *actions* performed by *agents*. Actions consist of sending, receiving, and rewriting data, and generating random values. Agents constitute processes in the underlying process calculus; in this case, they can be construed as strands [17], or as cords [11]. Roles and principals can then be modeled as classes of agents, sharing data or information: keys and names in the case of principals, or actions in the case of roles. The other way around, an agent may be thought of as a special instance of a role, or of a principal. We will concentrate on conclusions that can be derived from participation in challenge-response protocols, and use challenge-response as building blocks for more complex protocols.

The logic is built out of simple axioms describing the conclusions that a principal can draw from her observations of protocol actions, using the known axioms. These axioms are usually of the form: "If an agent performs certain sequence of actions, then she can conclude that some other sequence of actions by other parties also occurred". For instance, if A receives a message, then she can conclude that someone must have sent that message; if that message contains a term that only B can form, then she knows that B must have been on the path of the message.

The notational conventions are as follows. A language of terms t, which can be sent in messages, is assumed to be given. It includes variables for unknown terms or agents, and sufficient typing. The expressions $\langle t \rangle_A$, resp. $(t)_A$, denote the statements that the agent A has sent, resp. received the term t. The expressions $\langle\langle t \rangle\rangle_A$ resp. $((t))_A$, denote the statements that A has sent, resp. received a message *containing* t. An agent asserting such a containment statement may not be able to extract t, but must be able to establish its presence (e.g., as in the case of hashing). When the source and the destination of a message are relevant, we use the verbose forms $\langle\langle t : A \to B \rangle\rangle_C$ and $((t : A \to B))_C$, where A and B are respectively the purported source and destination fields. Like the the "To" and the "From" fields, they can be spoofed, whereas the subscripts C name the agent who actually performs the action. A further convenient abbreviation is $\langle\langle t \rangle\rangle_{C<}$, which means that C is the *originator* of the first message containing t [2]. In general, t may contain subterms generated by others, yet $\langle\langle t \rangle\rangle_{C<}$ asserts that no one before C had sent t itself. The expression (νm) describes the generation of a fresh nonce m. As usually in process calculus, it binds m to the right.

Atomic statements are generated over actions in one of the following forms:

- a – "*the action a has occurred*",
- $a < b$ – "*the action a has occurred before b*", and
- $a = b$ – "*the actions a and b are identical*".

The conditional precedence in the form "*if b occurs, then a must have occurred before*" is often used, so we abbreviate it as $a \prec b \iff b \Rightarrow a < b$.

When authenticating each other, agents reason from partial descriptions and unknown order of actions, towards total descriptions and order. The names a and b thus usually denote only partially determined actions. Thus, for instance

- $\langle t \rangle_A < (x)_Y$ – means that *some* action in the form $\langle t \rangle_A$ precedes *some* action in the form $(x)_Y$,
- $a = \langle t \rangle_A$ – means that the action denoted by a must be in the form $\langle t \rangle_A$; note that in the same session there may be $b \neq a$ with $b = \langle t \rangle_A$;
- $\langle U(t) \rangle_A = \langle V(t) \rangle_B$, where $U(t)$ and $V(t)$ are undetermined messages containing t – means that $U(t) = V(t)$ and $A = B$.

The state of each agent consists of what she has *seen* and *recorded*. In principle, she only sees her own actions. She can thus record (some of) the terms that she has sent, received, or computed, and the order of actions that she has performed. At each new state, an agent can draw new conclusions, applying the axioms, which constitute common knowledge, to the data seen or recorded. Each such derivation thus consists of three fields:

---

[2] Formally, $\langle\langle t \rangle\rangle_{C<}$ abbreviates $\exists c.\ c = \langle\langle t \rangle\rangle_C \wedge \forall b.\ b = \langle\langle t \rangle\rangle_B \Rightarrow b \leq c$.

- "A sees:..." – displaying A's state,
- "A knows:..." – displaying axioms and the previously derived facts,
- "A concludes:..." – displaying the new conclusions, following from the above.

We omit "sees", "knows", and "concludes" whenever confusion seems unlikely.

There are two basic axioms that express semantics of actions. All principals are assumed to know them.

$$(t) \implies \exists a. \; a = \langle t \rangle \wedge a < (t) \tag{rcv}$$

$$(\nu m)_M \implies \forall a_A. \; \Big(a = \langle\langle m \rangle\rangle \vee a = ((m)) \Rightarrow (\nu m) < a \; \wedge$$

$$A \neq M \Rightarrow (\nu m)_M < \langle\langle m \rangle\rangle_M < ((m))_A \leq a_A \Big) \tag{new}$$

The (rcv) axiom says that if a message is received, it must have been sent. The (new) axiom says that, if a fresh value is generated, then any action involving that fresh value must occur after its generation; moreover, if some principal other than the originator receives a message containing the fresh value, then the originator of the value must have sent a message containing it.

Axiom (cr) supports the reasoning of the initiator of a challenge-response protocol. It is formalized as follows:

$$A: \; (\nu m)_A \Big(\langle\langle c^{AB} m \rangle\rangle_A < ((r^{AB} m))_A$$

$$\implies \langle\langle c^{AB} m \rangle\rangle_A < ((c^{AB} m))_B < \langle\langle r^{AB} m \rangle\rangle_{B<} < ((r^{AB} m))_A \Big) \tag{cr}$$

The expression $c^{AB} m$ denotes a challenge function applied to m, while the expression $r^{AB} m$ denotes a response function applied to m. The axiom can be viewed as a specification of the requirement defining these two functions. It tells that A can be sure that if she issues a message containing a challenge $c^{AB} m$, and receives response containing $r^{AB} m$, then B must be the originator of that response. In other words, B is the only agent who could have transformed $c^{AB} m$ to $r^{AB} m$, given the A's own observed actions. This is the basic logical building block of authentications. The same idea is captured by Woo-Lam's correspondence statements [18], or by Guttman and Thayer's authentication tests [12].

In the various instances of axiom (cr), functions c and r satisfying the above specification, can be implemented in various ways, e.g. taking B's signature as the response, or B's public key encryption as the challenge. In each case, it will need to be proved that the particular implementation satisfies the specified requirement.

The logic also contains axioms for composing, refining and transforming protocols. A transformation or refinement usually adds a new property or functionality to the protocol, in which case it comes annotated with an axiom, leading to new conclusions. In authentication protocols, such axioms may expand principal's knowledge about the events in the run of the protocol that he is participating. For example, in the basic challenge-response axiom there is no indication that B intended its message as a response to A's particular challenge. This would need to be supplied by some refinement introducing a specific integrity token, such as computing a MAC.

While many formal details of our logical derivation of GDOI will have to be omitted, the axioms and the derivation steps do yield to a simple diagrammatic presentation without an essential loss of precision or insight. As usually, messages are represented by horizontal arrows from one principal to another. A vertical line corresponds to principal's internal change of state. If the principal creates a new value m, this is represented by putting νm next to the appropriate vertical line. Below, we describe a derivation of a simple challenge and response protocol, which we use to form the core of GDOI.

There are several properties of protocols that will be of interest here. One, known as *matching histories*, due to Diffie, van Oorschot, and Wiener [9], says that after two principals complete a protocol successfully, then they both should have the same history of messages sent. Another, due to Lowe [14], known as *agreement*, says that the principals should agree not only about the message histories, but also about the source and destination of each message.

Assumptions. A principal can be honest, and follow the protocol, or dishonest, and perform arbitrary actions. However, it is assumed that no principal, honest or dishonest, can compromise the private data used to authenticate him: they are securely bound to his identity, outside the considered protocols[3]. protocol cannot be to possession of authenticating We also tacitly assume strong typing. If a principal, for example, attempts to use a key in the place of a nonce, the message will be rejected. These assumptions are a matter of convenience, and can be discharged in a more detailed treatment. This is, indeed, needed when it comes, e.g., to perfect forward secrecy, which is of interest in GDOI, and describes the behavior of the protocol after a master key is compromised.

4   Deriving Core GDOI

In this section we derive the conclusions the principals can draw as a result of participating in Core GDOI, without Proof of Possession. This is done by first constructing a mutual hash-based challenge-response protocol, and then inserting key distribution. For reasons of space, we will only give a detailed presentation of the derivation of A's conclusions as the result of participating in the Hash-based Challenge-Response, while giving a broad overview of the rest. We hope that this is enough to give a flavor of the logic.

4.1   Hash-Based Challenge-Response

The derivation of GDOI begins with the basic protocol functionality, which is mutual authentication through hash-based challenge-response. It is obtained by

---

[3] The authentication data that cannot be denied or delegated are sometimes called fingerprints.

composing and binding two copies of the challenge-response protocol described above, with the challenge and response functions instantiated:

$$c^{AB} m = m \quad \text{and} \quad r^{AB} m = H^{BA} m$$

Here, the hash H^{AB} is axiomatized by

$$H^{AB} s = H^{AB} t \implies s = t \tag{hash1}$$

$$\langle\langle H^{AB} t \rangle\rangle_{X<} \implies X = A \vee X = B \tag{hash2}$$

$$H^{AB} t = H^{BA} t \implies A = B \tag{hash3}$$

The idea is that $H^{AB} m = h \circ q(\sigma^{AB}, A, B, m)$, where h is a given pseudorandom function, σ^{AB} a secret shared by A and B, and q a convenient projection, perhaps eliminating one of the identifiers. The axioms capture enough of this intended meaning, to ensure that the above instantiation of c^{AB} and r^{AB} validates axiom (cr), so that we can prove

$$A: \ (\nu m)_A \Big(\langle\langle m \rangle\rangle_A < ((H^{BA} \overline{m}))_A$$

$$\implies \langle\langle m \rangle\rangle_A < ((m))_B < \langle\langle H^{BA} \overline{m} \rangle\rangle_{B<} < ((H^{AB} \overline{m}))_A \Big) \tag{crh}$$

where $\overline{m}$ denotes a term containing[4] m. The proof makes use of (rcv) to conclude, if the message $H^{BA \, rather} \overline{m}$ was received, it must have been sent by somebody, and (hash2) to conclude that the sender must have been B. It then makes use of (new) to conclude that m must have been created and sent by A and received by B previous to B's sending the hash.

We now use (crh) to derive A's conclusions.

A sees : $\qquad (\nu m)_A < \langle m \rangle_A < (H^{BA} m)_A$

knows (crh) : $\ (\nu m)_A \Big(\langle\langle m \rangle\rangle_A < ((H^{BA} m))_A$

$$\implies \langle\langle m \rangle\rangle_A < ((m))_B < \langle\langle H^{BA} m \rangle\rangle_{B<} < ((H^{BA} m))_A \Big)$$

concludes : $\quad (\nu m)_A < \langle m \rangle_A < ((m))_B < \langle\langle H^{BA} m \rangle\rangle_{B<} < (H^{BA} m)_A$

So keyed hash can be used for ping authentication. But furthermore, it turns out that composing and binding two copies of such hash-based authentication allows both principals to derive the exact order of all of their joint actions, and thus arrive at matching records of the conversation. To derive this, we begin from the simple hash-based challenge response, the first diagram in fig. 1. The responder B learns little (only that someone has sent a message), but A learns that B received her challenge and responded to it. The second diagram is obtained by sequential composition of two copies of the first one. We only display the first copy. The second one is symmetric, with B as the initiator and A as responder.

---

[4] Like before, the agent asserting containment may not be able to extract m, but must be able to verify its presence.

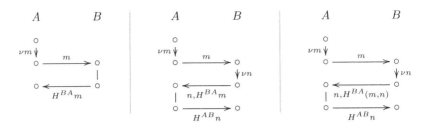

Fig. 1. Hash-based Challenge-Response: from one-way to mutual authentication

The conclusions that A and B can draw are the union of the conclusions that they could draw as initiator and responder of two independent protocols: A knows that it receives a response to B, and B knows that it received a response from A, but they are not able to derive much more than that. The reasoning for A is as follows:

A sees : $(\nu m)_A < \langle m \rangle_A < (n, H^{BA}m)_A < \langle H^{AB}n \rangle_A$

(crh) $(\nu m)_A \Big(\langle\langle m \rangle\rangle_A < ((H^{BA}m))_A$

$\qquad\qquad \Longrightarrow \langle\langle m \rangle\rangle_A < ((m))_B < \langle\langle H^{BA}m \rangle\rangle_{B<} < ((H^{BA}m))_A \Big)$

(rcv) $(t) \Longrightarrow \exists a.\ a = \langle t \rangle \wedge a < (t)$

A : $(\nu m)_A < \langle m \rangle_A < ((m))_B < \langle\langle H^{BA}m \rangle\rangle_{B<} < (n, H^{BA}m)_A < \langle H^{AB}n \rangle_A$
$\qquad \wedge \ \exists Y.\ \langle\langle n : B \to A \rangle\rangle_Y < (n, H^{BA}m : B \to A)_A$

The third protocol is obtained by binding the two one-way authentications by a simple protocol transformation, introducing responder's challenge into his response. In the logic, this is accompanied by the protocol specific definition of B's honesty:

$$A : B \text{ honest} \iff (x)_B \prec (\nu y)_B \prec \langle y, H^{BA}(x, y) \rangle_B \prec (H^{AB}y)_B$$

where A is an agent from the initiator role. This statement tells that, if A knows that any of the above events have occurred, then A knows that all of the preceding events must have occurred as well, in the described order – provided that B is honest, and acts according to the protocol. The reasoning now proceeds as follows.

A sees : $(\nu m)_A < \langle m \rangle_A < (n, H(m, n))_A < \langle Hn \rangle_A$

(crh) $(\nu m)_A \Big(\langle\langle m \rangle\rangle_A < ((H\overline{m}))_A$

$\qquad\qquad \Longrightarrow \langle\langle m \rangle\rangle_A < ((m))_B < \langle\langle H\overline{m} \rangle\rangle_{B<} < ((H\overline{m}))_A \Big)$

(rcv) $(t) \Longrightarrow \exists a.\ a = \langle t \rangle \wedge a < (t)$

A : $B \text{ honest} \iff (x)_B \prec (\nu y)_B \prec \langle y, H(x, y) \rangle_B \prec (Hy)_B$

Just as in the one-way authentications, the conclusion is

A (i) : $(\nu m)_A < \langle m \rangle_A < ((m))_B < \langle\langle H(m, n) \rangle\rangle_{B<} < (n, H(m, n))_A$

On the other hand, from the honesty assumption

$$A \text{ (ii)} : B \text{ honest} \wedge \langle\langle H\overline{x} \rangle\rangle_B \implies (x)_B < (\nu y)_B << \langle y, H(x,y) \rangle_{B<} = \langle\langle H\overline{m} \rangle\rangle_B$$

where, as we recall, $\overline{x}$ denotes a term containing x. Instantiating $x = m$ and $\overline{x} = (m, n)$, we get the antecedens that $\langle\langle H(m, n) \rangle\rangle_B$ has occurred. The consequens now tells that the action $\langle\langle H(m, n) \rangle\rangle_{B<}$ of (i) must be $\langle y, H(m, y) \rangle_B$ of (ii), with y fresh. From axiom (hash1), A derives that $n = y$ and thus

$$\begin{aligned} A : \quad & B \text{ honest} \implies (\nu m)_A < \langle m \rangle_A < \\ & (m)_B < (\nu n)_B < \langle n, H^{BA}(m, n) \rangle_B < (n, H^{BA}(m, n))_A < \langle H^{AB} n \rangle_A \end{aligned}$$

By similar reasoning, B reaches the same conclusion, just extended by $(H^{AB} n)_B$ at the end. The hash-based challenge-response thus yields the matching conversations authentication.

In fact, with the same assumptions, A can derive essentially more: not only that B has indeed sent the response that she has received, and generated the challenge that she has responded to – but also that B has *intended* his response and his challenge for her. More precisely, the above conclusion of A's can be extended by the desired source and destination of each message, $A \to B$, or $B \to A$. Indeed, assuming that B is honest,

- he must have received $(m : A \to B)_B$, because he would never form H^{BA} $(m \ldots)$ otherwise, and then
- he must have generated fresh n and sent $\langle n, H^{BA}(m, n) : B \to A \rangle_B$, again because the protocol and his honesty say so.

Formalizing this, A can first prove that the above definition of B's honesty is equivalent to a stronger formula:

$$\begin{aligned} A : B \text{ honest} \iff & (x : A \to B)_B \prec (\nu y)_B \prec \\ & \langle y, H^{BA}(x, y) : B \to A \rangle_B \prec (H^{AB} y : A \to B)_B \end{aligned}$$

and then strengthen the rest of her reasoning. Mutatis mutandis, the same holds for B. The principals thus agree not only about the order of their joint actions, but also about the intended sources and destinations of their messages, and about each other's identity. This stronger form of authentication is called *agreement* in Lowe's hierarchy [14]. While matching conversations authentication suffices for some purposes, we shall see in the sequel how it can lead to misidentification even in combination with agreement.

4.2   Towards GDOI: Hash-Based Authenticated Key Distribution

Towards authenticated key distribution, the hash-based mutual authentication protocol should now be composed with the hash-based key distribution protocol, identifying initiator's nonces used in the two components. The argument is essentially the same as that for hash-based challenge-response, so we omit it here. In the first diagram in fig. 2, we start with a protocol pattern in which

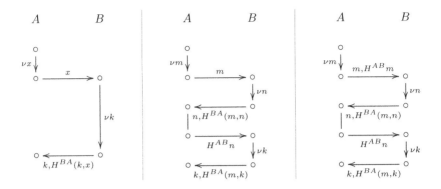

Fig. 2. Composition with hash-based key distribution

hash-based challenge-response is used to guarantee authentication of a key (or any other piece of data). As a result of this protocol, A can conclude that B sent the key in response to her challenge. In the second diagram, we compose the key distribution with the challenge-response diagram from fig. 1. Now A can conclude that B has responded to her challenge with challenge of his own, and later with a key. B can conclude that A was still participating in the protocol at the time he received the challenge (that is, that the first message that it received from A was not a replay). The last diagram in fig. 2 is a simple refinement that authenticates the initial challenge[5]. This step is independent, and can been introduced at any point in the derivation. In any case, it is not hard to prove that the authenticity properties, achieved in the hash-based challenge response, are preserved under the last two derivation steps. The same messages that appear in the hash-based challenge response also appear in the hash-based key distribution in the same order. So the same proof strategy works again.

Since the distributed key is also authenticated by hash, the resulting protocol – the core of GDOI – thus realizes the agreement authentication again. This means that each principal can exactly derive the order of all actions (except that the sender of the very last message cannot know that it is received) – *including* the correct source and the intended destination of each message.

5   Adding Second Authentication

In this section we describe the second way of authorizing group membership and leadership. This is done by passing a signed public key certificate with a new identity and additional authorizations. This can be done for either the group member, or the GCKS, or both. A principal is intended to prove possession of the private key corresponding to the public key contained in the certificate by using it to sign the two nonces. Thus we can think of GDOI with proof-of-possession (PoP) as the composition of two protocols: the core GDOI protocol and the PoP protocol.

---

[5] Omitting this would expose B to a denial-of-service.

5.1   Towards PoP: Signature-Based Challenge-Response

The PoP protocol is another implementation of the abstract challenge response template (cr), this time using signatures. The challenge is again just $c^{AB}m = m$, but the response is $r^{AB}m = C^B, S^B m$, where S^B is B's signature, axiomatized by

$$S^B t = S^B u \implies t = u \tag{sig1}$$

$$\langle\langle S^B t\rangle\rangle_{X<} \implies X = B \tag{sig2}$$

$$V^B(y, t) \iff y = S^B t \tag{sig3}$$

whereas C^B is B's certificate, with her identity bound to the signature verification algorithm V^B, and possibly containing additional authorization payload, used in GDOI. As usually, the integrity of this binding is assured by certifying authority. The derivation proceeds similarly as for the hash-based authentica-

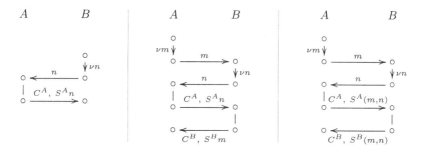

Fig. 3. Signature-based Challenge-Response: from one-way to mutual authentication

tion. The difference is that the second diagram in fig. 3 is a nested composition of two copies of the first, rather than a sequential composition, as in fig. 1. We only display the inner copy, while the outer one is symmetric, with A as the initiator, and B as responder. Like before, the third diagram is obtained by binding transformations, i.e. introducing each principal's own challenge into his response. The result is what we call the PoP protocol.

Properties and attacks. The proof of the matching conversation authenticity for the signature-based challenge response protocol closely follows the proof for the hash-based protocol, presented in sec. 4.1. However, while the latter proof readily extends to a proof of agreement, by extending the messages by $A \to B$ and $B \to A$, the former does not.

The reason is that the messages in the hash-based protocol carry enough information to ensure that an honest principal, say A, will send the messages to the correct destination B – whereas in the signature-based protocol they do not. More concretely, in the hash-based protocol, the assertion that A is honest and sends and receives the messages in correct order implies, as we have seen, that the sources and the destinations of the messages are also correct. In the simplest signature-based challenge response protocol, B's assumption that A is honest, B : A honest $\iff (n)_A \prec \langle\langle C^A, S^A n\rangle\rangle_A$ cannot be extended to $\langle C^A, S^A n : A \to B\rangle_A$. While the response $H^{AB}n$ must be for B if A is honest, the response $C^A, S^A n$ does not tell who A may have intended it for, honestly or not.

The signature-based challenge response protocols thus realize matching conversations authentication, but they do not realize agreement, and do allow identity confusion. Indeed, by spoofing the source of B's challenge, and the destination of A's response, an intruder I can convince B that he has authenticated a, while A believes that she has been authenticated by I, and knows nothing of B. This is illustrated in in the first diagram in fig. 4. The attack validates e.g. the following statement

$$B : \quad A \text{ honest} \implies (\nu n)_B < \langle n\rangle_B < (n)_A < \langle C^A, S^A n\rangle_A < (C^A, S^A n)_B$$
$$\wedge \neg\Big(B : A \text{ honest} \implies \langle C^A, S^A n : A \to B\rangle_A\Big)$$

which shows that it cannot validate agreement authentication. Now recall the derivation pattern displayed in fig. 3, used to derive a mutual authentication protocol by nested composition and binding of two copies of one way authentication. Applying this derivation pattern not to the one way authentication protocol itself, but to the attack on it – yields a similar attack on the resulting mutual authentication protocol. This attack is illustrated in the second diagram of fig. 4. A formula contradicting the agreement authentication, but asserting the matching conversation can be extracted just as above.

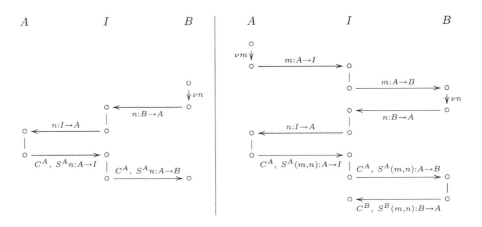

Fig. 4. Attacks Against Signature-Based Challenge-Response

To remove the attacks, one would need to provide grounds for the reasoning pattern that led to establishing the agreement authentication in sec. 4.1. Like there, the response function should thus be extended by peer's information, which would allow the extending honesty assertion by the source and destination fields. When anonymity of the initiator is not required, this can be achieved by taking $r^{AB}m = C^B, S^B(A, m)$

5.2   Composing Core GDOI with the PoP Option

We are now ready to compose core GDOI, derived in sec. 4, with the PoP protocol, derived above. This is shown in fig. 5, where we abbreviate $\Sigma^X = S^X(m, n)$.

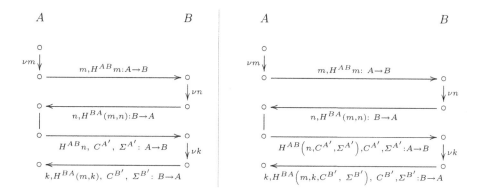

Fig. 5. Composition of Core GDOI with PoP

In the first diagram, we compose the hash-based protocol from sec. 4.2 with the signature-based protocol from sec. 5.1, identifying the fresh data. In the second diagram, we bind the two components using hashes. Note that the principal A claims both A and A' as her identities: one as the source field of her message, the other through the certificate, which she proves as hers by the signature. The principal B similarly claims both B and B'.

6   Attacks on GDOI with PoP and Its Defenses

When we attempted to prove the security of the composition of the core GDOI and POP, we found that the proofs derived for GDOI and for POP could not be composed, because the two components used two different identities. At a closer examination, it turned out that this fact not only preempted a proof of security of the composite protocol, but also allowed a derivation of an attack on it. A further attempt to prove security of an amended version then led to a derivation of an additional, more subtle attack. Defending the protocol against this attack, we arrived at the version supporting the agreement authentication. We shall now discuss these attacks and the defenses against them.

The first attack on the composite protocol is obtained by composing attack on the PoP component with the GDOI protocol. It can be specified by composing the vulnerability statement about PoP from sec. 5.1, with the statements derived about GDOI. The composition turns out to preserve the vulnerability. The second attack emerges from the interaction of the components, even after the attack on the PoP component has been eliminated.

6.1   Lifting the Attack from PoP

The attack on the PoP, presented in sec. 5.1, leaves the responder confused about who the initiator is actually trying to initiate contact with. To lift this attack to GDOI, we compose it with the core GDOI, as derived in sec. 4. This is step done in the same way as the PoP protocol itself was composed with core GDOI in sec. 5.2, to yield GDOI. The derivation of this attack on GDOI thus parallels the derivation of GDOI itself, up to the last step, when it introduces the attack on the PoP component, instead of the PoP itself. This is illustrated in fig. 6. We compose two copies of the GDOI protocol, one between A as initiator and I as responder, and the other between I as initiator and B as responder, with a copy of the attack on the signature protocol in sec. 5.1, in which I claims to B that A' is his identity, and proves this by certificate and signature. The notation $X_{A'}$ refers to the fact that the agent X claims the identity of A' (in this case by proving possession of the certificate belonging with this identity). The upshot of this attack is that a rogue GCKS I, who does not have the credentials to join the group managed by GCKS B, could hijack the credentials belonging to A under identity A' that she presents to I when joining I's group.

A solution? The simplest way to eliminate this composition is to eliminate the attack in fig. 4, i.e. to strengthen the signature-based authentication from

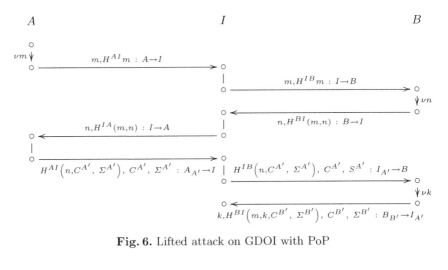

Fig. 6. Lifted attack on GDOI with PoP

matching conversations to agreement. As pointed out in sec. 5.1, this can be done by introducing the peer's identity under the signature, responding to the challenge, i.e. to replace $\Sigma^{A'}$ by $\Sigma_{B'}^{A'} = S^{A'}(B', m, n)$ We do the same for $\Sigma^{B'}$. However, eliminating the attack on the component is in this case not enough to solve the problem.

6.2   Emergent Attack

Even if the PoP protocol is modified as recommended, an attack can still emerges in composition. To see this, consider the modified version of GDOI with PoP, where $\Sigma^{A'}$ is replaced by $\Sigma_{B'}^{A'}$, and $\Sigma^{B'}$ by $\Sigma_{A'}^{B'}$. In order to allow A' to introduce the identity B' under her signature in the third message, this transformation must be enabled by moving the certificate $C^{B'}$ from the last message to the second one. The attack that nevertheless arises is presented in fig. 7. The attack still allows a correct hash-based mutual authentication between A and I (obtained by removing certificates and signatures), and a correct signature-based mutual authentication between A' and B' (obtained by removing hashes) yet putting these two authentications together leaves A believing that the identifiers I and B' belong to the same principal, and B believing that the identifiers I and A' belong to the same principal.

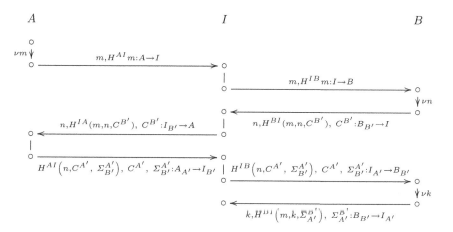

Fig. 7. Emergent Attack on modified GDOI

Suggested solution. A solution currently under discussion with the designers of GDOI is to introduce the shared secret σ^{AB} under the signatures, i.e. to replace $\Sigma^{A'} = S^{A'}(m, n)$ in fig. 5 by $\Sigma_{AB}^{A'} = S^{A'}(\sigma^{AB}, m, n)$, and symmetrically $\Sigma^{B'}$ by $\Sigma_{AB}^{B'}$. Alternatively, instead of σ^{AB}, one could use other identifying information, such as A's Phase 1 identity, could be used in place of σ^{AB}.

The responder's security argument now boils down to proving that, if either A or A' is honest, then $A = A'$. If A' is honest, then she will only sign the σ^{AB}

belonging to her, so B can conclude that $A' = A$. On the other hand, if A is honest, then, since $\Sigma_{AB}^{A'}$ appears in a hash computed with A's key σ^{AB}, B can conclude that A must have included the signature, which she only would have done if she herself had produced it using A''s private key. Therefore, B can again conclude that $A = A'$. A similar proof works for A's conclusions about B and B'.

One thing that the responder B cannot conclude is that $A = A'$ if both A and A' are dishonest. Even if A and A' do not share their long-term keys, we can produce a counterexample, albeit with a refined definition of digital signature. Note that the axiomitization in section 5.1 disallows message recovery. The recommended implementation of this uses a one-way hash of signed data. If this is captured in the axioms, then we can show that A can still pass the hash of (σ^{AB}, m, n) to A', without revealing its long-term key. After A' computes the signature, she can pass $\Sigma_{AB}^{A'} = S^{A'}(\sigma^{AB}, m, n)$ to A, who can then include it in her hashed message. Avoiding this collusion by signatures without hashing is cryptographically unsound, and opens up even more risks. So the problem of collusion remains open.

7 Conclusion

The presented results illustrate some of the features of a compositional protocol logic, and in particular the fragment for distributed reasoning in authentication protocols. The claim is that such logic not only supports incremental protocol design and analysis, but also facilitates the attack construction. The discovery of the compositional flaw in the GDOI group key exchange protocol, and the analyses of the various ways in which the protocol could be fixed and proven correct, provide evidence for this. The derivation system has not only been instrumental not only in protocol analysis and attack construction, but was also useful tool for communicating the issues to the GDOI authors and the Msec working group.

One might ask, how could this problem happen in the first place, since GDOI had already undergone a formal analysis with another tool, the NRL Protocol Analyzer? Indeed, the flaw that we found is very much of the type that the NPA can find. The answer is that the fact that certificate identities could be different from Phase 1 identities was missed by the authors of [16] when they were eliciting requirements. But, even if it had been caught, it would have not been trivial to go back and reverify the protocol with the NPA. With the derivational approach, we are able to verify only the parts that had changed.

Indeed, we note also that the approach of this logic addresses a growing problem in the design of cryptographic protocols: the problem of securely composing two or more different protocols. As Asokan et al. point out in [1], deploying a new protocol is expensive, and there is considerable pressure to reuse security protocols and security context databases by composing them with other protocols. However, the problem of securely reusing these protocols in new contexts is not well understood. Indeed, a man-in-the-middle attack of the sort described in [1] was found on the IETF's Extendible Authentication Protocol [4], and has much in common with the attack we found on Proof of Possession.

In conclusion, we believe that our approach offers the possibility of greatly facilitating the formal methods to cryptographic protocol analysis. Not only should it be possible to provide a complete verification of a protocol at one stage of its life, but to reverify the protocol as modifications are suggested and incorporated. Moreover, it facilitates the study of the growing problem of composition of protocols and protocol reuse.

Acknowledgements

We would like to thank Mark Baugher, Ran Canetti, Iliano Cervesato, Thomas Hardjono, and Brian Weis for helpful conversations and suggestions.

References

1. N. Asokan, V. Niemi, and K. Nyberg. Man-in-the-middle in tunnelled authentication protocols. In *2003 Cambridge Security Protocol Workshop*, April 2-4 2003.
2. M. Backes, B. Pfitzmann, and M. Waidner. A universally composable cryptographic library. Cryptology ePrint Archive, Report 2003/015, 2003. URL `http://eprint.iacr.org/`.
3. M. Baugher, B. Weis, T. Hardjono, and H. Harney. The group domain of interpretation. IETF RFC 3547, July 2003.
4. L. Blunk, J. Vollbrecht, B. Aboba, J. Carlson, and H. Levkowetz. Extensible authentication protocol (eap). IETF RFC 2284bis, November 27 2003.
5. Michael Burrows, Martín Abadi, and Roger Needham. A Logic of Authentication. *ACM Transactions in Computer Systems*, 8(1):18–36, February 1990.
6. R. Canetti. Universally composable security: A new paradigm for cryptographic protocols. In *Proceedings of the 42nd IEEE Symposium on the Foundations of Computer Science*. IEEE Computer Society Press, 2001.
7. A. Datta, A. Derek, J.C. Mitchell, and D. Pavlovic. A derivation system for security protocols and its logical formalization. In *IEEE Computer Security Foundations Workshop*, pages 109–125, Pacific Grove, CA, June 2003. IEEE Computer Society Press.
8. A. Datta, A. Derek, J.C. Mitchell, and D. Pavlovic. Secure protocol composition. In *Proceedings of ACM FMCS 2003*, pages 109–125, Washington, DC, October 2003. ACM.
9. W. Diffie, P. C. van Oorschot, and M.l J. Wiener. Authentication and Authenticated Key Exchanges. *Designs, Codes, and Cryptography*, 2:107–125, 1992.
10. N.A. Durgin, J.C. Mitchell, and D. Pavlovic. A compositional logic for proving security properties of protocols. *Journal of Computer Security*, 11(4):667–721, 2003.
11. Nancy Durgin, John C. Mitchell, and Dusko Pavlovic. A compositional logic for protocol correctness. In Steve Schneider, editor, *Proceedings of CSFW 2001*, pages 241 255. IEEE, 2001.
12. J. Guttman and F. J. Thayer. Authentication tests and the structure of bundles. *Theor. Comput. Sci.*, 283(2):333–380, 2002.
13. D. Harkins and D. Carrel. The Internet Key Exchange (IKE). IETF RFC 2409, November 1998.

14. G. Lowe. A hierarchy of authentication specifications. In *Proceedings of the 10th IEEE Computer Security Foundations Workshop*, pages 31–43. IEEE Computer Society Press, 1997.

15. P. Mateus, J.C. Mitchell, and A. Scedrov. Composition of cryptographic protocols in a probabilistic polynomial-time process calculus. In *Proceedings of 14-th International Conference on Concurrency Theory 2003*, volume 2761 of *Lecture Notes in Computer Science*, pages 327–349, Marseille, September 2003. Springer-Verlag.

16. C. Meadows, P. Syverson, and I. Cervesato. Formal specification and analysis of the Group Domain of Interpretation Protocol using NPATRL and the NRL Protocol Analyzer. *Journal of Computer Security*, 2004. To appear, currently available at `http://chacs.nrl.navy.mil/publications/CHACS/2003/2003meadows-gdoi.pdf`.

17. F. J. Thayer, J. Herzog, and J. Guttman. Strand Spaces: What Makes a Security Protocol Correct? *Journal of Computer Security*, 7:191–230, 1999.

18. Thomas Y. C. Woo and Simon S. Lam. A Semantic Model for Authentication Protocols. In *Proceedings IEEE Symposium on Research in Security and Privacy*. IEEE Computer Society Press, 1993.

Better Privacy for Trusted Computing Platforms
(Extended Abstract)

Jan Camenisch

IBM Research, Zurich Research Laboratory, CH-8803 Rüschlikon, Switzerland

Abstract. The trusted computing group (TCG) specified two protocols
that allow a trusted hardware device to remotely convince a communication partner that it is indeed a trusted hardware device. In turn, This
enables two communication partners to establish that the other end is
a secure computing platform and hence it is safe exchange data. Both
these remote identification protocols provide some degree of privacy to
users of the platforms. That is, the communication partners can only
establish that the other end uses some trusted hardware device but not
which particular one. The first protocol achieves this property by involving trusted third party called Privacy CA in each transaction. This party
must be fully trusted by all other parties. In practice, however, this is
a strong requirement that is hard to fulfill. Therefore, TCG proposed a
second protocol called direct anonymous attestation that overcomes this
drawback using techniques known from group signature schemes. However, it offers less privacy than the one involving the Privacy CA. The
reason for this is that the protocol needs to allow the verifier to detect
rogue hardware devices while before this detection was done by the Privacy CA. In this paper we show how to extend the direct anonymous
attestation protocols such that if offers the same degree of privacy as the
first solution but still allows the verifier to rogue devices.

1 Introduction

Consider a trusted hardware module, called the trusted platform module (TPM)
in the following, that is integrated into a platform such as a laptop or a mobile
phone. Assume that the user of such a platform communicates with a verifier
who wants to be assured that the user indeed uses a platform containing such a
trusted hardware module, i.e., the verifier wants the TPM to authenticate itself.
However, the user wants her privacy protected and therefore requires that the
verifier only learns that she uses a TPM but not which particular one – otherwise
all her transactions would become linkable to each other. This problem arose in
the context of the Trusted Computing Group (TCG). TCG is an industry standardization body that aims to develop and promote an open industry standard
for trusted computing hardware and software building blocks to enable more
secure data storage, online business practices, and online commerce transactions
while protecting privacy and individual rights (cf. [19]). TCG is the successor
organization of the Trusted Computing Platform Alliance (TCPA).

P. Samarati et al. (Eds.): ESORICS 2004, LNCS 3193, pp. 73–88, 2004.

In principle, the problem just described could be solved using any standard public key authentication scheme (or signature scheme): One would generate a secret/public key pair, and then embed the secret key into each TPM. The verifier and the TPM would then run the authentication protocol. Because all TPMs use the same key, they are indistinguishable. However, this approach would never work in practice: as soon as one hardware module (TPM) gets compromised and the secret key extracted and published, verifiers can no longer distinguish between real TPMs and fake ones. Therefore, detection of rogue TPMs needs to be a further requirement.

The solution first developed by TCG uses a trusted third party, the so-called privacy certification authority (Privacy CA), and works as follows [17]. Each TPM generates an RSA key pair called an Endorsement Key (EK). The Privacy CA is assumed to know the Endorsement Keys of all (valid) TPMs. Now, when a TPM needs to authenticate itself to a verifier, it generates a second RSA key pair called an Attestation Identity Key (AIK), sends the AIK public key to the Privacy CA, and authenticates this public key w.r.t. the EK. The Privacy CA will check whether it finds the EK in its list and, if so, issues a certificate on the TPM's AIK. The TPM can then forward this certificate to the verifier and authenticate itself w.r.t. this AIK. In this solution, there are two possibilities to detect a rogue TPM: 1) If the EK secret key was extracted from a TPM, distributed, and then detected and announced as a rogue secret key, the Privacy CA can compute the corresponding public key and remove it from its list of valid Endorsement Keys. 2) If the Privacy CA gets many requests that are authorized using the same Endorsement Key, it might want to reject these requests. The exact threshold on requests that are allowed before a TPM is tagged rogue depends of course on the actual environment and applications, and will in practise probably be determined by some risk-management policy.

This solutions has the obvious drawback that the Privacy CA needs to be involved in every transaction and thus highly available on the one hand but still as secure as an ordinary certification authority that normally operates off-line on the other hand. Moreover, if the Privacy CA and the verifier collude, or the Privacy CA's transaction records are revealed to the verifier by some other means, the verifier will still be able to uniquely identify a TPM. Similarly, the verifier needs to trust the Privacy CA not to issue certificate to just anybody, but only the genuine TPM. These trust relationships are in fact the more severe drawback as it is not clear who would provide such a Privacy CA service.

To overcome these problems, TCG included in the TPM v1.2 specification [18, 4] an alternative proposal called direct anonymous attestation. This new protocols draws on techniques that have been developed for group signatures [11, 8, 1], identity escrow [14], and credential systems [10, 5]. In fact, direct anonymous attestation can be seen as a group signature scheme without the capability to open signatures (or anonymity revocation) but with a mechanism to detect rogue members (TPMs in this case). More precisely, it also employs a suitable signature scheme to issue certificates on a membership public key generated by a TPM. Then, to authenticate as a group member, or valid TPM, a

TPM proves that it possesses a certificate on a public key for which it also knows the secret key. To allow a verifier to detect rogue TPMs, the TPM is further required to reveal and prove correct of a value $N_V = \zeta^f$, where f is its secret key and ζ is a generator of an algebraic group where computing discrete logarithms is infeasible. As in the Privacy-CA solution, there are two possibilities for the verifier to detect a rogue TPM: 1) By comparing N_V with $\zeta^{\tilde{f}}$ for all $\tilde{f}$'s that are known to stem from rogue TPMs. 2) By detecting whether he has seen the same N_V too many times. Of course, the second method only works if the verifier always uses the same ζ, or at least changes it only rarely. However, ζ should not be a fixed system parameter as otherwise the user gains almost no privacy – in the TCG specification it is proposed that either ζ be somehow derived from the verifier's name, e.g., using an appropriate hash function. However, this has the drawback that it allows the verifier to link transactions by perfectly honest users and hence drastically reduces the privacy offered by the direct anonymous attestation. In fact, in this respect, direct anonymous attestation is inferior to TCG's initial Privacy CA solution. There, a user can get a new certificate from the Privacy CA for each transactions and hence a verifier can not link the different transactions (unless it colludes with the Privacy CA).

In this paper we show how direct anonymous attestation can be modified such that it offers the same degree of privacy as the Privacy CA solution but it is still possible to detect rogue TPM. That is, it allows the verifier to check the frequency a TPM accesses some service but prevents it from doing profiling. The idea is to separate the frequency check from the request of the service. This can be done as follows: the verifier checks that the TPM's authentication as a genuine TPM using the direct anonymous attestation protocol, performs the frequency check and, if the check succeeds, issues an anonymous one-time certificate to the TPM/host instead of providing the service. In the following we will often call this anonymous one-time certificate a *frequency certificate*. Later, the TPM/host can then access the service using the anonymous one-time certificate. Of course, this frequency certificate must be such that

- the issuing of the certificate and its use cannot be linked,
- it can only be used a single time and with a single verifier, and
- it is tied to the particular TPM/host, i.e., cannot be transferred.

The first property can be achieved either by using so-called blind signatures [9] or by using an the approach similar to the one used for direct anonymous attestation and group signatures [8, 4]. The second property can be obtained by including the verifier's name and something like a serial number in the certificate. Finally, the third property is obtained by ensuring that the DAA attestation and the frequency certificate share a common value that is unique for each TPM. This value must of course be hidden from the verifier and the Privacy CA, but the TPM/host needs to prove to the verifier that the attestation certificate and the frequency certificate share such a values. Thus, the TPM/host need to convince the verifier not only that they have obtained the frequency certificate from the Privacy CA but also that they got attestation and that these two credentials share a common value. Of course, here the TPM/host must use a random base ζ when showing that they have obtained the attestation.

In this paper we will show how to implement all of this, using the same approach to issue and using frequency certificate that is used for anonymous attestation. For simplicity we assume that the frequency test are not performed by the verifier itself but by a third party which we will call Privacy CA. However, we stress that in the remainder of this document, the verifier can be the same entity as the Privacy CA without that any security and privacy property is compromised. We also note that the protocols we propose are compatible with the TCG TPM v1.2 specifications [18, 4]. That is, while we require some modification to the direct anonymous attestation protocol, the parts of it that are executed by the TPM (i.e., realized in hardware) need not to be modified!

Our protocols as well as direct anonymous attestation [18, 4] are based on prior work on group signatures and credential systems [1, 5, 6] that relies on the strong RSA assumption. While one could also base our protocol on the recently proposed groups signature scheme by Boneh, Boyen, Shacham [3] and Camenisch and Lysyanskaya [7] that use bi-linear maps, this seems not preferable as this would introduce additional computational assumptions to the ones already employed by direct anonymous attestation.

2   Informal Model

This section provides an informal model of what our protocols is supposed to achieve. A formal model is beyond the scope of this extended abstract. However, it is not too hard to modify and adapt the model provided in [4] to our purposes.

The parties in our model are several trusted platform modules (TPMs), several hosts, an attester, several Privacy CAs, and several verifiers. Each host has exclusive access to a TPM. As a TPM is embedded into a host, all communication to and from a TPM is routed via its host. We call the pair host and TPM also platform.

The systems consists of the following procedures.

Key Generation and Setup. There are key generation algorithms for the attester, the Privacy CA and the TPM. We assume that each of these parties has made its public key authentically available.

Attestation Protocol. This is a protocol involving the attester, a TPM and the corresponding host. The attester's input to the protocol is its secret and public keys as well as a list of public keys of valid TPMs, the inputs to the TPM consists of its secret and public keys and the public key of the attester, and the input to the host are the public keys of the attester and the TPM.
   If the protocol terminates successfully, the TPM and host will have obtained a attestation certificate from the attester.

Frequency-Certification Protocol. This is a protocol involving the a Privacy CA, a TPM, and the corresponding host. The Privacy CA's input to the protocol is its secret and public keys as well as the public key of the attester, the

inputs to the TPM consists of its secret and public keys, the public key of
the attester and an attestation certificate, and the input to the host are the
public keys of the attester, the Privacy CA, and the TPM and an attestation
certificate. Furthermore, the Privacy CA's input also contains a policy stating
how frequently a TPM is allowed to obtain a *frequency certificate* from it. The
inputs to the TPM consists of its secret and public keys, the public key of
the attester, and an attestation certificate. and the input to the host are the
public keys of the attester, the Privacy CA, and the TPM and an attestation
certificate.

If the protocol terminates successfully, the TPM and host will have obtained
a frequency certificate from the Privacy CA while the Privacy CA will have
obtained a pseudonym of the TPM.

Verify. This is a protocol involving a verifier, a TPM, and the corresponding
host. The input of the verifier consists of the public keys of the attester and a
Privacy CA, the inputs to the TPM consists of its secret and public keys, the
public key of the attester, an attestation certificate, and a frequency certificate.
and the input to the host are the public keys of the attester, the Privacy CA,
and the TPM, an attestation certificate, and a frequency certificate.

The security requirements are as follows.

Unforgeability. A TPM-host pair should only obtain a frequency certificate from
a Privacy CA if it has obtained an attestation certificate from the attester and
if it has not asked the same Privacy CA for too many frequency certificates
within a given time. This requires that a TPM-host pair can have only a single
pseudonym with a given Privacy CA. Furthermore, a frequency certificate
should be usable only once and with a single verifier.

Anonymity. All transactions by the TPM-host pair should be unlinkable, except
transactions with the same Privacy CA.

3   Preliminaries

Let $\{0,1\}^\ell$ denote the set of all binary strings of length ℓ. We often switch
between integers and their representation as binary strings, e.g., we write $\{0,1\}^\ell$
for the set $[0, 2^\ell - 1]$ of integers. Moreover, we often use $\pm\{0,1\}^\ell$ to denote the
set $[-2^\ell + 1, 2^\ell - 1]$.

We need some notation to select the high and low order bits of an integer. Let
$\mathrm{LSB}_u(x) := x - 2^u \lfloor \frac{x}{2^u} \rfloor$ and $\mathrm{CAR}_u(x) := \lfloor \frac{x}{2^u} \rfloor$. Let $(x_k \ldots x_0)_b$ denote the binary
representation of $x = \sum_{i=0}^k 2^i x_i$, e.g., $(1001)_b$ is the binary representation of the
integer 9. Also note that $x = \mathrm{LSB}_u(x) + 2^u \mathrm{CAR}_u(x)$.

In our scheme we will use various protocols to prove knowledge of and relations among discrete logarithms. To describe these protocols, we use notation
introduced by Camenisch and Stadler [8] for various proofs of knowledge of
discrete logarithms and proofs of the validity of statements about discrete log-
arithms. For instance, $PK\{(\alpha, \beta, \gamma) : y = g^\alpha h^\beta \ \wedge \ \tilde{y} = \tilde{g}^\alpha \tilde{h}^\gamma \ \wedge \ (u \le \alpha \le v)\}$

denotes a "*zero-knowledge* Proof of Knowledge *of integers* α, β, *and* γ *such that* $y = g^{\alpha} h^{\beta}$ *and* $\tilde{y} = \tilde{g}^{\alpha} \tilde{h}^{\gamma}$ *holds, where* $u \leq \alpha \leq v$," where $y, g, h, \tilde{y}, \tilde{g}$, and $\tilde{h}$ are elements of some groups $G = \langle g \rangle = \langle h \rangle$ and $\tilde{G} = \langle \tilde{g} \rangle = \langle \tilde{h} \rangle$. The convention is that Greek letters denote the quantities the knowledge of which is being proved, while all other parameters are known to the verifier. Using this notation, a proof protocol can be described by just pointing out its aim while hiding all details.

In the random oracle model, such protocols can be turned into signature schemes using the Fiat-Shamir heuristic [12, 16]. We use the notation $SPK\{(\alpha) : y = g^{\alpha}\}(m)$ to denote a signature obtained in this way and call it proof signature.

The Camenisch-Lysyanskaya Signature Scheme. The direct anonymous attestation scheme as well as our new scheme are both based on the Camenisch-Lysyanskaya (CL) signature scheme [6]. Unlike most signature schemes, this one is particularly suited for our purposes as it allows for efficient protocols to prove knowledge of a signature and to retrieve signatures on secret messages efficiently using discrete logarithm based proofs of knowledge [6]. As we will use somewhat different (and also optimized) protocols for these tasks than those provided in [6], we recall the signature scheme here and give an overview of discrete logarithm based proofs of knowledge in the following subsection.

Key generation. On input 1^k, choose a special RSA modulus $n = pq$, $p = 2p' + 1$, $q = 2q' + 1$. Choose, uniformly at random, $R_0, \ldots, R_{L-1}, S, Z \in QR_n$. Output the public key $(n, R_0, \ldots, R_{L-1}, S, Z)$ and the secret key p. Let ℓ_n be the length of n.

Signing algorithm. Let ℓ_m be a parameter. On input $(m_0, \ldots, m_{L-1})$ with $m_i \in \pm\{0,1\}^{\ell_m}$, choose a random prime number e of length $\ell_e > \ell_m + 2$, and a random number v of length $\ell_v = \ell_n + \ell_m + \ell_r$, where ℓ_r is a security parameter. Compute the value A such that $Z \equiv R_0^{m_0} \ldots R_{L-1}^{m_{L-1}} S^v A^e \pmod{n}$. The signature on the message $(m_0, \ldots, m_{L-1})$ consists of (e, A, v).

Verification algorithm. To verify that the tuple (e, A, v) is a signature on message $(m_0, \ldots, m_{L-1})$, check that $Z \equiv A^e R_0^{m_0} \ldots R_{L-1}^{m_{L-1}} S^v \pmod{n}$, and check that $2^{\ell_e} > e > 2^{\ell_e - 1}$.

Theorem 1 ([6]). *The signature scheme is secure against adaptive chosen message attacks [13] under the strong RSA assumption.*

The original scheme considered messages in the interval $[0, 2^{\ell_m} - 1]$. Here, however, we allow messages from $[-2^{\ell_m} + 1, 2^{\ell_m} - 1]$. The only consequence of this is that we need to require that $\ell_e > \ell_m + 2$ holds instead of $\ell_e > \ell_m + 1$.

The Direct Anonymous Attestation Protocol. In this section we review the idea underlying the direct anonymous attestation scheme. The idea is in fact similar to the one of the Camenisch-Lysyanskaya anonymous credential system [5, 6]: A trusted hardware module (TPM) chooses a secret "message" f, obtains a Camenisch-Lysyanskaya (CL) signature (aka attestation) on it from the attester via a secure two-party protocol, and then can convince a verifier that it got attestation anonymously by a proof of knowledge of a signature on a secret message. To allow the verifier to recognize rogue TPMs, a TPM must also provide a pseudonym N_V and a proof that the pseudonym is formed correctly, i.e., that it is derived from the TPM's secret f contained in the attestation and a base determined by the verifier. We discuss different ways to handle rogue TPMs later.

Let us now describe this more detailed. Let (n, S, Z, R_0, R_1, R_2) be the attester's public key for the CL signature scheme. First, for efficiency reasons, the TPM's secret f is split into two ℓ_f-bit messages to be signed. These (secret) messages are denoted by f_0 and f_1 (instead of m_0 and m_1). This split allows for smaller primes e as their size depends on the size of the messages that get signed, which will make issuing of signature more efficient. The two-party protocol to sign secret messages is as follows (cf. [6]). First, the TPM sends the attester a commitment to the message-pair (f_0, f_1), i.e., $U := R_0^{f_0} R_1^{f_1} S^{v'}$, where v' is a value chosen randomly by the TPM to "blind" the f_i's. Also, the TPM computes $N_I := \zeta_I^{f_0 + f_1 2^{\ell_f}} \bmod \Gamma$, where ζ_I is a quantity derived from the attester's name, and sends U and N_I to the attester. Next, the TPM convinces the attester that U and N_I correctly formed (using a proof of knowledge a representation of U w.r.t. the bases R_0, R_1, S and N_I w.r.t. ζ_I) and that the f_i's lie in $\pm\{0,1\}^{\ell_f + \ell_H + \ell_\varnothing + 2}$, where ℓ_f, ℓ_H, and $\ell_\varnothing$ are security parameters. This interval is larger than the one from which the f_i's actually stem because of the proof of knowledge we apply here. If the attester accepts the proof, it compares N_I with previous such values obtained from this TPM to decide whether it wants to issue a certificate to TPM w.r.t. N_I or not. (The attester might not want to grant too many credentials to the TPM w.r.t. different N_I, but should re-grant a credential to a N_I it has already accepted.) To issue a credential, the attester chooses a random ℓ_v-bit integer v'' and a random ℓ_e-bit prime e, signs the hidden messages by computing $A := \left(\frac{Z}{U S^{v''}}\right)^{1/e} \bmod n$, and sends the TPM (A, e, v''). The attester also proves to the TPM that she computed A correctly. The signature on (f_0, f_1) is then $(A, e, v := v' + v'')$, where v should be kept secret by the TPM (for f_0 and f_1 to remain hidden from the attester), while A and e can be public. This concludes the description of the *DAA-Join* protocol.

A TPM can now prove that it has obtained attestation by proving that it got a CL-signature on some values f_0 and f_1. This can be done by a zero-knowledge proof of knowledge of values f_0, f_1, A, e, and v such that $A^e R_0^{f_0} R_1^{f_1} S^v \equiv Z$ (mod n). Also, the TPM computes $N_V := \zeta^{f_0 + f_1 2^{\ell_f}} \bmod \Gamma$ and proves that the exponent here is related to those in the attestation, where $\zeta \in \langle \gamma \rangle$, i.e., the subgroup of $\mathbb{Z}_\Gamma^*$ of order ρ. This proof of knowledge is turned into a signature scheme using the Fiat-Shamir heuristic. The specification provides to modes for this signature scheme: in one mode, an arbitrary message can be signed, in the other mode an attestation identity key (AIK) generated by the TPM is signed. This ensures that the verifier can tell whether a signed AIK was indeed produced by and is held inside a TPM. The resulting procedure is called *DAA-Sign*.

The base ζ is either chosen randomly by the TPM or is generated from a basename value bsn_V provided by the verifier. As mentioned in the introductions, the value N_V serves two purposes. The first one is rogue-tagging: If a rogue TPM is found, the values f_0 and f_1 are extracted and put on a blacklist. The verifier can then check N_V against this blacklist by comparing it with $\zeta^{\hat{f}_0 + \hat{f}_1 2^{\ell_f}}$ for all pairs $(\hat{f}_0, \hat{f}_1)$ on the black list. Note that i) the black list can be expected to be short, ii) the exponents $\hat{f}_0 + \hat{f}_1 2^{\ell_f}$ are small (e.g., 200-bits), and iii) batch-verification techniques can be applied [2]; so this check can be done efficiently. Also note that the blacklist need not be certified, e.g., by a certificate revocation agency: whenever f_0, f_1, A, e, and v are discovered, they can be published and everyone can verify whether (A, e, v) is a valid signature on f_0 and f_1. The second purpose of N_V is its use as a pseudonym, i.e., if ζ is not chosen randomly by the TPM but generated from a basename then, whenever the same basename bsn_V is used, the TPM will provide the same value for N_V. This allows the verifier to link different transactions made by the same TPM while not identifying it, and to possibly reject a N_V if it appeared too many times. By defining how often a different basename is used (e.g., a different one per verifier and day), one obtains the full spectrum from full identification to pseudonymity to full anonymity. The way the basename is chosen, the frequency it is changed, and the threshold on how many times a particular N_V can appear before a verifier should reject it, is a question that depends on particular scenarios/applications and is outside of the scope of this paper.

The actual anonymous attestation protocols outsources some operations of the TPM to the host in which the TPM is embedded. In particular, these are operation that are related to hiding the TPM's identity but not to the capability of producing a proof-signature of knowledge of an attestation. The rationale behind this is that the host can always reveal a TPM's identity.

4   Better Privacy Using a Two Stage Authorization

In this section we describe how we can achieve better privacy if we combine the direct anonymous attestation protocols with the Privacy CA approach. We will first describe the solution on a high level, similarly to the description of the direct anonymous attestation in the previous section. We will then describe the different protocols of our new scheme in more detail.

High-Level Idea. Recall that using the DAA-join protocol, a TPM can get a certificate (A, e, v) from an attester such that $A^e R_0^{f_0} R_1^{f_1} S^v \equiv Z \pmod{n}$ holds, where f_0, f_1, and v are only known to the TPM and (R_0, R_1, S, Z, n) are values of the attester's public key. Using the DAA-sign protocol, a TPM can convince a verifier that it has obtained such a certificate without revealing any other information. That is, it can convince the verifier that it knows values A, e, f_0, f_1, and v such that the above equation holds.

Now for our scheme, we need to modify the DAA-Join protocol such that the attester not only signs the secret keys of the TPM but also some value k_t

the attester chooses such that it is unique for each TPM. That is, the certificate (A, e, v) the TPM/host obtains from an attester will satisfy

$$A^e R_0^{f_0} R_1^{f_1} R_2^{k_t} S^v \equiv Z \pmod{n} ,$$

and R_2 is an additional value of the attester's public key. From this is also follows that k_t should be an ℓ_f-bit value. Of course, the attester has to send k_t to the TPM. This value will then also be part of all other the certificates issued to the platform. The value of k_t could for instance be derived from the TPM's endorsement key EK or in some other way; there is no cryptographic requirement on how k_t is chosen such as requiring that k_t is a cryptographic hash of EK.

Let us now look at how a frequency certificate is issued. Let (n, S, Z, R_0, R_1, R_2) be the Privacy CA's public key for the CL signature scheme. Now, in order to get an anonymous frequency certificate from the Privacy CA, the TPM/host show the attestation certificate to the Privacy CA using a long-term named base ζ for the computation of N_V and, if N_V passes the Privacy CA's frequency test, they will obtain a frequency certificate (A, e, v) from the Privacy CA such that

$$\mathsf{A}^e \mathsf{R}_0^{k_0} \mathsf{R}_1^{k_1} \mathsf{R}_2^{k_t} \mathsf{R}_3^{\mathsf{exp\text{-}date}} \mathsf{S}^v \equiv \mathsf{Z} \pmod{\mathsf{n}}$$

holds, where k_t is the same values as in the attestation, k_0 and k_1 are values chosen by the host, and exp-date is an encoding of the expiration date of the certificate (the different possible values of exp-date should be small to guarantee privacy). In getting this certificate from the Privacy CA, the TPM will need to be only involved in showing the attestation but not in anything related to the frequency certificate. The k_0 and k_1 should identify the verifier and some random number in a cryptographically secure way, e.g., $k_0 := \mathsf{LSB}_{\ell_f}(H(\mathtt{verifier\text{-}name}\|\mathtt{ran}))$ and $k_1 := \mathsf{CAR}_{\ell_f}(H(\mathtt{verifier\text{-}name}\|\mathtt{ran}))$.

Finally, when the host wants to show a verifier that is has obtained a certificate from the Privacy CA, the TPM/host convince the verifier that 1) they have a valid attestation (using a random base ζ in this proof), 2) they have a certificate from the Privacy CA, 3) the attestation and the certificate are linked by a common values (i.e., k_t), and 4) the certificates contains verifier-name, ran, and exp-date. That it, the TPM/host jointly proof knowledge of values This can be done by a zero-knowledge proof of knowledge of values f_0, f_1, A, e, and v, k_t, A, e, v such that $A^e R_0^{f_0} R_1^{f_1} R_2^{k_t} S^v \equiv Z \pmod{n}$ and $\mathsf{A}^e \mathsf{R}_0^{k_0} \mathsf{R}_1^{k_1} \mathsf{R}_2^{k_t} \mathsf{R}_3^{\mathsf{exp\text{-}date}} \mathsf{S}^v \equiv \mathsf{Z}$ (mod n) hold (note that the verifier can compute k_0 and k_1 himself).

Security Parameters. Our protocol employ the same security parameters as the direct anonymous attestation protocol [4], i.e., ℓ_n, ℓ_f, ℓ_c, ℓ'_e, ℓ_v, $\ell_\varnothing$, $\ell_\mathcal{H}$, ℓ_r, ℓ_Γ, and ℓ_ρ, where ℓ_n (2048) is the size of the RSA modulus, ℓ_f (104) is the size of the f_i's (information encoded into the certificate), ℓ_e (368) is the size of the e's (exponents, part of certificate), ℓ'_e (120) is the size of the interval the e's are chosen from, ℓ_v (2536) is the size of the v's (random value, part of certificate), $\ell_\varnothing$ (80) is the security parameter controlling the statistical zero-knowledge property,

$\ell_{\mathcal{H}}$ (160) is the output length of the hash function used for the Fiat-Shamir heuristic, ℓ_r (80) is the security parameter needed for the reduction in the proof of security, ℓ_Γ (1632) is the size of the modulus Γ, and ℓ_ρ (208) is the size of the order ρ of the sub group of $\mathbb{Z}_\Gamma^*$ that is used for rogue-tagging (the numbers in parentheses are our proposal for these parameters). We require that: $\ell_e > \ell_\varnothing + \ell_{\mathcal{H}} + \max\{\ell_f + 4 , \ \ell_e' + 2\}$, $\ell_v > \ell_n + \ell_\varnothing + \ell_{\mathcal{H}} + \max\{\ell_f + \ell_r + 3 , \ \ell_\varnothing + 2\}$, and $\ell_\rho = 2\ell_f$.

The parameters ℓ_Γ and ℓ_ρ should chosen such that the discrete logarithm problem in the subgroup of $\mathbb{Z}_\Gamma^*$ of order ρ with Γ and ρ being primes such that $2^{\ell_\rho} > \rho > 2^{\ell_\rho - 1}$ and $2^{\ell_\Gamma} > \Gamma > 2^{\ell_\Gamma - 1}$, has about the same difficulty as factoring ℓ_n-bit RSA moduli (see [15]).

Finally, let $\mathcal{H}$ be a collision resistant hash function $\mathcal{H} : \{0,1\}^* \rightarrow \{0,1\}^{\ell_{\mathcal{H}}}$.

Key Generation and Setup. The attester runs the following key-generation algorithm.

1. It chooses a RSA modulus $n = pq$ with $p = 2p' + 1$, $q = 2q' + 1$ such that p, p', q, q' are all primes and n has ℓ_n bits.
2. It chooses a random element $g' \in_R \mathbb{Z}_n$ of order $p'q'$.
3. Next, it chooses random integers $x_0, x_1, x_2, x_z, x_s, x_h, x_g \in [1, p'q']$ and computes $g := g'^{x_g} \bmod n$, $h := g'^{x_h} \bmod n$, $S := h^{x_s} \bmod n$, $Z := h^{x_z} \bmod n$, $R_0 := S^{x_0} \bmod n$, $R_1 := S^{x_1} \bmod n$, $R_2 := S^{x_2} \bmod n$.
4. It produces a non-interactive proof *proof* that R_0, R_1, S, Z, g, and h are computed correctly, i.e., that $g, h \in \langle g' \rangle$, $S, Z \in \langle h \rangle$, and $R_0, R_1, R_2 \in \langle S \rangle$ (see [4] for how this is done).
5. Output the public key $(n, g', g, h, S, Z, R_0, R_1, R_2)$ and the secret key (p, q).

We denote the resulting public key for the attester by $PK_I := (n, g', g, h, S, Z, R_0, R_1, R_2)$. The Privacy CA runs the same key generation algorithm, except that it also generates a third base R_3 in the same way that $R_0, \ldots, R_2$ are generated. We denote the thus generated public key of the Privacy CA by $PK_P := (\mathsf{n, g', g, h, S, Z, R_0, R_1, R_2, R_3})$

The attester furthermore makes available a group $\langle \gamma \rangle$ of prime order ρ, i.e., it chooses primes ρ and Γ such that $\Gamma = r\rho + 1$ for some r with $\rho \nmid r$, $2^{\ell_\Gamma - 1} < \Gamma < 2^{\ell_\Gamma}$, and $2^{\ell_\rho - 1} < \rho < 2^{\ell_\rho}$. Choose a random $\gamma' \in_R \mathbb{Z}_\Gamma^*$ such that $\gamma'^{(\Gamma - 1)/\rho} \not\equiv 1 \pmod{\Gamma}$ and set $\gamma := \gamma'^{(\Gamma - 1)/\rho} \bmod \Gamma$.

Finally, each TPM has generated an endorsement key, i.e., an RSA encryption public key, and has made it available to the attester. We refer to the TCG TPM specification [18, 4] for how this is done.

The Attestation Protocol. Let $PK_I := (n, g', g, h, S, Z, R_0, R_1, R_2, \gamma, \Gamma, \rho)$ be the public key of the attester. Let $\zeta_I \equiv (H_\Gamma(1\|\mathsf{bsn}_I))^{(\Gamma - 1)/\rho} \bmod \Gamma$, where bsn_I is the attester's long-term base name.

We assume that the TPM somehow authenticates itself towards the attester using its endorsement key before the protocol below is run. We refer to the TCG TPM specification [18, 4] for how this is done.

The protocol's input to the TPM is $(n, R_0, R_1, S, \rho, \Gamma)$ and its input to the host is $(n, g', g, h, S, Z, R_0, R_1, R_2, \gamma, \Gamma, \rho)$.

1. The host computes $\zeta_I := (H_\Gamma(1\|\mathtt{bsn}_I))^{(\Gamma-1)/\rho} \bmod \Gamma$ and sends ζ_I to the TPM.
2. The TPM checks whether $\zeta_I^\rho \equiv 1 \pmod{\Gamma}$.
3. Let $i := \lfloor \frac{\ell_\rho + \ell_\varnothing}{\ell_\mathcal{H}} \rfloor$ (i will be 1 for values of the parameters selected in Section 4).
   The TPM computes

$$f := H(H(\mathtt{seed}\|H(PK_I'))\|\mathtt{cnt}\|0)\| \ldots \|$$
$$H(H(\mathtt{seed}\|H(PK_I'))\|\mathtt{cnt}\|i) \pmod{\rho} ,$$

$$f_0 := \mathtt{LSB}_{\ell_f}(f), \; f_1 := \mathtt{CAR}_{\ell_f}(f), \; v' \in_R \{0,1\}^{\ell_n+\ell_\varnothing}, \; U := R_0^{f_0} R_1^{f_1} S^{v'} \bmod n,$$

   and $N_I := \zeta_I^{f_0 + f_1 2^{\ell_f}} \bmod \Gamma$, and sends U and N_I to the attester.
4. The TPM proves to the attester knowledge of f_0, f_1, and v': it executes as prover the proof signature

$$SPK\{(f_0, f_1, v') : f_0, f_1 \in \{0,1\}^{\ell_f + \ell_\varnothing + \ell_\mathcal{H} + 2} \wedge v' \in \{0,1\}^{\ell_n + \ell_\varnothing + \ell_\mathcal{H} + 2} \wedge$$
$$U \equiv \pm R_0^{f_0} R_1^{f_1} S^{v'} \pmod{n} \wedge N_I \equiv \zeta_I^{f_0 + f_1 2^{\ell_f}} \pmod{\Gamma}\}$$

   with the attester as the verifier.
5. The attester chooses $\hat{v} \in_R \{0,1\}^{\ell_v - 1}$, a prime $e \in_R [2^{\ell_e - 1}, 2^{\ell_e - 1} + 2^{\ell_e' - 1}]$, and an appropriate and unique k_t, computes $v'' := \hat{v} + 2^{\ell_v - 1}$ and
   $A := (\frac{Z}{U R_2^{k_t} S^{v''}})^{1/e} \bmod n$, and sends (A, e, v'') and k_t to the host.
6. To convince the platform that A was correctly computed, the attester as prover runs the proof signature

$$SPK\{(d) : A \equiv \pm(\frac{Z}{U S^{v''} R_2^{k_t}})^d \pmod{n}\}$$

   with the host as verifier.
7. The host verifies whether e is a prime and lies in $[2^{\ell_e - 1}, 2^{\ell_e - 1} + 2^{\ell_e' - 1}]$. The host sends v'' to the TPM. The host stores A, e, and k_t.

The only change we have made to this protocol is that A is computed differently. That is, the term $R_2^{k_t}$ does not appear in the original DAA protocol in any of the computations of A. In particular, we did not modify anything that involves the TPM, so our modified protocol is compatible with the TCG TPM v1.2 specification [18, 4].

Obtaining a One-Time Certificate from the Privacy-CA. In this section we describe how the TPM/host convince the Privacy CA that the got an attestation certificate, how they obtain a frequency certificate from it, and how it is ensured that this certificate will also contain the value k_t that is contained on the attestation certificate. The protocol for this can be seen as a combination of the DAA-join protocol and the DAA-sign and DAA-verify algorithms.

Let $PK_P := (n, g', g, h, S, Z, R_0, R_1, R_2, R_3)$ be the public key of the Privacy CA. Let $n_p \in \{0, 1\}^{\ell_\mathcal{H}}$ be a nonce and $\mathtt{bsn}_P$ a base name value provided by the Privacy CA.

The input to the protocol for the TPM is $(n, R_0, R_1, R_2, S = S^{2^{\ell_s}}, \Gamma, \rho)$ and (f_0, f_1, v_1, v_2), and the host's input to the protocol is the certificate (A, e) and, $(n, g, g', h, R_0, R_1, R_2, S, Z, \gamma, \Gamma, \rho)$ and $(n, g', g, h, S, Z, R_0, R_1, R_2, R_3)$. The frequency certification protocol is as follows:

1. (a) The host computes $\zeta := (H_\Gamma(1\|\mathtt{bsn}_P))^{(\Gamma-1)/\rho} \bmod \Gamma$ and sends ζ to the TPM.
2. (a) The host picks random integers $w, r \in [1, \lfloor\frac{n}{4}\rfloor]$ and computes $T_1 := Ah^w \bmod n$ and $T_2 := g^w h^e (g')^r \bmod n$.
   (b) The TPM computes $N_P := \zeta^{f_0+f_1 2^{\ell_f}} \bmod \Gamma$ and sends N_P to the host.
   (c) Let $\mathtt{ran}$ be a sufficiently large random string chosen by the host, e.g., $\mathtt{ran} \in_R \{0, 1\}^{\ell_\mathcal{H}}$. Let $k_0 := \mathsf{LSB}_{\ell_f}(H(\mathtt{verifier\text{-}name}\|\mathtt{ran}))$ and $k_1 := \mathsf{CAR}_{\ell_f}(H(\mathtt{verifier\text{-}name}\|\mathtt{ran}))$. The host picks a random integer $\mathsf{v}' \in_R [0, \lfloor\frac{n}{4}\rfloor]$ and computes $\mathsf{U} := R_0^{k_0} R_1^{k_1} R_2^{k_t} S^{\mathsf{v}'} \bmod n$.
3. To prove that U was computed correctly, that the TPM/host has obtained attestation, and that it contains the same value of k_t as does U, the host/TPM jointly perform the following proof signature

$$SPK\{(f_0, f_1, v, e, w, r, k_t, k_0, k_1, \mathsf{v}') :$$
$$Z \equiv T_1^e R_0^{f_0} R_1^{f_1} R_2^{k_t} S^v h^{-ew} \pmod{n} \wedge T_2 \equiv g^w h^e g'^r \pmod{n} \wedge$$
$$1 \equiv T_2^{-e} g^{ew} h^{ee} g'^{er} \pmod{n} \wedge N_P \equiv \zeta^{f_0+f_1 2^{\ell_f}} \pmod{\Gamma} \wedge$$
$$\mathsf{U} \equiv R_0^{k_0} R_1^{k_1} R_2^{k_t} S^{\mathsf{v}'} \pmod{n} \wedge$$
$$f_0, f_1, k_t, k_0, k_1 \in \{0, 1\}^{\ell_f+\ell_\varnothing+\ell_\mathcal{H}+2} \wedge (e - 2^{\ell_e}) \in \{0, 1\}^{\ell_e'+\ell_\varnothing+\ell_\mathcal{H}+1}\}$$

as prover with the Privacy CA as verifier. We show in the full version of this paper how this can be done.
4. The Privacy CA checks whether $\zeta \overset{?}{\equiv} (H_\Gamma(1\|\mathtt{bsn}_P))^{(\Gamma-1)/\rho} \pmod{\Gamma}$.
5. For all (f_0, f_1) on the revocation list, check if $N_P \overset{?}{\not\equiv} (\zeta^{f_0+f_1 2^{\ell_f}}) \pmod{\Gamma}$.
6. The Privacy CA checks whether N_P has appeared too often lately, i.e., performs the frequency checks on N_P.
7. Let $\mathtt{exp\text{-}date} \in \{0, 1\}^{\ell_f}$ encode the certificate's expiration date. The Privacy CA chooses $\hat{v} \in_R \{0, 1\}^{\ell_v-1}$ and a prime $e \in_R [2^{\ell_e-1}, 2^{\ell_e-1} + 2^{\ell_e'-1}]$ and computes $v'' := \hat{v} + 2^{\ell_v-1}$ and $A := \left(\frac{Z}{\mathsf{UR}_3^{\mathtt{exp\text{-}date}} S^{v''}}\right)^{1/e} \bmod n$, and sends (A, e, v'') and $\mathtt{exp\text{-}date}$ to the host.
8. To convince the platform that A was correctly computed, the attester as prover runs the proof signature

$$SPK\{(d) : \quad A \equiv \pm\left(\frac{Z}{\mathsf{UR}_3^{\mathtt{exp\text{-}date}} S^{v''}}\right)^d \pmod{n}\}$$

with the host as verifier.

9. The host verifies whether e is a prime and lies in $[2^{\ell_e-1}, 2^{\ell_e-1} + 2^{\ell'_e-1}]$. The host computes $v := v'' + v'$, verifies $A^e R_0^{k_0} R_1^{k_1} R_2^{k_t} R_3^{\text{exp-date}} S^v \equiv Z \pmod{n}$ and stores (A, e, v) together with `verifier-name`, `ran`, and `exp-date`.

As mentioned this protocol can be seen as a merge of the DAA-Join and the DAA-Sign protocols. However, as far as the TPM is concerned it is basically the DAA-Sign protocol, all other operations are solely carried out on the host. This can be easily be seen for all steps of the protocol, apart from the step 3 where the TPM and host proof that they got an attestation certificate, that the value U was computed correctly, and that the attestation certificate and U both contained the same (secret) value k_t. How this proof is exactly done is described in the full version of this paper. The idea of it is that the TPM executes all its operations of the DAA-sign protocol, i.e., it basically executes the proof signature $SPK\{(f_0, f_1, v) : (Z/A^e) \equiv R_0^{f_0} R_1^{f_1} S^v \bmod n \wedge N_V \equiv \zeta^{f_0+f_1 2^{\ell_f}} \pmod{\Gamma}\}$, which the host then extends to the full proof of step 3. Note that this proof does not involve any terms related to the Privacy CA. Thus, our protocol is compatible with the DAA-Sign protocol as in the TCG TPM v1.2 specification [18, 4].

We finally remark that the expiration date selected by the Privacy CA will later also be shown to the verifier. Thus it, if it is chosen too fine-grained, the Privacy CA and the verifier could link the transactions by the expiration date. Specifying the expiration date in days should be fine for most applications Moreover, as the certificate can be used only one, there seems to be no strong reason to even have an expiration date at all. If no expiration date is required one can just set `exp-date` $= 0$, or just drop all terms $R_3^{\text{exp-date}}$.

Using the Certificate from the Privacy CA. In this section we finally provide the procedure for the TPM/host to convince that they got an attestation certificate and a frequency certificate. The procedure can be seen as running two instances of the DAA-sign protocol in parallel, one w.r.t. the attestation certificate and one w.r.t. the frequency certificate. In the latter instance, however, the TPM is not involved at all – here the host plays also the role of the TPM.

Let $n_v \in \{0, 1\}^{\ell_H}$ be a nonce provided by the verifier. Let b be a byte describing the mode of the protocol, i.e., $b = 0$ means that the message m is an AIK generated by the TPM and $b = 1$ means that the message m was input to the TPM.

The input to the protocol of for the TPM is m, $(n, R_0, R_1, S, S' = S^{2^{\ell_s}}, \Gamma, \rho)$ and (f_0, f_1, v_1, v_2), and the host's input to the protocol is m, the certificate (A, e) and, $(n, g, g', h, R_0, R_1, S, Z, \gamma, \Gamma, \rho)$;

Let $PK_P := (n, g', g, h, S, Z, R_0, R_1, R_2)$ be the public key of the Privacy CA. The signing algorithm is as follows.

1. The host sends the verifier `verifier-name`, `ran`, and `exp-date` who checks whether `verifier-name` is correct, whether `ran` is a value that he has not seen so far, and whether *exp-date* is still valid.
2. (a) The host chooses a random $\zeta \in_R \langle \gamma \rangle$ and sends ζ to the TPM.
   (b) The host receives N_V from the TPM (however, we don't use N_V in the following).

3. (a) The host picks random integers $w, r \in [1, \lfloor \frac{n}{4} \rfloor]$ and computes $T_1 := Ah^w \bmod n$ and $T_2 := g^w h^e (g')^r \bmod n$.

   (b) The host picks random integers $\mathsf{w}, \mathsf{r} \in [1, \lfloor \frac{n}{4} \rfloor]$ and computes $\mathsf{T}_1 := A\mathsf{h}^{\mathsf{w}} \bmod \mathsf{n}$ and $\mathsf{T}_2 := \mathsf{g}^{\mathsf{w}} \mathsf{h}^e (\mathsf{g}')^{\mathsf{r}} \bmod \mathsf{n}$.

4. The host sends $T_1, T_2, \mathsf{T}_1, \mathsf{T}_2$, exp-date, verifier-name, and ran to the verifier.

5. The verifier checks whether it has seen ran before. If that is the case, the verifier aborts. Otherwise, it computes

$$k_0 := \mathsf{LSB}_{\ell_f}(H(\texttt{verifier-name}\|\texttt{ran})) \tag{1}$$

$$k_1 := \mathsf{CAR}_{\ell_f}(H(\texttt{verifier-name}\|\texttt{ran})) \tag{2}$$

6. To prove that the TPM/host has obtained attestation, that it has obtained a one-time certificate from the Privacy CA that contains the values k_0, k_1 and exp-date as well some value (k_t) that is also contained in the attestation, the host/TPM jointly perform the following proof signature

$$\begin{aligned}
SPK\{(f_0, f_1, v, e, w, r, k_t, \mathsf{v}, \mathsf{e}, \mathsf{w}, \mathsf{r}) : \quad & T_2 \equiv g^w h^e g'^r \pmod{n} \wedge \\
Z \equiv T_1^e R_0^{f_0} R_1^{f_1} R_2^{k_t} S^v h^{-ew} \pmod{n} \wedge \quad & 1 \equiv T_2^{-e} g^{ew} h^{ee} g'^{er} \pmod{n} \wedge \\
\mathsf{T}_2 \equiv \mathsf{g}^{\mathsf{w}} \mathsf{h}^e \mathsf{g}'^{\mathsf{r}} \pmod{\mathsf{n}} \wedge \quad & \frac{Z}{R_0^{k_0} R_1^{k_1} R_3^{\texttt{exp-date}}} \equiv \mathsf{T}_1^e R_2^{k_t} S^{\mathsf{v}} \mathsf{h}^{-e\mathsf{w}} \pmod{\mathsf{n}} \wedge \\
1 \equiv \mathsf{T}_2^{-e} \mathsf{g}^{e\mathsf{w}} \mathsf{h}^{ee} \mathsf{g}'^{er} \pmod{\mathsf{n}} \wedge \quad & f_0, f_1, k_t \in \{0,1\}^{\ell_f + \ell_\varnothing + \ell_H + 2} \wedge \\
(e - 2^{\ell_e}), (\mathsf{e} - 2^{\ell_e}) & \in \{0,1\}^{\ell'_e + \ell_\varnothing + \ell_H + 1} \}(n_t \| n_p \| b \| m)
\end{aligned}$$

as prover with the Privacy CA as verifier, where n_t is a nonce generated by the TPM. We refer to the full version of this paper for the details on how the TPM and the host jointly compute this proof signature.

Apart from the proof signature in the last step of the protocol, it is clear that the TPM performs only the operations as it would in the DAA-sign protocol. In the full version of this paper, we show that also in order to generate this proof signature, it is sufficient if the TPM only executes the steps from the DAA-sign protocol. Thus, also this protocol does not requires any change to the TPM as specified [18].

Security Analysis. Providing a formal proof of security is beyond the scope of this extended abstract; we will only provide an informal discussion why the proposed protocol meet the requirements listed in Section 2. However, given the proof of security of the original direct anonymous attestation protocol [4], deriving a proof of security for the protocols described in this paper is not too hard.

We argue why the requirements from Section 2 are fulfilled.

Unforgeability. First note that due to the properties of the direct anonymous attestation scheme, a TPM/host pair can only generate a DAA-signature if it has obtained an attestation certificate. Furthermore, if the same base ζ is used in the signature, the pseudonym N_P (resp. N_V) contained in the signature will be the same for all DAA-signatures produced by the TPM/host. Thus a TPM-host pair can not have more than one pseudonym with the same Privacy CA and will only obtain a frequency certificate if it is indeed entitled to obtain one. Furthermore, a TPM-host pair can use a frequency certificate only once and only with a single verifier. This is ensured by deriving the k_0 and k_1 that are included into the frequency certificate from `verifier-name` and `ran`. Changing these values can only be done if one could forge frequency certificates or break the hash function. Thus, if the verifier only accepts certificates where k_0 and k_1 are derived from it's name and a random string `ran` that it had not seen before, a frequency certificate can only be used with a single verifier and only once.

Anonymity. Apart from the zero-knowledge proofs and the pseudonyms N_P, all values that the TPM-host pair ever reveal are information theoretic commitments, or values that appear only in a single transaction. For instance, a value `ran` will appears only in a transaction with a verifier in the clear; in the corresponding transaction with the Privacy CA it appears only in a commitment. Furthermore, it is not hard to show that all the proofs protocols employed are statistically zero-knowledge. Thus, the pseudonyms N_P are the only information that could be used to link transactions. However, if it is ensured that the Privacy CAs each use a different base ζ, then the only transaction by the same TPM-host pair that can be linked are those made with the same Privacy CA, provided the decisional Diffie Hellman assumption is true. Ensuring that each Privacy CA indeed uses a different base could for instance be done by requiring that it is derived by the Privacy CA's name using a hash function. Thus anonymity is guaranteed even if the attester, all Privacy CAs, and all verifiers collude.

This assumes of course that the TPM-host pairs do chose the time at which to run the protocol to obtain a frequency certificate and the protocol to show it such that these instances become not linkeable solely by the time they are executed.

We finally note that because of the anonymity property even holds if the verifiers and the Privacy CAs collude, the role of the Privacy CAs can assume by the verifiers. Thus our solution overcomes the main drawback of the original Privacy CA solution where the TPM/host needs to trust these parties not to collude and hence this separation was needed.

5   Conclusion

We have shown how to modify the direct anonymous attestation protocol as to provide the same level of privacy as the TCG's initial Privacy CA solution while avoiding all the drawbacks of it. In particular, in our solution the TPM-host pair no longer needs to trust the Privacy CA which drastically lowers the requirements for running such a Privacy CA. In fact, in our solution the Privacy CA and the verifier can be the same party without loosing any security properties.

References

1. G. Ateniese, J. Camenisch, M. Joye, and G. Tsudik. A practical and provably secure coalition-resistant group signature scheme. In *CRYPTO 2000*, vol. 1880 of *LNCS*, pp. 255–270. Springer Verlag, 2000.
2. M. Bellare, J. A. Garay, and T. Rabin. Fast batch verification for modular exponentiation and digital signatures. In *EUROCRYPT '98*, vol. 1403 of *LNCS*, pp. 236–250. Springer Verlag, 1998.
3. D. Boneh, X. Boyen, and H. Shacham. Short group signatures using strong Diffie Hellman. In *CRYPTO 2004*, *LNCS*, Springer Verlag, 2004.
4. E. Brickell, J. Camenisch, and L. Chen. Direct anonymous attestation. Technical Report Research Report RZ 3450, IBM Research Division, Mar. 2004.
5. J. Camenisch and A. Lysyanskaya. Efficient non-transferable anonymous multi-show credential system with optional anonymity revocation. In *EUROCRYPT 2001*, vol. 2045 of *LNCS*, pp. 93–118. Springer Verlag, 2001.
6. J. Camenisch and A. Lysyanskaya. A signature scheme with efficient protocols. In *SCN 2002*, vol. 2576 of *LNCS*, pp. 268–289. Springer Verlag, 2003.
7. J. Camenisch and A. Lysyanskaya. Signature schemes and anonymous credentials from bilinear maps. In *CRYPTO 2004*, *LNCS*, Springer Verlag, 2004.
8. J. Camenisch and M. Stadler. Efficient group signature schemes for large groups. In *CRYPTO '97*, vol. 1296 of *LNCS*, pp. 410–424. Springer Verlag, 1997.
9. D. Chaum. Blind signatures for untraceable payments. In *CRYPTO '82*, pp. 199–203. Plenum Press, 1983.
10. D. Chaum. Security without identification: Transaction systems to make big brother obsolete. *Communications of the ACM*, 28(10):1030–1044, Oct. 1985.
11. D. Chaum and E. van Heyst. Group signatures. In *EUROCRYPT '91*, vol. 547 of *LNCS*, pp. 257–265. Springer-Verlag, 1991.
12. A. Fiat and A. Shamir. How to prove yourself: Practical solutions to identification and signature problems. In *CRYPTO '86*, vol. 263 of *LNCS*, pp. 186–194, 1987.
13. S. Goldwasser, S. Micali, and R. Rivest. A digital signature scheme secure against adaptive chosen-message attacks. *SIAM Journal on Computing*, 17(2):281–308, Apr. 1988.
14. J. Kilian and E. Petrank. Identity escrow. In *CRYPTO '98*, vol. 1642 of *LNCS*, pp. 169–185, Berlin, 1998. Springer Verlag.
15. A. K. Lenstra and E. K. Verheul. Selecting cryptographic key sizes. *Journal of Cryptology*, 14(4):255–293, 2001.
16. D. Pointcheval and J. Stern. Security proofs for signature schemes. In *EUROCRYPT '96*, vol. 1070 of *LNCS*, pp. 387–398. Springer Verlag, 1996.
17. Trusted Computing Group. Trusted Computing Group (TCG) main specifcation, Version 1.1b, Available at www.trustedcomputinggroup.org, 2001.
18. Trusted Computing Group. TCG TPM specification 1.2. Available at www.trustedcomputinggroup.org, 2003.
19. Trusted Computing Group website. www.trustedcomputinggroup.org.

A Cryptographically Sound Dolev-Yao Style Security Proof of the Otway-Rees Protocol

Michael Backes

IBM Zurich Research Laboratory, Switzerland
mbc@zurich.ibm.com

Abstract. We present the first cryptographically sound security proof of the well-known Otway-Rees protocol. More precisely, we show that the protocol is secure against arbitrary active attacks including concurrent protocol runs if it is implemented using provably secure cryptographic primitives. Although we achieve security under cryptographic definitions, our proof does not have to deal with probabilistic aspects of cryptography and is hence in the scope of current proof tools. The reason is that we exploit a recently proposed ideal cryptographic library, which has a provably secure cryptographic implementation. Together with composition and preservation theorems of the underlying model, this allows us to perform the actual proof effort in a deterministic setting corresponding to a slightly extended Dolev-Yao model. Besides establishing the cryptographic security of the Otway-Rees protocol, our result also exemplifies the potential of this cryptographic library. We hope that it paves the way for cryptographically sound verification of security protocols by means of formal proof tools.

1 Introduction

Many practically relevant cryptographic protocols like SSL/TLS, IPSec, or SET use cryptographic primitives like signature schemes or encryption in a black-box way, while adding many non-cryptographic features. Vulnerabilities have accompanied the design of such protocols ever since early authentication protocols like Needham-Schroeder [34, 15], over carefully designed de-facto standards like SSL and PKCS [40, 13], up to current widely deployed products like Microsoft Passport [17]. However, proving the security of such protocols has been a very unsatisfactory task for a long time.

One way to conduct such proofs is the cryptographic approach, whose security definitions are based on complexity theory, e.g., [19, 18, 20, 10]. The security of a cryptographic protocol is proved by reduction, i.e., by showing that breaking the protocol implies breaking one of the underlying cryptographic primitives with respect to its cryptographic definition. This approach captures a very comprehensive adversary model and allows for mathematically rigorous and precise proofs. However, because of probabilism and complexity-theoretic restrictions, these proofs have to be done by hand so far, which yields proofs with faults and imperfections. Moreover, such proofs rapidly become too complex for larger protocols.

The alternative is the formal-methods approach, which is concerned with the automation of proofs using model checkers and theorem provers. As these tools currently cannot deal with cryptographic details like error probabilities and computational restrictions, abstractions of cryptography are used. They are almost always based on the

P. Samarati et al. (Eds.): ESORICS 2004, LNCS 3193, pp. 89–108, 2004.

so-called Dolev-Yao model [16]. This model simplifies proofs of larger protocols considerably and has given rise to a large body of literature on analyzing the security of protocols using various techniques for formal verification, e.g., [31, 29, 25, 14, 37, 1].

Among the protocols typically analyzed in the Dolev-Yao model, the Otway-Rees protocol [35], which aims at establishing a shared key between two users by means of a trusted third party, stands out as one of the most prominent protocols. It has been extensively studies in the past, e.g., in [36, 24, 37], and various new approaches and formal proof tools for the analysis of security protocols were validated by showing that they can prove the protocol in the Dolev-Yao model (respectively that they can find the well-known type-flaw attack if the underlying model does not provide sufficient typing itself; the model that our proof is based upon excludes this attack). However, all existing proofs of security of the Otway-Rees protocol are restricted to the Dolev-Yao model, i.e., no theorem exists which allows for carrying over the results of an existing proof to the cryptographic approach with its much more comprehensive adversary. Thus, despite of the tremendous amount of research dedicated to the Otway-Rees protocol, it is still an open question whether an actual implementation based on provably secure cryptographic primitives is secure under cryptographic security definitions. We close this gap by providing the first security proof of the Otway-Rees protocol in the cryptographic approach. We show that the protocol is secure against arbitrary active attacks if the Dolev-Yao-based abstraction of symmetric encryption is implemented using a symmetric encryption scheme that is secure against chosen-ciphertext attacks and additionally ensures integrity of ciphertexts. This is the standard security definition of authenticated symmetric encryption schemes [12, 11], and efficient symmetric encryptions schemes provably secure in this sense exist under reasonable assumptions [11, 39].

Obviously, establishing a proof in the cryptographic approach presupposes dealing with the mentioned cryptographic details, hence one naturally assumes that our proof heavily relies on complexity theory and is far out of scope of current proof tools. However, our proof is not performed from scratch in the cryptographic setting, but based on a recently proposed cryptographic library [8, 9, 7], which provides cryptographically faithful, deterministic abstractions of cryptographic primitives, i.e., the abstractions can be securely implemented using actual cryptography. Moreover, the library allows for nesting the abstractions in an arbitrary way, quite similar to the original Dolev-Yao model. While this was shown for public-key encryption and digital signatures in [8] and subsequently extended with message authentication codes in [9], the most recent extension of the library further incorporated symmetric encryption [7] which constitutes the most commonly used cryptographic primitive in the typical proofs with Dolev-Yao models, and also serves as the central primitive for expressing and analyzing the Otway-Rees protocol. However, as shown in [7], there are intrinsic difficulties in providing a sound abstraction from symmetric encryption in the strong sense of security used in [8]. Very roughly, a sound Dolev-Yao-style abstraction of symmetric encryption can only be established if a so-called *commitment problem* does not occur, which means that whenever a key that is not known to the adversary is used for encryption by an honest user then this key will never be revealed to the adversary. We will elaborate on the origin of this problem in more detail in the paper. While [7] discusses several solutions to this problem, the one actually taken is to leave it to the surrounding protocol to guarantee that the commitment problem does not occur, i.e., if a protocol that uses symmetric encryption should be faithfully analyzed, it additionally has to be shown that the protocol guarantees that keys are no longer sent in a form that might make them known to the adversary once an honest participant has started using them. Our proof shows that this is a manageable task that can easily be incorporated in the overall security proof without imposing a major additional burden on the prover.

Once we have shown that the Otway-Rees protocol does not raise the commitment problem, it is sufficient to prove the security of the Otway-Rees protocol based on the deterministic abstractions; then the result automatically carries over to the cryptographic setting. As the proof is deterministic and rigorous, it should be easily expressible in formal proof tools, in particular theorem provers. Even done by hand, our proof is much less prone to error than a reduction proof conducted from scratch in the cryptographic approach. We also want to point out that our result not only provides the up-to-now missing cryptographic security proof of the Otway-Rees protocol, but also exemplifies the usefulness of the cryptographic library [8] and their extensions [9, 7] for the cryptographically sound verification of cryptographic protocols.

Further Related Work. Cryptographic underpinnings of a Dolev-Yao model were first addressed by Abadi and Rogaway in [3]. However, they only handled passive adversaries and symmetric encryption. The protocol language and security properties handled were extended in [2, 26], but still only for passive adversaries. This excludes most of the typical ways of attacking protocols, e.g., man-in-the-middle attacks and attacks by reusing a message part in a different place or a concurrent protocol run. A full cryptographic justification for a Dolev-Yao model, i.e., for arbitrary active attacks and within arbitrary surrounding interactive protocols, was first given recently in [8] with extensions in [9, 7]. Based on the specific Dolev-Yao model whose soundness was proven in [8], the well-known Needham-Schroeder-Lowe protocol was proved in [6]. Besides the proof that we present in this paper, the proof in [6] is the only Dolev-Yao-style, computationally sound proof that we are aware of. However, it is considerably simpler than the one we present in this work since it only addresses integrity properties whereas our proof additionally establishes confidentiality properties; moreover, the Needham-Schroeder-Lowe protocols does not use symmetric encryption, hence the commitment problem does not occur there which greatly simplifies the proof. Another cryptographically sound proof of this protocol was concurrently developed by Warinschi [41]. The proof is conducted from scratch in the cryptographic approach which takes it out of the scope of formal proof tools.

Laud [27] has recently presented a cryptographic underpinning for a Dolev-Yao model of symmetric encryption under active attacks. His work enjoys a direct connection with a formal proof tool, but it is specific to certain confidentiality properties, restricts the surrounding protocols to straight-line programs in a specific language, and does not address a connection to the remaining primitives of the Dolev-Yao model. Herzog et al. [21, 22] and Micciancio and Warinschi [30] have recently also given a cryptographic underpinning under active attacks. Their results are considerably weaker than the one in [8] since they are specific for public-key encryption; moreover, the former relies on a stronger assumption whereas the latter severely restricts the classes of protocols and protocol properties that can be analyzed using this primitive. Section 6 of [30] further points out several possible extensions of their work which all already exist in the earlier work of [8].

Efforts are also under way to formulate syntactic calculi for dealing with probabilism and polynomial-time considerations, in particular [32, 28, 33, 23] and, as a second step, to encode them into proof tools. However, this approach can not yet handle protocols with any degree of automation. Generally it is complementary to, rather than competing with, the approach of proving simple deterministic abstractions of cryptography and working with those wherever cryptography is only used in a blackbox way.

Outline. Section 2 introduces the notation used in the paper and briefly reviews the aforementioned cryptographic library. Section 3 shows how to model the Otway-Rees protocol based on this library as well as how initially shared keys can be represented in the underlying model. Section 4 contains the security property of the Otway-Rees protocol in the ideal setting, and this property is proven in Section 5. Section 6 shows how to carry these results over to the cryptographic implementation of the protocol. Section 7 concludes.

2   Preliminaries

In this section, we give an overview of the ideal cryptographic library of [8, 9, 7] and briefly sketch its provably secure implementation. We start by introducing the notation used in this paper.

2.1   Notation

We write ":=" for deterministic and "←" for probabilistic assignment. Let $\downarrow$ denote an error element available as an addition to the domains and ranges of all functions and algorithms. The list operation is denoted as $l := (x_1, \ldots, x_j)$, and the arguments are unambiguously retrievable as $l[i]$, with $l[i] = \downarrow$ if $i > j$. A database D is a set of functions, called entries, each over a finite domain called attributes. For an entry $x \in D$, the value at an attribute att is written $x.att$. For a predicate $pred$ involving attributes, $D[pred]$ means the subset of entries whose attributes fulfill $pred$. If $D[pred]$ contains only one element, we use the same notation for this element.

2.2   Overview of the Ideal and Real Cryptographic Library

The ideal (abstract) cryptographic library of [8, 9, 7] offers its users abstract cryptographic operations, such as commands to encrypt or decrypt a message, to make or test a signature, and to generate a nonce. All these commands have a simple, deterministic semantics. To allow a reactive scenario, this semantics is based on state, e.g., of who already knows which terms; the state is represented as a database. Each entry has a type (e.g., "ciphertext"), and pointers to its arguments (e.g., a key and a message). Further, each entry contains handles for those participants who already know it. A send operation makes an entry known to other participants, i.e., it adds handles to the entry. The ideal cryptographic library does not allow cheating. For instance, if it receives a command to encrypt a message m with a certain key, it simply makes an abstract database entry for the ciphertext. Another user can only ask for decryption of this ciphertext if he has obtained handles to both the ciphertext and the secret key. To allow for the proof of cryptographic faithfulness, the library is based on a detailed model of asynchronous reactive systems introduced in [38] and represented as a deterministic machine $\mathsf{TH}_{\mathcal{H}}$, called *trusted host*. The parameter $\mathcal{H} \subseteq \{1 \ldots, n\}$ denotes the honest participants, where n is a parameter of the library denoting the overall number of participants. Depending on the considered set $\mathcal{H}$, the trusted host offers slightly extended capabilities for the adversary. However, for current purposes, the trusted host can be seen as a slightly modified Dolev-Yao model together with a network and intruder model, similar to "the CSP Dolev-Yao model" or "the inductive-approach Dolev-Yao model".

The real cryptographic library offers its users the same commands as the ideal one, i.e., honest users operate on cryptographic objects via handles. The objects are now real cryptographic keys, ciphertexts, etc., handled by real distributed machines. Sending a term on an insecure channel releases the actual bitstring to the adversary, who can do with it what he likes. The adversary can also insert arbitrary bitstrings on non-authentic channels. The implementation of the commands is based on arbitrary secure encryption and signature systems according to standard cryptographic definitions, with certain additions like type tagging and additional randomizations.

The security proof of [8] states that the real library is *at least as secure* as the ideal library. This is captured using the notion of *reactive simulatability* [38], which states that whatever an adversary can achieve in the real implementation, another adversary can achieve given the ideal library, or otherwise the underlying cryptography can be broken [38]. This is the strongest possible cryptographic relationship between a real and an ideal system. In particular it covers arbitrary active attacks. Moreover, a composition theorem exists in the underlying model [38], which states that one can securely replace the ideal library in larger systems with the real library, i.e., without destroying the already established simulatability relation.

2.3 Detailed Description of the State of the Cryptographic Library

We conclude this section with the rigorous definition of the state of the ideal cryptographic library. A rigorous definition of the commands of the ideal library used for modeling the Otway-Rees protocol and for capturing the slightly extended adversary capabilities can be found in the long version of this paper [4].

The machine $\mathsf{TH}_{\mathcal{H}}$ has ports $\mathsf{in}_u?$ and $\mathsf{out}_u!$ for inputs from and outputs to each user $u \in \mathcal{H}$ and for $u = \mathsf{a}$, denoting the adversary. The notation follows the CSP convention, e.g., the cryptographic library obtains messages at $\mathsf{in}_u?$ that have been output at $\mathsf{in}_u!$. Besides the number n of users, the ideal cryptographic library is parameterized by a tuple L of length functions which are used to calculate the "length" of an abstract entry, corresponding to the length of the corresponding bitstring in the real implementation. Moreover, L contains bounds on the message lengths and the number of accepted inputs at each port. These bounds can be arbitrarily large, but have to be polynomially bounded in the security parameter. Using the notation of [8], the ideal cryptographic library is a *system* $Sys_{n,L}^{\mathrm{cry,id}}$ that consists of several *structures* $(\{\mathsf{TH}_{\mathcal{H}}\}, S_{\mathcal{H}})$, one for each value of the parameter $\mathcal{H}$. Each structure consists of a set of machines, here only containing the single machine $\mathsf{TH}_\mathcal{H}$, and a set $S_\mathcal{H} := \{\mathsf{in}_u?, \mathsf{out}_u! \mid u \in \mathcal{H}\}$ denoting those ports of $\mathsf{TH}_\mathcal{H}$ that the honest users connect to. Formally, we obtain $Sys_{n,L}^{\mathrm{cry,id}} := \{(\{\mathsf{TH}_\mathcal{H}\}, S_\mathcal{H}) \mid \mathcal{H} \subseteq \{1, \ldots, n\}\}$. In the following, we omit the parameters n and L for simplicity[1].

The main data structure of $\mathsf{TH}_\mathcal{H}$ is a database D. The entries of D are abstract representations of the data produced during a system run, together with the information on who knows these data. Each entry in D is of the form (recall the notation in Section 2.1)

$$(ind, type, arg, hnd_{u_1}, \ldots, hnd_{u_m}, hnd_{\mathsf{a}}, len)$$

where $\mathcal{H} = \{u_1, \ldots, u_m\}$. For each entry $x \in D$:

- $x.ind \in \mathcal{INDS}$, called index, consecutively numbers all entries in D. The set $\mathcal{INDS}$ is isomorphic to $\mathbb{N}$ and is used to distinguish index arguments from others. The index is used as a primary key attribute of the database, i.e., we write $D[i]$ for the selection $D[ind = i]$.
- $x.type \in typeset$ identifies the *type* of x.
- $x.arg = (a_1, a_2, \ldots, a_j)$ is a possibly empty list of arguments. Many values a_i are indices of other entries in D and thus in $\mathcal{INDS}$. We sometimes distinguish them by a superscript "ind".
- $x.hnd_u \in \mathcal{HNDS} \cup \{\downarrow\}$ for $u \in \mathcal{H} \cup \{\mathsf{a}\}$ are handles by which a user or adversary u knows this entry. $x.hnd_u = \downarrow$ means that u does not know this entry. The set $\mathcal{HNDS}$ is yet another set isomorphic to $\mathbb{N}$. We always use a superscript "hnd" for handles.
- $x.len \in \mathbb{N}_0$ denotes the "length" of the entry; it is computed by applying the functions from L.

Initially, D is empty. $\mathsf{TH}_\mathcal{H}$ has a counter $size \in \mathcal{INDS}$ for the current size of D. For the handle attributes, it has counters $curhnd_u$ (current handle) initialized with 0.

3   The Otway-Rees Protocol

The Otway-Rees protocol [35] is a four-step protocol for establishing a shared secret encryption key between two users. The protocol relies on a distinguished trusted third party T, i.e., $\mathsf{T} \notin \{1, \ldots, n\}$, and it is assumed that every user u initially shares a secret key K_{ut} with T. Expressed in the typical protocol notation, the Otway-Rees protocol works as follows[2].

1. $u \to v : M, (N_u, M, u, v)_{K_{ut}}$
2. $v \to \mathsf{T} : M, (N_u, M, u, v)_{K_{ut}}, (N_v, M, u, v)_{K_{vt}}$
3. $\mathsf{T} \to v : M, (N_u, K_{uv})_{K_{ut}}, (N_v, K_{uv})_{K_{vt}}$
4. $v \to u : M, (N_u, K_{uv})_{K_{ut}}.$

---

[1] Formally, these parameters are thus also parameters of the ideal Otway-Rees system $Sys^{\mathrm{OR,id}}$ that we introduce in Section 3.2.

[2] For simplicity, we omit the explicit inclusion of u and v in the unencrypted part of the first and second message since the cryptographic library already provides the identity of the (claimed) sender of a message, which is sufficient for our purpose.

3.1 Capturing Distributed Keys in the Abstract Library

In order to capture that keys shared between users and the trusted third party have already been generated and distributed, we assume that suitable entries for the keys already exist in the database. We denote the handle of u to the secret key shared with v, where either $u \in \{1, \ldots, n\}$ and $v = \mathsf{T}$ or vice versa, as $skse_{u,v}^{hnd}$. More formally, we start with an initially empty database D, and for each user $u \in \mathcal{H}$ two entries of the following form are added (the first one being a public-key identifier for the actual secret key as described below in more detail):

$$(ind := pkse_u, type := \mathsf{pkse}, arg := (), len := 0);\,^3$$

$$(ind := skse_u, type := \mathsf{skse}, arg := (ind - 1),$$
$$hnd_u := skse_{u,\mathsf{T}}^{hnd}, hnd_\mathsf{T} := skse_{\mathsf{T},u}^{hnd}, len := \mathsf{skse\_len}^*(k)).$$

Here $pkse_u$ and $skse_u$ are two consecutive natural numbers; $\mathsf{skse\_len}^*(k)$ denotes the abstract length of the secret key which will not matter in the following.

The first entry has to be incorporated in order to reflect special capabilities that the adversary may have with respect to symmetric encryption schemes in the real world. For instance it must be possible for an adversary against the ideal library to check whether encryptions have been created with the same secret key since the definition of symmetric encryption schemes does not exclude this and it can hence happen in the real system. For public-key encryption, this was achieved in [8] by tagging ciphertexts with the corresponding public key so that the public keys can be compared. For symmetric encryption, this is not possible as no public key exists, hence this problem is solved by tagging abstract ciphertexts with an otherwise meaningless "public key" solely used as an identifier for the secret key. Note that the argument of a secret key points to its key identifier. In the following, public-key identifiers will not matter any further.

We omit the details of how these entries for user u are added by a command gen_symenc_key, followed by a command send_s for sending the secret key over a secure channel.

3.2 The Otway-Rees Protocol Using the Abstract Library

We now model the Otway-Rees protocol in the framework of [38] and using the ideal cryptographic library.

For each user $u \in \{1, \ldots, n\}$ we define a machine $\mathsf{M}_u^{\mathsf{OR}}$, called a *protocol machine*, which executes the protocol sketched above for participant identity u. It is connected to its user via ports $\mathsf{KS\_out}_u!$, $\mathsf{KS\_in}_u?$ ("KS" for "Key Sharing") and to the cryptographic library via ports $\mathsf{in}_u!$, $\mathsf{out}_u?$. We further model the trusted third party as a machine $\mathsf{M}_\mathsf{T}^{\mathsf{OR}}$. It does not connect to any users and is connected to the cryptographic library via ports $\mathsf{in}_\mathsf{T}!$, $\mathsf{out}_\mathsf{T}?$. The combination of the protocol machines $\mathsf{M}_u^{\mathsf{OR}}$, the trusted third party $\mathsf{M}_\mathsf{T}^{\mathsf{OR}}$, and the trusted host $\mathsf{TH}_\mathcal{H}$ is the *ideal Otway-Rees system $Sys^{\mathsf{OR,id}}$*. It is shown in Figure 1; H and A model the arbitrary joint honest users and the adversary, respectively.

---

[3] Treating public-key identifiers as being of length 0 is a technicality in the proof of [7] and will not matter in the sequel.

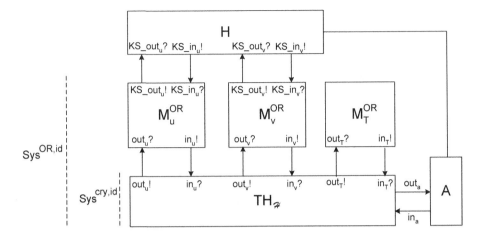

Fig. 1. Overview of the Otway-Rees Ideal System.

Using the notation of [8], we have $Sys^{\mathsf{OR,id}} := \{(\hat{M}_{\mathcal{H}}, S_{\mathcal{H}}) \mid \mathcal{H} \subseteq \{1, \ldots, n\}\}$, cf. the definition of the ideal cryptographic library in Section 2.3, where $\hat{M}_{\mathcal{H}} := \{\mathsf{TH}_{\mathcal{H}}\} \cup \{\mathsf{M}_u^{\mathsf{OR}} \mid u \in \mathcal{H} \cup \{\mathsf{T}\}\}$ and $S_{\mathcal{H}} := \{\mathsf{KS\_in}_u?, \mathsf{KS\_out}_u! \mid u \in \mathcal{H}\}$, i.e., for a given set $\mathcal{H}$ of honest users, only the protocol machines $\mathsf{M}_u^{\mathsf{OR}}$ with $u \in \mathcal{H}$ are actually present in a protocol run. The others are subsumed in the adversary.

The state of the protocol machine $\mathsf{M}_u^{\mathsf{OR}}$ consists of the bitstring u and a set $Nonce_u$ of pairs of the form $(n^{\mathsf{hnd}}, m^{\mathsf{hnd}}, v, j)$, where $n^{\mathsf{hnd}}, m^{\mathsf{hnd}}$ are handles, $v \in \{1, \ldots, n\}$, and $j \in \{1, 2, 3, 4\}$. Intuitively, a pair $(n^{\mathsf{hnd}}, m^{\mathsf{hnd}}, v, j)$ states that $\mathsf{M}_u^{\mathsf{OR}}$ generated the handle n^{hnd} in the j-th step of the protocol in a session run with v and session identifier m^{hnd}. The set $Nonce_u$ is initially empty. The trusted third party $\mathsf{M}_{\mathsf{T}}^{\mathsf{OR}}$ maintains an initially empty set SID_{T} to store already processed session IDs.

We now define how the protocol machine $\mathsf{M}_u^{\mathsf{OR}}$ evaluates inputs. They either come from user u at port $\mathsf{KS\_in}_u?$ or from $\mathsf{TH}_{\mathcal{H}}$ at port $\mathsf{out}_u?$. The behavior of $\mathsf{M}_u^{\mathsf{OR}}$ in both cases is described in Algorithm 1 and 3 respectively, which we will describe below. The trusted third party $\mathsf{M}_{\mathsf{T}}^{\mathsf{OR}}$ only receives inputs from the cryptographic library, and its behavior is described in Algorithm 2. We refer to Step i of Algorithm j as Step $j.i$. All three algorithms should immediately abort if a command to the cryptographic library does not yield the desired result, e.g., if a decryption requests fails. For readability we omit these abort checks in the algorithm descriptions; instead we impose the following convention on all three algorithms.

Convention 1 *For all $w \in \{1, \ldots, n\} \cup \{\mathsf{T}\}$ the following holds. If $\mathsf{M}_w^{\mathsf{OR}}$ enters a command at port $\mathsf{in}_w!$ and receives $\downarrow$ at port $\mathsf{out}_w?$ as the immediate answer of the cryptographic library, then $\mathsf{M}_w^{\mathsf{OR}}$ aborts the execution of the current algorithm, except if the command was of the form $\mathsf{list\_proj}$ or $\mathsf{send\_i}$.*

Protocol start. The user of the protocol machine $\mathsf{M}_u^{\mathsf{OR}}$ can start a new protocol with user $v \in \{1, \ldots, n\} \setminus \{u\}$ by inputting $(\mathsf{new\_prot}, \mathsf{Otway\_Rees}, v)$ at port $\mathsf{KS\_in}_u?$. Our security proof holds for all adversaries and all honest users, i.e., especially those that start

---

Algorithm 1 Evaluation of Inputs from the User (Protocol Start).

Input: $(\mathsf{new\_prot}, \mathsf{Otway\_Rees}, v)$ at $\mathsf{KS\_in}_u?$ with $v \in \{1, \ldots, n\} \setminus \{u\}$.

1: $n_u^{\mathsf{hnd}} \leftarrow \mathsf{gen\_nonce}()$.
2: $ID^{\mathsf{hnd}} \leftarrow \mathsf{gen\_nonce}()$.
3: $Nonce_u := Nonce_u \cup \{(n_u^{\mathsf{hnd}}, ID^{\mathsf{hnd}}, v, 1)\}$.
4: $u^{\mathsf{hnd}} \leftarrow \mathsf{store}(u)$.
5: $v^{\mathsf{hnd}} \leftarrow \mathsf{store}(v)$.
6: $l_1^{\mathsf{hnd}} \leftarrow \mathsf{list}(n_u^{\mathsf{hnd}}, ID^{\mathsf{hnd}}, u^{\mathsf{hnd}}, v^{\mathsf{hnd}})$.
7: $c_1^{\mathsf{hnd}} \leftarrow \mathsf{sym\_encrypt}(skse_{u,\mathsf{T}}^{\mathsf{hnd}}, l_1^{\mathsf{hnd}})$.
8: $m_1^{\mathsf{hnd}} \leftarrow \mathsf{list}(ID^{\mathsf{hnd}}, c_1^{\mathsf{hnd}})$.
9: $\mathsf{send\_i}(v, m_1^{\mathsf{hnd}})$.

---

protocols with the adversary (respectively a malicious user) in parallel with protocols with honest users. Upon such an input, $\mathsf{M}_u^{\mathsf{OR}}$ builds up the term corresponding to the first protocol message using the ideal cryptographic library according to Algorithm 1. The command gen_nonce generates the ideal nonce as well as the session identifier. $\mathsf{M}_u^{\mathsf{OR}}$ stores the resulting handles n_u^{hnd} and m^{hnd} in $Nonce_u$ for future comparison together with the identity of v and an indicator that these handles were generated in the first step of the protocol. The command store inputs arbitrary application data into the cryptographic library, here the user identities u and v. The command list forms a list and sym_encrypt is symmetric encryption. The final command send_i means that $\mathsf{M}_u^{\mathsf{OR}}$ sends the resulting term to v over an insecure channel. The effect is that the adversary obtains a handle to the term and can decide what to do with it (such as forwarding it to $\mathsf{M}_v^{\mathsf{OR}}$).

Evaluation of network inputs for protocol machines. The behavior of the protocol machine $\mathsf{M}_u^{\mathsf{OR}}$ upon receiving an input from the cryptographic library at port $\mathsf{out}_u?$ (corresponding to a message that arrives over the network) is defined similarly in Algorithm 3. By construction of $\mathsf{TH}_{\mathcal{H}}$, such an input is always of the form $(v, u, \mathsf{i}, m^{\mathsf{hnd}})$ where m^{hnd} is a handle to a list. To increase readability, and to clarify the connection between the algorithmic description and the usual protocol notation, we augment the algorithm with explanatory comments at its right-hand side to depict which handle corresponds to which Dolev-Yao term. We further use the naming convention that ingoing and outgoing messages are labeled m, where outgoing messages have an additional subscript corresponding to the protocol step. Encryptions are labeled c, the encrypted lists are labeled l, both with suitable sub- and superscripts.

$\mathsf{M}_u^{\mathsf{OR}}$ first determines the session identifier and aborts if it is not of type nonce. $\mathsf{M}_u^{\mathsf{OR}}$ then checks if the obtained message could correspond to the first, third, or fourth step of the protocol. (Recall that the second step is only performed by T.) This is implemented by looking up the session identifier in the set $Nonce_u$. After that, $\mathsf{M}_u^{\mathsf{OR}}$ checks if the obtained message is indeed a suitably constructed message for the particular step and the particular session ID by exploiting the contents of $Nonce_u$. If so, $\mathsf{M}_u^{\mathsf{OR}}$ constructs a message according to the protocol description, sends it to the intended recipient, updates the set $Nonce_u$, and possibly signals to its user that a key has been successfully shared with another user.

Algorithm 2 Behavior of the Trusted Third Party.

Input: $(v, \mathsf{T}, i, m^{\mathsf{hnd}})$ at out_T? with $v \in \{1, \ldots, n\}$.

1:   $ID^{\mathsf{hnd}} \leftarrow \mathsf{list\_proj}(m^{\mathsf{hnd}}, 1)$. $\{ID^{\mathsf{hnd}} \approx M\}$

2:   $type_1 \leftarrow \mathsf{get\_type}(ID^{\mathsf{hnd}})$.

3:   $c^{(3)^{\mathsf{hnd}}} \leftarrow \mathsf{list\_proj}(m^{\mathsf{hnd}}, 3)$. $\{c^{(3)^{\mathsf{hnd}}} \approx \{N_v, M, u, v\}_{K_{vt}}\}$

4:   $l^{(3)^{\mathsf{hnd}}} \leftarrow \mathsf{sym\_decrypt}(skse^{\mathsf{hnd}}_{\mathsf{T},v}, c^{(3)^{\mathsf{hnd}}})$. $\{l^{(3)^{\mathsf{hnd}}} \approx \{N_v, M, u, v\}\}$

5:   $y_i^{\mathsf{hnd}} \leftarrow \mathsf{list\_proj}(l^{(3)^{\mathsf{hnd}}}, i)$ for $i = 1, 2, 3, 4$.

6:   $y_i \leftarrow \mathsf{retrieve}(y_i^{\mathsf{hnd}})$ for $i = 3, 4$.

7:   **if** $(ID^{\mathsf{hnd}} \in SID_\mathsf{T}) \vee (type_1 \neq \mathsf{nonce}) \vee (y_2^{\mathsf{hnd}} \neq ID^{\mathsf{hnd}}) \vee (y_3 \notin \{1, \ldots, n\} \setminus \{v\}) \vee (y_4 \neq v)$ **then**

8:      Abort

9:   **end if**

10:   $SID_\mathsf{T} := SID_\mathsf{T} \cup \{ID^{\mathsf{hnd}}\}$.

11:   $c^{(2)^{\mathsf{hnd}}} \leftarrow \mathsf{list\_proj}(m^{\mathsf{hnd}}, 2)$. $\{c^{(2)^{\mathsf{hnd}}} \approx \{N_u, M, u, v\}_{K_{ut}}\}$

12:   $l^{(2)^{\mathsf{hnd}}} \leftarrow \mathsf{sym\_decrypt}(skse^{\mathsf{hnd}}_{\mathsf{T},y_3}, c^{(2)^{\mathsf{hnd}}})$. $\{l^{(2)^{\mathsf{hnd}}} \approx \{N_u, M, u, v\}\}$

13:   $x_i^{\mathsf{hnd}} \leftarrow \mathsf{list\_proj}(l^{(2)^{\mathsf{hnd}}}, i)$ for $i = 1, 2, 3, 4$.

14:   $type_2 \leftarrow \mathsf{get\_type}(x_1^{\mathsf{hnd}})$.

15:   $x_i \leftarrow \mathsf{retrieve}(x_i^{\mathsf{hnd}})$ for $i = 3, 4$.

16:   **if** $(type_2 \neq \mathsf{nonce}) \vee (x_2^{\mathsf{hnd}} \neq y_2^{\mathsf{hnd}}) \vee (x_3 \neq y_3) \vee (x_4 \neq y_4)$ **then**

17:      Abort

18:   **end if**

19:   $skse^{\mathsf{hnd}} \leftarrow \mathsf{gen\_symenc\_key}()$. $\{skse^{\mathsf{hnd}} \approx K_{uv}\}$

20:   $l_3^{(2)^{\mathsf{hnd}}} \leftarrow \mathsf{list}(x_1^{\mathsf{hnd}}, skse^{\mathsf{hnd}})$. $\{l_3^{(2)^{\mathsf{hnd}}} \approx \{N_u, K_{uv}\}\}$

21:   $c_3^{(2)^{\mathsf{hnd}}} \leftarrow \mathsf{sym\_encrypt}(skse^{\mathsf{hnd}}_{\mathsf{T},y_3}, l_3^{(2)^{\mathsf{hnd}}})$. $\{c_3^{(2)^{\mathsf{hnd}}} \approx \{N_u, K_{uv}\}_{K_{ut}}\}$

22:   $l_3^{(3)^{\mathsf{hnd}}} \leftarrow \mathsf{list}(y_1^{\mathsf{hnd}}, skse^{\mathsf{hnd}})$. $\{l_3^{(3)^{\mathsf{hnd}}} \approx \{N_v, K_{uv}\}\}$

23:   $c_3^{(3)^{\mathsf{hnd}}} \leftarrow \mathsf{sym\_encrypt}(skse^{\mathsf{hnd}}_{\mathsf{T},v}, l_3^{(3)^{\mathsf{hnd}}})$. $\{c_3^{(3)^{\mathsf{hnd}}} \approx \{N_v, K_{uv}\}_{K_{vt}}\}$

24:   $m_3^{\mathsf{hnd}} \leftarrow \mathsf{list}(ID^{\mathsf{hnd}}, c_3^{(2)^{\mathsf{hnd}}}, c_3^{(3)^{\mathsf{hnd}}})$. $\{m_3^{\mathsf{hnd}} \approx M, \{N_u, K_{uv}\}_{K_{ut}}, \{N_v, K_{uv}\}_{K_{vt}}\}$

25:   $\mathsf{send\_i}(v, m_3^{\mathsf{hnd}})$.

Behavior of the trusted third party. The behavior of $\mathsf{M}^{\mathsf{OR}}_\mathsf{T}$ upon receiving an input $(v, \mathsf{T}, i, m^{\mathsf{hnd}})$ from the cryptographic library at port out_T? is defined similarly in Algorithm 2. We omit an informal description.

3.3   On Polynomial Runtime

In order to use existing composition results of the underlying model, the protocol machines $\mathsf{M}^{\mathsf{OR}}_w$ and $\mathsf{M}^{\mathsf{OR}}_\mathsf{T}$ must be polynomial-time. Similar to the cryptographic library, we define that each of these machines maintains explicit polynomial bounds on the message lengths and the number of inputs accepted at each port.

4   The Security Property

In the following, we formalize the security property of the ideal Otway-Rees protocol. The property consists of a *secrecy property* and a *consistency property*. The secrecy

---

Algorithm 3 Evaluation of Inputs from $\mathsf{TH}_{\mathcal{H}}$ (Network Inputs).

Input: $(v, u, \mathsf{i}, m^{\mathsf{hnd}})$ at $\mathrm{out}_u?$ with $v \in \{1, \dots, n\} \setminus \{u\}$.

1: $ID^{\mathsf{hnd}} \leftarrow \mathsf{list\_proj}(m^{\mathsf{hnd}}, 1)$. $\{ID^{\mathsf{hnd}} \approx M\}$

2: $type_1 \leftarrow \mathsf{get\_type}(ID^{\mathsf{hnd}})$.

3: **if** $type_1 \neq \mathsf{nonce}$ **then**

4:     Abort

5: **end if**

6: **if** $v \neq \mathsf{T} \wedge \forall j, n^{\mathsf{hnd}} : (n^{\mathsf{hnd}}, ID^{\mathsf{hnd}}, v, j) \notin Nonce_u$ **then** {First Message is input}

7:     $c^{(2)^{\mathsf{hnd}}} \leftarrow \mathsf{list\_proj}(m^{\mathsf{hnd}}, 2)$. $\{c^{(2)^{\mathsf{hnd}}} \approx (N_v, M, v, u)_{K_{vt}}\}$

8:     $n_u^{\mathsf{hnd}} \leftarrow \mathsf{gen\_nonce}()$.

9:     $Nonce_u := Nonce_u \cup \{(n_u^{\mathsf{hnd}}, ID^{\mathsf{hnd}}, v, 2)\}$.

10:    $u^{\mathsf{hnd}} \leftarrow \mathsf{store}(u)$.

11:    $v^{\mathsf{hnd}} \leftarrow \mathsf{store}(v)$.

12:    $l_2^{(3)^{\mathsf{hnd}}} \leftarrow \mathsf{list}(n_u^{\mathsf{hnd}}, ID^{\mathsf{hnd}}, v^{\mathsf{hnd}}, u^{\mathsf{hnd}})$. $\{l_2^{(3)^{\mathsf{hnd}}} \approx N_u, M, v, u\}$

13:    $c_2^{(3)^{\mathsf{hnd}}} \leftarrow \mathsf{sym\_encrypt}(skse_{u,\mathsf{T}}^{\mathsf{hnd}}, l_2^{(3)^{\mathsf{hnd}}})$. $\{c_2^{(3)^{\mathsf{hnd}}} \approx (N_u, M, v, u)_{K_{ut}}\}$

14:    $m_2^{\mathsf{hnd}} \leftarrow \mathsf{list}(ID^{\mathsf{hnd}}, c^{(2)^{\mathsf{hnd}}}, c_2^{(3)^{\mathsf{hnd}}})$. $\{m_2^{\mathsf{hnd}} \approx M, (N_v, M, v, u)_{K_{vt}}, (N_u, M, v, u)_{K_{ut}}\}$

15:    $\mathsf{send\_i}(\mathsf{T}, m_2^{\mathsf{hnd}})$.

16: **else if** $v = \mathsf{T}$ **then** {Third Message is input}

17:    $c^{(2)^{\mathsf{hnd}}} \leftarrow \mathsf{list\_proj}(m^{\mathsf{hnd}}, 2)$. $\{c^{(2)^{\mathsf{hnd}}} \approx (N_v, K_{uv})_{K_{vt}}\}$

18:    $c^{(3)^{\mathsf{hnd}}} \leftarrow \mathsf{list\_proj}(m^{\mathsf{hnd}}, 3)$. $\{c^{(3)^{\mathsf{hnd}}} \approx (N_u, K_{uv})_{K_{ut}}\}$

19:    $l^{(3)^{\mathsf{hnd}}} \leftarrow \mathsf{sym\_decrypt}(skse_{u,\mathsf{T}}^{\mathsf{hnd}}, c^{(3)^{\mathsf{hnd}}})$. $\{l^{(3)^{\mathsf{hnd}}} \approx N_u, K_{uv}\}$

20:    $y_i^{\mathsf{hnd}} \leftarrow \mathsf{list\_proj}(l^{(3)^{\mathsf{hnd}}}, i)$ for $i = 1, 2$.

21:    $type_2 \leftarrow \mathsf{get\_type}(y_2^{\mathsf{hnd}})$.

22:    **if** $(\not\exists! w \in \{1, \dots, n\} \setminus \{u\} : (y_1^{\mathsf{hnd}}, ID^{\mathsf{hnd}}, w, 2) \in Nonce_u) \vee (type_2 \neq \mathsf{skse})$ **then**

23:      Abort

24:    **end if**

25:    $Nonce_u := (Nonce_u \setminus \{(y_1^{\mathsf{hnd}}, ID^{\mathsf{hnd}}, w, 2)\}) \cup \{(y_1^{\mathsf{hnd}}, ID^{\mathsf{hnd}}, w, 3)\}$.

26:    $m_4^{\mathsf{hnd}} \leftarrow \mathsf{list}(ID^{\mathsf{hnd}}, c^{(2)^{\mathsf{hnd}}})$. $\{m_4^{\mathsf{hnd}} \approx M, \{N_v, K_{uv}\}_{K_{vt}}\}$

27:    $\mathsf{send\_i}(w, m_4^{\mathsf{hnd}})$.

28:    Output $(\mathsf{ok}, \mathsf{Otway\_Rees}, w, ID^{\mathsf{hnd}}, y_2^{\mathsf{hnd}})$ at $\mathsf{KS\_out}_u!$.

29: **else if** $v \neq \mathsf{T} \wedge \exists! n^{\mathsf{hnd}} : (n^{\mathsf{hnd}}, ID^{\mathsf{hnd}}, v, 1)$ **then** {Fourth Message is input}

30:    $c^{(2)^{\mathsf{hnd}}} \leftarrow \mathsf{list\_proj}(m^{\mathsf{hnd}}, 2)$. $\{c^{(2)^{\mathsf{hnd}}} \approx \{N_u, K_{uv}\}_{K_{ut}}\}$

31:    $l^{(2)^{\mathsf{hnd}}} \leftarrow \mathsf{sym\_decrypt}(skse_{u,\mathsf{T}}^{\mathsf{hnd}}, c^{(2)^{\mathsf{hnd}}})$. $\{l^{(2)^{\mathsf{hnd}}} \approx \{N_u, K_{uv}\}\}$

32:    $x_i^{\mathsf{hnd}} \leftarrow \mathsf{list\_proj}(l^{(2)^{\mathsf{hnd}}}, i)$ for $i = 1, 2$.

33:    $type_3 \leftarrow \mathsf{get\_type}(x_2^{\mathsf{hnd}})$.

34:    **if** $x_1^{\mathsf{hnd}} \neq n^{\mathsf{hnd}} \vee type_3 \neq \mathsf{skse}$ **then**

35:      Abort

36:    **end if**

37:    $Nonce_u := (Nonce_u \setminus \{(x_1^{\mathsf{hnd}}, ID^{\mathsf{hnd}}, v, 1)\}) \cup \{(x_1^{\mathsf{hnd}}, ID^{\mathsf{hnd}}, v, 4)\}$.

38:    Output $(\mathsf{ok}, \mathsf{Otway\_Rees}, v, ID^{\mathsf{hnd}}, x_2^{\mathsf{hnd}})$ at $\mathsf{KS\_out}_u!$.

39: **else**

40:    Abort

41: **end if**

$\forall u, v \in \mathcal{H}, \forall t_1, t_2 \in \mathbb{N}:$ # *For all honest users u and v,*

$(t_1 : \mathsf{KS\_out}_u!(\mathsf{ok}, \mathsf{Otway\_Rees}, v, ID^{\mathsf{hnd}}, skse_u^{\mathsf{hnd}})$ # *if u has established a shared key with v*

$\Rightarrow$ # *then*

$t_2 : D[hnd_u = skse_u^{\mathsf{hnd}}].hnd_\mathsf{a} = \downarrow)$ # *the adversary never learns this key*

Fig. 2. The Secrecy Property Req^{Sec}.

$\forall u, v \in \mathcal{H}, \forall t_1, t_2 \in \mathbb{N}:$ # *For all honest users u and v,*

$t_1 : \mathsf{KS\_out}_u!(\mathsf{ok}, \mathsf{Otway\_Rees}, v, ID_u^{\mathsf{hnd}}, skse_u^{\mathsf{hnd}}) \wedge$ # *if u has established a key with v*

$t_2 : \mathsf{KS\_out}_v!(\mathsf{ok}, \mathsf{Otway\_Rees}, w, ID_v^{\mathsf{hnd}}, skse_v^{\mathsf{hnd}}) \wedge$ # *and v has established a key with w*

$t_1 : D[hnd_u = ID_u^{\mathsf{hnd}}] = t_2 : D[hnd_v = ID_v^{\mathsf{hnd}}]$ # *and the sessions are equal*

$\Rightarrow (u = w \Leftrightarrow$ # *then u is equal to w if and only if*

$t_1 : D[hnd_u = skse_u^{\mathsf{hnd}}] = t_2 : D[hnd_v = skse_v^{\mathsf{hnd}}])$ # *both keys are equal.*

Fig. 3. The Consistency Property Req^{Cons}.

property states that if two honest users successfully terminate a protocol session and then share a key, the adversary will never learn this key, which captures the confidentiality aspects of the protocol. The consistency property states that if two honest users establish a session key then both need to have a consistent view of who the peers to the session are, i.e., if an honest user u establishes a key with v, and v establishes the same key with user w, then u has to equal w. Moreover, we incorporate the correctness of the protocol into the consistency property, i.e., if the aforementioned outputs occur and $u = w$ holds, then both parties have obtained the same key[4]. In the following definitions, we write $t : D$ to denote the contents of database D at time t, i.e., at the t-th step of the considered trace, and $t : p?m$ and $t : p!m$ to denote that message m occurs at input port respectively output port p at time t.

The secrecy property Req^{Sec} is formally captured as follows: If an output $(\mathsf{ok}, \mathsf{Otway\_Rees}, v, ID^{\mathsf{hnd}}, skse_u^{\mathsf{hnd}})$ occurs at $\mathsf{KS\_out}_v!$ at an arbitrary time t_1, then the key corresponding to $skse_u^{\mathsf{hnd}}$ never gets an adversary handle, i.e., $t_2 : D[hnd_u = skse_u^{\mathsf{hnd}}].hnd_\mathsf{a} = \downarrow$ for all t_2. Figure 2 contains the formal definition of Req^{Sec}.

The *consistency property* Req^{Cons} is formally captured as follows: Assume that outputs $(\mathsf{ok}, \mathsf{Otway\_Rees}, v, ID_u^{\mathsf{hnd}}, skse_u^{\mathsf{hnd}})$ and $(\mathsf{ok}, \mathsf{Otway\_Rees}, w, ID_v^{\mathsf{hnd}}, skse_v^{\mathsf{hnd}})$ occur at $\mathsf{KS\_out}_u!$ respectively at $\mathsf{KS\_out}_v!$ at arbitrary times t_1 and t_2 for honest users u and v such that the session identifiers are the same, i.e., $t_1 : D[hnd_u = ID_u^{\mathsf{hnd}}] = t_2 : D[hnd_v = ID_v^{\mathsf{hnd}}]$. Then the handles $skse_u^{\mathsf{hnd}}$ and $skse_v^{\mathsf{hnd}}$ point to the same entry in the database, i.e., $t_1 : D[hnd_u = skse_u^{\mathsf{hnd}}] = t_2 : D[hnd_v = skse_v^{\mathsf{hnd}}]$ if and only if $u = w$. The formal definition of Req^{Cons} is given in Figure 3.

---

[4] A violation of the consistency property has been pointed out in [24] which arises since in their modeling the trusted third party creates multiple keys if it is repeatedly triggered with the same message. We explicitly excluded this in our definition of the trusted third party by storing the session IDs processed so far, cf. Step 7 and 10 in Algorithm 2.

The notion of a system Sys fulfilling a property Req essentially comes in two flavors [5]. *Perfect fulfillment*, $Sys \models^{\text{perf}} Req$, means that the property holds with probability one (over the probability spaces of runs, a well-defined notion from the underlying model [38]) for all honest users and for all adversaries. *Computational fulfillment*, $Sys \models^{\text{poly}} Req$, means that the property only holds for polynomially bounded users and adversaries, and only with negligible error probability. Perfect fulfillment implies computational fulfillment. The following theorem captures the security of the ideal Otway-Rees protocol.

Theorem 1. *(Security of the Otway-Rees Protocol based on the Ideal Cryptographic Library) Let $Sys^{\text{OR,id}}$ be the ideal Otway-Rees system defined in Section 3.2, and Req^{Sec} and Req^{Cons} the secrecy and consistency property of Figure 2 and 3. Then $Sys^{\text{OR,id}} \models^{\text{perf}} Req^{\text{Sec}} \wedge Req^{\text{Cons}}$.* □

5   Proof in the Ideal Setting

This section sketches the proof of Theorem 1, i.e., the proof of the Otway-Rees protocol using the ideal, deterministic cryptographic library. The complete proof can be found in the long version of this paper [4]. The proof idea is the following: If an honest user u successfully terminates a session run with another honest user v, then we first show that the established key has been created before by the trusted third party. After that, we exploit that the trusted third party as well as all honest users may only send this key within an encryption generated with a key shared between u and T respectively v and T, and we conclude that the adversary hence never gets a handle to the key. This shows the secrecy property, and the consistency property can also be easily derived from this. The main challenge was to find suitable invariants on the state of the ideal Otway-Rees system. This is somewhat similar to formal proofs using the Dolev-Yao model, and the similarity supports our hope that the new, sound cryptographic library can be used in the place of the Dolev-Yao models in automated tools.

The first invariants, *correct nonce owner* and *unique nonce use*, are easily proved and essentially state that handles x^{hnd} where $(x^{\text{hnd}}, \cdot, \cdot, \cdot)$ is contained in a set $Nonce_u$ indeed point to entries of type nonce, and that no nonce is in two such sets. The next two invariants, *nonce secrecy* and *nonce-list secrecy*, deal with the secrecy of certain terms. They are mainly needed to prove the invariant *correct list generation*, which establishes who created certain terms. The last invariant, *key secrecy*, states that the adversary never learns keys created by the trusted third party for use between honest users.

- *Correct Nonce Owner.* For all $u \in \mathcal{H}$, and for all $(x^{\text{hnd}}, \cdot, \cdot, \cdot) \in Nonce_u$, it holds $D[hnd_u = x^{\text{hnd}}] \neq \downarrow$ and $D[hnd_u = x^{\text{hnd}}].type = \mathsf{nonce}$.
- *Unique Nonce Use.* For all $u, v \in \mathcal{H}$, all $w, w' \in \{1, \dots, n\}$, and all $j \leq size$: If $(D[j].hnd_u, \cdot, w, \cdot) \in Nonce_u$ and $(D[j].hnd_v, \cdot, w', \cdot) \in Nonce_v$, then $(u, w) = (v, w')$.

Nonce secrecy states that the nonces exchanged between honest users u and v remain secret from all other users and from the adversary. For the formalization, note that the handles x^{hnd} to these nonces are contained as elements $(x^{\text{hnd}}, \cdot, v, \cdot)$ in the set $Nonce_u$.

The claim is that the other users and the adversary have no handles to such a nonce in the database D of $\mathsf{TH}_\mathcal{H}$:

- *Nonce Secrecy.* For all $u, v \in \mathcal{H}$ and for all $j \leq size$: If $(D[j].hnd_u, \cdot, v, \cdot) \in Nonce_u$ then $D[j].hnd_w \neq \downarrow$ implies $w \in \{u, v, \mathsf{T}\}$. In particular, this means $D[j].hnd_\mathsf{a} = \downarrow$.

Similarly, the invariant *nonce-list secrecy* states that a list containing such a handle can only be known to u, v, and T. Further, it states that the identity fields in such lists are correct. Moreover, if such a list is an argument of another entry, then this entry is an encryption created with the secret key that either u or v share with T. (Formally this means that this entry is tagged with the corresponding public-key identifier as an abstract argument, cf. Section 3.1.)

- *Nonce-List Secrecy.* For all $u, v \in \mathcal{H}$ and for all $j \leq size$ with $D[j].type = \mathsf{list}$:
  Let $x_i^{\mathsf{ind}} := D[j].arg[i]$ for $i = 1, 2, 3, 4$. If $(D[x_1^{\mathsf{ind}}].hnd_u, \cdot, v, l) \in Nonce_u$ then
  a) $D[j].hnd_w \neq \downarrow$ implies $w \in \{u, v, \mathsf{T}\}$ for $l \in \{1, 2, 3, 4\}$.
  b) If $l \in \{1, 4\}$ and $D[x_3^{\mathsf{ind}}].type = \mathsf{data}$, then $D[x_3^{\mathsf{ind}}].arg = (u)$ and $D[x_4^{\mathsf{ind}}].arg = (v)$.
  c) If $l \in \{2, 3\}$ and $D[x_3^{\mathsf{ind}}].type = \mathsf{data}$, then $D[x_3^{\mathsf{ind}}].arg = (v)$ and $D[x_4^{\mathsf{ind}}].arg = (u)$.
  d) for $l \in \{1, 2, 3, 4\}$ and for all $k \leq size$ it holds $j \in D[k].arg$ only if $D[k].type = \mathsf{symenc}$ and $D[k].arg[1] \in \{pkse_u, pkse_v\}$.

The invariant *correct list owner* states that certain protocol messages can only be constructed by the "intended" users respectively by the trusted third party.

- *Correct List Owner.* For all $u, v \in \mathcal{H}$ and for all $j \leq size$ with $D[j].type = \mathsf{list}$:
  Let $x_i^{\mathsf{ind}} := D[j].arg[i]$ for $i = 1, 2$ and $x_{1,u}^{\mathsf{hnd}} := D[x_1^{\mathsf{ind}}].hnd_u$.
  a) If $(x_{1,u}^{\mathsf{hnd}}, \cdot, v, l) \in Nonce_u$ and $D[x_2^{\mathsf{ind}}].type \neq \mathsf{sske}$, then $D[j]$ was created by $\mathsf{M}_u^{\mathsf{OR}}$ in Step 1.6 if $l = 1$ and in Step 3.12 if $l = 2$.
  b) If $(x_{1,u}^{\mathsf{hnd}}, ID_u^{\mathsf{hnd}}, v, l) \in Nonce_u$ and $D[x_2^{\mathsf{ind}}].type = \mathsf{sske}$, then $D[j]$ was created by $\mathsf{M}_\mathsf{T}^{\mathsf{OR}}$ in Step 2.22 if $l = 3$ and in Step 2.20 if $l = 4$. Moreover, we have $D[hnd_u = ID_u^{\mathsf{hnd}}] = D[hnd_\mathsf{T} = ID_\mathsf{T}^{\mathsf{hnd}}]$, where $ID_\mathsf{T}^{\mathsf{hnd}}$ denotes the handle that T obtained in Step 2.1 in the same execution.

Finally, the invariant *key secrecy* states that a secret key entry that has been generated by the trusted third party to be shared between honest users u and v can only be known to u, v, and T. In particular, the adversary will never get a handle to it. This invariant is key for proving the secrecy and the consistency property of the Otway-Rees protocol.

- *Key Secrecy.* For all $u, v \in \mathcal{H}$ and for all $j \leq size$ with $D[j].type = \mathsf{sske}$:
  If $D[j]$ was created by $\mathsf{M}_\mathsf{T}^{\mathsf{OR}}$ in Step 2.19 and, with the notation of Algorithm 2, we have that $y_3 = u$ and $y_4 = v$ in the current execution of $\mathsf{M}_\mathsf{T}^{\mathsf{OR}}$, then $D[j].hnd_w \neq \downarrow$ implies $w \in \{u, v, \mathsf{T}\}$.

6   Proof of the Cryptographic Realization

If Theorem 1 has been proven, it remains to show that the Otway-Rees protocol based on the real cryptographic library computationally fulfills corresponding secrecy and consistency requirements. Actually, different corresponding requirements can easily be derived from the proof in the ideal setting. Obviously, carrying over properties from the ideal to the real system relies crucially on the fact that the real cryptographic library is at least as secure as the ideal one. This has been established in [8, 7], but only subject to the side condition that the surrounding protocol, i.e., the Otway-Rees protocol in our case, does not raise a so-called *commitment problem*. Establishing this side condition is crucial for using symmetric encryption in abstract, cryptographically sound proofs. We explain the commitment problem in the next section to illustrate the cryptographic issue underlying the commitment problem, and we exploit the invariants of Section 5 to show that the commitment problem does not occur for the Otway-Rees protocol. As our proof is the first Dolev-Yao-style, cryptographically sound proof of a protocol that uses symmetric encryption, our result also shows that the commitment problem, and hence also symmetric encryption, can be conveniently dealt with in cryptographically sound security proofs by means of the approach of [7].

For technical reasons, one further has to ensure that the surrounding protocol does not create "encryption cycles" (such as encrypting a key with itself), which had to be required even for acquiring properties weaker than simulatability, cf. [3] for further discussions. This property is only a technical subtlety and clearly holds for the Otway-Rees protocol.

6.1   Absence of the Commitment Problem for the Otway-Rees Protocol

As the name suggests, a "commitment problem" in simulatability proofs captures a situation where the simulator commits itself to a certain message and later has to change this commitment to allow for a correct simulation. In the case of symmetric encryption, the commitment problem occurs if the simulator learns in some abstract way that a ciphertext was sent and hence has to construct an indistinguishable ciphertext, knowing neither the secret key nor the plaintext used for the corresponding ciphertext in the real world. To simulate the missing key, the simulator will create a new secret key, or rely on an arbitrary, fixed key if the encryption systems guarantees indistinguishable keys, see [3]. Instead of the unknown plaintext, the simulator will encrypt an arbitrary message of the correct length, relying on the indistinguishability of ciphertexts of different messages. So far, the simulation is fine. It even stays fine if the message becomes known later because secure encryption still guarantees that it is indistinguishable that the simulator's ciphertext contains a wrong message. However, if the secret key becomes known later, the simulator runs into trouble, because, learning abstractly about this fact, it has to produce a suitable key that decrypts its ciphertext into the correct message. It cannot cheat with the message because it has to produce the correct behavior towards the honest users. This is typically not possible.

The solution for this problem taken in [7] for the cryptographic library is to leave it to the surrounding protocol to guarantee that the commitment problem does not occur, i.e., the surrounding protocol must guarantee that keys are no longer sent in a form that might make them known to the adversary once an honest participant has started using them. To exploit the simulatability results of [7], we hence have to prove this condition for the Otway-Rees protocol. Formally, we have to show that the following property NoComm does not occur: "If there exists an input from an honest user that causes a symmetric encryption to be generated such that the corresponding key is not known to the adversary, then future inputs may only cause this key to be sent within an encryption that cannot be decrypted by the adversary". This event can be rigorously defined in the style of the secrecy and consistency property but we omit the rigorous definition due to space constraints and refer to [7]. The event NoComm is equivalent to the event "if there exists an input from an honest user that causes a symmetric encryption to be generated such that the corresponding key is not known to the adversary, the adversary never gets a handle to this key" but NoComm has the advantage that it can easily be inferred from the abstract protocol description without presupposing knowledge about handles of the cryptographic library. For the Otway-Rees protocol the event NoComm can easily be verified by inspection of the abstract protocol description, and a detailed proof based on Algorithms 1-3 can also easily be performed by exploiting the invariants of Section 5.

Lemma 1. *(Absence of the Commitment Problem for the Otway-Rees Protocol) The ideal Otway-Rees system $Sys^{OR,id}$ perfectly fulfills the property* NoComm, *i.e.,* $Sys^{OR,id} \models^{perf}$ NoComm. □

Proof. Note first that the secret key shared initially between a user and the trusted third party will never be sent by definition in case the user is honest, and it is already known to the adversary when it is first used in case of a dishonest user. The interesting cases are thus the keys generated by the trusted third party in the protocol sessions.

Let $j \leq size$, $D[j].type =$ skse such that $D[j]$ was created by M_T^{OR} in Step 2.19, where, with the notation of Algorithm 2, we have $y_3 = u$ and $y_4 = v$ for $y_3, y_4 \in \{1, \ldots, n\}$. If u or v were dishonest, then the adversary would get a handle for $D[j]$ after M_T^{OR} finishes its execution, i.e., in particular before $D[j]$ has been used for encryption for the first time, since the adversary knows the keys shared between the dishonest users and the trusted third party. If both u and v are honest, *key secrecy* then immediately implies that $t : D[j].hnd_a = \downarrow$ for all $t \in \mathbb{N}$, which finishes the proof. ■

6.2   Proof of Secrecy and Consistency

As the final step in the overall security proof, we show how to derive corresponding secrecy and consistency properties from the proofs in the ideal setting and the simulatability result of the underlying library.

We show this only for secrecy and sketch the proof for consistency. Note that the secrecy property Req^{Sec} specifically relies on the state of $TH_{\mathcal{H}}$, hence it cannot be used to capture the security of the real Otway-Rees system, where $TH_{\mathcal{H}}$ is replaced with the secure implementation of the cryptographic library. The natural counterpart of Req^{Sec} in the real system is to demand that the adversary never learns the key (now as an actual bitstring), which can be captured in various ways. One possibility that allows for a very convenient proof is to capture the property as a so-called *integrity property* in the sense of [5]. Integrity properties correspond to sets of traces at the in- and output ports connecting the system to the honest users, i.e., properties that can be expressed solely via statements about events at the port set $S_{\mathcal{H}}$; in particular, integrity properties do not rely on the state of the underlying machine. Integrity properties are preserved under simulatability, i.e., they carry from the ideal to the real system without any additional work. Formally, the following *preservation theorem* has been established in [5].

Theorem 2. *(Preservation of Integrity Properties (Sketch)) Let two systems* Sys_1, Sys_2 *be given such that* Sys_1 *is at least as secure as* Sys_2 *(written* $Sys_1 \geq^{poly}_{sec} Sys_2$*). Let* Req *be an integrity property for both* Sys_1 *and* Sys_2*, and let* $Sys_2 \models^{poly} Req$*. Then also* $Sys_1 \models^{poly} Req$. □

We can now easily rephrase the secrecy property Req^{Sec} into an equivalent integrity property that is well-defined for both the ideal and the real Otway-Rees system by employing standard techniques, e.g., by assuming that once the adversary has learned the shared key, the adversary sends the key to an honest user. Formally, we may augment the behavior the protocol machine M^{OR}_u so that if it receives a message (broken, $skse^{hnd}_u$) from a dishonest sender, it outputs this message to its user u at port KS_out$_u$!. The property Req^{Sec} can then be rewritten by replacing the statement $t_2 : D[hnd_u = skse^{hnd}_u].hnd_a = \downarrow$ with $t_2 : \mathsf{KS\_out}_u!m \implies m \neq$ (broken, $skse^{hnd}_u$). We call the resulting integrity property Req^{Sec}_{real}. If we denote the ideal Otway-Rees system based on these augmented protocol machines by $Sys'^{OR,id}$ then we clearly have $Sys^{OR,id} \models^{perf} Req^{Sec}$ if and only if $Sys'^{OR,id} \models^{perf} Req^{Sec}_{real}$ since a user may only receive a message (broken, $skse^{hnd}_u$) if the adversary already has a handle to $skse^{hnd}_u$, and conversely if an adversary has a handle to $skse^{hnd}_u$ it can create and send the message (broken, $skse^{hnd}_u$). This can easily be turned into a formal proof by inspection of the commands list and send_i offered by the trusted host. The preservation theorem now immediately allows us to carry over the secrecy property to the real Otway-Rees system.

Theorem 3. *(Security of the Real Otway-Rees Protocol) Let* $Sys'^{OR,real}$ *denote the Otway-Rees system based on the real cryptographic library and the protocol machines augmented for capturing the integrity property* Req^{Sec}_{real}*. Then* $Sys'^{OR,real} \models^{poly} Req^{Sec}_{real}$. □

Proof. Let $Sys^{cry,id}$ and $Sys^{cry,real}$ denote the ideal and the real cryptographic library from [8] augmented with symmetric encryption as introduced in [7]. In [8,7] it has already been shown that $Sys^{cry,real} \geq^{poly}_{sec} Sys^{cry,id}$ holds for suitable parameters in the ideal system, provided that neither the commitment problem nor encryption cycles occur. We have shown both conditions in the previous section. Let $Sys'^{OR,id}$ denote the ideal Otway-Rees system based on the augmented protocol machines. Since $Sys'^{OR,real}$ is derived from $Sys'^{OR,id}$ by replacing the ideal with the real cryptographic library, $Sys'^{OR,real} \geq^{poly}_{sec} Sys'^{OR,id}$ follows from the composition theorem of [38]. We only have to show that the theorem's preconditions are in fact fulfilled. This is straightforward, since the machines M^{OR}_u are polynomial-time (cf. Section 3.3). Now Theorem 1 implies $Sys^{OR,id} \models^{poly} Req^{Sec}$ which yields $Sys'^{OR,id} \models^{poly} Req^{Sec}_{real}$. Since Req^{Sec}_{real} is an integrity property Theorem 2 yields $Sys'^{OR,real} \models^{poly} Req^{Sec}_{real}$. ∎

Similar to the secrecy property, the consistency property Req^{Cons} specifically relies on the state of $\mathsf{TH}_{\mathcal{H}}$. The corresponding consistency property for the real Otway-Rees system can be defined by requiring that both handles point to the same bitstring, i.e., by replacing $t_1 : D[hnd_u = skse_u^{\mathsf{hnd}}] = t_2 : D[hnd_v = skse_v^{\mathsf{hnd}}$ with $t_1 : D_u[hnd_u = skse_u^{\mathsf{hnd}}].word = t_2 : D_v[hnd_v = skse_v^{\mathsf{hnd}}].word$ for the databases D_u and D_v of the real library. We omit a formal proof that the real Otway-Rees system computationally fulfills this property; the proof can be established similar to the proof of the secrecy property where one additionally exploits that if the real Otway-Rees protocol is run with an arbitrary adversary and we have $t_1 : D[hnd_u = skse_u^{\mathsf{hnd}}] = t_2 : D[hnd_v = skse_v^{\mathsf{hnd}}]$ then there always exist an adversary against the ideal Otway-Rees protocol such that $t_1 : D_u[hnd_u = skse_u^{\mathsf{hnd}}].word = t_2 : D_v[hnd_u = skse_u^{\mathsf{hnd}}].word$, cf. [8, 7].

6.3 Towards Stronger Properties

To conclude, we sketch that also stronger properties can be derived for the real Otway-Rees protocol from Theorem 1 and the proof of the simulatability result of the cryptographic library, e.g., a stronger notion of secrecy: There does not exist a polynomial-time machine that is able to distinguish the adversary's view in a correct protocol execution from the adversary's view in a protocol execution where all keys shared between honest users are replaced with a fixed message of equal length (which means that the adversary does not learn anything about these keys except for their lengths). It is easy to show that the real Otway-Rees protocol fulfills this property because one could otherwise exploit Theorem 1 to distinguish the ideal cryptographic library from the real one using standard techniques, which would yield a contradiction to the results of [8, 7].

The proof idea is as follows: In the simulatability proof of the cryptographic library, the simulator simulates all keys for which no adversary handle exists with a fixed message since it does not know the appropriate key [7]. Moreover, when run with the ideal system and the simulator, the adversary does not learn any information in the Shannon sense about those symmetric keys for which it does not have a handle [8, 7]. Hence Theorem 1 implies that these statements in particular hold for the secret keys shared between honest users. Now if an adversary $\mathsf{A_{Dis}}$ existed that violated the above property with not negligible advantage over pure guessing, we could define a distinguisher Dis for the ideal and real library by first triggering $\mathsf{A_{Dis}}$ as a black-box submachine with the obtained view and by then outputting the guess of $\mathsf{A_{Dis}}$ as a guess for distinguishing the ideal and the real library. It is easy to show that Dis provides a correct simulation for $\mathsf{A_{Dis}}$ and hence succeeds in distinguishing the ideal and the real library with not negligible probability.

7 Conclusion

We have proven the Otway-Rees protocol in the real cryptographic setting via a deterministic, provably secure abstraction of a real cryptographic library. Together with composition and preservation theorems from the underlying model, this library allowed us to perform the actual proof effort in a deterministic setting corresponding to a slightly extended Dolev-Yao model. We hope that it paves the way for the actual use of automatic proof tools for this and many similar cryptographically faithful proofs of security protocols.

References

1. M. Abadi and A. D. Gordon. A calculus for cryptographic protocols: The spi calculus. *Information and Computation*, 148(1):1–70, 1999.
2. M. Abadi and J. Jürjens. Formal eavesdropping and its computational interpretation. In *Proc. 4th International Symposium on Theoretical Aspects of Computer Software (TACS)*, pages 82–94, 2001.
3. M. Abadi and P. Rogaway. Reconciling two views of cryptography: The computational soundness of formal encryption. In *Proc. 1st IFIP International Conference on Theoretical Computer Science*, volume 1872 of *LNCS*, pages 3–22. Springer, 2000.
4. M. Backes. A cryptographically sound Dolev-Yao style security proof of the Otway-Rees protocol. Research Report RZ 3539, IBM Research, 2004.
5. M. Backes and C. Jacobi. Cryptographically sound and machine-assisted verification of security protocols. In *Proc. 20th Annual Symposium on Theoretical Aspects of Computer Science (STACS)*, volume 2607 of *LNCS*, pages 675–686. Springer, 2003.
6. M. Backes and B. Pfitzmann. A cryptographically sound security proof of the Needham-Schroeder-Lowe public-key protocol. In *Proc. 23rd Conference on Foundations of Software Technology and Theoretical Computer Science (FSTTCS)*, pages 1–12, 2003.
7. M. Backes and B. Pfitzmann. Symmetric encryption in a simulatable Dolev-Yao style cryptographic library. In *Proc. 17th IEEE Computer Security Foundations Workshop (CSFW)*, 2004.
8. M. Backes, B. Pfitzmann, and M. Waidner. A composable cryptographic library with nested operations (extended abstract). In *Proc. 10th ACM Conference on Computer and Communications Security*, pages 220–230, 2003. Full version in IACR Cryptology ePrint Archive 2003/015, Jan. 2003, http://eprint.iacr.org/.
9. M. Backes, B. Pfitzmann, and M. Waidner. Symmetric authentication within a simulatable cryptographic library. In *Proc. 8th European Symposium on Research in Computer Security (ESORICS)*, volume 2808 of *LNCS*, pages 271–290. Springer, 2003.
10. M. Bellare, A. Desai, D. Pointcheval, and P. Rogaway. Relations among notions of security for public-key encryption schemes. In *Advances in Cryptology: CRYPTO '98*, volume 1462 of *LNCS*, pages 26–45. Springer, 1998.
11. M. Bellare and C. Namprempre. Authenticated encryption: Relations among notions and analysis of the generic composition paradigm. In *Advances in Cryptology: ASIACRYPT 2000*, volume 1976 of *LNCS*, pages 531–545. Springer, 2000.
12. M. Bellare and P. Rogaway. Encode-then-encipher encryption: How to exploit nonces or redundancy in plaintexts for efficient constructions. In *Advances in Cryptology: ASIACRYPT 2000*, volume 1976 of *LNCS*, pages 317–330. Springer, 2000.
13. D. Bleichenbacher. Chosen ciphertext attacks against protocols based on the RSA encryption standard PKCS. In *Advances in Cryptology: CRYPTO '98*, volume 1462 of *LNCS*, pages 1–12. Springer, 1998.
14. M. Burrows, M. Abadi, and R. Needham. A logic for authentication. Technical Report 39, SRC DIGITAL, 1990.
15. D. E. Denning and G. M. Sacco. Timestamps in key distribution protocols. *Communications of the ACM*, 24(8):533–536, 1981.
16. D. Dolev and A. C. Yao. On the security of public key protocols. *IEEE Transactions on Information Theory*, 29(2):198–208, 1983.
17. D. Fisher. Millions of .Net Passport accounts put at risk. *eWeek*, May 2003. (Flaw detected by Muhammad Faisal Rauf Danka).
18. O. Goldreich, S. Micali, and A. Wigderson. How to play any mental game – or – a completeness theorem for protocols with honest majority. In *Proc. 19th Annual ACM Symposium on Theory of Computing (STOC)*, pages 218–229, 1987.

19. S. Goldwasser and S. Micali. Probabilistic encryption. *Journal of Computer and System Sciences*, 28:270–299, 1984.

20. S. Goldwasser, S. Micali, and C. Rackoff. The knowledge complexity of interactive proof systems. *SIAM Journal on Computing*, 18(1):186–207, 1989.

21. J. Herzog. *Computational Soundness of Formal Adversaries*. PhD thesis, MIT, 2002.

22. J. Herzog, M. Liskov, and S. Micali. Plaintext awareness via key registration. In *Advances in Cryptology: CRYPTO 2003*, volume 2729 of *LNCS*, pages 548–564. Springer, 2003.

23. R. Impagliazzo and B. M. Kapron. Logics for reasoning about cryptographic constructions. In *Proc. 44th IEEE Symposium on Foundations of Computer Science*, pages 372–381, 2003.

24. F. Javier Thayer, J. C. Herzog, and J. D. Guttman. Honest ideals on strand spaces. In *Proc. 11th IEEE Computer Security Foundations Workshop (CSFW)*, pages 66–77, 1998.

25. R. Kemmerer. Analyzing encryption protocols using formal verification techniques. *IEEE Journal on Selected Areas in Communications*, 7(4):448–457, 1989.

26. P. Laud. Semantics and program analysis of computationally secure information flow. In *Proc. 10th European Symposium on Programming (ESOP)*, pages 77–91, 2001.

27. P. Laud. Symmetric encryption in automatic analyses for confidentiality against active adversaries. In *Proc. 25th IEEE Symposium on Security & Privacy*, pages 71–85, 2004.

28. P. Lincoln, J. Mitchell, M. Mitchell, and A. Scedrov. A probabilistic poly-time framework for protocol analysis. In *Proc. 5th ACM Conference on Computer and Communications Security*, pages 112–121, 1998.

29. C. Meadows. Using narrowing in the analysis of key management protocols. In *Proc. 10th IEEE Symposium on Security & Privacy*, pages 138–147, 1989.

30. D. Micciancio and B. Warinschi. Soundness of formal encryption in the presence of active adversaries. In *Proc. 1st Theory of Cryptography Conference (TCC)*, volume 2951 of *LNCS*, pages 133–151. Springer, 2004.

31. J. K. Millen. The interrogator: A tool for cryptographic protocol security. In *Proc. 5th IEEE Symposium on Security & Privacy*, pages 134–141, 1984.

32. J. Mitchell, M. Mitchell, and A. Scedrov. A linguistic characterization of bounded oracle computation and probabilistic polynomial time. In *Proc. 39th IEEE Symposium on Foundations of Computer Science*, pages 725–733, 1998.

33. J. Mitchell, M. Mitchell, A. Scedrov, and V. Teague. A probabilistic polynominal-time process calculus for analysis of cryptographic protocols (preliminary report). *Electronic Notes in Theoretical Computer Science*, 47:1–31, 2001.

34. R. Needham and M. Schroeder. Using encryption for authentication in large networks of computers. *Communications of the ACM*, 12(21):993–999, 1978.

35. D. Otway and O. Rees. Efficient and timely mutual authentication. *Operation Systems Review*, 21(1):8–10, 1987.

36. L. Paulson. Mechanized proofs for a recursive authentication protocol. In *Proc. 10th IEEE Computer Security Foundations Workshop (CSFW)*, pages 84–95, 1997.

37. L. Paulson. The inductive approach to verifying cryptographic protocols. *Journal of Cryptology*, 6(1):85–128, 1998.

38. B. Pfitzmann and M. Waidner. A model for asynchronous reactive systems and its application to secure message transmission. In *Proc. 22nd IEEE Symposium on Security & Privacy*, pages 184–200, 2001.

39. P. Rogaway, M. Bellare, J. Black, and T. Krovetz. OCB: A block-cipher mode of operation for efficient authenticated encryption. In *Proc. 8th ACM Conference on Computer and Communications Security*, pages 196–205, 2001.

40. D. Wagner and B. Schneier. Analysis of the SSL 3.0 protocol. In *Proc. 2nd USENIX Workshop on Electronic Commerce*, pages 29–40, 1996.

41. B. Warinschi. A computational analysis of the Needham-Schroeder-(Lowe) protocol. In *Proc. 16th IEEE Computer Security Foundations Workshop (CSFW)*, pages 248–262, 2003.

A Formalization
of Anonymity and Onion Routing

S. Mauw[1], J.H.S. Verschuren[1,2], and E.P. de Vink[1,3]

[1] Dept of Math. and Comp. Sc., Technische Universiteit Eindhoven
P.O. Box 513, 5600 MB Eindhoven, the Netherlands
[2] TNO ITSEF, P.O. Box 96864, 2509 JG 's-Gravenhage, the Netherlands
[3] LIACS, Leiden University, Niels Bohrweg 1, 2333 CA Leiden, the Netherlands

Abstract. The use of formal methods to verify security protocols with respect to secrecy and authentication has become standard practice. In contrast, the formalization of other security goals, such as privacy, has received less attention. Due to the increasing importance of privacy in the current society, formal methods will also become indispensable in this area. Therefore, we propose a formal definition of the notion of anonymity in presence of an observing intruder. We validate this definition by analyzing a well-known anonymity preserving protocol, viz. onion routing.

1 Introduction

Nowadays there is a growing concern about one's privacy. The adoption of techniques like RFID and DRM may have severe consequences for the privacy of the individual [8, 6]. The widespread acceptance of electronic services, such as location based services, electronic tolling, loyalty schemes, may carry consequences on the user's privacy. As 'privacy' is becoming more of an issue, there is an increasing need for analysis of systems in relation to privacy requirements.

The so-called functional class in the Common Criteria (CC, [10]) distinguishes between four aspects of privacy: anonymity, pseudonymity, unlinkability and unobservability. Anonymity, which is the topic of our current research, ensures that a subject may use a resource or service without disclosing its user identity. Pseudonymity ensures that a user may use a resource or service without disclosing its identity, but can still be accountable for that use. Unlinkability ensures that a user may make multiple uses of resources or services without others being able to link these uses together. Unlinkability differs from pseudonymity in the sense that, although in pseudonymity the user is also not known, relations between different actions can be provided. Unobservability ensures that a user may use a resource or service without others, especially third parties, being able to observe that the resource or service is being used.

Such informal definitions are essential to the understanding of the different notions of privacy, but will only allow to investigate a system informally. However, in contrast to other security properties, such as confidentiality and authentication (see e.g. [14, 4]), privacy has hardly been studied from a formal

P. Samarati et al. (Eds.): ESORICS 2004, LNCS 3193, pp. 109–124, 2004.

methods point of view (see e.g. [12, 11, 3] for more or less informal approaches to anonymity). It is our aim to provide an appropriate formal definition of anonymity and validate this definition by analyzing the well-known onion routing protocol. In [14] a start is made to give a formal description of anonymity.

Our definition of anonymity is based on the above mentioned definition in the CC and on the definition of anonymity provided by Pfitzmann et al. [12], which reads "Anonymity is the state of being not identifiable within a set of subjects, the anonymity set." This anonymity group forms the basis of our definition. We say that a user u' is in the anonymity group of user u, if for every behaviour of the system that can be attributed to u, there is another possible behaviour of the system that can be attributed to u', such that an observer or intruder cannot tell the difference between these two behaviours. This means that an intruder cannot tell the difference between u and any other user in its anonymity group.

Onion routing was originally devised by Goldschlag, Reed, Syverson in [9, 17] as a solution for anonymous connections. Onion routing creates a layered data structure called an onion. As the data passes through each onion router along the way, one layer of encryption is removed according to the recipe contained in the onion. The Naval Research Lab has a test bed Onion Routing Network that is available for any one to use. While in operation, users in more than sixty countries initiated up to 1.5 million connections per month through the prototype system. This demand certainly shows an interest in the service. It also shows that it is feasible. Based on this success, a design for a second generation system was initiated [16].

Syverson et al. have performed an analysis of the second generation system for onion routing. In [16] different attacker models are considered, viz. single, multiple, roving and global adversary. A single and a multiple adversary point to a situation where only one core onion router, respectively, more core onion routers are compromised. In both cases the compromised onion routers are fixed. A roving adversary points to a situation where a fixed-bound size subset of core onion routers is compromised at any one time. At specific intervals, other core onion routers can become compromised or uncompromised. Syverson et al. rule out the global adversary (all core onion routers are compromised) as the onion routing infrastructure cannot realize any anonymity in that case. They compare the results with the protection provided by the Crowds model [13]. It is shown, that onion routing generally resists traffic analysis more effectively than any other published and deployed mechanisms for Internet communication.

Diaz et al. [5] and also Serjantov and Danezis [15] propose an information theoretic approach to measure the level of anonymity of a system. In their model the attacker will carry out a probabilistic attack: after observing the system, an attacker may assign some probabilities to each sender as being the originator of a message. This can be based on information the system is leaking, message lengths, traffic analysis, etc. Subsequently, the entropy is used as a tool to calculate the degree of anonymity achieved by the users of a system towards a particular attacker. Their measurement method is applied to analyze the degree of anonymity of crowds and onion routing.

We provide a possibilistic analysis of the onion routing protocol in a process algebraic framework. We aim at determining the anonymity groups of part taking users under different circumstances, such as conspiring routers. In order to appreciate the intricacies of the onion routing protocol, we have analyzed several weaker protocols too. In this paper we will only report on our findings with respect to a variation which we coined coconut routing.

Our paper is structured as follows. In Section 2 we provide a formal definition of anonymity in a trace model. In Section 3 we explain an abstraction of the onion routing protocol and give its formal specification in process algebra. We also provide an alternative characterization which will show helpful in the formal analysis of Section 4. In Section 5 we discuss conclusions and future research.

2   Formal Definitions

Intruder capabilities. In this section we define the notion of anonymity in presence of an eavesdropping intruder. In general, the intruder can overhear the communication, but can not interpret all the messages. Dependent on the set of keys known to the intruder, some behaviours of the system observed by the intruder can be distinguished while others can not. If the intruder can not, based on its eavesdropping capacities, distinguish between two users, these two users are in the same anonymity group.

We fix a set of users $\mathcal{U}$, a set of actions $\mathcal{A}$, a set of traces $\mathcal{T}$ and a set of keys $\mathcal{K}$. The set of actions $\mathcal{A}$ is split up into a subset of observable actions $\mathcal{A}_{\text{obs}}$ and a set of invisible actions $\mathcal{A}_{\text{inv}}$. For our purposes, the set of traces $\mathcal{T}$ consists of all finite and infinite words of actions from $\mathcal{A}$.

The actions come equipped with some syntactic structure, the details of which do not matter here. We assume that the set $\mathcal{A}$ can be viewed as the collection of terms of some signature that includes an operation $e, k \mapsto \{e\}_k$ for an expression e and key k. Let $K \subseteq \mathcal{K}$ be a set of keys. A tagging function $\theta \colon \mathcal{A} \to \mathcal{A}_\Theta$, with Θ some fixed set of tags, maps actions in $\mathcal{A}$, i.e. terms over the implicit signature, to tagged actions in $\mathcal{A}_\Theta$, i.e. terms over the implicit signature extended with the elements of Θ as new constants. The function θ is assumed to be injective; the idea is to replace undecryptable subterms by some tag, such that equal subterms are identified with the same tag. More concretely, the mapping $\theta_K \colon \mathcal{A} \to \mathcal{A}_\Theta$ has the property $\theta_K(\{e\}_k) = \{\theta_K(e)\}_k$ if the key k is in the set of keys K and $\theta_K(\{e\}_k) = \theta(\{e\}_k)$ if not. The mapping θ_K extends naturally from actions to traces.

We say that two traces $t_1, t_2 \in \mathcal{T}$ are K-equivalent, notation $t_1 \sim_K t_2$, if, for some bijection $\beta \colon \Theta \to \Theta$, it holds that $\theta_K(t_1) = (\beta \circ \theta)_K(t_2)$. The interpretation of $t_1 \sim_K t_2$ is that the traces t_1 and t_2 are equal for what can be observed, possibly after decryption with the keys in K, and there is a global correspondence between the parts that can not be decrypted. Suppose we have the actions $a = \{e_1\}_k$, $b = \{e_2\}_k$ and $c = \{e_3\}_k$, and actions $x = \{e\}_{k_1}$, $y = \{e\}_{k_2}$ and $z = \{e\}_{k_3}$. The tagging of traces is a means to express the capability of an intruder to distinguish, e.g., the 2-element traces $a \cdot b$ and $c \cdot c$ even if the intruder can not decrypt any of the terms . Likewise, we have $x \cdot y \not\sim_K z \cdot z$ irrespective of which of the keys k_1, k_2 and k_3 are known.

The above notion of tagging and renaming captures that not all information carried by a trace can be distinguished by the intruder. This even stretches a little further: some actions will not be visible at all. Although we assume, that the intruder can overhear all network activity, the internal activity of principals can not be observed. Therefore, we have means to restrict a trace t over $\mathcal{A}$ to a trace over $\mathcal{A}_{obs}$ of observable actions. The mapping $obs \colon \mathcal{T} \to \mathcal{T}$ is such that $obs(\varepsilon) = \varepsilon$, $obs(a \cdot t) = a \cdot obs(t)$ if $a \in \mathcal{A}_{obs}$ and $obs(a \cdot t) = obs(t)$ if not. We use the notation $t_1 \sim^K_{obs} t_2$ iff $obs(t_1) \sim_K obs(t_2)$. When the set of keys K is clear from the context, we simply write $t_1 \sim_{obs} t_2$. For the sake of simplicity, we treat K as a constant set of keys. This will suffice for the treatment of the onion routing protocol, where the intruder does not learn any new keys during operation. In general, however, a privacy protocol may leak encryption keys, requiring a dynamic modeling of K. This extension is rather straightforward and will not influence the main line of reasoning. Therefore, we will ignore this possibility.

User attribution. Next, we address the notion of attributing a trace to a user. As a trace can contain interaction of various sessions of many principals in different roles, we introduce a mechanism to focus on a particular action of a trace. In concrete situations we fix a so-called attribution function for each role that is of interest. Such an attribution function $\alpha \colon \mathcal{T} \times \mathbb{N} \to \mathcal{U}$ returns the user in the particular role, involved in the interaction corresponding to the n-th action $t[n]$ of the trace t. For example, in a four step key agreement protocol we can distinguish between the roles of initiator, responder and server. A trace t of a system with many users, acting both as initiator and responder, contains many sessions. There may be some communication at position n of t corresponding to the third step of the protocol. The attribution function for initiator then returns the initiator of the particular protocol session; the attribution function for the responder returns the responder of the particular session.

The attribution function $\alpha(\cdot, \cdot)$ does not take the intruder into account. In general, the intruder considers a particular occurrence of an action in a trace or part of a trace and tries to identify the user or users involved in this. However, the selection by the intruder of the action of interest is based on observable actions only. If two traces are observationally the same to the intruder, its analysis is focused on the same action. The traces generally differ in the number and/or position of invisible actions, so that the particular action can be at different positions in the two traces. Therefore, we introduce the partial mapping $obscnt \colon \mathcal{T} \times \mathbb{N} \xrightarrow{p} \mathbb{N}$, that returns for a position n in a trace t the corresponding position $obscnt(t, n)$ in the reduced trace, i.e. $obscnt(t, 0) = 0$, $obscnt(a \cdot t, n + 1) = obscnt(t, n) + 1$ if $a \in \mathcal{A}_{obs}$ and $obscnt(a \cdot t, n + 1) = obscnt(t, n) + 1$ if $a \notin \mathcal{A}_{obs}$, and $obscnt(\varepsilon, n + 1)$ is undefined.

Selection functions. Next, we introduce selection functions, that take only observables and relative positions of observables into account. A selection function reflects a specific preference of the intruder. Formally, a mapping $\sigma \colon \mathcal{T} \to \mathbb{N}$ is called a selection function, with respect to a set of keys K, if (i) $\sigma(t) \in dom(t)$, (ii) $t[\sigma(t)] \in \mathcal{A}_{obs}$, and (iii) if $t_1 \sim^K_{obs} t_2$ then $obscnt(t_1, \sigma(t_1)) = obscnt(t_2, \sigma(t_2))$. Thus, if traces t_1 and t_2 are the same to the intruder that knows about the keys in K, then the selection function σ points in t_1 and in t_2 to an observable action at corresponding positions. Given the choice of positions governed by a selection function σ, the attribution α_σ of users to a trace, induced by the selection function σ, is then simply defined as $\alpha_\sigma(t) = \alpha(t, \sigma(t))$. Note that, in general, we do not have $\alpha(t_1, \sigma(t_1)) = \alpha(t_2, \sigma(t_2))$.

Below, we have occasion to further restrict the selection function that we consider. Intuitively, it is clear that an intruder observing a system from its very first startup is more powerful, than an intruder viewing the same system from some moment in time onwards. Typically, we assume the selection functions to stem from a class Σ of selection functions that point at positions in traces beyond some initialization phase. Likewise, we only want to consider the traces of the system under consideration. Thus, for a given system $\mathcal{S}$ with the set of traces $Tr(\mathcal{S})$ as its behaviour, we restrict the choice of traces to $Tr(\mathcal{S})$ or a subset thereof (for example, fair traces). Thus, a selection function σ will have functionality $\sigma \colon Tr(\mathcal{S}) \to \mathcal{U}$ rather than $\sigma \colon \mathcal{T} \to \mathcal{U}$.

Anonymity. With this in mind, we are ready for the definition of an anonymity group of a user. For a user u, its anonymity group $AG(u)$ consists of all users u' that can not be distinguished from u by the intruder: u' is in the anonymity group of u with respect to an attribution α and selection function σ, if for any trace t that is attributed to u, i.e. $\alpha(t, \sigma(t)) = u$, we can find an observationally equivalent trace t', i.e. $t' \sim_{obs} t$, that is attributed to u'. So, given the observable behavior one can not tell whether u or any other user u' in its anonymity group was involved.

Definition 1. *Let $\mathcal{S}$ be a system, $\mathcal{A}_{obs} \subseteq \mathcal{A}$ a set of observable actions, $K \subseteq \mathcal{K}$ a set of keys, Σ a class of selection functions and α an attribution function. For a user $u \in \mathcal{U}$, its anonymity group $AG(u)$ is given by*

$$AG(u) = \{\, u' \in \mathcal{U} \mid \forall \sigma \in \Sigma \, \forall t \in Tr(\mathcal{S}) \, \exists t' \in Tr(\mathcal{S}) \colon$$
$$\alpha_\sigma(t) = u \to \alpha_\sigma(t') = u' \wedge t \sim_{obs} t' \,\}.$$

Clearly, the size of $AG(u)$ is an indication for the degree of anonymity user u has. Furthermore, note that, in general, we do not have $v \in AG(u) \Leftrightarrow u \in AG(v)$, so the set of anonymity groups does not form a partition of the set of users. In Section 4, we will exploit our definition of anonymity in a formal analysis of the onion routing protocol.

3   An Example: Onion Routing

We discuss the onion routing protocol for illustrating the formalization of privacy. After an informal explanation of the onion routing protocol, we provide a formal specification in ACP-style process algebra. We will also briefly discuss a weaker security protocol, which we call coconut routing. Next, we present an alternative characterization of the onion routing protocol which helps in proving our anonymity results in Section 4.

3.1   The Onion Routing Protocol

The onion routing protocol as devised by Syverson et al. [17] is a constellation of measures to establish anonymous connections between two agents. It is our intention to formally describe and analyze the smallest protocol based on the onion routing principle that still exhibits interesting privacy properties. Starting point is a network of routers. We assume that the network forms a connected graph, which means that there is a path from every router to every other router. Such a path may be comprised of a series of intermediate routers.

To every router we associate a collection of users. Connections between a user and its router are typically realized within a local network and will be considered secure, while connections between two routers are not controlled by either router and may belong to a global communication infrastructure such as the Internet. It is realistic to assume that remote routers and connections between routers may be compromised. Given this possibly hostile environment, the purpose of the onion routing protocol is to enable a user S to send a message to a user R without revealing the identity of S nor that of R.

In order to establish the above requirement, we assume the existence of a public key infrastructure for the routers. This means that every router (whether compromised or not) has a public/private key pair and that all routers know the public keys of all other routers. The Message Sequence Chart of Figure 1 explains how the protocol operates. Suppose that user S intends to send message m to user R. For S this simply means that it uses its router OS as a proxy to perform this task. Therefore, it sends message m and recipient R to OS. Next, its router determines a path leading to the router to which R belongs and packs the message in such a way that every node in the path can only deduce the next node in the path, but nothing else. Suppose the chosen path is $OS; O1; O2; OR$, then the message sent to $O1$ is $O1, \{O2, \{OR, \{R, m\}_{pk(OR)}\}_{pk(O2)}\}_{pk(O1)}$, i.e. a header identifying the intended intermediate recipient $O1$ and a payload of some content encrypted with the public key of $O1$. Since we expect that $O1$ only knows its own secret key, $O1$ can only peel off the outermost layer of this composite message. Therefore, $O1$ obtains message $O2, \{OR, \{R, m\}_{pk(OR)}\}_{pk(O2)}$ and learns that this message has to be passed through to router $O2$. Likewise, $O2$ and OR peel off their layer from the onion and, finally, OR knows that it has to send message m to its user R.

The reason why this protocol establishes privacy of the sender and receiver of a message lies in the fact that the messages leaving a router cannot be related to the messages that have entered a router. This unlinkability of incoming and outgoing messages requires that an attacker cannot trace an outgoing message back to an incoming message by simply trying the public keys of all routers. Therefore, we require randomized encryption, which means that the same message encrypted with the same key every time yields a different enciphered message.

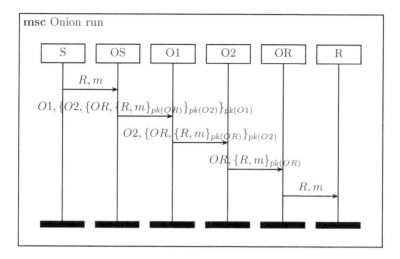

Fig. 1. Sample run of the onion routing protocol

This can be established e.g. by salting the input. Which conditions exactly guarantee which kind of privacy is subject of the formal analysis later in this paper.

3.2   Coconut Routing

The onion routing protocol works because the messages are packed in a series of shells, which are subsequently peeled off by the conveying routers. It is interesting to study weaker variants of this protocol and see how onion routing solves the weaknesses. To this end, we introduce a variation on onion routing, which we will call *coconut routing*. We will only conduct an informal analysis of this weaker protocol. A thorough analysis follows along the same steps as the analysis of the onion routing protocol above.

In the coconut routing protocol, the original message and the path are encrypted with a symmetric cryptographic key. This key is a secret shared by all routers. Figure 2 shows a sample run of the coconut routing protocol and suffices to understand its operation.

3.3   Formal Specification of Onion Routing

The above describes onion routing informally. Next, we define the onion routing protocol in ACP-style process algebra (see, e.g., [1, 7, 2]). We assume that the reader is familiar with the basics of this particular branch of process algebra. Nevertheless, our approach is independent of the chosen framework as long as it supports reasoning at a trace level.

Fix a set $\mathcal{R}$ of routers, a set $\mathcal{U}$ of user, a set $\mathcal{M}$ of messages and a set $\mathcal{K}$ of keys. The set $Path$ of paths is defined by $Path = \mathcal{R}^*$. We use r to range over $\mathcal{R}$, u and v to range over $\mathcal{U}$, and m and p to range over $\mathcal{M}$ and $Path$, respectively.

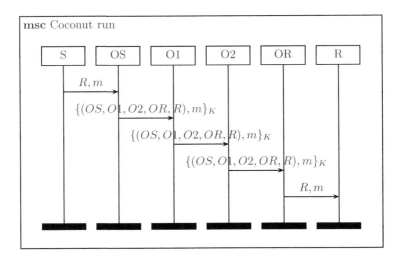

Fig. 2. Sample run of the coconut routing protocol

Fix a router assignment $\rho\colon \mathcal{U} \to \mathcal{R}$ that associates a router $\rho(u)$ with each user. We use $site(r)$ and $site(u)$ to denote the set of users u' such that $\rho(u') = r$ and $\rho(u') = \rho(u)$, respectively. We assume to be given a mapping $pk\colon \mathcal{R} \to \mathcal{K}$ to retrieve a public key $pk(r)$ of a router r. Furthermore, the topology of the router network is reflected by an undirected connected graph $\mathcal{N}$ having the set $\mathcal{R}$ as its nodes. The set $\mathcal{N}(r)$, the neighborhood of the router r, consists of all routers r' for which an edge connecting r and r' exists in the graph $\mathcal{N}$.

We use the notation $path(r, q)$ for the collection of those non-empty paths $r_1 \cdot r_2 \cdots r_n$ such that $\mathcal{N}(r, r_1)$, $\mathcal{N}(r_i, r_{i+1})$, for $1 \leq i < n$, and $r_n = q$. Onions are the basic objects that will be passed around in the onion routing protocol below. The set of onions $\mathcal{O}$, ranged over by o, is inductively given by

$$v \in \mathcal{U} \wedge m \in \mathcal{M} \implies \langle v, m \rangle \in \mathcal{O} \tag{1}$$

$$o \in \mathcal{O} \wedge r \in \mathcal{R} \implies \langle r, \{o\}_{pk(r)} \rangle \in \mathcal{O}. \tag{2}$$

The collection $\mathcal{O}_\perp = \mathcal{O} \cup \{\perp\}$ extends $\mathcal{O}$ with the dummy onion $\perp$. For a path p and onion o, the function $pack\colon Path \times \mathcal{O} \to \mathcal{O}$ is given by

$$pack(\varepsilon, o) = o \tag{3}$$

$$pack(r \cdot p, o) = \langle r, \{pack(p, o)\}_{pk(r)} \rangle. \tag{4}$$

The function $pack$ wraps the onion o with the public keys of the routers along the path p. In particular, for a path $p = r_1 \cdot r_2 \cdots r_n$, user v and plaintext m, we have $pack(p, \langle v, m \rangle) = \langle r_1, \{\langle r_2, \{\ldots \langle r_n, \{\langle v, m \rangle\}_{pk(r_n)} \rangle \ldots\}_{pk(r_2)} \rangle\}_{pk(r_1)} \rangle$. Conversely, the function $peel\colon \mathcal{O} \to \mathcal{O}_\perp$ is the inverse of packing, i.e., $peel(o) = o'$ if $o = \langle r, \{o'\}_{pk(r)} \rangle$ for some router r and delivers $\perp$ otherwise.

Node-oriented system description The basic building blocks in an onion routing system are the routers. We consider the process $Node_r$, with the subscript r

denoting the particular router, to come equipped with a buffer B that contains the onions that are still to be delivered. In general, $B \in Mul(\mathcal{O})$ is a multiset of onions. Possible actions for $Node_r$ are taken from the alphabet

$$\mathcal{A}_r = \{\; input(u,v,m), read(r',r,o), send(r,r'',o), output(v,m)$$
$$\mid u \in site(r), v \in \mathcal{U}, m \in \mathcal{M}, \mathcal{N}(r',r), \mathcal{N}(r,r''), o \in \mathcal{O}\;\}.$$

We fix the set of actions $\mathcal{A}$ to $\mathcal{A} = \bigcup\{\; \mathcal{A}_r \mid r \in \mathcal{R}\;\}$. A router r with buffer B can either

- input, from one of its users u, a new message m with destination v that can subsequently be forwarded along a path p from r to the router of v,
- store an onion o that is read from one of its neighboring router r' after peeling it off,
- take an onion $\langle r'', \{o'\}_{pk(r)}\rangle$ from the buffer for sending to another router r'', or
- deliver an onion $\langle v, m\rangle$ in the buffer to the user v.

Using the operators $+$ and $\sum$ to denote choice and $\cdot$ for sequential composition, we obtain the following recursive definition of the behaviour of a node:

$$Node_r(B) \;=$$
$$\sum\nolimits_{u\in site(r),v\in\mathcal{U},m\in\mathcal{M}} input(u,v,m)$$
$$\cdot \sum\nolimits_{p\in path(r,\rho(v))} Node_r(B \cup \{pack(p,v,m)\})$$
$$+ \sum\nolimits_{\mathcal{N}(r',r),o\in\mathcal{O}} read(r',r,o) \cdot Node_r(B \cup \{peel(o)\})$$
$$+ \sum\nolimits_{o=\langle r'',\{o''\}_{pk(r'')}\rangle\in B} send_{r,r''}(o) \cdot Node_r(B \setminus \{o\})$$
$$+ \sum\nolimits_{\langle v,m\rangle\in B} output(v,m) \cdot Node_r(B \setminus \{\langle v,m\rangle\}).$$

The communication function matches read and sent events, i.e.

$$read(r,r',o) \mid send(r,r',o) = comm(r,r',o)$$

for any two routers r, r' and onion o. The set H of encapsulated or forbidden actions is given by

$$H = \{\; read(r,r',o), send(r,r',o) \mid r,r' \in \mathcal{R}, o \in \mathcal{O}\;\}.$$

Finally, using ∂_H to encapsulate partial communications and $\|$ to denote parallel composition, the onion routing network ORN is defined by

$$ORN - (\partial_H(\|_{r\in\mathcal{R}} Node_r(\emptyset))).$$

Thus, the onion routing network consist of a number of routers, each with a local buffer. The system starts with all routers having an empty buffer, and evolves by routers getting from and delivering to their clients and exchanging onions with other routers. Because of the choice of the communication function and encapsulation, the system ORN does not exhibit unmatched *read* and *send* actions, but *input*, *output* and *comm* actions only.

A technical issue concerns the synchronization of read and send actions. In general, the environment can influence a non-deterministic choice over the index set $path(r, \rho(v))$ for a user v and message m, by offering only a selection of reads that can match the send action that executes to the sending of $pack(p, v, m)$ to the first router along the path. This way an intruder could get control over the choice of the path connecting r and v (and, e.g., direct it via some compromised router). To prevent this, the usual trick is to insert a so-called silent action, *skip* say, just in front of $Node_r(B + \{pack(p, v, m)\})$ in the first summand. This would clutter up the further analysis dramatically, with a distinction between nodes that have or have not taken the *skip*-step after an input and path-selection. As we consider in this paper mainly an intruder model with eavesdropping capabilities only, we suppress this technicality in the remainder.

Path-oriented system description As alternative to the above node-oriented description of the network as a collection of nodes, one can follow an activity-driven approach. The node-oriented description is not very appealing from a global point of view. It is hard to identify the flow triggered by an intent of sending a message m from a user u to a user v over the network. Therefore, we view an onion routing network as a parallel composition of the process of the sending of a message by an initiating user, the passage of the associated onion along a certain path of routers, and the receipt of the message by the designated user. In order to capture the above intuition, we define processes $Comm(r, p, o)$, for a router r, path p and an onion o, to reflect that the onion o resides in packed form at the router r and still has to travel along the path p. Also, for usage in Section 4, we define processes $OR(u, v, m, p)$ representing the sending of message m from user u to v along the path p. Thus

$$OR(u, v, m, p) = input(u, v, m) \cdot Comm(r, p, \langle v, m \rangle) \cdot output(v, m)$$
$$Comm(r, \varepsilon, o) = \varepsilon \quad \text{if } o = \langle v, m \rangle \text{ and } v \in site(r)$$
$$Comm(r, r' \cdot p, o) = comm(r, r', \langle r', pack(r' \cdot p, o) \rangle) \cdot Comm(r', p, o)$$
$$\text{if } r' \in \mathcal{N}(r), \, Comm(r', p, o) \neq \delta$$
$$Comm(r, p, o) = \delta \quad \text{otherwise}$$

where, in the right-hand side, ε and δ are the successfully terminating process and unsuccessfully terminating or deadlocking process, respectively. The resulting system ORN' is then given by

$$ORN' = \sum_{r \in \mathcal{R}, u \in site(r), v \in \mathcal{U}, m \in \mathcal{M}, p \in path(r, \rho(v))} input(u, v, m) \cdot$$
$$\big(ORN' \parallel Comm(r, p, \langle v, m \rangle) \cdot output(v, m)\big).$$

Note the recurrence of ORN' at the right-hand side. After the displayed input action, the system continues with the processing of the input in component $Comm(r, p, \langle v, m \rangle)$, but is also ready to initiate the sending of new messages.

Next, we would like to have that the node-oriented and path-oriented description of onion routing coincide. The former is closest to the informal description; for the latter it is immediate what its traces look like.

Theorem 1. *The systems ORN and ORN' have the same traces.*   □

For a proof of Theorem 1, one introduces some auxiliary concepts, viz. that of a distributed buffer state β and of a global communication state γ. Using these one shows, for some suitable relation C, that $C(\beta, \gamma)$ implies that the generalized systems $ORN(\beta)$ and $ORN'(\gamma)$ have the same traces. Since, in particular, it holds that $C(\emptyset, \emptyset)$ and $ORN = ORN(\emptyset)$, $ORN' = ORN'(\emptyset)$, the result follows. The characterization of Theorem 1 will be exploited in the next section, where we establish anonymity results for onion and coconut routing.

4   Anonymity Properties of Onion Routing

In this section, we determine the anonymity group for senders and receivers engaged in a message exchange via onion routing based on the formal definition presented in Section 2. For the instantiation of Definition 1 we have to pick a system, a subset of observable actions, a set of compromised keys, a class of selection functions and a user attribution. The system under consideration is ORN with set of traces $Tr(ORN)$. We split the set of actions by considering inputs and outputs to be invisible and communications to be observable, thus $\mathcal{A}_{\mathrm{obs}} = \{\, comm(r, r', o) \mid r, r' \in \mathcal{R}, o \in \mathcal{O} \,\}$. Furthermore, we fix a set $CN \subseteq \mathcal{R}$ of compromised nodes, i.e., a set of routers r of which the secret key corresponding to the public key $pk(r)$ is known to the intruder. Hence, the set K of compromised keys consists of $\{\, pk(r) \mid r \in CN \,\}$ that are no longer safe to use. The anonymity analysis below is with respect to the observational equivalence $\sim_{\mathrm{obs}}$ induced by the observables $\mathcal{A}_{\mathrm{obs}}$ and bad keys K.

The selection functions, that select the observable action of interest in a trace, are restricted to functions that point beyond a proper initialization prefix. More concretely, part of the anonymity results below depend on the fact that a router has both been recorded as a receiving and as a sending host in the trace, earlier than the selected subtrace. So, we want to distinguish an index N_t such that

$$\forall r \in \mathcal{R} \exists n_1, n_2 < N_t \colon t[n_1] = comm(r_1, r, o_1) \wedge t[n_2] = comm(r, r_2, o_2)$$

for some routers $r_1, r_2 \in \mathcal{R}$, $o_1, o_2 \in \mathcal{O}$. For such an index N_t to exist at all, we assume a fairness condition stating that every input and communication action have a successor action (communication or output) in the trace. In terms of the causality relation $\prec_t$, to be defined in a minute, we require, for a trace t of ORN, to hold that

$$\forall i \in \mathbb{N} \colon t[i] \neq output(\cdot, \cdot) \rightarrow \exists j \in \mathbb{N} \colon i \prec_t j.$$

The requirement is not only technically convenient, but, more importantly, it is plausible as well. For it is realistic to postulate, that the intruder can not oversee a whole infinite trace, but only a finite part of it. Therefore, it is safe to start from the assumption that finite subprocesses will terminate within an infinite trace.

The alternative characterization of ORN captured by Theorem 1 states that a trace t of ORN is an interleaving of subtraces of the form $OR(u, v, m, p)$ for users u and v, message m and path $p \in path(\rho(u), \rho(v))$. In general, this does not provide a unique decomposition of the trace t. There are multiple ways to merge the finite subtraces $OR(u, v, m, p)$ into an infinite trace t. Even more so, if, e.g. due to retransmission, actions can have several occurrences in a trace. For our purposes it suffices to choose, for every position n of t, a particular subtrace $w = OR(u, v, m, p)$ such that $n \in dom(w)$ (exploiting the partial function interpretation of traces). More precisely, define for a trace t the relation $\prec_t$ on $\mathbb{N}$ by

$$
\begin{aligned}
n \prec_t m \iff\ & t[n] = input(u, v, m),\ t[m] = Comm(r, p, \langle v, m \rangle)[1], \\
& u, v \in \mathcal{U}, m \in \mathcal{M}, r = \rho(u), q = \rho(v), p \in path(r, q),\ \text{or} \\
& t[n] = Comm(r, p, o)[i],\ t[m] = Comm(r, p, o)[i + 1], \\
& r \in \mathcal{R}, p \in path(r), o \in \mathcal{O}, i \in \mathbb{N},\ \text{or} \\
& t[n] = Comm(r, p, \langle v, m \rangle)[k],\ t[m] = output(v, m), \\
& r \in \mathcal{R}, v \in \mathcal{U}, m \in \mathcal{M}, k = len(Comm(r, p, \langle v, m \rangle)), \\
& q = \rho(v), p \in path(r, q)
\end{aligned}
$$

such that $\forall \ell, n < \ell < m\colon t[\ell] \neq t[m]$. Then $w = OR(u, v, m, p)$, with finite domain $dom(w) = \{\, i_0, i_1, \ldots, i_k, i_{k+1} \,\}$, is the subtrace of t for position n if $n \in dom(w)$, $i_0 \prec_t i_1 \prec_t \cdots \prec_t i_k \prec_t i_{k+1}$, $[i_0] = input(u, v, m)$, $t[i_1, \ldots, i_k] = Comm(r, p, \langle v, m \rangle)$, and $t[i_{k+1}] = output(v, m)$.

We define, for a selection function σ, the sender attribution function α_σ^s and receiver attribution function α_σ^r, in full $\alpha_\sigma^s, \alpha_\sigma^r\colon Tr(ORN) \to \mathcal{U}$ by $\alpha_\sigma^s(t) = u$ and $\alpha_\sigma^r(t) = v$ if $OR(u, v, m, p)$ is the subtrace of t for position $\sigma(t)$.

Having observational equivalence and attribution in place, we continue with discussing two properties of onion routing that will be used in the proofs of anonymity results below. The first property states how a sequence of communications can be cut in two. See Figure 5.

Lemma 1 (path decomposition). *Let $r, r' \in \mathcal{R}$, $p \in path(r, r')$. Let q be a router on p such that $p = p_1 \cdot q \cdot p_2$ for suitable path p_1 and p_2. Then it holds that $Comm(s, p, o) = Comm(s, p_1 \cdot q, pack(p_2, o)) \cdot Comm(q, p_2, o)$.* $\square$

The second property that we will exploit in the analysis below, states that if an outgoing communication $comm(r, r', o)$ from a router r does not originate from an input of a user of r, then there must be an earlier incoming communication $comm(r'', r, o')$ such that the outgoing onion o is obtained from the incoming onion o' by peeling off one skin. See Figure 4.

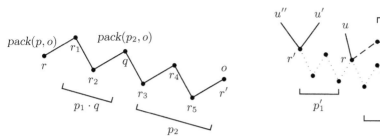 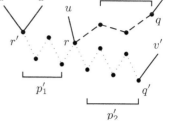

Fig. 3. path decomposition   **Fig. 4.** cross over

Lemma 2 (cross over). *Let $r \in \mathcal{R}$, σ a selection function and t a trace such that $\sigma(t) = i$, $t[i] = \mathrm{comm}(r, r', o)$.*

(a) If $\alpha_\sigma^s(t) \notin \mathrm{site}(r)$, then $j \prec_t i$, $t[j] = \mathrm{comm}(r'', r, o')$ and $o' = \mathrm{pack}(r', o)$ for some $j < i$, r'' and o'.

(b) If $\alpha_\sigma^r(t) \notin \mathrm{site}(r')$, then $i \prec_t k$, $t[k] = \mathrm{comm}(r', r'', o')$ and $o = \mathrm{pack}(r', o')$ for some $i < k$, r'' and o'. □

We first consider the case of anonymity for senders. We distinguish between the situation where the key of router of the site is or is not compromised. As a consequence of Theorem 2 we have that, no matter how many keys have been leaked, the anonymity of a user is save as long as the key of its router is.

Theorem 2. *For a set of compromised nodes CN, onion routing has the following anonymity groups for senders: $AG_s(u) = U$ if $\rho(u) \notin CN$, and $AG_s(u) = \mathrm{site}(u)$ otherwise.* □

The proof of the theorem exploits Lemma 1, in case $\rho(u) \notin CN$, to construct, for any trace t of ORN with $\alpha_\sigma^s(t) = u$, an alternative trace t' of ORN such that $\alpha_\sigma^s(t') = u'$. If $\rho(u) \in CN$, then, we construct a particular trace t with $\alpha_\sigma^s(t) = u$ and use Lemma 2 to rule out that any observational equivalent trace t' can be attributed to a user u' not in $\mathrm{site}(u)$.

Next, we turn to the receiver. In the proof of Theorem 2 we exploited the initialization condition which helps in prepending subbehaviour to the subtrace under consideration. For the case of the receiver we call upon the fairness assumption in order to find subbehaviour that extends the particular subtrace.

Theorem 3. *For a set of compromised nodes CN, onion routing has the following anonymity groups for receivers: $AG_r(v) = \mathcal{U}$ if $\mathrm{router}(v) \notin CN$, and $AG_r(v) = \{v\}$ otherwise.* □

The proof of Theorem 3 is in the same vein as that of Theorem 2.

For comparison, we next consider the coconut case. Recall that in our model for coconut routing, packets are decrypted but not encrypted again at the node. Instead, the original encrypted packet is forwarded.

Theorem 4. *Coconut routing has for senders the anonymity groups* $AG_s(u) = site(u)$, *and, for receivers the anonymity groups* $AG_r(v) = site(v)$ *if the key* k *is not compromised, but* $AG_r(v) = \{v\}$ *otherwise.* □

Theorem 4, which can be proven along the same line as its onion routing counterparts, shows the weakness of our artificial coconut routing scheme. However, if incoming messages are decrypted and encrypted again using a randomized symmetric encryption schema the above reasoning does not apply. Then, the difference of onion routing vs. coconut routing lies in the robustness. If the single symmetric key is leaked, coconut routing breaks down, whereas for onion routing users at uncompromised sites remain anonymous.

The above analysis establishes the anonymity groups given the choice of parameters to the problem. A number of variations have been considered by way of experiments for our definition of anonymity groups. For example, instead of restricting the selection functions to the class Σ one can allow arbitrary selections, but demanding that each router sends itself a fake message over a random path. This does not affect the anonymity results. However, the sender anonymity drops to an isolated site for senders, but not for receivers if such a randomized initialization phase does not take place and general selection functions are allowed. Another line of variation is in the fairness assumptions or in the definition itself. A concrete alternative is to consider 'windows of observation', leading to a set-up that is simpler than the one with selection functions, but unintuitive results (as one can claim behavior just outside the window of the intruder). In fact, one could argue that the selection functions form a generalization of considering finite prefixes. A protocol, that we baptized kiwi-routing employs symmetric keys that are shared among pairs of routers. This protocol is weaker than coconut routing (whence the naming) in the sense that it breaks down as soon as one of the many shared keys gets compromised.

5 Conclusion

The achievements of our research are twofold. First of all, we have given a general and formal definition of anonymity in a trace model. Main parameters of this definition are the attribution function which assigns to each trace a user, and the capabilities of the intruder. This allows us to calculate a user's anonymity group, i.e. the collection of other users that cannot be distinguished from this user by the intruder. Our definition is of a qualitative nature and discards quantitative aspects. This means that we only consider statements such as "could this behaviour be attributed to some other user", rather than "what is the chance that this behaviour is caused by some other user". It is our believe that a formal quantitative analysis of a security protocol can only be achieved after first having developed a proper qualitative analysis methodology. In future research we wish to investigate the use of tool support to analyze privacy protocols and to adapt our approach to a quantitative setting.

The second result of our research is the formalization of a basic onion routing protocol and its analysis. By abstracting from several details we were able to concentrate on what we consider the protocol proper and to formalize some of the insights expressed by the designers of the protocol. By varying over the user attribution function we could analyze the anonymity of both the receiver and sender of some intercepted message. Reasoning about different attribution functions, such as "did u ever send a message", follows the same line. Due to the restrictions on the intruder's choice function, we were able to express conditions on the initialization of the protocol that guarantee full privacy. It is not the case that during this initialization phase senders of messages can be traced back. The size of a user's anonymity group expands during this phase until it comprises all other users. It would be interesting to express the anonymity group of each user during initialization as a closed expression.

One of our aims was to understand why the onion routing protocol has its current shape and under which conditions its privacy properties are satisfied. Thereto we compared it to several weaker protocols, of which we have discussed the coconut routing protocol here only. This comparison explains what the implications are of simplifying the layered messages. Coconut routing hardly guarantees privacy. While performing our analysis, it turned out quite naturally that the onion routing protocol requires randomized encryption to guarantee full privacy. Without such randomization the protocol is vulnerable to guessing attacks, when the intruder seeks to relate incoming and encryptions of outgoing traffic.

It would be interesting to analyze more complex versions of the onion routing protocol, such as an extension of the protocol with connections, like in the original onion routing protocol. Further validation of our methodology would not only require to consider other protocols, but also stronger intruder models. In the case of the onion routing protocol it is conjectured that an active intruder could not threaten privacy more than a passive (eavesdropping) intruder. Since denial-of-service attacks is a topic of research of its own, we will not consider these attacks in the course of our privacy research.

A final topic of future research is the formalization of other privacy notions, such as unlinkability, pseudonymity and unobservability. Initial research indicates that their formalization follows the same line as the formalization of anonymity.

References

1. J.C.M. Baeten and W.P. Weijland. *Process Algebra*, volume 18 of *Cambridge Tracts in Theoretical Computer Science*. Cambridge University Press, 1990.
2. J.A. Bergstra, A. Ponse, and S. A. Smolka. *Handbook of Process Algebra*. Elsevier, 2001.
3. R. Clarke. Introduction to dataveillance and information privacy, and definitions of terms. http://www.anu.edu.au/people/Roger.Clarke/DV/Intro.html, 1999.
4. C.J.F. Cremers, S. Mauw, and E.P. de Vink. Defining authentication in a trace model. In T. Dimitrakos and F. Martinelli, editors, *Proc. FAST 2003*, 1st International Workshop on Formal Aspects in Security and Trust, pages 131–145, Pisa, 2003. IIT-CNR technical report.

5. C. Díaz, J. Claessens, S. Seys, and B. Preneel. Information theory and anonymity. In B. Macq and J.-J. Quisquater, editors, *Proc. 23rd Symposium on Information Theory in the Benelux*, pages 179–186. Université Catholique de Louvain, 2002.
6. EPIC. Comments of the Electronic Privacy Information Center. www.epic.org/privacy/drm/, 2002.
7. W.J. Fokkink. *Introduction to Process Algebra*. Texts in Theoretical Computer Science, an EATCS Series. Springer, 2000.
8. Association for Automatic Identification and Mobility. Rfid.org. www.aimglobal.org/technologies/rfid/, 2004.
9. D.M. Goldschlag, M.G. Reed, and P.F. Syverson. Hiding routing information. In R.J. Anderson, editor, *Proc. 1st International Workshop on Information Hiding*, pages 137–150, Cambridge, 1996. LNCS 1174.
10. ISO. Common Criteria–ISO/IEC/15408. http://csrc.nist.gov/cc/, 1999.
11. M. Korkea-aho. Anonymity and privacy in the electronic world, 1999. Seminar on Network Security, Helsinki University of Technology.
12. A. Pfitzmann and M. Köhntopp. Anonymity, unobservability, and pseudonymity. In H. Federrath, editor, *Designing Privacy Enhancing Technologies*, pages 1–9. LNCS 2009, 2001.
13. M.K. Reiter. Crowds: Anonymity for web transactions. *ACM Transactions on Information and System Security*, pages 66 – 92, 1998.
14. S. Schneider and A. Sidiroupoulos. CSP and anonymity. In *Proc. ESORICS'96*, pages 198–218. LNCS 1146, 1996.
15. A. Serjantov and G. Danezis. Towards an information theoretic metric for anonymity. In H. Federrath, editor, *Proc. PET 2002*, pages 41–53. LNCS 2482, 2003.
16. P. Syverson, G. Tsudik, M. Reed, and C. Landwehr. Towards an analysis of onion routing security. In H. Federrath, editor, *Designing Privacy Enhancing Technologies*, pages 96–114. LNCS 2009, 2001.
17. P.F. Syverson, D.M. Goldschlag, and M.G. Reed. Anonymous connections and onion routing. In *IEEE Symposium on Security and Privacy*, pages 44–54, Oakland, California, 1997.

Breaking Cauchy Model-Based JPEG Steganography with First Order Statistics

Rainer Böhme and Andreas Westfeld

Technische Universität Dresden
Institute for System Architecture
01069 Dresden, Germany
{rainer.boehme,westfeld}@mail.inf.tu-dresden.de

Abstract. The recent approach of a model-based framework for steganography fruitfully contributes to the discussion on the security of steganography. In addition, the first proposal for an embedding algorithm constructed under the model-based paradigm reached remarkable performance in terms of capacity and security. In this paper, we review the emerging of model-based steganography in the context of decent steganalysis as well as from theoretical considerations, before we present a method to attack the above-mentioned scheme on the basis of first order statistics. Experimental results show a good detection ratio for a large test set of typical JPEG images. The attack is successful because of weaknesses in the model and does not put into question the generalised theoretical framework of model-based steganography. So we discuss possible implications for improved embedding functions.

1 Introduction

Steganography is the art and science of hiding information such that its presence cannot be detected. Unlike cryptography, where anybody on the transmission channel notices the flow of information but cannot read its content, steganography aims to embed a confidential message in unsuspicious data, such as image or audio files [18]. Like in cryptography, the Kerckhoffs principle [16] also applies to steganography: Security relies on publicly known algorithms that are parameterised with secret keys.

Steganalysis is the task to attack steganographic systems. For a successful attack, it is sufficient for an adversary to prove the existence of a hidden message in a carrier even if she cannot decrypt the content. Whereas in most cases the existence of steganography can only be expressed in probabilities, the literature suggests a somewhat weaker notion for successful attacks. A steganographic algorithm is considered as broken if there exists a method that can determine whether or not a medium contains hidden information with a success rate better than random guessing.

1.1 Related Embedding Schemes and Successful Attacks

Judging from the set of available steganographic tools, digital images are the most popular carrier for steganographic data, likely because of being both op-

P. Samarati et al. (Eds.): ESORICS 2004, LNCS 3193, pp. 125–140, 2004.

erable and plausible. The plausibility of steganographic target formats increases with the amount of data transmitted in the respective format. Regarding the WWW and E-mail, JPEG images are widely used, and therefore they are an ideal target format.

Jsteg [22], released in 1993, is probably the first steganographic tool to embed into JPEG images. Embedding is accomplished by replacing the least significant bits of quantised coefficients that describe the image data in the frequency domain. Even though, this simple method can be reliably detected with the Chi-square attack (χ^2) [26]. This attack exploits the pair wise dependencies of adjacent bins in the histogram, which occur after embedding of uniformly distributed message bits.

To prevent this attack, the algorithm F5 [24] uses a different embedding function, adapting the least significant bits to the message by decreasing the coefficients' absolute values. In addition, F5 implements two steganographic techniques to lower the risk of detection for messages below the full capacity. *Matrix encoding* [4] minimises the amount of modifications per message bit by carefully selecting the modified coefficients. A *permutative straddling* function spreads the message equally over the whole image.

OutGuess [19], another algorithm, also replaces the least significant bits, but additionally introduces correction bits to preserve the first order statistics. Thus, it is not vulnerable to the Chi-square attack. OutGuess voluntarily limits the maximum steganographic content to 6 % of the file size (about half as much as the before mentioned algorithms support) in order to realise *plausible deniability*: At first, a secret message is embedded together with error correction codes. Then, a second harmless message can be embedded, which acts as alibi for the case that the concealed communication is actually discovered.

Both OutGuess and F5 can be detected by computing *calibrated statistics*. Uncompressing a JPEG image and re-compressing it after a slight transformation in the spatial domain accomplishes this. A comparison of both marginal statistics, of the examined image and of the re-compressed image, reveals the existence of a hidden message [10, 11].

Apart from targeted attacks, which are constructed for particular embedding functions, *blind attacks* [17, 7] do not assume knowledge about the functionality of particular algorithms. Blind methods extract a broad set of statistical features, which might be subject to changes due to embedding. Then, a classifier is trained with a large number of typical images, both pristine carriers and stegotexts. Although suffering from lower prediction reliability than targeted attacks, blind attacks have the advantage of easy adaptability to new embedding functions. While in this case targeted attacks have to be altered or redesigned, blind attacks just require a new training.

1.2 Towards Model-Based Steganography

There have been several attempts to formalise the security of steganographic systems from an information theoretic point of view. Based on Anderson and Petitcolas' [1] initial idea to argue with entropy measures of carrier, stegotexts, and hidden messages, Zöllner et al. [29] show that information theoretical secure steganography is not feasible in general. As a result, they introduce the notion of an *in-deterministic steganographic function*. This concept implies that the steganographic carrier, represented as random variable $X = (X_{det}, X_{indet})$, can be split up into a deterministic part X_{det} and an in-deterministic part X_{indet}. Zöllner et al. assume that an adversary has knowledge about deterministic parts of a carrier, ranging from general assumptions about marginal distributions – for example, the typical macro structures of natural images – to specific information about an actual carrier, such as the possibility to verify the accuracy of a digitised photograph by comparing it to the depicted scene. Hence, the deterministic part must not be altered to carry steganographic data. The in-deterministic part, however, is assumed to be uniformly distributed random noise, which has been introduced, for example, by quantising the signal with an analogue-digital converter. Apart from meta-information, such as proportion and marginal distribution, the adversary has no knowledge about the actual shape of X_{indet}. Under this assumption, X_{indet} can be replaced with a similar distributed payload message X^*_{indet} (i. e., compressed data can be considered as uniformly distributed) to compose a stegotext $X^* = (X_{det}, X^*_{indet})$.

Though this approach sounds simple in theory, its practical application suffers from the problem to separate X_{indet} from X_{det}. This separation is not only complicated by the varying qualitative assumptions about which information an adversary can gain about the carrier – in more general terms, this is a question of the adversary model –, but also by the difficulty to consider all possible dependencies between

1. the "noise" and the structure of a carrier, and
2. the intra-dependencies within the "noise" part[1].

So, most attempts to separate X_{det} from X_{indet} are rather naive. The most widely used one is *least significant bit* (LSB) embedding, which implicitly assumes the k LSBs as X_{indet}, and the remaining bits as X_{det}. A couple of successful attacks against this scheme [5, 9, 12, 26, 28] proves the inadequacy of this approach.

Also arguing with information theory, Cachin [3] describes the relation of the relative entropy between the probability distributions of carrier data and stegotexts to the error probabilities in a hypothesis test of a passive adversary. He introduces the concept of ε-security, denoting an upper bound for the binary relative entropy $d(\alpha, \beta) \leq \varepsilon$. In steganographic hypothesis tests, α is the probability that the adversary falsely suspects a hidden message in a pristine carrier (also *false positives*, or *type I error*), and β is probability that the adversary does not detect a hidden message (*misses*, or *type II error*).

These information theoretic considerations, however, seemed to have only marginal influence on the design of specific steganographic algorithms. Eventually, Sallee's work [21] contributes to remedy this unsatisfactory situation. His proposal of a *model-based* approach to steganography can be interpreted as an

---

[1] We put the term *noise* in inverted commas, because if it were *real* (i.e., uncorrelated) noise, we would not face the described problems.

evolutionary combination of the above mentioned concepts coupled with strong implications for the design of steganographic algorithms.

Model-based steganography adapts the division of the carrier into a deterministic random variable X_det and an in-deterministic one X_indet[2]. In contrast to the previous approaches, model-based steganography does not assume X_indet to be independently and uniformly distributed. Therefore the developers propose to find suitable models for the distribution of X_indet, which reflect the dependencies with X_det. The general model is parameterised with the actual values of X_det of a concrete cover medium, which leads to a cover specific model. The purpose of this model is to determine the conditional distributions $P(X_\mathrm{indet}|X_\mathrm{det} = x_\mathrm{det})$. Then, an arithmetic decompression function[3] is used to fit uniformly distributed message bits to the required distribution of X_indet, thus replacing X_indet by X_indet^*, which has similar statistic properties and contains the confidential message. Figure 1 shows a block diagram of the general model-based embedding process.

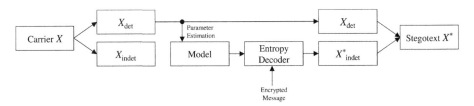

Fig. 1. Block diagram of the principles of model-based steganography

In addition to these general considerations, the initial work on model-based steganography contains a proposal for a concrete embedding function for JPEG images in the frequency domain. The purpose of this paper is to point to weaknesses of this concrete model, which allow an adversary to separate stegotexts from innocuous images.

The remainder of this paper is structured as follows: In the next section we explain the functionality of the actual embedding scheme, before we discuss its weaknesses in Section 3 in order to construct an operable attack. In Section 4, we report experimental results evaluating the performance of the presented detection method. In the final Section 5, we discuss the insights in a more general context and derive implications towards ever more secure steganography.

2   Model-Based Steganography for JPEG Images

In this section, we briefly explain the steganographic algorithm for JPEG images proposed in [21]. As we acknowledge the theoretical framework of the model-based approach, we expect further development under the new framework. So,

---

[2] Sallee [21] denotes X_indet as X_α and X_det as X_β. We do not follow this convention because the symbols α and β usually stand for error probabilities and might lead to confusion in other contexts.

[3] The idea of employing a decompression functions to generate arbitrary target distributions has been described in the literature as *mimic function* [23].

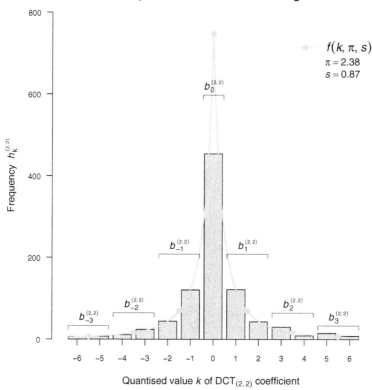

Fig. 2. Typical histogram of JPEG coefficients and approximated Cauchy distribution with data points. The frequency of the low precision bins $b_k^{(i,j)}$ is not modified during embedding

we will refer to the examined method as MB1, because it was the first one derived from the general considerations of model-based steganography.

Standardised JPEG compression cuts a greyscale image into blocks of 8×8 pixels, which are separately transformed into the frequency domain by a two dimensional *discrete cosine transformation* (DCT). The resulting 64 DCT coefficients, $(i, j) : i, j = 1, \ldots, 8$, are quantised with a quality dependent quantisation step size and further compressed by a lossless Huffman entropy encoder. The MB1 algorithm, as most steganographic schemes for JPEG files, embeds the steganographic semantic by modifying the quantised values. This ensures a lossless transmission of the hidden message bits.

Since individual modifications are not detectable without knowledge of the original values, an attacker reverts to the marginal statistics over all blocks of an image. Hence, the MB1 algorithm has been designed to preserve these distributions. Figure 2 depicts an example histogram of a selected $DCT_{(2,2)}$ coefficient. The histogram shape is typical for all JPEG DCT coefficients except $DCT_{(1,1)}$, which are therefore excluded from embedding (i. e., the $\text{DCT}_{(1,1)}$ coefficients belong to X_{det}).

Let us denote $h_k^{(i,j)}$ as the number of quantised $\text{DCT}_{(i,j)}$ coefficients equal to k in a given image. We will further refer to this quantity as the k-th *high precision bin* of the histogram $h^{(i,j)}$. By contrast, the *low precision bins* comprise several high precision bins. Without restricting generality, we focus on the case when a low precision bin $b_k^{(i,j)}$ ($k \neq 0$) contains exactly two high precision bins, so that

$$b_k^{(i,j)} = \begin{cases} h_{2k+1}^{(i,j)} + h_{2k}^{(i,j)} & \text{for } k < 0 \\ h_0^{(i,j)} & \text{for } k = 0 \\ h_{2k-1}^{(i,j)} + h_{2k}^{(i,j)} & \text{for } k > 0 . \end{cases}$$

To avoid the case differentiation and simplify the notation, we will write further equations only for $k > 0$. Furthermore, $q \in [0,1]$ denotes the quality parameter of a JPEG compression that is used to compute the quantisation tables.

The MB1 algorithm defines the size of the low precision bins $b_k^{(i,j)}$ as part of X_{det}, while the distribution within the low precision bins (i. e., the corresponding high precision bins $h_{2k-1}^{(i,j)}$ and $h_{2k}^{(i,j)}$) is considered as part of X_{indet}. The embedding function alters the quantised DCT coefficients, so that

1. the new values belong to the same low precision bin, and
2. the conditional distribution of $h_{2k-1}^{(i,j)}$ and $h_{2k}^{(i,j)}$ from a given $b_k^{(i,j)}$ keeps coherent according to a model.

This is accomplished by altering coefficient values of $2k-1$ to $2k$ and vice versa. In contrast to simple LSB overwriting, the conditional probabilities of occurrence $P(X_{\text{indet}}|X_{\text{det}} = x_{\text{det}})$, actually $P(h_{2k-1}^{(i,j)}|b_k^{(i,j)})$, are derived from the model in dependency of the low precision bin $b_k^{(i,j)}$. As it is obvious that the probabilities for all high precision bins sum up to 1 in each low precision bin,

$$P(h_{2k-1}^{(i,j)}|b_k^{(i,j)}) + P(h_{2k}^{(i,j)}|b_k^{(i,j)}) = 1, \qquad \forall\, i, j, k,$$

we further refer only to the $P(h_{2k-1}^{(i,j)}|b_k^{(i,j)})$ as $p_k^{(i,j)}$. The required $p_k^{(i,j)}$ is adjusted to the shape of a Modified Generalised Cauchy (MGC) distribution $f(k, \pi, s)$:

$$p_k^{(i,j)} = \frac{f(2k-1, \pi, s)}{f(2k-1, \pi, s) + f(2k, \pi, s)}$$

The density function of the MGC distribution applied is defined as follows:

$$f(k, \pi, s) = \frac{p-1}{2s}(|k/s| + 1)^{-\pi}$$

The scale parameter s and the location parameter π are computed separately for all DCT modes by a maximum likelihood estimation over the low precision bins $b^{(i,j)}$. Then, $p_k^{(i,j)}$ is determined for all low precision bins $b_k^{(i,j)}$, $k \neq 0$ of each DCT mode, but $\mathrm{DCT}_{(1,1)}$ coefficients and zero value coefficients $b_0^{(i,j)}$ are excluded from embedding. An arithmetic entropy decoder [27, cited from [21]] is used to fit the compressed and encrypted – thus uniformly distributed – message bits $m \sim U$ to a discrete vector with defined symbol probabilities $p_k^{(i,j)}$ and $1 - p_k^{(i,j)}$ [4]. As $b^{(i,j)}$ is not modified due to embedding, the receiver can recompute the model parameters and thus extract the message.

One way to evaluate the performance of an embedding algorithm is the embedding efficiency. According to [24], the embedding efficiency in JPEG files can be defined as the average message bits encoded per change of a coefficient. The application of an arithmetic decoder is an elegant way to achieve an exceptionally high embedding efficiency. Sallee reports embedding efficiencies between 2.06 and 2.16 bits per change for test images with $q = 80\,\%$ [21]. Other decent algorithms achieve values between 1.0 and 2.0 (OutGuess), or just under 2.0 (F5)[5]. Also in terms of capacity, MB1 performs on the upper end of the range. The capacity is defined as ratio of message bits per transmitted bits. MB1 reaches values of just under 14 %, which is slightly better than F5 and Jsteg (about 13 % and 12 %, respectively), and clearly above OutGuess (below 7 %).

Being explicitly designed as proof of concept, the developers of MB1 concede that the simple model does not include higher order statistics. However, they claim it to be "resistant to first order statistical attacks" [21, p. 166]. First order statistics are all measures describing data regardless of the inter-dependencies between observations, such as mean, variance, and histograms. Higher order statistics consider the relationship between observations and their position in the dataset; for example correlations between adjacent pixels in an image. As a rule of thumb, if the results of a statistical measure are invariant to any permutation of the data, then it is first order statistics.

Until today, none of the existing attacks against other algorithms also works on MB1, and no targeted attack has been published. Though, it is not surprising that a blind attack with special second order features, such as blockiness measures and co-occurrence tables, can discriminate between plain carriers and MB1 stegotexts [7]. But according to the outlook in the initial paper, we soon expect improved methods also taking into account some second order statistics. Whereas research clearly goes into this direction, it is somewhat important and also surprising that MB1 steganography is also vulnerable from the believed safe side: In the following section, we present a detection method which is completely based on first order statistics.

---

[4] The use of a *de*-coder might sound surprising, however, entropy considerations suggest that the length of the symbol stream increases with the skewness of the target distribution. For all $p_k^{(i,j)} \neq 0.5$ the amount of symbols and of consumed coefficients dominates the length of the message bit stream.

[5] Matrix encoding in F5 leads to higher efficiencies if the capacity is not fully used.

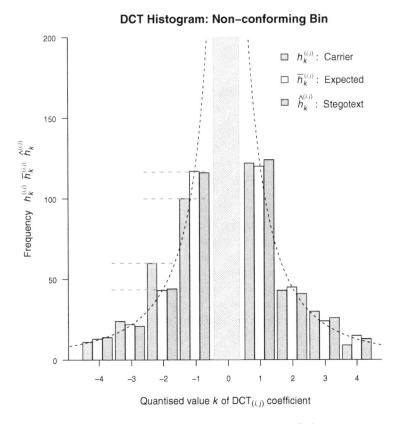

Fig. 3. Example DCT histogram with non-conforming bin $b_{-1}^{(i,j)}$. The divergences in the carrier between actual frequency and Cauchy-based expected frequencies disappear after MB1 embedding

3 Detection Method

The main idea of the proposed attack can be summarised as follows: Although the Cauchy distribution generally fits well to the DCT histograms, there are outlier bins in natural images. After embedding, these non-conforming bins are adjusted to the density function of the model distribution.

The construction of an attack can be structured into two steps: First, a test discriminates non-conforming bins from conforming ones. The test is run on all independent low precision bins of a particular JPEG image. Second, the count of positive test results is compared to an empirical threshold value for natural carrier images. If a questionable image contains less non-conforming bins than plain carrier images usually have, it is likely that the histograms are smoothed by the MB1 embedding function and thus, the image is classified as steganogram.

Figure 3 depicts a DCT histogram with a typical outlier in the low precision bin b_{-1}. The bins $b_0^{(i,j)}$ are excluded from embedding, so the respective bars are blanked out in the histogram. It is clearly visible that the original frequencies h_{-1} and h_{-2} (left bars of the triples) differ from the expected frequencies (middle bars). The expected frequencies and the frequencies in the stegotext (right bars) are fitted to the same level.

The differences can be measured by a contingency test between the observed frequencies and expected frequencies of both high precision bins represented in one low precision bin. To calculate the expected frequencies, we model the symbol output of the arithmetic decoder as a Bernoulli distributed random variable $Y(p)$ with $p = p_k^{(i,j)}$ [6]. So the high precision histogram bins of stegotexts $\hat{h}^{(i,j)}$ follow a Binomial distribution

$$\hat{h}_{2k-1}^{(i,j)} \sim B(b_k^{(i,j)}, p_k^{(i,j)}) \qquad , \text{and}$$

$$\hat{h}_{2k}^{(i,j)} \sim B(b_k^{(i,j)}, 1 - p_k^{(i,j)}).$$

The expected frequencies $\bar{h}^{(i,j)}$ are given by the expected values of B:

$$\bar{h}_{2k-1}^{(i,j)} = E(B(b_k^{(i,j)}, p_k^{(i,j)})) = b_k^{(i,j)} \cdot p_k^{(i,j)}.$$

An adversary can compute these values by refitting the model for $p_k^{(i,j)}$ because the low precision bins are not altered. Then a contingency table is used to perform Pearsons's χ^2-test, whether or not individual low precision bins are conform to the model (see Table 1). The distribution function $Q(\chi^2, \mathrm{df})$ of the χ^2 distribution gives an error probability for the null hypothesis that the contrasted frequencies are independent. The test will reject the null for non-conforming bins if $p < p_{\lim}$.

Table 1. Contingency test for non-conforming low precision bins

	High precision bin		
	left	right	$\sum$
Observed frequencies	$h_{2 \cdot k-1}^{(i,j)}$	$h_{2 \cdot k}^{(i,j)}$	$b_k^{(i,j)}$
Expected frequencies	$\bar{h}_{2 \cdot k-1}^{(i,j)}$	$\bar{h}_{2 \cdot k}^{(i,j)}$	$b_k^{(i,j)}$
$p = Q(\chi^2, \mathrm{df} = 1)$			

To explore the average count of non-conforming bins in typical JPEG images, contingency tests are run on the low precision bins $b_1^{(i,j)}$ and $b_{-1}^{(i,j)}$ for 63 DCT modes of a set of 100 JPEG images (altogether 126 tests per image). These images were randomly drawn from a large number of digital photographs with the

---

[6] The assumption that the symbol output is drawn from a Bernoulli distribution is a worst case assumption. Any "better" arithmetic decoding algorithm would – apart from reducing the entropy – on average fit the stegotext bin sizes closer to the expected sizes and thus lead to more arbitrable contingency tests.

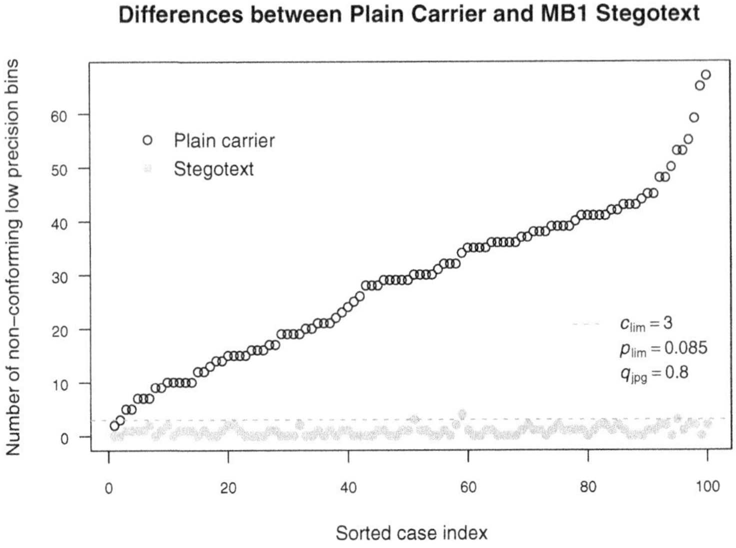

Differences between Plain Carrier and MB1 Stegotext

Fig. 4. Non-conformities with the assumed Cauchy distribution are typical for JPEG images. MB1 is detectable because it erases these particularities

resolution 800×600 and a JPEG quality parameter of $q = 0.8$. Figure 4 contrasts the results to 100 full capacity stegotexts created from the same carriers. It is obvious that a threshold of, say, $c_{lim} = 3$ can quite reliably discriminate the two sets.

At last, two more details of the contingency test are worth to mention: First, as the test is unreliable for low frequency numbers in any of the cells, tables with a minimal cell value below 3 are excluded from the evaluation. Second, the reliability of the test depends on the number of DCT coefficients unequal to zero. Since this number varies both with the size of the test image and with the quantisation step size derived from q, the critical probability p_{lim} has to be adjusted to the above mentioned parameters. This method allows an optimal differentiation in terms of low error probabilities α and β of the stegotext detection.

4   Experimental Results

The reliability of the proposed detection method was assessed using a test database of about 300 images from a digital camera[7]. To reduce unwanted influences or atypical artefacts due to previous JPEG compression [8], all images were scaled down to a resolution of 800×600 pixels and stored as JPEG with six different quality settings, $q = 0.4, 0.5, \ldots, 0.9$. In all experiments, only the luminance component of colour images has been regarded. All analyses were accomplished with the R *Project for Statistical Computing* [20, 14].

---

[7] Sony Cybershot DSC-F55E, 2.1 mega-pixel.

To generate comparable histogram sets of plain carrier and steganograms, 63 DCT histograms were extracted from all images. The plain carrier histograms were transformed to equivalent stegotext histograms by replacing the high precision bins with random numbers drawn from a Binomial distribution, using before determined parameters from the model:

$$\hat{h}_{2k-1}^{(i,j)} = R_{\text{binom}}(b_k^{(i,j)}, p_k^{(i,j)})$$

$$\hat{h}_{2k}^{(i,j)} = b_k^{(i,j)} - \hat{h}_{2k-1}^{(i,j)}$$

Furthermore it is obvious that limiting capacity leads to smaller changes in the histograms and thus shorter messages are less detectable. To estimate this effect we also varied the capacity usage in 10 levels from full capacity down to 10 % for all test images and quality factors. This leads to a set of 1.2 M stegotext DCT histograms (equivalent to 18,120 stegotext images), which were compared to the same amount of plain carrier histograms. Explorative analyses of suitable bins for the contingency test revealed that the bins $b_{-1}^{(i,j)}$ and $b_1^{(i,j)}$ yielded to the best results for all DCT modes. So, all other bins were excluded from the evaluation.

In a first experiment, the proposed attack was run on a subset of this database with 100 % capacity usage and $q = 0.8$. Here, all images could be correctly classified with $p_{\text{lim}} = 0.014$ (corresp. $\chi^2 = 6$, $df = 1$). The threshold $c_{\text{lim}} = 2$ was fixed in all experiments. Attacks on steganograms with lower capacity usage or lower q cause misclassifications. The number of false positives (α) and misses (β) depends on the choice of the threshold parameters.

To further explore the relationship between α and β, the attack was repeated multiple times with different $p_{\text{lim}} \in [0.0001, 0.2]$ [8], and the resulting error rates were plotted in a *receiver operating characteristics* (ROC) diagram shown in Figure 5. Here again, we reached good discriminatory power for capacity usages higher than 80 %, and still acceptable detection rates for capacities above 50 %. Hence, we can state that the MB1 algorithm is broken with first order statistics.

The qualitative interpretation of the shape of ROC curves can be quantified in an aggregated measure of the reliability of a detection method. Unfortunately, different quality measures in the literature complicate comparisons between different studies. Some authors argue with the probability $(1 - \beta)$ for a fixed proportion of false positives, say $\alpha = 1 \%$ [17]. Others compare α values for a fixed detection rate of $\beta = 1 - \beta = 50 \%$ [15]. In this paper, we follow the third approach from [7], which reflects both α and β: The detection reliability ρ is defined as $\rho = 2A - 1$, where A is the area under the ROC curve. It is normalised, so that $\rho = 0$ indicates no discriminatory power at all (i. e., random guessing) and $\rho - 1$ stands for a perfect detection.

Table 2 reports the empirical ρ values derived from the test images for different allocations of capacity, and different quantisation factor q. The minimum

---

[8] In fact, varying the underlying χ^2 threshold leads to equivalent results since the (computing intensive) transformation function Q is strictly monotonic decreasing.

Receiver Operating Characteristics

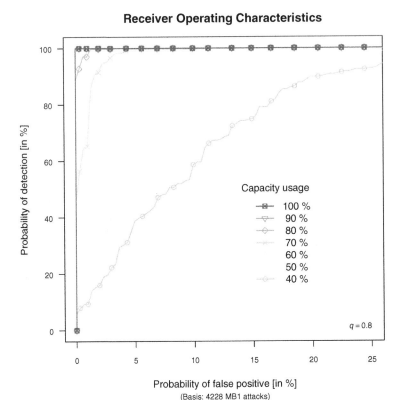

Fig. 5. Dicriminatory power of attacks on MB1 for different capacity usages

embedding rate that is detectable under the arbitrary definition of 'reliablility' stated in [15], namely $\alpha = 5\,\%$ and $\beta = 50\,\%$, is about 45 % of the capacity of JPEG images with $q = 0.8$. Note that these figures reflect average estimations. The actual detectability is likely to vary for certain carrier images.

5   Discussion and Conclusion

It is important to emphasise that this vulnerability of the MB1 scheme is rather a problem of the specific model used in the scheme, than a weakness of the general approach of model-based steganography. Having said this, the successful attack is still somewhat surprising, because the theoretical considerations given in the original paper [21, p. 166] suggest that possible vulnerabilities come from analyses of higher order statistics, which are not reflected in the model. However, the proposed detection method only uses characteristics of first order statistics, which were considered as safe.

The remainder of this section addresses three open subjects. First, we point to limits of the proposed attack and propose future improvements. Then, we discuss

Table 2. Experimental attacks: Detection reliablility ρ

Capacity usage	Avg. message size per file size	JPEG quality q					
		0.9	0.8	0.7	0.6	0.5	0.4
100 %	13.1 %	**1.0000**	**1.0000**	**0.9999**	**1.0000**	**1.0000**	**0.9979**
90 %	11.8 %	**1.0000**	**1.0000**	**0.9997**	**1.0000**	**0.9996**	**0.9963**
80 %	10.5 %	**0.9989**	**0.9982**	**0.9949**	**0.9970**	**0.9940**	**0.9826**
70 %	9.2 %	**0.9890**	**0.9850**	**0.9797**	**0.9777**	**0.9740**	**0.9596**
60 %	7.9 %	**0.9593**	**0.9527**	**0.9440**	**0.9322**	**0.9292**	**0.9202**
50 %	6.6 %	**0.9012**	**0.8898**	**0.8782**	0.8615	0.8552	0.8519
40 %	5.2 %	0.8057	0.7906	0.7796	0.7624	0.7509	0.7516
30 %	3.9 %	0.6576	0.6476	0.6457	0.6185	0.6063	0.6180
20 %	2.6 %	0.4568	0.4549	0.4583	0.4295	0.4214	0.4362
10 %	1.3 %	0.2289	0.2294	0.2357	0.2160	0.2133	0.2252

The ROC curves for values printed bold-face meet a reliability criterium of more than 50 % detection rate with less than 5 % false positives.

possible countermeasures to prevent this attack, before we finally conclude with more general implications for the design of new and better embedding functions.

This attack is considered as proof of concept and as first step towards more precise attacks. It has been mainly driven by the feeling that an embedding algorithm offering a payload capacity of about 13 % of the transferred data is very likely to be detectable with a targeted attack. Similar to the evolution of attacks against LSB steganography after the publication of [26], we expect that this existential break will lead to far better attacks, which shall be able to estimate the hidden message length and thus will even detect tiny messages.

A possible extension to this attack can be the anticipation of common image processing steps. As the experiments were run on a limited set of test images directly loaded from a digital camera, we cannot generalise our results to all kind of carrier data. At first, computer generated images may have different characteristics than natural images. This is a reason why the literature suggests that this type of carrier should be avoided for steganography [18]. Even though, natural images are often subject to image manipulation. It is likely that some of these algorithms, e. g. blurring, also result in smoother DCT histograms. The challenge to detect these manipulations in advance and thus reduce the number of false positives, or even to distinguish between "white collar" image processing and "black hat" Cauchy-based steganography, is subject to further research.

Thinking about possible countermeasures, the ad hoc solution is as old as digital steganography, namely a reduction in capacity usage. Nevertheless it is an interesting research question, how this limitation can be optimally accomplished for model-based steganography. Whereas the conditional distributions for individual bins depend on the deterministic part X_{det}, a careful selection of the skipped bins or coefficients may lead to a far better ratio between security and capacity, than random selection. A similar approach is described in [6]. This method exactly preserves the low precision bins without a model – albeit in the spatial domain of losslessly compressed images, and in a less optimal manner. Therefore it is not vulnerable to attacks on first order statistics, but still detectable due to other flaws [2].

Refining the model could be another promising countermeasure. As a rather fussy preservation of the properties of the actual carrier is often superfluous and also complicates the embedding function, we could imagine to model a certain amount of non-conforming bins, and to randomly intersperse the stegotext with outliers.

Despite the specific obstacles of MB1, the model-based approach offers a promising framework for the design of adaptive steganographic algorithms. The clear link between information theoretic considerations and the design of actual algorithms contributes to structure the research area. A generalisation from the concrete vulnerabilities suggests two implications for the design of more secure embedding functions.

First, it is dangerous to give up the information superiority of the colluding communication partners. The described attack on MB1 is successful, because an adversary can re-compute the model parameters. If the adversary had no access to the Cauchy distribution, she would not be able to compute the expected frequencies. Hence, future algorithms should either consider to make the parameter retrieval key dependant, or perform an embedding operation which does not require the receiver to know the exact model. The recently developed *wet paper codes* [13] seem to be a promising technique to tackle this problem.

Second, the reliability of statistical attacks increases with the amount of observations. Although MB1 already computes distinct models for each of the 63 usable DCT modes, an even more detailed segmentation of individually modelled – and maybe even locally correlated – statistics breaks the steganalyst's advantage of large numbers. Apart from including second order dependencies into the models, the challenge to harden future algorithms against the here discussed weaknesses can be accomplished by modelling the carrier medium with a multiple of key dependent models.

To conclude, as it is common sense that the ultimate and provable secure model cannot exist [1, 21, 29], the core contribution of this paper is pointing out that future models should reflect the particularities that made this attack successful.

Acknowledgement

The work on this paper was supported by the Air Force Office of Scientific Research under the research grant number FA8655-03-1-3A46. The U.S. Government is authorised to reproduce and distribute reprints for Governmental purposes notwithstanding any copyright notation there on. The views and conclusions contained herein are those of the authors and should not be interpreted as necessarily representing the official policies, either expressed or implied, of the Air Force Office of Scientific Research, or the U.S. Government.

References

1. Anderson, R., Petitcolas, F. A. P.: On the Limits of Steganography. *IEEE Journal of Selected Areas in Communications* **16** (1998) 474–481
2. Böhme, R., Westfeld, A.: Exploiting Preserved Statistics for Steganalysis. Paper presented at the Sixth Workshop on Information Hiding, Toronto, Canada (2004, May)
3. Cachin, C.: An Information-Theoretic Model for Steganography. In: Aucsmith, D. (ed.): Information Hiding. Second International Workshop, LNCS 1525, Springer-Verlag, Berlin Heidelberg (1998) 306–318
4. Crandall, R.: Some Notes on Steganography. Posting to a mailing list on steganography (1998) `http://os.inf.tu-dresden.de/~westfeld/crandall.pdf`
5. Dumitrescu, S., Wu, X., Wang, Z.: Detection of LSB Steganography Via Sample Pair Analysis. In: Petitcolas, F. A. P. (ed.): Information Hiding. Fifth International Workshop, LNCS 2578, Springer-Verlag, Berlin Heidelberg (2003) 355–372
6. Franz, E.: Steganography Preserving Statistical Properties. In: Petitcolas, F. A. P. (ed.): Information Hiding. Fifth International Workshop, LNCS 2578, Springer-Verlag, Berlin Heidelberg (2003) 278–294
7. Fridrich, J.: Feature-based Steganalysis for JPEG Images and its Implications for Future Design of Steganographic Schemes. Paper presented at the Sixth Workshop on Information Hiding, Toronto, Canada (2004, May)
8. Fridrich, J., Goljan, M., Du, R.: Steganalysis Based on JPEG Compatibility. In: Tescher, A. G., Vasudev, B., Bove,V. M., Jr. (eds.): Proceedings of SPIE, Multimedia Systems and Applications IV, Denver, CO (2001) 275–280
9. Fridrich, J., Goljan, M., Du, R.: Reliable Detection of LSB Based Image Steganography. Proceedings of the ACM Workshop on Multimedia and Security (2001) 27–30
10. Fridrich, J., Goljan, M., Hogea, D.: Attacking the OutGuess. Proceedings of the ACM Workshop on Multimedia and Security (2002)
11. Fridrich, J., Goljan, M., Hogea, D.: Steganalysis of JPEG Images: Breaking the F5 Algorithm. In: Petitcolas, F. A. P. (ed.): Information Hiding. Fifth International Workshop, LNCS 2578, Springer-Verlag, Berlin Heidelberg (2003) 310–323
12. Fridrich, J., Goljan, M., Soukal, D.: Higher-order Statistical Steganalysis of Palette Images. In: Delp, E. J., Wong, P. W. (eds.): Proceedings of SPIE, Security and Watermarking of Multimedia Contents V (2003) 178–190
13. Fridrich, J., Goljan, M., Soukal, D.: Perturbed Quantization Steganography Using Wet Paper Codes. Paper to be presented at the ACM Workshop on Multimedia and Security, Magdeburg, Germany (2004, September 20–21)
14. Ihaka, R., Gentlemen, R.: R – A Language for Data Analysis and Graphics. *Journal of Computational Graphics and Statistics* **5** (1996) 299–314
15. Ker, A.: Improved Detection of LSB Steganography in Grayscale Images. Paper presented at the Sixth Workshop on Information Hiding, Toronto, Canada (2004, May)
16. Kerckhoffs, A.: La cryptographie militaire. *Journal des sciences militaires* **XI** (1883) 5–38, 161–191, `http://www.cl.cam.ac.uk/~fapp2/`
17. Lyu, S., Farid, H.: Detecting Hidden Messages Using Higher-Order Statistics and Support Vector Machines. In: Petitcolas, F. A. P. (ed.): Information Hiding. Fifth International Workshop, LNCS 2578, Springer-Verlag, Berlin Heidelberg (2003) 340–354

18. Petitcolas, F. A. P., Anderson, R. J., Kuhn, M. G.: Information Hiding – A Survey. *Proceedings of the IEEE* **87** (1999) 1062–1078
19. Provos, N.: OutGuess – Universal Steganography (2001) http://www.outguess.org/
20. The R Project for Statistical Computing, http://www.r-project.org/.
21. Sallee, P.: Model-Based Steganography. In: Kalker, T., et al. (eds.): International Workshop on Digital Watermarking, LNCS 2939, Springer-Verlag, Berlin Heidelberg (2004) 154–167
22. Upham, D: Jsteg (1993) http://ftp.funet.fi/pub/crypt/cypherpunks/applications/jsteg/
23. Wayner, P.: Mimic Functions. *Cryptologia* **16** (1992) 193–214
24. Westfeld, A.: F5 – A Steganographic Algorithm. High Capacity Despite Better Steganalysis. In: Moskowitz, I. S. (ed.): Information Hiding. Fourth International Workshop, LNCS 2137, Springer-Verlag, Berlin Heidelberg (2001) 289–302
25. Westfeld, A.: Detecting Low Embedding Rates. In: Petitcolas, F. A. P. (ed.): Information Hiding. Fifth International Workshop, LNCS 2578, Springer-Verlag, Berlin Heidelberg (2003) 324–339
26. Westfeld, A., Pfitzmann, A.: Attacks on Steganographic Systems. In: Pfitzmann, A. (ed.): Information Hiding. Third International Workshop, LNCS 1768, Springer-Verlag, Berlin Heidelberg (2000) 61–76
27. Witten, I. H., Neal, R., M., Cleary, J. G.: Arithmetic Coding for Data Compression. *Communications of the ACM* **20** (1987) 520–540
28. Zhang, X., Wang, S., Zhang, K.: Steganography with Least Histogram Abnormality. In: Gorodetsky et al. (eds.): MMM-ACNS 2003, LNCS 2776, Springer-Verlag, Berlin Heidelberg (2003) 395–406
29. Zöllner, J., Federrath, H., Klimant, H., Pfitzmann, A., Piotraschke, R., Westfeld, A., Wicke, G., Wolf, G.: Modelling the Security of Steganographic Systems. In: Aucsmith, D. (ed.): Information Hiding. Second International Workshop, LNCS 1525, Springer-Verlag, Berlin Heidelberg (1998) 334–354

Comparison Between Two Practical Mix Designs

Claudia Díaz[1], Len Sassaman[2], and Evelyne Dewitte[1]

[1] K.U. Leuven ESAT-COSIC
Kasteelpark Arenberg 10, B-3001 Leuven-Heverlee, Belgium
{claudia.diaz,dewitte}@esat.kuleuven.ac.be
[2] rabbi@abditum.com

Abstract. We evaluate the anonymity provided by two popular email mix implementations, Mixmaster and Reliable, and compare their effectiveness through the use of simulations which model the algorithms used by these mixing applications. Our simulations are based on actual traffic data obtained from a public anonymous remailer (mix node). We determine that assumptions made in previous literature about the distribution of mix input traffic are incorrect: in particular, the input traffic does not follow a Poisson distribution. We establish for the first time that a lower bound exists on the anonymity of Mixmaster, and discover that under certain circumstances the algorithm used by Reliable provides no anonymity. We find that the upper bound on anonymity provided by Mixmaster is slightly higher than that provided by Reliable.

We identify flaws in the software in Reliable that further compromise its ability to provide anonymity, and review key areas that are necessary for the security of a mix in addition to a sound algorithm. Our analysis can be used to evaluate under which circumstances the two mixing algorithms should be used to best achieve anonymity and satisfy their purpose. Our work can also be used as a framework for establishing a security review process for mix node deployments.

1 Introduction

The Internet was initially perceived as a rather anonymous environment. Now we know that it can be a powerful surveillance tool: anyone capable of listening to the communication links can spy on Internet users, while data mining techniques are becoming increasingly powerful and more widely accessible.

Preserving privacy does not only mean keeping information confidential; it also means not revealing information about who is communicating with whom. Anonymous remailers (also called *mixes*) allow their users to send emails without disclosing the identity of the recipient to a third party. They also allow the sender of a message to stay anonymous to the recipient.

The objective of this work is to have quantitative results on the anonymity actually provided by two mix software implementations in wide deployment, to test the actual anonymity provided to the users of the remailer service, and to compare the two different designs. We evaluate anonymity in a single-node

P. Samarati et al. (Eds.): ESORICS 2004, LNCS 3193, pp. 141–159, 2004.
© Springer-Verlag Berlin Heidelberg 2004

context. To assess the anonymity provided by the entire remailer network, additional considerations are necessary. As individual nodes are the basic component to the network of mixes, we aim to provide information to be considered when choosing this component. We have used as input real-life data gathered from a popular remailer, and simulated the behavior of the mix.

2   Mixes

Mixes are the essential building block of anonymous email services. A mix is a router that hides the relationship between incoming and outgoing messages. The mix changes the appearance and the flow of the message traffic. In order to make messages indistinguishable from each other the mix uses techniques such as padding and encryption, which provide bitwise unlinkability between inputs and outputs. Techniques such as reordering messages delaying them, and generating dummy traffic are used to modify the flow of messages. This modification of the traffic flow is needed to prevent timing attacks that could disclose the relationship between input and output messages by observing the time the messages arrived at and left from the mix.

The idea of mixes was introduced by Chaum [Cha81]. This first design was a *threshold mix*, a mix that collects a certain number of messages and then flushes them. Since then, variants on this first design have been proposed in the literature. In this paper, we focus on two practical mix designs that have been implemented and are part of the Mixmaster remailer network [Cot95], which has been providing anonymous email services since 1995.

The first design is called "Mixmaster" (as the remailer network) because it is descended from the original software program designed by Cottrell [Cot,MCPS03]. The second design, called "Reliable", uses a different reordering strategy [RPr99]. The details of the two remailers are explained in the following sections. We compare version 3.0 of the Mixmaster software and version 1.0.5 of Reliable.

2.1   Mixmaster

Mixmaster[1] is a *pool* mix. Pool mixes process the messages in batches. They collect messages for some time, place them in the pool (memory of the mix), and select some of them for flushing in random order when the flushing condition is fulfilled. Mixmaster is a timed mix that has a *timeout* of 15 minutes. During this period of time, it collects messages that are placed in the pool of the mix. When the timeout expires, the mix takes a number of messages from the pool

---

[1] Mixmaster version 3.0, as well as Reliable, also optionally supports the older "Cypherpunk" remailer message format. For the purposes of this paper, we are assuming that the remailers are being operated without this support. As anonymity sets for the two protocols generally do not overlap, this does not impact our results. The Cypherpunk remailer protocol is known to contain numerous flaws, and should not be used if strong anonymity is required [Cot,DDM03].

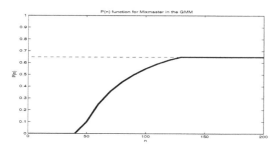

Fig. 1. Mixmaster in the GMM

that are forwarded to their next destination, which may be another mix or a final recipient. The number s of messages sent in a *round* (one cycle of the mix) is a function of the number n of messages in the pool:

```
if (n<45) s=0;
else if (0.35*n < 45) s=n-45;
else s=0.65*n;
```

Mixmaster is represented in the generalized mix model (GMM) proposed by Díaz and Serjantov [DS03b] as shown in Figure 1. In this model, the mix is represented at the time of flushing. The function $P(n)$ represents the probability that a message is flushed by the mix, as a function of the number n of messages in the pool. Note that $P(n) = s/n$.

2.2   Reliable

Reliable is loosely based on the Stop-and-Go (*S-G Mix*) mix proposed by Kesdogan *et al.* in [KEB98]. In S-G mixes (also called *continuous mixes*), the users generate a random delay from an exponential distribution. The mix holds the message for the specified delay and then forwards it. The messages are reordered by the randomness of the delay distribution. This mix sends messages continuously: when it has been kept for the delay time it is sent out by the mix.

Reliable interoperates with Mixmaster on the protocol level by using the Mixmaster message format for packet transfer. Reliable uses a variant of the *S-G mix* design[2].

---

[2] The theoretical S-G mix design assumes that the delay parameter adapts to the traffic load, that is, the users should set the delay parameter according to the amount of input traffic the mix is receiving. This feature is not implemented in Reliable, which has a static delay parameter. True S-G mixes also implement timestamps in order to prevent active attacks ($n-1$ attacks in particular). Previous work has argued that this method is unlikely to be effective, since the senders be able to determine the appropriate delay for each mix in the path [SDS]. True S-G mixes would require a service provide such information. Regardless, as the message protocol was originally designed with only a pool mix network in mind, these timestamps are not used. Reliable thus does not provide any resistance to this kind of active attack.

In Reliable, the delay may be chosen by the sender from an exponential distribution of mean one hour. If the sender does not provide any delay to the mix, then the mix itself picks a delay from a *uniform* distribution of one and four hours. Note that these parameters of the delay distributions are configurable, and therefore many remailer operators may set them lower to provide a faster service.

2.3   Dummy Traffic

A dummy message is a *fake* message introduced into the mix network to make it more difficult for an attacker to deploy attacks that compromise the anonymity of a message. The dummy messages are produced by the mixes, and use a chain of mix nodes that terminates at a mix instead of a real recipient.

Dummies are indistinguishable from real messages as they travel in the mix network. Since they are introduced to prevent traffic analysis, the dummy policy should maximize the number of possible destinations for the messages flushed by the mix. Dummy traffic has an impact when analyzing the mix network as a whole. We have made measurements that show that the impact of dummies on the anonymity provided by a single mix is very small. To make the comparison of Mixmaster and Reliable easier, we have not taken into account the dummy policies of these two mixes in the results presented in this paper.

Dummy Policy of Mixmaster. Each time a message is received by Mixmaster, d_1 dummies are generated and inserted in the pool of the mix. The number d_1 of dummies generated follow a geometrical distribution whose parameter has the default value of $1/10$. In addition, each time Mixmaster flushes messages, it generates a number d_2 of dummies that are sent along with the messages. The number d_2 of dummies follows a geometrical distribution whose parameter has the default value $1/30$.

Dummy Policy of Reliable. Reliable's default dummy policy consists of the generation of 25 dummies every 6 hours. The time these dummies are kept in the mix is selected from a uniform distribution whose minimum value is 0 and maximum is 6 hours.

3   Anonymity Metrics

In this section we introduce the anonymity metrics for mixes and we present the attack model that we have considered. Let us first define anonymity in this context. *Anonymity* was defined by Pfitzmann and Köhntopp [PK00] as *"the state of being not identifiable within a set of subjects, the anonymity set".*

The use of the information theoretical concept of entropy as a metric for anonymity was simultaneously proposed by Serjantov and Danezis in [SD02] and by Díaz *et al.* in [DSCP02]. The difference between the two models for measuring anonymity is that in [DSCP02] the entropy is normalized with respect to the number of users. In this paper we will use the non-normalized flavor of the metric.

The anonymity provided by a mix can be computed for the incoming or for the outgoing messages. We call this *sender anonymity* and *recipient anonymity*.

Sender Anonymity. To compute the sender anonymity, we want to know the effective size of the anonymity set of senders for a message output by the mix. Therefore, we compute the entropy of the probability distribution that relates our target outgoing message with all the possible inputs.

Recipient Anonymity. To compute the effective recipient anonymity set size of an incoming message that goes through the mix, we have to compute the entropy of the probability distribution that relates the chosen input with all possible outputs.

Note that in these two cases, the metric computes the anonymity of a *particular* input or output message; it does not give a general value for a mix design and it is dependent on the traffic pattern. The advantage of this property is that mixes may offer information about the *current* anonymity they are providing. The disadvantage is that it becomes very difficult to compare theoretically different mix designs. Nevertheless, it is possible to measure on real systems (or simulations) the anonymity obtained for a large number of messages and provide comparative statistics, as we do in this paper.

To measure Mixmaster's sender and recipient anonymity, we have applied the formulas provided by Díaz and Preneel in [DP04]. The anonymity of Reliable has been measured using the formulas presented in Appendix A. Note that we could not apply the method used by Kesdogan [KEB98] because we did not make any assumption on the distribution of the mix's incoming traffic (Kesdogan assumes incoming Poisson traffic).

3.1   Attack Model

The anonymity metric computes the uncertainty about the sender or the recipient of a message, given that some information is available. In our case, we assume that the mix is observed by a passive attacker, who can see the incoming and outgoing messages of the mix. The attacker knows all internal parameters of the mix so he can effectively compute the anonymity set size for every incoming and outgoing message.

Previous work by Serjantov *et al.* [SDS] has focused on active attacks on several mix designs. We refer to this paper for complementary information on the resistance of several mixes to active attackers.

4   Simulators

We have implemented Java simulators for Reliable and Mixmaster. We have fed the simulated mixes with real input, obtained by logging a timestamp each time a message arrived to a working Mixmaster node (note that the information we logged does not threaten the anonymity of the users of the mix). We have used four months of incoming traffic (July-November 2003) to obtain the results presented in Section 5.

In order to make a fair comparison, we have set the mean of the exponential delay of Reliable (default 1 hour) to be the same as provided by Mixmaster for the given four months of input (43 minutes)[3]. We have assumed users choose their delays from an exponential distribution. The mix-chosen uniform delay option has not been taken into account, due to the infeasibility of implementing algorithms that compute the anonymity for such a delay distribution without making assumptions on the traffic pattern, as explained in Appendix A.

The simulators log the delay and the anonymity for every message. Mixes are empty at the beginning of the simulation. The first message that is taken into account for the results is the one that arrives when the first input has been flushed with 99% probability. All messages flushed after the last arrival to the mix are also discarded for the results. This is done in order to eliminate the transitory initial and final phases. In our simulations, the number of rounds discarded in the initial phase is 3, and the number of rounds discarded in the final phase is 39. The total number of rounds for our input traffic is 11846.

5   Results

In this section we present and analyze the results we have obtained with the simulations.

5.1   Analysis of the Input Traffic

It is a common assumption in the literature that the arrivals at a mix node follow a Poisson process. We have analyzed the input traffic, and found that it does not follow a Poisson distribution nor can it be modeled with a single time-independent parameter.

A Poisson process is modeled by a single parameter λ representing the expected amount of arrivals per (fixed) time interval. If the arrivals to a mix are assumed to follow a Poisson process with an average of λ arrivals per time interval Δt and we denote the number of arrivals in such a time interval by X, then X is Poisson distributed with parameter λ: $X \sim \text{Poiss}(\lambda)$. It is important to note that λ is *time-independent*.

In our statistical analysis we first *assumed* that the process of arrivals *was* a Poisson process and we estimated the parameter λ. The latter was done by taking the maximum likelihood estimate given the number of arrivals per time interval $\Delta t = 15$ minutes ($N = 11800$). We also constructed a 95% confidence interval for this estimate. In this way we found $\hat{\lambda} = 19972$ with confidence region $[19891; 20052]$. Then we performed a goodness-of-fit test to determine if we can reject the hypothesis

---

[3] We have made some simulations for Reliable with mean 1 hour, and the results obtained do not differ significantly from the ones presented in this paper (i.e., some messages do not get any anonymity at all). We do not include these figures here due to a lack of space, but they will be added to an extended abstract version of the paper.

H_0 : the number of arrivals per time interval $\sim$ Poiss($\bar{\lambda}$) ,

where $\bar{\lambda}$ varies over the constructed confidence interval. The goodness-of-fit test we used is the well-known Chi-square test (df=$n-1$=11802). Using a significance level of 0.01, the null hypothesis gets rejected (Chi-value=826208)!

In the left part of Figure 2 we show the number of messages received by the mix per hour. The right part of Figure 2 shows the evolution of the arrivals per day. We can observe that the traffic that arrived at the mix during the first month is much heavier than in the following three months. This shows that the input traffic pattern that gets to a mix node is highly unpredictable and that the assumption of lambda being time-independent cannot hold.

Figure 3 shows the frequency in hours and in days of receiving a certain number of arrivals. We can see that in most of the hours the mix receives less than 20 messages.

5.2   Analysis of Mixmaster

We have simulated a Mixmaster node as explained in Section 4. Mixmaster is a pool mix and processes messages in batches. The recipient anonymity of each message in a given round is the same. Equivalently, all outputs of a round have the same sender anonymity value. In this section we show the results obtained in our simulation.

In Figure 4 we show the correlation between the recipient anonymity and the delay for every message. Figure 4 shows the same for sender anonymity.

The first conclusion we come to when observing the figures is that there is a lower bound to the anonymity of Mixmaster. It is worth noting that, so far, we do not know any theoretical analysis of pool mixes able to predict the anonymity a pool mix provides, and prior to this analysis there were no figures on the anonymity that Mixmaster was actually providing. With this simulation, we can clearly see that Mixmaster guarantees a minimum sender and recipient anonymity of about 7. This means that the sender (recipient) of a message gets a minimum anonymity equivalent to perfect indistinguishability among $2^7 = 128$ senders (recipients).

We can see that the minimum anonymity is provided when the traffic (arrivals) is low. As the traffic increases, anonymity increases, getting maximum values of about 10 (i.e., equivalent to perfect indistinguishability among $2^{10} = 1024$) senders or recipients. We also observe that the delays of the messages don't take high values, unless the traffic load getting to the mix is very low.

In order to study the behavior of the mix under different traffic loads, we have plotted values of delay and anonymity obtained in the simulation for the rounds with few arrivals (low traffic), intermediate number of arrivals (medium traffic), and many arrivals (high traffic).

We have selected the low, medium, and high traffic taking into account the data statistics of the arrival process:

Low traffic: all rounds where the number of arrivals was between the first and third quartile ($1 \leq$ data ≤ 17); hence 50 percent of the rounds are denoted as normal traffic.

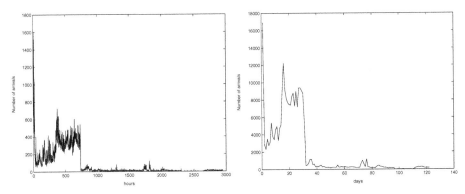

Fig. 2. Incoming traffic patterns

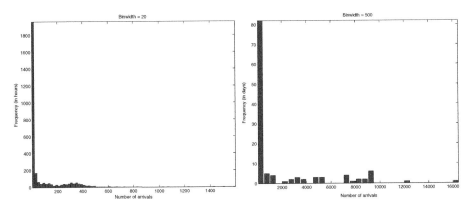

Fig. 3. Frequency analysis of inputs

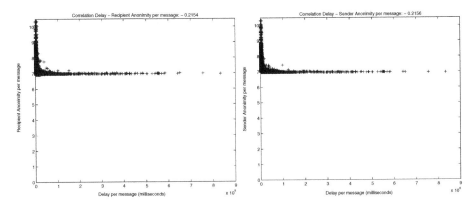

Fig. 4. Correlation Delay-Anonymity for Mixmaster

Medium traffic: all rounds where the number of arrivals was greater than the third quartile but lower than the outlier bound ($17 <$ data $\leq$ 41).

High traffic: all rounds with outlier values for the incoming messages (data > 41).

In Figure 5 we show the minutes of delay of every message (the x-axis indicates the evolution in time). We can see that the delay only takes high values when the traffic is low. The fact that some messages appear as having a delay close to zero in the low traffic figure is due to the fact that we have more samples, so there are messages that arrive just before the flushing and are forwarded immediately. In Figure 6 we show the recipient anonymity of every message (the sender anonymity presents very similar characteristics). We can see that as the traffic increases, the anonymity provided takes higher values. No matter how low the traffic load is, the anonymity provided by Mixmaster is always above 7.

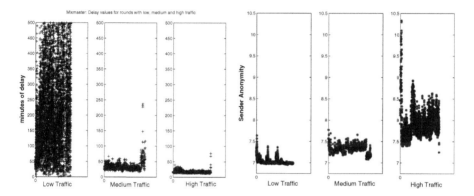

Fig. 5. Delay values for Mixmaster   **Fig. 6.** Anonymity values for Mixmaster

5.3   Analysis of Reliable

The theoretical method proposed in [KEB98] that gives a probabilistic prediction on the anonymity provided by Reliable is based on the assumption of Poisson traffic. As we have seen, this assumption is definitely not correct for email mix traffic.

We have simulated a Reliable mix as explained in Section 4. Reliable treats every message independently: when it receives a message it delays it for a predetermined amount of time (selected from an exponential distribution) and then forwards it. We represent a star, '*', per message.

In Figure 7 we present the sender and recipient anonymity provided by Reliable for the real stream of inputs we have considered. We can see that the anonymity takes minimum values close to zero, which means that some of the messages can be trivially traced by a passive attacker. The maximum values of Reliable's anonymity for this input are lower than Mixmaster's maximums. Figure 8 shows the highly correlated values of sender and recipient anonymity for both Reliable and Mixmaster. We can clearly see that for Reliable some of

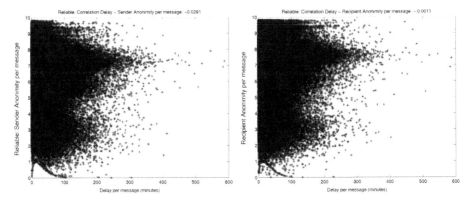

Fig. 7. Correlation Delay-Anonymity for Reliable

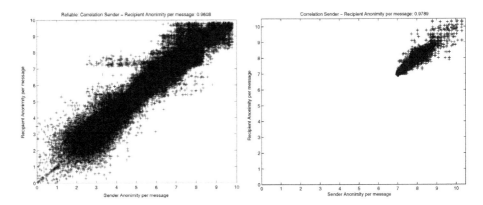

Fig. 8. Correlation Sender-Recipient Anonymity for Reliable and Mixmaster

the messages get nearly no anonymity, while the ones of Mixmaster get at least sender and recipient anonymity 7.

5.4   Mixmaster vs. Reliable

As we have shown in the previous two sections, Mixmaster and Reliable have very different behaviors for the same traffic stream. Note that we have modified the default (1 hour) mean delay of Reliable, so that the average delay is the same as Mixmaster for comparison purposes.

Mixmaster priorizes the anonymity over the delay, and it provides a minimum recipient (sender) anonymity of around 7, equivalent to perfect indistinguishability among $2^7 = 128$ input (output) messages. When the traffic load decreases, Mixmaster provides a larger latency to keep the anonymity at high levels.

Reliable delays messages according to an exponential distribution, regardless of the traffic load. This has an effect on the anonymity, in that it will only have high values when there is a high traffic load. When the traffic load decreases, the anonymity provided by Reliable drops to very low values. In some cases of very low load, Reliable does not provide anonymity at all.

Our conclusion is that a continuous mix like Reliable is not appropriate to provide anonymous services for applications that do not have real-time requirements (like email). A pool mix like Mixmaster should be used instead.

Continuous mixes like Reliable may be useful for real-time applications with tight delay constraints (like web browsing). Nevertheless, in order to provide acceptable levels of anonymity, the traffic load should be kept high.

6   Other Factors That Influence Anonymity

We have evaluated the anonymity strength of the mixing algorithms implemented in Mixmaster and Reliable. Additional factors have a direct impact on the anonymity provided by the system. Concerns such as the security of the underlying operating system, host server integrity, proper implementation of the cryptographic functions provided by the remailer software, and likelihood of administration mistakes all contribute to the overall anonymity these software packages can provide. We assume that no active attacks against the software occurred during the development or compilation process, though additional concerns are present in that area [Tho84].

This paper does not aim to be an in-depth analysis of the full spectrum of host-attacks against remailer nodes. Nevertheless, it is important to mention some significant differences between Reliable and Mixmaster that may affect their ability to provide adequate anonymity for their users.

6.1   Host Server Integrity

The security of an operating mix is dependent on the security of the underlying host server. Many factors can impact the underlying system's security. Some considerations include shared access to the system by untrusted users, access to key material on disk or in memory, and the ability to insert shims to intercept dynamically loaded libraries called by the remailer software [Tha03].

Reliable is limited to operation on the Windows platform. Mixmaster is portable, and has been known to run on a wide variety of operating systems[4].

Host server security is ultimately the responsibility of the remailer operator.

6.2   UI Issues

In a privacy application client, an intuitive user interface is essential in order to ensure that the software is used consistently and correctly [Sas02]. A greater level of skill can safely be assumed when designing privacy software that is intended to be operated as a service, however. Most anonymity systems, including mix

---

[4] There have been instances of remailers based on the Mixmaster 3.0 codebase operating on SunOS, Solaris, SunOS, AIX, Irix, BeOS, MacOS X, Windows NT (natively and through the use of Cygwin), Windows 2000 (natively and through the use of Cygwin), Windows XP (through the use of Cygwin), FreeBSD, NetBSD, OpenBSD, and multiple versions of Linux.

implementations, do imply a significant degree of complexity. Since the operation of a public Internet service involves the correct configuration and maintenance of the host server, this necessary complexity is acceptable as long as the operator's skill level is sufficient. The level of skill required to properly install, configure, and operate a mix node should not exceed that required to properly install, configure, and operate the server itself.

The software packages we evaluated differed with regard to their interface complexity in a number of areas.

In general, Reliable has a greater "ease of use" factor with respect to its interface. Mixmaster automates many important tasks, such as adaptive dummy generation, key rotation and key expiration announcement, and integrates more easily with the host MTA[5]. Reliable's installation process is easier, but its build process requires the use of third-party commercial applications and assumes experience with Windows development, so most users will install a pre-compiled binary. Compilation of Mixmaster is performed through a simple shell script.

At first glance, it appears that Reliable will be easier for hobbyists to operate than Mixmaster. However, Mixmaster's difficulty does not rise above the difficulty of maintaining a secure Internet-connected server, and thus has little effect on the overall security of a mix node deployment.

6.3   Programming Language

While the most critical factor in the creation of secure code is the manner in which it is written, some languages lend themselves to greater risk of exploitable mistakes. An inexperienced or unskilled programmer will always be in danger of making an application insecure. The choice of programming language merely sets the bar for the required level of experience and ability necessary to develop applications in that language safely. Thus, when evaluating the likelihood of the existence of exploitable code in an application, it is worthwhile to consider the programming language used to create that application. Mixmaster is written in C, while Reliable is written in Visual Basic. Since neither Mixmaster nor Reliable was written by seasoned software developers, we assume a level of experience that would allow for simplistic security mistakes[6].

6.4   Source Code Documentation

To facilitate source code review and verification of an application's correctness with regard to its implementation of a protocol, it is beneficial for there to

---

[5] Mail Transport Agent, e.g. sendmail or postfix

[6] The bulk of the code for Mixmaster 3.0 was written by Ulf Möller as his first major software development project while completing his undergraduate computer science degree [MÖ2]. He has since gained respect as a skilled cryptographic software developer for his open source and proprietary development projects. Reliable was authored under a pseudonym, and we can only speculate about the level of experience of its author. (There has been no known communication with the author of Reliable since February, 2000).

be both good commenting in the source code and a clear specification for its behavior.

While neither program is sufficiently commented or written clearly enough to allow a reviewer to easily learn how either system works by reading the source code alone, there exists a complete specification of the Mixmaster node behavior [MCPS03]. No such specification or description exists for Reliable.

6.5   Included Libraries

In addition to the standard POSIX libraries provided by the compilation OS, Mixmaster 3.0 (the version of Mixmaster evaluated in this paper) requires that the zlib [DG96] and OpenSSL [CEHL] libraries be included. Optionally, Mixmaster also links against pcre [Haz] and ncurses [BHRPD].

Reliable requires many native Windows system calls as well as the third-party application, Mixmaster 2.0.4[7].

6.6   Cryptographic Functions

Both Mixmaster and Reliable avoid direct implementation of cryptographic algorithms when possible. Mixmaster 3.0 relies strictly on OpenSSL for these cryptographic functions. Any attackable flaws in the cryptographic library used to build Mixmaster that affect the security of the algorithms[8] used by Mixmaster may be an attack against Mixmaster as well.

Reliable abstracts the cryptographic operations one step further. To support the Mixmaster message format, Reliable acts as a wrapper around the DOS version of Mixmaster 2.0.4. Thus, any attack against the Mixmaster message format due to implementation flaws in Mixmaster 2.0.x will work against Reliable as well. Mixmaster 2.0.4 relies on the cryptographic library OpenSSL or its predecessor SSLeay for the MD5, EDE-3DES, and RSA routines[9].

6.7   Entropy Sources

The quality of the entropy source plays an extremely important role in both the pool mix and S-G mix schemes. In pool mix systems, the mixing in the pool must be cryptographically random in order to mix the traffic in a non-deterministic

---

[7] Mixmaster 2.0.x has an entirely different codebase than that of Mixmaster 3.0. While Reliable relies on the Mixmaster 2.0.4 binary for some of its functionality, Reliable is an independent application in its own right, and should not be considered a mere extension to the Mixmaster codebase.

[8] It is understood that flaws in the cryptographic algorithms will affect the security of software that relies upon those algorithms. However, since most attacks on cryptographic applications are due to flaws in the implementation, care must be taken when evaluating the shared cryptographic libraries.

[9] Prior to the expiration of the RSA patent, versions of Mixmaster 2.0.x offered support for the RSAREF and BSAFE libraries as well. Use of these versions of Mixmaster is largely abandoned.

way. The timestamps that determine how long a message should be held by an S-G mix implementation must also be from a strong entropy source for the same reasons. In addition, the Mixmaster message format specifies the use of random data for its message and header padding.

Software is dependent on its underlying operating system for a good source of entropy. Cryptographic quality entropy is a scarce resource on most systems[10], and therefore the entropy sources provided by most modern operating systems actually provide PRNG output which has been seeded with truly-random data.

Mixmaster uses OpenSSL's rand_ functions[11]. Reliable uses the standard Windows system call, Rnd(), when obtaining entropy, with the exception of message and header padding (which is done by the supporting Mixmaster 2.0.4 binary). The Rnd() function is not a cryptographically strong source of entropy [Cor]. Rnd() starts with a seed value and generates numbers which fall within a limited range. Previous work has demonstrated that systems that use a known seed to a deterministic PRNG are trivially attackable [GW96]. While its use of Rnd() to determine the latency for a message injected into the mix is the most devastating, Reliable uses Rnd() for many other critical purposes as well.

6.8   Network Timing Attacks

By analyzing the input and output traffic of a mix, a skilled attacker may be able to deduce the value of pool variables by timing observation. This affects pool mixes more than S-G mixes, and possibly aids an attacker in some non-host based active attacks such as $(n-1)$ attacks. The anonymity strength of a remailer should not require pool values to be hidden, and countermeasures to this class of active attacks should be taken [DS03a].

7   Conclusions and Future Work

In this paper we have analyzed the traffic pattern of a real traffic stream going through a working mix node and found that the traffic is not Poisson, as it is commonly assumed in the literature. The traffic pattern is highly unpredictable. Therefore, no assumptions on the traffic should be made when designing a mix.

We measure the anonymity of the pool mix scheme used in Mixmaster by applying a metric previously proposed in the literature. We provide our own metric for evaluating the anonymity of the S-G mix variant used in Reliable that does not assume a Poisson traffic pattern.

Our comparison of the two predominant mixing applications shows that Mixmaster provides superior anonymity, and is better suited for the anonymization of email messages than Reliable. Mixmaster provides a minimum level of anonymity at all times; Reliable does not. Reliable's anonymity drops to nearly zero if the

---

[10] Systems that employ the use of noisy diodes or other plentiful sources of entropy have less of a concern for entropy pool exhaustion.

[11] OpenSSL relies on its internal PRNG seeded with various system sources to provide cryptographically strong entropy.

traffic is very low. In high-traffic situations, Mixmaster provides a higher maximum anonymity than Reliable for the same stream of input: 10.5 of Mixmaster versus 10 of Reliable. We have shown that Mixmaster provides higher average anonymity than Reliable for the same input and same average delay. Due to its nature as a pool mix, Mixmaster provides higher delays than Reliable in low traffic conditions. Comparatively, due to the nature of S-G mixes, Reliable's delay is not dependent on the traffic.

In addition, we have identified a number of key points of attack and weakness in mix software to which anonymity software designers need to pay particular attention. In addition to the areas of theoretical weakness that we have identified, we discovered a fatal flaw in the use of randomness in Reliable, which diminishes its ability to provide anonymity, independent of our findings with regard to the S-G mix protocol.

We can conclude from our analysis of the mixing algorithms used by these mix implementations that S-G mix variants such as the one used in Reliable are not suitable for use with systems that may have occurrences of low traffic on the network. While such S-G mixes may be an appropriate solution for systems with a steady input rate, they are not suited for systems with variable input traffic. Pool mixes such as Mixmaster should be preferred for systems with fluctuating traffic loads and relaxed latency contraints.

Acknowledgments

Claudia Díaz is funded by a research grant of the K.U.Leuven. This work was also partially supported by the IWT STWW project on Anonymity and Privacy in Electronic Services (APES), and by the Concerted Research Action (GOA) Mefisto-2000/06 of the Flemish Government.

Evelyne Dewitte is a research assistant with the I.W.T. (Flemish Institute for Scientific and Technological Research in Industry). Research supported by Research Council KUL: GOA-Mefisto 666, several PhD/postdoc & fellow grants; Flemish Government: FWO: PhD/postdoc grants, projects, G.0240.99 (multilinear algebra), G.0407.02 (support vector machines), G.0197.02 (power islands), G.0141.03 (identification and cryptography), G.0491.03 (control for intensive care glycemia), G.0120.03 (QIT), research communities (ICCoS, ANMMM); AWI: Bil. Int. Collaboration Hungary/ Poland; IWT: PhD Grants, Soft4s (softsensors), Belgian Federal Government: DWTC (IUAP IV-02 (1996-2001) and IUAP V-22 (2002-2006)), PODO-II (CP/40: TMS and Sustainability); EU: CAGE; ERNSI; Eureka 2063-IMPACT; Eureka 2419-FliTE; Contract Research/agreements: Data4s, Electrabel, Elia, LMS, IPCOS, VIB.

The authors also wish to thank Jasper Scholten for an assessment of the feasibility of some simulation algorithms; Peter Palfrader for his comments on our conclusions, as well as assistance with the gathering of input data for our simulations; members of The Shmoo Group for discussion of secure programming issues; and Roger Dingledine, Ben Laurie and the anonymous reviewers for valuable comments.

A   Method to Compute the Anonymity of Reliable

To formalize the behavior of the mixes, we define:

- X_s : an incoming message arriving at time s;
- Y_t : an outgoing message leaving at time t;
- D : the amount of time a message has been delayed.

We know that the mixes delay the messages exponentially and we have set the mean to 1 hour: $D \sim \exp(1)$:

$$\text{pdf} : f(d) = e^{-d} \qquad \text{for all } d \geq 0 \ ;$$

$$= 0 \qquad \text{elsewhere } ;$$

$$\text{cdf} : F(d) = P(D \leq d) = 1 - e^{-d} \qquad \text{for all } d \geq 0 \ ;$$

$$= 0 \qquad \text{elsewhere } .$$

All delay times are independent.

Crucial to note in this setup is that the sequence of outgoing messages is not a Poisson process. This would only be true if all inputs would arrive at the same time, hence belong to the mix when the delaying starts or if the sequence of arrivals are a Poisson process. But in our case, messages arrive at distinct moments in time, each being exponentially delayed upon their arrival times.

Mixes flush at fixed time moments which are observed by the attacker:

$$t \in \{\text{out}_1, \ \text{out}_2, \ \ldots, \ \text{out}_M\}.$$

He also observes the arrival times:

$$s \in \{\text{in}_1, \ \text{in}_2, \ \ldots, \ \text{in}_N\}.$$

If a message leaves the mix at time t, what are then the probabilities for the arrival times? Suppose the departure time $t = out$ is fixed. We then look for the probability that the message that left at time out is the same message as the one that entered the mix at time s:

$$P(Y_{\text{out}} = X_s) = P(D = \text{out} - s) \ .$$

We can hence rephrase the problem in terms of the delay: which values for the delay times are the most probable? Clearly, negative delay is impossible so only arrival times prior to out are probable. These arrival times form a set $\{\text{in}_1, \ \text{in}_2, \ \ldots, \ \text{in}_k\}$ with $\text{in}_k < out$. The matching delay times are then $\{$ out-in_1, out-in_2,$\ldots$, out-in_k $\}$ to which we will refer to as $\{d_1, d_2, \ldots, d_k\}$. Note that $d_1 > d_2 > \ldots > d_k$. We are almost at the solution as the density function of the delay times is known! Caution has to be taken however as the exponential function is a continuous function which means that the probability of the delay taking a single value is zero: $P(D = d_1) = \ldots = P(D = d_k) = 0!$

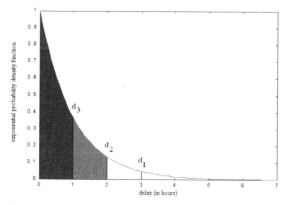

Fig. 9. An example of an exponential probability density function

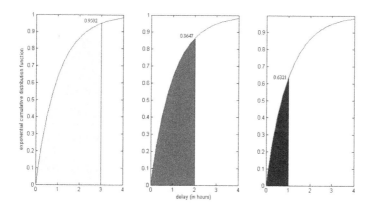

Fig. 10. The matching exponential cumulative density function

How can we then calculate the probabilities of the delay times? To make this clear, let us look at Figure 9 and suppose that we only have three arrival times prior to *out*. We have thus three possible delays $d_1 > d_2 > d_3$. Let us now assume for simplicity reasons that $d_1 = 3$ hours, $d_2 = 2$ hours and $d_3 = 1$ hour. The variable delay is continuous and can theoretically take every value in the interval $[0, 3]$. However, we know that we only flush at three particular times and that hence only three particular delays can occur. We can exploit this knowledge in the following way:

$$P(D = d_1) \approx P(d_2 < D \le d_1) = \text{ light surface ;}$$
$$P(D = d_2) \approx P(d_3 < D \le d_2) = \text{ medium surface ;}$$
$$P(D = d_3) \approx P(0 < D \le d_3) = \text{ dark surface .}$$

In this way one can clearly see that the biggest surface corresponds to the most probable delay! This is straightforward for more than three delays. For computation we make use of the cumulative distribution function (cdf) which is graphed in Figure 10. Cumulative probabilities are listed in tables and known in statistical software. For reasons of simplicity we put the mean of the exponential to be 1 hour (easy parameterization):

$$P(D = d_1) \approx F(d_1) - F(d_2) = 0.9502 - 0.8647 = 0.0855 \; ;$$
$$P(D = d_2) \approx F(d_2) - F(d_1) = 0.8647 - 0.6321 = 0.2326 \; ;$$
$$P(D = d_3) \approx F(d_3) = 0.6321 \; .$$

In our little example, the message corresponds most likely with the one that entered the mix 1 hour before *out*. You can also clearly see this on Figure 9. In practical applications however, many possible delays will occur so that visual inspections will not be efficient and calculations have to made and compared.

A.1   Uniform Delays

Reliable allows for mix-chosen uniform delays if the users do not specify any delay for their messages.

We have found a method to compute the anonymity provided by a mix that delays inputs uniformly from a distribution $U[a, b]$. The method consists in creating a tables with all inputs and outputs. Then we search for all possible combinations input-output that are possible from an external observer's point of view (i.e., those that assign to every input that arrives at time T an output that leaves between $T + a$ and $T + b$). Let us call the total number of combinations C.

Then, to compute the recipient (sender) anonymity of message m_i, we need to find the distribution of probabilities that link this input (output) to all outputs (inputs).

If input m_i appears matching output s_j in P combinations, then the probability assigned to s_j is P/C.

The probability of an input of matching an output is computed as possible cases divided by total cases. From this distribution, the sender and recipient anonymity can be computed for every message.

Unfortunately, due to the large amount of messages considered, the implementation of this algorithm in our case is not feasible.

References

[BHRPD] Z. Ben-Halim, E. Raymond, J. Pfeifer, and T. Dickey. Ncurses.
[CEHL]   M. Cox, R. Engelschall, S. Henson, and B. Laurie. The OpenSSL Project.
[Cha81] David Chaum. Untraceable electronic mail, return addresses, and digital pseudonyms. *Communications of the ACM*, 4(2):84–88, February 1981.
[Cor]   Microsoft Corporation. Visual basic language reference–Rnd function. *MSDN Library*.
[Cot]   Lance Cottrell. Mixmaster and remailer attacks.
[Cot95] Lance Cottrell. Announcement: Mixmaster 2.0 remailer release! Usenet post, May 1995.

[DDM03]   George Danezis, Roger Dingledine, and Nick Mathewson. Mixminion: Design of a Type III Anonymous Remailer Protocol. In *Proceedings of the 2003 IEEE Symposium on Security and Privacy*, May 2003.

[DG96]   P. Deutsch and J-L. Gailly. ZLIB Compressed Data Format Specification version 3.3. Request for Comments: 1950, May 1996.

[DP04]   Claudia Diaz and Bart Preneel. Reasoning about the anonymity provided by pool mixes that generate dummy traffic. In *proceedings of the 6th Information Hiding Workshop (IH2004)*, LNCS, Toronto (Canada). May 2004.

[DS03a]   George Danezis and Len Sassaman. Heartbeat traffic to counter (n-1) attacks. In *Proceedings of the Workshop on Privacy in the Electronic Society (WPES 2003)*, Washington, DC, USA, October 2003.

[SDS]   Andrei Serjantov, Roger Dingledine and Paul Syverson. From a trickle to a flood: Active attacks in several mix types. In *Proceedings of Information Hiding Workshop (IH 2002)*, LNCS 2578. October 2002.

[DS03b]   Claudia Diaz and Andrei Serjantov. Generalising mixes. In *Privacy Enhancing Technologies*, LNCS 2760, Dresden, Germany, April 2003.

[DSCP02] Claudia Diaz, Stefaan Seys, Joris Claessens, and Bart Preneel. Towards measuring anonymity. In Roger Dingledine and Paul Syverson, editors, *Proceedings of Privacy Enhancing Technologies Workshop (PET 2002)*. Springer-Verlag, LNCS 2482, April 2002.

[GW96]   Ian Goldberg and David Wagner. Randomness and the Netscape browser. *Dr. Dobb's Journal*, January 1996.

[Haz]   Philip Hazel. Perl compatible regular expressions.

[KEB98]   Dogan Kesdogan, Jan Egner, and Roland Büschkes. Stop-and-go MIXes: Providing probabilistic anonymity in an open system. In *Proceedings of Information Hiding Workshop (IH 1998)*. Springer-Verlag, LNCS 1525, 1998.

[MÖ02]   Ulf Möller. Personal communication. Private email to Len Sassaman, August 2002.

[MCPS03] Ulf Möller, Lance Cottrell, Peter Palfrader, and Len Sassaman. Mixmaster Protocol – Version 2. `http://www.abditum.com/mixmaster-spec.txt`, July 2004.

[PK00]   Andreas Pfitzmann and Marit Kohntopp. Anonymity, unobservability and pseudonymity – a proposal for terminology. In *Designing Privacy Enhancing Technologies: Proceedings of the International Workshop on the Design Issues in Anonymity and Observability*, pages 1–9, July 2000.

[RPr99]   RProcess. Selective denial of service attacks. Usenet post, September 1999.

[Sas02]   Len Sassaman. The promise of privacy. Invited talk, LISA XVI, November 2002.

[SD02]   Andrei Serjantov and George Danezis. Towards an information theoretic metric for anonymity. In Roger Dingledine and Paul Syverson, editors, *Proceedings of Privacy Enhancing Technologies Workshop (PET 2002)*. Springer-Verlag, LNCS 2482, April 2002.

[Tha03]   Rodney Thayer. SlimJim: shared library shimming for password harvesting. Presentation, ToorCon 2003, September 2003.

[Tho84]   K. Thompson. Reflections on trusting trust. *Communications of the ACM*, 27(8), August 1984.

Signature Bouquets: Immutability for Aggregated/Condensed Signatures

Einar Mykletun, Maithili Narasimha, and Gene Tsudik

Computer Science Department
School of Information and Computer Science
University of California, Irvine
{mykletun,mnarasim,gts}@ics.uci.edu

Abstract. Database outsourcing is a popular industry trend which involves organizations delegating their data management needs to an external service provider. Since a service provider is almost never fully trusted, security and privacy of outsourced data are important concerns. This paper focuses on integrity and authenticity issues in outsourced databases. Whenever someone queries a hosted database, the returned results must be demonstrably authentic: the querier needs to establish – in an efficient manner – that both integrity and authenticity (with respect to the actual data owner) are assured. To this end, some recent work [19] examined two relevant signature schemes: a condensed variant of batch RSA [3] and an aggregated signature scheme based on bilinear maps [6]

In this paper, we introduce the notion of **immutability** for aggregated signature schemes. Immutability refers to the difficulty of computing new valid aggregated signatures from a set of other aggregated signatures. This is an important feature, particularly for outsourced databases, since lack thereof enables a frequent querier to eventually amass enough aggregated signatures to answer other (un-posed) queries, thus becoming a *de facto* service provider. Since prior work does not offer immutability, we propose several practical techniques to achieve it.

1 Introduction

Database outsourcing is a prominent example of the more general commercial trend of outsourcing non-core competencies. In the Outsourced Database (ODB) Model, a third-party database service provider offers adequate software, hardware and network resources to host its clients' databases as well as mechanisms to efficiently create, update and access outsourced data.

The ODB model poses numerous research challenges which influence overall performance, usability and scalability. One of the biggest challenges is the security of hosted data. A *client* stores its data (which is usually a critical asset) at an external, and only partially trusted, database service provider. It thus becomes important to secure outsourced data from potential attacks not only by malicious outsiders but also from the service provider itself.

P. Samarati et al. (Eds.): ESORICS 2004, LNCS 3193, pp. 160–176, 2004.

The two pillars of data security are privacy and integrity. (We use the term integrity in a somewhat broad sense, encompassing both *data integrity* and *authentication of origin*.) The need for data privacy in the ODB model has been recognized and addressed, to some degree, in prior work by Hacigümüş, et al. [14]. The central problem in the context of privacy is allowing a client to efficiently query its own data hosted by a third-party service provider (referred to as simply "server" from here on) while revealing to the latter neither the actual query nor the data over which the query is executed.

Other relevant prior work [10][15] examined integrity issues in outsourced databases and suggested some limited solutions[1]. Recently, more general techniques were investigated in [19] where two signature schemes were proposed for efficient integrity and authenticity support in querying outsourced databases. One scheme is a simple variant of batch RSA and the other – the aggregated signature scheme based on bilinear maps [6]. Each scheme enables bandwidth- and computation-efficient integrity verification for any possible query reply. However, as shown below in more detail, the schemes in [19] (as well as those in [10]) are mutable, i.e., any entity in possession of multiple authentic query replies can derive other, equally authentic query replies.

We view mutability not as a flaw of the underlying signature schemes but rather as an issue with their specific application in the ODB model. In this paper, we focus on providing a feature that we term *immutability* for aggregated signature schemes.

Contributions: This work makes two contributions. First, it informally defines the notion of immutability for aggregated signatures which is, at some level, equivalent to adaptive attack resistance for aggregated signature schemes. Second, it demonstrates some simple add-on techniques for schemes considered in [19]. These techniques provide, at a little additional cost (as illustrated in Section 6), immutability for the respective signature schemes.

Organization: In section 2, we describe the ODB model in more detail. Section 3 motivates the need for immutable aggregated signature schemes. Next, section 4 describes the variant of RSA that allows aggregation of signatures by a single signer and the aggregated signature scheme by Boneh et al. [6] which allows aggregation of signatures by multiple signers. Section 5 then presents some techniques to achieve *immutability* for these two schemes. Section 6 discusses the overhead associated with the proposed techniques, followed by section 7 which overviews relevant prior work. The paper concludes with the summary of our results in section 8.

2   System Model

The ODB model is an example of the well-known Client-Server paradigm. In ODB, a *Database Service Provider* (which we refer to as a server) has the in-

---

[1] See section 7 for the discussion of this and other related work.

frastructure to host outsourced databases and provides efficient mechanisms for remote clients to create, store, update and query their databases.

Clients are assumed to trust the server to faithfully maintain outsourced data. Specifically, the server is relied upon for replication, backup and availability of outsourced databases. However, the server is not assumed to be trusted with the integrity of the actual database contents. This lack of trust is crucial as it brings up new security issues and serves as the chief motivation for our work. Specifically, we want to prevent the server from making unauthorized modifications to the data stored in the database.

Depending on the types of clients involved, we distinguish among three flavors of the ODB model:

1. **Unified Client:** a database is owned by a single client which is also the only entity querying the same database. This is the simplest ODB scenario with relatively few security challenges (in terms of integrity).
2. **Multi-querier:** a database is owned by a single client but multiple *queriers* are allowed to query the hosted database. This scenario is very similar to authentic third-party publication [10].
3. **Multi-owner:** a database is jointly owned by multiple clients and multiple queriers are allowed to query the hosted database. This scenario is typical in many organizational settings where multiple users/entities are allowed to own a subset of records within the same database. (Consider, for example, a sales database where each salesperson owns all records for the transactions that she performed.)

Since the integrity issues in the Unified Client scenario are few and easily handled with standard textbook techniques, in the remainder of this paper, we focus on the Multi-Querier and Multi-Owner scenarios.

We assume that a querier may be a device (or an entity) limited in all or some of: computation, communication and storage facilities. A cellphone, a wireless PDA or a computer communicating over a slow dial-up line are all examples of such *anemic* queriers. Limited amount of battery power may be an additional, yet orthogonal, issue.

All of these constraints incentivize new techniques that optimize (i.e., minimize) both communication and computation overhead for the queriers in the ODB model. To this end, the recent work in [19] considered two signature schemes: Condensed-RSA and Aggregated-BGLS – both of which allow the server to return to the querier a set of records[2] matching the query predicate along with a single *aggregated* signature. Condensed-RSA is very efficient but only permits aggregation of signatures produced by a single signer. In contrast, Aggregated-BGLS is less efficient but supports aggregation of signatures produced by multiple signers. Hence, Condensed-RSA is more suitable for the Multi-Querier, and Aggregated-BGLS – for the Multi-Owner, scenario.

---

[2] In our setting, the client's database is a typical relational database (RDBMS) where data is organized in tables (or relations). Each table has multiple rows and columns. A column represents an attribute of the table and a row (or a record) is an instance of the table.

3   Motivation

Although both techniques explored in [19] are fairly practical, each exhibits a potentially undesirable *mutability* feature. *Mutability* means that anyone in possession of multiple aggregated signatures can derive new and valid (authentic) aggregated signatures which may correspond to un-posed queries. For example, consider a database with two relations *employee* and *department* with the following respective schemas: *employee(empID, name, salary, deptID)* and *department(deptID, managerID)*. We now suppose that two SQL queries are posed, as shown in Figure 1. The first (Q1) asks for names and salaries of all managers with salary $> 100K$ and the second (Q2) asks for the same information for all managers with salary $\geq 140K$.

Q1.   *SELECT e.name, e.salary*
       FROM employee e, department d
       WHERE e.empID = d.managerID AND e.salary > 100000

Q2.   *SELECT e.name, e.salary*
       FROM employee e, department d
       WHERE e.empID = d.managerID AND e.salary $\geq$ 140000

Q3.   *SELECT e.name, e.salary*
       FROM employee e, department d
       WHERE e.empID = d.managerID AND
              e.salary BETWEEN 100000 AND 140000

Fig. 1. SQL Queries

A querier who previously posed queries Q1 and Q2 and obtained corresponding replies along with their aggregated signatures S1 and S2, can compute, on her own, a valid new signature for the un-posed query Q3, as shown in Figure 1. In essence, the reply to Q3 is $(Q1 - Q2)$, i.e., information about all managers who earn between 100K and 140K. The specifics of computing a new signature from a set of existing signatures depend on the underlying aggregated signature scheme, as described in the next section.

We note that the above example is not specific to the use of aggregated signature schemes for integrity purposes in the ODB context. If, instead of aggregated signatures, plain record-level signatures were used (e.g., DSA or RSA), a single SELECT-style query would cause the server to compose a query reply containing a set of records matching the query predicate, each accompanied by its signature. The querier can then easily construct legitimate and authentic query replies for un-posed queries, since she is free to manipulate individual record-level signatures. Furthermore, other methods, such as the constructs based on Merkle Hash Trees (MHTs) suggested by Devanbu, et al. [10], are equally susceptible to mutability of authentic query replies. (In [10], a querier obtains a set of records matching a posed query along with a set of of non-leaf nodes of an MHT. The exact composition of this set depends on the type of a query.) We now consider a few concrete scenarios where mutability is undesirable.

Paid Database Services: Mutability is undesirable when the data owner wants to offer *paid database services* in association with the server. (This clearly applies only to the Multi-Querier and Multi-Owner ODB scenarios.) In essence, a server can be viewed as an *authorized re-distribution agent* for the information contained in, or derived from, the outsourced database. Consequently, one reason for avoiding mutability is to prevent *unauthorized splitting and re-distribution* of authentic query replies. For example, consider the case of data owner and/or server who wish to charge a fee for each query over the outsourced database. Consequently, it might be important to prevent queriers from deriving new valid aggregated signatures from prior query reply sets and re-selling information that has not been paid for.

To make the example more specific, consider an on-line authorized music distributor with a large database of songs, each digitally signed by the artist. Suppose that the distributor only wishes to sell complete albums (compilations) and not individual songs. The distributor (server) can then simply aggregate the signatures of individual tracks to provide its clients a unified proof of authenticity and integrity for the entire album. In this case, signature aggregation gives the distributor the means to *mix and match* the songs to make various compilations.

One concern that would arise in this scenario (due to the mutability of the underlying aggregated signature scheme) is that clients could potentially start their own music distribution services with the goal of reselling individual songs at higher cost per song than that of the original distributor (who only sells complete albums).

Content Access Control: Consider the ODB scenario where the owner wants the server to enforce a certain content access control mechanism: for each client (or a group of clients) access is restricted to a specific subset of the database. A client who poses a query only gets back the data that she is entitled to see based on her specific *privileges*. If the database is a collection of individually signed records, the server can aggregate individual record signatures to construct a single proof of authenticity and integrity for the entire query reply.

Two colluding clients (each with different access control privileges) can share their respective query replies. If the aggregated signature scheme is mutable, the two clients, by further aggregating the two query replies into a single quantity, can convince others that they have more privileges than they really have. In other words, a client can *combine* two aggregated signatures to produce a new and authentic aggregated signature that can act as proof that she has higher access privileges. This can have undesirable implications.

4   Aggregated Signature Schemes

In this section, we take a closer look at the two signature schemes considered in [19] and illustrate their respective mutability properties.

4.1 Condensed-RSA

The RSA [20] signature scheme is multiplicatively homomorphic which makes it suitable for combining multiple signatures generated by a single signer into one *condensed* signature[3]. A valid condensed signature assures its verifier that each individual signature contained in the condensed signature is valid, i.e., generated by the purported signer. Aggregation of single-signer RSA signatures can be performed incrementally by anyone in possession of individual RSA signatures. By incrementally, we mean that the signatures can be combined in any order and the aggregation need not be carried out in a single operation.

RSA Signature Scheme: We first describe the setup of the standard RSA signature scheme. A party has a public key $pk = (n, e)$ and a secret key $sk = (n, d)$, where n is a k-bit modulus formed as a product of two $k/2$-bit primes p and q. Both public and private exponents $e, d \in Z_n^*$ and satisfy $ed \equiv 1 \mod \phi(n)$, where $\phi(n) = (p - 1)(q - 1)$. The minimum currently recommended k is 1024. The security of the RSA cryptosystem is based on the conjectured intractability of the large integer factorization problem.

In practice, an RSA signature is computed on the hash of an input message. Let $h()$ denote a cryptographically strong hash function (such as, SHA-1) which takes a variable length input m and produces a fixed-length output denoted as $h(m)$. A standard RSA signature on message m is computed as: $\sigma = h(m)^d$ (mod n). Verifying a signature involves checking that $\sigma^e \equiv h(m) \mod n$. Both signature generation and verification involve computing one modular exponentiation.

Condensed-RSA Signature Scheme: Given t different messages $\{m_1, ..., m_t\}$ and their corresponding signatures $\{\sigma_1, ..., \sigma_t\}$ generated by the same signer, a Condensed-RSA signature is computed as the product of all t individual signatures:

$$\sigma_{1,t} = \prod_{i=1}^{t} \sigma_i \pmod{n}$$

The resulting aggregated (or condensed) signature $\sigma_{1,t}$ is of the same size as a single standard RSA signature. Verifying an aggregated signature requires the verifier to multiply the hashes of all t messages and checking that:

$$(\sigma_{1,t})^e \equiv \prod_{i=1}^{t} h(m_i) \pmod{n}$$

Security of Condensed-RSA: [19] describes the security of Condensed-RSA by demonstrating that it is at least as secure as Batch verification of RSA [3]. Batch verification of RSA signatures was shown to be secure (in [3]) under the assumption that RSA is a collection of one-way functions. The proof assumes

---

[3] We use the term *condensed* in the context of a single signer and *aggregated* in the context of multiple signers. Clearly, the former is a special case of the latter.

that the individual RSA signatures are generated using a full-domain hash function (FDH) in place of a standard hash function (such as SHA-1), as described in [5]. An FDH is a hash function which takes arbitrary length input and produces an output that is an element of Z_n^*, i.e., $H_{FDH} : \{0,1\}^* \to Z_n^*$

Mutability of Condensed RSA: Given two condensed signatures: $\sigma_{1,i}$ on messages $\{m_1, ..., m_i\}$ and $\sigma_{1,j}$ on messages $\{m_1, ..., m_j\}$ where $j < i$, it is possible to obtain a new condensed signature $\sigma_{j+1,i}$ on messages $\{m_{j+1}, ..., m_i\}$ by simply dividing $\sigma_{1,i}$ by $\sigma_{1,j}$ (modulo n).

$$(\sigma_{j+1,i}) \equiv (\sigma_{1,i})/(\sigma_{1,j}) \pmod{n}$$

Similarly, given two condensed signatures $\sigma_{1,i}$ on messages $\{m_1, ..., m_i\}$ and $\sigma_{i+1,j}$ on messages $\{m_{i+1}, ..., m_j\}$, anyone can obtain a new condensed signature $\sigma_{1,j}$ on messages $\{m_1, ..., m_i, m_{i+1}, ..., m_j\}$ (assuming all messages are distinct) by multiplying $\sigma_{1,i}$ and $\sigma_{i+1,j}$:

$$(\sigma_{1,j}) \equiv (\sigma_{1,i}) \times (\sigma_{i+1,j}) \pmod{n}$$

4.2   BGLS

Boneh, et al. in [6] construct an interesting signature scheme that allows incremental aggregation of signatures generated by multiple signers on different messages into one short signature based on elliptic curves and bilinear maps. This scheme (BGLS) operates in a Gap Diffie-Hellman group (GDH) – a group where the Decisional Diffie-Hellman problem (DDH) is easy while the Computational Diffie-Hellman problem (CDH) is hard. The first instance of such a group was illustrated in [17]. Before describing BGLS, we briefly overview the necessary parameters:

- G_1 is a cyclic additive group with generator g_1
- G_2 is a cyclic multiplicative group
- e is a computable bilinear map $e : G_1 \times G_1 \to G_2$ as described below

A bilinear map $e : G_1 \times G_1 \to G_2$, where $|G_1| = |G_2|$, satisfies the following two properties.

1. Bilinearity: $\forall P, Q \in G_1$ and $a, b \in \mathbb{Z}$, $e(aP, bQ) = e(P, Q)^{ab}$
2. Non-degenerativity: $e(g_1, g_1) \neq 1$

These two properties imply that, for any $P_1, P_2, Q \in G_1, e(P_1 + P_2, Q) = e(P_1, Q) \cdot e(P_2, Q)$; and, for any $P, Q \in G_1, e(\psi(P), Q) = e(\psi(Q), P)$.

BGLS Signature Scheme: BGLS requires the use of a full-domain hash function $h() : \{0,1\}^* \to G_1$ that maps binary strings to non-zero points in G_1. Key generation involves picking a random $x \in \mathbb{Z}_p$, and computing $v = xg_1$. The public key is $v \in G_1$ and the secret key is $x \in \mathbb{Z}_p$. Signing a message m involves computing $H = h(m)$, where $H \in G_1$ and $\sigma = xH$. The signature is σ. To verify a signature one needs to compute $H = h(m)$ and check that $e(\sigma, g_1) = e(H, v)$.

BGLS Aggregated Signature Scheme: To aggregate t BGLS signatures, one computes the point-addition operation (on the elliptic curve) of the individual signatures as follows: $\sigma_{1,t} = \sum_{i=1}^{t} \sigma_i$, where σ_i corresponds to the signature of message m_i. The aggregated signature $\sigma_{1,t}$ is of the same size as a single BGLS signature, i.e., $|p|$ bits. Similar to Condensed-RSA, the aggregation of signatures can be performed incrementally and by anyone.

Verification of an aggregate BGLS signature $\sigma_{1,t}$ involves computing the point-addition of all hashes and verifying that:

$$e(\sigma_{1,t}, g_1) = \prod_{i=1}^{t} e(H_i, v_i)$$

Due to the properties of the bilinear maps, we can expand the left hand side of the equation as follows:

$$e(\sigma_{1,t}, g_1) = e\left(\sum_{i=1}^{t} x_i H_i, g_1\right) = \prod_{i=1}^{t} e(H_i, g_1)^{x_i} = \prod_{i=1}^{t} e(H_i, x_i g_1) = \prod_{i=1}^{t} e(H_i, v_i)$$

Mutability of Aggregated BGLS: Similar to Condensed-RSA, aggregated BGLS signatures can be manipulated to obtain new and valid signatures that correspond to un-posed query replies. Specifically, it is possible to either (or both) add and subtract available aggregated signatures to obtain new ones.

For example, given 2 aggregated BGLS signatures $\sigma_{1,i}$ on messages $\{m_1, ..., m_i\}$ and $\sigma_{i+1,j}$ on messages $\{m_{i+1}, ..., m_j\}$, if the messages $\{m_1, ..., m_i\}$ and $\{m_{i+1}, ..., m_j\}$ are all distinct (i.e.,the two queries do not overlap), the verifier can obtain a new BGLS signature $\sigma_{1,j}$ on messages $\{m_1, ..., m_i, m_{i+1}, ...m_j\}$ by adding $\sigma_{1,i}$ and $\sigma_{i+1,j}$.

$$(\sigma_{1,j}) \equiv (\sigma_{1,i}) + (\sigma_{i+1,j}) \pmod{p}$$

5   Immutable Signature Schemes

In this section, we propose extensions that strengthen previously described signature schemes and make them *immutable*.

5.1   Immutable Condensed RSA (IC-RSA)

To make condensed-RSA signatures immutable, we use the technique that can be broadly classified as a zero-knowledge proof of knowledge of signatures. The server, instead of revealing the actual aggregated signature for a posed query, reveals only the proof of knowledge of that signature. We present two variants: one that requires interaction, based on the well-known Guillou-Quisquater scheme, and the other that is non-interactive, based on so-called "signatures of knowledge".

Interactive Variant. This technique uses the well-known Guillou-Quisquater (GQ) identification scheme [13] which is among the most efficient follow-ons to the original Fiat-Shamir zero-knowledge identification Scheme [2]. The version we present is an interactive protocol between the server (Prover) and the querier (Verifier) that provides the latter with a zero-knowledge proof that the Prover has a valid Condensed-RSA signature corresponding to the records in the query result set.

Basically, the server returns to the querier the result set along with a *witness*. The querier then sends a random *challenge* to which the server replies with a valid *response*. The *response* together with the *witness* convince the querier of server's knowledge of the Condensed-RSA signature, without revealing any knowledge about the Condensed-RSA signature itself. The actual protocol is shown in Figure 2. We use the terms *Prover* (P) and *Verifier* (V) instead of Server and Querier, respectively, since the protocol is not specific to the ODB setting[4]. Let $X = \sigma_{1,t} = \prod_{i=1}^{t} \sigma_i \pmod{n}$ be the condensed-RSA signature computed as shown above. Recall that (e, n) is the public key of the original data-owner which all concerned parties are assumed to possess. Let $M \equiv \prod_{i=1}^{t} h(m_i) \pmod{n}$ and $X^e = (\sigma_{1,t})^e \equiv M \pmod{n}$.

In step 0, the querier poses a query (not shown in figure 2). In step 1, the server (prover) replies with the result set for that query as well as a commitment Y. Note that $Y = r^e \pmod{n}$ where r is a randomly chosen element in $\mathbb{Z}_n^*$ and n is the RSA modulus of the data owner who generated the individual RSA signatures corresponding to the records in the result set[5] and e, the corresponding public exponent. In step 2, the verifier (querier) sends back a challenge v that is chosen randomly from $\{0, 1\}^{l(k)}$ where $l(k)$ is the bit-length of the public exponent e. In Step 3, server, upon receiving the challenge v, computes the response $z = rX^v \pmod{n}$ where X is the Condensed-RSA signature of the result set. In Step 4, the verifier accepts the proof if $z \neq 0$ and $z^e \equiv YM^v \pmod{n}$ where M is the product of (hashes of) all messages in the result set. Checking $z \neq 0$ precludes a malicious server from succeeding by choosing $r = 0$. Note that $z^e \equiv (rX^v)^e \equiv r^e X^{ev} \equiv Y(X^e)^v \equiv YM^v \pmod{n}$. Hence the protocol works.

Security Considerations: GQ is RSA-based; the protocol is known to be honest-verifier zero-knowledge and is secure against impersonation under passive attacks, assuming RSA is one-way [13]. Subsequently, it is also proven secure against impersonation under active attacks in [4].

Forgery: The public exponent e defines the security level, i.e., a cheating prover can convince the verifier, and thus defeat the protocol with probability $1/e$, by correctly guessing the value of the *challenge* v a priori. Therefore, the bit-length of v (and, therefore, e since $v \in_R \{0, 1\}^{l(k)}$ where $l(k)$ is the bit-length of e)

---

[4] The original GQ scheme proposed in [13] is *identity-based* since it is used by the Prover to prove his "identity" to the verifier. However, in the current scenario, we present a version that is not id-based and does not require a key generation phase since the server uses the public key of the data owner to prove knowledge of the condensed-RSA signature by that data owner.

[5] Recall that Condensed-RSA allows only single signer aggregation.

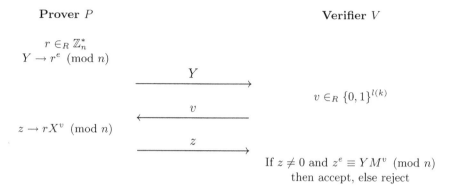

Fig. 2. IC-RSA GQ-based Interactive Technique

should be large enough. Note that the above protocol can be run multiple times for commensurably lower probability of successful forgery. In general, if it is run t times, the probability of forgery is e^{-t}.

Security Assumptions: The security of the protocol is based on the hardness of the RSA problem (i.e., computing e-th roots mod a composite integer n which is formed as a product of two large primes.)

Non-interactive Immutable Condensed-RSA. The second, non-interactive, variant uses the technique of *Signatures of Knowledge* first popularized by Camenisch and Stadler in [8]. Specifically, we use the so-called **SKROOTLOG** primitive which can be used to prove knowledge of an e-th root of the discrete logarithm of a value to a given base. Before presenting the details, we briefly describe how this technique is used in our scenario. Conceptually, the server reveals all records matching the query as well as a signature of knowledge for the actual condensed-RSA signature corresponding to these records. A querier verifies by checking the SKROOTLOG proof. However, since the querier never actually gets the condensed signature, she can not exploit the mutability of Condensed-RSA to derive new signatures. In general, the querier can not derive proofs for any other queries by using proofs for any number of previously posed queries.

SKROOTLOG Details: Let $G = < g >$ be a cyclic group of order n. An e-th root of the discrete logarithm of $y \in G$ to the base g is an integer α satisfying $g^{(\alpha^e)} = y$ if such a α exists. If the factorization of n is unknown, for instance if n is an RSA modulus, computing e-th roots in $\mathbb{Z}_n^*$, is assumed to be infeasible. A signature of knowledge of an e-th root of the discrete logarithm of y to the base g is denoted $SKROOTLOG[\alpha : y = g^{\alpha^e}](m)$.

Below, we briefly outline an efficient version of SKROOTLOG proposed in [8] which is applicable when the public exponent e is a small value (for instance, this efficient SKROOTLOG version is applicable when the value of e is set to 3).

Definition 1. *If e is small, it is possible to show the proof of knowledge of the e-th root of the discrete log of $y = g^{\alpha^e}$ to the base g by computing the following $e - 1$ values:*

$$y_1 = g^\alpha, y_2 = g^{\alpha^2}, \ldots, y_{e-1} = g^{\alpha^{e-1}}$$

and showing the signature of knowledge:

$$U = SKREP[\alpha : y_1 = g^\alpha \wedge y_2 = y_1^\alpha \wedge \ldots \wedge y = y_{e-1}^\alpha]$$

that the discrete logarithms between two subsequent values in the list g, y_1, ..., y_{e-1} are all equal (to α) and known (to the prover).

Below, we give the formal definition of SKREP as in [8]:

Definition 2. *A signature of the knowledge of representations of $y_1, \ldots, y_w$ with respect to bases $g_1, \ldots, g_v$ on the message m is defined as follows:*

$$SKREP\left[(\alpha_1, \ldots, \alpha_u) : \left(y_1 = \prod_{j=1}^{l_1} g_{b_{1j}}^{\alpha_{e_{1j}}}\right) \wedge \ldots \wedge \left(y_w = \prod_{j=1}^{l_w} g_{b_{wj}}^{\alpha_{e_{wj}}}\right)\right](m)$$

where the indices $e_{ij} \in \{1, \ldots, u\}$ refer to the elements $\alpha_1, \ldots, \alpha_u$ and the indices $b_{ij} \in \{1, \ldots, v\}$ refer to the base elements $g_1, \ldots, g_v$.
The signature consists of an $(u+1)$ tuple $(c, s_1, \ldots, s_u) \in \{0,1\}^k \times \mathbb{Z}_n^*$ satisfying the equation

$$c = \mathcal{H}\left(m||y_1|| \ldots ||y_w||g_1|| \ldots ||g_v||\{\{e_{ij}, b_{ij}\}_{j=1}^{l_i}\}_{i=1}^w ||y_1^c \prod_{j=1}^{l_1} g_{b_{1j}}^{s_{e_{1j}}}|| \ldots ||y_w^c \prod_{j=1}^{l_w} g_{b_{wj}}^{s_{e_{wj}}}\right)$$

SKREP can be computed easily if the u-tuple $(\alpha_1, \ldots, \alpha_u)$ is known. Prover first chooses $r_i \in_R \mathbb{Z}_n$ for $i = 1, \ldots, u$, computes c as

$$c = \mathcal{H}\left(m||y_1|| \ldots ||y_w||g_1|| \ldots ||g_v||\{\{e_{ij}, b_{ij}\}_{j=1}^{l_i}\}_{i=1}^w || \prod_{j=1}^{l_1} g_{b_{1j}}^{r_{e_{1j}}} || \ldots || \prod_{j=1}^{l_w} g_{b_{wj}}^{r_{e_{wj}}}\right)$$

and then sets $s_i = r_i - c\alpha_i \pmod{n}$ for $i = 1, \ldots, u$

Non-interactive IC-RSA: The server executing a client query is required to perform the following:

1. select records that match the query predicate;
2. fetch the signatures corresponding to these records;
3. aggregate the signatures (by multiplying them modulo n, as mentioned above) to obtain the condensed RSA signature σ;
4. send the individual records $\mathcal{M} = \{m_1, \ldots, m_t\}$ back to the querier along with a proof of knowledge of σ which is essentially a SKROOTLOG proof showing that the server knows the e-th root of g^{σ^e}. In other words, SKROOTLOG proof shows that the server knows the e-th root of $g^{\prod m_i}$. In order to show this, the server sends g^σ, g^{σ^2} and[6] the SKREP proof computed as above.

---

[6] Note that the server need not send $g^{\sigma^3} = g^{\prod m_i}$ explicitly since the querier can compute this value knowing g and the individual m_i-s

Security Considerations: In practice, the efficient version of the SKROOTLOG proof which was described in the previous section cannot be used as is. This is because the values $y_1 \ldots y_{e-1}$ that are required for the SKREP proofs leak additional information about the secret. Hence a randomized version that is proposed in [8] needs to be used. The interactive protocol corresponding to the above definition of SKROOTLOG is proven honest-verifier zero-knowledge in [7]. For brevity, we skip the details of this discussion and refer interested readers to [8]. However, we would like to note that the security of the SKROOTLOG protocol is based on the difficulty of the discrete logarithm problem and the RSA problem. In addition, SKREP is based on the security of Schnorr signature scheme. The Non-Interactive IC-RSA, which in essence is the SKROOTLOG primitive, is therefore honest-verifier zero-knowledge [7]. This implies that the querier who is given only the proof of the condensed RSA signature, can not derive new signatures. In addition, the querier can not derive new proofs for any other queries by using proofs for any number of previously posed queries.

Discussion. In this section, we compare the two techniques presented above.

- **Initialization and Parameter Generation:** Non-Interactive technique (SKROOTLOG based) requires an elaborate parameter generation phase at the server. For each data owner whose RSA public key is (n, e), the server needs to generate a large prime $p' = j * n + 1$ (where n is the RSA modulus and j is some integer) and an element $g \in \mathbb{Z}_p'^*$ such that order of g is n. On the other hand, Interactive (GQ based) technique requires no additional parameter generation at the server since the server only requires to have knowledge of each data owner's RSA public key (n, e).
- **Verifiability:** In the Non-Interactive technique, the SKROOTLOG proof provided by the server is universally verifiable (or in other words, the proof is self authenticating and hence transferable). On the other hand, the Interactive (GQ-based) technique provides guarantees only to the interactive verifier who poses the challenge and the proof of knowledge in this case is non-transferrable. This is perhaps the biggest difference between the two techniques.
- **Communication Rounds:** Since SKROOTLOG based technique requires no interaction with the verifier for the proof, it requires no additional rounds of communication. In other words, the server executes the query and returns the result set as well as the proof of knowledge of the corresponding unified Condensed-RSA signature. On the other hand, the Interactive technique requires two additional rounds of communication with the verifier.

5.2   Immutable BGLS (iBGLS)

The extension to aggregated BGLS to achieve immutability is very simple: The server computes its own signature on the whole query reply and aggregates it with the aggregated BGLS signature of the owners. In other words, for a given query whose result includes messages $\{m_1, m_2, \ldots, m_k\}$, the server computes

$\mathcal{H} = h(m_1 || m_2 ... || m_k ||$ other information[7]) where $||$ denotes concatenation, and signs this hash $\mathcal{H}$ using its own private key x_s to obtain $x_s \mathcal{H}$ and computes:

$$\sigma = \sigma_{1,t} + x_s \mathcal{H}$$

where $\sigma_{1,t}$ is the aggregated BGLS signature of t messages obtained as described above.

Now, a valid and authentic query reply comprises of the records in the result set along with an authentic iBGLS signature on the entire result set. Due to this simple extension, it is no longer feasible for anybody to manipulate the existing iBGLS signatures to obtain new and authentic ones or get any information about individual component BGLS signatures. Verification of an iBGLS signature σ involves computing the individual hashes H_i-s of each message as well as computing the hash of the concatenation of all the messages $\mathcal{H}$ and verifying the following equality: $e(\sigma, g_1) = \prod_{i=1}^{t} e(H_i, v_i).e(\mathcal{H}, v_s)$ where v_s is the server's public key. Due to the properties of the bilinear mapping, we can expand the left hand side of the equation as follows:

$$
\begin{aligned}
e(\sigma, g_1) &= e(\textstyle\sum_{i=1}^{t} x_i H_i + x_s \mathcal{H}, g_1) \\
&= e(\textstyle\sum_{i=1}^{t} x_i H_i, g_1).e(x_s \mathcal{H}, g_1) \\
&= \textstyle\prod_{i=1}^{t} e(H_i, g_1)^{x_i}.e(\mathcal{H}, g_1)^{x_s} \\
&= \textstyle\prod_{i=1}^{t} e(H_i, x_i g_1).e(\mathcal{H}, x_s g_1) \\
&= \textstyle\prod_{i=1}^{t} e(H_i, v_i).e(\mathcal{H}, v_s)
\end{aligned}
$$

Security Considerations: iBGLS is a direct application of the original aggregate BGLS signature scheme (see section 4.2). The security of BGLS relies upon a Gap-Diffie Hellman group setting and specifically requires that each message included in the aggregated signature be unique. Below we argue, informally, the security of our construction of iBGLS signatures.

Let r_i denote database record i. An iBGLS signature σ is then constructed as follows: $\sigma = \sum_{i=1}^{t+1} x_i h(m_i)$, where messages $m_1, m_2, ..., m_t$ correspond to the selected records $r_1, r_2, ..., r_t$ and $m_{t+1} = (r_1 || r_2 || ... || r_t)$, i.e., the concatenation of the these records. $x_1, x_2, ..., x_t$ are the data owner's private keys and x_{t+1} is the server's key. We then claim that these $t + 1$ messages are distinct. Each database record r_i contains a unique record identifier, resulting in messages $m_1, m_2, ..., m_t$ being distinct. m_{t+1} will be unique for each record set returned as it consists

---

[7] BGLS aggregation is secure only when the messages signed are all distinct. Therefore, if the server signed only the result set, it can potentially create a problem if the result set to a particular query contained a single record (message). Note that if the result set contained only one message then the owner's message as well as the server's message would be the same since server computes its signature on the entire result set. In order to avoid such situations, we require that the server add some additional information to the message that he signs. For example, the server may include query and/or querier specific information, timestamp etc.

exactly of the selected records, and moreover, it will be different than any m_j where $j < t + 1$. Therefore, all $t + 1$ messages are distinct.

The immutability property of the above scheme relies upon the inability of an adversary to forge the server's signature. This, in turn, implies that such an adversary cannot use an aggregate BGLS signature to generate a new iBGLS signature that verifies. In other words, the iBGLS signature construction is resistant to mutations assuming that BGLS signatures are unforgeable.

6   Performance Analysis

In this section, we present and discuss the experimental results for immutable signature schemes. We mainly consider the overheads introduced by the extensions we made to the Condensed-RSA and BGLS signature schemes to achieve immutability. Since these signature schemes were not implemented in their entirety, we provide rough estimates on the running costs by showing the number of additional basic cryptographic operations (such as modular exponentiations and multiplications) required by the extensions and also point out any additional communication overheads. We then present the actual cost (time) required to carry out these additional operations.

Table 1 enlists the computational as well as communication overheads associated with the various techniques we propose in this paper. We use the following notation to describe the various basic cryptographic operations: $Mult^t(k) \leftarrow t$ modular multiplications with modulus of size $|k|$; $Exp_l^t(k) \leftarrow t$ modular exponentiations with modulus of size $|k|$ and exponent of size $|l|$; $BM(t) \leftarrow t$ bilinear mappings; $MTP(t) \leftarrow t$ Map-To-Point operations which are $h() : \{0,1\}^* \rightarrow G_1$ that map binary strings to non-zero points in G_1; $SPM(t) \leftarrow t$ Scalar-Point-Multiplications.

Table 1. Cost comparison of techniques for Immutability

	Computation		Communication
	at Client	at Server	
GQ	$Mult^1(n) + Exp_e^2(n)$	$Mult^1(n) + Exp_e^2(n)$	2
SKROOTLOG	$Exp_n^4(p') + Mult^3(p')$	$Exp_n^4(p') + Exp_2^1(n)$ $+Mult^1(n)$	0
iBGLS	$BM(1)$	$MTP(1) + SPM(1)$	0

Table 2 gives the actual time required to generate a single signature and also the time required to verify a single signature, multiple signatures by a single signer, and multiple signatures by multiple signers in both condensed RSA and BGLS schemes. We set the RSA public exponent e to 3 for SKROOTLOG and set $e = (2^{30} + 1)$ for GQ. Note that it is essential to have a large e for GQ since e in this case is also the security parameter. Further, we have used a 1024 bit modulus n and the Chinese Remainder Theorem to speed up the signing procedure. All computations were carried out on an Intel Pentium-3 800 MHz processor with 1GB memory. The results for BGLS are obtained by using the

Table 2. Cost comparison (time in msec): Verification and signing

		Condensed-RSA		BGLS
		$e = 3$	$e = 2^{30} + 1$	
Sign	1 signature	6.82	6.82	12.0
Verify	1 signature	0.14	0.56	77.4
	t = 1000 sigs, k = 1 signer	44.12	45.531	12085.4
	t = 100 sigs, k = 10 signers	45.16	50.31	12320.2

MIRACL library [1] and the elliptic curve defined by the equation $y^2 = x^3 + 1$ over $\mathbb{F}_p$ where p is a 512 bit prime and q is a 160 prime factor of $p-1$. In the table k denotes the total number of signers and t denotes the number of signatures generated by each signer.

The next table (3) gives the time required to generate and verify an immutable signature under the two different RSA-based techniques as well as the BGLS extension. In this table, we only measure the **overhead** associated with the immutability extensions. Therefore, the costs do not include the original condensed-RSA or BGLS costs. In addition, we also do not count the communication delays introduced by the protocols, particularly in the case of GQ which is multi-round protocol.

Table 3. Cost comparison (time in msec): Immutable Signature Schemes

Technique Used	Computation at Client	Computation at Server	Total Overhead
GQ	0.309	0.309	0.618
SKROOTLOG	48.88	46.489	89.369
iBGLS	37.2	12.0	49.2

We also would like to mention at this point that SKROOTLOG, in addition to the above mentioned costs, also incurs additional setup costs. These costs are necessary to set the parameters prime p' and element g of order n. Further, it is also worth noting that since condensed-RSA only enables single-signer aggregation, it is necessary for the server to set up multiple sets of parameters: one for each signer. (In other words, since n-s of distinct owners are different, it becomes necessary to find distinct pairs (p', g) for each n).

7   Related Work

Database security has been studied extensively within the database as well as cryptographic research communities. Specifically, the problem of data privacy for outsourced databases has been investigated by many. Hacigümüş, et al. examined various challenges associated with providing database as a service in [16]. In our work, we used a very similar system model.

Private Information Retrieval (PIR) [9, 11] deals with the exact matching problem and has been explored extensively in the cryptographic literature. However, most of current PIR techniques aim for very strong security bounds and, consequently, remain unsuitable for practical purposes. Song et al. [21] develop a more pragmatic scheme to search on data encrypted using a secret symmetric key. In summary, searching on encrypted data is becoming an increasingly popular research topic with such recent interesting results as [21, 12]. However, the aforementioned schemes only support exact-match queries, i.e., the server returns data matching either a given address or a given keyword. Hacigümüş, et al. in [14] explore how different types of SQL queries can be executed over encrypted data Specifically, they support *range* searches and *joins* in addition to exact-match queries.

On a more related topic, [15] investigated integrity issues in the ODB model: data encryption is used in combination with manipulation detection codes to provide integrity. As mentioned earlier [19] mainly focuses on the use of digital signatures in order to facilitate efficient integrity assessment. The work of [10] explores the applicability of Merkle Hash Tree-s (MHT-s) as a technique for providing authenticity and integrity in third-party data publication settings. The use of authenticated data structures for providing data integrity in general has been studied extensively in [18].

8   Conclusions

In this paper, we introduced the notion of **immutability** for aggregated signature schemes. Some aggregated signature schemes suitable for providing data integrity and origin authentication for outsourced databases were considered recently in [19]. We constructed add-on techniques to provide immutability for these schemes. We also performed a detailed comparison and performance analysis of the proposed techniques.

Acknowledgments

The authors would like to thank Claude Castelluccia, Stanislaw Jarecki and Moti Yung for helpful comments and discussions. We thank Nitesh Saxena and Jeong Hyun Yi for providing timing measurements of BGLS-related crypto operations. Finally, the authors would like to thank the anonymous reviewers for their insightful comments.

References

1. MIRACL Library. http://indigo.ie/˜mscott
2. Fiat, A., Shamir, A.: How to prove yourself: practical solutions to identification and signature problems. Advances in Cryptology - Crypto (1987) 186–194
3. Bellare, M., Garay, J., Rabin, T.: Fast Batch Verification for Modular Exponentiation and Digital Signatures. Eurocrypt, volume 1403 (1998) pages 191–2048
4. Bellare, M., Palacio, A.: GQ and Schnorr Identification Schemes: Proofs of Security against Impersonation under Active and Concurrent Attacks. Advances in Cryptology - Crypto (1992) 162–177

5. Bellare, M., Rogaway, P.: Random oracles are practical: a paradigm for designing efficient protocols. ACM Press (1993) 62–73
6. Boneh, D., Gentry, C., Lynn, B., Shacham, H.: Aggregate and Verifiably Encrypted Signatures from Bilinear Maps. Eurocrypt (1993)
7. Camenisch, J.: Group Signature Schemes and Payment Systems Based on the Discrete Logarithm Problem. Vol. 2 of ETH-Series in Information Security an Cryptography, ISBN 3-89649-286-1, Hartung-Gorre Verlag, Konstanz (1998)
8. Camenisch, J., Stadler, M.: Efficient Group Signature Schemes for Large Groups. Advances in Cryptology - Crypto (1997) 410–424
9. Chor, B., Goldreich, O., Kushilevitz, E., Sudan, M.: Private Information Retrieval. Journal of ACM (1998) 965–981
10. Devanbu, P., Gertz, M., Martel, C., Stubblebine, S.: Authentic third-party data publication. 14th IFIP Working Conference in Database Security (2000) 101–112
11. Gertner, Y., Ishai, Y., Kushilevitz, E., Malkin, T.: Protecting Data Privacy in Private Information Retrieval Schemes 30th Annual Symposium on Theory of Computing (STOC) ACM Press (1998)
12. Goh, E.: Secure Indexes for Efficient Searching on Encrypted Compressed Data. Cryptology ePrint Archive, Report 2003/216 (2003)
13. Guillou L., Quisquater, J.: A "Paradoxical" Identity-Based Signature Scheme Resulting from Zero-Knowledge. Advances in Cryptology - Crypto (1998) 216–231
14. Hacigümüş, H., Iyer, B., Li, C., Mehrotra, S.: Executing SQL over Encrypted Data in the Database-Service-Provider Model. ACM SIGMOD Conference on Management of Data (2002) 216–227
15. Hacigümüş, H., Iyer, B., Mehrotra, S.: Encrypted Database Integrity in Database Service Provider Model. International Workshop on Certification and Security in E-Services (2002)
16. Hacigümüş, H., Iyer, B., Li, C., Mehrotra, S.: Providing Database as a Service. International Conference on Data Engineering (2002)
17. Joux, A., Nguyen, K.: Separating decision Diffie-Hellman from Diffie-Hellman in cryptographic groups. Cryptology ePrint Archive, Report 2001/003 (2001)
18. Martel, C., Nuckolls, G., Devanbu, P., Gertz, M., Kwong, A., Stubblebine, S.: A General Model for authenticated data structures. Algorithmica, Volume 39 (2004)
19. Mykletun, E., Narasimha, M., Tsudik, G.: Authentication and Integrity in Outsourced Databases. ISOC Symposium on Network and Distributed Systems Security (2004) 205–214
20. Rivest, R., Shamir, A., Adleman, L.: A Method for Obtaining Digital Signatures and Public-Key Cryptosystems. Communications of the ACM (1978) 120–126
21. Song, D., Wagner, D., Perrig, A.: Practical Techniques for Searches on Encrypted Data. IEEE Symposium on Security and Privacy (2000) 44–55

Towards a Theory of Data Entanglement[*]
(Extended Abstract)

James Aspnes[**], Joan Feigenbaum[***],
Aleksandr Yampolskiy[†], and Sheng Zhong[‡]

Department of Computer Science, Yale University, New Haven CT 06520-8285, USA
aspnes@cs.yale.edu,
{joan.feigenbaum,aleksandr.yampolskiy,sheng.zhong}@yale.edu

Abstract. We give a formal model for systems that store data in entangled form. We propose a new notion of entanglement, called **all-or-
nothing integrity** (AONI) that binds the users' data in a way that
makes it hard to corrupt the data of any one user without corrupting
the data of all users. AONI can be a useful defense against negligent or
dishonest storage providers who might otherwise be tempted to discard
documents belonging to users without much clout. We show that, if all
users use the standard recovery algorithm, we can implement AONI using a MAC, but, if some of the users adopt the adversary's non-standard
recovery algorithm, AONI can no longer be achieved. However, even for
the latter scenario, we describe a simple entangling mechanism that provides AONI for a restricted class of destructive adversaries.

1 Introduction

Suppose that I provide you with remote storage for your most valuable information. I may advertise various desirable properties of my service: underground
disk farms protected from nuclear attack, daily backups to chiseled granite mon-
uments, replication to thousands of sites scattered across the globe. But what
assurance do you have that I will not maliciously delete your data as soon as
your subscription check clears?

If I consider deleting the data of a rich or powerful customer, I may be de-
terred by economic, social, or legal repercussions. The small secret joy I might
experience from the thought of the loss will not compensate me for losing a
posted bond, destroying my reputation, or being imprisoned. But if you are an
ordinary customer who does not have much clout, and I see a lucrative opportu-
nity in altering – or simply neglecting to keep – your data, then deterrence loses

---

[*] This work was supported by the DoD University Research Initiative (URI) ad-
ministered by the Office of Naval Research under Grant N00014-01-1-0795.
[**] Supported in part by NSF grants CCR-0098078 and CNS-0305258.
[***] Supported in part by ONR grant N00014-01-1-0795 and NSF grants ITR-0219018
and ITR-0331548.
[†] Supported by NSF grants CCR-0098078 and ANI-0207399.
[‡] Supported by NSF grant CCR-0208972.

P. Samarati et al. (Eds.): ESORICS 2004, LNCS 3193, pp. 177–192, 2004.

its effectiveness. Consequently, data of powerful customers end up being more protected than data of average customers. To convince an average customer that she will not lose her data at my random whim, I might offer stronger technical guarantees that I cannot destroy her data without serious costs. One way to do this would be to link the fate of her documents to the documents of enough other users that I cannot hope to offend them all with impunity. We shall call such documents **entangled**.

Data entanglement was initially suggested as a mechanism for increasing censorship-resistance in document-storage systems, *e.g.*, Dagster [21] and Tangler [22]. These systems split data into blocks in such a way that a single block becomes part of several documents. New documents are represented using some number of existing blocks, chosen randomly from the pool, combined with new blocks created using exclusive-or (Dagster) or 3-out-of-4 secret sharing [19] (Tangler). Dagster and Tangler use entanglement as one of many mechanisms to prevent a censor from tampering with unpopular data; others involve disguising the ownership and contents of documents and (in Tangler) storing documents redundantly.

It is not clear that data entanglement is actually useful for censorship resistance. Instead of having to specifically attack a target document, a censor only needs to damage any document entangled with the target to achieve his goal. Instead, we consider data entanglement for a different purpose: protecting the data from an untrusted storage provider that might be tempted to damage or destroy the data through negligence or malice. Entanglement provides an incentive for the storage provider to take extra care in protecting average users' documents by increasing the cost of errors.

We begin in Section 2 by analyzing the intuitive notion of entanglement provided by Dagster and Tangler. We show that entanglement as provided by Dagster and Tangler is not by itself sufficiently strong to deter a dishonest storage provider from tampering with data, because not enough documents get deleted on average when destroying a block of a typical document. This motivates our efforts to obtain a stronger form of an entanglement than the ones provided by these systems.

In Section 3, we define our general model of entanglement in an untrusted storage system. Our goal here is to model the entanglement operation itself, and we do not address the question of where in the system entanglement occurs. However, we do assume that the storage provider does *not* carry out the entangling operation itself, as giving it the users' raw data would allow it to store copies that it could selectively return later, even if the entangled store were lost or damaged. Instead, some trusted third party is assumed to carry out the entangling operation, and a negligent or malicious storage provider is modeled separately as a "tamperer" that has access only to the entangled store.

Section 4 contains our definitions of **document dependency**, where a document cannot be recovered if any document it depends on is lost, and **all-or-nothing integrity**, where no document can be recovered if any document is lost. These definitions allow a system-independent description of the binding between entangled documents. We then consider how different levels of attacks on the common data store do or do not prevent enforcement of document dependency or all-or-nothing integrity.

In particular, we show that, if all clients use a standard algorithm to recover their data, then all-or-nothing integrity requires only the ability to detect tampering using a MAC (Section 5.1); in this model, the standard recovery algorithm is too polite to return any user's data if any other user's data has been lost. Relying on such fastidiousness provides only a weak guarantee; what we really want is that all data becomes irretrievable even by non-standard algorithms if any is lost. We show that this goal is impossible if an adversary is allowed to both tamper with the common store arbitrarily and provide a replacement recovery algorithm (Section 5.2). Despite such **upgrade attacks**, it is still possible to provide a weaker guarantee that we call **symmetric recovery**, in which each document is equally likely to be destroyed (Section 5.3). Furthermore, if we restrict the adversary to **destructive tampering**, which reduces the amount of information in the common store, all-or-nothing guarantees are possible even with upgrade attacks (Section 5.4).

These results provide a first step toward understanding document dependency. Suggestions for further work are given in Section 6.

Because of space limitations, many proofs are omitted from this extended abstract. Complete proofs can be found in the full version, available as a Yale CS technical report [2].

1.1   Related Work

Entanglement is motivated by the goal of deterring data tampering by untrusted servers, a more general problem that has been studied extensively. Entanglement has been used specifically in Dagster [21] and Tangler [15], as we describe in Section 2. Other approaches to preventing or deterring tampering include replication across global networks of tamper-resistant servers [1, 4, 5, 9, 17, 23] or tamper detection [6–8, 12–14, 20] using digital signatures and Merkle hash trees [16]. Replication protects against data loss if a small number of servers are compromised; tamper detection prevents data loss from going unnoticed. Both techniques complement the entanglement approach considered here.

All-or-nothing integrity as defined in the present work is related to the guarantee provided by the **all-or-nothing transform** proposed by Rivest [18]. An all-or-nothing transform is an invertible transform that guarantees that no bits of the preimage can be recovered if ℓ bits of the image are lost. All-or-nothing transforms are not directly applicable to our problem, because we consider the more general case in which the image may be corrupted in other ways, such as by superencryption or alteration of part or all of the common store.

2   Dagster and Tangler

We now review how Dagster [21] and Tangler [22] work, concentrating on their operations at a block level and omitting details of how documents are divided into blocks. We then analyze the resulting entangling effects and show their shortcomings for protecting data from a negligent storage provider, motivating our stronger notions of entanglement in Section 4.

2.1 Dagster

The Dagster storage system may run on a single server or on a P2P overlay network. Each document in Dagster consists of $c + 1$ server blocks: c blocks of older documents and one new block, an exclusive-or of previous blocks with the document. The $c + 1$ blocks that must be XORed to recover the document are listed in a **Dagster Resource Locator**.

2.2 Tangler

The Tangler storage system uses (3, 4) Shamir secret sharing [19] to entangle the data: Each document is represented by four server blocks, any three of which are sufficient to reconstruct the original document. The blocks get replicated across a subset of Tangler servers. Hashes of blocks are recorded in a data structure, similar to Dagster Resource Locator, called an **inode**.

2.3 Analysis of Entanglement

At a given point in time, a Dagster or Tangler server contains a set of blocks $\{C_1, \ldots, C_m\}$ comprising documents $\{d_1, \ldots, d_n\}$ of a group of users. (Here $m, n \in \mathbb{N}$ and $m \geq n$.) Data are partitioned in a way that each block becomes a part of several documents. We can draw an **entanglement graph** (see Figure 1), which has an edge (d_j, C_k) if block C_k belongs to document d_j. This connection is rather tenuous – even if (d_j, C_k) is in the graph, it may still be possible to reconstruct d_j from blocks excluding C_k. Document nodes in Dagster's entanglement graph have an out-degree $c + 1$, and those in Tangler's have out-degree 4. Entangled documents share one or more server blocks. In Figure 1, documents d_1 and d_2 are entangled because they share server block C_1; meanwhile, documents d_1 and d_2 are not entangled.

This shared-block notion of entanglement has several drawbacks. Even if document d_j is entangled with a specific document, it may still be possible to delete d_j from the server without affecting that particular document. For example, knowing that d_n is entangled with d_1 (as in Figure 1), and that d_1 is owned by some Very Important Person, may give solace to the owner of d_n, who might assume that no adversary would dare incur the wrath of the VIP merely to destroy d_n. But in the situation depicted in the figure, the adversary can still delete server blocks C_2 and C_m and corrupt d_n but not d_1.

The resulting dependence between documents is thus very weak. In the full paper, we show:

Theorem 1. *In a Dagster server with n documents, where each document is linked with c pre-existing blocks, deleting a block of a random document destroys on average $O(c)$ other documents.*

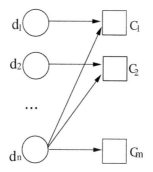

Fig. 1. An entanglement graph is a bipartite graph from the set of documents to the set of server blocks. Edge (d_j, C_k) is in the graph if server block C_k can be used to reconstruct document d_j.

Theorem 2. *In a Tangler server with n documents, deleting two blocks of a random document destroys on average $O\left(\frac{\log n}{n}\right)$ other documents.*

Even a small chance of destroying an important document will deter tampering to some extent, but some tamperers might be willing to run that risk. Still more troubling is the possibility that the tamperer might first flood the system with junk documents, so that almost all real documents were entangled only with junk. Since our bounds show that destruction of a typical document will on average affect only a handful of others in Dagster and almost none in Tangler, we will need stronger entanglement mechanisms if entanglement is to deter tampering by itself.

3   Our Model

In Section 3.1, we start by giving a basic framework for systems that entangle data. Specializing the general framework gives specific system models, differentiated by the choice of recovery algorithms and restrictions placed on the adversary. We discuss them in Section 3.2.

Our model abstracts away many details of storage and recovery processes. It concentrates on a single entanglement operation, which takes documents of a finite group of users and intertwines these documents to form a common store. In practice, the server contents would be computed as an aggregation of common stores from multiple entanglement operations. We defer analyzing this more complex case to later work; see the discussion of possible extensions to the model in Section 6.

3.1   Basic Framework

The model consists of an **initialization phase**, in which keys are generated and distributed to the various participants in the system; an **entanglement**

phase, in which the individual users' data are combined into a common store; a **tampering phase**, in which the adversary corrupts the store; and a **recovery phase**, in which the users attempt to retrieve their data from the corrupted store using one or more recovery algorithms. For simplicity of notation, we number the users $\{1, \ldots, n\}$, where every user i possesses a document d_i that he wants to publish.

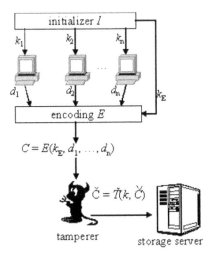

Fig. 2. Initialization, entanglement, and tampering stages.

An encoding scheme consists of three probabilistic Turing machines, (I, E, R), that run in time polynomial in the size of their inputs and a security parameter s. The first of these, the **initialization algorithm** I, hands out the keys used in the encoding and recovery phases. The second, the **encoding algorithm** E, combines the users' data into a common store using the encoding key. The third, the **recovery algorithm** R, attempts to recover each user's data using the appropriate recovery key.

Acting against the encoding scheme is an adversary $(\check{I}, \check{T}, \check{R})$, which also consists of three probabilistic polynomial-time Turing machines. The first is an **adversary-initialization algorithm** $\check{I}$; like the good initializer I, the evil $\check{I}$ is responsible for generating keys used by other parts of the adversary during the protocol. The second is a **tampering algorithm** $\check{T}$, which modifies the common store. The third is a **non-standard recovery algorithm** $\check{R}$, which may be used by some or all of the users to recover their data from the modified store.

We assume that $\check{I}$, $\check{T}$ and $\check{R}$ are chosen after I, E, and R are known but that a single fixed $\check{I}$, $\check{T}$, and $\check{R}$ are used for arbitrarily large values of s and n. This is necessary for polynomial-time bounds on $\check{T}$ and $\check{R}$ to have any effect.

Given an encoding scheme (I, E, R) and an adversary $(\check{I}, \check{T}, \check{R})$, the **storage protocol** proceeds as follows (see also Figure 2):

1. **Initialization.** The initializer I generates a combining key k_E used by the encoding algorithm and recovery keys $k_1, k_2, \ldots k_n$, where each key k_i is used by the recovery algorithm to recover the data for user i. At the same time, the adversary initializer $\check{I}$ generates the shared key $\check{k}$ for $\check{T}$ and $\check{R}$.

$$k_E, k_1, k_2, \ldots k_n \leftarrow I(1^s, n),$$
$$\check{k} \leftarrow \check{I}(1^s, n).$$

2. **Entanglement.** The encoding algorithm E computes the combined store C from the combining key k_E and the data d_i:

$$C \leftarrow E(k_E, d_1, d_2, \ldots d_n).$$

3. **Tampering.** The tamperer $\check{T}$ alters the combined store C into $\check{C}$:

$$\check{C} \leftarrow \check{T}(\check{k}, C).$$

4. **Recovery.** The users attempt to recover their data. User i applies his recovery algorithm R_i to k_i and the changed store $\check{C}$. Each R_i could be either the standard recovery algorithm R, supplied with the encoding scheme, or the non-standard algorithm $\check{R}$, supplied by the adversary, depending on the choice of the model.

$$d'_i \leftarrow R_i(k_i, \check{C})$$

We say that user i **recovers** his data if the output of R_i equals d_i.

3.2   Adversary Classes

We divide our model on two axes: one bounding the users' choices of reconstruction algorithms and the other bounding the adversary's power to modify the data store. With respect to recovery algorithms, we consider three variants on the basic framework (listed in order of increasing power given to the adversary):

- In the **standard-recovery-algorithm model**, the users are restricted to a single standard recovery algorithm R, supplied by the system designer. Formally, this means $R_i = R$ for all users i; The adversary's recovery algorithm $\check{R}$ is not used. This is the model used to analyze Dagster and Tangler.
- In the **public-recovery-algorithm model**, the adversary not only modifies the combined store, but also supplies a single non-standard recovery algorithm $\check{R}$ to all of the users. Formally, we have $R_i = \check{R}$ for each i. The original recovery algorithm R is not used[1]. We call this an **upgrade attack** by analogy to the real life situation of a company changing the data format of documents processed by its software and distributing a new version of the

---

[1] Though it may seem unreasonable to prevent users from choosing the original recovery algorithm R, any R can be rendered useless in practice by superencrypting the data store and distributing the decryption key only with the adversary's $\check{R}$. We discuss this issue further in Section 5.2.

software to read them. We believe such an attack is a realistic possibility, because most self-interested users will be happy to adopt a new recovery algorithm if it offers new features or performance, or if the alternative is losing their data.

– In the **private-recovery-algorithm model**, the adversary may choose to supply the non-standard recovery algorithm $\check{R}$ to only a subset of the users. The rest continue to use the standard algorithm R. Formally, this model is a mix of the previous two models: $R_i = R$ for some i and $R_i = \check{R}$ for others.

We also differentiate between two types of tamperers:

– An **arbitrary tamperer** can freely corrupt the data store and is not restricted in any way. Most real-life systems fit into this category as they place no restrictions on the tamperer.

– A **destructive tamperer** can only apply a transformation to the store whose range of possible outputs is substantially smaller than the set of inputs. The destructive tamperer can superimpose its own encryption on the common store, transform the store in arbitrary ways, and even add additional data, provided that the cumulative effect of all these operations is to decrease the entropy of the data store. Though a destructive tampering assumption may look like an artificial restriction, it subsumes natural models of block deletion or corruption, and either it or some similar assumption is needed to achieve all-or-nothing integrity in the private-recovery-algorithm model.

An **adversary class** specifies what kind of tamperer $\check{T}$ is and which users, if any, receive $\check{R}$ as their recovery algorithm. Altogether, we consider 6 $(= 3 \times 2)$ adversary classes, each corresponding to a combination of constraints on the tamperer and the recovery algorithms.

4   Dependency and All-or-Nothing Integrity

We now give our definition of document dependency for a particular encoding scheme and adversary class. We first discuss some basic definitions and assumptions in Section 4.1. Our strong notions of entanglement, called **dependency** and **all-or-nothing integrity**, are defined formally in Section 4.2.

4.1   Preliminaries

Because we consider protocols involving probabilistic Turing machines, we must be careful in talking about probabilities. Fix an encoding (I, E, R), an adversary $A = (\check{I}, \check{T}, \check{R})$, and the recovery algorithm R_i for each user i. An **execution** of the resulting system specifies the inputs k_i and d_i to E, the output of E, the tamperer's input $\check{k}$ and output $\check{C}$, and the output of the recovery algorithm R_i $(R(k_i, \check{C})$ or $\check{R}(\check{k}, k_i, \check{C})$ as appropriate) for each user i. The set of possible executions of the storage system is assigned probabilities in the obvious way: the probability of an execution is taken over the inputs to the storage system and the coin tosses of the encoding scheme and the adversary. It will be convenient to consider multiple adversaries with a fixed encoding scheme. In this case, we use $\Pr_A(Q)$ to denote the probability that an event Q occurs when A is the adversary.

During an execution of the storage system, the tamperer alters the combined store from C into $\check{C}$. As a result, some users end up recovering their documents while others do not. We summarize which users recover their documents in a **recovery vector**, which is a vector-valued random variable $\boldsymbol{r}$ in which $r_i = 1$ if $R_i(k_i, \check{C}) = d_i$ (i.e., if user i recovers his document) and 0 otherwise. For example, if the server contains documents d_1, d_2, and d_3 and in an execution we recover only d_1 and d_2, then $\boldsymbol{r} = 110$.

4.2   Our Notions of Entanglement

In Section 2, we observed that the block-sharing notion of entanglement provided by Dagster and Tangler is not adequate for our purposes. This motivates us to propose the notion of **document dependency**, which formalizes the idea that "if my data depends on yours, I can't get my data back if you can't." In this way, the fates of specific documents become linked together: specifically, if document d_i depends on document d_j, then whenever d_j cannot be recovered neither can d_i.

Given just one execution, either users i and j each get their data back or they don't. So how can we say that the particular outcome for i depends on the outcome for j? Essentially, we are saying that we are happy with executions in which either j recovers its data (whether or not i does) or in which j does not recover its data and i does not either. Executions in which j does not recover its data but i does are bad executions in this sense. We will try to exclude these bad executions by saying that they either never occur or occur only with very low probability. Formally:

Definition 1. *A document d_i **depends on** a document d_j with respect to a class of adversaries $\mathcal{A}$, denoted $d_i \overset{\mathcal{A}}{\hookrightarrow} d_j$, if, for all adversaries $A \in \mathcal{A}$,*

$$\Pr_A[r_i = 0 \vee r_j = 1] \geq 1 - \epsilon.$$

Remark 1. Hereafter, ϵ refers to a negligible function of the security parameter s [2].

The ultimate form of dependency is **all-or-nothing integrity**. Intuitively, a storage system is all-or-nothing if either every user i recovers his data or no user does:

---

[2] A function $\epsilon : \mathbb{N} \mapsto (0, 1)$ is **negligible** if for every $c > 0$, for all sufficiently large s, $\epsilon(s) < 1/s^c$. See any standard reference, such as [10], for details.

Definition 2. *A storage system is **all-or-nothing** with respect to a class of adversaries $\mathcal{A}$ if, for all $A \in \mathcal{A}$,*

$$\Pr_A[\boldsymbol{r} = 0^n \vee \boldsymbol{r} = 1^n] \geq 1 - \epsilon.$$

It is easy to show that

Theorem 3. *A storage system is all-or-nothing with respect to a class of adversaries $\mathcal{A}$ if and only if, for all users i, j, $d_i \overset{\mathcal{A}}{\hookrightarrow} d_j$.*

All-or-nothing integrity is a very strong property. In some models, we may not be able to achieve it, and we will accept a weaker property called **symmetric recovery**. Symmetric recovery requires that all users recover their documents with equal probability:

Definition 3. *A storage system has **symmetric recovery** with respect to a class of adversaries $\mathcal{A}$ if, for all $A \in \mathcal{A}$ and all users i and j,*

$$\Pr_A[r_i = 1] = \Pr_A[r_j = 1].$$

Symmetric recovery says nothing about what happens in particular executions. For example, it is consistent with the definition for exactly one of the data items to be recovered in every execution, as long as the adversary cannot affect which data item is recovered. This is not as strong a property as all-or-nothing integrity, but it is the best that can be done in some cases.

5   Possibility and Impossibility Results

The possibility of achieving **all-or-nothing integrity** (abbreviated AONI) depends on the class of adversaries we consider. In Sections 5.1 through 5.3, we consider adversaries with an **arbitrary tamperer**. We show that AONI cannot always be achieved in this case. Then in Section 5.4, we look at adversaries with a **destructive tamperer**. We give a simple interpolation scheme that achieves all-or-nothing integrity for a destructive tamperer in all three recovery models.

5.1   Possibility of AONI for Standard-Recovery-Algorithm Model

In the standard-recovery-algorithm model, all users use the standard recovery algorithm R; that is $R_i = R$ for all users i.

This model allows a very simple mechanism for all-or-nothing integrity based on Message Authentication Codes (MACs)[3]. The intuition behind this mechanism is that the encoding algorithm E simply tags the data store with a MAC

---

[3] Informally, a **MAC** consists of a key generator GEN, a tagging algorithm TAG that associates a tag σ with message m, and a verification algorithm VER that can be used to check if (m, σ) is a valid message/tag pair. A MAC is **existentially unforgeable** under chosen message attacks if the adversary cannot forge a valid message/tag pair even after interacting polynomially many times with a signing oracle (see [11] for details).

using a key known to all the users, and the recovery algorithm R returns an individual user's data only if the MAC on the entire database is valid.

We now give an encoding scheme (I, E, R) based on a MAC scheme (GEN, TAG, VER):

Initialization. The initialization algorithm I computes $k_{MAC} = GEN(1^s)$. It then returns an encoding key $k_E = k_{MAC}$ and recovery keys $k_i = (i, k_{MAC})$.

Entanglement. The encoding algorithm E generates an n-tuple $m = (d_1, d_2, \ldots, d_n)$ and returns $C = (m, \sigma)$ where $\sigma = TAG(k_{MAC}, m)$.

Recovery. The standard recovery algorithm R takes as input a key $k_i = (i, k_{MAC})$ and the (possibly modified) store $\check{C} = (\check{m}, \check{\sigma})$. It returns $\check{m}_i$ if $VER(k_{MAC}, \check{m}, \check{\sigma}) = $ accept and returns a default value $\perp$ otherwise.

The following theorem states that this encoding scheme achieves all-or-nothing integrity with standard recovery algorithms:

Theorem 4. *Let (GEN, TAG, VER) be a MAC scheme that is existentially unforgeable against chosen message attacks, and let (I, E, R) be an encoding scheme based on this MAC scheme as above. Let $\mathcal{A}$ be the class of adversaries that does not provide non-standard recovery algorithms $\check{R}$. Then there exists some minimum s_0 such that for any security parameter $s \geq s_0$ and any inputs $d_1, \ldots, d_n$ with $\sum |d_i| \leq s$, (I, E, R) is all-or-nothing with respect to $\mathcal{A}$.*

5.2 Impossibility of AONI
for Public and Private-Recovery-Algorithm Models

In both these models, the adversary modifies the common store and distributes a non-standard recovery algorithm $\check{R}$ to the users (either to all users or only to a few select accomplices). Let us begin by showing that all-or-nothing integrity cannot be achieved consistently in either case:

Theorem 5. *For any encoding scheme (I, E, R), if $\mathcal{A}$ is the class of adversaries providing non-standard recovery algorithms $\check{R}$, then (I, E, R) is not all-or-nothing with respect to $\mathcal{A}$.*

The essential idea of the proof is to have the adversary supply a defective recovery algorithm $\check{R}$ that fails randomly with probability $1/n$. This yields a constant probability converging to $1/e$ that some document is not returned, while all others are.

This proof is rather trivial, which suggests that letting the adversary substitute an error-prone recovery algorithm in place of the standard one gives the adversary far too much power. But it is not at all clear how to restrict the model to allow the adversary to provide an improved recovery algorithm without allowing for this particular attack. Allowing users to apply the original recovery algorithm R can be defeated by superencrypting the data store and burying the decryption key in the error-prone $\check{R}$; defeating this attack would require analyzing $\check{R}$ to undo the superencryption and remove the errors, a task that is likely to be difficult in practice[4].

On the other hand, we do not know of any general mechanism to ensure that no useful information can be gleaned from $\check{R}$, and it is not out of the question that there is an encoding so transparent that no superencryption can disguise it for sufficiently large inputs, given that both $\check{R}$ and the adversary's key $\check{k}$ are public.

5.3 Possibility of Symmetric Recovery for Public-Recovery-Algorithm Model

As we have seen, if we place no restrictions on the tamperer, it becomes impossible to achieve all-or-nothing integrity in the public-recovery-algorithm model. We now show that we can still achieve symmetric recovery.

Because we cannot prevent mass destruction of data, we will settle for preventing targeted destruction. The basic intuition is that if the encoding process is symmetric with respect to permutations of the data, then neither the adversary nor its partner, the non-standard recovery algorithm, can distinguish between different inputs. Symmetry in the encoding algorithm is not difficult to achieve and basically requires not including any positional information in the keys or the representation of data in the common store. One example of a symmetric encoding is a trivial mechanism that tags each input d_i with a random k_i and then stores a sequence of (d_i, k_i) pairs in random order.

Symmetry in the data is a stronger requirement. We assume that users' documents d_i are independent and identically distributed (i.i.d.) random variables. If documents are not i.i.d (in particular, if they are fixed), we can use a simple trick to make them appear i.i.d.: Each user i picks a small number r_i independently and uniformly at random, remembers the number, and computes $d'_i = d_i \oplus G(r_i)$, where G is a pseudorandom generator. The new d'_i are also uniform and independent (and thus computationally indistinguishable from i.i.d.). The users can then store documents d'_i $(1 \leq i \leq n)$ instead of the original documents d_i. To recover d_i, user i would retrieve d'_i from the server and compute $d_i = d'_i \oplus G(r_i)$.

We shall need a formal definition of symmetric encodings:

Definition 4. *An encoding scheme (I, E, R) is **symmetric** if, for any s and n, any inputs $d_1, d_2, \ldots d_n$, and any permutation π of the indices 1 through n, if the joint distribution of $k_1, k_2, \ldots, k_n$ and C in executions with user inputs $d_1, d_2, \ldots d_n$ is equal to the joint distribution of $k_{\pi_1}, k_{\pi_2}, \ldots, k_{\pi_n}$ and C in executions with user inputs $d_{\pi_1}, d_{\pi_2}, \ldots d_{\pi_n}$.*

---

[4] Whether it is difficult from a theoretical perspective depends on how well $\check{R}$ can be obfuscated; though obfuscation is impossible in general [3], recovering useful information from $\check{R}$ is likely to be difficult in practice, especially if the random choice to decrypt incorrectly is not a single if-then test but is the result of accumulating error distributed throughout its computation.

Using this definition, it is easy to show that any symmetric encoding gives symmetric recovery:

Theorem 6. *Let (I, E, R) be a symmetric encoding scheme. Let $\mathcal{A}$ be a class of adversaries as in Theorem 5. Fix s and n, and let $d_1, \ldots, d_n$ be random variables that are independent and identically distributed. Then (I, E, R) has symmetric recovery with respect to $\mathcal{A}$.*

5.4 Possibility of AONI for Destructive Adversaries

Given the results of the previous sections, to achieve all-or-nothing integrity we need to place some additional restrictions on the adversary.

A tampering algorithm $\check{T}$ is **destructive** if the range of $\check{T}$ when applied to an input domain of m distinct possible data stores has size less than m. The amount of destructiveness is measured in bits: if the range of $\check{T}$ when applied to a domain of size m has size r, then $\check{T}$ destroys $\lg m - \lg r$ bits of entropy. Note that it is not necessarily the case that the outputs of $\check{T}$ are smaller than its inputs; it is enough that there be fewer of them.

Below, we describe a particular encoding, based on polynomial interpolation, with the property that after a sufficiently destructive tampering, the probability that *any* recovery algorithm can reconstruct a particular d_i is small. While this is trivially true for an unrestrained tamperer that destroys all $\lg m$ bits of the common store, our scheme requires only that with n documents the tamperer destroy slightly more than $n \lg(n/\epsilon)$ bits before the probability that any of the data can be recovered drops below ϵ (a formal statement of this result is found in Corollary 1). Since n counts only the number of users and not the size of the data, for a fixed population of users the number of bits that can be destroyed before all users lose their data is effectively a constant independent of the size of the store being tampered with.

The encoding scheme is as follows. It assumes that each data item can be encoded as an element of Z_p, where p is a prime of roughly s bits.

Initialization. The initialization algorithm I chooses $k_1, k_2, \ldots k_n$ independently and uniformly at random *without replacement* from Z_p. It sets $k_E = (k_1, k_2, \ldots, k_n)$ and then returns $k_E, k_1, \ldots k_n$.

Entanglement. The encoding algorithm E computes, using Lagrange interpolation, the coefficients $c_{n-1}, c_{n-2}, \ldots c_0$ of the unique degree $(n-1)$ polynomial f over Z_p with the property that $f(k_i) = d_i$ for each i. It returns $C = (c_{n-1}, c_{n-2}, \ldots c_0)$.

Recovery. The standard recovery algorithm R returns $f(k_i)$, where f is the polynomial whose coefficients are given by C.

Intuitively, the reason the tamperer cannot remove too much entropy without destroying all data is that it cannot identify which points $d = f(k)$ correspond to actual user keys. When it maps two polynomials f_1 and f_2 to the same corrupted store $\check{C}$, the best that the non-standard recovery algorithm can do is return one of $f_1(k_i)$ or $f_2(k_i)$ given a particular key k_i. But if too many polynomials are mapped to the same $\check{C}$, the odds that $\check{R}$ returns the value of the correct polynomial will be small.

A complication is that a particularly clever adversary could look for polynomials whose values overlap; if $f_1(k) = f_2(k)$, it doesn't matter which f the recovery algorithm picks. But here we can use that fact that two degree $(n-1)$ polynomials cannot overlap in more than $(n-1)$ places without being equal. This limits how much packing the adversary can do.

As in Theorem 6, we assume that the user inputs $d_1, \ldots, d_n$ are chosen independently and have identical distributions. We make a further assumption that each d_i is chosen uniformly from Z_p. This is necessary to ensure that the resulting polynomials span the full p^n possibilities[5].

Theorem 7. *Let (I, E, R) be defined as above. Let $A = (\check{I}, \check{T}, \check{R})$ be an adversary where $\check{T}$ is destructive: for a fixed input size and security parameter, there is a constant M such that for each key $\check{k}$,*

$$|\{\check{T}(\check{k}, f)\}| \leq M,$$

where f ranges over the possible store values, i.e. over all degree-$(n-1)$ polynomials over Z_p. If the d_i are drawn independently and uniformly from Z_p, then the probability that at least one user i recovers d_i using $\check{R}$ is

$$\Pr_A[\boldsymbol{r} \neq 0^n] < \frac{2n^2 + nM^{1/n}}{p},$$

even if all users use $\check{R}$ as their recovery algorithm.

We can use Theorem 7 to compute the limit on how much information the tamperer can remove before recovering any of the data becomes impossible:

Corollary 1. *Let (I, E, R) and $(\check{I}, \check{T}, \check{R})$ be as in Theorem 7. Let $\epsilon > 0$ and let $p > 4n^3/\epsilon$. If for any fixed $\check{k}$, tamperer $\check{T}$ destroys at least $n \lg(n/\epsilon) + 1$ bits of entropy, then*

$$\Pr_A[\boldsymbol{r} = 0^n] \geq 1 - \epsilon.$$

6   Conclusion and Future Work

Our results are summarized below:

	Destructive Tamperer	Arbitrary Tamperer
Standard Recovery	all-or-nothing	all-or-nothing
Public Recovery	all-or-nothing	symmetric recovery
Private Recovery	all-or-nothing	no guarantees possible

---

[5] The assumption that the documents are i.i.d. does not constrain the applicability of our results much, because the technique to get rid of it described in Section 5.2 can also be used here.

They show that it is possible in principle to achieve all-or-nothing integrity with only mild restrictions on the adversary. Whether it is possible in practice is a different question. Our model abstracts away most of the details of the storage and recovery processes, which hides undesirable features of our algorithms such as the need to process all data being stored simultaneously and the need to read every bit of the data store to recover any data item. Some of these undesirable features could be removed with a more sophisticated model, such as a round-based model that treated data as arriving over time, allowing combining algorithms that would touch less of the data store for each storage or retrieval operation at the cost of making fewer documents depend on each other. The resulting system might look like a variant of Dagster or Tangler with stronger mechanisms for entanglement. But such a model might permit more dangerous attacks if the adversary is allowed to tamper with data during storage, and finding the right balance between providing useful guarantees and modeling realistic attacks will be necessary. We have made a first step towards this goal in the present work, but much still remains to be done.

References

1. R. J. Anderson. The eternity service. In *Proceedings of PRAGOCRYPT 96*, pages 242–252, 1996.
2. J. Aspnes, J. Feigenbaum, A. Yampolskiy, and S. Zhong. Towards a theory of data entanglement. Technical Report YALEU/DCS/TR-1277, March 2004. Available at `http://www.cs.yale.edu/~aspnes/entanglement-abstract.html`.
3. B. Barak, O. Goldreich, S. Rudich, A. Sahai, S. Vadhan, and K. Yang. On the (im)possibility of obfuscating programs. In *Advances in Cryptology - Proceedings of CRYPTO 2001*, 2001.
4. M. Castro and B. Liskov. Practical Byzantine fault tolerance. In *Proceedings of the 3rd Symposium on Operating Systems Design and Implementation*, pages 173–186, 1999.
5. I. Clarke, O. Sandberg, B. Wiley, and T. Hong. Freenet: A distributed information storage and retrieval system. In *Designing Privacy Enhancing Technologies: International Workshop on Design Issues in Anonymity and Unobservability*, volume 2009 of *Lecture Notes in Computer Science*, pages 46–66, 2000.
6. K. Fu, F. Kaashoek, and D. Mazieres. Fast and secure distributed read-only file system. In *Proceedings of the 4th Symposium on Operating Systems Design and Implementation*, pages 181–196, 2000.
7. G. A. Gibson, D. F. Nagle, K. Amiri, J. Butler, F. W. Chang, H. Gobioff, C. Hardin, E. Riedel, D. Rochberg, and J. Zelenka. A cost-effective, high-bandwidth storage architecture. In *Proceedings of the 8th International Conference on Architectural Support for Programming Languages and Operating Systems*, pages 92–103, 1998.
8. E. Goh, H. Shacham, N. Mdadugu, and D. Boneh. Sirius: Securing remote untrusted storage. In *Proceedings of the Internet Society (ISOC) Network and Distributed Systems Security (NDSS) Symposium*, pages 131–145, 2003.
9. A. Goldberg and P. Yianilos. Towards an archival intermemory. In *Proceedings of the IEEE International Forum on Research and Technology, Advances in Digital Libraries (ADL '98)*, pages 147–156. IEEE Computer Society, 1998.

10. S. Goldwasser and M. Bellare. Lecture notes on cryptography. Summer Course "Cryptography and Computer Security" at MIT, 1996–1999, 1999.
11. S. Goldwasser, S. Micali, and R. Rivest. A digital signature scheme secure against adaptive chosen message attack. *SIAM Journal on Computing*, 17(2):281–308, 1988.
12. U. Maheshwari and R. Vingralek. How to build a trusted database system on untrusted storage. In *Proceedings of the 4th Symposium on Operating Systems Design and Implementation*, pages 135–150, 2000.
13. D. Mazieres and D. Shasha. Don't trust your file server. In *Proceedings of the 8th IEEE Workshop on Hot Topics in Operating Systems*, pages 99–104, 2001.
14. D. Mazieres and D. Shasha. Building secure file systems out of Byzantine storage. In *Proceedings of the Twenty-First Annual ACM Symposium on Principles of Distributed Computing*, pages 108–117, 2002.
15. D. Mazieres and M. Waldman. Tangler : A censorship-resistant publishing system based on document entanglements. In *Proceedings of the 8th ACM Conference on Computer and Communications Security*, pages 126–135, 2001.
16. R. Merkle. Protocols for public key cryptosystems. In *IEEE Symposium on Security and Privacy*, pages 122–134, 1980.
17. Mojo Nation. Technology overview. Online at `http://www.mojonation.net/docs/technical_overview.shtml`, 2000.
18. R. Rivest. All-or-nothing encryption and the package transform. In *Fast Software Encryption*, volume 1267 of *Lecture Notes in Computer Science*, pages 210–218, 1997.
19. A. Shamir. How to share a secret. *Communications of the ACM*, 22(11):612–613, 1979.
20. J. Strunk, G. Goodson, M. Scheinholtz, C. Soules, and G. Ganger. Self-securing storage: Protecting data in compromised systems. In *Proceedings of the 4th Symposium on Operating Systems Design and Implementation*, pages 165–180, 2000.
21. A. Stubblefield and D. S. Wallach. Dagster: Censorship-resistant publishing without replication. Technical Report TR01-380, Rice University, 2001.
22. M. Waldman and D. Mazieres. Tangler: A censorship-resistant publishing system based on document entanglements. In *Proceedings of the 8th ACM Conference on Computer and Communications Security*, pages 126–135, 2001.
23. M. Waldman, A. Rubin, and L. Cranor. Publius: A robust, tamper-evident, censorship-resistant, web publishing system. In *Proccedings of 9th USENIX Security Symposium*, 2000.

Portable and Flexible Document Access Control Mechanisms*

Mikhail Atallah and Marina Bykova

Computer Sciences Department and CERIAS
Purdue University
{mja,mbykova}@cs.purdue.edu

Abstract. We present and analyze portable access control mechanisms for large data repositories, in that the customized access policies are stored on a portable device (e.g., a smart card). While there are significant privacy-preservation advantages to the use of smart cards anonymously created and bought in public places (stores, libraries, etc), a major difficulty is that, for huge data repositories and limited-capacity portable storage devices, it is not possible to represent any possible access configuration on the card. For a customer whose card is supposed to contain a subset S of documents, access to all of S must be allowed. In some situations a small enough number of "false positives" (which are accesses to non-S documents) is acceptable to the server, and the challenge then is to minimize the number of false positives implicit to any given card. We describe and analyze schemes for both unstructured and structured collections of documents. For these schemes, we give fast algorithms for efficiently using the limited space available on the card. In our model the customer does not know which documents correspond to false positives, the probability of a randomly chosen document being a false positive is small, and information about false positives bound to one card is useless for any other card even if both of them permit access to the same set of documents S.

1 Introduction

In this work we consider a very large collection of documents or other objects, and do not limit the customers to rigid menus of pre-defined sets of items to which they may have access. With the rapid recent increase in the number and the level of maturity of on-line document collections (digital libraries and the like) that provide payment-based access to their documents, this model has emerged as an appropriate way of dealing with this explosive growth. To make this model as flexible and convenient for the customer as possible, we allow each customer to choose a custom set of documents to be included in his subscription order.

---

* Portions of this work were supported by Grants IIS-0325345, IIS-0219560, IIS-0312357, and IIS-0242421 from the National Science Foundation, Contract N00014-02-1-0364 from the Office of Naval Research, by sponsors of the Center for Education and Research in Information Assurance and Security, and by Purdue Discovery Park's e-enterprise Center.

P. Samarati et al. (Eds.): ESORICS 2004, LNCS 3193, pp. 193–208, 2004.
© Springer-Verlag Berlin Heidelberg 2004

As stated above, this model might not appear interesting or challenging to implement: each customer receives a unique policy configuration that allows him to access the documents requested. What makes it intriguing are the additional requirements that we impose: we wish to fit such customer policy configurations into a limited amount of space, yet still be able to provide access to large data sets. This requirement becomes important in our era of portable devices such as smart cards and sensors that are space and/or battery-limited.

One might argue that putting the access policies on limited-storage smart cards is not a sound approach to portable access rights, that one can instead store the access policies on the server end. For privacy reasons, instead of storing customers' real identity, the server and the smart card could then store only a random ID (a pseudonym) while the access policies associated with that ID are kept at the server. In this case, the customer gets privacy without any need for storing the access policies on the card itself. This, however, has the disadvantage that tracking and profiling of a random ID's document access patterns is still possible; the danger then is that, if even once the random card ID is associated with an event (e.g., access from a particular IP address) that is linked to the customer's real identity, the whole access history of that individual becomes known to the server. This problem does not occur when the access policies are on the card itself. As both a metaphor and an example, we envision a customer, who walks into a bookstore; selects a number of items from a large universe of books, articles, and newspapers; pays with cash; and receives a smart card that provides him private access to the selected items at many terminals in various locations at stores, libraries, etc.

Storing access rights on the card itself has another advantage in that the entity that issues the card can be distinct from the entity that provides access to the data. In other words, the customer policy configuration can be constructed and written on the card by the data owner, while access to the data is performed by a third-party data publisher (possibly not completely trusted). Digital Rights Management (DRM) opens another avenue for utilizing digital portable access rights that the card can carry (see [2] for an overview of DRM techniques). For example, a card can manage access to a large collection of multi-media objects while using only a limited local storage space.

As we attempt to reduce the storage requirements of access policies, we lose the ability to represent all possible subsets of the documents in a deterministic way. Some documents or subsets of documents might have to share the same access policies which means that, given a configuration policy, a customer might unintentionally receive access to more documents that was originally requested; we refer to these accessible yet not requested (hence not paid for) documents as "false positives." Companies can clearly not charge their customers for such false positives, yet they will need to minimize them and the losses they cause. One of our main goals is therefore minimizing these additional "false positive costs" caused by the limited storage space. To prevent dishonest customers from sharing information learned about the false positives implicit to their card, we also require policy representations to be unique to each card, even if they correspond to the same set of documents. It is the constraints such as this minimization and the requirement of unique policy representations that make this problem very different from a mere data compression problem. Another (more minor) reason why we cannot use compression is that the access policies representations must be usable "as is" without uncompressing them first: There is no room in the smart card for that, and using server memory to uncompress would throw us back into the lack of privacy-preservation that we sought to avoid.

Our contributions are as follows: (i) For an unstructured collection of documents, we give and analyze a scheme that is based on generating a "good" random permutation for the documents in a subscription and is suitable for any arbitrary subset of the documents. We provide analysis of time complexity and cost of the scheme. (ii) For a structured collection of documents, we give a scheme similar to the random permutations one which has been modified to appropriately suit the structured data. We provide analysis of its time complexity.

This paper is organized as follows: Section 2 provides an overview of prior work. Section 3 gives a detailed problem specification and requirements that we impose on any solution. In section 4, we describe our solution for an unstructured collection of documents and provide efficient algorithms for card generation. That section also discusses viability of our scheme and analyzes it with respect to our design goals. In section 5, we describe a solution for the (more difficult) case of structured data, namely hierarchies, and provide algorithms for them as well. Finally, section 6 concludes the paper and gives directions for future work.

2   Related Work

Most literature on digital libraries does not explore the problem of access control, and many deployed systems nowadays provide only a single or otherwise a few inflexible subscription types. Payette and Lagoze [19] recognized this problem and proposed a way of solving it by introducing a spectrum of policy enforcement models which range from system-wide to object-specific and are capable of providing very flexible access control. They, however, give only a general framework for specifying policy enforcement mechanisms but do not deal with the problem of policy assignment itself.

Work conducted on XML [23] explores the problem of access control for online documents. Recently, there has been extensive work on securing access to XML documents and using XML as a tool for specifying security policies [6–8, 13, 14]. Bertino et al. [5] use binary strings to represent both customer policy configurations and document policies in the third-party publisher model, i.e., the model in which the roles of the *data owner* (who assigns policy configurations to its customers) and *data publishers* (who provide the service and enforce access control) are separate. We consider binary strings to be the most space efficient and precise way of policy representation and adopt policies in the form of binary strings in our work. Bertino et al., however, allocate one bit per policy on the assumption that there will be a limited number of different subscription types, and their approach becomes inefficient as the data repository grows in size and each customer chooses a customized document subscription set. Therefore, we need a new method of representing policy strings so as to be able to store and use them on space-limited media.

The idea of achieving space efficiency at the cost of a small probability of false positives was introduced in Bloom [9]. The Bloom filter is a clever randomized data structure for concisely representing a set to support approximate membership queries and is widely used in a broad spectrum of applications ([10, 15, 18], to name a few). The queries never result in false negatives (i.e., a query result never says that an item is not a member of the set if it, in fact, is a member) but might result in false positives with a small probability, which is acceptable for many applications. This approach achieves a better space utilization than a simpler representation with one hash function, but even in the case of Bloom filters, the filter length (which in our case corresponds to the card capacity) should be larger than the total number of items in the set n to result in a reasonable performance. This is not suitable for the problem we are trying to solve and therefore the Bloom filter approach cannot be used "as is" for our problem. Customized Bloom filters also do not appear to provide acceptable results.

The problem of policy assignment of minimal cost for a set of homogeneous objects within a large data repository was explored in more detail in Bykova and Atallah [11], and their problem is very close to the one we are considering. The present paper adds two new dimensions to the problem, and ends up with very different solutions from [11]: (i) it considers hierarchically structured collections of documents, and (ii) it is inherently resilient to collusive attacks by users. In the schemes of [11], the policy assignment algorithm is static and the pattern of false positives is preserved over all subscription orders and customers. This means that once a customer has learned that a particular combination of documents results in free access to another document (false positive), he can enable a different customer with the same subscription set to also obtain the same false positive.

Recent techniques for the problem of software license management through portable limited-storage card-based access rights [4, 3] do not apply to our problem, mainly because we cannot afford to avail ourselves of resources external to the card (as was the case in [4, 3]).

Work on unlinkability and untraceability was started by Chaum [12] and has been explored more extensively in recent years. In particular, work on unlinkability includes anonymous group authentication ([21, 17, 20, 16] and others) and unlinkable serial transactions [22] for subscription-based services. Prior work, however, does not account for the fact that descriptions of access rights (or service types) may be long and required to be portable, while we describe a scheme that combines compact policy representation with transaction unlinkability.

3   Problem Specification

The goal is to design an access control scheme for the following specifications:

1. We are given a large data collection of n items (documents, multimedia objects, etc.).

2. A customer can request access to any subset of the items in the repository (m documents) and is charged according to the set of documents selected.
3. Access policy configuration is stored on a card of limited capacity of k cells, each cell having $O(\log n)$ bits such that $k \log n < n$ and $k < m$ [1].

Below are the properties that guide our design decisions and which we seek in any solution:

1. **Low rate of false positives.** One of our main goals is to design a scheme with a reasonably low rate of false positives meaning that, given a subscription order for m documents, the number of documents m' that the customer can unintentionally access for free is bounded by some suitably low value. The threshold could be defined as a function of m', m, and/or n, but in all cases must be tolerably low to the service provider.

2. **Transaction untraceability.** For customer privacy, transactions should not be linked back to the customer who is making a request to access a document.

3. **Transaction unlinkability.** To provide further customer privacy, two transactions by a single customer should not be linked together, thus making customer profiling impossible. This desired property does not allow us to permanently store complete customer orders at the service provider, and it is desirable that an order is processed by a separate entity (e.g., the data owner) and discarded after it has been processed.

4. **Unforgeability.** It should be impossible for an entity other than the legal service provider to issue cards that will allow access to the document repository. This means that all terminals that read smart cards will ask a smart card to present evidence of authenticity of the card (evidence that only the service provider can initially issue).

5. **Unique policy representation.** In order to lower damage caused by dishonest customers that collaborate to discover as many free documents (false positives) as possible, we would like our scheme to be resistant to such behavior. This requires not only that false positives depend on the subscription order but they uniquely differ from one request to another even when the set of requested documents stays unchanged over multiple orders. With such a scheme in place, no correlation between free documents in different orders is possible, and any gain to customers who collude is eliminated. All a dishonest customer can do is to try to discover for himself the free documents for his particular order, which, combined with some penalty mechanism, can be prohibitively inefficient for him to do.

6. **No additional sources of information.** All information needed to perform access control verification should be stored on the card itself. No other sources of additional storage may be required (such as storage space of a home workstation in case of software license management), as there is no single place where such information can be stored.

---

[1] If $k \geq m$, the list of selected documents can be explicitly stored on the card.

7. **Fast access verification.** Policy enforcement and access verification should be performed in real time and thus expensive computations should be avoided.

8. **In-house card generation.** The card generation process should be relatively short. It might be performed on a powerful computer, but within a certain time limit. For example, a card can be generated while the customer is waiting in a line for the cashier at a bookstore.

   A case can be made for relaxing this last constraint if there exists a scheme that requires an extended amount of time for card generation but is much more efficient and less costly (compared to other models that obey this constraint). In this case, a card is delivered to the customer when its processing completes (like an order at a pharmacy, that usually involves a wait).

9. **Forward compatibility.** An old card does not lose its validity as the repository grows.

4   Solution for Unstructured Data

We now present our approach for an unstructured collection of documents and provide its analysis. In what follows and in the rest of this paper we use to the term *order* to refer to a subscription order of m documents for which the customer pays and receives a card that permits access to those documents. We use the term *request* to refer to a request to access a document by a customer who already possesses a card and wishes to view a document.

Our solution consists of generating random permutations of documents included into an order until they are clustered in such a way that the cost (in terms of false positives) of storing the permuted documents on a smart card is below a certain threshold (defined later). After generating the subsequent permutation of the documents, we run the evaluation algorithm to compute the cost of the optimal solution for that particular set of permuted documents. If the cost is acceptable, the algorithm terminates and the solution is written to the card; and a new permutation is generated and tested otherwise. Information written on the card includes the data that can be used to reproduce the permutation, as well as a number of document intervals that indicate access to which documents should be granted. The intervals include all documents from the subscription order and as few additional documents (i.e., not from the original order) as possible. Consider an oversimplified example where the repository has a size of 10, our card can store 2 intervals, and we receive a customer subscription order for documents 1, 5, 7, and 9. Suppose that after permuting the documents we obtain set $\{2, 3, 6, 8\}$, so the best option in this case is to use intervals 2–3 and 6–8 for storing the set on the card. The cost of a solution is computed as the number of false positives (in the example above, the cost of the permutation is equal to 1).

Both the random permutation seed and the document intervals are a subject to the card's storage constraints. Since a smart card's capacity is $O(k \log n)$, we can use it to store $O(k)$ numbers within the range $\{1, \ldots, n\}$, or k intervals. The permutation seed can be up to $O(k \log n)$ bits long.

Every interval included in a solution can be either *positive*, i.e., specifies a range of documents to which access should be granted, or *negative*, i.e., specifies a range of documents to which access should be denied. In the case of unstructured data, negative ranges do not improve the result by decreasing the cost of a solution, as the lemma below shows (but, as we show later on, they are necessary for structured data).

Lemma 1. *For unstructured data, for every solution of cost C expressed using both positive and negative ranges there is a solution of cost C' expressed using only positive ranges, such that $C' \leq C$.*

Proof. Omitted due to space limitations and can be found in [1].   □

In the rest of this section, we use $r = \{r_1, \ldots, r_m\}$ to compactly represent a customer order of m documents. Each r_i uniquely identifies a single document in the repository (i.e., it is a number in the range $\{1, \ldots, n\}$) and all r_i's are sorted in increasing order such that $r_i < r_{i+1}$ for $1 \leq i < m$. We first present an algorithm for producing a suitable encoding to be placed on a card (given in section 4.1). This is a high level algorithm that tries different solutions until the conditions corresponding to the policies are satisfied. It uses two additional algorithms as its subroutines: an algorithm to produce a permutation (discussed in section 4.3) and a linear-time algorithm to compute a cost of a permutation (given in section 4.2). We give asymptotic bounds of our solution and also discuss possibilities for generating a random permutation. Later in this section we explore this approach in terms of its economic feasibility (section 4.5), and the next section (section 5) provides an extension to it that covers structured data.

4.1   Algorithm for Producing a Solution

To find a suitable encoding for a customer order, we might have to try numerous permutations of n elements until one that satisfied certain criteria is found. These criteria can be expressed in terms of the cost of a solution (e.g., the number of false positives for the permutation produced falls below a certain threshold), in terms of a time interval during which a solution should be computed, or some other requirements. These rules are examined in more detail in section 4.5.

The algorithm we provide below takes a subscription order of m documents and a set of rules, which tell the algorithm to stop when they are satisfied. It runs until a suitable solution is found and returns an encoding to be stored on a smart card, which consists of a permutation seed s and k intervals that optimally represent the requested documents r.

Input: The repository size n, a customer order of m documents $r = \{r_1, \ldots, r_m\}$, and a set of stopping criteria $\tau = \{\tau_1, \ldots, \tau_t\}$.

Output: A seed s for generating a permutation and k intervals to be stored on a smart card.

Algorithm 1:

1. Seed the permutation algorithm with a random number s.
2. Permute the m documents to get $p_i = \pi_s(r_i)$ for each document $r_i \in r$.
3. Sort the p_i's ($O(m \log(m))$ time).
4. Run the evaluation algorithm to find the cost of the permutation ($O(m)$ time, per section 4.2).
5. Apply the evaluation rules τ to the result: if a sufficient subset $\tau' \subseteq \tau$ of them, $1 \le |\tau'| \le t$, is satisfied, output the solution. Otherwise go to step (1).

The asymptotic bound of a single run of the algorithm depends on the choice of the permutation function (discussed in section 4.3). The total running time of the algorithm depends on the evaluation criteria and cannot be expressed as a function of the input parameters in the general case. The upper bound of the algorithm is $O(n^k)$ loop invocations, but typical values are lower. This time is constrained by the space available for storing a random seed s: there are $O(2^{k \cdot \log n}) = O(n^k)$ possible seed values that can be stored on the card.

4.2   Algorithm for Computing the Cost of a Permutation

The algorithm given in this section corresponds to step 4 of Algorithm 1. As the input, it expects a set of m distinct permuted documents sorted in increasing order $p = \{p_1, \ldots, p_m\}$ and computes k disjoint intervals of the minimal cost that include all of the p_i's and as few other documents as possible. Our algorithm works by computing distances between the documents in the set p and excluding the largest $k - 1$ of them, so that the overall cost of the covering is minimized.

Input: The repository size n and a sorted set of m elements $p = \{p_1, \ldots, p_m\}$.

Output: k disjoint intervals that contain all of the p_i's and as few other elements as possible.

Algorithm 2:

1. Let x be the value of p_1, y the value of p_m. Compute $c_1, \ldots, c_{m-1}$, where c_i is the number of documents between the elements p_i and p_{i+1} not including either p_i or p_{i+1}. For example, c_1 is computed as $c_1 = p_2 - p_1 - 1$.
2. In $O(m)$ time select a $(k - 1)^{\text{th}}$ largest among $c_1, \ldots, c_{m-1}$ (say it is c_j).
3. In $O(m)$ time go through $c_1, \ldots, c_{m-1}$ and choose $k - 2$ entries that are $\ge c_j$. Those entries and c_j correspond to the $k - 1$ "gaps" between the optimal k intervals, i.e., they define the optimal k intervals.

Note that the "cost" of the solution is $C = c_1 + \ldots + c_{m-1} -$ (sum of the largest $k - 1$ c_i's), which also proves the correctness of the algorithm because $c_1 + \ldots + c_{m-1}$ is the number of documents between positions x and y other than the elements of p, and the best that can be done is by "excluding" the large c_i's from the chosen intervals. It is also clear that the algorithm runs in $O(m)$ time since every step (1)–(3) runs in $O(m)$ time.

The actual monetary damage caused by the false positives might not be linear in the number of false positives, but instead could be some other (possibly arbitrary) function specified by the service provider. In this case, however, the algorithm will still produce correct results, and the cost function itself can be incorporated into the set of stopping rules τ, as we explain in section 4.5.

4.3   Algorithms for Producing a Permutation

There are several well-known methods for computing random permutations. Any method that has the following properties should be suitable for our approach:

- The permutation can be specified by a seed, i.e., given a seed value, the permutation could be reproduced from it. Recall that the set of storable seeds does not "access" all possible permutations of n elements, but only a random subset of $O(n^k)$ of these permutations[2]. This turns out to be enough in practical situations (cf. discussion in section 4.5).
- The algorithm allows concurrent computing of a mapping for a single element. It is then not necessary to compute the permutation mappings for $O(n)$ documents of the data collection at the access verification time just to obtain one of them that we are interested in. We can also directly compute the mappings for the m documents included in the order during card creation time without having to generate all of the n mappings.

For discussion and an example of a permutation algorithm satisfying these requirements (omitted from this paper due to space constraints) see [1].

4.4   Card Operation

The algorithms presented above describe card generation, but they imply a corresponding operational use of the card, which we sketch here. We assume that the card is tamper-resistant, so that the unforgeability constraint is satisfied; techniques for achieving tamper-resistance can be found in the literature and are beyond the scope of this paper. Also, the card must authenticate itself, e.g., by sharing secret keys with the server (a secret key is not unique to a card) and/or using other known means of low-computation anonymous authentication suitable for smart cards. Policy enforcement by using the policy encoding placed on a card is performed as follows. Given a document index i, access to which is being requested from the server, and a card that stores a permutation seed s and k intervals, the verification process takes the following steps:

- The card computes a permuted value of i as $p_i = \pi_s(i)$.
- The card searches its k intervals for p_i to determine whether p_i is covered by one of them. Since we can sort all intervals before storing them on the card, this step can be done in $O(\log k)$ time using binary search.

---

[2] In cases where a sequence of random numbers is needed by the permutation algorithm, the seed can be used to initialize a pseudo-random number generator.

- If p_i is covered by one of the k intervals, the card requests the document i from the server. Otherwise, it notifies the user about access denial.

One can see from the above that the untraceability and unlinkability constraints of our design (goals (2) and (3) in section 3) are satisfied: Each card anonymously authenticates itself and does not send any information to server that might happen to be unique and used to link two transactions together. The card also does not require any additional sources of information to enforce proper access control (goal (6)) and uses an efficient method for such enforcement (goal (7)).

4.5 Economic Analysis

This section analyzes the practicability of the scheme described above. We explore the possibility of using the scheme under different settings, and examine what policies a service provider might specify in order to use the model as efficiently as possible. We also make the "stopping criteria" mentioned in the previous section that govern permutation selection process more precise.

Values of interest. As input, we are given the size of data repository n and the number of documents in a customer order m [3]. Other parameters of use for determining what an acceptable cost is are:

$c_{card}(m)$ – price a customer pays for an order of m documents, which can be a possibly arbitrary function of the documents that comprise the order.

$t(m)$ – maximum number of requests to documents access to which was denied. Each card can count the number of attempts to view documents that were denied. When a customer requests a document not bound to the card, not only is the access denied, but also the permitted limit of unsuccessful requests is decremented. After t such attempts, the count reaches zero and the card is self-invalidated (i.e., the policy here is "t strikes and you are out"). This is to prevent customers from probing their cards for false positives, e.g., by trying all documents in the data repository. With this mechanism in place, each customer should be informed about t at the time of purchasing the card and should be given an explicit list of the documents included into his order.

$m'(n, m)$ – number of documents that come for free with a card (i.e., the "false positives"). This value is computed as a by-product of Algorithm 2, and implicitly reflects the card's capacity k.

$n'(n, m)$ – number of documents in which an attacker is interested (other than the m he ordered). This value is useful in measuring the attacker's economic gain in case of discovering free accesses to documents. In the worst case, any free document can be valuable to the attacker. In the best case, the attacker has zero interest in anything outside the m documents he ordered.

---

[3] In reality, we have the entire order $r = \{r_1, \ldots, r_m\}$ as an input parameter. For simplicity of presentation we assume that the cost of each document is the same and m can be treated as a sufficient representation of the set. Similar analysis can be carried out when document prices differ from one to another. Then each derived value that takes m as a parameter can be computed as a function of the set r itself.

Policy alternatives. Each service provider deploying this approach might have one or more varying criteria that define an acceptable "false positives" cost of a card. Below we list policies that can be used during card generation to govern execution of Algorithm 1:

1. **Threshold for the number of false positives** m' a card contains. This policy might dictate that the absolute value of the number itself is constrained (e.g., $f(m') \leq m'_{max}$), or its ratio to the number of documents in the repository or to the number of documents in the order is constrained by some threshold (e.g., $f\left(\frac{g(m')}{h(n)}\right) \leq m'_{max}$ or $f\left(\frac{g(m')}{h(m)}\right) \leq m'_{max}$, where $f(x)$, $g(x)$ and $h(x)$ are arbitrary functions of argument x). We may consider a policy that lists several conditions but requires satisfying a subset of them.

2. **Constraints on the gain from cheating.** In this type of policies, we perform analysis of cheating in terms of the attacker's loss vs. his gain after attempting to access t' out of the $n - m$ documents not included in his order. Suppose that $t' > t$. The expected gain from the attack in this case is the difference between the cost of the documents acquired for free from the list of n' documents of interest, and the cost of losing the card due to this behavior. The gain is then computed as the probability of successfully getting a free access to a document multiplied by the document cost, while the loss is computed as the probability of losing the card multiplied by the cost of the card:

$$E(gain) \simeq t' \cdot \frac{c(m')}{n-m} \cdot \frac{n'}{n-m} - c_{card} \cdot Q \simeq \frac{t' c(m') n'}{(n-m)^2} - c_{card} \sum_{t''=t}^{t'} \binom{t'}{t''} q^{t''} p^{t'-t''}$$

where $c(m')$ is the cost of having access to m' documents computed according to some pricing function. Here $p = \frac{m'}{n-m}$ specifies the probability of not being caught, while $q = 1 - p$ is the probability of begin caught.

Similarly, we can compute the expected gain when the number of unauthorized attempts is kept below the maximum, i.e., $t' \leq t$. In this case, the expected gain is computed based on the probability of getting free access, and there is no loss for the attacker:

$$E(gain) \simeq t' \cdot \frac{c(m')}{n-m} \cdot \frac{n'}{n-m} \tag{1}$$

In the worst-case scenario, the attacker might be interested in and benefit from any document acquired for free, i.e., $n' = n - m$, and we can also assume that $t' \simeq t$, to maximize the gain. Then equation (1) becomes:

$$E(gain) \simeq t \cdot \frac{c(m')}{n-m}$$

To keep the attacker's gain low, we might constrain the value by some threshold. Equation (2) gives such a constraint where the coefficient α plays the role of a threshold value that keeps the card's loss within a specified bound.

$$\frac{t \cdot c(m')}{n-m} \leq \alpha \cdot c_{card} \tag{2}$$

3. **Timeout.** Under some policies, the card creation process might have to be carried within a certain period of time. Then if no suitable permutation is found during that interval, the best permutation tried so far is used.

Based on the policies listed above, we create a set of stopping criteria by possibly combining two or more conditions in such a way that the card produced always satisfies the card issuer. A sample policy that we provide in [1] and which is omitted here shows that our model can accommodate a wide range of reasonable policies without requiring lengthy and heavy computations for card creation.

4.6   Analysis of the Approach

Our proposed solution is compliant with the desired design properties and minimizes the total number of false positives bound to a card. More precisely, the design of our scheme ensures that goals (2)–(7) listed in section 3 are met. Goal (9) is achieved by using unique policy representations that "capture" the state of the repository at the time of card generation and are self-contained. As we add more documents to the repository, the old cards can still be used, for instance, to reproduce permutations of the documents from the previous state of the repository and provide access to the documents from customer subscriptions.

Our permutation approach also guarantees a low rate of false positives (goal (1)), especially if this constraint is a part of the algorithm's termination criteria. Depending on the policies enforced by the service provider, the scheme can be evaluated on its time requirements, i.e., how long, on average, it might take to generate a card. Thus, it might or might not comply with goal (8). If the service provider employs a policy that includes a timeout, then in-house card generation is always achievable. If, on the other hand, he places more weight on minimizing the number of false positives, then this constraint might be relaxed.

5   Structured Data

This section explores the possibility of extending our approach to structured data such as trees. In many data repositories documents are stored in hierarchies, which makes it possible to utilize the repository structure and reduce the number of false positives in the solution computed.

5.1   Tree Structure

Suppose we are given a tree of n documents and a subscription order of m documents. The card's capacity is still $O(k \log n)$ bits or $O(k)$ records, but in this case each record, in addition to two numbers that specify a range, might contain some other information. We consider both positive and negative ranges for encoding documents on a card. We also consider two different types of placements: When a positive or negative assignment is placed on a node v, it can either affect the entire subtree rooted at v – we denote this case as *recursive* – or affect only the node on which the assignment is placed – we denote this assignment as *local*. The case where a depth parameter can be stored at v, so as to limit the depth of the subtree included, will be considered later in this section (such a depth parameter limits the depth of the nodes influenced by that range, so that nodes that are farther than that depth below v are not affected). When two ranges overlap, the more specific (= lower in the tree) wins. Finally, the word "cost" in the rest of this section is used as "cost of the false positives" (not the dollar cost paid by the customer).

Throughout our algorithm, we use the following notations. For each node v, a cost of the subtree rooted at v can be computed in two different contexts: positive and negative. If a node v is evaluated in the positive context (the cost is denoted by $C^+(v)$), this means that a positive range has been specified at its parent or above the parent in the tree. In this case, if no new range is placed at v or below, the entire subtree will be included in the final solution. In this context, only negative ranges placed at v or below have effect. Similarly, if a node v is evaluated in the negative context (the cost is denoted by $C^-(v)$), then it means that a negative range has been specified at its parent or above, and by default the entire subtree will be excluded from the solution. If no context has been specified, we start in the negative context and assume that no nodes are included in the solution unless explicitly specified.

As with any dynamic programming approach, the cost of an optimal solution at any given node v needs to be calculated for a number of cases that differ in the number of encoding slots available. Thus, we use $C^+(v, j)$ and $C^-(v, j)$ to mean the cost of encoding the tree rooted at v in positive and negative contexts, respectively, with j storage slots available, where $0 \leq j \leq k$.

Here we provide an algorithm for binary trees, which can naturally be extended to work for more general t-ary trees with $t \geq 2$. When working with binary trees, we typically use nodes u and w as child nodes of v. In order to compute a cost of a subtree rooted at node v, we need to consider two cases: computation of $C^+(v, j)$ and $C^-(v, j)$, which we describe subsequently. Let us consider non-leaf nodes first and then proceed with leaves of the tree. Time complexity of the algorithm for both binary and arbitrary t-ary trees is given later in this section.

Non-leaf Nodes

Case of $C^+(v, j)$: When the cost is computed in the positive context, we need to consider three different cases.

Case 1: No record is placed at v. Then $C^+(v, j)$ is computed as:
$$C^+(v, j) = \min\{C^+(u, i) + C^+(w, j - i) + c_1|\ 0 \leq i \leq j\},$$
where c_1 is 1 if v is not in the order, and 0 otherwise.

Case 2: A negative recursive record is placed at v. This case cannot happen if v is included in the order. We compute the value as:
$$C^+(v, j) = \min\{C^-(u, i) + C^-(w, j - i - 1)|\ 0 \leq i \leq j - 1\}.$$

Case 3: A negative local record is placed at v. This case also cannot happen if v is included in the order. To compute $C^+(v, j)$, we use:
$$C^+(v, j) = \min\{C^+(u, i) + C^+(w, j - i - 1)|\ 0 \leq i \leq j - 1\}$$
After computing all of the values above, $C^+(v, j)$ is assigned the minimum of the three values.

Case of $C^-(v, j)$: For the negative context there are also three possible cases.

Case 1: No record is placed at v. This case cannot happen if v is included in the order. The formula for computing $C^-(v, j)$ is as follows:
$$C^-(v, j) = \min\{C^-(u, i) + C^-(w, j - i)|\ 0 \le i \le j\}$$
Case 2: A positive recursive record is placed at v. In the formula below, c_1 is set to 1 if v was not included in the order, and it is 0 otherwise:
$$C^-(v, j) = \min\{C^+(u, i) + C^+(w, j - i - 1) + c_1|\ 0 \le i \le j\}$$
Case 3: A positive local record is placed at v. This case normally does not happen when v is not in the order. To compute $C^-(v, j)$, we use:
$$C^-(v, j) = \min\{C^+(u, i) + C^+(w, j - i - 1) + c_1|0 \le i \le j\}$$
Analogously to the previous case, $C^-(v, j)$ receives the value of the minimum of the three values computed in these cases.

Leaf Nodes

Case of $C^+(v, j)$: If $j > 0$ and v is not in the order, then we can exclude the node from the solution by placing a negative record at it. In this case, the cost $C^+(v, j)$ is 0. Otherwise, no record can be placed at the node; the cost $C^+(v, j)$ is 0 if v is included in the order, and 1 otherwise.

Case of $C^-(v, j)$: If $j = 0$ and v is included in the order, then $C^-(v, j)$ should be set to $+\infty$ to prevent this configuration from being chosen, as it does not satisfy the algorithm's requirements. In all other cases, $C^-(v, j)$ is 0.

Complexity analysis. To compute the cost of an order, we use the above rules to compute $C^-(root, k)$. Every documents i included in the order is taken into account at the time of computing the cost of the subtree rooted at node i. For a tree of n documents and card's capacity of k slots, this algorithm runs in $O(n \cdot k^2)$ time for binary trees. For arbitrary t-ary trees the algorithm gives $O(n \cdot k^t)$ time.

An extension to records of variable depth. Let h be the height of the tree. The dynamic programming approach we have can be extended to include all possible heights for each node v. This means that when we compute a cost of a subtree $C^+(v, j)$ or $C^-(v, j)$, we now can specify the depth of the record placed at v, which can vary from 1 to the height of the subtree rooted at v. In this case, there is no need to distinguish between local and recursive nodes any more, as they are replaced by a single record in which the desired depth is specified. We do not include the algorithm's details in the paper due to space considerations.

For a t-ary tree, this modification implies a factor of h (but not h^t) because any record placed at the parent covers one child's subtree at same depth as for another child's subtree. Thus, this adds an extra h to the time complexity.

Note. Currently, the tree algorithm is static because no permutation for the tree structure is used. To make this scheme viable, more research needs to be done to make each solution unique by means other than permutation, e.g., false positives are randomized for each order but are kept below a certain threshold.

6   Conclusions and Future Work

In this work we presented a problem of fine-grained document access control under space restrictions. Our solution preserves customer anonymity, uses efficient algorithms to perform access control, and at the same time minimizes loss caused by policy compression. We gave a full-grown solution for unstructured data and provided a method for evaluating the cost of a solution for hierarchically structured repositories. Future directions include providing more thorough (possibly empirical) analysis of our scheme and building a solid framework for hierarchical data.

This work can be extended to cover other types of structured data. In particular, grids can be of practical interest in the context of Geographic Information Systems (GIS) subscriptions where land is partitioned into cells of a standard size. A customer can subscribe to a cell and receive information about temperature, humidity, precipitation, and other meteorological data relevant to the area. Each subscriber selects cells of his interest and pays to get access to a customized area of his choice. Access control is enforced through the use of cheap cards of limited capacity. An algorithm to compute the optimal cost of a subscription in this case will model geometric algorithms for approximate representation of a polygon. A difference from the standard approximation methods here is that the requested area must be included entirely in the card, while the number of other cells stored on the card should be minimized.

Acknowledgments

We would like to thank anonymous reviewers for their valuable comments.

References

1. M. Atallah and M. Bykova. "Portable and Flexible Document Access Control Mechanisms," *CERIAS Technical Report TR 2004-24, Purdue University,* Jun. 2004.
2. M. Atallah, K. Frikken, C. Black, S. Overstreet, and P. Bhatia. "Digital Rights Management," *Practical Handbook of Internet Computing,* Munindar Singh (Ed.), CRC Press, 2004.
3. M. Atallah and J. Li. "Enhanced Smart-card based License Management," *IEEE International Conference on E-Commerce (CEC),* Jun. 2003, pp. 111–119.
4. T. Aura and D. Gollmann. "Software license management with smart cards," *USENIX Workshop on Smart Card Technology,* USENIX Association, May 1999.
5. E. Bertino, B. Carminati, E. Ferrari, B. Thuraisingham, and A. Gupta. "Selective and Authentic Third-party Distribution of XML Documents," *Working Paper,* Sloan School of Management, MIT, 2002,
   http://papers.ssrn.com/sol3/papers.cfm?abstract_id=299935.
6. E. Bertino, S. Castano, and E. Ferrari. "On Specifying Security Policies for Web Documents with an XML-based Language," *ACM Symposium on Access Control Models and Technologies (SACMAT'01),* May 2001.

7. E. Bertino, S. Castano, and E. Ferrari. "Securing XML Documents with Author-X," *IEEE Internet Computing*, Vol. 5, No. 3, pp. 21–31, 2001.

8. E. Bertino and E. Ferrari. "Secure and Selective Dissemination of XML Documents," *ACM Transactions on Information and System Security*, Vol. 5, No. 3, Aug. 2002, pp. 290–331.

9. B. Bloom. "Space/time trade-offs in hash coding with allowable errors." *Communications of the ACM*, Vol. 13, No. 7, pp. 422–426, 1970.

10. A. Broder and M. Mitzenmacher. "Network Applications of Bloom Filters: A Survey," *Allerton Conference*, 2002.

11. M. Bykova and M. Atallah. "Succinct Specifications of Portable Document Access Policies," *ACM Symposium on Access Control Models and Technologies (SACMAT'04)*, Jun. 2004.

12. D. Chaum. "Untraceable Electronic Mail, Return Addresses, and Digital Pseudonyms," *Communications of the ACM*, Vol. 24, No. 2, Feb. 1981, pp. 84–88.

13. D. Damiani, S. De Capitani Di Vimercati, S. Paraboschi, and P. Samarati. "A Fine-Grained Access Control System for XML Documents," *ACM Transactions on Information and System Security*, Vol. 5, No. 2, May 2002, pp. 169–202.

14. P. Devanbu, M. Gertz, A. Kwong, C. Martel, and G. Nuckolls. "Flexible Authentication of XML Documents," *ACM Conference on Computer and Communications Security (CCS'01)*, Nov. 2001.

15. L. Fan, P. Cao, J. Almeida, and A. Broder. "Summary Cache: A Scalable Wide-Area Web Cache Sharing Protocol," *IEEE/ACM Transactions on Networking*, Vol. 8, No. 3, pp. 281–293, 2000.

16. J. Kim, S. Choi, K. Kim, and C. Boyd. "Anonymous Authentication Protocol for Dynamic Groups with Power-Limited Devices," *Symposium on Cryptography and Information Security (SCIS'03)*, Vol. 1/2, pp. 405–410, Jan. 2003.

17. C. Lee, X. Deng, and H. Zhu. "Design and Security Analysis of Anonymous Group Identification Protocols," *Public Key Cryptography (PKC'02)*, LNCS, Vol. 2274, pp. 188–198, Feb. 2002.

18. M. Mitzenmacher. "Compressed Bloom Filters," *ACM symposium on Principles of Distributed Computing*, Aug. 2001.

19. S. Payette and C. Lagoze. "Policy-Carrying, Policy-Enforcing Digital Objects," *Research and Advanced Technology for Digital Libraries, 4th European Conference (ECDL'00)*, Vol. 1923, pp. 144–157, 2000.

20. P. Persiano and I. Visconti. "A Secure and Private System for Subscription-Based Remote Services," *ACM Transactions on Information and System Security*, Vol. 6, No. 4, Nov. 2003, pp. 472–500.

21. S. Schechter, T. Parnell, and A. Hartemink. "Anonymous Authentication of Membership in Dynamic Groups," *Financial Cryptography*, LNCS, Vol. 1648, pp. 184–195, 1999.

22. S. Stubblebine, P. Syverson, and D. Goldschlag. "Unlinkable Serial Transactions," *ACM Transactions on Information and System Security*, Vol. 2, No. 4, Nov. 1999, pp. 354–389.

23. World Wide Web Consortium. Extensible Markup Language (XML) 1.0 (second edition), October 2000, W3C Recommendation, http://www.w3.org/TR/REC-xml.

Possibilistic Information Flow Control
in the Presence of Encrypted Communication[*]

Dieter Hutter and Axel Schairer

German Research Center for Artificial Intelligence (DFKI GmbH)
Stuhlsatzenhausweg 3, 66123 Saarbrücken, Germany
{hutter,schairer}@dfki.de

Abstract. Distributed systems make increasing use of encrypted channels to enable confidential communication. While non-interference provides suitable means to investigate the flow of information within distributed systems, it has proved to be rather difficult to capture the notion of encrypted channels in such a framework. In this paper, we extend the framework MAKS for possibilistic information flow in order to distinguish between the information flow due to the fact that a message has been sent and the flow that is due to the actual content of a message. We introduce an equivalence relation on observable events to identify those events an observer cannot distinguish and provide reduction techniques that enable us to prove the security of such systems with the help of exisiting unwinding techniques.

1 Introduction

Information flow control (e.g. [7, 16, 11, 5]) relies on the idea of modeling confidentiality (and dually: privacy) of data as restrictions on the flow of information between different domains of a system. Starting with the work of Goguen and Meseguer [2, 3], the restrictions on information flow for deterministic systems have been formalized as independence properties between actions and observations of domains: Alice's actions are confidential wrt. Charly if his observations are independent of her actions, i.e. if Alice changes her actions this does not cause different observations for Charly. In this case Alice is said to be non-interfering with Charly. For non-deterministic systems, the intuition works backwards: Alice is possibilistically non-interfering with Charly if the observations of Charly can be explained by several, different behaviors of Alice. Thus, Charly's observation does not reveal which actions Alice has chosen.

Consider, for example, that Alice has stored a personal identification number (PIN) on her computer and suppose Charly is monitoring her internet connections. Alice's PIN is confidential for Charly if his observations of Alice's actions are explicable with both, Alice's actual PIN and another arbitrary PIN. If we assume that Charly can only observe messages going from and to Alice's computer then Alice's PIN is secure if no message leaving her computer depends on the PIN. However, once Alice uses her PIN when communicating with her bank, Charly can observe a message which depends on Alice's PIN; i.e. using a different PIN would result in a different observable message. Hence,

---

[*] This work was supported by the German Federal Ministry of Education and Research (BMBF) and the German Research Foundation (DFG)

analyzing the security of this scenario with the help of strict information flow control techniques would reveal a leak of information. In practice however, Charly is not able to infer the PIN if we assume perfect cryptography. There are specialized techniques to investigate and verify properties of cryptographic protocols (e.g. [8, 1, 9]). They investigate how an attacker can deduce secret information (only) by analyzing, intercepting or forging messages and assume fixed capabilities of an attacker (Dolev-Yao model).

In the past intransitive information flow techniques (cf. [12, 10, 13]) have been advocated to deal with modeling encrypted communications. Encryption is considered as an explicit downgrading that renders the confidential message into a visible (encrypted) one. However, while this approach simply *assumes* that Charly cannot infer the PIN by observing visible encrypted messages, our approach will allow us to *prove* this property provided that Charly cannot, in fact, distinguish different encrypted messages. In particular, we will be able to detect security leakages arising from traffic analysis.

Encryption, or more generally one-way functions, have been studied in the context of language based security, e.g. [4], [15]. These approaches provide assumptions about the probabilistic properties of encryption. They give syntactic conditions for programs that ensure there is no probabilistic information flow from the initial values of high variables to the final values of low variables, once the program has been run. In contrast, we are interested in what an observer can learn from messages that are exchanged between parties in the system in an ongoing computation, where the observer may or may not be one of the parties.

We base our techniques on the framework MAKS [6] developed to specify and verify possibilistic information flow policies. In this paper we extend the framework by techniques which enable its application also when specifying and verifying the security of systems containing encrypted communication. They allow us to model the property that an observer cannot distinguish different encrypted messages without knowing the key. Regardless whether Alice sends the encrypted 4711 or the encrypted 4712 to her bank, Charly will see a bit-stream. He might suspect to see an encrypted PIN but (unless he knows the key) he has no information which encrypted PIN he sees. Both events cause the same flow of information for Charly: some encrypted PIN has been sent to the bank. In the formal analysis of such a system we will identify these events when inspecting the security of the system from Charly's point of view by introducing equivalence classes of events. We assume that Charly is not able to distinguish different representatives within an equivalence class by presuming perfect cryptography.

After a brief introduction to the framework MAKS in Sect. 2, we illustrate how generic security predicates (defined in MAKS) are adjusted to the new setting. In Sect. 3 we exemplify this approach by translating two basic security predicates into new security predicates and show that we can reduce these predicates to the original predicates for a transformed system. This allows us to make use of the original verification techniques, i.e. the unwinding theorems, to verify these predicates as presented in Sect. 4.

2   Preliminaries

In this section we will introduce concepts and notation and briefly present the parts of MAKS [6] that we use in this paper. Systems are described by an *event system ES* =

(E,I,O,Tr), which consists of a set E of events, two sets $I,O \subseteq E$ of input and output events, respectively, and the set $Tr \subseteq 2^{E^*}$ of possible system traces. The set Tr of finite sequences of events is required to be closed under prefixes, i.e. $\alpha.\beta \in Tr$ implies $\alpha \in Tr$, where we write $\alpha.\beta$ for the sequence resulting from concatenating the sequences α and β. We write $\langle e_1,\ldots,e_n \rangle$ for the sequence consisting of the events $e_1,\ldots,e_n$.

In MAKS, *security properties* are closure properties of sets of possible system traces (parametrized over an arbitrary set of events E) that are described by a conjunction of *basic security predicates* (BSPs) and a *view*. A view $\mathcal{V} = (V,N,C)$ for E is a disjoint, exhaustive partition of E and formalises an observer or attacker: C comprises those events whose occurrence or non-occurrence should be confidential for the observer, V represents those events that are directly visible for the observer, and N are all other events. An event system satisfies a security property if each BSP holds for the view and the set of possible system traces. BSPs that we will be using as examples in this paper are *BSD* and *BSIA*[1] defined as

$$BSD_{\mathcal{V}}(Tr) \iff [\forall \alpha,\beta \in E^*, c \in C. \ (\beta.\langle c \rangle.\alpha \in Tr \land \alpha|_C = \langle \rangle \tag{1}$$
$$\implies \exists \alpha' \in E^*, \tau' \in Tr. \ (\beta.\alpha' = \tau' \land \alpha'|_V = \alpha|_V \land \alpha'|_C = \langle \rangle))]$$

$$BSIA_{\mathcal{V}}^{\rho}(Tr) \iff [\forall \alpha,\beta \in E^*, c \in C. \ (\beta.\alpha \in Tr \land \alpha|_C = \langle \rangle \land Adm_{\mathcal{V}}^{\rho}(Tr,\beta,c) \tag{2}$$
$$\implies \exists \alpha' \in E^*, \tau' \in Tr. \ (\beta.\langle c \rangle.\alpha' = \tau' \land \alpha'|_V = \alpha|_V \land \alpha'|_C = \langle \rangle))]$$

where $\tau|_D$ is the projection of τ to the events in $D \subseteq E$. $Adm_{\mathcal{V}}^{\rho}(Tr,\beta,c)$ holds if the confidential event c is admissible after the trace β, when only events in the set $\rho(\mathcal{V})$ are considered, i.e. for all functions ρ from views over E to sets of events, we have $\forall \beta \in E^*, c \in C. \ Adm_{\mathcal{V}}^{\rho}(Tr,\beta,c) \iff \exists \gamma \in E^*. \ \gamma.\langle c \rangle \in Tr \land \gamma|_{\rho(\mathcal{V})} = \beta|_{\rho(\mathcal{V})}$.

A *state-event system* $SES = (E,I,O,S,s_0,T)$ consists of a set of events E, in- and output events I and O, a set of states S, an initial state $s_0 \in S$, and a transition relation $T \subseteq S \times E \times S$. T is required to be a partial function on $S \times E$, i.e. for each given state s and for each given event e there is at most one successor state s' for which $T(s,e,s')$, which we also write as $s \xrightarrow{e}_T s'$. We also write $s \xrightarrow{\alpha}_T s'$ if $\alpha = \langle \rangle$ and $s' = s$ or $\alpha = \langle e \rangle.\beta$ and there is a state s'' such that $s \xrightarrow{e}_T s''$ and $s'' \xrightarrow{\beta}_T s'$, and say that α is enabled in s, that s' is reachable from s, and write *reachable*(SES,s') if s' is reachable from s_0. $SES = (E,I,O,S,s_0,T)$ *induces* $ES = (E,I,O,Tr)$ iff $Tr = \{\alpha \mid \alpha$ enabled in s_0 for $SES\}$.

MAKS provides *unwinding conditions* that allow the local verification of BSPs. As examples for *unwinding theorems* [6], we have

- $lrf_{\mathcal{V}}(SES,\ltimes)$ and $osc_{\mathcal{V}}(SES,\ltimes)$ imply $BSD_{\mathcal{V}}(Tr)$ and
- $lrbe_{\mathcal{V}}^{\rho}(SES,\ltimes)$ and $osc_{\mathcal{V}}(SES,\ltimes)$ imply $BSIA_{\mathcal{V}}^{\rho}(Tr)$

where $\ltimes$ is an arbitrary relation over $S \times S$ and

$$osc_{\mathcal{V}}(SES,\ltimes) \iff \forall s_1,s_1',s_2' \in S, e \in E \setminus C. \tag{3}$$
$$reachable(SES,s_1) \land reachable(SES,s_1') \land s_1' \xrightarrow{e}_T s_2' \land s_1' \ltimes s_1$$
$$\implies \exists s_2 \in S, \delta \in (E \setminus C)^*. \ \delta|_V = \langle e \rangle|_V \land s_1 \xrightarrow{\delta}_T s_2 \land s_2' \ltimes s_2$$

---

[1] BSD stands for backwards-strict deletion and BSIA for backwards-strict insertion of admissible events.

$$lrf_{\mathcal{V}}(SES, \ltimes) \iff \forall s, s' \in S, c \in C.\ reachable(SES, s) \wedge s \xrightarrow{c}_T s' \implies s' \ltimes s \quad (4)$$

$$lrbe^{\rho}_{\mathcal{V}}(SES, \ltimes) \iff \forall s \in S, c \in C. \quad\quad\quad\quad\quad\quad\quad\quad\quad\quad\quad\quad (5)$$

$$reachable(SES, s) \wedge En^{\rho}_{\mathcal{V}}(SES, s, c) \implies \exists s' \in S.\ s \xrightarrow{c}_T s' \wedge s \ltimes s',$$

where $En^{\rho}_{\mathcal{V}}$, similarly to $Adm^{\rho}_{\mathcal{V}}$, models that the event c is enabled in state s:

$$\forall s \in S, c \in C.\ En^{\rho}_{\mathcal{V}}(SES, s, c) \Leftrightarrow \exists \beta, \gamma \in E^*, \bar{s}, \bar{s}' \in S.\ s_0 \xrightarrow{\beta} s \wedge \gamma|_{\rho(\mathcal{V})} = \beta|_{\rho(\mathcal{V})} \wedge s_0 \xrightarrow{\gamma}$$
$$\bar{s} \wedge \bar{s} \xrightarrow{c} \bar{s}'.$$

3   Non-interference Modulo

In MAKS a basic security predicate Θ is defined as a closure property on sets of traces. The idea behind using closure properties is the following. Suppose an attacker observes the visible events of a system run (while the confidential ones are invisible). We assume that attackers know all possible system runs, thus they know the set of all possible system runs which might have caused the observed behavior. In particular, an attacker knows the confidential events occurring in these possible runs, and can try to deduce constraints on the confidential events that must have occurred in the observed run. Information flow happens if the attacker is able to deduce knowledge about the occurrence or non-occurrence of confidential events beyond the knowledge already deducible from knowing the system specification, by inspecting the set of runs that are consistent with the observed behavior. A system is secure if this set of runs contains a *sufficient* variety of different possible sequences of confidential events. Closure properties are used to describe this variety because, intuitively, they demand that if there is a possible system run τ satisfying some precondition, then there is also another possible system run τ' such that the attacker cannot distinguish both. Suppose τ' in turn satisfies the precondition. Then we can inductively deduce the existence of another trace τ'' and so on. To assess the security of a system satisfying some basic security predicates we need to understand the guaranteed variance of traces wrt. confidential events being in the transitive closure $\{\tau, \tau', \tau'', \ldots\}$ of an observed system run τ.

3.1   An Example

As an example suppose, Alice uses e-banking, and she is required to change her authorization PIN periodically. For this purpose she uses a web interface to edit the PIN and to send it to the bank via some encrypted channel. The bank checks the new PIN and accepts it if it has been changed and rejects it if the new PIN is identical to the old one. We simplify this example by assuming that -1 is the old PIN. Figure 1 illustrates the possible traces of the corresponding system. The set V of visible events consists of all the messages that Alice exchanges with her bank: $V = \{\text{Send}(\text{enc}(i)) \mid i \in \mathbb{N} \cup \{-1\}\} \cup \{\text{Repl}(\text{enc}(\text{acc})), \text{Repl}(\text{enc}(\text{rej}))\}$. $C = \{\text{SetPIN}(i) \mid i \in \mathbb{N}\}$ is the set of confidential events that represent Alice changing her PIN to $i \neq -1$. The set of non-visible but deducible events N is empty. Let us now discuss three different scenarios depending on how the bank reacts to Alice's change requests.

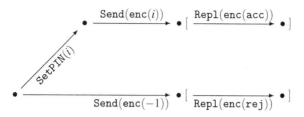

Fig. 1. Traces of Examples 1, 2, and 3

Example 1. Suppose the bank responds to all attempts of Alice to change her PIN. Thus the set of traces Tr is the smallest set with $\langle \text{SetPIN}(i), \text{Send}(\text{enc}(i)), \text{Repl}(\text{enc}(\text{acc})) \rangle$ $\in Tr$ for all $i \in \mathbb{N}$, $\langle \text{Send}(\text{enc}(-1)), \text{Repl}(\text{enc}(\text{rej})) \rangle \in Tr$, and Tr is closed under prefixes. Since in all cases Charly only sees two encrypted messages between Alice and her bank, he can never say whether Alice has changed her PIN. However, neither $BSD_{\mathcal{V}}$ nor $BSIA^{\rho}_{\mathcal{V}}$ (with $\rho(\mathcal{V}) = V$) hold for the system and the view $\mathcal{V} = (V, N, C)$. Consider for instance BSD: if we remove the confidential event $\text{SetPIN}(5)$ from the admissible trace $\langle \text{SetPIN}(5), \text{Send}(\text{enc}(5)) \rangle$ we end up in a non-admissible trace $\langle \text{Send}(\text{enc}(5)) \rangle$.

Example 2. Suppose now that the bank only rejects Alice's message $\text{Send}(\text{enc}(-1))$ and does not answer to any other message. Then the non-occurrence of a confidential event $\text{SetPIN}(i)$ is leaked, even if all the messages are encrypted: when Charly sees the second visible event, which is the encrypted reject, he knows that Alice has not changed her PIN.

Example 3. Finally suppose that the bank only acknowledges correct PINs by sending only $\text{Repl}(\text{enc}(\text{acc}))$ but no $\text{Repl}(\text{enc}(\text{rej}))$-messages, then the occurrence of a confidential event $\text{SetPIN}(i)$ is leaked. If Charly sees the second visible event, he knows that Alice has changed her PIN.

In the following we will use these three scenarios as running examples to illustrate our approach.

3.2   Definition of BSP Modulo $\approx$

While MAKS allows arbitrary closure properties as BSPs, all concrete instances are given in a more constructive way: they describe in a declarative way how to manipulate confidential events of the system run τ in order to obtain the confidential events of the postulated run τ'. Our examples, BSD and BSIA, simply add or remove, respectively, a single confidential event in τ to obtain τ' (*perturbation*), and they additionally allow the adjustment of the non-visible events of τ (*corrections*) to obtain a new possible trace τ'. Since we are only interested in traces which are consistent with a particular observed system behavior, τ and τ' have to cause the same observation for the attacker, i.e. $\tau|_V = \tau'|_V$.

   BSPs of this form can be represented with the help of two predicates, P and Q. P is used to select those runs τ that imply the existence of other runs τ'. Q is used to describe or analyze the form of the postulated τ'. We use $\bar{y}$ and $\bar{z}$ as technical means to refer to structural information about the related traces τ and τ' obtained by the predicates P and Q. Based on this structural information, the two functions $comp_\tau$ and $comp_{\tau'}$ construct or synthesize the traces from these substructures. Technically, all concrete BSPs in [5] satisfy the following pattern:

$$\Theta_{\mathcal{V}}(Tr) \longleftrightarrow \forall \bar{y} \in \bar{Y}.\ comp_\tau(\bar{y}) \subset Tr \wedge P(\bar{y}) \tag{6}$$
$$\implies \exists \bar{z} \in \bar{Z}.\ comp_{\tau'}(\bar{y}, \bar{z}) \in Tr \wedge Q(\bar{y}, \bar{z})$$

Roughly speaking, the basic security predicates Θ requires that if there is a trace $\tau = comp_\tau(\bar{y})$ in Tr satisfying some precondition $P(\bar{y})$, then there is also some trace $\tau' = comp_{\tau'}(\bar{y}, \bar{z})$ in Tr satisfying some postcondition $Q(\bar{y}, \bar{z})$.

3.3 Event Classes

We formalize the idea of non-distinguishable events by introducing an equivalence relation $\approx$ on visible events that identifies exactly those visible events that an observer cannot distinguish. In our examples we choose $\texttt{Send}(\texttt{enc}(i)) \approx \texttt{Send}(\texttt{enc}(j))$ for all $i, j \in \mathbb{N} \cup \{-1\}$ and $\texttt{Repl}(\texttt{enc}(\texttt{acc})) \approx \texttt{Repl}(\texttt{enc}(\texttt{rej}))$. Furthermore, our observer is also not able to identify two encrypted messages having the same content. Technically, this requirement can be obtained by implementing the encryption by using a so-called "salt". Then, encrypting the same message twice results in different ciphertexts.

We extend $\approx$ to the set E of events in the canonical way and write $e_\approx$ for the equivalence class of an event e. We also extend this notation to other sets that are uniformly constructed in terms of the set E, e.g. if $\langle e_1, \ldots, e_n \rangle \in E^*$ we write $\tau_\approx = \langle e_{1\approx}, \ldots, e_{n\approx} \rangle \in (E_\approx)^* = E_\approx^*$ for the sequence consisting of the equivalence classes of the events that occurred in τ and similarly for tuples $(e_1, \ldots, e_n)_\approx = (e_{1\approx}, \ldots, e_{n\approx})$ and sets $\{e_1, \ldots, e_n\}_\approx = \{e_{1\approx}, \ldots, e_{n\approx}\}$. $\mathcal{V}_\approx$ is always a view over $E_\approx$ given by $\mathcal{V}_\approx = (V_\approx, C_\approx, N_\approx)$ because $\approx$ only identifies events in V. Let $\omega \subseteq (E_\approx)^*$, then by abuse of notation we write $\alpha \in \omega$ for $\alpha_\approx = \omega$.

As mentioned before, the concrete BSPs in [5] are based on a fixed semantics of visibility. The closure property will guarantee the existence of different traces having identical sequences of visible events. However, this semantics is too restrictive for our purposes since we assume that an observer cannot distinguish between visible events in the same equivalence class. Hence, we adjust the definitions of BSPs in a uniform way to be in line with the changed semantics of visibility. First, a BSP Θ requires for all system traces τ that some constructed sequence τ' is also a system trace. While using the same functions $comp_\tau$ and $comp_{\tau'}$ to synthesize τ and τ' as in the original BSP, we weaken the requirements that τ' be a system trace: we only require that there is a system trace τ'' that is equivalent to τ' wrt. $\approx$. Since $\approx$ identifies only visible events, τ' and τ'' will coincide in their confidential and non-visible events. They only differ in the plain text of encrypted messages, a difference that an observer cannot notice by assumption. In general we also have to adjust the predicates P and Q to the changed semantics of visibility resulting in some predicates $\tilde{P}$ and $\tilde{Q}$. For example, when translating $BSIA^\rho$ in Def. 3 we have to adjust the notion of admissibility Adm such that we do not require the existence of a system trace $\alpha.\langle c \rangle$ but only the existence of a system trace that is *equivalent* to $\alpha.\langle c \rangle$. In general, we obtain the following pattern for a BSP modulo $\approx$:

$$\widetilde{\Theta}_\mathcal{V}(Tr) \iff \forall \bar{y} \in \overline{Y}.\ comp_\tau(\bar{y}) \in Tr \wedge \widetilde{P}(\bar{y}) \tag{7}$$
$$\implies \exists \bar{z} \in \overline{Z}.\ \exists \tau'' \in Tr.\ comp_{\tau'}(\bar{y},\bar{z}) \approx \tau'' \wedge \widetilde{Q}(\bar{y},\bar{z})\ .$$

As a first example consider the closure property *BSD*, cf. (1) on page 211. Since *BSD* does not involve additional pre- or postconditions, we can apply the pattern straightforwardly which results in the following modified basic security property:

Definition 1.

$$\widetilde{BSD}_\mathcal{V}(Tr) \iff [\forall\alpha,\beta \in E^*, c \in C.\ (\beta.\langle c\rangle.\alpha \in Tr \wedge \alpha|_C = \langle\rangle$$
$$\implies \exists\alpha' \in E^*, \tau' \in Tr.\ (\beta.\alpha' \approx \tau' \wedge \alpha'|_V = \alpha|_V \wedge \alpha'|_C = \langle\rangle))] \tag{8}$$

Let us apply the definition of $\widetilde{BSD}_\mathcal{V}$ to our examples. Consider all traces $\beta.\langle c\rangle.\alpha$ in which confidential events occur. This implies $c = \texttt{SetPIN}(i)$ for some $i \in \mathbb{N}$ and $\beta = \langle\rangle$, since a confidential event occurs only as the first event of a trace. Then, $\widetilde{BSD}_\mathcal{V}$ demands in our example that there is a system trace equivalent to α in which the PIN is not changed. In Example 1, Charly will observe an encrypted message from Alice to her bank and a response of the bank to Alice, regardless of whether Alice had changed her PIN or not. Formally, α is a prefix of $\langle\texttt{Send(enc}(i)),\texttt{Repl(enc(acc))}\rangle$. Let $\alpha' = \alpha$ and τ' the corresponding prefix of $\langle\texttt{Send(enc}(-1)),\texttt{Repl(enc(rej))}\rangle$ then $\beta.\alpha' = \tau'$ and $\widetilde{BSD}$ holds.

In Example 2, the bank only replies if Alice uses her old PIN. Observing the trace in which Alice changes her PIN, Charly is not able to distinguish this trace from the prefix of a trace in which Alice uses her old PIN. Formally, in this case α is a prefix of $\langle\texttt{Send(enc}(i))\rangle$. Again let $\alpha' = \alpha$ and τ' be the corresponding prefix of $\langle\texttt{Send(enc}(-1))\rangle$ then $\beta.\alpha' = \tau'$ and $\widetilde{BSD}$ holds. In Example 3, the bank acknowledges the changed PIN. Charly can observe this encrypted response and deduce that Alice has changed her PIN. Therefore, $\widetilde{BSD}$ is not satisfied: if we choose $\alpha = \langle\texttt{Send(enc}(i)),$ $\texttt{Repl(enc(acc))}\rangle$ we cannot find an appropriate α' which satisfies the requirement of $\widetilde{BSD}$. The only non-empty trace would be $\langle\texttt{Send(enc}(-1))\rangle$ which can be easily distinguished from α by the observer. Hence, $\widetilde{BSD}$ reveals that in Example 3 information about the occurrence of a high-level event is leaked. As expected it does not reveal the information leak about the non-occurrence of a confidential event in Example 2. For this purpose, the framework MAKS provides BSPs for inserting events, e.g. $BSIA^\rho_\mathcal{V}$ which is used to detect information leakages about the non-occurrence of confidential events. Thus, let us consider $BSIA^\rho_\mathcal{V}$ which involves a non-trivial $P(Tr,\beta,c) = Adm^\rho_\mathcal{V}(Tr,\beta,c)$.

Definition 2. *Let ρ be a function mapping views on $E = V \cup C \cup N$ to subsets of E and $\approx$ be an equivalence relation on V. ρ is compatible with $\approx$ iff for all views $\mathcal{V}$: $e_1 \approx e_2$ implies $e_1 \in \rho(\mathcal{V}) \iff e_2 \in \rho(\mathcal{V})$. If ρ is compatible with $\approx$ then we write $\rho_\approx$ for the uniquely defined function that maps views on $E_\approx = V_\approx \cup C_\approx \cup N_\approx$ to subsets of $E_\approx$ by $\rho_\approx(\mathcal{V}_\approx) = (\rho(\mathcal{V}))_\approx$. Let ρ be compatible with $\approx$ then $\widetilde{Adm}^\rho_\mathcal{V}$ is defined by:*

$$\forall\beta \in E^*, c \in C.\ \widetilde{Adm}^\rho_\mathcal{V}(Tr,\beta,c) \iff \exists\gamma \in E^*.\ \gamma.\langle c\rangle \in Tr\ and\ \gamma|_{\rho(\mathcal{V})} \approx \beta|_{\rho(\mathcal{V})}$$

Definition 3.

$$\widetilde{BSIA}^\rho_\mathcal{V}(Tr) \iff [\forall \alpha, \beta \in E^*, c \in C. (\beta.\alpha \in Tr \wedge \alpha|_C = \langle\rangle \wedge \widetilde{Adm}^\rho_\mathcal{V}(Tr, \beta, c) \quad (9)$$
$$\implies \exists \alpha' \in E^*, \tau' \in Tr. (\beta.\langle c\rangle.\alpha' \approx \tau' \wedge \alpha'|_V = \alpha|_V \wedge \alpha'|_C = \langle\rangle))]$$

Let us discuss this definition within our examples. Roughly speaking, $\widetilde{BSIA}$ requires that we can insert "admissible" confidential events into system traces and obtain again system traces. In our example, we only have SetPIN(i) as confidential events, and these are only admissible at the beginning of a trace. Thus, $\widetilde{Adm}^\rho_\mathcal{V}(Tr, \beta, c)$ is true iff $\beta = \langle\rangle$ and $c = $ SetPIN(i). Hence, for all $\alpha \in Tr$ we have to find a trace $\tau' \in Tr$ which produces the same visible behavior as $\langle$SetPIN(i)$\rangle.\alpha$ (since $N = \emptyset$, α and α' must be equal). In Example 1, α is a prefix of $\langle$Send(enc(-1)),Repl(enc(rej))$\rangle$, and with τ' being the corresponding prefix of $\langle$Send(enc(i)),Repl(enc(acc))$\rangle$, $\widetilde{BSIA}^\rho_\mathcal{V}$ is satisfied. In Example 3, α is a prefix of $\langle$Send(enc(-1))$\rangle$, and with τ' being a prefix of $\langle$Send(enc(i))$\rangle$, $\widetilde{BSIA}^\rho_\mathcal{V}$ is satisfied. However in Example 2, $\widetilde{BSIA}^\rho_\mathcal{V}$ does not hold: let $\alpha = \langle$Send(enc(-1)),Repl(enc(rej))$\rangle$ then there is no corresponding trace τ' producing the same observable behavior, because only prefixes of $\langle$SetPIN(i),Send(enc(i))$\rangle$ are possible traces. Thus, $\widetilde{BSIA}^\rho_\mathcal{V}$ reveals the information leakage in Example 2. Selecting the conjunction of $\widetilde{BSD}$ and $\widetilde{BSIA}^\rho_\mathcal{V}$ as the security predicate of our example reveals that both Examples 2 and 3 are insecure while Example 1 is secure.

3.4 Reduction of Θ Modulo $\approx$

In order to prove the security (in the meaning of information flow) of a given system we specify the security predicate as a conjunction of basic security predicates and prove each BSP, e.g., by using appropriate unwinding techniques. We can cope with encrypted messages by defining an appropriate equivalence relation on visible events and using the individual corresponding $\Theta_\approx$ instead of Θ.

Although each property $\Theta_\approx$ is itself a closure property of traces and, therefore, a BSP, it is not a member of those BSPs presented in [5]. Thus, *a priori* no unwinding result exists for $\Theta_\approx$. Rather than developing our own unwinding theorems for proving $\Theta_\approx$, we will reduce the problem of proving $\Theta_\approx$ in a given system to the problem of proving the related Θ in a transformed system. We obtain the transformed system by operating on classes of events instead of operating on individual events. Hence we define:

Definition 4. *Let $ES = (E, I, O, Tr)$ be an event system with $E = V \cup C \cup N$ and $\approx$ be an equivalence relation on V. Then, $ES_\approx$, the event system ES modulo $\approx$ is defined by $ES_\approx = \{E_\approx, I_\approx, O_\approx, Tr_\approx\}$ (with $Tr_\approx = \{\tau_\approx | \tau \in Tr\}$).*

Obviously, $ES_\approx$ is itself an event system. Note that the set of input and output events of $ES_\approx$ might not be disjoint, even if I and O are disjoint. However, input and output events are not required to be disjoint for event systems anyway.

Since $ES_\approx$ is an event system over the set of events $E_\approx$, we can require it to satisfy a given BSP relative to a view for $E_\approx$. We will now investigate the relationship between

ES satisfying $\widetilde{\Theta}_{\mathcal{V}}$ and $ES_{\approx}$ satisfying $\Theta_{\mathcal{V}_{\approx}}$. In particular we are interested in BSPs for which the two are equivalent.

Definition 5. *Let* Θ *and* Θ' *be two closure properties of traces, ES an event system,* $\mathcal{V}$ *a view, and* $\approx$ *an equivalence relation over V. We say that* Θ' *is* $\approx$*-reducible to* Θ *iff*
$$\Theta'_{\mathcal{V}}(Tr) \iff \Theta_{\mathcal{V}_{\approx}}(Tr_{\approx}).$$

In the rest of this section we will show that $\widetilde{BSD}$ is $\approx$-reducible to BSD, and similarly for $\widetilde{BSIA}$ and $BSIA$ with some restriction on admissible relations $\approx$.

Lemma 1. *Let* $D \subseteq E$ *be a set of events. Then*[2]
$$\forall \omega, \mu \in E_{\approx}^*. \ \omega|_{D_{\approx}} = \mu|_{D_{\approx}} \implies \forall \alpha \in \omega. \ \exists \alpha' \in \mu. \ \alpha|_D = \alpha'|_D . \tag{10}$$

Proof. By induction on the length of $\omega|_{D_{\approx}}$. *Base case*: let $\omega|_{D_{\approx}} = \langle \rangle = \mu|_{D_{\approx}}$. Thus $\omega, \mu \in (E_{\approx} \setminus D_{\approx})^*$ and $\alpha \in (E \setminus D)^*$. Let $\alpha' \in \mu$, then $\alpha' \in (E \setminus D)^*$ and $\alpha'|_D = \langle \rangle = \alpha|_D$. *Induction step*: let $\omega|_{D_{\approx}} \neq \langle \rangle$. Thus, there are $\omega_1, \omega_2 \in E_{\approx}^*$ and $u \in D_{\approx}$ such that $\omega = \omega_1.\langle u \rangle.\omega_2$ and $\omega_1|_{D_{\approx}} = \langle \rangle$. Analogously, we decompose μ by $\mu = \mu_1.\langle u \rangle.\mu_2$ with $\mu_1|_{D_{\approx}} = \langle \rangle$. Hence, $\alpha = \alpha_1.\langle e \rangle.\alpha_2$ with $\alpha_1 \in \omega_1$, $e \in u$ and $\alpha_2 \in \omega_2$. Let $\alpha'' \in \mu$. Thus $\alpha'' = \alpha_1''.\langle e' \rangle.\alpha_2''$ with $\alpha_1''|_D = \langle \rangle$, $e' \in u$ and $\alpha_2'' \in \mu_2$. Since $\omega_2|_{D_{\approx}} = \mu_2|_{D_{\approx}}$ and $\alpha_2 \in \omega_2$ the induction hypothesis implies that there is an $\alpha_2' \in \mu_2$ with $\alpha_2|_D = \alpha_2'|_D$. Let $\alpha' = \alpha_1''.\langle e \rangle.\alpha_2'$ then $(\alpha_1''.\langle e \rangle.\alpha_2')_{\approx} = \mu_1.\langle u \rangle.\mu_2 = \mu$ and $\alpha_1''.\langle e \rangle.\alpha_2'|_D = \langle \rangle.\langle e \rangle.\alpha_2'|_D = \alpha_1|_D.\langle e \rangle.\alpha_2|_D = \alpha|_D$. $\square$

Theorem 1. *Let* $\approx$ *be an equivalence relation on V then* $\widetilde{BSD}$ *is* $\approx$*-reducible to BSD.*

Proof. "$\Leftarrow$": Suppose, $ES_{\approx}$ satisfies $BSD_{\mathcal{V}_{\approx}}$ which means that for all $\omega, \mu \in E_{\approx}^*$ and $z \in C_{\approx}$, $(\mu.\langle z \rangle.\omega \in Tr_{\approx} \wedge \omega|_{C_{\approx}} = \langle \rangle)$ implies that there is a $\omega' \in E_{\approx}^*$ such that $\mu.\omega' \in Tr_{\approx} \wedge \omega'|_{V_{\approx}} = \omega|_{V_{\approx}} \wedge \omega'|_{C_{\approx}} = \langle \rangle$ holds. Let $\beta.\langle c \rangle.\alpha \in Tr$ for some $\alpha, \beta \in E^*$ and $c \in C$ such that $\alpha|_C = \langle \rangle$. Thus $\beta_{\approx}.\langle c_{\approx} \rangle.\alpha_{\approx} \in Tr_{\approx}$ and $\alpha_{\approx}|_{C_{\approx}} = \langle \rangle$. Since $ES_{\approx}$ satisfies $BSD_{\mathcal{V}}$ there is some $\omega' \in E_{\approx}^*$ with $\beta_{\approx}.\omega' \in Tr_{\approx}$, $\omega'|_{V_{\approx}} = \alpha_{\approx}|_{V_{\approx}}$, and $\omega'|_{C_{\approx}} = \langle \rangle$. Since $\omega'|_{V_{\approx}} = \alpha_{\approx}|_{V_{\approx}}$ and $\alpha \in \alpha_{\approx}$ Lemma 1 implies the existence of $\alpha'' \in \omega'$ such that $\alpha|_V = \alpha''|_V$. Since $\beta_{\approx}.\omega' \in Tr_{\approx}$ there are also $\alpha', \beta' \in E^*$ such that $\beta'.\alpha' \in Tr$, $\beta' \in \beta_{\approx}$, and $\alpha' \in \omega'$. Thus, first $\beta.\alpha'' \in \beta_{\approx}.\omega' = \beta'_{\approx}.\alpha'_{\approx} = (\beta'.\alpha')_{\approx}$. Second, $\alpha''|_V = \alpha|_V$ and finally, $\alpha''|_C = \alpha_{\approx}|_{C_{\approx}} = \langle \rangle$.

"$\Rightarrow$": Suppose, ES satisfies $\widetilde{BSD}_{\mathcal{V}}$ which means for all $\alpha, \beta \in E^*$ and $c \in C$, $(\beta.\langle c \rangle.\alpha \in Tr \wedge \alpha|_C = \langle \rangle)$ implies that there are $\alpha' \in E^*$ and $\tau' \in Tr$ such that $\beta.\alpha' \approx \tau'$, $\alpha'|_V = \alpha|_V$ and $\alpha'|_C = \langle \rangle$. Let $\omega, \mu \in E_{\approx}^*$ and $z \in C_{\approx}$ such that $\mu.\langle z \rangle.\omega \in Tr_{\approx}$ and $\omega|_{C_{\approx}} = \langle \rangle$. Thus, there are $\alpha, \beta \in E^*$ and $c \in C$ such that $\beta.\langle c \rangle.\alpha \in \mu.\langle z \rangle.\omega$, $\beta.\langle c \rangle.\alpha \in Tr$ and $\alpha|_C = \langle \rangle$. Since ES satisfies $\widetilde{BSD}_{\mathcal{V}}$, there is a $\alpha' \in E^*$ and a $\tau' \in Tr$ such that $\beta.\alpha' \approx \tau'$, $\alpha'|_V = \alpha|_V$, and $\alpha'|_C = \langle \rangle$. Therefore, $\beta_{\approx}.\alpha'_{\approx} = (\beta.\alpha')_{\approx} = \tau'_{\approx} \in Tr_{\approx}$, $\alpha'_{\approx}|_{V_{\approx}} = \alpha_{\approx}|_{V_{\approx}}$ and $\alpha'_{\approx}|_{C_{\approx}} = \langle \rangle$. $\square$

Lemma 2. *Let* ρ *be a function mapping views in E to subsets of E that is compatible with an equivalence relation* $\approx$ *on V. Then, for all* $Tr \subseteq E^*$*, for all* $\beta \in Tr$ *and* $c \in C$*:*
$$\widetilde{Adm}_{\mathcal{V}}^{\rho}(Tr, \beta, c) \iff Adm_{\mathcal{V}_{\approx}}^{\rho_{\approx}}(Tr_{\approx}, \beta_{\approx}, c_{\approx}).$$

---

[2] Remember that by definition $D_{\approx} = \{e_{\approx} | e \in D\} = \{\mu \in E_{\approx} | \mu \cap D \neq \emptyset\}$.

Proof. Suppose $\widetilde{Adm}^{\rho}_{\mathcal{V}}(Tr,\beta,c)$ holds for some $Tr \subseteq E^*$, $\beta \in Tr$, and $c \in C$ which means there is a $\gamma \in E^*$ such that $\gamma . \langle c \rangle \in Tr$ and $\gamma|_{\rho(\mathcal{V})} \approx \beta|_{\rho(\mathcal{V})}$. Then obviously, $\gamma_\approx . \langle c_\approx \rangle \in Tr_\approx$ and $\gamma_\approx|_{\rho_\approx(\mathcal{V}_\approx)} = \beta_\approx|_{\rho_\approx(\mathcal{V}_\approx)}$ such that $Adm^{\rho_\approx}_{\mathcal{V}_\approx}(Tr_\approx,\beta_\approx,c_\approx)$ holds.

Suppose $Adm^{\rho_\approx}_{\mathcal{V}_\approx}(Tr_\approx,\beta_\approx,c_\approx)$ holds which means there is a $\mu \in E^*_\approx$ such that $\mu . \langle c_\approx \rangle \in Tr_\approx$ and $\mu|_{\rho_\approx(\mathcal{V}_\approx)} = \beta|_{\rho_\approx(\mathcal{V}_\approx)}$. Since $\mu . \langle c_\approx \rangle \subset Tr_\approx$ there is some $\beta' \subset E^*$ with $\beta' . \langle c \rangle \subset Tr$ and $\beta' \in \mu$. Thus, $\beta'|_{\rho(\mathcal{V})_\approx} = \mu|_{\rho_\approx(\mathcal{V}_\approx)} = \beta_\approx|_{\rho_\approx(\mathcal{V}_\approx)}$ which implies $\beta'|_{\rho(\mathcal{V})} \approx \beta|_{\rho\mathcal{V}}$. $\square$

Theorem 2. *Let $\approx$ be an equivalence relation on V and ρ be compatible with $\approx$, then $\widetilde{BSIA}^{\rho}$ is $\approx$-reducible to $BSIA^{\rho_\approx}$.*

Proof. "$\Leftarrow$": Suppose, $ES_\approx$ satisfies $BSIA^{\rho_\approx}_{\mathcal{V}_\approx}$. Thus for all $\omega,\mu \in E^*_\approx$ and $z \in C_\approx$, $(\mu.\omega \in Tr_\approx \wedge \omega|_{C_\approx} = \langle \rangle \wedge Adm^{\rho_\approx}_{\mathcal{V}_\approx}(Tr_\approx,\mu,z))$ implies that there is a $\omega' \in E^*_\approx$ such that $\mu . \langle z \rangle . \omega' \in Tr_\approx \wedge \omega'|_{V_\approx} = \omega|_{V_\approx} \wedge \omega'|_{C_\approx} = \langle \rangle$ holds. Let $\beta.\alpha \in Tr$, $\alpha|_C = \langle \rangle$ and $\widetilde{Adm}^{\rho}_{\mathcal{V}}(Tr,\beta,c)$. Thus, $\beta_\approx.\alpha_\approx \in Tr_\approx$, $\alpha_\approx|_{C_\approx} = \langle \rangle$ and $Adm^{\rho_\approx}_{\mathcal{V}_\approx}(Tr_\approx,\beta_\approx,c_\approx)$ hold. Since $ES_\approx$ satisfies $BSIA^{\rho_\approx}_{\mathcal{V}_\approx}$ there is a $\omega' \in E^*_\approx$ such that $\beta_\approx . \langle c_\approx \rangle . \omega' \in Tr_\approx$, $\omega'|_{V_\approx} = \alpha_\approx|_{V_\approx}$ and $\omega'|_{C_\approx} = \langle \rangle$. Hence, we can find $\beta',\gamma \in E^*$ with $\beta' . \langle c \rangle . \gamma \in Tr$ such that $\beta' \in \beta_\approx$ and $\gamma \in \omega'$. This implies that $\gamma_\approx|_{V_\approx} = \alpha_\approx|_{V_\approx}$ which guarantees the existence of some $\gamma' \in \gamma_\approx$ with $\gamma'|_V = \alpha|_V$. Finally, $\beta . \langle c \rangle . \gamma' \approx \beta' . \langle c \rangle . \gamma \in Tr$ and $\gamma'|_V = \alpha|_V$ and $\gamma'|_C = \gamma'_\approx|_{C_\approx} = \gamma_\approx|_{C_\approx} = \omega'|_{C_\approx} = \langle \rangle$.

"$\Rightarrow$": Suppose, ES satisfies $\widetilde{BSIA}^{\rho}_{\mathcal{V}}$. Thus for all $\alpha,\beta \in E^*$ and $c \in C$, $(\beta.\alpha \in Tr \wedge \alpha|_C = \langle \rangle \wedge \widetilde{Adm}^{\rho}_{\mathcal{V}}(Tr,\beta,c))$ implies that there is some $\alpha' \in E^*$ and $\tau' \in Tr$ such that $\beta . \langle c \rangle . \alpha' \approx \tau'$ with $\alpha'|_V = \alpha|_V$ and $\alpha'|_C = \langle \rangle$. Let $\mu.\omega \in Tr_\approx$, $\omega|_{C_\approx} = \langle \rangle$ and $Adm^{\rho_\approx}_{\mathcal{V}_\approx}(Tr_\approx,\mu,z)$ for some $z \in C_\approx$. Then there are $\alpha,\beta \in E^*$ such that $\beta.\alpha \in Tr$, $(\beta.\alpha) \in \mu.\omega$ and $\alpha|_C = \langle \rangle$. Let $c \in z$. Then Lemma 3 implies $\widetilde{Adm}^{\rho}_{\mathcal{V}}(Tr,\beta,c)$. Since ES satisfies $\widetilde{BSIA}^{\rho}_{\mathcal{V}}$ there exist $\alpha' \in E^*, \tau' \in Tr$ such that $\beta . \langle c \rangle . \alpha' \approx \tau'$, $\alpha'|_V = \alpha|_V$ and $\alpha'|_C = \langle \rangle$. Thus $(\beta . \langle c \rangle . \alpha')_\approx = \beta_\approx . \langle z \rangle . \alpha'_\approx = \mu . \langle z \rangle . \alpha'_\approx$, $\alpha'_\approx|_{V_\approx} = \alpha_\approx|_{V_\approx}$, and $\alpha'_\approx|_{C_\approx} = \langle \rangle$. $\square$

Corollary 1. *Let $\approx$ be an equivalence relation on V, then $\widetilde{BSI}$ is $\approx$-reducible to BSI.*

Proof. Easy consequence of Theorem 2 with $\rho(\mathcal{V}) = E$. $\square$

We believe that for each BSP Θ of MAKS a corresponding $\widetilde{\Theta}$ can be defined such that $\widetilde{\Theta}$ is $\approx$-reducible to Θ for most equivalence relations $\approx$, but we have not checked the details yet.

4   Unwinding

In the previous section we have given a definition of security predicates modulo an equivalence relation $\approx$ on visible events. We have also shown that security predicates modulo $\approx$ can equivalently be expressed as security predicates applied to an event system transformed by $\approx$. This means that all results for given security predicates can be used to reason about security predicates modulo $\approx$. This applies, e.g., to compositionality results or unwinding results. In this section we will investigate the details of how unwinding results for a BSP Θ are used for $\widetilde{\Theta}$.

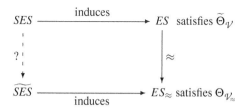

Fig. 2. Unwinding Θ modulo $\approx$.

Suppose, $SES = (E,I,O,S,s_0,T)$ is a state-event system that induces an event system $ES = (E,I,O,Tr)$. To prove that ES satisfies a BSP Θ wrt. a view $\mathcal{V}$ we have to show that, for some chosen unwinding relation $\ltimes$ on the set of states S, the unwinding conditions corresponding to Θ and $\mathcal{V}$ hold. Now we are interested in whether ES satisfies Θ, which – for $\approx$-reducible BSPs – can be reduced to the problem of proving that $ES_\approx$ satisfies Θ wrt. $\mathcal{V}_\approx$. We can show this property by unwinding if we find a state event system $\widetilde{SES}$ that induces $ES_\approx$ and for which we can show the unwinding conditions corresponding to $ES_\approx$, $\mathcal{V}_\approx$, and Θ, cf. Fig. 2 for a visualisation of this.

4.1 Unwinding for $\widetilde{SES}$

We are left with the construction of an appropriate state-event system $\widetilde{SES}$ that induces $ES_\approx$. Since the states in the original state-event system SES usually express the intuition about the system under consideration we construct the state-event system $\widetilde{SES}$ by using simply the set of states introduced for SES.

Definition 6. *Let* $SES = (E,I,O,S,s_0,T)$ *be a state-event system such that* $\widetilde{T}$ *defined by* $\forall s_1, s_2 \in S, u \in E_\approx.\ \widetilde{T}(s_1,u,s_2) \iff \exists e \in u.\ T(s_1,e,s_2)$ *is a partial function on* $S \times E_\approx$. *Then, the state-event system SES modulo* $\approx$, *is defined as* $\widetilde{SES} = (E_\approx, I_\approx, O_\approx, S, s_0, \widetilde{T})$.

Theorem 3. *For each* $\omega \in E_\approx^*$, ω *is enabled in* $\widetilde{SES}$ *iff* $\omega \in Tr_\approx$, *i.e.* $\widetilde{SES}$ *induces* $ES_\approx$.

To prove this we need the following lemma.

Lemma 3. *For all* $s \in S$ *and* $\omega \in E_\approx^*$, $s_0 \xrightarrow{\omega}_{\widetilde{T}} s$ *iff there is a* $\tau \in E^*$ *with* $\tau_\approx = \omega$ *such that* $s_0 \xrightarrow{\tau}_T s$.

Proof. By induction on the length of ω. *Base case:* trivial since $\omega = \langle\rangle$ and $\tau = \langle\rangle$. *Induction step:* assume that $\omega = \mu.\langle u \rangle$. The induction hypothesis yields that for all states $s' \in S$, $s_0 \xrightarrow{\mu}_{\widetilde{T}} s'$ iff there is an $\alpha \in E^*$ with $\alpha_\approx = \mu$ such that $s_0 \xrightarrow{\alpha}_T s'$. By Def. 6, $\widetilde{T}(s',u,s)$ iff there is an event $e \in u$ such that $T(s',e,s)$. Thus, $s_0 \xrightarrow{\mu.\langle u \rangle}_{\widetilde{T}} s$ iff there are α, e such that $e \in u$, $\alpha_\approx = \mu$, and $s_0 \xrightarrow{\alpha.\langle e \rangle}_T s$. $\square$

Proof (of Theorem 3). "$\Rightarrow$": ω is enabled in $\widetilde{SES}$, thus there is some $s \in S$ such that $s_0 \xrightarrow{\omega}_{\widetilde{T}} s$, which implies that there is some $\tau \in \omega$ with $s_0 \xrightarrow{\tau}_T s$ (by Lemma 3), and

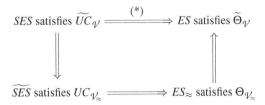

Fig. 3. Direct unwinding. Arrows represent logical implication.

because *SES* induces *ES* this implies $\tau \in Tr$, and finally $\omega = \tau_\approx \in Tr_\approx$ by definition of $Tr_\approx$.

"$\Leftarrow$": $\omega \in Tr_\approx$ implies there is some $\tau \in \omega$ with $\tau \in Tr$, thus $s_0 \xrightarrow{\tau}_T s$, which implies $s_0 \xrightarrow{\tau_\approx}_{\widetilde{T}} s$, and because of $\tau_\approx = \omega$, this implies that ω is enabled in $\widetilde{SES}$.   □

Now, existing unwinding theorems for Θ are directly applicable and we obtain the following theorem.

Theorem 4. *Let $\widetilde{SES}$ be a state-event system SES modulo $\approx$ and Θ be a $\approx$-reducible BSP with associated unwinding conditions UC_Θ. If $\widetilde{SES}$ satisfies UC_Θ wrt. $\mathcal{V}_\approx$ then ES satisfies Θ wrt. $\mathcal{V}$.*

The theorem allows us to lift all unwinding results for BSPs in MAKS to unwinding results for BSPs modulo $\approx$ provided the transition relation $\widetilde{T}$ of $\widetilde{SES}$ is functional. Suppose $\widetilde{T}$ is (in contrast to T) *not* a partial function. Thus, there is a state s that has several successor states wrt. a (visible) event $v_\approx$. This represents a spontaneous choice that is, on one hand, independent of the confidential behavior of the system but, on the other hand, hidden from the observer by the encryption. If the choice is not confidential, then there is no need to encrypt the event. But if the choice is confidential there should be a confidential event representing the choice and resolving the indeterminism. Thus we claim that the restriction of $\widetilde{T}$ being a partial function is not a serious restriction in practice. Netherless, if there should be realistic examples which require a non-functional $\widetilde{T}$, there is still the possibility to lift the approach to state-event systems with non-functional transition relations.

4.2   Direct Unwinding of Θ Modulo $\approx$

Given a state-event system *SES*, a view $\mathcal{V}$, an equivalence relation $\approx$ on V, and a $\approx$-reducible BSP Θ, Theorem 4 allows us to show that *SES* satisfies the security property Θ modulo $\approx$ wrt. $\mathcal{V}$ by unwinding. However, the unwinding conditions are properties of the state-event system $\widetilde{SES}$ involving universal quantifications over equivalence classes of events. For practical reasons, we would like to use unwinding conditions $\widetilde{UC}$ formulated on the *original* state event system *SES* as it is indicated by the arrow (*) in Fig. 3. In this case, we do not need to explicitly specify or construct $ES_\approx$ or $\widetilde{SES}$. Also, we do not even need to be able to express the construction of $ES_\approx$ or $\widetilde{SES}$ from *SES* in the specification language or mechanism we use. Furthermore, we can reason within the system that we have specified and, presumably, have some intuition about. Similarly to the argument in Sect. 3.4 we show for *BSD* and *BSIA* how direct unwinding relations are derived for specific BSPs. An analogous construction can be done for other BSPs.

We can show that a given system *SES* satisfies $BSD_{\mathcal{V}}$ modulo $\approx$ using Theorem 4, which is applicable if $\approx$ is an equivalence relation over V and $\widetilde{SES}$ is well-defined (i.e. T is such that $\widetilde{T}$ is functional according to Def. 6). The unwinding conditions that we have to show for *BSD* are $lrf_{\mathcal{V}_{\approx}}(\widetilde{SES}, \ltimes_1)$ and $osc_{\mathcal{V}_{\approx}}(\widetilde{SES}, \ltimes_1)$ for some arbitrary relation $\ltimes_1 \subseteq S \times S$ (cf. Sect. 2). Similarly, for $BSIA^{\rho}_{\mathcal{V}}$, we need to show that $\approx$ is an equivalence relation, that $\widetilde{T}$ is functional, that ρ is compatible with $\approx$ (cf. Theorem 2), and that the unwinding conditions $lrbe^{\rho_{\approx}}_{\mathcal{V}_{\approx}}(\widetilde{SES}, \ltimes_2)$ and $osc_{\mathcal{V}_{\approx}}(\widetilde{SES}, \ltimes_2)$ hold for some arbitrary relation $\ltimes_2 \subseteq S \times S$.

We can expand the definition of $SES_{\approx}$ in these conditions, and rewrite them so that they are formulated entirely in terms of *SES* and the equivalence relation $\approx$. As sufficient conditions for $BSD_{\mathcal{V}}$ we then get:

1. $\approx$ is an equivalence relation over V.
2. $\widetilde{T}$ is a partial function:

$$\forall s, s_1, s_2 \in S, e_1, e_2 \in E.\ e_1 \approx e_2 \wedge T(s, e_1, s_1) \wedge T(s, e_2, s_2) \implies s_1 = s_2\ .$$

3. The unwinding conditions *osc* (11) and *lrf* (12) hold:

$$\forall s_1, s'_1, s'_2 \in S, e \in E \setminus C. \tag{11}$$
$$reachable(SES, s_1) \wedge reachable(SES, s'_1) \wedge s'_1 \xrightarrow{e}_T s'_2 \wedge s'_1 \ltimes_1 s_1$$
$$\implies \exists s_2 \in S, \delta \in (E \setminus C)^*.\ \delta|_V \approx \langle e \rangle|_V \wedge s_1 \xrightarrow{\delta}_T s_2 \wedge s'_2 \ltimes_1 s_2 \quad \text{and}$$

$$\forall s, s' \in S, c \in C.\ reachable(SES, s) \wedge s \xrightarrow{c}_T s' \implies s' \ltimes_1 s\ . \tag{12}$$

Similarly, for $BSIA^{\rho}_{\mathcal{V}}$, we get Conditions 1. and 2. as above, and additionally we get:

3'. The unwinding conditions *osc* (11) with $\ltimes_1$ replaced by $\ltimes_2$, and *lrbe* (13) hold:

$$\forall s \in S, c \in C.\ reachable(SES, s) \wedge \widetilde{En}^{\rho}_{\mathcal{V}}(SES, s, c) \implies \tag{13}$$
$$\exists s' \in S.\ s \xrightarrow{c}_{\widetilde{T}} s' \wedge s \ltimes s'$$

with

$$\dot{En}^{\rho}_{\mathcal{V}}(SES, s, c) \iff$$
$$\exists \beta, \gamma \in E^*, s_1, s_2 \in S.\ s_0 \xrightarrow{\beta}_T s \wedge \gamma|_{\rho(\mathcal{V})} \approx \beta|_{\rho(\mathcal{V})} \wedge s_0 \xrightarrow{\gamma}_T s_1 \wedge s_1 \xrightarrow{c}_T s_2$$

All these conditions do no longer refer to the equivalence classes and can directly be formulated in the language and formalism in which the original state-event system was formulated.

4.3 An Example

We return to Example 1 presented in Sect 3.1, for which a specification in form of a state-event system can be given as follows. Let $S = (\mathbb{N} \cup \{-1\}) \times (\mathbb{N} \cup \{-1, \bot\}) \times$

$\{0,1,\perp\}$, and write $\{\mathtt{pin}=i;\mathtt{sent}=j;\mathtt{answered}=k\}$ for $(i,j,k)\in S$. The start state is $s_0=(-1,\perp,\perp)=\{\mathtt{pin}=-1;\mathtt{sent}=\perp;\mathtt{answered}=\perp\}$. The transition relation T is given by the following pre-/postcondition (PP) statements [6], where, e.g., the first one means that $T(s,\mathtt{SetPIN}(i),s')$ iff $s=(-1,j,k)$ and $s'=(i,j,k)$ (for $i\in\mathbb{N}$ and any j,k).

- $\mathtt{SetPIN}(i:\mathbb{N})$: modifies pin; pre: $\mathtt{pin}=-1$; post: $\mathtt{pin}'=i$.
- $\mathtt{Send}(\mathtt{enc}(i:\mathbb{N}\cup\{-1\}))$: modifies sent;
$$\text{pre: }\mathtt{sent}=\perp\wedge\mathtt{pin}=i;\text{ post: }\mathtt{sent}'=i.$$
- $\mathtt{Repl}(\mathtt{enc}(\mathtt{acc}))$: modifies answered;
$$\text{pre: }\mathtt{sent}\in\mathbb{N};\text{ post: }\mathtt{answered}=1.$$
- $\mathtt{Repl}(\mathtt{enc}(\mathtt{rej}))$: modifies answered;
$$\text{pre: }\mathtt{sent}=-1;\text{ post: }\mathtt{answered}=0.$$

It is easy to check that T is a partial function and that this SES induces the ES given in Example 1. Define $\approx$ to be the smallest relation such that $\mathtt{Send}(\mathtt{enc}(x))\approx\mathtt{Send}(\mathtt{enc}(y))$ for all x,y and $\mathtt{Repl}(\mathtt{enc}(\mathtt{acc}))\approx\mathtt{Repl}(\mathtt{enc}(\mathtt{rej}))$.

We now show conditions 1.–3. and 3' given in the preceding section. $\approx$ is trivially an equivalence relation, so Condition 1. holds. $\widetilde{T}$ is a partial function provided that the successor states s' are uniquely determined by the relations $\widetilde{T}(s,\mathtt{Send}(\ldots)_{\approx},s')$ and $\widetilde{T}(s,\mathtt{Repl}(\mathtt{enc}(\mathtt{acc}))_{\approx},s')$. Since two events $\mathtt{Send}(\mathtt{enc}(i))$ and $\mathtt{Send}(\mathtt{enc}(j))$ with $i\neq j$ are never both enabled in the same state (which also holds for $\mathtt{Repl}(\mathtt{enc}(\mathtt{acc}))$ and $\mathtt{Repl}(\mathtt{enc}(\mathtt{rej}))$), also $\widetilde{T}$ is a partial function, and Condition 2 holds.

Finding a viable unwinding relation is relatively easy in this case: for proving *BSD*, since s_0 is reachable and $\mathtt{SetPIN}(i)$ enabled, *lrf* requires that for $i\in\mathbb{N}$

$$\{\mathtt{pin}=i,\mathtt{sent}=\perp,\mathtt{answered}=\perp\}\bowtie_1\{\mathtt{pin}=-1,\mathtt{sent}=\perp,\mathtt{answered}=\perp\}$$

and similar consideration with *osc* yield that we also have $(i,i,\perp)\bowtie_1(-1,-1,\perp)$ and $(i,i,1)\bowtie_1(-1,-1,0)$. In the specific case, we can make $\bowtie$ symmetric and include unreachable state-pairs in the relation – this will later allow us to reuse the relation for proving *BSIA*. We will therefore use the following symmetric definition of $\bowtie$ for $\bowtie_1$ and $\bowtie_2$ (and write $\bowtie$ instead of $\bowtie_i$).

$$(i_1,j_1,k_1)\bowtie(i_2,j_2,k_2)\iff$$
$$(j_1=j_2=\perp)\text{ or }(k_1=k_2=\perp\wedge j_1\neq\perp\wedge j_2\neq\perp)\text{ or }(k_1\neq\perp\wedge k_2\neq\perp).$$

The unwinding conditions can now be shown to hold for the $\bowtie$ that we have defined.

- *lrf*: Let c be a confidential event, and let s be a reachable state, in which c is enabled. This fixes c to be of the form $\mathtt{SetPIN}(i)$ and $s=s_0$. In the result state s', we have sent and answered unchanged equal to $\perp$, so $s'\bowtie s_0$, and *lrf* holds.
- *lrbe^p*: Similarly, the only state in which a confidential event is enabled is s_0, and the successor state s' again has sent and answered unchanged equal to $\perp$, i.e. we have $s_0\bowtie s'$ and *lrbe^p* holds.
- *osc*: We have to look at all states and all non-confidential events that are enabled. Case distinction over non-confidential events:

- $e = \mathtt{Send}(\mathtt{enc}(i))$ is enabled in s'_1 only if $\mathtt{sent} = \bot$, and in the successor state s'_2 we will have $\mathtt{sent} \neq \bot$ but $\mathtt{answered} = \bot$ unchanged. For any other state $s_1 \bowtie s'_1$ we also have $\mathtt{sent} = \bot$, and in the successor state s_2 we thus have $\mathtt{sent} \neq \bot$ but $\mathtt{answered} = \bot$ unchanged, and this yields $s'_2 \bowtie s_2$.
- $e = \mathtt{Repl}(\mathtt{enc}(\mathtt{acc}))$ is enabled if $\mathtt{sent} = i$ (for $i \in \mathbb{N}$) and $\mathtt{answered} = \bot$ (by reachability). Any reachable state in relation $\bowtie$ will also have $\mathtt{answered} = \bot$ but might have $\mathtt{sent} = -1$, in which case $\mathtt{Repl}(\mathtt{enc}(\mathtt{rej})) \approx e$ is enabled. In any case, the successor states will both have $\mathtt{answered} \neq \bot$ and will therefore be in relation $\bowtie$.
- $e = \mathtt{Repl}(\mathtt{enc}(\mathtt{rej}))$ is similar, except that $\mathtt{Repl}(\mathtt{enc}(\mathtt{acc}))$ and $\mathtt{Repl}(\mathtt{enc}(\mathtt{rej}))$ are exchanged.

Note that for Example 2 (without the $\mathtt{Repl}(\mathtt{enc}(\mathtt{acc}))$-event) or Example 3 (without $\mathtt{Repl}(\mathtt{enc}(\mathtt{rej}))$), we fail to prove *osc*. This is consistent with the earlier observation that Example 1 is secure while Examples 2 and 3 are not.

5 Conclusion

We presented an approach to investigate possibilistic information flow security for systems that include the exchange of encrypted messages. The work was motivated by open problems arising in an investigation [14] of information flow security for a scenario of comparison shopping agents. The idea of the approach is to identify events corresponding to messages that an observer cannot distinguish because of the encryption. It has been integrated into an existing framework for possibilistic information flow control which now allows its application to a wider range of scenarios.

Compared to modeling encrypted channels using intransitive information flow policies, we can investigate whether the encryption actually prevents confidential information from leaking, or whether the occurrence of encrypted messages provides a covert channel. In the future we intend to apply our approach to further examples. Also we are interested in a combination of our approach with security protocol analysis, in particular in how our assumptions about confidential keys relates to the results of the other technique.

Acknowledgements

We would like to thank Serge Autexier, Heiko Mantel, and the anonymous reviewers for helpful comments on previous versions of this paper.

References

1. R. Focardi, A. Ghelli, and R. Gorrieri. Using non interference for the analysis of security protocols. In *Proceedings of the DIMACS Workshop on Design and Formal Verification of Security Protocols*, Rutgers University, 1997.
2. J. A. Goguen and J. Meseguer. Security policies and security models. In *Proceedings of the IEEE Symposium on Security and Privacy*. IEEE Computer Society, 1982.

3. J. A. Goguen and J. Meseguer. Inference control and unwinding. In *Proceedings of the IEEE Symposium on Security and Privacy*. IEEE Computer Society, 1984.

4. P. Laud. Handling encryption in an analysis for secure information flow. In *Proceedings of the 12th European Symposium on Programming*, volume 2618 of *LNCS*. Springer, 2003.

5. H. Mantel. Possibilistic definitions of security – an assembly kit. In *Proceedings of the IEEE Computer Security Foundations Workshop*. IEEE Computer Society, 2000.

6. H. Mantel. *A Uniform Framework for the Formal Specification and Verification of Information Flow Security*. PhD thesis, Universität des Saarlandes, 2003. Published as a manuscript.

7. J. D. McLean. Proving noninterference and functional correctness using traces. *Journal of Computer Security*, 1(1):37–57, 1992.

8. C. Meadows. The NRL protocol analyzer: An overview. *Journal of Logic Programming*, 26(2):113–131, 1996.

9. L. C. Paulson. Proving security protocols correct. In *Proceedings the 14th Annual IEEE Symposium on Logic in Computer Science*. IEEE Computer Society, 1999.

10. S. Pinsky. Absorbing covers and intransitive non-interference. In *Proceedings of IEEE Symposium on Security and Privacy*. IEEE Computer Society, 1995.

11. A.W. Roscoe and M.H. Goldsmith. What is intransitive noninterference. In *Proceedings of the 12th IEEE Computer Security Foundations Workshop*. IEEE Computer Society, 1999.

12. J. Rushby. Noninterference, transitivity, and channel-control security policies. Technical Report CSL-92-02, SRI International, Menlo Park, CA, 1992.

13. P.Y.A. Ryan and S.A Schneider. Process algebra and non-interference. *Journal of Computer Security*, 9(1/2):75–103, 2001.

14. I. Schaefer. Information flow control for multiagent systems - a case study on comparison shopping. Master's thesis, Universität Rostock / DFKI, September 2003.

15. D. M. Volpano. Secure introduction of one-way functions. In *Proceedings of the 13th IEEE Computer Security Foundations Workshop,*. IEEE Computer Society, 2000.

16. A. Zakinthinos and E. S. Lee. A general theory of security properties. In *Proceedings of the IEEE Symposium on Security and Privacy*. IEEE Computer Society, 1997.

Information Flow Control Revisited: Noninfluence = Noninterference + Nonleakage

David von Oheimb

Siemens CT IC Sec, Munich

Abstract. We revisit the classical notion of noninterference for state-based systems, as presented by Rushby in 1992. We strengthen his results in several ways, in particular clarifying the impact of transitive vs. intransitive policies on unwinding. Inspired partially by Mantel's observations on unwinding for event systems, we remove the restriction on the unwinding relation to be an equivalence and obtain new insights in the connection between unwinding relations and observational preorders.
Moreover, we make two major extensions. Firstly, we introduce the new notion of nonleakage, which complements noninterference by focusing not on the observability of actions but the information flow during system runs, and then combine it with noninterference, calling the result noninfluence. Secondly, we generalize all the results to (possibilistic) nondeterminism, introducing the notions of uniform step consistency and uniform local respect. Finally, we share our experience using nonleakage to analyze the confidentiality properties of the Infineon SLE66 chip.
Like Rushby's, our theory has been developed and checked using a theorem prover, so there is maximal confidence in its rigor and correctness.

1 Introduction

Noninterference, a very strong, abstract and mathematically elegant way of expressing secrecy, has been introduced more than two decades ago by Goguen and Meseguer [GM82,GM84]. Since then, a large body of work ([Sut86,Fol87,McC90], [Rya90,McL94,ZL97,Man00], etc.) has grown generalizing noninterference to non-deterministic systems, leading to a variety of definitions that partially coincide or exhibit subtle differences. A systematic overview is given by Mantel [Man03].

A further dimension of generalization is towards information flow policies that are not transitive, used for describing downgrading, information filters and channel control. The notion of *intransitive noninterference* [HY86,Rus92,Pin95] has caused some difficulties and debate. Also Roscoe and Goldsmith [RG99] motivate and explain intransitive noninterference, but on the other hand add new confusion: they criticize the classical definition via the *ipurge* function, giving examples of wrongly implemented downgraders and attributing the problem to limitations of the expressiveness of purging, yet the actual problem is at least in part due to the semantical discrepancies (i.e., the implementation errors) that they assume and not due to intransitivity. Nevertheless, we believe that intransitive noninterference is a notion both valid and practically useful, thus we make sure not to limit ourselves to the transitive case.

P. Samarati et al. (Eds.): ESORICS 2004, LNCS 3193, pp. 225–243, 2004.

Many approaches focus on event systems and therefore typically use variants of process algebras like CSP as the underlying system model. Yet most systems that appear in practice are heavily state-oriented. Consequently, when it comes to their security, the flow of information contained in the system state often is the only thing that really matters or is at least as important as the visibility of actions or I/O events. Though state-oriented systems can be described in event-oriented formalisms, we feel that this is not very natural. Our aim is to have a theory of secure information flow as simple and abstract as possible that models state-oriented systems directly, hence we use plain state automata as the underlying system model. Furthermore, we require verification techniques like unwinding theorems implemented in a theorem proving system usable for practical security analysis. Moreover, we want to cover both deterministic and (non-total) nondeterministic systems and both transitive and intransitive policies. We are not aware of a theory that meets all these requirements – for instance, both McCullough's restrictiveness [McC90] and the contemporary language-based security [SM03] handle deterministic and nondeterministic state-based systems but not intransitive policies. So we decided to develop our own theory.

Rushby's work [Rus92], using simple automata and handling intransitive non-interference yet not nondeterminism, appeared as a good starting point. We have implemented a slight variant of his theory, using the state-of-the-art theorem prover Isabelle/HOL [NPW02], removing some unnecessary limitations, extending it as straightforwardly as possible to nondeterministic systems, and introducing a hierarchy of variants of noninterference that concentrate to various extents on information flow between domains. The complete theory sources including proofs are available online [Ohe04]. There is some closely related work by Mantel [Man01,Man03] that also handles nondeterminism and unwinding for intransitive noninterference. It deals with a large number of variants of noninterference in a systematic way, but is event-oriented and not implemented in a theorem prover. We give more comments on the similarities and differences to his approach in the course of presenting our development.

2   System Model

We use two simple automaton models for describing systems as deterministic or nondeterministic state machines. Each action a of type $action$ transforms the $state$ via a total transition function $step(a)$, following Rushby [Rus92], or a (possibly partial and nonfunctional) transition relation $Step(a)$, respectively[1].

$step : \; action \; \times \; state \; \rightarrow \; state$
$Step : \; action \; \rightarrow \; \wp(state \; \times \; state)$

Runs of a system are described by lifting steps over action sequences.

$run : \; action^* \; \times \; state \; \rightarrow \; state$
$Run : \; action^* \; \rightarrow \; \wp(state \; \times \; state)$

---

[1] Whenever there is a direct correspondence between the deterministic and the non-deterministic case, we use the same names except that the versions for the latter case are capitalized in part.

They are defined by straightforward primitive recursion:

def $run([], s) \equiv s$
def $run(a \frown \alpha, s) \equiv run(\alpha, step(a, s))$
def $Run([]) \equiv \{(s, s) \mid True\}$
def $Run(a \frown \alpha) \equiv \{(s, t) \mid \exists s'. \ (s, s') \in Step(a) \ \wedge \ (s', t) \in Run(\alpha)\}$

In the above definitions, '$[]$' stands for the empty sequence and '$a \frown \alpha$' denotes the action sequence α with the action a prepended to it.

The initial system state, used for defining classical noninterference even in the nondeterministic case, is denoted by s_0.

Each action is associated with a security *domain* used to describe both restrictions on its own visibility and the portion of the state it may read from.

$$dom : \ action \ \to \ domain$$

There is an output function defined on *state* yielding some value(s) of type *output*. Output is not associated with an action but with the state alone, i.e., we model systems as Moore automata. In order to express the observations possible for each security domain, the output function receives an extra parameter of type *domain*. In this respect, we deviate slightly from Rushby's system model which uses Mealy automata where output depends on the security domain indirectly via the domain associated with actions.

$$output : \ domain \ \times \ state \ \to \ output$$

We use *domain* instead of *action* as the extra parameter of *output* because this slightly simplifies some formulations and allows both a more direct interpretation of access control and an easier comparison with nonleakage.

3   Generic Notions

3.1   Policies

Central to noninterference and its derivatives is the notion of a *policy*,

$$\cdot \rightsquigarrow \cdot : \ \wp(domain \ \times \ domain)$$

also called *interference relation*. It expresses that information is allowed to flow from the first domain to the second. The complementing relation, $\not\rightsquigarrow$, is called *noninterference relation*. Classical multi-level security policies induce a transitive interference relation, but others are intransitive: they allow indirect information flow via privileged channels like a censoring downgrader or an encryption engine while a direct (short-circuit) flow is prohibited.

As usual, we globally assume reflexivity of policies: $\forall u. \ u \rightsquigarrow u$. Other assumptions are of local nature. For instance, for part of our results, transitivity of policies is required (but only where explicitly stated).

3.2   Allowed Source Domains

In order to express the allowed information flow between domains for (in general) intransitive policies, we employ the auxiliary function *sources* [Rus92]. It takes a sequence of actions α and a target domain u and yields the set of domains that are allowed to pass information to u immediately or indirectly via (a subsequence of) α. The following definition is equivalent to the classical one:

$$sources : action^* \times domain \rightarrow \wp(domain)$$

def $sources([], u) \equiv \{u\}$

def $sources(a \frown \alpha, u) \equiv sources(\alpha, u) \cup$
$$\{w| \; \exists v. \; dom(a) = w \; \wedge \; w \rightsquigarrow v \; \wedge \; v \in sources(\alpha, u)\}$$

For example, a sufficient condition for $v \in sources(a_1 \frown a_2 \frown a_3 \frown a_4 \frown [], u)$ is $v = dom(a_2) \; \wedge \; dom(a_2) \rightsquigarrow dom(a_4) \; \wedge \; dom(a_4) \rightsquigarrow u$ (even if $v \not\rightsquigarrow u$).

For defining weak nonleakage in §5.3, we will use a second variant called *chain*. It can be derived from the above definition by leaving out the restriction $dom(a) = w$ on the chain elements. This variant yields all domains connected with the given domain via the relation $\{(u, u)| \; True\} \cup \rightsquigarrow \cup (\rightsquigarrow)^2 \cup \ldots \cup (\rightsquigarrow)^n$ where n is the length of the action sequence given as the first argument.

Obviously, *sources* yields a subset of the result of *chain*, i.e. $sources(\alpha, u) \subseteq chain(\alpha, u)$. Moreover, in the case of transitive policies, *chain* yields a subset of $\rightsquigarrow$, in the sense that $chain(\alpha, u) \subseteq \{w| \; w \rightsquigarrow u\}$.

3.3   Unwinding Relations

Central for both the well-known unwinding results and our extensions is the *unwinding relation* on states, parameterized by the observing domain u:

$$\cdot \overset{\cdot}{\sim} \cdot : \; domain \rightarrow \wp(state \times state)$$

Classically, this relation is a *view-partitioning* equivalence [Rus92,ZM01] expressing indistinguishability of states from u's perspective. In most applications, it is simply a pointwise equation on the contents of those variables that u may observe. Zdancewic and Myers [ZM01] call this a *view* of a system S and use it for defining an observational equivalence, $S[\approx]$, on stuttering-equivalent traces. In order to maintain confidentiality of information contained in the system state, the unwinding relation is to be preserved locally by every computation step.

Regarding the unwinding relation to be an equivalence is intuitive and valid for most cases, yet Mantel pointed out that unwinding does not really require symmetry [Man00], neither reflexivity nor transitivity [Man03], and that in some applications the relation is e.g. intransitive[2]. Inspired partially by his results, we allow for arbitrary unwinding relations as long as they imply the observational equivalence (or preorder, respectively) induced by the *output* function. Only for the unwinding theorems of noninterference, it has to be assumed that for all observers the initial state is in unwinding relation with itself: $\forall u. \; s_0 \overset{u}{\sim} s_0$

The unwinding relation is lifted in the canonical way to sets of domains, inheriting any reflexivity, symmetry, and transitivity properties.

$$\cdot \overset{\cdot}{\approx} \cdot : \; \wp(domain) \rightarrow \wp(state \times state)$$

def $s \overset{U}{\approx} t \equiv \forall u \in U. \; s \overset{u}{\sim} t$

---

[2] This is not to be confused with intransitivity of the information flow policy.

4   Noninterference

In this section, we slightly improve the theory of noninterference as presented by Rushby in [Rus92]. Moreover, we extend the results to nondeterministic systems. Also in the two subsequent sections introducing nonleakage and noninfluence, we will handle both the deterministic and the nondeterministic case, displaying the inherent parallelism between the two cases as far as appropriate.

4.1   Purging

We define the classical purge function filtering out confidential events with respect to (generally) intransitive policies, as introduced in [Rus92]:

$$ipurge : domain \times action^* \rightarrow action^*$$
def $ipurge(u, []) \equiv []$
def $ipurge(u, a \frown \alpha) \equiv if \; dom(a) \in sources(a \frown \alpha, u)$
$$then \; a \frown ipurge(u, \alpha) \; else \; ipurge(u, \alpha)$$

For example, $ipurge(a_1 \frown a_2 \frown a_3 \frown a_4 \frown [], u) = a_2 \frown a_4 \frown []$ if a_1 and a_3 may not directly nor indirectly (i.e., via any of their successors in the given chain of actions) influence u, but if a_4 does so directly (i.e., $dom(a_4) \rightsquigarrow u$ holds) and a_2 indirectly, via $dom(a_2) \rightsquigarrow dom(a_4)$. Generally, $ipurge$ enjoys properties like

lemma $sources\_ipurge : sources(ipurge(u, \alpha), u) = sources(\alpha, u)$
lemma $ipurge\_idempotent : ipurge(u, ipurge(u, \alpha)) = ipurge(u, \alpha)$

If we replace the condition $dom(a) \in sources(a \frown \alpha, u)$ by $dom(a) \rightsquigarrow u$, we obtain the simpler variant typically used for transitive policies, which we call $tpurge$. It can be shown that there is a very intuitive characterization of $tpurge$, namely: $tpurge(u, \alpha)$ removes from α all actions a with $dom(a) \not\rightsquigarrow u$. Moreover, as already stated by Rushby, $tpurge$ coincides with $ipurge$ in the case of transitive policies. Therefore, in the following we will use only $ipurge$ because it covers both the transitive and the general (possibly intransitive) case.

4.2   The Deterministic Case

General version. The essence of noninterference is that an observer cannot tell the difference between any system run and the variant of it obtained by removing ("purging") all events that he is not allowed to notice directly or indirectly. In order to formulate this notion and its derivatives in a concise way, we first define an *observational equivalence* relation on the state with an associated action sequence. The equivalence is parameterized by the observing domain and is induced by the *output* function applied to the final state after executing the respective action sequence.

$$\cdot \triangleleft \cdot \overset{\cdot}{\simeq} \cdot \triangleleft \cdot : domain \rightarrow \wp(state \times action^* \times state \times action^*)$$
def $s \triangleleft \alpha \overset{u}{\simeq} t \triangleleft \beta \equiv output(u, run(\alpha, s)) = output(u, run(\beta, t))$

Using this relation, classical noninterference can be written as

def $noninterference \equiv \forall \alpha \; u. \; s_0 \triangleleft \alpha \overset{u}{\simeq} s_0 \triangleleft ipurge(u, \alpha)$

Unwinding reduces this global security property to a set of local, step-wise properties, in particular the two complementing ones introduced in [Rus92]:

- *step consistency* : $s \overset{u}{\sim} t \longrightarrow step(a,s) \overset{u}{\sim} step(a,t)$, preserves the unwinding relation for each action a. Its meaning is that the effects of executing a on s and t as far as observable by the domain u, expressed by $step(a,s) \overset{u}{\sim} step(a,t)$, may depend on the previous values in the states s and t observable by u, expressed by $s \overset{u}{\sim} t$, but on nothing else. This property is used in the case that the domain of the action to be performed, $dom(a)$, is allowed to interfere with the observing domain u, i.e. $dom(a) \rightsquigarrow u$.
- *local respect* : $dom(a) \not\rightsquigarrow u \longrightarrow s \overset{u}{\sim} step(a,s)$ handles the opposite case.

We weaken (thus effectively generalize) Rushby's definition of step consistency:

def *weakly_step_consistent* $\equiv$ [3]
$$\forall a\, u\, s\, t.\ dom(a) \rightsquigarrow u\ \wedge\ s \overset{dom(a)}{\sim} t\ \wedge\ s \overset{u}{\sim} t \longrightarrow step(a,s) \overset{u}{\sim} step(a,t)$$

by adding two premises which make step consistency easier to establish in applications. Firstly, $dom(a) \rightsquigarrow u$ states that action a is allowed to interfere with the observing domain u. This is just an enhancement of convenience because in the other case, $dom(a) \not\rightsquigarrow u$, the property can be obtained from local respect.

Secondly, the premise $s \overset{dom(a)}{\sim} t$ is present not only in the intransitive case, as it was before. It allows that the effects of a depend also on the observables of $dom(a)$, the "official" input domain that the action a may read from. In Figure 1,

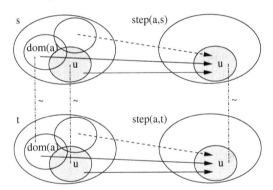

Fig. 1. data flow if $dom(a) \rightsquigarrow u$

the large ovals give an extensional view of all variables in the system state. The small ovals describe (possibly overlapping) subsets of them – the standard interpretation of security domains. The solid arrows depict allowed information flow into the domain u induced by a, while the dashed arrow depicts forbidden flow. Since the information flow from $dom(a)$ additionally allowed here is both very natural and important in applications, the "ordinary" step consistency is too strong. Adding the extra premise also for the transitive case is sound, as our main unwinding theorem confirms. Rushby does not state this sharpened result, although he compares the transitive and the intransitive case in detail.

---

[3] We adopt the convention that '$\wedge$' binds stronger than '$\longrightarrow$'

Like Mantel [Man00], we split Rushby's notion of local respect into a left-hand and right-hand variant, which allows us to remove the symmetry constraint on the unwinding relation. Moreover, we transform local respect such that it preserves rather than introduces the unwinding relation. This not only relieves us from requiring transitivity of the unwinding relation, but also yields a stronger observational preorder for the nondeterministic case than Mantel's (see §5.6).

def $local\_respect\_left \equiv \forall a\ u\ s\ t.\ dom(a) \not\rightsquigarrow u\ \wedge\ s \overset{u}{\sim} t \longrightarrow step(a,s) \overset{u}{\sim} t$

def $local\_respect\_right \equiv \forall a\ u\ s\ t.\ dom(a) \not\rightsquigarrow u\ \wedge\ s \overset{u}{\sim} t \longrightarrow s \overset{u}{\sim} step(a,t)$

def $local\_respect \equiv local\_respect\_left\ \wedge\ local\_respect\_right$

One can show easily that under the assumption that the unwinding relation is an equivalence, these definitions coincide with the classical one recalled above.

In the proof of the unwinding theorem for both noninterference and nonleakage, a consequence of local respect is used that is structurally very similar to step consistency, but handles the case $dom(a) \not\rightsquigarrow u$. We call it *step respect*.

def $step\_respect \equiv \forall a\ u\ s\ t.\ dom(a) \not\rightsquigarrow u\ \wedge\ s \overset{u}{\sim} t \longrightarrow step(a,s) \overset{u}{\sim} step(a,t)$

Obviously, the combination of the left-hand and right-hand variants of local respect implies step respect: $local\_respect \longrightarrow step\_respect$

Assuming $\forall u.\ s_0 \overset{u}{\sim} s_0$ and employing *output consistency*, which is defined as

def $output\_consistent \equiv \forall u\ s\ t.\ s \overset{u}{\sim} t \longrightarrow output(u,s) = output(u,t)$

we can prove the main unwinding theorem for noninterference:

theorem *noninterference* :
$weakly\_step\_consistent \wedge local\_respect \wedge output\_consistent \longrightarrow noninterference$

This theorem is essentially the same as [Rus92, Theorem 7] except that is not (unnecessarily) restricted to intransitive policies. Appendix A gives an abstract example of using its extra strength.

Strong version. Strictly speaking, the classical notion of noninterference only states that an observer cannot deduce that the subsequence of all actions that he is not allowed to see has occurred. This is because purging *removes all* unsuitable actions from a given sequence, but not *part of* them, and neither *adds* any such actions. This shortcoming can be repaired by using the canonical strong version of noninterference (cf. e.g. [McC90,Rya90]) that handles arbitrary insertion and deletion of secret actions:

def $strong\_noninterference \equiv$
$$\forall \alpha\ u\ \beta.\ ipurge(u,\alpha) = ipurge(u,\beta) \longrightarrow s_0 \lhd \alpha \overset{u}{\sim} s_0 \lhd \beta$$

Taking $\beta = ipurge(u,\alpha)$, it is easy to see from the idempotence of purging that this version implies the original version of noninterference. On the other hand, one can derive the strong version of noninterference from the standard right-hand one, exploiting symmetry and transitivity of the observational equivalence. Thus one can conclude that in the deterministic case, the strong version is not strictly stronger than the classical one.

The just mentioned proof scheme does not work for the nondeterministic case because there the observational preorder (see below) is not symmetric. Therefore, we prefer to prove the corresponding "strong" unwinding theorem directly.

theorem *strong_noninterference* : *weakly_step_consistent* $\wedge$
  local_respect $\wedge$ *output_consistent* $\longrightarrow$ *strong_noninterference*

4.3   The Nondeterministic Case

After having elaborated classical noninterference and unwinding in the case of automata with total deterministic transitions, we now generalize these results to partial nondeterministic transitions, trying to parallel the above development as far as possible. This kind of transitions is the one that typically occurs in the abstract system models that we develop during our security analysis projects. It imposes two extra challenges to security: because of partiality, the enabledness of action sequences now plays a role in observations, and because of nonfunctionality, preservation of the unwinding relation becomes more difficult.

For the reasons just given, we extend the observational equivalence of §4.2 with the preservation of enabledness, obtaining an *observational preorder*:

$$\cdot \triangleleft \cdot \overset{\cdot}{\underset{\sim}{\rightarrow}} \cdot \triangleleft \cdot : domain \;\rightarrow\; \wp(state \times action^* \times state \times action^*)$$
def $s \triangleleft \alpha \overset{u}{\underset{\sim}{\rightarrow}} t \triangleleft \beta \equiv \forall s'. \; (s, s') \in Run(\alpha) \;\longrightarrow$
$$\exists t'. \; (t, t') \in Run(\beta) \;\wedge\; output(u, s') = output(u, t')$$

Using this relation, we define noninterference for nondeterministic systems by the canonical generalization of strong noninterference (cf. [McC90, III]):

def $Noninterference \equiv \forall \alpha \; u \; \beta. \; ipurge(u, \alpha) = ipurge(u, \beta) \longrightarrow s_0 \triangleleft \alpha \overset{u}{\underset{\sim}{\rightarrow}} s_0 \triangleleft \beta$

Simple version. The immediate generalization of step consistency, step respect, and local respect for nondeterministic systems is straightforward[4]. Here we define only "ordinary" rather than weak step consistency, for reasons given below. There is some similarity of these definitions with weak bisimulation, as explained e.g. in [Rya01, §10].

def $Step\_consistent \equiv \forall a \; u \; s \; s' \; t. \; dom(a) \rightsquigarrow u \;\wedge$
  $(s, s') \in Step(a) \;\wedge\; s \overset{u}{\sim} t \;\longrightarrow\; (\exists t'. \; (t, t') \in Step(a) \;\wedge\; s' \overset{u}{\sim} t')$

def $Step\_respect \equiv \forall a \; u \; s \; s' \; t. \; dom(a) \not\rightsquigarrow u \;\wedge$
  $(s, s') \in Step(a) \;\wedge\; s \overset{u}{\sim} t \;\longrightarrow\; (\exists t'. \; (t, t') \in Step(a) \;\wedge\; s' \overset{u}{\sim} t')$

def $Local\_respect\_left \equiv$
  $\forall a \; u \; s \; s' \; t. \; dom(a) \not\rightsquigarrow u \;\wedge s \overset{u}{\sim} t \;\wedge\; (s, s') \in Step(a) \longrightarrow s' \overset{u}{\sim} t$
def $Local\_respect\_right \equiv$
  $\forall a \; u \; s \; t. \; dom(a) \not\rightsquigarrow u \;\wedge s \overset{u}{\sim} t \;\longrightarrow\; (\exists t'. \; (t, t') \in Step(a) \;\wedge\; s \overset{u}{\sim} t')$

Obviously, *Local_respect_left* and *Local_respect_right* implies *Step_respect*.

---

[4] Actually, it would be sufficient to state them only for reachable states s and t. We refrain from doing so in order to avoid extra clutter in the presentation.

Note that for consistency with the preservation of enabledness, the left-hand variant assumes the transition between the two states while the right-hand variant requires it to be shown. If the unwinding relation is reflexive and transitive, our definitions of local respect essentially coincide with those given in [Man01]:

$lrf : \forall a\ u\ s\ s'\ t.\ dom(a) \not\rightsquigarrow u \longrightarrow (s,s') \in Step(a) \longrightarrow s' \overset{u}{\sim} s$ and

$lrb : \forall a\ u\ s\ t.\ dom(a) \not\rightsquigarrow u \longrightarrow \exists t'.\ (t,t') \in Step(a) \wedge t \overset{u}{\sim} t'$

Unwinding can be proved essentially as for the deterministic case.

theorem $simple\_Noninterference : Step\_consistent \wedge Local\_respect\_left \wedge Local\_respect\_right \wedge output\_consistent \longrightarrow Noninterference$

Uniform version. Unfortunately, the classical unwinding results concerning weak step consistency cannot be directly transferred to the nondeterministic case. This is due to the two premises of weak step consistency, $s \overset{u}{\sim} t$ and $s \overset{dom(a)}{\sim} t$, which require an inductive argument that in each unwinding step the unwinding relation is preserved simultaneously for more than one domain:

$(s,s') \in Step(a) \wedge s \overset{sources(a \frown \alpha, u)}{\approx} t \longrightarrow (\exists t'.\ (t,t') \in Step(a) \wedge s' \overset{sources(\alpha, u)}{\approx} t')$

Without uniformity, (weak) step consistency etc. only guarantee that for each $v \in sources(\alpha, u)$ there is a suitable t', but not necessarily a single t' for all v.

The problem can be circumvented by requiring that the relation $Step(a)$ is functional for all actions a, as done in [Man01]. This means that every transition for a with nondeterministic outcome has to be replaced by a set of transitions with distinguished actions a', a'', ..., where the choice between these actions is nondeterministic. We would like to avoid requiring such a transformation on system descriptions. This is possible, namely by resorting to the stronger notions of *uniform step consistency*, *uniform step respect*, etc. They generalize their counterparts by replacing the unwinding relation for single domains by the variant lifted over arbitrary sets of domains.

def $uni\_Step\_consistent \equiv \forall U\ a\ s\ s'\ t.\ (\exists u \in U.\ dom(a) \rightsquigarrow u) \wedge s \overset{dom(a)}{\sim} t \wedge$
$\quad (s,s') \in Step(a) \wedge s \overset{U}{\approx} t \longrightarrow (\exists t'.\ (t,t') \in Step(a) \wedge s' \overset{U}{\approx} t')$

def $uni\_Step\_respect \equiv \forall U\ a\ s\ s'\ t.\ \neg(\exists u \in U.\ dom(a) \rightsquigarrow u) \wedge U \neq \emptyset \wedge$
$\quad (s,s') \in Step(a) \wedge s \overset{U}{\approx} t \longrightarrow (\exists t'.\ (t,t') \in Step(a) \wedge s' \overset{U}{\approx} t')$

def $uni\_Local\_respect\_right \equiv \forall U\ a\ s\ t.\ \neg(\exists u \in U.\ dom(a) \rightsquigarrow u) \wedge U \neq \emptyset \wedge$
$\quad s \overset{U}{\approx} t \longrightarrow (\exists t'.\ (t,t') \in Step(a) \wedge s \overset{U}{\approx} t')$

def $uni\_Local\_respect \equiv Local\_respect\_left \wedge uni\_Local\_respect\_right$

$uni\_Local\_respect$ implies $uni\_Step\_respect$, as well as $uni\_Local\_respect\_right$ implies $Local\_respect\_right$. A uniform version of $Local\_respect\_left$ is not required because one can show

lemma $uni\_Local\_respect\_leftD : Local\_respect\_left \longrightarrow$
$\quad (s,s') \in Step(a) \wedge \neg(\exists u \in U.\ dom(a) \rightsquigarrow u) \wedge s \overset{U}{\approx} t \longrightarrow s' \overset{U}{\approx} t$

With the help of the uniform variants of step consistency and step respect, the remaining notions and lemmas carry over from the deterministic variants, essentially retaining their structure, and we obtain

theorem $Noninterference : uni\_Step\_consistent \land$
$uni\_Local\_respect \land output\_consistent \longrightarrow Noninterference$

In applications of this theorem, in general it will take more effort to prove the uniform variants of step consistency and local respect. Yet in the important special case of a two-level hierarchy of domains $\{H, L\}$, to which every transitive policy may be reduced, the only non-trivial case is $\{L\}$, which happens to be the single standard case that has to be considered also for the non-uniform variants.

If in an application the relation $Step(a)$ is functional from the outset or has been transformed to be functional for every a, i.e. $\forall s\ t\ t'.\ (s, t) \in Step(a) \land (s, t') \in Step(a) \longrightarrow t = t'$, the original and the uniform variants of step consistency and step respect etc. coincide and therefore it is sufficient to prove only the simpler original versions.

5   Nonleakage

Classical noninterference is concerned with the visibility of *events*, or to be more precise, with the secrets that events introduce in the system state and that are possibly observed via outputs. While this is the adequate notion for some sorts of applications, there are many others where the concern is not to hide the fact that some secret event has (or has not) occurred but to prevent that initially present secret information leaks out of the domain(s) it is intended to be confined to. The most important of them apparently is language-based information-flow security where type systems give sufficient conditions for confidentiality; see [SM03] for an up-to-date survey. Its semantical core is that variations of high-level *data* (input) should not cause a variation of low-level data (output). In our notation, assuming that $s \overset{L}{\sim} t$ means that the low-level portions of the two states s and t are equal, this can be written as $s \overset{L}{\sim} t \longrightarrow step(a, s) \overset{L}{\sim} step(a, t)$ which is nothing but the common structure of step consistency and step respect.

Language-based security typically handles only the two-level domain hierarchy $\{H, L\}$ and in particular does not address intransitive policies. Inspired by our results on noninterference, we generalize it to arbitrary multi-domain policies. As already argued in §4.2 and depicted by Figure 1, it then becomes important to take into account the domain an action or transition (which in the automata-oriented setting is the analogon to atomic statements in the programming language setting) is allowed to read from. Therefore, the above formula has to be generalized to $(dom(a) \rightsquigarrow u \longrightarrow s \overset{dom(a)}{\sim} t) \land s \overset{u}{\sim} t \longrightarrow step(a, s) \overset{u}{\sim} step(a, t)$, which is nothing but the conjunction of weak step consistency and step respect. The conjunction of the two premises can equivalently be written as $s \overset{sources(a \frown [], u)}{\approx} t$, and further generalizing this idea from a single step to an arbitrary sequence of actions, we arrive at the new notion of *nonleakage*.

5.1   Notion

A system is said to be *nonleaking* iff for any pair of states s and t and observing domain u, the two states resulting from running any action sequence α on s and t are indistinguishable for u if s and t have been indistinguishable for all domains that may (directly or indirectly) interfere with u during the run of α:

$$\mathbf{def}\ nonleakage \equiv \forall \alpha\ s\ u\ t.\ s \overset{sources(\alpha,u)}{\approx} t \longrightarrow s \triangleleft \alpha \overset{u}{\approx} t \triangleleft \alpha$$

Or put in other words, for any sequence α of actions performed by the system, the outcome of u's observations is independent of variations in all domains except for those in $sources(\alpha, u)$, from which (direct or indirect) information flow in the course of α is allowed. Therefore, the relation in the premise is not simply the unwinding relation $s \overset{u}{\sim} t$ as for language-based security but the conjunction of all $s \overset{v}{\sim} t$ where $v \in sources(\alpha, u)$.

As motivated above, nonleakage can also be seen as the global criterion on allowed vs. actual information flow between domains that is induced by the local criteria of weak step consistency and step respect depicted by Figure 1.

Note that in comparison to the theory of noninterference, purging is not needed, and we do not relate the outcome of runs of different action sequences on the same initial state s_0 but of the same action sequence on two states suitably related at the beginning. Moreover, the unwinding relation is used not only as part of the proof technique, but also for specifying what a domain is allowed to observe. Indeed, it is a rather common approach (cf. [RG99]) to define noninterference in terms of an unwinding relations.

The above notion that initially present secrets do not leak can be simulated using noninterference: by prepending all system runs with a sequence of secret actions that produce the secrets in question and considering all subsequent actions non-secret such that they will not be purged. After the initial sequence, the two intermediate states reached in the purged and in the non-purged run are thus handled by noninterference in the same way as by nonleakage. Still we believe that is worthwhile to have the simpler, independent notion of nonleakage that expresses the desired information flow property directly.

5.2   Unwinding

For nonleakage and its descendants introduced below, the unwinding techniques are analogous to those for noninterference. From the above introduction of nonleakage, it is easy to see that nonleakage is implied by weak step consistency, step respect, and output consistency, whereas local respect is not required:

theorem *nonleakage* :

$weakly\_step\_consistent \wedge step\_respect \wedge output\_consistent \longrightarrow nonleakage$

Apart from the fact that nonleakage can handle an arbitrary number of domains and arbitrary interference relations between them, the other major difference to language-based security is that, due to the more general automata-theory setting, we cannot give a type system that allows for static checks of confidentiality (provided the type system is sound). Instead, unwinding gives local semantic conditions for confidentiality, which are harder to verify but on the other hand are (presumably) complete.

5.3 Weak Nonleakage

The assignment of domains to actions and the resulting relation $\overset{sources(\alpha,u)}{\approx}$ gives a very fine-grained control over the information flow caused by action sequences α. Often this is not actually needed (or possible), namely if actions are not distinguished or else domains are not assigned to them, such that individual input domains of transitions cannot be specified. Replacing $sources(\alpha, u)$ with supersets not referring to particular actions, we obtain weaker variants of nonleakage.

Using $chain(\alpha, u)$, the set of all domains that may interfere with u via a chain of domains whose length is at most the length of α, we obtain *weak nonleakage*:

def $weak\_nonleakage \equiv \forall \alpha\; s\; u\; t.\; s \overset{chain(\alpha,u)}{\approx} t \longrightarrow s \triangleleft \alpha \overset{u}{\simeq} t \triangleleft \alpha$

For any action sequence α, any domain u may be influenced only by domains linked to u via $\rightsquigarrow$, up to a chain length given by α. One can understand this notion as an inductive, multi-domain generalization of language-based security, interpreting atomic statements as unclassified actions and attributing program variables a domain structure with a possibly intransitive interference relation.

As $sources(\alpha, u)$ is a subset of $chain(\alpha, u)$, *nonleakage* implies *weak_nonleakage*. Due to the use of *chain*, in unwinding proofs it suffices to use very weak versions of step consistency and step respect that allow one to assume that the unwinding relation holds for all domains that may influence the current domain u. Moreover, since the domains of actions do not longer play a role, step consistency and step respect collapse into a single notion:

def $weak\_step\_consistent\_respect \equiv$
$\qquad \forall s\; u\; t.\; s \overset{\{w|\; w\rightsquigarrow u\}}{\approx} t \longrightarrow \forall a.\; step(a, s) \overset{u}{\sim} step(a, t)$

This notion can also be seen as the direct generalization of language-based security to transitive multi-domain policies. Here we use it for unwinding, as follows:

theorem $weak\_nonleakage :$
$weak\_step\_consistent\_respect \wedge output\_consistent \longrightarrow weak\_nonleakage$

5.4 Transitive Weak Nonleakage

If actions do not have domains associated with them and additionally the length of a $\rightsquigarrow$ -chain is not of interest, for instance if the interference relation is transitive, we can further replace $chain(\alpha, u)$ with the even simpler $\{w|\; w \rightsquigarrow u\}$:

def $trans\_weak\_nonleakage \equiv \forall s\; u\; t.\; s \overset{\{w|\; w\rightsquigarrow u\}}{\approx} t \longrightarrow \forall \alpha.\; s \triangleleft \alpha \overset{u}{\simeq} t \triangleleft \alpha$

Transitive weak nonleakage expresses that if two states are initially indistinguishable for all domains that may influence u, then u cannot tell them apart after any sequence of actions. We share our experience using it (for the nondeterministic case) in §7. Actually, the application described there had motivated our research on noninterference and its variants presented in this article.

For transitive policies, *weak_nonleakage* implies *trans_weak_nonleakage*, hence we obtain

theorem *trans_weak_nonleakage* :
weak_step_consistent_respect $\wedge$ *output_consistent* $\longrightarrow$ *trans_weak_nonleakage*

Note the strong similarities between the global property of transitive weak non-leakage and the associated local criterion *weak_step_consistent_respect*.

5.5   The Nondeterministic Case

All results on nonleakage generalize to the nondeterministic case in analogy with noninterference. We give the formal details without further ado in Appendix B.

5.6   Observation and Unwinding Relations

The notion of nonleakage and its connection with the proof of unwinding properties gives rise to some new insights on observational equivalence (or preorders) and their connection with unwinding relations.

The observational equivalence $s \triangleleft \alpha \stackrel{u}{\simeq} t \triangleleft \alpha$ can be seen as equal outcome of tests on s and t: an attacker belonging to domain u tries to distinguish the two states on their secret contents by attending and/or executing actions α. This is closely related to the passive and active attacks defined by Zdancewic and Myers [ZM01].

Recall that in the deterministic case, the observed outcome of tests is solely $output(u, run(\alpha, s))$ and $output(u, run(\alpha, t))$, respectively. In the nondeterministic case, where we use the observational preorder $s \triangleleft \alpha \stackrel{u}{\rightarrow} t \triangleleft \alpha$, the outcome is additionally the enabledness of the event sequence α. If *output* respects the unwinding relation $\stackrel{u}{\sim}$, our observational equivalence seems to be equivalent to $S[\approx]$ defined in [ZM01]. Since any output may be encoded by the enabledness of certain "probing" actions, our observational preorder is in fact also very similar to the one implicitly used by Mantel [Man03, Remark 5.2.2], namely, preservation of enabledness for every sequence α of visible events. The only difference is that this preorder is weaker because it restricts α to non-secret events (from u's perspective), i.e. there is no chance for "higher-level" events accidentally helping u to distinguish the two states. One can – and we do – allow for an arbitrary mixture of secret and non-secret events because the unwinding relation is preserved not only by (weak) step consistency dealing with the visible actions, but also by step respect dealing with the invisible ones.

Mantel states that preservation of enabledness (for sequences of visible events) is implied by the unwinding relation, which in the above sense is analogous to output consistency requiring that equality of outputs is implied by unwinding.

As already mentioned, neither Mantel's nor our theory requires that the unwinding relation is reflexive, symmetric, or transitive, while the observational equivalence (or preorder) is weaker and necessarily reflexive and transitive. One could regard the latter as the reflexive and transitive closure of the former, and for many applications, both relations even coincide.

6 Noninfluence

As Mantel and Sabelfeld [MS01] point out, it is important to combine language-based security (of information flow in local computations) and the secrecy of (inter-process communication) events. They achieve this by translating a multi-threaded while-language with variables labeled either *high* or *low* to state-event systems with deterministic transitions and prove the two corresponding notions of security equivalent. We can also deal with both worlds (even for intransitive policies and unrestrictedly nondeterministic systems) by combining noninterference and nonleakage, obtaining a new security notion that we call *noninfluence*:

$$\textbf{def } noninfluence \equiv \forall \alpha \; s \; u \; t. \; s \stackrel{sources(\alpha,u)}{\approx} t \longrightarrow s \triangleleft \alpha \stackrel{u}{\doteq} t \triangleleft ipurge(\alpha,u)$$

Note that here no translation between system descriptions is needed.
Noninfluence is the adequate security notion for state-oriented systems if both
  - the occurrence of certain events, which may introduce new secrets, should not be observed, as with classical noninterference, and
  - initially present secret data should not be leaked. Allowing for any two indistinguishable initial states s and t rather than the same (and fixed) initial states s_0 gives the extra strength of noninfluence over noninterference.

One could also define a variant of noninfluence resembling the stronger formulation of noninterference allowing arbitrary insertion and deletion of actions.

It is interesting to observe that the proof of the main unwinding theorem for noninterference (cf. §4.2) uses a lemma which already states essentially the above formula (apart from applying the *output* function on the result of *run*), namely $s \stackrel{sources(\alpha,u)}{\approx} t \longrightarrow run(\alpha,s) = run(ipurge(u,\alpha),t)$. Rushby uses it too [Rus92, Lemma 5], yet he does not attribute to it an independent value. Its extra strength is needed to get through the main induction in the proof, though later it is specialized to $s = t = s_0$ to deduce noninterference. Thus, noninfluence implies noninterference if $\forall u. \; s_0 \stackrel{u}{\sim} s_0$ holds.

In the light of the new notion of noninfluence, both noninterference and nonleakage are just special cases where either leakage of initial secrets or the visibility of secret events does not play a role. Nevertheless, it makes sense to keep both of them because they are simpler than noninfluence, and nonleakage does not require local respect.

From the observation in the last paragraph it will be clear that the unwinding theorem for noninfluence requires only those preconditions already used for for noninterference, even though the conclusion is stronger – it simply makes the strength already contained in [Rus92, Lemma 5] available as a security property in its own right. Recall that technically it is even slightly stronger because unwinding may be an arbitrary (even nonreflexive) relation rather than an equivalence.

theorem *noninfluence* :
$weakly\_step\_consistent \wedge local\_respect \wedge output\_consistent \longrightarrow noninfluence$

The generalization to the nondeterministic case is given in Appendix B.

7   Security of the Infineon SLE66

As a concrete example of applying the purely state-based notion of nonleakage, we sketch an extended security analysis of the Infineon SLE66 smart card processor. The main security objective for this device is that part of the chip-internal security mechanisms and secret data like the master encryption key is not leaked to any non-authorized observer or manipulator, called "spy".

In the course of the evaluation of the chip according to ITSEC and Common Criteria, an abstract formal security model, the so-called "LKW model" [LKW00] has been developed and later machine-checked [OL02] using the ISM approach and toolset [ON02]. This model takes a rather naive view of information leakage: a secret value is revealed to the spy if and only if its representation appears on the external interface of the chip. This interpretation does not account for partial or indirect leakage of information that may be used to deduce at least certain properties of the secret values.

We have improved the security analysis using transitive weak nonleakage (for nondeterministic systems). This is the adequate notion for the SLE66 because the observability of actions does not play a role, but the information flow between domains. Only two security domains, *Sec* and *NSec*, are distinguished, so the interference relation is trivially transitive and we have to show *weak_uni_Step_consistent_respect* only for $U = \{NSec\}$, as explained at the end of §4.3. Since encryption is not explicit in the model, we do not have to deal with bogus "interference" of secret keys with encrypted outputs, though this would be possible by stating an intransitive information flow via the encryption unit.

For the unwinding relation we choose an equivalence that states equality for all parts of the chip state that is allowed to be observed from outside, namely the phases of the chip life-cycle, the availability of chip functionality (see below), and all non-secret data values. Once the right relation has been chosen, the proof is rather schematic and in this case not very difficult. The only complication is that the property holds only for reachable states for which suitable invariants hold, but we can re-use the invariants that we had already shown during the previous analysis.

Conducting the proof, we obtained the following results.

– It is crucial that chip functions do not internally leak secret data or give them away via the chip interface. Since chip functionality is heavily underspecified, this auxiliary property cannot be proved but has to be provided as an axiom.
– The possibility that at most one (encrypted) secret data value or the encryption key itself gets leaked is explicitly allowed by the chip designers because there is no practical means to prevent this. This leakage is actually found during the proof. Yet it does not do harm because immediately thereafter the chip gets completely locked such that no more values can be obtained and thus not both some encrypted data and the key are known to the spy.
– The chip cannot avoid leaking the availability even of those functions that are considered to be secret (whereas their actual code is not leaked).
– Apart from the exceptions just given, no secret information, not even any partial information about secret data, can be leaked.

8   Conclusion

We have refined Rushby's work on noninterference by rectifying its minor short-comings concerning transitive vs. intransitive policies and the requirements on the unwinding relation. This opens a wider range of applications and enables stronger results like in Appendix A. We have significantly extended Rushby's theory to handle nondeterministic systems, introducing uniform step consistency.

We have introduced notions of information flow security that have not been considered before but naturally arise from re-interpreting Rushby's unwinding lemmas, and gained new insights in the nature of unwinding and observability. Nonleakage has a high application potential because it generalizes language-based security to arbitrary policies and state-transforming systems. Noninfluence combines this with classical event-oriented noninterference.

It should be worthwhile conducting further theoretical investigations, e.g. on completeness of the unwinding conditions and the comparison with related notions like (robust) declassification and bisimulation.

Our theory has been implemented in the interactive theorem proving system Isabelle/HOL. As the example of the SLE66 shows, it is ready to be applied in the formal security analysis of state-oriented systems.

Acknowledgments. We thank John Rushby, Heiko Mantel, Peter Ryan, Volkmar Lotz, Stephan Merz, Tamara Rezk, and several anonymous referees for their encouragement and feedback on drafts of this paper.

References

[Fol87]   Simon N. Foley. A universal theory of information flow. In *IEEE Symposium on Security and Privacy*, pages 116–122, 1987.

[GM82]   J. A. Goguen and J. Meseguer. Security policies and security models. In *Symposium on Security and Privacy*. IEEE Computer Society Press, 1982.

[GM84]   J. A. Goguen and J. Meseguer. Unwinding the inference control. In *Symposium on Security and Privacy*. IEEE Computer Society Press, 1984.

[HY86]   J. Haigh and W. Young. Extending the non-interference version of MLS for SAT. In *Proc. of the Symposium on Security and Privacy*, pages 232–239. IEEE Computer Society Press, 1986.

[LKW00]   Volkmar Lotz, Volker Kessler, and Georg Walter. A Formal Security Model for Microprocessor Hardware. In *IEEE Transactions on Software Engineering*, volume 26, pages 702–712, August 2000.

[Man00]   Heiko Mantel. Unwinding possibilistic security properties. In *Proc. of ESORICS*, volume 1895 of *LNCS*, pages 238 – 254. Springer, 2000.

[Man01]   Heiko Mantel. Information Flow and Applications – Bridging a Gap. In *Proc. of FME 2001: Formal Methods for Increasig Software Productivity*, volume 2021 of *LNCS*, pages 153 – 172. Springer, 2001.

[Man03]   Heiko Mantel. *A Uniform Framework for the Formal Specification and Verification of Information Flow Security*. PhD thesis, Univ. d. Saarlandes, 2003.

[McC90]   Darly McCullough. A hookup theorem for multilevel security. In *IEEE Transactions on Software Engineering*, pages 563–568, 1990.

[McL94]   John McLean. A general theory of composition for trace sets closed under selective interleaving functions. In *IEEE Symposium on Security and Privacy*, pages 79–93, 1994.

[MS01]   Heiko Mantel and Andrei Sabelfeld. A Generic Approach to the Security of Multi-threaded Programs. In *Proc. of 14th CSFW*, pages 126–142, Cape Breton, Nova Scotia, Canada, 2001. IEEE Computer Society.

[NPW02]   Tobias Nipkow, Lawrence C. Paulson, and Markus Wenzel. *Isabelle/HOL – A Proof Assistant for Higher-Order Logic*, volume 2283 of *LNCS*. Springer, 2002. See also http://isabelle.in.tum.de/docs.html.

[Ohe04]   David von Oheimb. *Isabelle theory sources: Noninfluence = Noninterference + Nonleakage*, 2004. http://ddvo.net/HOL/NI/.

[OL02]   David von Oheimb and Volkmar Lotz. Formal Security Analysis with Interacting State Machines. In Dieter Gollmann, Günter Karjoth, and Michael Waidner, editors, *Proc. of the 7th European Symposium on Research in Computer Security (ESORICS)*, volume 2502 of *LNCS*, pages 212–228. Springer, 2002. http://ddvo.net/papers/FSA_ISM.html.

[ON02]   David von Oheimb and Sebastian Nanz. *ISM Homepage: Documentation, sources and distribution*, 2002. http://ddvo.net/ISM/.

[Pin95]   Sylvan Pinsky. Absorbing covers and intransitive non-interference. In *IEEE Symposium on Security and Privacy*, pages 102–113, 1995.

[RG99]   A.W. Roscoe and M.H. Goldsmith. What is intransitive noninterference? In *12th Computer Security Foundations Workshop*, pages 228–238. IEEE Computer Society Press, 1999.

[Rus92]   John Rushby. Noninterference, Transitivity, and Channel-Control Security Policies. Technical Report CS-92-02, SRI International, 1992.

[Rya90]   Peter Ryan. A CSP formulation of non-interference and unwinding. In *Proc. of IEEE CSFW-3*. Cipher, 1990.

[Rya01]   Peter Y. A. Ryan. Mathematical models of computer security. In Riccardo Focardi and Roberto Gorrieri, editors, *Foundations of Security Analysis and Design: Tutorial Lectures*, volume 2171 of *LNCS*. Springer, 2001.

[SM03]   A. Sabelfeld and A. C. Myers. Language-based information-flow security. *IEEE J. on Selected Areas in Communications*, 21(1):5–19, January 2003.

[Sut86]   D. Sutherland. A model of information. In *Proc. National Computer Security Conference*, pages 175–183, 1986.

[ZL97]   Aris Zakinthinos and E. Stewart Lee. A general theory of security properties. In *Computer Society Symposium on Research in Security and Privacy*, 1997.

[ZM01]   Steve Zdancewic and Andrew C. Myers. Robust Declassification. In *14th IEEE Computer Security Foundations Workshop (CSFW)*, 2001.

A   Access Control Interpretation

As a (rather abstract) application of our strengthened noninterference theory, we give an improvement of Rushby's access control interpretation [Rus92, §2.1].

Employing our unwinding theorem which works for both transitive and intransitive interference relations, we only have to show weak step consistency. Doing so, we have stronger preconditions and thus can dispense with the monotonicity condition $u \rightsquigarrow v \longrightarrow observe(u) \subseteq observe(v)$, which, according to Rushby, had forced the transitive completion of the policy. In effect, we generalize his access control interpretation to the general (possibly intransitive) case.

In order to express access control, the system model is extended by adding structure to the state, which now becomes a function that maps names to values:

$$contents :\ state \times name\ \to\ value$$

Policies are refined accordingly, associating each domain with a set of names of objects that it is allowed to read and write, respectively:

$$observe :\ domain\ \to\ \wp(name)$$
$$alter\ \ :\ domain\ \to\ \wp(name)$$

Following Rushby, for the application of the unwinding theorem, we use the canonical unwinding relation induced by *contents* and *observe*,

def $s \overset{u}{\sim} t \equiv \forall n \in observe(u).\ contents(s,n) = contents(t,n)$

which happens to be an equivalence, though we do not take advantage of this.

Rushby introduces three *reference monitor assumptions*. The first of them is the already introduced output consistency:

def $RMA_1 \equiv output\_consistent$

As a matter of fact, if the output function yields all values observable for the given domain, i.e. $output(u,s) \equiv \{contents(s,n)\ |n|\ n \in observe\ u\}$, output consistency is fulfilled immediately.

Rushby's second reference monitor assumption states that if an action a changes the value at some location n, the new value depends only on $dom(a)$. Due to our observation that weak step consistency is sufficient in any case, we can use a weaker variant of it, offering the extra premises $dom(a) \rightsquigarrow u$, $s \overset{u}{\sim} t$, and $n \in observe\ u$ which allow information flow into n from any domain u that is allowed to observe n and that may be influenced by the input domain of a.

def $RMA_2 \equiv \forall a\ u\ s\ t\ n.\ s \overset{dom(a)}{\sim} t \wedge dom(a) \rightsquigarrow u \wedge s \overset{u}{\sim} t \wedge n \in observe\ u\ \wedge$
$$(contents(step(a,s),n) \neq contents(s,n)\ \vee$$
$$contents(step(a,t),n) \neq contents(t,n))\ \longrightarrow$$
$$contents(step(a,s),n) = contents(step(a,t),n)$$

Interestingly, weak step consistency can now be derived from the second reference monitor assumption alone: $RMA_2 \longrightarrow weakly\_step\_consistent$

The third assumption, stating that any changes must be granted by *alter*,

def $RMA_3 \equiv$
$$\forall a\ s\ n.\ contents(step(a,s),n) \neq contents(s,n) \longrightarrow n \in alter(dom(a))$$

in conjunction with the remaining condition of Rushby's Theorem 2,

def $AC\_policy\_consistent \equiv \forall u\ v.\ alter(u)\ \cap\ observe(v)\ \neq \emptyset \longrightarrow u \rightsquigarrow v$

implies local respect: $RMA_3\ \wedge\ AC\_policy\_consistent\ \longrightarrow\ local\_respect$

Hence, we can prove enforcement of access control

theorem $access\_control\_secure$:
$$RMA_1\ \wedge\ RMA_2\ \wedge\ RMA_3\ \wedge\ AC\_policy\_consistent\ \longrightarrow\ noninterference$$

under weaker assumptions than Rushby does: we do *not* require that

- *observe* and *alter* induce a transitive information flow policy,
- granted information flow induces a hierarchy of observable locations, nor
- information flow into a location n from any domain that is allowed to observe n and that may be influenced by the input domain of the current action does not occur.

B   Nondeterministic Nonleakage and Noninfluence

Nonleakage.

def $Nonleakage \equiv \forall \alpha \ s \ u \ t. \ s \overset{sources(\alpha,u)}{\approx} t \longrightarrow s \triangleleft \alpha \overset{u}{\rightharpoonup} t \triangleleft \alpha$

theorem $Nonleakage$:
$uni\_Step\_consistent \wedge uni\_Step\_respect \wedge output\_consistent \longrightarrow Nonleakage$

Weak nonleakage.

def $weak\_Nonleakage \equiv \forall \alpha \ s \ u \ t. \ s \overset{chain(\alpha,u)}{\approx} t \longrightarrow s \triangleleft \alpha \overset{u}{\rightharpoonup} t \triangleleft \alpha$

As above, $Nonleakage \longrightarrow weak\_Nonleakage$.

def $weak\_uni\_Step\_consistent\_respect \equiv \forall U \ a \ s \ s' \ t. \ U \neq \emptyset \ \wedge$
$\quad (s,s') \in Step(a) \wedge (\forall u \in U. \ s \overset{\{w| \ w \rightsquigarrow u\}}{\approx} t) \longrightarrow (\exists t'. \ (t,t') \in Step(a) \wedge s' \overset{U}{\approx} t')$

theorem $weak\_Nonleakage$:
$weak\_uni\_Step\_consistent\_respect \wedge output\_consistent \longrightarrow weak\_Nonleakage$

Transitive weak nonleakage.

def $trans\_weak\_Nonleakage \equiv \forall s \ u \ t. \ s \overset{\{w| \ w \rightsquigarrow u\}}{\approx} t \longrightarrow \forall \alpha. \ s \triangleleft \alpha \overset{u}{\rightharpoonup} t \triangleleft \alpha$

For transitive policies, $weak\_Nonleakage \longrightarrow trans\_weak\_Nonleakage$, hence

theorem $trans\_weak\_Nonleakage$:
$\quad weak\_uni\_Step\_consistent\_respect \ \wedge \ output\_consistent \longrightarrow$
$\quad trans\_weak\_Nonleakage$

Noninfluence.

Paralleling the deterministic case as far as possible, we define

def $Noninfluence \equiv$
$\quad \forall \alpha \ \beta \ s \ u \ t. \ s \overset{sources(\alpha,u)}{\approx} t \ \wedge \ ipurge(u,\alpha) = ipurge(u,\beta) \longrightarrow s \triangleleft \alpha \overset{u}{\rightharpoonup} t \triangleleft \beta$

and obtain

theorem $Noninfluence$:
$uni\_Step\_consistent \wedge uni\_Local\_respect \wedge output\_consistent \longrightarrow Noninfluence$

Security Property Based Administrative Controls

Jon A. Solworth and Robert H. Sloan

University of Illinois at Chicago
Dept. of Computer Science
Chicago, IL 60607
solworth@cs.uic.edu, sloan@uic.edu

Abstract. Access control languages which support administrative controls, and thus allow the ordinary permissions of a system to change, have traditionally been constructed with first order predicate logic or graph rewriting rules. We introduce a new access control model to implement administrative controls directly in terms of the security properties – we call this *Security Property Based Administrative Controls (SPBAC)*. Administrative approval is required only when a security property is changed (violated) relative to the current configuration. We show that in the case of information flow, and its effects on both integrity and confidentiality, SPBACs are implementable, and the necessary administrative approvals exactly determinable.

1 Introduction

In sufficiently static protection systems, such as Lattice-Based Access Controls (LBAC) [1] or Type Enforcement (TE) [2, 3], security properties such as allowed information flow are decidable.

Unfortunately, such systems are inflexible. For LBAC, consider the two most important security models, Bell-LaPadula [4] and Biba [5]. Both of these provide absolute security properties: In Bell-LaPadula, the security property ensures that the readership of information (i.e., the confidentiality) is never enlarged, and hence information is never disclosed beyond its original readership. In Biba, the quality ("integrity") of an object is bounded by its lowest quality input, ensuring that lower quality information does not pollute higher quality information.

In real systems, the security properties are not uniformly applicable. For example, even military security systems require the ability to declassify information, overriding the confidentiality security property of Bell-LaPadula. Similarly, information flow integrity is not limited by Biba Integrity considerations: It is possible to increase the ultimate quality of information beyond the worst quality input by cross checking the information. Unfortunately these overrides, while necessary, are not part of the LBAC model.

On the other hand, TE does not have these restrictions. TE controls are sufficient to enforce these properties yet flexible enough to selectively not enforce them. We believe that this is a significant advantage over LBAC and one of

P. Samarati et al. (Eds.): ESORICS 2004, LNCS 3193, pp. 244–259, 2004.

the primary reasons that TE is gaining in popularity. TE also enables other security properties to be enforced which are difficult or impossible to enforce with LBAC, such as specifying the executables allowed to read or write an object of a specific type. Our concern here, however, is only with information flow security properties.

TE's flexibility is limited since there is no provision for modifications to the protection scheme, and hence there is very limited control over whether or how the protection system can change. In contrast, with LBAC the lattice can be augmented in well controlled ways ensuring that the security properties can be maintained – for example, by adding another category or compartment. But since TE selectively enforces security properties, it is not clear when making changes whether a given security property should hold in that part of the system (e.g., confidentiality) or whether it can be violated (e.g., declassification).

We note that although both Bell-LaPadula and Biba have their genesis in military security, they apply selectively to *all* environments. For example, an owner of a personal computer may want to ensure that her credit card number is not disclosed outside a limited number of trusted vendors[1]. Or a medical practice may want to ensure that information entered into patient files is from a hospital, lab, or staff trusted to provide such information. While it is always safe to maintain such security properties, real systems cannot impose these properties uniformly across the entire system.

It seems desirable to combine the elegant security properties of LBAC, and their implications for how the system can evolve over time, with the flexibility of selective application of security properties. To enable security properties to hold selectively, *administrative controls* – those which enable changes to ordinary permissions – are needed. We call the class of administrative controls introduced here *Security Property Based Administrative Controls (SPBAC)*.

In this paper, we describe a decidable mechanism for administrative controls which ensures that administrative approval is required exactly when information flow security properties are violated. Although there are other security properties besides information flow, the information flow based security properties are both interesting and important. For example, these administrative controls can be configured to ensure:

1. Approval is *never* granted to violate a specific information flow security property at a fine grain. That is, the information flow security property may be inviolate in some parts of the system but not others or
2. Approval may require specific individuals (specified in terms of groups) to concur in the approval.

The protection system's initial configuration defines not only the ordinary permissions, but also the administrative controls to enable a security property to be selectively enforced. Changes to the ordinary protection requires administrative approval only if it modifies some existing security properties.

---

[1] The mechanisms discussed here are *the access control part* of providing such protections; they need appropriate network authentication mechanisms to be complete.

Trivial changes to the protection system, that have no impact on the security properties, do not require *any* approval[2]. This significantly simplifies the mechanism needed while ensuring that security properties are maintained.

The paper is organized as follows: In Section 2 we review related work. In Section 3 we describe the mechanisms of our model to support *ordinary* – that is, non-administrative activities. Of particular interest is a new permission we call *mayFlow*. In Section 4 we describe the administrative controls and their rationale. In Section 5 we show that the administrative approvals necessary can be exactly determined, identifying the security properties which are violated and requiring the appropriate administrators to concur in a change to the system. Finally, we conclude in Section 6.

2   Related Work

One of the problems that occurs with sufficiently dynamic protection systems is that security properties can be undecidable: Harrison, Ruzzo, and Ullman first showed that a security property, *safety* was undecidable in their model [6].

Sandhu's Typed Access Model (TAM) [7] associates a fixed type with each subject and each object. Although TAM has the same undecidable safety property as HRU, Sandhu showed that if TAM is restricted to be *monotonic* then the problem is decidable. More recently, Soshi [8] showed that a different, non-monotonic restriction, Dynamic TAM, also has a decidable safety property, under the restriction that the number of objects in a system is bounded.

Take-grant can be used to represent information flow issues which are decidable [9], but does not support administrative controls..

RBAC models have traditionally been constructed using either first order predicate logic or graph transformation rules. Unfortunately, either of these constructions can lead to undecidability results. For example, both RBAC'96 [10] and ARBAC'97 [11] are undecidable [12,13]. The most vexing problems for decidability seem to arise from administrative controls.

Tidswell and Jaeger created Dynamic Typed Access Control (DTAC) which extends TE to dynamic types and is capable of implementing administrative controls [14,15]. These were implemented as runtime checks in the operating system to ensure that various safety properties are not violated [16]. In this paper, we show how security properties can be enforced statically and enable administrators to understand when and where they are being violated.

Koch and colleagues described a model based on graph transformations, and showed that it was decidable if no step both added and deleted parts of the graph [17,18]. This means that no command may both remove and add privileges. This restriction can be viewed as a somewhat milder form of monotonicity. Take-Grant also obeys this restriction.

We have recently shown that administrative controls for classical DAC systems can be implemented in a decidable language [19]. The SPBAC model here uses both the groups and unary permissions of the DAC model. The full SPBAC information flow model is also decidable [20].

---

[2] Some simple approval might be necessary to prevent creation of superfluous entities.

As with Foley, Gong, and Qian [21] we make extensive use of relabeling to encode protection state: Foley et al. allow a user to relabel an object to one she cannot access. In our case, relabels are used to change group membership and are associated with permissions.

We note that while we discuss information flow, we do not consider covert flows, which in any event are tied to the execution model.

3 Ordinary Privileges

Our model consists of users, objects, labels, permissions, and groups. Each user is authenticated and individuals who can use the system are one-to-one with users. A process derives its authority to perform an operation from the user on whose behalf the process executes.

3.1 Unary and *mayFlow* Privileges

Privileges to access an object are based on the label of that object. Each label l and privilege p is mapped to a group of users who have privilege p on objects with that label. This mapping is defined when the label is created and thus the *group* is fixed, although the group's *membership can change*. Each label is mapped to three groups:

- $r(l)$: the group which can read objects labeled l.
- $w(l)$: the group which can write, that is, create or modify, objects labeled l. Write privileges do not imply read privileges.
- $x(l)$: the group which can execute objects labeled l^3.

A new binary privilege, *mayFlow* is introduced to control information flow:

- *mayFlow*(l, l'): the group that can write l' after having read l. This is a necessary, but not sufficient condition since *mayFlow* does not include privileges to read l or write l'.

Therefore, for a process executing on behalf of user u to read l and then write l', the following must hold: $u \in r(l) \sqcap w(l') \sqcap mayFlow(l, l')$. Note that the above must hold for *each* l read prior to writing l'.

MayFlow need not be defined on *all* label pairs. For pairs on which *mayFlow* is not yet defined, the specified flow may not occur. Unlike with lattices, *mayFlow* is not transitive, so each allowed flow must be individually specified.

Bell-LaPadula Example. Consider the diamond lattice shown below. Let *cleared$_x$* be the group of users whose clearance level is x or above. Bell-LaPadula for this lattice can be represented with *mayFlows* as follows:

---

[3] Execute privileges are included here for completeness; they do not play any further role in this paper.

For all x, y such that in the lattice $x \le y$:

$$mayFlow(x, y) = cleared_L$$

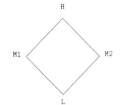

All other *mayFlows* have the value of the empty group.
In addition, for all clearances x:

$$r(x) = w(x) = cleared_x$$

The user groups are defined taking advantage of the ability of our model to construct hierarchical groups (see the next subsection). Hence, $cleared_L \subseteq cleared_{M1} \subseteq cleared_H$ and $cleared_L \subseteq cleared_{M2} \subseteq cleared_H$. Note, for example, that a process which reads objects labeled respectively M1 and H cannot then write an object labeled M1 since $mayFlow(H,M1)$ is the empty group.

We note that Bell-LaPadula does not specify access control rules but rather describes constraints which must be satisfied by the access control rules. Many variants of Bell-LaPadula can be constructed by modifying the above rules or group construction.

3.2   Groups

The group structure is summarized here and is based upon Solworth and Sloan [19] where more details and examples can be found.

A *group set* defines a collection of related groups. The structure of the group set enables relationships to be maintained between its constituent groups such as hierarchy of groups or partitioning of users between groups. Instead of using constraints to maintain relationships, our mechanism relies on permissions.

Group objects are 1-for-1 with users in the group set. Each group set contains 0 or more *group objects* with labels $\langle U, G \rangle$ where U is a user ID and G is a group tag which is unique to the group set (the object does not have any contents, only its label is of interest). At any given time, for each group set and for all users U, there is at most one label whose first component is U.

Group membership is defined using a set of patterns applied to the group object labels. Each pattern is of the form $\langle *u, G \rangle$ – matching any user with group tag G, or of the form $\langle U, G \rangle$ – matching user U and group tag G. *Group relabels* change group tags and hence group membership.

Changing a user's group membership within the group set's groups is controlled by relabel permissions. The permission $Relabel(G, G') = g$ enables a member of group g (the *membership secretary*) to change a group object labeled $\langle U, G \rangle$ to $\langle U, G' \rangle$, for any U.

When adding a new user U to the system, U can be automatically added to the group set. The group set's new user rule specifies an optional tag G. When U is added to the system, the group mechanism creates a group object with label $\langle U, G \rangle$. Group objects can only be created by the group mechanism, and only when initializing the group set or when adding a new user.

A user U is removed by permanently disabling their login, after which U's group objects can be garbage collected.

The general properties of group sets are:

- A *group* determines a set of users and each group is in some *group set*.
- A group's membership is controlled by a membership secretary which is itself a group.
- New users can be automatically added to a group set (and to its groups) as a consequence of creating the user.
- Changes in group membership can be constrained by relabel rules.
- Groups in a group set can be constructed so that the groups have relative structure, such as hierarchy (one group always contains another) or partition (a user cannot be simultaneously a member of two separate groups).

The *membership secretary* mechanism constrains group membership and is independent of the security property administrative controls discussed in Section 4.

This completes the definition of groups but there is an issue which arises when a user U is removed from a group g via a relabel. Under this condition, to maintain the relative structure properties on group sets, all processes running on behalf of U and having used privileges based on membership in g are terminated.

4   Administrative Privileges

Conceptually, the system is configured, verified, and then made operational, or goes "live". Before the system goes live, entities such as groups, labels, objects, permissions, and users may be created.

After the system goes live, instances of each of these entities can still be created. To create entities after the system goes live which modify the security properties, security property approval must be given appropriate both to the security properties changed and to the part of the system where the changes occur.

We distinguish three separate levels of actions that can be performed in our model:

Ordinary. These actions are governed by the mechanism described in Section 3, and include (1) create, read, and write objects and (2) change membership of groups (including the addition of new users)[4].

SysAdmin Actions. Actions performed by system administrators (except for adding new users) but which do not violate any security property. These actions include the (1) creation of new groups, (2) definition of new *mayFlows* not requiring security property approval, and (3) the creation of new labels.

Security Property Approvals. Actions performed by administrators which require approval because they directly or indirectly effect security properties. When security property approvals are requested, an administrator is

---

[4] The rationale here is that since any user could be in a membership secretary and therefore change group membership, and since new users only gain privileges through group membership, it is logically consistent to have in the same category everything about how a group evolves.

given all the information needed to make a decision. The security property approvals include (1) integrity relations and (2) *mayFlows* which violate existing security properties.

The idea here is that SysAdmin Actions can be delegated to technical administrators because they do not effect the core security properties of the system.

In Figure 1, our SPBAC hierarchy is shown. The layered design ensures a given layer's implementation only depends upon lower layers; hence there can be no loops in the layer dependencies. As a consequence of our layered design, administrative controls have no effect over groups, and in particular over group membership. Hence, security property approvals need to be resilient across all future group memberships. (The group membership mechanism restricts group membership, so this is a meaningful goal).

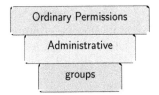

Fig. 1. Access Control Hierarchy

Our primary focus shall be on the effect of defining new *mayFlows*. (Note that existing permissions cannot be changed[5] once established). Secondarily, we shall be concerned with the issues that effect future approval of *mayFlows*.

In subsection 4.1 we will describe the administrative entities that need to be added, beyond what is necessary for ordinary permission, to support changes to the information flow properties of the system. In subsection 4.2 we describe how we keep track of the relevant past actions. In subsection 4.3, we describe the conditions under which security property approvals are required.

4.1 Administrative Entities

We introduce here the entities to support administration of information flow security properties. These are the administrative permissions associated with labels and integrity relations on pairs of labels.

Administrative permissions associated with labels. For information flow, all security property approval is associated with labels. In particular, for each label we define three administrative permissions at the time of label creation:

ac(l) The (administrative) group which can approve exceptions to confidentiality for label l;

---

[5] However, existing permissions can be added incrementally by defining a new *mayFlow*.

ai(l) The (administrative) group which can approve exceptions to integrity for label l. These exceptions either allow flows violating current integrity relations or create additional integrity relations; and

af(l) The (administrative) group which can approve flows into or out of l.

We note that the first two permissions, $ac(l)$ and $ai(l)$, are for security property approvals while the last permission, $af(l)$ does not effect security properties.

We shall require that *administrative groups* – those used for administrative permissions – are distinct from *ordinary groups* – those used for ordinary permissions. Furthermore each administrative group is the only group defined in its group set. These properties hold not only for the administrative group, but also for its membership secretary (and recursively for their membership secretaries, etc.). The purpose of these restrictions on groups is to ensure that (i) administrative permissions don't interact with ordinary permissions and (ii) that there is no interaction between administrative groups in which a group being nonempty requires another group to be empty.

Integrity relations. Each ordered pair of labels can (optionally) be associated with an integrity relationship. (If no integrity relationship is defined between a pair of labels, we must assume the worst case). From an integrity standpoint, it is always safe to include information from an object with greater integrity into one with lower integrity. Hence, no integrity security property approvals are required to allow a write to an object with integrity level i after having read only objects whose integrity levels are at or above i.

Definition 1. *The **relative integrity** of two labels, l and l' is written $geqIntegrity(l, l')$, meaning that the integrity level of l is at least as high as l'. The transitive closure of the relationship geqIntegrity is called the **effective integrity** and is denoted $l \succeq l'$. It is reflexive and transitive.*

Note that the effective integrity is *not* a partial order, because there can exist two *distinct* labels $l \neq l'$ with both $geqIntegrity(l, l')$ and $geqIntegrity(l', l)$. Instead, effective integrity is a poset of integrity *levels*, where multiple labels may correspond to one integrity level.

4.2   Tracking Past Actions

The analysis provided in section 5 will consider future actions. In order for this to track all flows, we also need to track past actions. The information on past actions is all relative to the flows over a defined $mayFlow(l, l')$.

We define $\textbf{\textit{didFlow}}(l, l')$ to be the set of labels that could have actually flowed across $mayFlow(l, l')$. The set $didFlow(l, l')$ tracks the actual flows, and is updated every time a process writes l' after having read l.

Let $flowed(l) = \bigcup_{l' \in \text{system}} didFlow(l', l) \cup \{l\}$. Then:

$$didFlow(l, l') \leftarrow didFlow(l, l') \cup flowed(l)$$

Note that the granularity of information is at the label level – not the object level – and hence forms an upper bound on information flow. We next define *flow along* $\mathcal{P}$ to capture past flows.

Definition 2. *Let $\mathcal{P}$ be path $[l_1, l_2, \ldots, l_n]$. There was a* (**past**) **flow along** $\mathcal{P}$ *if $l_1 \in didFlow(l_i, l_{i+1})$ for $0 < i < n$.*

4.3 Security Property Approvals

We now consider actions which might require security property approval.

As described in Section 3.1, if $mayFlow(l, l')$ is not defined, then information cannot directly flow from l to l', absent an action to create a $mayFlow$ edge.

The $mayFlow$ relation describes a permission. We shall use the the term *can flow* to denote the flows that are *actually possible without any SysAdmin actions or security property approvals.* That is, *information can flow from l to l'* if and only if there is a sequence of labels $[l = l_1, l_2, \ldots, l' = l_n]$ such that in sequential order for $i = 1 \ldots n - 1$ some user u_i can (1) read l_i, (2) write l_{i+1}, and (3) $mayFlow$ l_i to l_{i+1}. Such a sequence of labels is called a *can flow path*. Can flows denote possible future flows. To get all possible flows, actual past and possible future flows must be combined. Hence given a past flow along $[l_1, l_2, \ldots, l_k]$ and a can flow $[l_k, l_{k+1}, \ldots, l_n]$ there is an *extended can flow* $[l_1, l_2, \ldots, l_n]$, because that information has flown from l_1 to l_k and could flow to l_n.

Now we consider the requirements for security property approval to add a $mayFlow$ definition for a pair of labels. In an SPBAC, security property approval is needed for exactly those changes that affect the security properties of the system. The effect can be either direct or indirect. For example, adding a $mayFlow$ definition changes the "extended can-flow paths" in the system and so obviously is directly related to security properties. Other operations, such as defining an integrity relation, are indirectly related to the security properties since their definition is used in determining whether the security property holds.

Confidentiality depends on both the extended can-flow paths and on the readership. The readership is totally defined by the read permissions on a label (i.e., $r(l)$) together with the group definition. Defining confidentiality in terms of extended can flow paths means that the extended can flow path $[l_1, l_2, l_3]$ is different from $[l_1, l_4, l_3]$ *even if the only readership which can be less than l_3 is l_1.* The rationale is that l_1's administrator may trust the group who can write l_2 (after reading l_1) to remove sensitive information when doing so, but is unwilling to similarly trust the corresponding groups for l_4. This example is shown graphically in Figure 2. It is exactly the violation of security properties (such as information flow) which must be examined by administrators to determine appropriate trust. These trust issues are external to the system – that is, they must rely on the judgment of the trustworthiness of groups – and hence can only be decided by administrators.

Integrity is, as usual, more subtle than confidentiality. Biba captures the integrity issues arising from the quality of inputs[6]. The quality of the inputs cannot be determined from the access controls but must be separately specified.

---

[6] The various implementations of Biba, including low-water mark and ring integrity, do not vary in *what* information may flow but only in *how* the processes are labeled and whether objects are relabeled.

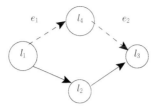

Fig. 2. Path based approval where edges indicate can flow

Integrity security property approval is needed only on information which flows from l_i to l_n where $l_i \not\preceq l_n$ and for which the extended can-flow path used have not been previously approved. Such a flow is reasonable only in limited circumstances – that is, when there is some action which increases the quality of the output over the input. Hence, any time "questionable" inputs are incorporated somewhere along the chain, $ai(l_n)$ must give security property approval. For example, integrity can be raised by a user with sufficient judgment and/or knowledge to vet the information or by cross checking against various sources. The entity that so raises the level can either be a user or a program. Once again the particular extended can-flow path is critical, because only the path ensures that the integrity has been raised in an appropriate way.

We next give formal requirements of security property approval. Adding a new $mayFlow(l, l')$ gives rise to a new set of extended can-flow paths. If there exists a new extended can-flow path $\mathcal{P} = [l_1, l_2, \ldots, l_n]$ such that:

Confidentiality. It is possible that $r(l_n) \not\subseteq r(l_1)$ then approval by $ac(l_1)$ is needed.

Integrity. The condition $l_1 \not\preceq l_n$ holds then approval by $ai(l_n)$ is needed.

In addition, approval is required by $af(l)$ and by $af(l')$, but these are not security property approvals, they are merely SysAdmin actions. We are also interested in any indirect effect which would change the approvals needed by a direct effect. There is only one indirect effect which arises from adding an integrity relationship.

Add integrity relationship. Unlike confidentiality, which is defined implicitly via the read permission, integrity must be defined separately from permissions. Hence, to define this new relationship $geqIntegrity(l, l')$ all labels whose integrity is effected by the relationship must agree.

It is flow from higher integrity levels to lower integrity levels which requires no approval. Hence, establishing a relationship $geqIntegrity(l, l')$ that induces $l_0 \succeq l_1$ must be approved by $ai(l_1)$, since l_1 is agreeing to accept future flows from l_0 without question so it must approve the new relationship.

5   Formal Results on System Properties

In this section, we give a number of formal results about our system showing that the security property approvals can be exactly computed. We begin with a discussion of an appropriate state space to represent such a system. Next we show that the *mayFlow* system is reasonable in the sense the we can exactly determine:

- The can flow and extended can-flow paths;
- The security property approvals needed for confidentiality and integrity for a new *mayFlow* definition; and
- The flows possible without any security property approvals.

Together, these show that everything needed to implement our administrative controls can be implemented.

5.1   State Space of SPBAC

Definition 3. *A **state** of a system includes the following information about the system: set of current users, the set of current groups and their memberships, the set of current labels, the assigned permissions and integrity levels. The **state space** $SS(s_0)$ is a directed graph on states that includes s_0 and every state reachable from s_0 by a sequence of legal changes to the system, and has an edge (s, s') exactly when s' is a legal successor state to s. The **ordinary state space**, $SSo(s_0)$ is the subset $SS(s_0)$ reachable from s_0 using only ordinary actions. The **approvaless state space**, $SSa(s_0)$ is the subset $SS(s_0)$ reachable from s_0 without any security property approvals.*

The possible changes from one state to the next include: a user being removed or added to a group (including a new user being added to a group when added to the system), any SysAdmin actions, and any actions requiring security property approvals.

Definition 4. *A sequence of labels $sl = [l_1, l_2, \ldots, l_n]$ (e.g., a can-flow path) **can be embedded** in $SS(s_0)$ (respectively $SSa(s_0)$, $SSo(s_0)$) **(for information flow)** if there exists a sequence of states $ss = [t_0 = s_0, t_1, t_2, \ldots, t_{n-1}]$, where for each $0 < j < n$:*

- *either $t_j = t_{j-1}$ or t_j is a successor of t_{j-1} in $SS(s_0)$ (respectively $SSa(s_0)$, $SSo(s_0)$) and*
- *in state t_j there exists a user who can (1) read l_j, (2) write l_{j+1}, and (3) mayFlow(l_j, l_{j+1}).*

Notice that a sequence of labels that can be embedded in $SSo(s_0)$ is a can-flow path.

Determining Approvals for a *mayFlow*

Confidentiality or integrity security property approval is needed when defining a new mayFlow(l, l') if the definition would add a new extended can-flow path that violates the confidentiality or integrity relation described in Section 4.3. We next exhibit an algorithm to determine this, developed in a series of lemmas.

The key to determining approvals is generating the set of all can-flow paths. From this, we will then show how to calculate the *new* extended can-flow paths.

Lemma 1. *There is an algorithm to determine which can-flow paths exist in a given state s_0 of the system.*

Proof. We first show how to construct a finite state space from $\mathcal{SS}o(s_0)$ – unfortunately, $\mathcal{SS}o(s_0)$ is not finite because of the addition of new users. The constructed state space contains only information about the groups, and in particular two kinds of information about the groups: which groups are empty (for membership secretary) and whether there is a particular user who is simultaneously a member of various read, write, and *mayFlow* groups for information flow.

Then we show that a bounded algorithm can compute all the can-flow paths.

The representation of $\mathcal{SS}o(s_0)$ is an extension of the form used in [19]. We use a tuple of sets, one set for each group tag that exists in state s_0. The elements of these sets can be any or all of: (1) initial user IDs (for users existing in state s_0); (2) $L-1$ newly minted user IDs, where L is the number of labels; and (3) the special symbol $\top$, representing an arbitrary number of new users. (As we shall see, the reason that L-1 newly minted user IDs are needed is that an existing can flow path will require at most $L-1$ *mayFlow* traversals.)

In our representation of the initial state of s_0, the elements of g's group tag set include all users U such that a group label $\langle U, G \rangle$ exists in state s_0. Additionally, the newly minted user IDs and the element $\top$ are in G's group tag set if some group set contains a rule for adding new users with tag G. The $\top$ indicates an unbounded number of group labels with tag G (one for each new user) could be added at any time after state s_0; the new IDs represent named new users.

To determine successor states, we will need to know whether various groups in the current state are nonempty. Group g_0 is nonempty in a state if and only if there is some group tag G such that group g_0's pattern contains either

1. the pair $\langle *u, G \rangle$ and the group tag set of G is nonempty, or
2. the pair $\langle U, G \rangle$ and initial user U is in the group tag set of G.

Now we compute successor states. Each relabel rule for group labels is of the form "For any user U, a group label $\langle U, G \rangle$ can be changed to $\langle U, G' \rangle$ by any member of group m." Such a rule leads to new states if both the membership secretary group m is nonempty in the current state, and G's group tag set is nonempty. In this case, for each user ID U in G's set, there is a successor state in which U is removed from G's set and added to G''s set. Additionally, if G's set contains $\top$ and G''s set does not contain $\top$, then there is a successor state in which both contain $\top$. This is because if there is an unbounded number of G group tags for added users, then using relabels we can create an unbounded number of G' group tags while still retaining an unbounded number of G group tags. Since we added new users to every initial group that could get new users in the initial state, we need not worry about the introduction of new users later.) There are only finitely many possible states, so the construction must halt.

Now we need to compute the set of can-flow paths from this finite representation of $\mathcal{SS}o(s_0)$. A flow between two different labels l and l' can occur in a state s of $\mathcal{SS}o(s_0)$ if and only if there is a user – either initial or named new user – who is in all three groups $r(l)$, $w(l')$, and $mayFlow(l, l')$ in state s. (The $L-1$ newly minted users are needed because it may be that no initial user could ever become a member of $r(l) \cap w(l') \cap mayFlow(l, l')$ but that a newly added user could. In the worst case, we would need $L-1$ such newly added users, one for each edge of a flow path containing all L labels.) Now we compute for every state which ordered pairs of labels can have flow in that state.

Now $cf = [l_1, \ldots, l_n]$ can be embedded in $SSo(s_0)$ if and only if there is a path through the state space starting at the initial state and passing through states where each can-flow edge (l_i, l_{i+1}) is possible, in order for $1 \le i \le n-1$, with no repeated states between any two can-flows (because we could delete such a cycle). (It is possible that multiple successive can-flow edges could all be located in one state.)

Corollary 1. *For any two fixed system state s_0 and s_1, there is an algorithm to determine which extended can-flow paths exist in s_1 and not in s_0.*

Proof Sketch. First, for each of the two states, calculate all the can-flow paths. Next, for each of the two states, for each possible path $\mathcal{P}$, determine whether there was a past flow along $\mathcal{P}$ using the *didFlow* information. For each of the two states, a path is an extended can-flow path if it can be formed as the concatenation of a path with past flow and a can-flow path. Finally, take the difference of the two sets of extended can-flow paths.

Lemma 2. *For a fixed state of the system s_0, there is an algorithm to determine which integrity security property approvals, if any, are needed to approve a request to define $mayFlow(l_a, l_b) = g$.*

Proof. Calculate which new extended can-flow paths approving the request would add using Corollary 1. Without SysAdmin actions, the labels and the effective integrity relation are fixed. So for each new extended can-flow path, $cf = [l_1, \ldots, l_n]$, check if $l_1 \succeq l_n$. If not, $ai(l_n)$ must approve.

Lemma 3. *For a fixed state of the system s_0, there is an algorithm to determine which confidentiality security property approvals, if any, are needed to approve a request to define $mayFlow(l_a, l_b) = g$.*

Proof. Similarly to the proof the Lemma 2, calculate which new extended can flow paths would be added by approving $mayFlow(l_a, l_b) = g$. For each new $\mathcal{P} = [l_1, l_2, \ldots, l_n]$, security property approval by $ac(l_1)$ is needed if in any state reachable from t_{n-1}, $r(l_n) \not\subseteq r(l_1)$.

We are now ready to state:

Theorem 1. *The exact security property approvals needed to define $mayFlow$ $(l_a, l_b) = g$ are computable.*

Proof. It follows immediately from Lemmas 2 and 3.

Finally, we show that we can analyze which information flows are possible with no security property approval. That is, which flows could occur in the approvaless state space (using only ordinary actions and SysAdmin actions that do not require security property approval). This is an extension of Theorem 1.

Theorem 2. *Given any state s_0, it is decidable whether information can flow from label l to l' without any security property approvals.*

Proof. First, observe that we can still ignore the addition of new labels. Without any security property approvals, a new label will have no integrity relation to any other label, and in that case it cannot have any flow in or out without security property approval of a *mayFlow*.

We argue that the only new groups needed are all the constant one-user groups. With no new labels, the only place new groups could be used would be to define new *mayFlows*. It might be that a "good" choice of group for a *mayFlow* would limit the number of new can-flow paths, and hence extended can flow paths, created. However, it suffices to consider constant groups that are as small as possible, and changing groups that have some relation (e.g., disjoint) to existing groups. For the second case, the groups must be in the same group set. (This argument is elaborated in [20].)

We next extend the construction of $\mathcal{SS}o(s_0)$ in Lemma 1 to construct a representation of $\mathcal{SS}a(s_0)$. In particular we must consider for each state whether there is a successor state which defines a new *mayFlow*.

First add to each state the set of currently defined *mayFlow* permissions. The construction is similar to that in the lemma, with the addition that for each state and each currently undefined $mayFlow(l_a, l_b)$ in the state, we add a successor state which contains $mayFlow(l_a, l_b) = r(l_a)$ if it can be done approvalessly. The determination of whether the *mayFlow* definition is approvaless can be done by Theorem 1.

6   Conclusions

In this paper, we have introduced a new access control model called *Security Property Based Administrative Controls (SPBAC)*. A SPBAC system seeks to maintain security properties, such as confidentiality and integrity, by:

- determining the effect on security properties of proposed (administrative) changes to the ordinary (non-administrative) part of the protection systems and
- seeking appropriate administrative approvals for those security properties which are violated.

An SPBAC allows selective violation of security properties, easy approval of changes which do not effect security properties, and localized (that is, distributed) control of the system by different administrators.

We believe, and give some evidence here, that the security properties violated in an SPBAC are exactly those that need reasoning about the trust placed in individuals to perform sensitive functions. These are the issues that an administrator should be thinking about when making changes to a system.

For information flow, we show how the security properties we develop implement Biba Integrity and Bell-LaPadula Confidentiality. We describe the design of such a system and its rationale, in particular a permission we call *mayFlow* and administrative groups associated with labels.

We show that the properties needed to perform administrative controls are decidable: (1) That we can exactly determine information flows (can-flow path), (2) that we can tell what security properties are violated and hence what administrative approvals would be necessary, and (3) we can determine all the flows that would be possible without violating any security property.

Our proofs rely on a state space construction. However, the state space is needed only to perform exact analysis. For administrative approvals it is certainly possible to tradeoff more approvals against much faster computation of the approvals requested.

SPBACs security properties are decidable [20] in a domain where access control methods have historically not been – that is administrative controls. Moreover we believe, and give some evidence in this paper, that they are nonrestrictive in the sense that they can represent all (or almost all) the relevant properties of one or more security properties.

Acknowledgments

The authors would like to thank Manigandan Radhakrishnan for his comments on an earlier draft and the referees for their many thoughtful comments. Robert Sloan was partially supported by NSF grant CCR-0100336.

References

1. Denning, D.E.: A lattice model of secure information flow. Communications of the ACM **19** (1976) 236–243
2. Boebert, W.E., Kain, R.: A practical alternative to hierarchical integrity policies. In: 8th National Computer Security Conference, Gaithersburg, MD (1985) 18–27
3. O'Brien, R., Rogers, C.: Developing applications on LOCK. In: Proc. 14th NIST-NCSC National Computer Security Conference. (1991) 147–156
4. Bell, D.E., LaPadula, L.J.: Secure computer systems: Mathematical foundations and model. Technical Report M74-244, Mitre Corporation, Bedford MA (1973)
5. Biba, K.: Integrity considerations for secure computer systems. Technical Report TR-3153, MITRE Corp, Bedford, MA (1977)
6. Harrison, M.A., Ruzzo, W.L., Ullman, J.D.: On protection in operating system. In: Symposium on Operating Systems Principles. (1975) 14–24
7. Sandhu, R.S.: The typed access matrix model. In: Proceedings of the IEEE Symposium on Security and Privacy. (1992) 122–136
8. Soshi, M.: Safety analysis of the dynamic-typed access matrix model. In Cuppens, F., Deswarte, Y., Gollmann, D., Waidner, M., eds.: 6th European Symposium on Research in Computer Security (ESORICS 2000). Volume 1895 of Lecture Notes in Computer Science., Toulouse, France, Springer-Verlag (2000) 106–121

9. Bishop, M., Snyder, L.: The transfer of information and authority in a protection system. In: Proceedings of the seventh ACM symposium on Operating systems principles, ACM Press (1979) 45–54

10. Sandhu, R.S., Coyne, E.J., Feinstein, H.L., Youman, C.E.: Role-based access control models. IEEE Computer **29** (1996) 38–47

11. Sandhu, R., Bhamidipati, V., Munawer, Q.: The ARBAC97 model for role-based administration of roles. ACM Transactions on Information and System Security **2** (1999) 105–135

12. Munawer, Q., Sandhu, R.: Simulation of the augmented typed access matrix model (ATAM) using roles. In: INFOSECU99: International Conference on Information Security. (1999)

13. Crampton, J.: Authorizations and Antichians. PhD thesis, Birkbeck College, Univ. of London, UK (2002)

14. Tidswell, J.F., Jaeger, T.: Integrated constraints and inheritance in DTAC. In: Proceedings of the 5th ACM Workshop on Role-Based Access Control (RBAC-00), N.Y., ACM Press (2000) 93–102

15. Tidswell, J., Jaeger, T.: An access control model for simplifying constraint expression. In Jajodia, S., Samarati, P., eds.: Proceedings of the 7th ACM Conference on Computer and Communications Security (CCS-00), N.Y., ACM Press (2000) 154–163

16. Jaeger, T., Tidswell, J.E.: Practical safety in flexible access control models. ACM Transactions on Information and System Security (TISSEC) **4** (2001) 158–190

17. Koch, M., Mancini, L.V., Parisi-Presicce, F.: A graph-based formalism for RBAC. ACM Transactions on Information and System Security (TISSEC) **5** (2002) 332–365

18. Koch, Mancini, Parisi-Presicce: Decidability of safety in graph-based models for access control. In: ESORICS: European Symposium on Research in Computer Security, LNCS, Springer-Verlag (2002) 229–243

19. Solworth, J.A., Sloan, R.H.: A layered design of discretionary access controls with decidable properties. In: Security and Privacy 2004, IEEE (2004) 56–67

20. Solworth, J.A., Sloan, R.H.: Decidable administrative controls of security properties (2004) submitted for publication.

21. Foley, S., Gong, L., Qian, X.: A security model of dynamic labeling providing a tiered approach to verification. In: IEEE Symposium on Security and Privacy, Oakland, California, IEEE Computer Society Press (1996) 142–154

A Vector Model of Trust
for Developing Trustworthy Systems

Indrajit Ray and Sudip Chakraborty

Colorado State University
Fort Collins, CO 80523, USA
{indrajit,sudip}@cs.colostate.edu

Abstract. All security services rely to a great extent on some notion of trust. However, even today, there is no accepted formalism or technique for the specification of trust and for reasoning about trust. Secure systems have been developed under the premise that concepts like "trusted" or "trustworthy" are well understood, unfortunately without even agreeing to what "trust" means, how to measure it, how to compare two trust values and how to combine two trust values. In this work we propose a new vector model of trust. Our model proposes the notion of different degrees of trust, differentiates between trust and distrust and formalizes the dependence of trust on time. We believe that our model will help answer some of the questions posed earlier.

1   Introduction

Confidentiality, integrity and availability of systems and information resources are increasingly becoming critical in our everyday life. To protect such resources it is important that we are able to determine the appropriate security policies. The notion of *trust* plays a critical role for the proper formulation of security policies. However, even today, there are no accepted formalisms or techniques for the specification of trust and for reasoning about trust. Secure systems have been built under the premise that concepts like "trustworthiness" or "trusted" are well understood, unfortunately without even agreeing on what "trust" means, how to measure it, how to compare two trust values and how to compose the same. This creates a number of problems in building secure systems, particularly those that are composed from several different components.

Consider, for example, the operational information base in a large corporation. Typically, this is generated with the accumulation of information from several sources. Some of these sources are under the direct administrative control of the corporation and thus are considered trustworthy. Other sources are "friendly" sources and information originating directly from them are also considered trustworthy. However, these "friendly" sources may have derived information from their own sources which the corporation does not have any first hand knowledge about; if such third-hand information is made available to the corporation, then the corporation has no real basis for determining the quality of that information. It will be rather naive for the corporation to trust this information to the same extent that it trusts information from sources under its direct control. Similarly not trusting this information at all is also too simplistic. Existing binary models of trust (where trust has only two values, "no trust" and "complete trust" and which

P. Samarati et al. (Eds.): ESORICS 2004, LNCS 3193, pp. 260–275, 2004.

are the ones most widely used in computer systems) will, nonetheless, categorize the trust value to one of these two levels. Existing trust models (even those that associate multiple levels to trust) do not provide satisfactory answers to questions such as: (i) What expectations can the corporation reasonably have about the usefulness of such information? (ii) What are the activities that the corporation can expect such information to fulfill without much problem? (iii) What are the activities that the corporation does not want to fulfill using this information?

The above observations prompt us to propose a new model of trust in which trust is defined as a vector of numeric values. Each element of the vector is a parameter in determining the value of trust. We identify three such parameters in our model. We propose methods to determine the values corresponding to these parameters. Substituting values for each of these parameters in the trust vector provides a value for trust of a certain degree. To make the concept of different degrees of trust more intuitive, we associate a numeric value in the range $[-1, 1]$ with the trust vector. The value in the positive region of this range is used to express trust and that in the negative region is used to express distrust. Uncertainty about trust and distrust is expressed using the value zero. We define operators to map a trust vector to a trust value within this range and also from a trust value to a trust vector. We investigate the dynamic nature of trust – how trust (or distrust) changes over time. Finally we observe that trust depends on trust itself – that is a trust relationship established at some point of time in the past will influence the computation of trust at the current time. We formalize this notion in our model.

The rest of the paper is organized as follows: In section 2 we briefly describe some of the more important works in the area of trust models. In section 3 we present our model of trust. We begin this section with the definition of trust that we use in the rest of the work. We define the parameters that contribute towards a value for trust. In sections 3.3, 3.4 and 3.5 we derive expressions to estimate each of these parameters. Then in section 3.6 we introduce the concept of normalized trust followed by, in section 3.7, the definition of the concept of value of trust. Section 3.8 deals with trust dynamics – the dependence of trust on time. In section 4 we define the dominance relation between two trust relationships that allow us to identify how two trust relationships compare. Finally section 5 concludes with a discussion of our future work.

2   Related Work

A number of logic-based formalisms of trust have been proposed by researchers. Almost all of these view trust as a binary relation. Forms of first order logic [1–3] and modal logic or its modification [4] have been variously used to model trust in these cases. Simple relational formulae like *A* trusts *B* are used to model trust between two entities. Each formalism extends this primitive construct to include features such as temporal constraints and predicate arguments. Given these primitives and the traditional conjunction, disjunction, negation and implication operators, these logical frameworks express trust rules in some language and reason about these properties. Abdul-Rahman and Hailes [3] propose a trust model, based on "reputation" that allows artificial agents to reason about trustworthiness and allows real people to automate that process. Jones and Firozabadi [5] models trust as the issue of reliability of an agent's transmission.

They use a variant of modal logic to model various trust scenarios. They also use their language to model the concepts of deception and an entity's trust in another entity.

Yahalom et al. [6, 7] propose a formal model for deriving new trust relationships from existing ones. In [6] the authors propose a model for expressing trust relations in authentication protocols, together with an algorithm for deriving trust relations from recommendations. In [7] rules and algorithms for obtaining public keys based on trust relationships are developed. Neither of these works define what is meant by trust. Beth et al. [8] extend the ideas presented by Yahalom et al. to include relative trust. This work proposes a method for extracting trust values based on experiences and recommendations and also a method for deriving new trust values from existing ones within a network of trust relationships. Jøsang [9–11] proposes a model for trust based on a general model for expressing relatively uncertain beliefs about the truth of statements. Trust is an opinion, which is expressed as a triplet $< b,d,u >\in \{b,d,u\}$. Here b, d, and u are respectively measures of one's belief, disbelief, and uncertainty in a proposition. A major shortcoming of this model is that it has no mechanism for monitoring trust relationships to re-evaluate their constraints. Cohen et al. [12] propose an alternative, more differentiated conception of trust, called Argument-based Probabilistic Trust model (APT). The most important use of APT is to chart how trust varies, from one user to another, from one decision aid to another, from one situation to another, and across phases of decision aid use.

Xiong and Liu [13] present a coherent adaptive trust model for quantifying and comparing the trustworthiness of peers based on a transaction-based feedback system. They propose three basic trust parameters – peer feedback through transactions, total number of transactions a peer performs, and credibility of the feedback sources. The authors address factors that influence peer-to-peer trust, like reputation systems and misbehavior of peers by giving false feedback. The authors also provide a trust metric for predicting a given peer's likelihood of a successful transaction in the future. Purser [14] presents a simple, graphical approach to model trust. He points out the relationship between trust and risk and argues that for every trust relationship, there exists a risk associated with a breach of the trust extended. Trust relationships are modeled as directed graphs where trust is an unidirectional directed edge from the trusting entity to the trusted entity. The author includes context (to define scope of trust), associated confidence level, associated risk and transitivity value. Bacharach and Gambetta [15] embark on a re-orientation of the theory of trust. They define trust as a particular belief, which arises in games with a certain payoff structure. They also identify the source of the primary trust problem in the uncertainty about the payoffs of the trustee. According to the authors, the trustor must judge whether apparent signs of trustworthiness are themselves to be trusted.

3   Our Model

We adopt the definition of trust as provided by Grandison and Sloman [16].

Definition 1. *Trust is defined to be the firm belief in the competence of an entity to act dependably, reliably and securely within a specific context.*

In the same work, Grandison and Sloman define *distrust* as the "lack of firm belief in the competence of an entity to act dependably, securely and reliably". However, we believe distrust is somewhat stronger than just "lacking a belief". Grandison and Sloman's definition suggests the possibility of ambivalence in making a decision regarding distrust. We choose to be more precise and thus define distrust as follows.

Definition 2. *Distrust is defined as the firm belief in the incompetence of an entity to act dependably, securely and reliably within a specific context.*

Trust is specified as a trust relationship between a truster – an entity that trusts the target entity – and a trustee – the entity that is trusted. The truster is always an active entity (for example, a human being or a subject). The trustee can either be an active entity or a passive entity (for example, a piece of information or a software). We use the following notation to specify a trust relationship – $(A \xrightarrow{c} B)_t^N$. We call this the *normalized* trust relationship. It specifies A's *normalized* trust on B at a given time t for a particular context c. This relationship is obtained from the simple trust relationship $- (A \xrightarrow{c} B)_t -$ by combining the latter with a normalizing factor. We also introduce a concept called the *value* of a trust relationship. This is denoted by the expression $\mathbf{v}(A \xrightarrow{c} B)_t^N$ and is a number in $[-1, 1]$ that is associated with the normalized trust relationship.

3.1   Trust Context

A trust relationship between a truster, A, and a trustee, B, is never absolute [16]. Always, the truster trusts the trustee with respect to its ability to perform a specific action or provide a specific service. For example, an entity A may trust another entity B about the latter's ability to keep a secret. However, this does not mean if A wants a job done efficiently, A will trust B to it. Similarly, if we want to compare two trust values, we just cannot compare two arbitrary trust values. We need to compare the values for trust which serves similar purposes. This leads us to associate a notion of *context* with a trust relationship. We begin by defining the notion of *atomic purpose* of a trust relationship.

Definition 3. *The* atomic purpose *of a trust relationship* $(A \xrightarrow{c} B)_t$ *is one of*

1. **TS-1** *The truster trusts a trustee to* access resources *that the truster controls.*
2. **TS-2** *The truster trusts the trustee to* provide a service *that does not involve access to the truster's resources.*
3. **TS-3** *The truster trusts the trustee to* make decisions *on its behalf.*

The truster may also trust the trustee for some combination of these atomic purposes. For example the truster may trust the trustee to provide a service and make decisions.

Definition 4. *The* purpose *of a trust relationship is defined as follows.*

1. *An atomic purpose is a purpose of a trust relationship.*
2. *The negation of a purpose denoted by "not" purpose, is a purpose.*
3. *Two purposes connected by the operator "and" form a purpose.*
4. *Two purposes connected by the operator "or" form a purpose.*
5. *Nothing else is a purpose.*

We are interested in three *aspects* – dependability, security and reliability – of the trustee. Combining the concepts of trust purposes and trustee aspects, we define the notion of trust *context* as the interrelated conditions in which trust exists or occurs. For example, let a truster, A, trust a trustee, B's dependability to provide a service and make a decision. The "dependability to provide a service and make a decision" is considered to be the trust context. Let S denote the set of trust purposes and $\mathcal{A}$, the set of trustee aspects identified above. Then a trust context is defined as follows.

Definition 5. *The* context, *$c(T)$, of a trust relationship T is defined as a function that takes a trust relationship as an input and returns a sequence of tuples of the form $< s_1, a_1 > | < s_2, a_2 > | \dots$ where*

1. $s_i : S \times S \to S$ *and*
2. $a_i : \mathcal{A} \times \mathcal{A} \to \mathcal{A}$

3.2   Trust Evaluation

We define a trust value in terms of a vector of numbers. Each element in the trust vector represents a parameter that contributes towards the trust value. Before we formally define these trust parameters, we would like to point to two characteristics of trust (or distrust). The first is the dynamic nature of trust. Trust changes over time. Even if there is no change in the underlying factors that influence trust over a time period, the value of trust at the end of the period is not the same as that at the beginning of the period. Irrespective of our initial trust or distrust decision, over a period of time we gradually become non-decisive or uncertain about the trust decision. This leads us to claim that trust (and alternately distrust) decays over time - both tends towards a non-decisive value over time.

The second characteristic is, what is often called the *propensity* to trust [16]. Given the same set of values for the factors that influence trust, two trusters may come up with two different trust values for the same trustee. We believe that there are two main reasons for this. First, during evaluation of a trust value, a truster may assign different weights to the different factors that influence trust. The weights will depend on the trust evaluation policy of the truster. So if two different trusters assign two different sets of weights, then the resulting trust value will be different. The second reason is applicable only when the truster is a human being and is completely subjective in nature – one person may be more trusting than another. We believe that this latter concept is extremely difficult to model. We choose to disregard this feature in our model and assume that all trusters are trusting to the same extent. We capture the first factor using the concept of a *trust evaluation policy vector*, which is simply a vector of weight values.

We begin by identifying three different parameters that influence trust values.

Definition 6. *The* experience *of a truster about a trustee is defined as the measure of the cumulative effect of a number of events that were encountered by the truster with respect to the trustee in a particular context and over a specified period of time.*

The trust value of a truster on a trustee can change because of the truster's *experiences* with the trustee in the particular context. Each experience that can influence the degree of trust is interpreted by the truster as either a *trust-positive experience* or a *trust-negative experience*. A trust-positive experience contributes towards a gain in trust degree whereas a trust-negative experience contributes towards a loss in trust degree.

Definition 7. *The* knowledge *of the truster regarding a trustee for a particular context is defined as a measure of the condition of awareness of the truster through acquaintance with, familiarity of or understanding of a science, art or technique.*

The trust value of a truster on a trustee can change because of some *knowledge* that the truster comes to posses regarding the trustee for the particular context. Knowledge can be of two types – *direct knowledge* and *indirect knowledge*. Direct knowledge is one which the truster acquires by itself. It may be obtained by the truster in some earlier time for some purpose or, it may be a piece of information about the trustee for which the truster has a concrete proof to be true. Indirect knowledge, on the other hand, is something that the truster does not acquire by itself. The source of indirect knowledge is the *reputation* of the trustee in the context. The truster may get the idea about the reputation of trustee from various sources like reviews, journals, news bulletin, people's opinion etc. As with experience, we can have *trust-positive knowledge* and *trust-negative knowledge*.

Definition 8. *A* recommendation *about a trustee is defined as a measure of the subjective or objective judgment of a recommender about the trustee to the truster.*

The trust value of a truster on a trustee can change because of a *recommendation* for the trustee. We can have a *trust-positive recommendation* and a *trust-negative recommendation*. Moreover, recommendation can be obtained by the truster from more than one source.

To compute a trust relationship we assume that each of these three factors is expressed in terms of a numeric value in the range $[-1, 1]$. A -ve value for the component is used to indicate the *trust-negative* type for the component, whereas a +ve value for the component is used to indicate the *trust-positive* type of the component. A 0 (zero) value for the component indicates neither positive effect nore negative effect on the trust value.

3.3 Evaluating Experience

We model experience in terms of the number of events encountered by a truster, A, regarding a trustee, B in the context c within a specified period of time $[t_0, t_n]$. We assume that A has a record of the events since time t_0. An event can be either trust-positive or trust-negative depending whether it contributes towards a trust-positive experience or a trust-negative experience.

Let N denote the set of natural numbers. The set of time instances $\{t_0, t_1, \ldots, t_n\}$ is a totally ordered set ordered by the temporal relation $\prec$ (called the *precedes-in-time* relation) as follows: $\forall i, j \in N, t_i \prec t_j \Leftrightarrow i < j$. We use the symbol $t_i \preceq t_j$ to signify either $t_i \prec t_j$ or $t_i = t_j$. Let also e_k denote the kth event. Events happen at time instances. We define the concept *event-occurrence-time* as follows:

Definition 9. Event-occurrence-time ET *is a function that takes an event e_k as input and returns the time instance, t_i at which the event occurred. Formally, $ET : e_k \rightarrow t_i$.*

We divide the time period $[t_0,t_n]$ over which the events have occurred into a set $\mathcal{T}$ of n intervals, $[t_0,t_1]$, $[t_1,t_2]$, ..., $[t_{n-1},t_n]$ such that for any interval $[t_i,t_j]$, $t_i \prec t_j$. A particular interval, $[t_{k-1},t_k]$, is referred to as the kth interval. We extend the $\prec$ relation on $\mathcal{T}$ and the time intervals are also totally ordered by the $\prec$ relation as follows – $\forall i,j,k,l \in N$, $[t_i,t_j] \prec [t_k,t_l] \Leftrightarrow t_j \prec t_k$. Finally, the intervals are non-overlapping, that is, $\forall i,j,k,l \in N$, $[t_i,t_j] \cap [t_k,t_l] = \phi$.

Definition 10. *Let $\mathcal{E}$ denote the set of all events. A* sequence of events, C_E, *is the set of events e_1, e_2, ..., e_n, $e_i \in \mathcal{E}$, such that $\forall i,j$, $ET(e_i) \in [t_k,t_l] \Leftrightarrow ET(e_j) \in [t_k,t_l]$ and such that $\forall i,j \in N$, $e_i \prec e_j \Leftrightarrow i < j$.*

Let P denote the set of all trust-positive events and Q denote the set of all trust-negative events (that is, $\mathcal{E} = \{P \cup Q\}$). We assign equal numeric weights to all events, trust-positive or trust-negative, within a given interval. Let v_{k_i} be the weight of the kth event in the ith interval. We assign a weight of +1 if an event is in the set P and -1 if the event is in the set Q. Thus,

$$v_{k_i} = \begin{cases} +1 & \text{, if } e_{k_i} \in P \\ -1 & \text{, if } e_{k_i} \in Q \end{cases}$$

Definition 11. *The* incidents I_i, *corresponding to the ith time interval is the sum of the values of all the events, trust-positive or trust-negative for the time interval. It is given by $I_i = \sum_{k=1}^{n_i} v_{k_i}$ where n_i is the number of events occurred in the ith time interval.*

Typically, events far back in time does not count just as strongly as very recent events. To accommodate this we assign a *non-negative* weight w_i to the ith interval such that $w_i > w_j$ whenever $j < i$, $i,j \in N$. We then define *experience* as follows:

Definition 12. *The* experience *of an entity A about another entity B for a particular context c, is the accumulation of all trust-positive and trust-negative events that A has with regards to B over a given period of time $[t_0,t_n]$, scaled to be in the range $[-1,1]$.*

To ensure that the value of experience is within this range $[-1,1]$ we define the weight w_i for the ith interval as

$$w_i = \frac{i}{S} \quad \forall i = 1,2,\ldots,n \text{ where } S = \frac{n(n+1)}{2} \tag{1}$$

Then the experience of A with regards to B for a particular context c is given by

$$_A E_B^c = \frac{\sum_{i=1}^{n} w_i I_i}{\sum_{i=1}^{n} n_i} \tag{2}$$

To illustrate our concept of experience we use the following example. We use the symbol "+" to denote positive events and the symbol "-" to denote negative events.

Example 1. Consider the following happening of events over time period $t_0 - t_7$.

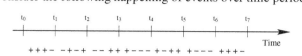

We divide the time period into the intervals – $[t_0,t_1], \ldots [t_6,t_7]$. Applying our theory, we have the following incidents: I_0 for interval $[t_0,t_1] = +2$, $I_1 = 0$, $I_2 = 0$, $I_3 = -2$, $I_4 = +2$, $I_5 = -2$ and $I_6 = +2$.

The weights assigned to each time interval are as follows – w_0 (for interval $[t_0,t_1]$) $= 0.04$, $w_1 = 0.07$, $w_2 = 0.11$, $w_3 = 0.14$, $w_4 = 0.18$, $w_5 = 0.21$ and $w_6 = 0.25$ (for interval $[t_6,t_7]$. Thus the value for experience over the period $[t_0,t_7]$ is 0.00857.

Example 2. Consider the second set of events over the same time period $t_0 - t_7$.

The difference between this set of events and the one in example 1 is that we have more negative events that have happened recently. The total number of trust-positive and trust-negative events are the same in both. We get a value of 0.00286 for experience with this set of events.

3.4 Evaluating Knowledge

The parameter, knowledge, is more difficult to compute and is, to some extent, subjective. To begin with, each truster must define its own criteria for gradation of knowledge regarding a particular entity. To assign a value to the *knowledge* component, the truster must come up with two values between -1 and +1 for direct knowledge as well as indirect knowledge or reputation. How the values are assigned, depends on the scheme and policy of the truster. Also the truster is solely responsible to assign the relative weights for these two types of knowledge. We represent this as, $_A K_B^c = w_1 d + w_2 r$, where $d, r \in [-1, 1]$ and $w_1 + w_2 = 1$. d and r are the values corresponding to direct knowledge and reputation respectively. The weights w_1 and w_2 are determined by the underlying policy where $w_i \in [0, 1] \ \forall i = 1, 2$.

The truster needs not have values for both the components. That is, there may be situation where either $d = 0$ or $r = 0$. A may not have any knowledge at all about B in the context. For these types of cases, where the truster does not have any information regarding the trustee in the context c, we assign $_A \mathbf{K}_B^c = 0$ where '0' represents 'no knowledge' about B in context c. This is the situation when both d and r are zero.

3.5 Evaluating Recommendation

An initial recommendation, V_R, is a value in the range [-1,1] that is provided to the truster by the recommender. To assist the recommender in generating this value, the truster provides a questionnaire to the recommender. The recommender uses the positive range to express his faith in the trustee while uses the negative range to express his discontent. If the recommender has no conclusive decision, he uses a zero value for recommendation.

Now, a truster A will often have a trust relationship with the recommender R. The context of this trust relationship will be to act "reliably to provide a service (recommendation, in this case)". This trust relationship will have an effect on the value of the recommendation provided by the recommender. For example, let us say that A trusts R to quite a great extent to provide an appropriate recommendation for B but does not trust C as much as R. R provides a recommendation value of -0.5 to A and C also provides the same recommendation value. To A, R's -0.5 value will have more weightage for computing the trust value on B than C's, although A will consider both the values. To model this scenario we use the trust of the truster on the recommender as a weight factor to the initial recommendation value returned by the recommender. We had introduced the expression $\mathbf{v}(A \xrightarrow{c} B)_t^N$ earlier in section 3 to denote the *value* of a normalized trust relationship. This is a value in the range $[-1,1]$. We use the absolute value of this value as the weight factor. At this stage we do not specify how we generate this value. We leave that to a later section. At this stage we express the *recommendation* $_CR_B$ of a recommeder C for an entity B to the truster A as $_CR_B = |\mathbf{v}(A \xrightarrow{rec} C)_t^N| V_R$.

Finally, the truster A may get recommendations about the trustee B from many different recommenders not just one. Thus the recommendation value that the truster uses to compute the trust in the trustee is specified as the sum of all recommendations scaled to the range $[-1,1]$. This is given by the equation

$$\psi R_B^c = \frac{\sum_{j=1}^n |\mathbf{v}(A \xrightarrow{rec} j)_t^N| \cdot V_j}{\sum_{j=1}^n |\mathbf{v}(A \xrightarrow{rec} j)_t^N|} \tag{3}$$

where, Ψ is a group of n recommenders.

3.6 Normalization of Trust Vector

Having determined the values for each component of the trust vector we specify the simple trust relationship between the truster A and the trustee B in a context c as $(A \xrightarrow{c} B)_t = [_AE_{B,A}^c K_{B,\psi}^c R_B^c]$

As mentioned earlier in section 3.2, a truster may give more weight to one of the parameters than other in computing a trust relationship. For example, a truster A may choose to lay more emphasis on experience than recommendation in computing trust. Or for example, a truster may be quite sceptical regarding recommendations about the trustee. In that case the truster may want to consider the recommendation factor to a lesser extent in computing trust than experience and knowledge about the trustee. Which particular component needs to be emphasized more than the others, is a matter of trust evaluation policy of the truster. The policy is represented by the truster as a trust policy vector.

Definition 13. *The trust policy vector, $\mathbf{W}$ is a vector that has the same dimension as the simple-trust vector. The elements are real numbers in the range $[0,1]$ and the sum of all elements is equal to 1.*

The normalized trust relationship between a truster A and a trustee B at a time t and for a particular context c is given by

$$(A \xrightarrow{c} B)^N_t = \mathbf{W} \odot (A \xrightarrow{c} B)_t \qquad (4)$$

The $\odot$ operator represents the normalization operator. Let $(A \xrightarrow{c} B)_t = [_AE^c_B, _AK^c_B, _\psi R^c_B]$ be a trust vector such that $_AE^c_B, _AK^c_B, _\psi R^c_B \in [-1,1]$. Let also $\mathbf{W} = [W_e, W_k, W_r]$ be the corresponding trust policy vector such that $W_e + W_k + W_r = 1$ and $W_e, W_k, W_r \in [0,1]$. The $\odot$ operator generates the normalized trust relationship as

$$
\begin{aligned}
(A \xrightarrow{c} B)^N_t &= \mathbf{W} \odot (A \xrightarrow{c} B)_t \\
&= [W_e,\ W_k,\ W_r] \odot [_AE^c_B,\ _AK^c_B,\ _\psi R^c_B] \\
&= [W_e \cdot _AE^c_B,\ W_k \cdot _AE^c_B,\ W_r \cdot _\psi R^c_B] \\
&= [_A\hat{E}^c_B,\ _A\hat{K}^c_B,\ _\psi\hat{R}^c_B]
\end{aligned}
$$

It follows from above that each element $_A\hat{E}^c_B, _A\hat{K}^c_B, _\psi\hat{R}^c_B$ of the normalized trust vector also lies within $[-1,1]$.

3.7 Value of the Normalized Trust Vector

So far we have defined a trust relationship in terms of a vector which is *normalized* by a trust policy. Recall, however, from section 3.5 that there is at least one scenario in which we need to use a trust value as a weight for a real number (namely recommendation). Thus it seems appropriate to define the concept of a *value* corresponding to the normalized trust vector. Moreover, although we had previously argued against using a single value for trust, there is a big advantage of using a single value. A single value is more intuitive than a vector. In the next section we also show how such a single value helps us in assessing the dynamics of trust.

Definition 14. *The* value *of a normalized trust relationship* $(A \xrightarrow{c} B)^N_t = [_A\hat{E}^c_B, _A\hat{K}^c_B, _\psi\hat{R}^c_B]$ *is a number in the range* $[-1,1]$ *and is defined as*

$$v(A \xrightarrow{c} B)^N_t = _A\hat{E}^c_B + _A\hat{K}^c_B + _\psi\hat{R}^c_B \qquad (5)$$

Having defined the value for a trust relationship we revise the terms "trust" and "distrust" as follows:

1. If the value, T, of a normalized trust relationship is such that $0 < T \le 1$ then it is trust.
2. If the value, T, of a normalized trust relationship is such that $-1 \le T < 0$ then it is distrust.
3. If the value, T, is 0 then it is neither trust nor distrust.

3.8 Trust Dynamics

Trust (and distrust) changes over time. Let us suppose that we have initially computed a trust relationship T_{t_i} at time t_i, based on the values of the underlying parameters at that time. Suppose now that we try to recompute the trust relationship T_{t_n} at time t_n. We claim that even if the underlying parameters do not change between times t_i and t_n, the trust relationship will change. This change of trust over time is often called *trust dynamics*.

To model trust dynamics we refer to the old adage – Time the great healer. The general tendency is to forget about past happenings. This leads us to claim that trust (and distrust) tends towards neutrality as time increases. Initially, the value does not change much; after a certain period the change is more rapid; finally the change becomes more stable as the value approaches the neutral (value = 0) level. Also we assert the following:

$$\lim_{t \to \infty} \mathbf{v}(T_t) = 0$$

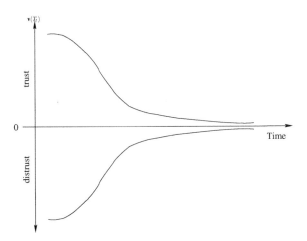

Fig. 1. Graph Showing the Nature of Trust Dynamics

How fast trust (or distrust) will decay over time, is, we believe, dependent on the truster's policy. The truster may choose to forget about trust relationships which are 3 years old or 5 years old. The model cannot dictate this. Our goal is to provide a basis by which the truster can at least estimate, based on the truster's individual perception about this, the trust at time t_n. We further believe that trust relationship at present time is not only dependent on the values of the underlying parameters, but also on the "decayed" value of the previous trust. We discuss this in more details in the next section.

Let $\mathbf{v}(T_{t_i})$, be the value of a trust relationship, T_{t_i}, at time t_i and $\mathbf{v}(T_{t_n})$ be the decayed value of the same at time t_n. Then the *time-dependent value* of T_{t_i} is defined as follows.

Definition 15. *The* time-dependent value *of a trust relationship T_{t_i} from time t_i, computed at present time t_n, is given by*

$$v(T_{t_n}) = v(T_{t_i})e^{-(v(T_{t_i})\Delta t)^{2k}} \tag{6}$$

where $\Delta t = t_n - t_i$ and k is any small integer ≥ 1.

The value of k determines the rate of change of trust with time and is assigned by the truster based on its perception about the change. If $\Delta t = 0$ that is at $t_n = t_i$, $e^{-(\mathbf{v}(T_{t_i})\Delta t)^{2k}} = 1$ and hence $\mathbf{v}(T_{t_n}) = \mathbf{v}(T_{t_i})$. When $\Delta t \to \infty$, then $e^{-(T_i\Delta t)^{2k}} \to 0$ and hence $\mathbf{v}(T_{t_n}) \to 0$. This corroborates the fact the time-dependent value of the last known trust value is asymptotic to zero at infinite time.

To obtain the trust vector T_{t_n} at time t_n, we distribute the value $\mathbf{v}(T_{t_n})$ obtained in equation (6) evenly over the components. The rational behind this is that between t_i and t_n we do not have sufficient information to assign different weights to the different components. Thus we have the time-dependent vector as

$$T_{t_n} = [\frac{\mathbf{v}(T_{t_n})}{3}, \frac{\mathbf{v}(T_{t_n})}{3}, \frac{\mathbf{v}(T_{t_n})}{3}]$$

3.9 Trust Vector at Present Time

As indicated earlier, the trust of a truster A on a trustee B in a context c at time t_n depends not only on the underlying components of the trust vector but also on the trust established earlier at time t_i. Consider for example that at time t_i Alice trusts Bob to the fullest extent (value = 1). At time t_n Alice re-evaluates the trust relationship and determines the value to be -0.5 (distrust). However, we believe that Alice will lay some importance on the previous trust value and will not distrust Bob as much as a -0.5 value. So, the normalized trust vector at t_n is a linear combination of time-dependent trust vector and the normalized trust vector calculated at present time. The weight Alice will give to old trust vector and present normalized trust vector is, again, a matter of policy. However, this leads us to refine the expression for normalized trust vector at time t_n as follows. Let $\hat{T}$ be the time-dependent trust vector derived from $\mathbf{v}(T_{t_i})$ at time t_n. Also, let α and β are the weights corresponding to present normalized vector and time-dependent vector, respectively.

Definition 16. *The normalized trust relationship between a truster A and a trustee B at time t_n in a particular context c is given by*

$$(A \xrightarrow{c} B)_{t_n}^N = \begin{cases} [_A\hat{E}_B^c, \; _A\hat{K}_B^c, \; _\psi\hat{R}_B^c] \\ \quad \text{if } t_n = 0 \\ [\frac{v(\hat{T})}{3}, \; \frac{v(\hat{T})}{3}, \; \frac{v(\hat{T})}{3}] \\ \quad \text{if } t_n \neq 0 \text{ and } _A\hat{E}_R^c = _A\hat{K}_R^c = _\psi\hat{R}_R^c = 0 \\ [_A\hat{E}_B^c, \; _A\hat{K}_B^c, \; _\psi\hat{R}_B^c] \oplus [\frac{v(\hat{T})}{3}, \; \frac{v(\hat{T})}{3}, \; \frac{v(\hat{T})}{3}] \\ \quad \text{if } t_n \neq 0 \text{ and at least one of} \\ \quad _A\hat{E}_B^c, _A\hat{K}_B^c, _\psi\hat{R}_B^c \neq 0 \end{cases} \quad (7)$$

The $\oplus$ operator is defined as follows.

$$[_A\hat{E}_B^c, _A\hat{K}_B^c, _\psi\hat{R}_B^c] \oplus [\frac{\mathbf{v}(\hat{T})}{3}, \frac{\mathbf{v}(\hat{T})}{3}, \frac{\mathbf{v}(\hat{T})}{3}] = \alpha \cdot [_A\hat{E}_B^c, _A\hat{K}_B^c, _\psi\hat{R}_B^c] + \beta \cdot [\frac{\mathbf{v}(\hat{T})}{3}, \frac{\mathbf{v}(\hat{T})}{3}, \frac{\mathbf{v}(\hat{T})}{3}]$$

$$= [\alpha \cdot _A\hat{E}_B^c + \beta \cdot \frac{\mathbf{v}(\hat{T})}{3}, \; \alpha \cdot _A\hat{K}_B^c + \beta \cdot \frac{\mathbf{v}(\hat{T})}{3}, \; \alpha \cdot _\psi\hat{R}_B^c + \beta \cdot \frac{\mathbf{v}(\hat{T})}{3}]$$

where $\alpha, \beta \in [0, 1]$ and $\alpha + \beta = 1$.

4   Comparison Operation on Trust Vectors

In many real life scenarios we need to determine the relative trustworthiness of two trustees. Consider the following example. Suppose entity A gets two conflicting pieces of information from two different sources B and C. In this case A will probably want to compare its trust relationships with entities B and C and accept the information that originated from the "more" trustworthy entity. This lead us to define a comparison operator on trust relationships.

Let $T = (A \xrightarrow{\dot{c}} B)_t^N$ and $T' = (A \xrightarrow{\ddot{c}} C)_t^N$ be two normalized trust relationships – between A and B, and between A and C respectively – at a particular time t. We have the following definition.

Definition 17. *Two trust relationships, T and T' are said to be* compatible *if the trust relationships have been defined under the same policy vector and the context $c(T)$ for the trust relationship T is the same as the context $c(T')$ for T', that is $c(T) = c(T')$. Otherwise the two trust relationships are called* incompatible.

Note that to determine if two trust relationships are compatible or not we do not make any assumptions about the truster and the trustee involved in the relationships nor about the time instances of the relationships. In order to be able to compare the two trust relationships T and T' from above it has to be the case that the two contexts $\dot{c}$ and $\ddot{c}$ are the same.

The most intuitive way to compare two trust relationships T and T' is to compare the values of the trust relationships in a numerical manner. Thus for A to determine the relative levels of trustworthiness of B and C, A evaluates $\mathbf{v}(A \xrightarrow{c} B)_t^N$ and $\mathbf{v}(A \xrightarrow{c} C)_t^N$. If $\mathbf{v}(A \xrightarrow{c} B)_t^N > \mathbf{v}(A \xrightarrow{c} C)_t^N$, then A trust B more than C in the context c. We say that T *dominates* T', given by $T \succ T'$.

However, if $\mathbf{v}(A \xrightarrow{c} B)_t^N = \mathbf{v}(A \xrightarrow{c} C)_t^N$, A cannot judge the relative trustworthiness of B and C. This is because there can be two vectors whose individual component values are different but their scalar values are the same. For such cases we need to compare the individual elements of the two trust relationships to determine the relative degree of trustworthiness.

Let $(A \xrightarrow{c} B)_t^N = [{}_A\hat{E}_B^c, \ {}_A\hat{K}_B^c, \ {}_\psi\hat{R}_B^c]$ and $(A \xrightarrow{c} C)_t^N = [{}_A\hat{E}_C^c, \ {}_A\hat{K}_C^c, \ {}_\psi\hat{R}_C^c]$ such that $\mathbf{v}(A \xrightarrow{c} B)_t^N = \mathbf{v}(A \xrightarrow{c} C)_t^N$. Let also the underlying trust policy vector be given by $W = (w_1, \ w_2, \ w_3)$ where $w_1 + w_2 + w_3 = 1$ and $w_i \geq 0 \ \forall i = 1,2,3$. To determine the dominance relation between T and T' we first determine the *ordered* trust relationships $\bar{T}$ corresponding to T.

Definition 18. *The* ordered *trust relationship $\bar{T}$ is generated from a trust relationship T as follows:*

1. *Order the w_i's in the trust policy vector corresponding to T in descending order of magnitude.*
2. *Sort the components of the trust vector T according to the corresponding weight components.*

We compare the two ordered trust relationships $\bar{T}$ and $\bar{T}'$, corresponding to T and T', componentwise to determine the dominance relation between the two. Note that we assume that the same underlying trust policy vector has been used to determine the trust relationships. If the first component of $\bar{T}$ is numerically greater than the first component of $\bar{T}'$ then $T \succ T'$. Else if the first components are equal then compare the second components. If the second component of $\bar{T}$ is greater than the second component of $\bar{T}'$ then $T \succ T'$, and so on. If we cannot conclude a dominance relation between the two trust relationship, then we say that the two trust relationships are *incomparable*. This is formalized by the following definition.

Definition 19. *Let T and T' be two trust relationships and $\bar{T}$ and $\bar{T}'$ be the corresponding ordered trust relationships. Let also $\bar{T}_i$ and $\bar{T}_i'$ represent the ith component of each ordered trust relationships and w_i represent the ith weight component in the corresponding trust policy vector. T is said to dominate T' if any one of the following holds.*

1. *$v(T) > v(T')$; or*
2. *if $\forall\, i,j,\ i \neq j,\ (w_i = w_j)$ then $\forall\, i,\ \bar{T}_i > \bar{T}_i'$; or*
3. *if $\exists\, i, \bar{T}_i > \bar{T}_i'$ and for $k = 0 \ldots (i-1),\ \bar{T}_{i-k} \not\prec T_{i-k}^{\bar{7}}$*

Otherwise T is said to be incomparable *with T'.*

5   Conclusions and Future Work

In this paper we introduce a new model of trust which we term the vector model. Trust is specified as a trust relationship between a truster and a trustee at a particular time instance and for a particular context. We identify three parameters namely, experience, knowledge and recommendation that contribute towards defining this trust relationship. We propose expression for evaluating these factors. Next we introduce the concept of normalized trust. We show how to factor in a notion of trust policy in computing the trust vector. We also model the notion of trust dynamics, that is the change of trust with time. Incorporating all these different notions we finally provide an expression to compute a trust vector that also includes the effect of a previous trust relationship between the same truster, trustee in the same context. We also define ways by which we can compare two trust vectors.

To our knowledge our model is the first to (1) formally differentiate between trust and distrust, (2) address explicitly the contributions of different factors towards formation of a trust relationship, (3) explore and formalize the dynamic nature of trust and (4) address the influence of a previous trust relationship in computing the current trust relationship. A novel feature of our model is that it is easily adaptable if the underlying parameters are changed to include more than the current three parameters (the parameters all need to be orthogonal to each other.).

A lot of work remains to be done. We are currently extending this model to define trust combination operators so that we can formulate the trust relationships between many trusters and many trustees beginning with simple trust relationships between one truster and one trustee as in this work. We also plan to formalize the notion of trust chains in the context of our model. In the current work we have not addressed the issue of determining trust policy. We have assumed that there is an underlying trust policy that helps us assign weights to the various components of the model. How to assign these weights? What will be an appropriate guideline for that? These are some of the issues we will address in future. This will be followed by a formal language to manage and manipulate trust relationships. We are looking towards an SQL like language for this purpose. Finally we plan to develop a complete trust management framework based on our model.

Acknowledgment

This work was partially supported by the U.S. Air Force Research Laboratory (AFRL) and the Federal Aviation Administration (FAA) under contract F30602-03-1-0101. The views presented here are solely those of the authors and do not necessarily represent those of the AFRL or the FAA.

References

1. Burrows, M., Abadi, M., Needham, R.: A logic of authentication. ACM Transactions on Computer Systems **8** (1990) 18–36
2. Jajodia, S., Samarati, P., Subrahmanian, V.: A logical language for expressing authorizations. In: Proceedings of the 1997 IEEE Symposium on Security and Privacy, Oakland, California, USA, IEEE Computer Society (1997) 31–42
3. Abdul-Rahman, A., Hailes, S.: Supporting trust in virtual communities. In: Proceedings of the 33rd Annual Hawaii International Conference on System Sciences (HICSS-33), Maui, Hawaii, USA, IEEE Computer Society (2000) 1769–1777
4. Rangan, P.: An axiomatic basis of trust in distributed systems. In: Proceedings of the 1988 IEEE Computer Society Symposium on Security and Privacy, Oakland, California, USA, IEEE Computer Society (1988) 204–211
5. Jones, A., Firozabadi, B.: On the characterization of a trusting agent – aspects of a formal approach. In C.Castelfranchi, Y.Tan, eds.: Trust and Deception in Virtual Societies. Kluwer Academic Publishers (2000) 163–174
6. Yahalom, R., Klein, B., Beth, T.: Trust relationship in secure systems: A distributed authentication perspective. In: Proceedings of the IEEE Computer Society Symposium on Security and Privacy, Oakland, California, USA, IEEE Computer Society (1993) 150–164
7. Yahalom, R., Klein, B.: Trust-based navigation in distributed systems. Computing Systems **7** (1994) 45–73
8. Beth, T., Borcherding, M., Klein, B.: Valuation of trust in open networks. In Gollmann, D., ed.: Proceedings of the 3rd European Symposium on Research in Computer Security - ESORICS '94. Volume 875 of Lecture Notes in Computer Science., Brighton, UK, Springer-Verlag (1994) 3–18
9. Jøsang, A.: Artificial reasoning with subjective logic. In: Proceedings of the Second Australian Workshop on Commonsense Reasoning, Perth, Australia (1997)
10. Jøsang, A.: A subjective metric of authentication. In Quisquater, J.J., et al., eds.: Proceedings of the 5th European Symposium on Research in Computer Security (ESORICS'98). Volume 1485 of Lecture Notes in Computer Science., Louvain-la-Neuve, Belgium, Springer-Verlag (1998) 329–344

11. Jøsang, A.: An algebra for assessing trust in certification chains. In: Proceedings of Network and Distributed Systems Security Symposium(NDSS'99), San Diego, California, USA, Internet Society (1999)

12. Cohen, M., Parasuraman, R., Serfaty, R., Andes, R.: Trust in decision aids:a model and a training strategy. Technical Report USAATCOM TR 97-D-4, Cognitive Technologies Inc., Fort Eustis, Virginia, USA (1997)

13. Li, L.X., Liu, L.: A reputation-based trust model for peer-to-peer ecommerce communities. In: Proceedings of IEEE Conference on E-Commerce (CEC'03), Newport Beach, California, USA, IEEE Computer Society (2003) 275–284

14. Purser, S.: A simple graphical tool for modelling trust. Computers & Security **20** (2001) 479–484

15. Bacharach, M., Gambetta, D.: Trust as type identification. In Castelfranchi, C., Tan, Y., eds.: Trust and Deception in Virtual Societies. Kluwer Academic Publishers (2000) 1–26

16. Grandison, T., Sloman, M.: A survey of trust in internet applications. IEEE Communications Surveys and Tutorials **3** (2000) 2–16

Parameterized Authentication*

Michael J. Covington, Mustaque Ahamad, Irfan Essa, and H. Venkateswaran

College of Computing, Georgia Institute of Technology, Atlanta, Georgia USA

Abstract. We describe an approach to sensor-based authentication that can adapt to accommodate incomplete, unreliable, or inaccurate input provided to the system. *Parameterized Authentication* moves beyond the traditional approach to security by acknowledging that identity verification cannot always produce perfect results. Our model addresses such inherent imperfections by introducing a metric, the Authentication Parameter, that captures the overall "quality" of authentication. We define authentication "quality" in terms of sensor trustworthiness and the accuracy of sensor measurements. Using the Authentication Parameter, we are able to enforce and enhance the principle of least privilege by ensuring that the authentication process provides credentials that are sufficient but not stronger than the access level required by the requested operation. This approach is particularly well-suited to meet the demands of a context-aware and pervasive computing environment in which authentication may be performed using passive and non-intrusive techniques. Our model supports the transparent capture of authentication-relevant information from the environment and provides a foundation for generating dynamic credentials for sources of requests. We present our model, discuss its contributions, and illustrate how it can be used to support rich access control policies.

1 Introduction

Authentication is a fundamental building block in any system that enforces a security policy; it enables "principals" to identify themselves to the system and provides a foundation for access control. For the purposes of this paper, the principals we consider are users, though their attributes such as location, role, or history may also be relevant in authorization decision-making. All authentication schemes follow the same basic approach: known identification information about a principal is compared with information received from the source claiming to be that principal. Authentication is successful if both pieces of information match; however, authentication failure will result if a match cannot be produced.

Pervasive computing environments strive to provide transparent access to resources and services. For example, the Aware Home [1], a prototype "home of the future" that has been built at Georgia Tech, is exploring a variety of emerging applications that range from remote appliance management (e.g., Cyberfridge [2]) to "awareness" and the active-monitoring of each resident's activities and

---

* This work was supported, in part, by NSF awards ITR-0081276 and ITR-0121643.

P. Samarati et al. (Eds.): ESORICS 2004, LNCS 3193, pp. 276–292, 2004.

needs. The prototype home has a rich computation and communication infrastructure and will eventually be connected to other homes and institutions in the community. A variety of sensors are used to infer the activities of the home's residents and various applications use this information to help improve the quality of life for residents.

Clearly, the assumption that a principal's identity can be verified with absolute certainty is impractical in real world scenarios, even when explicit interaction is required. The Aware Home is an example of an environment in which sensors will be used for user identification and verification purposes. Homeowners are forced to balance authentication quality with financial limitations and a tolerance for being inconvenienced. For example, the Smart Floor [3] is currently being deployed into the Aware Home despite its less-than-perfect accuracy because it is non-intrusive and easy-to-use.

Non-binary authentication could be used to limit the damage that may result from an erroneous authentication. We have designed a model that can be used to produce an authentication measure from incomplete, unreliable, or inaccurate identification information that is provided by a set of sensors. We accomplish this by providing a quality measure for authentication. In addition, we provide a method for computing an authentication value by combining inputs from multiple sources; by reinforcing authentication and forming a consensus, our authentication framework is more robust and than those that rely on a single source for authentication. We refer to this approach as *parameterized authentication*.

This paper is organized as follows: Section 2 presents related work. In section 3, we discuss the various logical components that comprise our model, identify a set of design principles that guide the development of our model, and introduce the *Authentication Parameter*. Sect. 4 details our approach to managing trust and accuracy in the system and illustrates how these measures are used to produce the Authentication Parameter. We revisit our design principles in section 5 to discuss how well our model meets these principles. We discuss several outstanding issues and related research contributions in section 6.

2   Related Work

Our approach to computing an Authentication Parameter (AP) value makes use of techniques that have been explored in diverse research areas, including distributed authentication, sensor matching and fusion, and trust and reputation management. In this section, we introduce relevant background material necessary for understanding the research contributions described in the remainder of this document.

Distributed Authentication. In sensor-based authentication, identification information is collected from multiple sensors that may be trusted to different degrees. In distributed system environments that span multiple trust domains, authentication may rely on certificates that are issued by certification authorities (CAs) that also have different levels of trust associated with them. Several researchers have explored such models where an authentication measure based on the trust level of the CAs is derived. Beth et al. [4] present a model where trust can be combined from multiple CAs. Reiter and Stubblebine [5] explore the design principles that must be followed by such a model. Maurer [6], Jøsang [7] and others have explored additional techniques to compute an authentication metric based on paths or chains of CAs that are used for authentication. These techniques primarily focus on trust of the relevant CAs and do not address accuracy of identification information.

Sensor Matching and Fusion. In interactive intelligent environments such as the home, biometric technologies are often used to obtain user identification with minimal explicit input. Unfortunately, many of the biometric devices widely available today cannot guarantee very high quality identification. This is typically a result of noise that interferes with sensor readings, limitations of the processing methods or the variability in both the biometric characteristic as well as its presentation [8]. For instance, biometric device test reports [9, 10] discuss biometric sensors that can be easily defeated, including a fingerprint sensor that can misinterpret imprints in a Gummi Bear candy as a valid fingertip scan and a vision system that can be defeated by a photograph of an authorized user. Such weaknesses in biometric technology create opportunities for an impostor to "mimic" the actions of a legitimate user and, in essence, trick the system into believing that they are someone else.

Sensor fusion refers to the combining of multiple identification "inputs" in order to produce a single identification metric. For example, one research group has recently incorporated speaker identification and speech recognition systems with a person tracking system to accurately locate a speaker and identify the speaker and what they are saying [11]. This form of sensor fusion yields a more reliable metric in case of uncertainty from an individual sensor. In addition to combined input, sensor fusion allows the system to reason about the fidelity of the composite information. This measure can be used to enhance the strength of the authentication service.

Despite the "stronger" authentication results produced through sensor fusion, they still do not reflect the overall quality of the authentication process. Instead, the results are binary, thus allowing the user to either receive all access rights or none at all. Parameterized authentication provides a more novel approach by incorporating a notion of trust (in individual sensors) into the authentication process and, ultimately, providing a metric that indicates the quality of the authentication process. This metric can be used to adjust the level of authentication. For instance, a user can be authenticated into a role that is based on the strength of her identification, thus ensuring that a user is never allowed to have more access than the evidence provided by them for authentication.

Trust and Reputation Management. Trustworthiness is often viewed as the expectation of cooperative behavior and can be based on previous experiences with the same party. However, it is often necessary to evaluate the trustworthiness of an entity without having any prior direct interactions. In such situations, a participant can place trust based on the latter's "reputation" among others in the system. This approach bases reputation on the collection of evidence that supports certain claims of good or bad behavior. In parameterized authentication, reputation or sensor trustworthiness can be based on whether a sensor's input led to correct authentication or a breach of security.

eBay and other similar Internet communities are practical examples of reputation management systems. On eBay's site, for example, sellers receive feedback $(+1, 0, -1)$ for their reliability in an online auction. Reliability is computed using the feedback values that are collected over a period of several months.

In similar work, Kamvar et al. [12] describe a trust-based algorithm that identifies malicious entities in a peer-to-peer environment and isolates them from the network. Their reputation system, called EigenTrust, identifies inauthentic files on a network and even handles conditions where malicious peers cooperate in an attempt to deliberately compromise the system. Likewise, work by Beth et al. [4] presents a method for the valuation of trustworthiness based on experiences and recommendations.

The mathematical foundations for reputation management are firmly rooted in probability and statistics. Our work draws heavily from Bayesian statistics in which a mechanism for combining evidence is presented.

3   System Model

Our model for parameterized authentication is based on information obtained from a distributed network of sensors. The model is composed of the following logical components: users, sensors, a user-attribute database, an attribute-matching service, a trust analysis engine, an audit service and the authentication service. A high-level overview of our adaptive authentication architecture is given in figure 1. In the following sections, we detail the functionality of these components and describe how they interact with one another.

3.1   Users

Our approach to user authentication assumes an open-world model in which there exist two classes of *Users* – those that are "known" (identifiable) by the system, and those that are not. A user is defined by a collection of *traits*, or properties, that are either non-intrusively captured by sensors or explicitly provided as input to the system. While some users may have similar traits, it is the collection of properties that define a user. By definition, no two collections are equal. Our model can make use of four fundamental trait types: physiological, knowledge-based, object-based and historical.

3.2   Sensors

Our system model consists of distributed sensors that collect identity information that is ultimately provided to an authentication service. Sensors are mechanisms

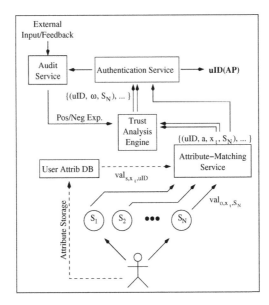

Fig. 1. Overview of Authentication Model

designed to observe and capture user-specific traits from the environment. Some sensors require explicit user participation to complete the capture, while others are less intrusive and can record information without the user's knowledge or active participation. These sensors observe user traits and forward relevant values to the authentication service where the information is interpreted and used to authenticate users. For example, in figure 1, sensor S_N provides a measured value of trait x_t.

Our authentication framework gathers information from a variety of sensors to infer user characteristics. Examples of sensor technologies being deployed into the Aware Home include the Smart Floor, vision systems (ranging from facial recognition to movement sensors) and voice-recognition. Such sensors can non-intrusively gather user information, albeit less-than-perfect, from the environment.

3.3   User-Attribute Database

We assume the existence of a user-attribute database that maintains, for each user in the system, a collection of traits that define that user. We can think of the traits for user u as a t-dimensional trait vector x_u, where $x_u = (x_{u1}, x_{u2}, \ldots, x_{ut})$. In the Aware Home, trait vectors are used to create profiles for each user of the Smart Floor. Traits, in this scenario, are derived from a biomechanics measure known as the ground reaction force (GRF). The trait vector consists of ten footstep profile features that are later used to match unknown footsteps against user's configured in the database.

3.4   Attribute-Matching Service

The Attribute-Matching Service is responsible for collecting and assembling a trait vector from sensor output, and then computing accuracy by comparing the assembled trait vector with the stored definition for a user. If a collection of sensors assemble a trait vector y, it can be compared directly to the associated values stored in x to determine how well the observed features match those stored in the system.

3.5   Trust Analysis Engine

We define *trust* as a measure of the system's confidence in a particular sensor; it reflects the quality of the information provided by a given sensor in the system. Clearly, this measure can only be refined over time, through a series of experiences that are recorded with the sensor.

We have identified three possible outcomes that can result from an authentication process. *Positive user identification* captures instances in which the correct user is identified or in which an unauthorized user is prevented from obtaining credentials from the system. A *denial of service* results when a legitimate user is prevented from being authenticated due to malicious tampering with sensors or authentication data. Similarly, a *compromise* has taken place when a user obtains credentials belonging to another user. Any interaction that leads to a denial of service or a system compromise is considered to be a negative experience and the trust measures that contribute to a negative experience are subsequently degraded. Likewise, the system attempts to reinforce positive experiences by assigning higher trust values to sensors that consistently provide data to the authentication service which leads to correct authentication.

3.6   Audit Service

On-line scrutiny of all authentication decisions may not be possible for a number of reasons. Therefore, selective authentication decisions may be logged to enable subsequent off-line examination. For example, if a security violation is detected, a log can be used to reconstruct the sequence of interactions that led up to the violation. This would allow the system to revise the experience values associated with the sensors that contributed to the incorrect authentication; instead of contributing to a positive experience, the sensors would receive a negative rating for the interaction. In addition, the audit service would be responsible for processing log information to produce feedback that is sent to the Trust Analysis Engine. This feedback is used to maintain evolving trust values for each of the sensors.

3.7   Authentication Service

The authentication service receives input from the Trust Analysis Engine and the Attribute-Matching Service that is combined to derive the Authentication Parameter. The output from this service is based on input supplied by one or more sensors. We identify a set of useful design principles that guide the derivation of an Authentication Parameter from the information received.

Principle 1: Accuracy of a sensor. Accuracy measures the similarity between a stored trait value and the value of a trait observed by a single sensor. The accuracy measure should address the need for normalized results so comparisons can be made.

Principle 2: Evolution of Trust through experience. Trust is a measure of confidence held by the authentication service in a particular sensor; it represents a reputation that is established through consistent behavior and observed over a series of experiences, both positive and negative. Trust should increase slowly to allow reputation to build between the authentication service and sensor. Likewise, once negative experiences are detected, trust should decrease quickly to defeat malicious or compromised sensors that attempt to improve their reputation through a short-run of positive performance.

Principle 3: Combining Trust and Accuracy. When trying to determine a user's authenticity, the authentication service analyzes input provided by each sensor. The authentication service forms an opinion by taking sensor input and adjusting it to reflect the current level of trust associated with each sensor. This opinion, generated for each sensor, should reflect both certainties and uncertainties with regard to user identity, giving both trust and accuracy important roles in generating the opinion.

Principle 4: Consensus of Opinions. Once a set of individual opinions have been collected, they must be combined to generate the authentication parameter. When sensor opinions are in agreement, certainty should increase. Conflicts in opinion should be indicated through increased lack of confidence in the authentication decision.

Principle 5: Evaluation order independence. The derived conclusions of the model, namely the Authentication Parameter, should be independent of the order in which sensor input is considered. This principle allows additional sensor inputs to be factored into an Authentication Parameter that has already been computed.

Principle 6: Property dependence and feedback. The value of the model's trust and accuracy parameters should impact the feedback cycle in which trust is recomputed and returned to the system.

Principle 7: Robustness. The authentication parameter should be designed to be resilient to long-term manipulation of its model by misbehaving entities, and its sensitivity to various forms of misbehavior should be made explicit.

4   Deriving the AP

The authentication service builds an authentication opinion by collecting input from one or more sensors with information relevant to the current user or request. An opinion is formed for each source of input and has two measures that impact its outcome. The first measure, *accuracy*, measures the similarity between a user trait that is observed by a sensor and the value of the same trait that is stored in a user signature. The second measure, *trust*, represents the reputation a sensor has with the authentication service; it measures consistency between past results and the output of an individual sensor. In this section, we further describe accuracy and trust and show how they can be combined to produce the Authentication Parameter.

4.1   Accuracy

In our model, *accuracy* is defined as a similarity measure between a stored trait value and an observed trait value. When a sensor provides input to the system, that input data is compared with stored identity data to determine if a match exists. In order to account for variations between stored and observed data, a perfect match is not always required by the system. The closeness or quality of a match, therefore, is reflected in the accuracy value.

In order to assess how well an observed trait x^o matches a stored trait x^s, we consider a distance measure $d(x^o, x^s)$ such that

$$d(x^o, x^s) = \begin{cases} large \text{ when } x^o, x^s \Rightarrow \text{mismatched traits} \\ small \text{ when } x^o, x^s \Rightarrow \text{similar traits} \end{cases}$$

The most obvious measure of similarity (or dissimilarity) between two measurements is the distance between them. Similarity and distance measures have been explored in a variety of domains (e.g., [13, 14] and can be used to compare one or more identifying features. Some comparison studies exist among similarity measures and indicate that different similarity measures perform best when coupled with the appropriate set of attributes. Clearly, the method for computing accuracy is implementation-specific.

An example of accuracy measurements being used in the Aware Home can be found in the Smart Floor. In modeling each individual's footsteps, the Smart Floor designers chose ten footstep profile features to use as markers in an overall user profile. References are made to a combination of user, foot, and shoe type as a condition (e.g., "Joe's left foot while he was wearing tennis shoes"). One instance of a user's footstep constitutes one cluster of data in a training set. This cluster is then used to calculate a Euclidean distance from an unidentified footstep. The identity of the cluster with the lowest average distance is chosen as the identity of the unknown footstep.

There are many approaches for computing distances in order to obtain an accuracy measure. Some instances will require that the attribute-matching service produce a distance measure between only two points. Other instances will require that a collection of identifiers or traits be used in the computation. For instance, a vision-based sensor will attempt to collect a series of traits that are combined to produce a single user identifier. This collection forms a vector that is compared with one stored by the system. Other sensors will produce more primitive output that will require less intensive comparisons.

4.2   Trust

The authentication service, when taking input from multiple sensors, may be presented with conflicting information that could either represent a compromised sensor, a failed sensor or a malicious agent trying to access the system. We make use of techniques from Bayesian statistics to derive and maintain the trust metrics for individual sensors. Bayes' theorem is based on the subjective definition of probability as "degrees of belief." This approach assigns probabilities to hypotheses, allowing for the combination of *a priori* judgments and experimental information. Trust, as defined in our model, is not a static value; it involves a set of uncertainties that are refined over time through experiences and interactions. This makes Bayesian logic a natural mechanism for evolving trust values in our model.

After defining the initial hypothesis and the associated probability for each sensor, Bayes' approach attempts to refine trust by calculating the effect of a correlated event on the original hypothesis. Our model focuses on an event E that captures the outcome of an authentication experience. We define E to be a binary event that is either *positive* or *negative*. The experience is positive if the sensor produces output that is correct (e.g., correctly identifies a user) and is negative if the sensor produces output that is incorrect (e.g., identifies an intruder as a known, authorized user). We then compute the following probability using Bayes' theorem, where T is the hypothesis or current trust value, and E is the value of the experience:

$$P(T|E) = \frac{P(E|T) \cdot P(T)}{P(E|T) \cdot P(T) + P(E|\neg T) \cdot P(\neg T)}$$

If the event is positive then $P(E|T) = P(+E|T)$ which is defined to be a, where a is the accuracy associated with the reading. Likewise, for a negative experience, $P(E|T) = P(-E|T)$ which is defined to be $(1 - a)$.

Similarly, we define $P(E|\neg T)$ in terms of the experience. If the experience is positive we define $P(+E|\neg T) = \alpha$. If the experience is negative we define $P(-E|\neg T) = (1 - \alpha)$. The value for $P(E|\neg T)$ reflects the probability that a (positive/negative) event will occur, even when the sensor is *not* trustworthy (e.g., when the hypothesis is invalid). The value for α is predetermined and indicates a lower-bound threshold for untrusted activity. Our model assumes that a compromised sensor will provide some positive experiences as it attempts to evade detection and exclusion. A high value for α implies that when a sensor is compromised, its malicious behavior will be caught quickly and it will no longer be used in authentication decisions. Thus, if a compromised sensor wants to damage the system over a longer period of time, it must limit incorrect results that it provides and behave more like a good sensor.

Once $P(T|E)$ is computed, it provides a revised trust value for a given sensor. This updated measure replaces the current trust value, $P(T)$, and is used in future refinements under the Bayes approach. We previously defined Design Principle 6 in which we detailed a "feedback cycle" for recomputing trust and returning it to the system. Our approach to evolving trust by computing $P(T) = P(T|E)$ provides this essential feedback cycle and allows us to react accordingly when sensors malfunction or misbehave.

In practice, determining the quality of E is difficult. We currently rely on both consensus results and an out-of-band audit analysis to determine the quality of an experience. For instance, if multiple sensors produce output for a single authentication request and a majority of those sensors support a similar user profile, those in the minority will be flagged as providing a negative experience. Likewise, if an out-of-band audit log review determines that a compromise has occurred, the sensors that contributed to the false authentication will have their trust values degraded through a negative experience.

Furthermore, evaluating and revising T after every authentication event may be impractical or impossible. If a sensor is overwhelmed with incoming authentication requests, recomputing T after each one may slow response time. Furthermore, it is difficult to determine the quality of an experience in real-time as the system may require information from outside sources (e.g., audit logs).

Using our function for trust evolution, the trust after n experiences (t_n), out of which k are positive and m are negative, can be written as follows. The base trust value t_0 is assigned to each individual sensor by the security administrator.

$$t_n = \frac{(\prod_{i=1}^{k} a_i) \cdot (\prod_{j=1}^{m}(1 - a_j)) \cdot t_0}{(\prod_{i=1}^{k} a_i) \cdot (\prod_{j=1}^{m}(1 - a_j)) \cdot t_0 + \alpha^k \cdot (1 - \alpha)^m \cdot (1 - t_0)}$$

4.3 Authentication Parameter

Jøsang defines a framework for artificial reasoning called Subjective Logic [7] that consists of a belief model called opinion space. Subjective Logic was developed to mathematically describe and manipulate subjective beliefs; it is an extension of standard logic that uses continuous uncertainty and belief parameters instead of only discrete truth values. We have used the Subject Logic framework for Parameterized Authentication as it provides a foundation for the handling of uncertainties and the forming of conclusions based on insufficient evidence.

Similar to Jøsang's approach, we assume that knowledge about the world (obtained through a sensor) is never perfect and it may be impossible to verify a user's identity with absolute certainty. Given this imperfect knowledge, it is impossible to know authoritatively whether a user has been properly identified, so a sensor can only have an opinion about the observation. For a single opinion about a user's authentication, we assume that

$$b \mid d \mid u = 1, \quad [b, d, u] \subset [0, 1]$$

where b, d, and u represent belief, disbelief and uncertainty respectively. A situation in which there is zero uncertainty is equivalent to the traditional probability model.

Our method for assigning values to the $\{b, d, u\}$-tuple differs from that proposed by Jøsang. His approach involves mapping the opinion space to an evidence space that consists of a probability certainty density function. Our evidence space, however, consists of trust and accuracy measures obtained from sensors. Therefore, we let $\omega_x = \{b_x, d_x, u_x\}$ be a single sensor's opinion about the authentication of user x. We now define ω_x as a function of trust and accuracy measures that have been obtained from the sensor:

$$\omega_x = \begin{cases} b_x = t \cdot a \\ d_x = t \cdot (1-a) \\ u_x = (1-t) \end{cases}$$

Here, t is a measure of trust for the sensor that is providing the authentication data and a is the accuracy of the observed trait. Our definition for ω_x makes it clear that belief and disbelief are functions of both accuracy and trust, whereas uncertainty results from the lack of trustworthiness. For example, belief will be high only when both match accuracy and sensor trust are high.

Subjective Logic contains several different operations, with the most relevant to our work being *consensus*. A consensus opinion consists of combining two or more independent opinions about the same proposition (e.g., "The user's identity as *Bob* can be verified") into a single opinion.

The Authentication Parameter is found in the final ω_x after consensus has been computed for all relevant opinions. The value of interest is the b_x that reflects the overall belief in the user's authenticity based on input from multiple sensors. However, this value alone is insufficient to describe the quality of authentication. The entire $\{b, d, u\}$-tuple is retained for a variety of reasons, including the addition of supplemental input through the consensus operation and the comparison of results.

5 Validation

Ideally, validation is done by using actual sensors deployed in a real environment in which users are authenticated based on sensor-obtained data. Unfortunately, we currently do not have access to such an infrastructure. We discuss the validity of our approach by examining how well it met the original design principles that were presented by us in section 3.7.

Design Principle 1: Accuracy of a Sensor. The accuracy measure we define is the distance measure between an observed trait and a stored trait. The open method presented in section 4.1 to compute authentication accuracy meets the guidelines presented in our model's design principles. We do not restrict the design of an accuracy function and acknowledge that implementations will vary widely depending on the sensor technology being used.

Design Principle 2: Evolution of Trust Through Experience. The following figures (figure 2 for positive experiences and figure 3 for negative experiences) demonstrate how trust evolves for various sensor "types" as experiences are encountered over a period of time. In figures 2 and 3, a sensor is defined with an initial trust value of $t = 0.9$, a sensor reading rated with accuracy $a = 0.9$, and an administrative α-value set to $\alpha = 0.6$. The solid line in the plot shows how trust changes when experiences are encountered with the sensor. Likewise, the dotted line shows a similar evolution process for trust with a lower setting of the initial trust value.

As illustrated through these figures, trust is slow to build and quick to degrade. These results follow in line with the expectations set forth in the second

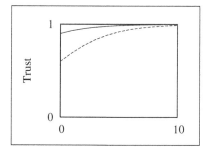

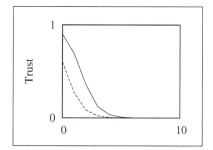

Fig. 2. 10 Positive Experiences   **Fig. 3.** 10 Negative Experiences

design principle. These properties allow for trust reputation to build over time, while quickly punishing any malicious or compromised components.

Figure 4 provides a look at trust evolution when both positive and negative experiences are encountered in a single sensor. The solid line illustrates how trust is increased when a series of 5 consecutive positive experiences are encountered and, subsequently, how trust is quickly degraded when it is followed by 5 consecutive negative experiences. The dotted line shows how trust is decreased during the time period when a random collection of experiences occur (e.g., an equal number of alternating positive and negative experiences). As above, these properties remain consistent with our design principles: trust is slow to build, quick to fall, and our model always errs on the side of caution – random experiences reflect an inconsistency with the sensor and cause trust to degrade.

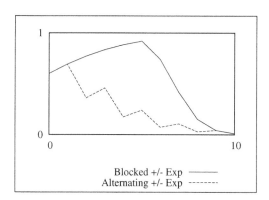

Fig. 4. 10 Alternating Positive/Negative Experiences

Design Principle 3: Combining Trust and Accuracy. By utilizing the Subjective Logic framework, our model is capable of describing and manipulating subjective beliefs, or sensor opinions. Our evidence space is comprised of the trust values maintained for each sensor and the accuracy of the each sensor output.

The consensus operation described in section 4.3 allows for the combination of two independent opinions. Clearly, an opinion consists of more than just trust and accuracy. By generating belief, disbelief and uncertainty values, the resulting tuple reflects a multitude of information that could not be conveyed with a single value. Combining trust and accuracy in this manner reflects both certainties and uncertainties, without placing any undue weight or emphasis on a particular component of the model. These properties are aligned with the design principles that govern the combination of trust and accuracy.

Design Principle 4: Consensus of Opinions. Using Jøsang's model for consensus [7] we can compute how an authentication parameter is effected when more sensors are used to compute an authentication decision. A "good" sensor is one with a high trust, or belief, value. A "bad" sensor is one that has low trust and high distrust. With both sensor types, uncertainty results from the lack of perfect trust in sensors and perfect accuracy from their readings.

The results from the consensus operation are consistent with design principle 4 in that certainty only goes up when the majority of opinions are in agreement. Any conflicts or increased disbelief cause a decline in confidence and, as a result, a lowering of the belief value in the authentication parameter.

Design Principle 5: Evaluation Order Independence. The fifth design principle can be validated by showing that order does not matter in evaluating trust. In section 4.2, we demonstrated that the trust after n experiences can be expressed as a function, with k positive and m negative experiences. This approach enables us to produce a trust value that is based on multiple experiences and computed in any order. Since trust is based on the collection of experiences, regardless of order, this design principle applies to our model and ensures that trust can be computed efficiently.

Design Principle 6: Property Dependence and Feedback. Our approach for managing trust using Bayesian statistics takes into account current trust values and accuracy readings. In addition, the model provides a feedback loop that evaluates the quality of an experience and incorporates this into an evolving trust value. By allowing trust parameters to evolve and accuracy readings to impact feedback cycles, our model is protected from misbehaving and malfunctioning sensors.

Design Principle 7: Robustness. This design principle aims to produce a resilient authentication parameter that is not subject to long-term manipulations by misbehaving entities. Figure 5 shows the result of a consensus operation that has been performed by one form of misbehavior – a "random," or inconsistent, sensor. In this example, a random sensor is defined as one with an initial trust value of $t = 0.5$ and an accuracy reading of $a = 0.5$. These values yield a "random opinion" of:

$$\omega_x = \begin{cases} b_x = t \cdot a = 0.25 \\ d_x = t \cdot (1 - a) = 0.25 \\ u_x = (1 - t) = 0.50 \end{cases}$$

Our future research will focus on building a more robust model for parameterized authentication. We intend to extend this work by investigating outstanding issues such as the impact of byzantine adversaries on our model.

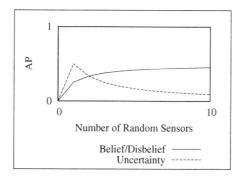

Fig. 5. 10 Random Sensors forming Consensus

As indicated in the figure, uncertainty decreases as more random sensors contribute an opinion to the authentication process. However, the randomness of the sensors results in an equal, but slow, rise of belief and disbelief values. Given the relatively low accuracy and trust values associated with a random sensor, the consensus operation does not allow these sensors to have a significant impact on the overall AP that results. In fact, the AP value does not increase beyond 0.5 even when many sensors are polled.

6   Discussion

We have introduced the concept of Parameterized Authentication and detailed the process for computing a measure that captures the overall quality of an authentication process. In this section, we present some noteworthy aspects of parameterized authentication that did not receive sufficient discussion in previous sections.

6.1   Authentication Paradigms and Historical Data

We believe that the use of historical state information would supplement and enhance the accuracy of a security subsystem. In essence, we propose an *authentication cache* that would allow authentication decisions to be based on identification information currently stored in the system. Traditional implementations of caching technology were able to store often-requested information at the edge of the network, therefore speeding up site performance and lowering connection costs. Given the overwhelming success of caching, we propose that similar technology be applied to the security services in interactive environments such as the home.

Such a cache would pull user identification information from sensors in the environment and use it when making future access control decisions. For example, in the Aware Home users will be identified using a number of devices and technologies. Suppose that *Alice* swipes a smart card in order to gain access to the house via the front door. As she enters, a camera is able to identify her with 86% accuracy and the Smart Floor is able to track her movements and maintain a positive identification as she moves throughout the house. When *Alice* attempts to access a restricted resource, the system is able to use all of the historical state information, including the data obtained via the smart card's key signature, the camera, and the Smart Floor, to obtain a positive identification, and therefore an accurate authentication, for *Alice*, a legitimate resident and authorized user of the resource.

To our knowledge, the use of historical information in security-related decisions has never been included as an enhancement to the overall system. Instead, historical data has been viewed as stale and inconsequential because security parameters and policies are subject to dynamic change and variability. However, in the case of the Aware Home and other computationally rich environments, historical data can offer something that is highly desirable – more timely and efficient access to critical information. In addition, historical information can act as a supplement in cases where the current or active data set is inaccurate or incomplete.

6.2   Authentication Refinement

Other authentication services, such as Kerberos [15], enforce session limits that force tickets or credentials to expire after a specified period of time has elapsed. We provide a mechanism to enforce similar session limitations, but use a method of enforcement that compliments our model for parameterized authentication. Since the user credential, or AP, is actually a consensus of input from multiple sources that could potentially be collected over a period of time, credentials cannot simply timeout. Also, it may be desirable to have a credential based on a lower AP value expire before one that was based on more reliable sensor input.

To address these concerns, our model provides a decay function that decrease the authentication value over time to enforce session limits and ensure the authenticity of user credentials. The effect of this decay on an AP's value can be modeled using a decay function $f(n)$ such that the AP decreases after some specified time has passed; the rate of decay should increase as more time passes. Higher AP values (e.g., those based on more trustworthy or accurate sensor inputs) are typically more reliable than lower AP values. After t time-periods, the AP value will be equal to y. This approach guarantees that access to restricted resources is provided only to users with sufficient authentication credentials that are current, accurate and trustworthy.

6.3   Application Scenario

To best illustrate our approach, we have built a secure implementation of AudioIM, an instant messaging (IM) application in the Aware Home, that uses parameterized authentication. AudioIM is one member of a family of applications [16] that are being used to explore how technology can enhance distributed conversation among family and close friends. Similar to text-based IM, which is used in the office to start semi-synchronous talks, AudioIM extends IM into the home with a touchscreen interface and audio messaging. AudioIM strives to provide instant messaging services where desktops are not suitable.

In order to identify users interacting with the system, the original AudioIM application provides a password verification scheme. The login component requires the user to authenticate herself with a username and password combination. This approach uses a desktop-centric authentication model for an application that was designed specifically for pervasive computing environments.

The enhanced application no longer requires the user to explicitly provide login information. Instead, a request to access a restricted function triggers the authentication service to collect identification information from the appropriate sensor(s) in the home. Consider an example in which the AudioIM application is physically located near a Smart Floor and a computer vision system. The Smart Floor's output identifies the user as *Alice* with an accuracy reading of *90%*. The second sensor also identifies the user as *Alice* but with an accuracy of *85%*. Using this identification information and previously established trust values, the authentication service generates an opinion for each sensor. If the Smart Floor and vision system each had a trust value of 0.9 prior to this experience, the following sensor opinions are computed using our approach described in 4.3.

$$\omega_{\text{Floor}} = \begin{cases} b = 0.81 \\ d = 0.09 \\ u = 0.1 \end{cases} \text{ and } \omega_{\text{Vision}} = \begin{cases} b = 0.765 \\ d = 0.135 \\ u = 0.1 \end{cases}$$

These results are then used to obtain the value of the consensus operation $\omega_{\text{Floor}} \oplus \omega_{\text{Vision}}$. In this example, the resulting consensus has a belief value $b = 0.829$. If this authentication parameter of 83% is sufficient to meet the requirements of the access control policy, no explicit communication is necessary to obtain user credentials. Furthermore, if the authentication of Alice is determined to be correct, each sensor's trust value will be recomputed to incorporate this positive experience.

7   Conclusion

We have introduced a new model for user authentication and have described how it can be used to secure dynamic applications in pervasive computing environments. The major benefit provided by this authentication model is its ability to provide quantitative measure for an authentication parameter when faced with incomplete, inaccurate or unreliable information.

We introduced the concept of *parameterized authentication* and have illustrated how it can allow continued functionality in a damaged, compromised or fundamentally inaccurate system. Furthermore, our authentication scheme is not limited by being binary in nature – users who cannot be fully authenticated by the system may still be given access rights based on their role and the level of confidence the system has in their identification.

Our notion of parameterized authentication provides a metric, the authentication parameter, that is based on *trust* and *accuracy* values associated with each authentication sensor and the output provided by those sensors. The authentication parameter is used to provide knowledge of the authentication process to an authorization service as a single, well-understood metric. We have presented several design principles that guided the design of our model and have used those principles to evaluate the model itself.

Our ongoing work focuses on improving the model for parameterized authentication. This includes further refinement of the robustness design principle, an exploration of session management in pervasive computing environments, and the design of a more timely feedback cycle.

References

1. Georgia Tech Broadband Institute: The Aware Home research initiative (1999-2004) http://www.cc.gatech.edu/fce/ahri/.
2. Mankoff, J., Abowd, G.: Domisilica: Providing ubiquitous access to the home. Technical Report GIT-GVU-97-17, College of Computing, Georgia Institute of Technology (1997)
3. Orr, R.J., Abowd, G.D., Salber, D.: The smart floor: A mechanism for natural user identification and tracking. In: Proceedings of the 2000 Conference on Human Factors in Computing Systems (CHI). (2000)
4. Beth, T., Borcherding, M., Klein, B.: Valuation of trust in open networks. In Coppersmith, D., ed.: Proceedings of ESORICS. Lecture Notes in Computer Science 875, Springer-Verlag (1994) 3–18
5. Reiter, M.K., Stubblebine, S.G.: Authentication metric analysis and design. ACM Transactions on Information and System Security (1999)
6. Maurer, U.: Modelling a public-key infrastructure. In Bertino, E., ed.: Proceedings of ESORICS, Lecture Notes in Computer Science (LNCS), Springer-Verlag (1996)
7. Jøsang, A.: Artificial reasoning with subjective logic. In: Australian Workshop on Commonsense Reasoning, In conjunction with the Tenth Australian Joint Conference on Artificial Intelligence (1997)
8. Pankanti, S., Jain, A.: Biometrics: The future of identification. In: IEEE Computer. IEEE (2000) 46–49
9. Thalheim, L., Krissler, J., Ziegler, P.M.: Körperkontrolle — Biometrische Zugangssicherungen auf die Probe gestellt. c't 8 (2002) 114 English translation: http://heise.de/ct/english/02/11/114/.
10. Matsumoto, T., Matsumoto, H., Yamada, K., Hoshino, S.: Impact of artificial gummy fingers on fingerprint systems. In: Proceedings of SPIE. Volume 4677, Optical Security and Counterfeit Deterrence Techniques IV. (2002)
11. Gardner, A., Essa, I.: Prosody analysis for speaker affect determination. In: Proceedings of Perceptual User Interfaces Workshop. (1997)
12. Kamvar, S.D., Schlosser, M.T., Garcia-Molina, H.: The EigenTrust algorithm for reputation management in P2P networks. In: Proceedings of the Twelfth International World Wide Web Conference. (2003)
13. Chellappa, R., Wilson, C., Sirohey, S.: Human and machine recognition of faces: A survey. Proceedings of IEEE 83 (1995) 705–740
14. Ross, A., Jain, A., Reisman, J.: A hybrid fingerprint matcher. In: Proceedings of the International Conference on Pattern Recognition (ICPR). (2002)
15. Kohl, J.T., Neuman, B.C., T'so, T.Y.: The evolution of the Kerberos authentication system. Distributed Open Systems (IEEE Computer Society Press) (1994)
16. Nagel, K., Kidd, C.D., O'Connell, T., Dey, A., Abowd, G.D.: The family intercom: Developing a context-aware audio communication system. In Abowd, G.D., Brumitt, B., Shafer, S.A.N., eds.: Ubicomp, Lecture Notes in Computer Science (LNCS), Springer-Verlag (2001) 176–183

Combinatorial Design of Key Distribution Mechanisms for Wireless Sensor Networks

Seyit A. Çamtepe and Bülent Yener

Department of Computer Science, Rensselaer Polytechnic Institute,
Troy, NY 12180, USA
{camtes,yener}@cs.rpi.edu

Abstract. Key distribution is one of the most challenging security issues in wireless sensor networks where sensor nodes are randomly scattered over a hostile territory. In such a sensor deployment scenario, there will be no prior knowledge of post deployment configuration. For security solutions requiring pairwise keys, it is impossible to decide how to distribute key pairs to sensor nodes before the deployment. Existing approaches to this problem are to assign more than one key, namely a key-chain, to each node. Key-chains are randomly drawn from a key-pool. Either two neighboring nodes have a key in common in their key-chains, or there is a path, called key-path, among these two nodes where each pair of neighboring nodes on this path has a key in common. Problem in such a solution is to decide on the key-chain size and key-pool size so that every pair of nodes can establish a session key directly or through a path with high probability. The size of the key-path is the key factor for the efficiency of the design. This paper presents novel, *deterministic* and *hybrid* approaches based on *Combinatorial Design* for key distribution. In particular, several *block design* techniques are considered for generating the key-chains and the key-pools.

Comparison to probabilistic schemes shows that our combinatorial approach produces better connectivity with smaller key-chain sizes.

1 Introduction and Problem Definition

In this work, we consider a sensor network in which sensor nodes need to communicate with each other for data processing and routing. We assume that the sensor nodes are distributed to the target area in large numbers and their location within this area is determined randomly. These type of sensor networks are typically deployed in adversarial environments such as military applications where a large number of sensors may be dropped from airplanes.

In this application, secure communication among sensor nodes requires authentication, privacy and integrity. In order to establish this, there must be a *secret key* shared between a pair of communicating sensor nodes. Because the network topology is unknown prior to deployment, a key pre-distribution scheme is required where keys are stored into ROMs of sensors before the deployment. The keys stored must be carefully selected so to increase the probability that

P. Samarati et al. (Eds.): ESORICS 2004, LNCS 3193, pp. 293–308, 2004.

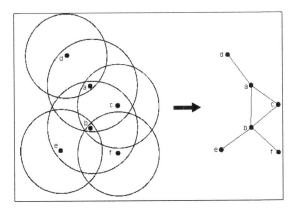

Fig. 1. A Wireless Sensor Network

two neighboring sensor nodes have at least one key in common. Nodes that do not share a key directly may use a path where each pair of nodes on the path shares a key. The length of this path is called *key-path* length. Average *key-path* length, is an important performance metric and design consideration. Consider sample sensor network given in Figure-1. Assume that only sensor nodes a and b does not share a key. Nodes a and c can establish secure communication where the key-path length is 1. Node c and b also have key-path length of one. However, nodes a and b can only use the path a-c-b to communicate securely with key-path length of two.

The common approach is to assign each sensor node multiple keys, *randomly* drawn from a *key-pool*, to construct a *key-chain* to ensure that either two neighboring nodes have a key in common in their key-chain, or there is a key-path. Thus the challenge is to decide on the key-chain size and key-pool size so that every pair of nodes can establish a session key directly or through a path. Key-chain size is limited by the storage capacity of the sensor nodes. Moreover, very small key-pool increases the probability of key share between any pair of sensor nodes by decreasing the security in that, the number of the keys needed to be discovered by the adversary decreases. Similarly, very large key-pool decreases the probability of key share by increasing the security.

Eschenauer *et al.* in [14] propose a *random key pre-distribution scheme* where tens to hundreds of keys are uploaded to sensors before the deployment. In their solution, initially a large key pool of P and the key identities are generated. For each sensor, k keys are randomly drawn from the key-pool P without replacement. These k keys and their identities form a *key-chain* which is loaded in to the memory of the sensor node. Two neighboring nodes compare list of identities of keys in their key-chain. Since only the identities are exchanged, this process can take place without any privacy mechanism. Eschenauer *et al.* also propose to employ *Merkle Puzzle* [20] similar approach to secure key identities. After key identity exchange, common key(s) are used to secure the link in between two sensor nodes. It may be the case that some of the neighboring nodes may not be able to find a key in common. These nodes may communicate securely through other nodes, through other secured links. Chan *et al.* in [6] propose a modification to the basic scheme of Eschenauer *et al.* They increase the amount of key overlap required for key-setup. That is, q common keys are needed instead of one to be able to increase the security of the communication between two neighboring nodes. In [33], common keys in the key-chains are used to establish multiple logical paths over which *threshold key sharing scheme* is used to agree on a new secret.

Random-pairwise key scheme in [6] is a modification of the pairwise key scheme. It is based on *Erdos and Renyi's* work; to achieve probability p of any two nodes are connected, in a network of n nodes, each node needs to store only a random set of np pairwise keys instead of $n - 1$. Slijepcevic *et al.* [24] propose that each sensor node shares a list of master keys, a random function and a seed. Every sensor uses shared random function and shared seed to select a network wise or group wise master key. In [3, 18], polynomial-based key pre-distribution protocol proposed for group key pre-distribution. In [19], polynomial pool-based key pre-distribution is used for pairwise key establishment. For each sensor, random or a grid based pre-distribution scheme is used to select set of polynomials from a pool.

In [2], Blom proposes a λ-secure key pre-distribution system where a public matrix P and a private symmetric matrix S over a finite field $GF(q)$ is used. Rows of the matrix $A = (S.P)^T$ is distributed to users. Blom's scheme is a deterministic scheme where any pair of nodes can find a common secret key. Du *et al.* in [9] use Blom's scheme with multiple spaces to increase resilience. In [10], Du *et al.* first model node deployment knowledge in a wireless sensor network and then develop a key pre-distribution scheme based on this model.

In [23, 30, 11, 12, 7, 5, 34] a network architecture where there are one or more base-stations is considered. These base-stations are considered as powerful in resource and sensor nodes are clustered around them. Each sensor node shares a key with each base-station to secure sensor node to base-station and base-station to sensor node unicast communication. Authentication mechanism for the broadcasts from base-station to sensor nodes is addressed in [23, 11, 12, 17, 7]. They propose modified versions of *TESLA* where a verifiable key, which is used to encrypt a message, is disclosed later then the message broadcasted.

1.1   Our Contributions and Organization of This Work

The main contribution of this work is the *deterministic* and *hybrid* approaches to the key distribution problem. In particular, we bring in a novel construction methodology from *Combinatorial Design Theory* to address this problem. Although there are some applications of Combinatorial Designs in cryptography [26–28], and in network design [32, 29], best to our knowledge this work is the first to apply design theory to key distribution. Our analysis indicate that deterministic approach has strong advantages over the randomized ones since it (i) increases the probability that two nodes will share a key, and (ii) decreases the key-path length.

This paper is organized as follows: In Section 2 we provide a brief background to the combinatorial designs used in this work without exceeding the scope of this paper. In Section 3 we introduce our key distribution construction and explain the mapping from design theory to this practical problem. In Section 4 we address scalability issues. In Section 5, we present our analysis and comparison with randomized methods. Finally, in Section 6 we conclude.

2   Background on Combinatorial Designs

A *Balanced Incomplete Block Design (BIBD)* is an arrangement of v distinct objects into b blocks such that each block contains exactly k distinct objects, each object occurs in exactly r different blocks, and every pair of distinct objects occurs together in exactly λ blocks. The design can be expressed as (v, k, λ), or equivalently (v, b, r, k, λ), where: $\lambda\,(v-1)\;=\;r\,(k-1)$ and $b\,k\;=\;v\,r$.

2.1   Symmetric BIBD

A *BIBD* is called *Symmetric BIBD* or *Symmetric Design* when $b = v$ and therefore $r = k$ [8,1,15,31]. A *Symmetric Design* has four properties: every block contains $k = r$ elements, every element occurs in $r = k$ blocks, every pair of elements occurs in λ blocks and every pair of blocks intersects in λ elements.

In this paper, we are interested in a subset of Symmetric Designs, called a *Finite Projective Plane*. A *Finite Projective Plane* consists of a finite set P of points and a set of subsets of P, called lines. For an integer n where $n \geq 2$, *Finite Projective Plane* of order n has four properties: (i) every line contains exactly $n + 1$ points, (ii) every point occurs on exactly $n + 1$ lines, (iii) there are exactly $n^2 + n + 1$ points, and (iv) there are exactly $n^2 + n + 1$ lines. If we consider lines as blocks and points as objects, then a *Finite Projective Plane* of order n is a *Symmetric Design* with parameters $(n^2 + n + 1, n + 1, 1)$ [8,1].

Given a block design $D = (v, k, \lambda)$ with a set S of $|S| = v$ objects and $B = \{B_1, B_2, \ldots, B_b\}$ of $|B| = b$ blocks where each block includes exactly k objects, *Complementary Design* $\overline{D}$ has the complement blocks $\overline{B_i} = S - B_i$ as its blocks for $1 \leq i \leq b$. $\overline{D}$ is a block design with parameters $(v, b, b - r, v - k, b - 2r + \lambda)$ where $(b - 2r + \lambda > 0)$ [1, Theorem 1.1.6]. If $D = (v, k, \lambda)$ is a *Symmetric Design*, then $\overline{D} = (v, v - k, v - 2r + \lambda)$ is also a *Symmetric Design* [1, Corollary 1.1.7].

2.2   Finite Generalized Quadrangle

A *Finite Generalized Quadrangle (GQ)* is an incidence structure $S = (P, B, I)$ where P and B are disjoint and nonempty sets of points and lines respectively, and for which I is a symmetric point-line incidence relation satisfying the following axiom:

1. Each point is incident with $t + 1$ lines ($t \geq 1$) and two distinct points are incident at most one line,

2. Each line is incident with $s + 1$ points $(s \geq 1)$ and two distinct lines are incident with at most one point,
3. If x is a point and L is a line not incident (I) with x, then there is a unique pair $(y, M) \in PXB$ for which $x\ I\ M\ I\ y\ I\ L$.

In this work, we are interested in three known GQ's as defined in [21, 13, 16, 22]: two GQs are from the *Projective Space* $PG(4, q)$ and $PG(5, q)$ of order q, third one is from $PG(4, q^2)$ of order q^2. Let function f be an *irreducible binary quadratic*, then the three GQs can be defined as follows:

1. $GQ(s, t) = GQ(q, q)$ from $PG(4, q)$ with canonical equation $x_0^2 + x_1 x_2 + x_3 x_4 = 0$:
   $GQ(q, q) \Rightarrow s = t = q, v = b = (q + 1)(q^2 + 1)$.
2. $GQ(s, t) = GQ(q, q^2)$ from $PG(5, q)$ with canonical equation $f(x_0, x_1) + x_2 x_3 + x_4 x_5 = 0$:
   $GQ(q, q^2) \Rightarrow s = q, t = q^2, v = (q + 1)(q^3 + 1), b = (q^2 + 1)(q^3 + 1)$.
3. $GQ(s, t) = GQ(q^2, q^3)$ from $PG(4, q^2)$ with canonical equation $x_0^{q+1} + x_1^{q+1} + ... + x_d^{q+1} = 0$:
   $GQ(q^2, q^3) \Rightarrow s = q^2, t = q^3, v = (q^2 + 1)(q^5 + 1), b = (q^3 + 1)(q^5 + 1)$.

Consider $GQ(s, t) = GQ(q, q)$ in which lines are mapped to blocks and points to objects. Thus, there are $v = b = (q + 1)(q^2 + 1)$ blocks and objects where each block contains $s + 1 = q + 1$ objects and where each object is contained in $t + 1 = q + 1$ blocks.

3   Combinatorial Design to Key Distribution

In the following two sections, we describe how *Symmetric Designs* and *Generalized Quadrangles* are used to generate key-chains for the sensors in a sensor network.

3.1   Mapping from Symmetric Design to Key Distribution

In this work, we are interested in *Finite Projective Plane* of order n which is a *Symmetric Design (Symmetric BIBD)* with parameters $(n^2 + n + 1, n + 1, 1)$.

Mapping: We assume a distributed sensor network where there are N sensor nodes. Sensor nodes communicate with each other and require pairwise keys to secure their communication. Each sensor has a *key-chain* of K keys which is stored to its ROM before the deployment. Keys are selected from a set P of *key-pool*. To secure the communication between them, a pair of sensor nodes need to have χ keys in common in their key-chain. Based on this, we define mapping given in Table-1

For a sensor network of N nodes, with total of N key-chains, a Symmetric Design with $b \geq N$ blocks needs to be constructed by using set S with $|S| = v = b$ objects. That means, $b = v = n^2 + n + 1 \geq N$ for a prime power n [8, 1]. Each object in S can be associated with a distinct random key, and each block can be

Table 1. Mapping from Symmetric Design to Key Distribution

Symmetric Design		Key Distribution
Object Set (S)	$\rightarrow$	Key-Pool (P)
Object Set Size $(\|S\| = v = n^2 + n + 1)$	$\rightarrow$	Key-Pool Size $(\|P\|)$
Blocks	$\rightarrow$	Key-Chains
# Blocks $(b = n^2 + n + 1)$	$\rightarrow$	# Key-Chains (N)
# Blocks $(b = n^2 + n + 1)$	$\rightarrow$	# Sensor Nodes (N)
# Objects in a Block $(k = n + 1)$	$\rightarrow$	# Keys in a Key-Chain (K)
# Blocks that an Object is in $(r = n + 1)$	$\rightarrow$	# Key-Chains that a Key is in
Two Blocks share $(\lambda = 1)$ Objects	$\rightarrow$	Two Key-Chains share (χ) Keys

used as a key-chain. That provides $b \geq N$ key-chains each having $K = k = n+1$ keys. Symmetric Design guarantees that any pair of blocks has λ objects in common, meaning that any pair of key-chains, or equivalently sensor nodes, has $\chi = \lambda$ keys in common.

Construction: There are several methods to construct *Symmetric Designs* of the form $(n^2 + n + 1, n + 1, 1)$. In this project, we use a *complete set* of $(n - 1)$ *Mutually Orthogonal Latin Squares (MOLS)*. A *Latin Square* on n symbols is an $n \times n$ array such that each of the n symbols occurs exactly once in each row and each column. The number n is called the *order of the square*. If $A = (a_{ij})$ and $B = (b_{ij})$ are any two $n \times n$ arrays, the *join* of A and B is a $n \times n$ array whose $(i, j)^{th}$ element is the pair (a_{ij}, b_{ij}). The Latin Squares A and B of order n are *Orthogonal* if all entries of the join of A and B are distinct. Latin Squares $A_1, A_2, ..., A_r$ are *Mutually Orthogonal (MOLS)* if they are orthogonal in pairs. For prime power n, a set of $(n - 1)$ MOLS of order n is called a *Complete Set* [8, 1]. A complete set of $(n - 1)$ MOLS can be used to construct *Affine Plane* of order n which is an $(n^2, n, 1)$ design. *Affine Plane* of order n can be converted to *Projective Plane* of order n which is a $(n^2 + n + 1, n + 1, 1)$ *Symmetric Design*. The construction algorithm can be summarized as follows:

1. Given a network size of N, find a prime power n where $n^2 + n + 1 \geq N$,
2. Generate a complete set of $(n - 1)$ MOLS of order n [1, Theorem 5.1.1],
3. Construct the Affine Plane of order n from the MOLS [1, Theorem 1.3.5],
4. Construct the Projective Plane of order n from the Affine Plane [1, Theorem 1.2.5].

Analysis: Symmetric Design has a very nice property that, any pair of blocks shares exactly one object. Probability of key share between any pair of nodes is $P_{SYM} = 1$, so that *Average Key Path Length* is 1.

Symmetric Design of the form $(n^2 + n + 1, n + 1, 1)$ is not a scalable solution itself. Given a fixed key-chain size $k = n + 1$, it can support network sizes of N where $N \leq n^2 + n + 1$. For networks smaller than $n^2 + n + 1$, simply some of blocks may not be used still preserving key sharing probability $P_{SYM} = 1$. For the networks where $N > n^2 + n + 1$, key-chain size must be increased, that is, n must be increased to next prime power. Due to the memory limitations in a

Table 2. The $GQ(s,t)$ parameters

GQ(s,t)	s	t	b	v
$GQ(q,q)$	q	q	$q^3 + q^2 + q + 1$	$q^3 + q^2 + q + 1$
$GQ(q,q^2)$	q	q^2	$q^5 + q^3 + q^2 + 1$	$q^4 + q^3 + q + 1$
$GQ(q^2,q^3)$	q^2	q^3	$q^8 + q^5 + q^3 + 1$	$q^7 + q^5 + q^2 + 1$

Table 3. Mapping from GQ to Key Distribution

Generalized Quadrangle $GQ(s,t)$		Key Distribution
Point Set (P)	$\rightarrow$	Key-Pool (P)
Point Set Size ($|S| = v = (s+1)(st+1)$)	$\rightarrow$	Key-Pool Size ($|P|$)
Line Set (B)	$\rightarrow$	Key-Chains
# Lines ($|B| = b = (t+1)(st+1)$)	$\rightarrow$	# Key-Chains (N)
# Lines ($|B| = b = (t+1)(st+1)$)	$\rightarrow$	# Sensor Nodes (N)
# Points on a Line ($s+1$)	$\rightarrow$	# Keys in a Key-Chain (K)
# Lines that a Point is incident ($t+1$)	$\rightarrow$	# Key-Chains that a Key is in
Two Lines share (≤ 1) points	$\rightarrow$	Two Key-Chains share (χ) Keys

sensor node, this may not be a good solution. Moreover, such an increase in n may produce designs which can support much bigger networks than required. In probabilistic key distribution schemes, it is always possible to increase size of key-pool for a fixed key-chain size to increase the number of key-chains. But, such an approach sacrifices key share probability and requires better connectivity at underlying physical network. It is possible to merge deterministic and probabilistic designs to inherit advantages of both. Later in Section-4, we propose *Hybrid* of Symmetric and Probabilistic Designs to cope with scalability problems. Basically, we use $n^2 + n + 1$ blocks of the Symmetric Design and select uniformly at random remaining $N - (n^2 + n + 1)$ blocks among the ($k = n + 1$)-subsets of the Complementary Symmetric Design.

3.2   Mapping from Generalized Quadrangles to Key Distribution

In this work, we are interested in three known $GQ(s,t)$: $GQ(q,q)$, $GQ(q,q^2)$ and $GQ(q^2,q^3)$. Table-2 gives details about their parameters.

Mapping: Consider a sensor network of N nodes where each node requires a *key-chain* having K keys coming from a *key-pool* P. Assume also that, not all pairs of neighboring nodes need to share a key directly, they can communicate through a secure path on which every pair of neighboring nodes shares a key. GQ can be used to generate key-chains for such networks. Namely, points in GQ can be considered as the keys and lines as the key-chains. Mapping between GQ and Key Distribution is given in Table-3.

In GQ, there are $(t+1)$ lines passing through a point, and a line has $(s+1)$ points. That means, a line shares a point with exactly $t(s+1)$ other lines.

Table 4. Projective Space equations

GQ	PG	Points	Canonical Equation for PG
$GQ(q, q)$	$PG(4, q)$	$(x_0, x_1, x_2, x_3, x_4)$	$x_0^2 + x_1 x_2 + x_3 x_4 = 0$
$GQ(q, q^2)$	$PG(5, q)$	$(x_0, x_1, x_2, x_3, x_4, x_5)$	$f(x_0, x_1) + x_2 x_3 + x_4 x_5 = 0$
$GQ(q^2, q^3)$	$PG(4, q^2)$	$(x_0, x_1, x_2, x_3, x_4)$	$x_0^{q+1} + x_1^{q+1} + x_2^{q+1} + x_3^{q+1} + x_4^{q+1} = 0$

Moreover, if two lines, say lines A and B, do not share a point, then for each point pt_A on line A, there is a point pt_B on line B such that there exist a line C passing through both points pt_A and pt_B. That means, if two lines A and B do not share a point, there are $(s + 1)$ distinct lines which share a point with both lines A and B. In terms of Key Distribution, it means that, a block shares a key with $t(s + 1)$ other blocks. Additionally, if two blocks do not share a key, there are $(s + 1)$ other blocks sharing a key with both.

Construction: The three $GQ(s, t)$'s used in this work are incidence relations between points and lines in a *Projective Space* $PG(d, q)$ and $PG(d, q^2)$ with dimension d. Points of the space are vectors with $(d + 1)$ elements of the form $(x_0, x_1, x_2, \ldots, x_d)$ where $x_i < q$ for $PG(d, q)$ and $x_i < q^2$ for $PG(d, q^2)$. They hold the projective plane equations given in Table-4.

We use irreducible binary quadratic $f(x_0, x_1) = dx_0^2 + x_0 x_1 + x_1^2$ for $GQ(q, q^2)$ as given in Table-4. Our construction algorithm can be summarized as follows:

1. Given network size of N, find a prime power q where:
   $b = q^3 + q^2 + q + 1 \geq N$ for $GQ(q, q)$.
   $b = q^5 + q^3 + q^2 + 1 \geq N$ for $GQ(q, q^2)$.
   $b = q^8 + q^5 + q^3 + 1 \geq N$ for $GQ(q^2, q^3)$.
2. Find all points in Projective Space $PG(4, q)$ for $GQ(q, q)$, $PG(5, q)$ for $GQ(q, q^2)$ and $PG(4, q^2)$ for $GQ(q^2, q^3)$. That is, find all points holding given canonical equation.
3. Construct bilinear groups of size $s + 1$ from v points, that is, find $s + 1$ points which are on the same line. Note that each point is incident to $t + 1$ lines.

Analysis: In a $GQ(s, t)$, there are $b = (t + 1)(st + 1)$ lines and a line intersects with $t(s + 1)$ other lines. Thus, in a design generated from a GQ, a block shares an object with $t(s + 1)$ other blocks. Probability P_{GQ} that two blocks shares at least one object, or equivalently, probability P_{GQ} that a pair of nodes share at least one key is:

$$P_{GQ} = \frac{t(s + 1)}{b} = \frac{t(s + 1)}{(t + 1)(st + 1)} .$$

Table-5 lists key share probabilities for the three GQ.

Probabilistic key distribution is the simplest and most scalable solution when compared to GQ and Symmetric Designs. Next, in Section-4, we propose Hybrid Symmetric and GQ Designs which provide solutions as scalable as probabilistic key distribution schemes, yet taking advantages of underlying GQ and Symmetric Designs.

Table 5. Pairwise Key Sharing Probabilities

GQ	Pairwise Key Sharing Probability
$GQ(q,q)$	$P_{QQ} = \frac{q^2+q}{q^3+q^2+q+1}$
$GQ(q,q^2)$	$P_{QQ^2} = \frac{q^3+q^2}{q^5+q^3+q^2+1}$
$GQ(q^2,q^3)$	$P_{Q^2Q^3} = \frac{q^5+q^3}{q^8+q^5+q^3+1}$

Table 6. Parameters k, r, v, b for Symmetric, GQ and their Complementary Designs

Design	k	r	b	v
Symmetric	$n+1$	$n+1$	n^2+n+1	n^2+n+1
Complementary Symmetric	n^2	n^2	n^2+n+1	n^2+n+1
$GQ(n,n)$	$n+1$	$n+1$	n^3+n^2+n+1	n^3+n^2+n+1
Complementary $GQ(n,n)$	n^3+n^2	n^3+n^2	n^3+n^2+n+1	n^3+n^2+n+1
$GQ(n,n^2)$	$n+1$	n^2+1	$n^5+n^3+n^2+1$	n^4+n^3+n+1
Complementary $GQ(n,n^2)$	n^4+n^3	n^5+n^3	$n^5+n^3+n^2+1$	n^4+n^3+n+1
$GQ(n^2,n^3)$	n^2+1	n^3+1	$n^8+n^5+n^3+1$	$n^7+n^5+n^2+1$
Complementary $GQ(n^2,n^3)$	n^7+n^5	n^8+n^5	$n^8+n^5+n^3+1$	$n^7+n^5+n^2+1$

4   Hybrid Designs for Scalable Key Distributions

The main drawback of the combinatorial approach comes from the difficulty of
their construction. Given a desired number of sensor nodes or a desired number
of keys in the pool, we may not be able to construct a combinatorial design for
the target parameters.

In this work, we present a novel approach called *Hybrid Design* which combines deterministic core and probabilistic extensions. We will consider two Hybrid Designs: *Hybrid Symmetric Design* and *Hybrid GQ Design*. By using Symmetric or GQ Design and its complement, we preserve nice properties of combinatorial design yet take advantages of flexibility and scalability of probabilistic
approaches to support any network sizes.

4.1   Mapping

Consider a sensor network where there are N nodes, therefore N key-chains
are required. Due to memory limitations, key-chains can have at most K keys
coming from key-pool P. We can employ Hybrid Design for the cases where there
is no known combinatorial design technique to generate design with N nodes for
the given key-chain size K. Basically, Hybrid Design finds largest prime power
n such that $k \leq K$ and generates N blocks of size k where objects come from
object set S of size $|S| = v$. The b of N blocks are generated by base Symmetric
or GQ Design and $N - b$ blocks are randomly selected among k-subsets of the
Complementary Design blocks. We define mappings as in Table-7.

Table 7. Mapping from Hybrid Design to Key Distribution

Hybrid Symmetric Design	Key Distribution
Object Set (S)	→ Key-Pool (P)
Object Set Size ($|S| = v$)	→ Key-Pool Size ($|P|$)
Blocks of base design and selected (k)-subsets from Complementary Design	→ Key-Chains
# blocks from base design (b) + # selected (k)-subsets ($N - b$)	→ # Key-Chains (N)
# blocks from base design (b) + # selected (k)-subsets ($N - b$)	→ # Sensor Nodes (N)
# Objects in a Block ($k \leq K$)	→ # in a Key-Chain (K)
Two Blocks share zero or more Objects	→ Two Key-Chains share (χ) Keys

4.2   Construction

For a given key-chain size K and network size N, Hybrid Design first generates the Base Symmetric or GQ Design with largest possible prime power n where $k \leq K$. Base Symmetric or GQ Design has b blocks of size k. Table-6 lists the relations between block size k and number of blocks b for the prime power n. Next step is to generate Complementary Design where there are b blocks of size $v - k$. Table-6 lists the parameters of the Complementary Designs. Due to the fact that $v - k > k$ for Symmetric and GQ designs, blocks of the Complementary Design can't be used as the key-chains, but their subsets can. To scale the base design up to given network size, Hybrid Design randomly selects remaining $N - b$ blocks uniformly at random among k-subsets of the Complementary Design blocks. Selected k-subsets along with the blocks of the base design form the Hybrid Design blocks. Algorithm can be summarized as follows:

1. Given N sensor nodes where each can store key-chain of size K, find largest possible prime power n such that $k \leq K$ for k values given in Table-6.
2. Generate base design (Symmetric or GQ):
   - Generate object pool $P = \{a_1, a_2, ..., a_v\}$ of size v,
   - Generate blocks $B = \{B_1, B_2, ..., B_b\}$ where $|B_i| = k$ for $1 \leq i \leq b$ and $B_i \subset P$.
3. Generate Complementary Design from the base design:
   - Generate blocks $\overline{B} = \{\overline{B_1}, \overline{B_2}, ..., \overline{B_b}\}$ where $\overline{B_i} = P - B_i$ and $|\overline{B_i}| = v - k$ for $1 \leq i \leq b$.
4. Generate $N - b$ hybrid blocks H=$\{H_1, H_2, ..., H_{N-b}\}$ of size $|H_i| = k$ ($1 \leq i \leq N - b$) from the Complementary Design $\overline{B} = \{\overline{B_1}, \overline{B_2}, ..., \overline{B_b}\}$. Use variable s_i to hold index of the block in $\overline{B}$ from which block H_i is obtained:
   - Consider all k-subsets of all blocks in $\overline{B}$,
   - Randomly select $N - b$ distinct k-subsets to generate the set H,
   - For each selected k-subset H_i ($1 \leq i \leq N - b$), find the block $\overline{B_j} \in \overline{B}$ ($1 \leq j \leq b$) from which block H_i is obtained. Set $s_i = j$.
5. Blocks of the Hybrid Design are $B \cup H$.

Example 1: Assume that we would like to generate key-chains for a network with $N = 10$ nodes. Assume also that nodes have very limited memories, so that they can store at most $K = 3$ keys in their key-chains. Hybrid Symmetric Design can be used to generate design for this network. Symmetric Design $(v, k, \lambda) = (7, 3, 1)$ can be used as the base design to generate $b = 7$ blocks out of $v = 7$ objects where block size is $k = 3$. Blocks of Symmetric Design form the set B={{1,2,3}, {1,4,5}, {1,6,7}, {2,4,6}, {2,5,7}, {3,4,7}, {3,5,6}}. Remaining $N - b = 3$ blocks are selected uniformly at random among the 3-subsets of the Complementary Symmetric Design $\overline{B} = \{\{4,5,6,7\}, \{2,3,6,7\}, \{2,3,4,5\}, \{1,3,5,7\}, \{1,3,4,6\}, \{1,2,5,6\}, \{1,2,4,7\}\}$. Assume that selected blocks are {4,5,6}, {2,3,6} and {1,5,7} which are the 3-subsets of the sets {4,5,6,7}, {2,3,6,7} and {1,3,5,7} respectively. These blocks (3-subsets) form the set H={{4,5,6}, {2,3,6}, {1,5,7}}. The blocks of the Hybrid Symmetric Design is then $B \cup H$= {{1,2,3}, {1,4,5}, {1,6,7}, {2,4,6}, {2,5,7}, {3,4,7}, {3,5,6}, {4,5,6}, {2,3,6}, {1,5,7}}.

4.3   Analysis

In this section, we analyze some important properties of Hybrid Symmetric and Hybrid GQ Designs. We will look for some useful properties coming from underlying combinatorial design. Based on these properties, we will analyze object share probabilities between any pair of blocks in Hybrid Design $B \cup H$, where B is the set of blocks of the base (Symmetric or GQ) design and H is the set of blocks which are uniformly at random selected among k-subsets of the complement design blocks $\overline{B}$ (variable s_i holds index of the block in $\overline{B}$ from which block $H_i \in H$ is obtained).

Hybrid Symmetric Design

Property 1. Given Hybrid Design $B \cup H$, $\forall \beta \in B$ and $\theta \in H$, $\exists b \in \beta | b \notin \theta$.   □

Proof. For the proofs of this property and the others please refer to [4].

Property 1 doesn't hold among the blocks in H. To see that, consider two such distinct blocks $H_i \in H$ and $H_j \in H$ where $s_i \neq s_j$. Complementary Design of a Symmetric Design has the property that, any pair of blocks has $n^2 - n$ objects in common. For $n > 2$, when $(n^2 - n) > (n + 1)$, it can be the case that randomly selected blocks (k-subsets) H_i and H_j are equivalent.

Property 2. Given key chain size $k = n + 1$, Hybrid Symmetric Design can support network sizes up to:
$$\binom{v}{k} = \binom{n^2+n+1}{n+1} .$$
   □

This is the maximum network size that simple probabilistic key pre-distribution scheme can support for key-chain size $k = n+1$ and key-pool size $v = n^2+n+1$. Probabilistic scheme can go beyond this limit by simply increasing the key-pool size v for a fixed key-chain size k. To provide the same scalability, we employ

Hybrid GQ Designs which is analyzed in the next section. For fixed key chain size $k = n + 1$, $GQ(n, n^2)$ will be able to generate designs for networks up to:

$$\binom{v}{k} = \binom{n^4 + n^3 + n + 1}{n + 1} .$$

This is the upper limit of our deterministic algorithms. Numerically, for key chain size of 4, our Hybrid $GQ(n, n^2)$ Design supports network sizes up to $6, 210, 820$. It supports (2.54×10^{14}) nodes for $k = 6$, (8.08×10^{22}) nodes for $k = 8$, (1.18×10^{32}) nodes for $k = 10$, (5.78×10^{41}) nodes for $k = 12$ and so on.

Theorem 1. *Probability P_{HSYM} that any pair of blocks shares a key in Hybrid Symmetric Design is:*

$$P_{HSYM} \leq \frac{b(b-1)}{N(N-1)} \times 1 + \frac{2b(N-b)}{N(N-1)} \times \frac{n^2+2}{n^2+n+1} + \frac{(N-b)(N-2b)}{bN(N-1)} \times P_H + \frac{(b-1)(N-b)^2}{bN(N-1)} \times 1 .$$

$$P_{HSYM} \geq \frac{b(b-1)}{N(N-1)} \times 1 + \frac{2b(N-b)}{N(N-1)} \times \frac{\frac{1}{2}n^2+\frac{3}{2}n+1}{n^2+n+1} + \frac{(N-b)(N-2b)}{bN(N-1)} \times P_H + \frac{(b-1)(N-b)^2}{bN(N-1)} \times 1 .$$

Where $P_H = \left[1 - \frac{\binom{n^2-n-1}{n+1}}{\binom{n^2}{n+1}} \right] .$ □

Hybrid GQ Designs

Property 3. Given key chain size $k = n + 1$, Hybrid GQ Design can support network sizes up to:

$$\binom{v}{s+1} = \binom{(s+1)(st+1)}{s+1} .$$ □

Theorem 2. *Probability P_{HGQ} that any pair of blocks shares a key in Hybrid GQ Design is:*

$$P_{HGQ} \leq \frac{b(b-1)}{N(N-1)} \times P_{GQ} + \frac{2b(N-b)}{N(N-1)} \times \frac{(st-s+t+2)}{(t+1)(st+1)} + \frac{(N-b)(N-2b)}{bN(N-1)} \times P_H + \frac{(b-1)(N-b)^2}{bN(N-1)} .$$

$$P_{HGQ} \geq \frac{b(b-1)}{N(N-1)} \times P_{GQ} + \frac{2b(N-b)}{N(N-1)} \times \frac{(s+1)(t-s/2+1)}{(t+1)(st+1)} + \frac{(N-b)(N-2b)}{bN(N-1)} \times P_H + \frac{(b-1)(N-b)^2}{bN(N-1)} .$$

Where P_{GQ} is given in Table-5 and $P_H = \left[1 - \frac{\binom{(s+1)(st-1)}{s+1}}{\binom{st(s+1)}{s+1}} \right] .$ □

5   Computational Results

We have implemented *Random Key Pre-distribution Scheme* by Eschenauer *et al.* [14], *Symmetric Design*, $GQ(q, q)$, $GQ(q, q^2)$, *Hybrid Symmetric Design*, and compared them with each other. In random key pre-distribution scheme, we initially generate a large pool of P keys and their identities. For each sensor, we uniformly at random draw k keys from the key-pool P without replacement. These k keys and key identities form the *key-chain* for a sensor node.

Basically, for a network of size N, we generate N key-chains and assign them to N sensor nodes. Then, we uniformly randomly distribute N nodes in to a 1×1 unit grid. Every wireless sensor has a coverage of radius r where $r = d(ln N)/N$, every node within this coverage area is assumed to be a neighbor. Note that,

Table 8. Symmetric Design vs Random Key Pre-distribution

Pool Size (P)	Key Chain Size(k)	Number Sensor Nodes	Random Prob.	Symmetric Prob.	Random Avg. Key Path	Symmetric Avg. Key Path	Avg. Node Degree
100807	318	100807	0.634	1.0	−	1.0	−
10303	102	10303	0.639	1.0	1.35	1.0	56
5113	72	5113	0.642	1.0	1.35	1.0	51
2863	54	2863	0.645	1.0	1.35	1.0	47
1407	38	1407	0.651	1.0	1.34	1.0	42
553	24	553	0.663	1.0	1.33	1.0	35

parameter d can be used to play with radius r and therefore average degree of the network.

After the deployment, two neighboring nodes compare the keys in their key-chains by using the key id's. If they have a key in common, it is used to secure the communication. If there is no key in common, they try to find a shortest possible path where each pair of nodes on the path shares a key. Length of this path is called *Key Path Length* where *Key Path Length* for two nodes directly sharing a key is 1. *Average Key Path Length* is one of the metrics that we use to compare random key pre-distribution scheme with our Combinatorial and Hybrid Design schemes.

Probability p that two key-chains share at least one key is another metric we use in comparison. For random key pre-distribution scheme, for a given key-pool size P and key-chain size k, Eschenauer *et al.* [14] approximate probability p as:
$$P_{RAND} = \left[1 - \frac{(1-\frac{k}{P})^{2(P-k+1/2)}}{(1-\frac{2k}{P})^{(P-2k+1/2)}}\right].$$

In Symmetric Design, $P_{SYM} = 1$ since any pair of key-chains shares exactly one key. In $GQ(s,t)$, probability of key share P_{QQ} for $GQ(q,q)$, P_{QQ^2} for $GQ(q,q^2)$ and $P_{Q^2Q^3}$ for $GQ(q^2,q^3)$ is given in Table-5.

Probability of key share P_{HSYM} is given in analysis section of the Hybrid Symmetric Design. Similarly, probability of key share P_{HGQ} for Hybrid GQ Design is given in analysis section of the Hybrid GQ Designs.

Tables 8, 9 and 10 summarize the computational results: (i) analytical solution for probability p that two key-chains share at least one key, and (ii) simulation results for *Average Key Path Length*.

Symmetric Design is compared with Random Key Pre-distribution scheme in Table-8. For the same network size, key-chain size and pool-size, Symmetric Design provides better probability of key share between any two key-chains. Simulation results for average key path length supports this advantage. In Random Key Pre-distribution scheme, a pair of nodes requires to go through a path of 1.35 hops on average to share a key and communicate securely. This path length is 1 for Symmetric Design.

$GQ(q,q)$ is compared with Random Key Pre-distribution scheme in Table-9. $GQ(q,q)$ decreases key-chain size, causing a small decrease in key sharing probability. Analytical solution shows that random key pre-distribution scheme

Table 9. Generalized Quadrangle $GQ(q, q)$ vs Random Key Pre-distribution

Pool Size (P)	Key Chain Size(k)	Number Sensor Nodes	Random Prob.	$GQ(q,q)$ Prob.	Random Avg. Key Path	$GQ(q,q)$ Avg. Key Path	Avg. Node Degree
7240	20	7240	0.053	0.052	2.68	2.69	205
5220	18	5220	0.060	0.058	2.89	2.88	148
2380	14	2380	0.079	0.076	3.17	3.18	88
1464	12	1464	0.094	0.090	2.73	2.71	81
400	8	400	0.150	0.140	3.61	3.49	32
156	6	156	0.212	0.192	2.82	2.53	25

Table 10. Hybrid Symmetric Design vs Random Key Pre-distribution

Pool Size (P)	Key Chain Size(k)	Number Sensor Nodes	Random Prob.	Hybrid Sym. Prob.	Random Avg. Key Path	Hybrid Sym. Avg. Key Path	Avg. Node Degree
10303	102	10500	0.632	0.99	1.36	1.01	56
5113	72	5250	0.632	0.99	1.35	1.01	51
2863	54	3000	0.628	0.98	1.35	1.03	47
1407	38	1500	0.627	0.97	1.34	1.04	42
553	24	750	0.547	0.89	1.33	1.15	37
183	14	250	0.563	0.89	1.31	1.14	29

provides slightly better probability of key share between key-chains, but $GQ(q, q)$ is still competitive to random key pre-distribution scheme. When two key-chains do not share a key, $GQ(q, q)$ guarantees existence of third one which shares a key with both.

Hybrid Symmetric Design is compared with Random Key Pre-distribution Scheme in Table-10. Hybrid Symmetric Design makes use of Symmetric Design, yet taking advantages of the scalability of probabilistic approach. Given target network size N and key chain size k for which there is no known design, computational results shows that Hybrid Symmetric Design shows better performance than Probabilistic Design.

6   Conclusions

In this work we presented novel approaches to the key distribution problem in large scale sensor networks. In contrast with prior work, our approach is combinatorial based on Combinatorial Block Designs. We showed how to map from two classes of combinatorial designs to deterministic key distribution mechanisms. We remarked the scalability issues in the deterministic constructions and proposed hybrid mechanisms. Hybrid constructions combine a deterministic core design with probabilistic extensions to achieve key distributions to any network size.

The analysis and computational comparison to the randomized methods show that the combinatorial approach has clear advantages: (i) it increases the probability of a pair of sensor nodes to share a key, and (ii) decreases the key-path length while provides scalability with hybrid approaches.

References

1. I. Anderson, "Combinatorial Designs: Construction Methods," Ellis Horwood Limited, 1990.
2. R. Blom, "An optimal class of symmetric key generation systems," EUROCRYPT 84, 1985.
3. C. Blundo, A. De Santis, A. Herzberg, S. Kutten, U. Vaccaro, M. Yung, "Perfectly-secure key distribution for dynamic conferences," In Advances in Cryptography - CRYPTO'92, 1993.
4. S. A. Camtepe, B. Yener, "Combinatorial Design of Key Distribution Mechanisms for Wireless Sensor Networks," RPI Computer Science Department, Technical Report 04-10, www.cs.rpi.edu/research/tr.html, 2004.
5. D.W. Carman, B.J. Matt and G.H. Cirincione, "Energy-efficient and Low-latency Key Management for Sensor Networks", In Proceedings of 23rd Army Science Conference, 2002.
6. H. Chan, A. Perrig and D. Song, "Random Key Predistribution Schemes for Sensor Networks," In 2003 IEEE Symposium on Research in Security and Privacy, 2003.
7. M. Chen, W. Cui, V. Wen and A. Woo, "Security and Deployment Issues in a Sensor Network," Ninja Project, A Scalable Internet Services Architecture, Berkeley, http://citeseer.nj.nec.com/chen00security.html, 2000.
8. C.J. Colbourn, J.H. Dinitz, "The CRC Handbook of Combinatorial Designs," CRC Press, 1996.
9. W. Du, J. Deng, Y. S. Han, P. Varshney, "A Pairwise Key Pre-distribution Scheme for Wireless Sensor Networks," In Proceedings of the 10th ACM Conference on Computer and Communications Security (CCS), 2003.
10. W. Du, J. Deng, Y. S. Han, S. Chen, P. K. Varshney, "A Key Management Scheme for Wireless Sensor Networks Using Deployment Knowledge," INFOCOM, 2004.
11. J. Deng, R. Han and S. Mishra, "Enhancing Base Station Security in Wireless Sensor Networks," Technical Report CU-CS-951-03, Department of Computer Science, University of Colorado, 2003.
12. J. Deng, R. Han, and S. Mishra, "A Performance Evaluation of Intrusion-Tolerant Routing in Wireless Sensor Networks," 2nd International Workshop on Information Processing in Sensor Networks (IPSN '03), 2003.
13. P. Dembowski, "Finite Geometries," Springer Verlag, 1968.
14. L. Eschenauer, V. D. Gligor, "A key-management scheme for distributed sensor networks", Proceedings of the 9th ACM conference on Computer and communications security, 2002.
15. M. Hall, "Combinatorial Theory," Blaisdell Publishing Company, 1967.
16. J.W.P. Hirschfeld, "Projective Geometries Over Finite Fields," Clarendon Press Oxford, 1979.
17. D. Liu and P. Ning, "Efficient Distribution of Key Chain Commitments for Broadcast Authentication in Distributed Sensor Networks", The 10th Annual Network and Distributed System Security Symposium, February 2003

18. D. Liu, P. Ning, K. Sun, "Efficient self-healing group key distribution with re-vocation capability," Proceedings of the 10th ACM conference on Computer and communication security, 2003.
19. D. Liu, P. Ning, "Establishing pairwise keys in distributed sensor networks," Pro-ceedings of the 10th ACM conference on Computer and communication security, 2003.
20. R. Merkle, "Secure Communication over insecure channels," Communications of the ACM, 1978.
21. S. E. Payne, J. A. Thas, "Finite Generalized Quadrangles," Research Notes in Mathematics, Pitman Advanced Publishing Program, 1984.
22. D. Pedoe, "An introduction to Projective Geometry," Oxford, 1963.
23. A. Perrig, R. Szewczyk, V. Wen, D. Culler and J. D. Tygar, "SPINS: Security Protocols for Sensor Networks," Wireless Networks Journal (WINE), 2002.
24. S. Slijepcevic, M. Potkonjak, V. Tsiatsis, S. Zimbeck, M. B. Srivastava, "On com-munication Security in Wireless Ad-Hoc Sensor Network," Eleventh IEEE Interna-tional Workshops on Enabling Technologies: Infrastructure for Collaborative En-terprises (WETICE'02), 2002.
25. F. Stajano, R. Anderson, "The resurrecting duckling: security issues for ad-hoc wireless networks," AT&T software symposium, 1999.
26. D. R. Stinson, S. A. Vanstone, "A combinatorial approach to threshold schemes,", Advances in Cryptology - CRYPTO '87, 1987.
27. D. R. Stinson, "A construction for authentication / secrecy codes from certain combinatorial designs," Advances in Cryptology - CRYPTO '87, 1987.
28. D. R. Stinson, "Combinatorial characterizations of authentication codes," Ad-vances in Cryptology - CRYPTO '91, 1991.
29. Y. Song, A. Wool, B. Yener, "Combinatorial Design of Multi-ring Networks with Combined Routing and Flow Control," in Computer Networks Vol.3 No: 3, pp 247-267, 2003.
30. J. Undercoffer, S. Avancha, A. Joshi, and J. Pinkston, "Security for Sensor Net-works," CADIP Research Symposium, 2002.
31. W.D. Wallis, "Combinatorial Desing," Marcel Dekker Inc., 1988.
32. B. Yener, Y. Ofek, M. Yung, "Combinatorial Design of Congestion Free Networks," In IEEE/ACM Transactions on Networking, Vol. 5, No. 6, pages: 989-1000, De-cember 1997.
33. S. Zhu, S. Xu, S. Setia, S. Jajodia, "Establishing Pairwise Keys for Secure Commu-nication in Ad Hoc Networks: A Probabilistic Approach," 11th IEEE International Conference on Network Protocols (ICNP'03), 2003.
34. S. Zhu, S. Setia, S. Jajodia, "LEAP: efficient security mechanisms for large-scale distributed sensor networks," Proceedings of the 10th ACM conference on Com-puter and communication security, 2003.

Hindering Eavesdropping
via IPv6 Opportunistic Encryption

Claude Castelluccia[1], Gabriel Montenegro[2],
Julien Laganier[2,3], and Christoph Neumann[1]

[1] INRIA Rhône-Alpes, 655 Avenue de l'Europe, 38334 Saint Ismier CEDEX, France
{claude.castelluccia,christoph.neumann}@inrialpes.fr
[2] Sun Labs, Europe, 180 Avenue de l'Europe, 38334 Saint Ismier CEDEX, France
{gab,ju}@sun.com
[3] LIP (UMR #5668 CNRS/ENS Lyon/INRIA/UCB Lyon)
46, Allée d'Italie, 69007 Lyon, France

Abstract. This paper presents an opportunistic encryption scheme strictly layered on top of IPv6. Assuming that a node needs to send data toward another node, our proposal enables the dynamic configuration of an encrypted tunnel between the two nodes' IPsec gateways. The main contribution of this paper is to propose a solution that is fully distributed and does not rely on any global Trusted Third Party (such as DNSSEC or a PKI). The IPsec gateways are discovered using IPv6 anycast, and they derive authorization from authorization certificates and Crypto-Based Identifiers (CBIDs). The result is a robust and easily deployable opportunistic encryption service for IPv6.

Keywords: Security, IPv6, Opportunistic Encryption, IPsec, CBID, delegation, IKE.

1 Introduction

Because of its massive and widespread use, it is easy to overlook that the Internet remains a very hostile environment. Given that most of the packets are sent in the clear, there is a strong incentive both for legitimate as well as illegitimate reasons to install wiretaps [1] or to carry out passive eavesdropping. While end-to-end encryption is arguably the best solution for those concerned, currently it is not practical for several reasons: (1) most of the current hosts do not implement any encryption algorithms, (2) these can be quite expensive and prohibitive for constrained devices, and (3) end-to-end encryption requires a key management infrastructure which does not exist today.

Opportunistic encryption is a practical solution to this problem. It allows secure (encrypted, authenticated) communication without connection-by-connection pairwise pre-arrangement. To accomplish further ease-of use, instead of end-to-end encryption special security gateways can intercept packets and encrypt them for their traversal over the general Internet. The main idea is that the local security gateway intercepts an outgoing packet addressed to a remote

P. Samarati et al. (Eds.): ESORICS 2004, LNCS 3193, pp. 309–321, 2004.
© Springer-Verlag Berlin Heidelberg 2004

host, and quickly negotiates an IPsec tunnel to that host's security gateway. As a result, packets sent by the hosts are encrypted as they traverse the Internet (i.e. between the security gateways). Although end-to-end encryption is preferable and more secure, this flavor of opportunistic encryption is easier to deploy as it requires modifying only the gateways, not the vastly more numerous end systems. The goal of opportunistic encryption is to increase the percentage of encrypted versus cleartext packets in the Internet. Security in existing schemes, such as the FreeSWAN system [2], relies on a *Trusted Third Party* (TTP), a globally-rooted security infrastructure such as DNSSEC [3] or a *Public Key Infrastructure* (PKI). As detailed in Section 2, relying on a TTP has major drawbacks in terms of security, deployment and robustness. The main contribution of this paper is to propose a solution for IPv6 that is opportunistic in a "gateway-to-gateway" manner, and that does not rely on any TTP. Our proposal relies on IPv6 Anycast, Authorization certificates and Crypto-Based Identifiers (CBID) to provide secure and easily deployable *opportunistic encryption* in IPv6.

The paper is structured as follows: Section 2 presents the concept of opportunistic encryption and provides an overview of the related work. Section 3 discusses the motivations of our work. Section 4 details our proposal and its different components. Section 5 presents the *Opportunistic SUCV* protocol, an opportunistic extension to the SUCV protocol [4]. Section 6 assesses the security of our proposal. Section 7 concludes the paper. Finally, we include implementation details and a description of how to integrate our scheme in IKEv2 [5] in the appendix.

2   Opportunistic Encryption: Concept and Related Work

Concept Overview: The main idea of opportunistic encryption is to deploy IPsec security gateways at site borders such that they are dynamically discoverable and usable by remote security gateways instead of requiring pre-configuration between specific sites. Such gateways (1) intercept an outgoing packet from a *source* aimed at a remote host (the *destination*), (2) dynamically discover the destination's security gateway, and (3) negotiate an IPsec tunnel with the destination's gateway (the *responder*).

Once an administrator configures its site's gateway(s) to support opportunistic encryption, the security services afforded by such an arrangement are (1) encrypted and authenticated communication *between the gateways* via IPsec without site-by-site pair-wise pre-arrangement, and, (2) protection from eavesdroppers (in particular, from the Internet at large).

In this paper, opportunistic encryption does not necessarily provide end-to-end security. For example, opportunistic encryption does not provide end-to-end authentication: A node that receives packets from a given IP address does not have the guarantee that these packets were actually sent by this IP address or even that the packets have not been modified on their way. The main goal of opportunistic encryption is to improve privacy on the Internet by enabling message privacy as a default. It aims at hindering eavesdropping on the Internet by encrypting packets at intermediate gateways.

The Design Challenges: Apart from careful attention to detail in various areas, there are three crucial design challenges for opportunistic encryption:

1. *Remote Gateway Discovery.* The local security gateway needs a way to quickly and securely discover the IP address of the remote Security Gateway for the packet that prompted the negotiation.
2. *Remote Gateway Authentication and Authorization.* The local security gateway needs to authenticate the other Security Gateway. This authentication needs to ensure that the other Security Gateway is who it claims to be and that it is authorized to represent the client for which it claims to be the gateway. Without this authorization phase, a malicious host could pretend to be the gateway of a node and eavesdrop on its packets.
3. *Tunnel Establishment.* The security gateways need to establish a secure tunnel in a way that guarantees to reach agreement, without any explicit pre-arrangement or preliminary negotiation.

FreeSWAN System: The most recognizable opportunistic encryption system is certainly the one designed by the FreeSWAN project [2]. This system heavily relies on DNSSEC to solve the *Remote Gateway Discovery* and *Remote Gateway Authentication and Authorization* phase. It uses IKE [5] for the *Tunnel Establishment* phase. FreeSWAN assumes that each end-node publishes in the reverse DNS tree its authorized security gateway(s), and their respective public key(s).

These two pieces of information are combined into a single IPSECKEY DNS Resource Record [6], stored in the reverse DNS tree (in-addr.arpa, or ip6.arpa). Lookups in the reverse DNS tree should be secured by DNSSEC in order to protect against active attacks. Note that a single node might publish several such IPSECKEY RRs with different precedence values for failover or load-balancing (similarly to what is done for mail servers with MX records). This solution has the following limitations:

- The availability of the opportunistic encryption service depends on the availability of the DNS service.
- The security of the system depends on DNS security [7] (DNSSEC) and its deployment, currently, a significant limitation. Using FreeSWAN without DNSSEC, while possible, renders the whole system vulnerable to spoofed DNS replies. Additionally, the full-scale deployment of DNSSEC may be as troublesome as that of a large-scale PKI [8].
- It assumes that each host has an entry in the DNS reverse tree, and has control over it. This is a very heavy constraint, in particular, for dynamic environments and the associated devices (e.g., a mobile node visiting a foreign network might use a care-of address that is not registered in its DNS).
- It introduces significant latencies. A security gateway must process some secure DNS requests and replies (i.e., perform some signature verifications) before establishing a tunnel with the remote gateway.
- It creates several new opportunities for DoS attacks. For example, a malicious host could send packets with forged source address. For each packet, the Responder security gateway would perform a secure DNS lookup.

3   Motivations

The motivation and objective of our work is to propose a model for IPv6 opportunistic encryption that is fully distributed and does not rely on higher level services. We aim to develop a *secure* opportunistic encryption system. By *secure*, we mean that the local gateway must be able to *discover* one of the gateways associated with the remote host, *authenticate* it, and verify that it has been *authorized* to act as a gateway for the remote host. The identity of the communicating hosts must be protected over the (insecure) Internet. *We impose the additional requirement that the gateways must be able to establish the opportunistic tunnel without relying on any kind of infrastructure nor any higher level services (such as DNS or PKI).*

Finally we make the assumption that the path between the source and the initiator, being within an intranet, is much more secure than the outside segment between initiator and responder (e.g. there is a pre-existing tunnel or the source and initiator belong to the same organization). This is the "hard outside shell, soft interior" security model. We believe that while this is not always true, the risk of eavesdropping on outside packets is so much larger that it deserves more immediate attention. Finally, in a security-conscious intranet, the existence of a homogeneous administrative domain makes it operationally much more possible for locally associated systems (e.g., a source and its initiator gateway) to be able to secure their traffic. In such a situation it is much more straightforward to obtain a security association using more traditional IPsec and key exchange mechanisms.

4   IPv6 Opportunistic Encryption

4.1   Proposal Overview

Our proposal relies on three mechanisms: *anycast addresses*, *Crypto-Based Identifiers (CBID)* and *authorization certificates*. Anycast is used to identify the remote security gateway. CBIDs are used for authentication and authorization certificates are used by the remote gateway to prove that it has been authorized by the destination host to act as a security gateway on its behalf.

The contribution of our work is to effectively combine these three mechanisms together with a key establishment protocol, such as IKE [5] or sucvP [4], to propose an opportunistic encryption system that is able to establish IPsec tunnels between two security gateways securely and without relying on higher layer support. This system is also very easily deployable because all of these mechanisms are already (almost) available and our system does not require any changes in the existing Internet architecture.

The rest of this section describes these three basic entities and then presents our proposal in more details.

IPv6 Anycast Review: An IPv6 Anycast address is an address that is assigned to more than one interface. Thus an IPv6 Anycast address defines a group but as opposed to multicast group a packet sent to an Anycast address is not routed to all members of the group but only to the source's "nearest" one [9]. All interfaces belonging to an Anycast address usually reside within a topological region defined by an address prefix, P. Within this region, each member must be advertised as a separate "host route" entry in the routing system. A *router* that is member of an Anycast group will advertise its membership using the routing protocol (RIP, OSPF, BGP, etc). A *host* that wants to join an Anycast group will have to use a group membership protocol, such as MLD [10], to register with the local router(s) that will then propagate this registration to the region using the routing protocol. From outside the region, such a reserved subnet anycast address can be aggregated into the routing entry for prefix P.

Crypto-Based Identifiers (CBID): Crypto-Based Identifiers and Addresses [4, 11, 12], otherwise known as Crypto-Based Identifiers (CBID's), are identifiers derived from the hash of a public key.

We use the term *CBID* to refer to either of the two following entities derived from a host's public key as follows:

- Crypto-Generated Address (CGA): an IPv6 address whose leftmost 64 bits are set to a valid prefix (as per normal IPv6 usage), and whose rightmost 64 bits (interface identifier) are set to a 64-bit entity obtained as follows: *hmac_64(imprint, PK)*.
- Crypto-Based Identifier (CBI): a fixed length cryptographic token obtained as follows: *hmac_x(imprint, PK)*, where x is the size of the identifier.

Where *imprint* is a 64-bit field and PK is the host's public key. The imprint is a quantity used to limit certain types of brute-force attacks [4]. In this work, it is assumed to be equal to the IPv6 64-bit network prefix for CGA (in agreement with [12]), and ignored (e.g., set to 0) for CBI.

These identifiers have two very important properties [4]:

- They are *statistically unique*, because of the collision-resistance property of the cryptographic hash function used to generate them.
- They are *securely bound to a given node*, because a node, N, can prove ownership of its CBID

A node can prove ownership of its *CBID* by revealing the public key, *PK*, and the imprint value, *imprint*, used to generate the CBID and by proving that it knows the corresponding private key, *SK*. This can be performed by signing a message.

Any other node can verify that a given node owns its *CBID* by recomputing it and verifying the signature. Note that this verification does not rely on any centralized security service such as a PKI or Key Distribution Center.

Review of Authorization Certificates: Authorization certificates are used to express delegation. We choose to use SPKI [13] in this paper even though Keynote2 [14] or potentially X.509 Attribute Certificates for Authorization [15] could also be used. The main principles of SPKI can be summarized as follows:

- a certificate has 5 fields: (1) issuer (who is giving the authorization), (2) subject (who is acquiring the permission), (3) delegation (set if the subject can delegate the permission), (4) authorization (specifies the permission being communicated) and (5) validity.
- SPKI is *key-oriented*. No (name, key) binding, and therefore no Certification Authority (CA), is necessary. The entities possessing, delegating and receiving access rights are cryptographic key pairs. A certificate can in short be written as: $(PK', R, t, PK)_{SK}$: PK gives the right R to PK' and the validity period is t, where PK and PK' are two public key. The certificate is signed with SK, where SK is the private key corresponding to PK.
- A certificate has a validity period.
- Delegation certificates differ from traditional access control schemes in that any key may issue certificates. There is no central or trusted authority.
- A key may delegate rights to services it controls, it may also re-delegate rights it received by delegation from other keys.

Note that a full certificate is composed of a sequence of three objects [16]: the *public-key object* that contains the issuer public key, the *certificate object* that defines the authorization and *a signature object* that contains the signature.

4.2   Proposal Description

System Configuration: In our proposal each host is configured with a Cryptographically Generated Address (CGA) as its default IPv6 unicast address. Each security gateway is configured with a Crypto-Based Identifier (CBI).

Additionally, each security gateway of a given network is reachable by a reserved IPv6 subnet anycast address, the OEGW (Opportunistic Encryption Gateway) Anycast address to be defined by the IANA [17]. This address must be configured and each authorized security gateway must join it.

Each security gateway must also be authorized by the hosts that it is serving as a security gateway for them. For this, each host issues a SPKI certificate to each security gateway it wants to authorize to act as a security gateway. This certificate specifies that the host, identified by its CGA address, authorizes the security gateway, identified by its CBI to act as a security gateway. This certificate is signed by the host[1]. The format of the authorization certificate (actually of the certificate object) is the following:

```
(cert
   (issuer  (addr <host_cga>)
   (subject (addr <GW_cbi>)
   (tag ( OEauthorization)
   (not-before <date1>)
   (not-after  <date2>)
)
```

---

[1] The gateway needs to keep one certificate per host. Note however that the certificates do not need to be stored locally but can be stored on a local server. This is just a *storage* server, not a TTP since it does not need to be trusted.

This certificate authorizes the security gateway, defined by its CBI, GW_cbi, to act as a security gateway for the host defined by its CGA, $host\_cga$. This certificate is only valid after $date1$ and before $date2$, and is signed by the host.

Protocol Overview: This section describes the message exchange of the proposed protocol. We assume that the application (at the Source) knows the destination IP CGA. The specific means of obtaining this destination IP address are not specific to (and out of scope of) our proposal, and may use any of various methods including: lookups (DNS/DNSSEC, LDAP, NIS, etc.), manual configuration, dynamic referrals and redirects, etc. Also possible are user-friendly exchanges using secure side channels such as SCEAU [4].

Our protocol works as follows[2].

1. The Source initiates a packet exchange (TCP, SCTP, DCCP, UDP, ICMP, etc) with the Destination.

2. The Source's security gateway, referred as the *Initiator*, intercepts the packet, and verifies that it is authorized to act as gateway by the Source's address CGA_S (by matching CGA_S against its available list of authorization certificates). If an adequate certificate is found, based upon the packet's destination address prefix, the Initiator gateway calculates the reserved subnet OEGW anycast address according to normal IPv6 usage [17]. The Initiator gateway then sends an "OEGW request" ($OEGW\_REQ$) to that anycast address. This packet contains the Source's CGA (CGA_S), the Source's Public Key (PK_S), the Destination's CGA (CGA_D), the Initiator's CBI (CBI_I), the Initiator's IP address (IP_I), the Initiator's Public Key (PK_I), the imprint value used by the Source to generate its CGA ($imprint_S$), the imprint value used by the Initiator to generate its CBI ($imprint_I$) and the SPKI certificate issued by the Source to the Initiator's CBI ($SPKI_S(I)$). This message is signed by the Initiator.

3. Upon reception of this message, one of the destination node's security gateway, the *Responder*, (1) verifies that the Initiator owns its CBI (i.e. the Initiator's CBI was generated from its public key and imprint and $OEGW\_REQ$'s signature is correct), and (2) that the SPKI certificate is valid (it is signed by the source and it does authorize the Initiator's CBI to act as a gateway). Upon this verification, the Responder has the assurance that it is talking with a legitimate and authorized security gateway. It then replies to the Initiator with a "OEGW reply" ($OEGW\_REP$) message that contains its CBI (CBI_R), its IP address (IP_R), its public key (PK_R), its imprint ($imprint_R$), and the SPKI certificate signed by the destination host ($SPKI_D(R)$). This message is signed by the Responder.

4. Upon reception of the $OEGW\_REP$, the initiator (1) verifies that the responding Gateway owns its CBI (i.e. the $OEGW\_REP$'s signature is correct and the responder's CBI was generated from its public key and imprint) and (2) that the SPKI certificate is valid (it is signed by the destination host and that it actually authorizes the responder to act as a gateway).

---

[2] This protocol has been intentionally simplified for clarity.

Upon this verification, the Initiator has the assurance that it is talking with a legitimate and authorized security gateway.

5. The Responder and the Initiator engage into a key establishment exchange (such as IKE [5] or sucvP [4]) to establish an IPsec Security Association.

The simplified message exchange described above is vulnerable to several DoS attacks. However, the above protocol should not be used as it is but must be integrated within a key establishment protocol, such as IKE or sucvP, as described in Section 5.

5 osucvP: Opportunistic Statistically Unique and Verifiable Protocol

This section presents *osucvP* (Opportunistic Statistically Unique and Verifiable Protocol), the protocol that is used between security gateways to establish secure channels. This protocol relies on the *sucvP* protocol described in [4]. We have selected *sucvP* because we believe that its design, based on simplicity and limited negotiation capabilities in order to facilitate interoperability, fits very well to the requirements of our system. *OsucvP* is very similar to the ISO protocol described and analysed in [18]. The security on this protocol can be based on the analytical work of [19] where it is shown that the ISO protocol is a secure key establishment protocol. *OsucvP* provides perfect forward secrecy via a Diffie-Hellman exchange authenticated with digital signatures.

Recently, the $IKEv2$ [20] protocol has been selected as the replacement for the current IKE (v1) standard. We describe in the Appendix how $IKEv2$ could be used with our OE scheme.

Using the same notation as in [4], our protocol is defined by the four following messages (illustrated by Fig. 1):

- *osucvP1* $(I \rightarrow OEGW\, Anycast Address)$:
  $N1, CGA_D, CGA_S$
- *osucvP2* $(R \rightarrow I)$:
  $N1, puzzle\ request, CBI_R, g^r$
- *osucvP3* $(I \rightarrow R)$:
  $N1, puzzle\ reply, CBI_I, g^i, CGA_S, CGA_D, SPKI_S(I), PK_I, SPI,$
  $lifetime_I, SIG_{SK_I}(N1, puzzle\ reply, CBI_R, CBI_I, SPKI_S(I), PK_I, g^i,$
  $g^r, CGA_S, CGA_D, SPI, lifetime_I)$
- *osucvP4* $(R \rightarrow I)$:
  $N1, SPKI_D(R), PK_R, SPI, lifetime_R, SIG_{SK_R}(N1, puzzle\ reply, CBI_R,$
  $CBI_I, SPKI_S(I), SPKI_D(R), PK_I, PK_R, g^i, g^r, CGA_S, CGA_D, SPI,$
  $lifetime_R)$

The first message (*osucvP1*) is the $OEGW\_REQ$ request that is sent by the source's security gateway (Initiator I) to the destination node's OEGW anycast address. Upon reception of this message, one security gateway (Responder R) serving the destination node replies with a *osucvP2* message. This message

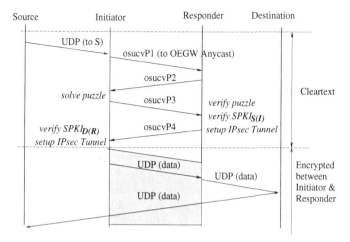

Fig. 1. Opportunistic SUCV Protocol

contains the nonce $N1$ that was sent in *osucvP1*, a client puzzle request, a Diffie-Hellman component and a session key lifetime. Upon reception of this message, I solves the puzzle and sends *osucvP3* back to R. This message is signed with SK_I, the private key whose corresponding public key, PK_I, was used to generate CBI_I. The four fields, CBI_I, CGA_D, CGA_S and $SPKI_S(I)$, have been added in *osucvP3* instead of *osucvP1* because in *sucvP* R does not commit any resource before *osucvP3* (as a DoS protection). Hence, it is useless to send this information before *osucvP3*. Upon reception of *osucvP3*, R verifies the signature and $SPKI_S(I)$, as described in the previous section, computes the IPsec session key, *Skey_ipsec*, using Diffie-Hellman key exchange protocol and establishes an IPsec tunnel with I. It then replies with *osucvP4*. This message is signed with SK_R, the private key whose corresponding public key, PK_R, was used to generate CBI_R. The messages *osucvP3* and *osucvP4* are signed to authenticate the DH exchange and to solve the key-identity binding problem described in [18]. The three fields, CBI_R, PK_R and $SPKI_D(R)$ are sent in *osucvP4* instead of *osucvP2* because R does not commit any resource until it verified the puzzle reply contained in *osucvP3*, to protect against DoS attacks. R could actually send them in *osucvP2* but since this message is not signed, I will not be able to make use of them before *osucvP4*. Upon reception of *osucvP4*, I verifies the signature and $SPKI_S(R)$, as described in the previous section, computes the IPsec session key, *Skey_ipsec*, using Diffie-Hellman key exchange protocol and establishes an IPsec tunnel with R.

Thereafter, the packets are encrypted between I and R, i.e. when they traverse the Internet.

6   Security Analysis

The security analysis of the sucvP protocol is detailed in [4]. In this section we assess the security of the extension that we added in the sucvP protocol to support opportunistic encryption.

6.1 Impersonation Attacks

CGA impersonation: A malicious host can attack a host, defined by a CGA, if it can find a public/private pair whose public key hashes to the target's CGA. It can then issue fake SPKI certificates and impersonate the target host's gateway. As a result of this attack, the malicious host can then wiretap the target's packets. To complete this attack the malicious host must attempt 2^{62} (i.e. approximately 4.8×10^{18}) tries to find a public key that hashes to the CGA. If the malicious host can do 1 million hashes per second it needs 142,235 years. If the malicious host can hash 1 billion hashes per second it still needs 142 years[3].

CBI impersonation: A malicious host can attack a security gateway, defined by a CBI, if it can find a public/private pair whose public key hashes to the target's CBI. If it succeeds, the malicious host can then wiretap the traffic of all hosts supported by the target security gateway. This attack is therefore more severe than the previous one. Fortunately this attack is much more difficult to perform. In fact, in order to complete it the malicious host must attempt 2^{128} (i.e. approximately 3.4×10^{38}) tries to find a public key that hashes to the CBI. If the malicious host can perform 1 million hashes per second it needs 10^{25} years. If the malicious host can hash 1 billion hashes per second it still needs 10^{22} years. Brute-force attacks are nearly impossible.

6.2 DoS Attacks

Fake (or malicious) Initiator: a malicious host (or a set of malicious hosts) could attack a Responder by bombing it with fake *osucvP* messages. In *osucvP* (as in sucvP), a Responder does not commit any resource before *osucvP3*. This is done in order to detect Initiator that uses spoofed address (in this case they won't receive *osucvP2*). So this attack is not very severe and probably not worse than just bombing the Initiator with regular packets.

A set of Initiators (using a DDoS type of attack) could also attack a target Responder by establishing a lot of opportunistic tunnels with it just for the sake of exhausting its resource. Notice that the responder cannot be forced to participate in the tunnel creation unless the responder had a certificate from the packet destination. The same family of attacks exists with SSL, the main difference being that the target of the attack is the destination in the SSL case, whereas it is authorized by the destination in the OE case. The solution is, for *osucvP*, to increase the number of security gateways and perform some load-balancing.

Fake (or malicious) Destination: A malicious host can attack an Initiator by sending packets to a lot of different destinations through it. For each of this packet, the Initiator will establish an IPsec tunnel and consume a lot of resource. To prevent this attack the Initiator must only establish tunnels for trusted sources. How this trust relationship is established is out of the scope of this paper. Ingress filtering might be enough in most of the cases. An Initiator will only establish tunnels for packets that come from the internal network.

---

[3] As shown in [12], the security of a CGA address can easily be increased if needed.

7   Conclusion

The main contribution of this paper is to propose a solution for IPv6 that is opportunistic in a "gateway-to-gateway" manner, and that does not rely on any Trusted Third Party (such as a Public Key Infrastructure or DNSSEC). We have obtained a solution that is fully distributed thanks to a judicious combination of IPv6 anycast, authorization certificates (or delegation) and Crypto-Based Identifiers (CBIDs), which rely on an inherent cryptographic binding between the identity of the entities and their public keys. This efficient combination is scalable, robust, efficient and easier to deploy.

Acknowledgements

We thank the anonymous reviewers for their valuable comments. Special thanks to Alberto Escudero-Pascual for his valuable help and many constructive suggestions.

References

1. Bellovin Steve, "Wiretapping the net," The Bridge, National Academy of Engineering., 2000.
2. M. Richardson and R. Redelmeier, *Opportunistic Encryption unsing the Internet Key Exchange (IKE)*, IETF, draft-richardson-ipsec-opportunistic-13.txt, February 2004.
3. R. Arends, M. Larson, D. Massey, and S. Rose, *DNS Security Introduction and Requirements*, IETF, draft-ietf-dnsext-dnssec-intro-02, July 2002.
4. Gabriel Montenegro and Claude Castelluccia, "Crypto-based identifiers (CBIDs): Concepts and applications," *ACM Transactions on Information and Systems Security (TISSEC)*, vol. 7, no. 1, February 2004.
5. D. Harkins and D. Carrel, *The Internet Key Exchange (IKE)*, IETF, RFC2409, November 1998.
6. Michael Richardson, *A Method for Storing IPsec Keying Material in DNS*, IETF, draft-ietf-ipseckey-rr-09.txt, Feb 2004.
7. Steven Bellovin, "Using the domain name system for system break-ins," in *Fifth Usenix UNIX Security Symposium*, July 1995.
8. C. Ellison and B. Schneier, "Ten risks of PKI: What you're not being told about public key infrastructure," *Computer Security Journal*, vol. 16, no. 1, pp. 1–7, 2000.
9. B. Hinden and S. Deering, *IP Version6 Addressing Architecture*, IETF, RFC3513, April 2003.
10. B. Haberman and D. Thaler, *Host-based Anycast using MLD*, IETF, draft-haberman-ipngwg-host-anycast-00.txt, February 2001.
11. Greg O'Shea and Michael Roe, ""Child-proof Authentication for MIPv6 (CAM)," *ACM Computer Communications Review*, April 2001.
12. Tuomas Aura, "Cryptographically generated addresses (CGA)," in *6th Information Security Conference (ISC'03*, Bristol, UK, October 2003, vol. 2851, pp. 29–43, LNCS.
13. C. Ellison and etc., *SPKI Certificate Theory*, IETF, RFC 2693, September 1999.

14. M. Blaze, J. Feigenbaum, J. Ioannidis, and A. Keromytis, *The KeyNote Trust-Management System Version 2*, IETF, RFC2704, September 1999.
15. S. Farrel and R. Housley, *An Internet Attribute Certificate Profile for Authorization*, IETF, RFC3281, April 2002.
16. C. Ellison and etc., *SPKI Examples*, IETF Internet Draft, Internet Draft, Available at http://world.std.com/cme/examples.txt, March 1998.
17. D. Johnson and S. Deering, *Reserved IPv6 Subnet Anycast Addresses*, IETF, RFC2526, March 1999.
18. Hugo Krawczyk, "SIGMA: The SIG-and-MAc approach to authenticated diffie-hellman and its use in the ike protocols," in *CRYPTO*, Santa Barbara, August 2003.
19. R. Canetti and H. Krawczyk, "Analysis of key-exchange protocols anf their use for building secure channels," in *Eurocrypt*, 2001, vol. 2045.
20. C. Kaufman, *Internet Key Exchange IKEv2 Protocol*, IETF, draft-ietf-ipsec-ikev2-13.txt, March 2004.
21. D. McDonald, C. Metz, and B. Phan, *PF_KEY Key Management API, Version 2*, IETF, RFC2367, July 1998.

Appendix A: Implementation

We implemented IPv6 opportunistic encryption on the FreeBSD-4.7 platform, which incorporates most of the KAME IPv6 stack.

Our implementation consists of two parts:

- a user level daemon (*sucvPd*) for (1) proof of ownership and verification of CBID's (CBI's and CGA's), (2) exchange and verification of SPKI delegation certificates and (3) key exchange via the sucvP ([4]) protocol.
- kernel level modification of the IPv6 outbound IPsec tunnel mode routine (*ipsec6_output_tunnel*), which does not interfere with regular IPsec behavior.

Prior to the sucvP transaction, the local security gateway is unaware of the remote OEGW's address. Accordingly, an opportunistic encryption SPD entry has the unspecified address (i.e., *::0*) as its remote tunnel endpoint.

The sucvP daemon communicates with the IPsec stack through the *PFKEY_V2* API [21]. It listens for an *SADB_ACQUIRE* message with the unspecified address as its remote tunnel endpoint, indicating that an OEGW needs to be discovered. To better understand this mechanism, let's look at the normal tunnel mode processing. Usually when a packet matches an SPD entry specifying that IPsec tunnel mode is required, the stack sends an *SADB_ACQUIRE* message to the key management daemon, thus requesting a key exchange between the tunnel endpoints (indeed, the two OEGW's). However, with opportunistic encryption the remote tunnel endpoint is not known at this moment. It needs to be discovered.

We defined a new kernel variable (*net.inet6.ipsec6.sucv_oe*) whose intent is to provide a user level means to modify the behavior of the IPsec stack when dealing with OE SPD entries.

When this variable is set to 0, the IPsec stack behaves like a regular FreeBSD implementation, i.e., a packet matching an opportunistic encryption SPD entry would trigger a regular *SADB_ACQUIRE* with the unspecified address as its remote tunnel endpoint (in the destination *SADB_ADDRESS* payload). Obviously, this will not progress any further, since there is not enough information for the key management daemon to know with which entity it should negotiate.

When this variable is set to 1, a packet matching an SPD entry will trigger a special *SADB_ACQUIRE* message in which the two *SADB_ADDRESS* payloads contain (1) the source, and (2) the destination addresses of the original packet (instead of the IPsec tunnel endpoints as in the previous case). Thus, the key management daemon knows the real destination of the packet, and uses it to derive the anycast address of the remote security gateway *OEGW*.

The key management daemon can identify this *SADB_ACQUIRE* message as one triggered by opportunistic encryption (as opposed to a regular one), because the first *SADB_ADDRESS* payload does not contain a source address assigned to the gateway itself (indeed, it contains the source address of the packet which triggered this message). This causes discovery and authorization verification of the remote *OEGW*, and, finally, key-exchange. If all the previous steps succeed, the key exchange daemon sends an *SADB_X_POLICY* message to the IPsec subsystem. This requests protection of subsequent communications between this source and destination via IPsec tunnel mode using the previously discovered OEGW as its tunnel remote endpoint.

Appendix B: Integration with IKE

No changes to the usual IKEv2 message exchanges are required. Rather, when configuring an opportunistic tunnel via IKEv2, an OEGW must use ISAKMP payloads in a specific manner to achieve CBI proof-of-ownership during the initial *IKE_AUTH*, and to prove, during the subsequent *CREATE_CHILD_SA* exchange, that the OEGW is authorized to provide opportunistic gateway service on behalf of a CGA.

An ID payload of type *ID_IPV6_ADDR* would not trigger any verification by the peer of the binding between the public key and the CBI. Hence, a new *ID* type of *ID_CBID_128* is needed.

When performing an opportunistic IKE exchange, two certificates needs to be carried, in two separate *CERT* payloads: (1) An OEGW wanting to prove CBI ownership must send a *CERT* payload (e.g., X.509) that contains the public key used when generating its CBI, and (2) an OEGW wanting to prove that it is authorized to act as such for a given CGA must send the corresponding *CERT* payload (e.g., SPKI)

The Traffic Selector (*TS*) Payload contains headers used to identify IP packet flows which need IPsec processing. In the case of opportunistic encryption, those flows will fly between two CGA's. Hence, we require that the *TS* payloads used contain CGA's. This implies that the TS Type is set to *TS_IPV6_CGADDR*, causing the CGAs used as traffic selectors to be validated against the CGAs which issue (and sign) the SPKI authorization certificates contained in the exchanged CERT payloads.

On the Role of Key Schedules in Attacks on Iterated Ciphers

Lars R. Knudsen[1] and John E. Mathiassen[2]

[1] Department of Mathematics, Technical University of Denmark
[2] Department of Informatics, University of Bergen, Norway

Abstract. This paper considers iterated ciphers and their resistance against linear and differential cryptanalysis. In the theory of these attacks one assumes independence of the round keys in the ciphers. Very often though, the round keys are computed in a key schedule algorithm from a short key in a nonrandom fashion. In this paper it is shown by experiments that ciphers with complex key schedules resist both attacks better than ciphers with more straightforward key schedules. It is well-known that by assuming independent round keys the probabilities of differentials and linear hulls can be modeled by Markov chains and that for most such ciphers the distribution of the probabilities of these converge to the uniform distribution after some number of rounds. The presented experiments illustrate that some iterated ciphers with very simple key schedules will never reach this uniform distribution. Also the experiments show that ciphers with well-designed, complex key schedules reach the uniform distribution faster (using fewer rounds) than ciphers with poorly designed key schedules. As a side result it was found that there exist ciphers for which the differential of the highest probability for one fixed key is also the differential of the highest probability for any other key. It is believed that this is the first such example provided in the literature.

1   Introduction

Most block ciphers today are so-called iterated ciphers. Here the ciphertext is computed as a function of the plaintext and the user-selected key, K, in a number of iterations. Typically, the user-selected key is input to a key scheduling algorithm, which returns a series of r keys, $K_1, \ldots, K_r$. Let $g(\cdot, \cdot)$ be a function which is a bijective mapping, when the second argument is fixed. Then the ciphertext is computed as c_r, where

$$c_i = g(c_{i-1}, K_i),$$

c_0 is the plaintext and the K_is are the so-called round keys. This is called an r-round iterated cipher. Since g is assumed to be injective for fixed K_i,

$$c_{i-1} = g^{-1}(c_i, K_i),$$

and the plaintext can be computed from the ciphertext and the round keys by inverting the encryption process.

P. Samarati et al. (Eds.): ESORICS 2004, LNCS 3193, pp. 322–334, 2004.

Differential cryptanalysis [2] and linear cryptanalysis [9] are the most effective short-cut attacks against iterated secret-key (block) ciphers today. The attacks have been applied to a wide range of ciphers and are applicable particularly to iterated block ciphers where a weak function is iterated a number of times.

The crucial step in differential and linear cryptanalysis is the search for so-called characteristics covering sufficiently many rounds of the cipher. An r-round characteristic is a tool to predict with a high probability some values of the ciphertext after each of the r rounds given some values of a plaintext blocks. In differential cryptanalysis one looks at differences between two plaintexts and their corresponding ciphertexts, in linear cryptanalysis one looks at linear relations between the bits in a plaintext, the key used and in the corresponding ciphertext. Characteristics over several rounds are constructed by combining characteristics over one round, which are usually easy to find by brute force. This combination of probabilities is only valid when the characteristics for single rounds are independent, which usually will be the case by assuming independent round keys, but which is almost never the case for practical ciphers.

An r-round differential [8] is a tool to predict with some probability some difference in a pair of ciphertexts after r rounds of encryption given some difference in two plaintexts. Thus, the probability of a differential will in general be higher than for a corresponding characteristic predicting the same ciphertext bits given the same plaintext bits. To prove resistance against differential attacks or to conclude to have found the best differential attack one must be able to bound or find the best differentials; a bound on the best characteristics is not sufficient. For all existing ciphers it is impossible to find the best differentials, e.g. for a 64 bit block cipher like the DES [16] there are $(2^{64})^2$ possible differentials.

The equivalent notion of a differential versus a characteristic for linear cryptanalysis is that of an r-round linear hull [13]. To prove resistance against linear attacks one must be able to bound or find the best linear hulls. This is also a hard problem for most practical ciphers.

[8] introduces the notion of a Markov cipher, for which a probability of an r-round differential characteristic can be found from the probabilities of the involved one-round characteristics, if it is assumed that the round keys are independent and uniformly random. Most iterated ciphers in use today are Markov ciphers. The theory of Markov ciphers for linear cryptanalysis was described in [14]. For both attacks it was shown that for almost all iterated ciphers, which are Markov ciphers, the distribution of the probabilities of differentials and of linear hulls converge to the uniform distribution after some number of rounds.

For many Markov ciphers it is possible to find the highest probabilities of characteristics for both differential and for linear cryptanalysis. [10] and [17] describe results of such a search algorithm for various ciphers, e.g., for the DES. However, it should be stressed that the search assumes that the round keys involved are independent. However, all practical ciphers take a relative small key and expand it to a series of dependent round keys. It remains an open problem to find an algorithm which efficiently computes the probabilities of characteristics over several rounds for iterated ciphers with such key schedules.

To explore this problem a series of tests were conducted on several small ciphers. The method is as follows. A cipher was chosen together with a number of different key schedules. Then for different numbers of rounds the probabilities of all differentials and all linear hulls were computed and various quantities recorded from the tests.

This paper is organised as follows. §2 describes our experiments in more detail and §3 discusses the results obtained. In §4 we discuss some possible future work and open problems and §5 gives some concluding remarks.

2   Experiments

In this section we describe some experiments made on small Feistel ciphers with n-bit blocks and n-bit keys. A key schedule is introduced which take the n-bit key as input and which returns a series of round keys.

The test cipher is an eight-bit Feistel cipher, where eight text bits and four key bits are input to each round. Let X_L^i and X_R^i denote the left most respectively rightmost four bits of the eight bit text input to the ith round and K_i the ith round key, then the text output from the round function is calculated:

$$(X_L^{i+1}, X_R^{i+1}) = (X_R^i, F(X_R^i \oplus K_i) \oplus X_L^i)$$

where $F : \{0,1\}^4 \rightarrow \{0,1\}^4$ is a four to four bit nonlinear function and K_i is a four-bit round key.

Two versions of this cipher were chosen. One where F is a bijection and one where F is a randomly chosen mapping. The functions are

$$F_1 : \{10, 3, 11, 7, 5, 13, 2, 6, 8, 0, 4, 9, 12, 14, 1, 15\}$$

and

$$F_2 : \{5, 11, 9, 4, 7, 13, 8, 1, 1, 15, 7, 14, 2, 7, 9, 9\}$$

where the notation used means $F_1[0] = 10$, $F_1[1] = 3$, $F_1[2] = 11$ etc.

Five different key schedules were developed for our experiments. The first four key schedules all take an eight bit key K as input and produce r 4-bit round keys K_i for $i = 1, \ldots, r$. All four algorithms take the user-selected key and divide it into two 4-bit halves, K^L and K^R.

The first key schedule is defined as follows.

Key schedule 1:

Input: $K = K^L \mid K^R$

For $i = 1$ **to** $r/2$ **do**
$\quad K_{2i-1} = K^L$
$\quad K_{2i} \;\;\; = K^R$
For $i = 0$ **to** r **do** $K_i = K_i$ XOR i

Here the round keys are constructed simply by repeating the user-selected key halves over the rounds. It is well-known that such key schedules leaves the cipher very vulnerable to so-called related-key attacks[6, 1] and the slide attacks [3]. To avoid these attacks, a round constant is added to the round keys. However, the key schedule is still weak, in that the even-numbered rounds in the cipher depend only on one key half and the odd-number rounds in the cipher depend only on the other key half. To avoid this symmetry the second key schedule uses the key halves in a different order over the rounds.

Key schedule 2:

Input: $K = K^L \mid K^R$

For $i = 1$ **to** $r/4$ **do**
$K_{4i-3} = K^L$
$K_{4i-2} = K^R$
$K_{4i-1} = K^R$
$K_{4i} \quad = K^L$
For $i = 0$ **to** r **do** $K_i = K_i$ XOR i

As before, a round constant is added to the round keys. The two first schedules use the 4-bit halves of K directly, that is, the least significant bit of a round key depends only on the least significant bit of the two halves of the input key. To avoid such properties the third schedule uses rotations to spread the bits of K over all positions in the round keys.

Key schedule 3:

Input: $K = K^L \mid K^R$

$K_1 = K^L$
$K_2 = K^R$
$K_3 = \text{LeftShift}(K^L, 2) + \text{RightShift}(K^R, 2)$
$K_4 = \text{LeftShift}(K^R, 2) + \text{RightShift}(K^L, 2)$

For $i = 5$ **to** r **do** $K_i = \text{Rotate}(K_{i-3}, 1)$
For $i = 1$ **to** r **do** $K_i = K_i$ XOR i

Leftshift takes the two least significant bits of its input and shift these two positions to the left. *Rightshift* takes the two most significant bits of its input and shift these two positions to the right. As a consequence, the third round key K_3 depends on two bits from K^L and two bits from K^R, whereas the fourth round key K_4 depends on the remaining four bits from K^L and K^R. Then the remaining round keys are generated as rotated versions of previous round keys. To avoid trivial symmetries and weak keys, a round constant is exclusive-ored to all round keys.

The fourth schedule is yet more complex. Here a series of temporary round keys $TK_1, \ldots, TK_r$ are generated in manner similar to the previous one. Then these round keys are used in the cipher in question to generate the (real) round keys for the experiments. The cipher is used in counter mode and the resulting ciphertext halves are exclusive-ored to generate the (real) round keys $K_1, \ldots, K_r$.

Key schedule 4:
Input: $K = K^L \mid K^R$

$$TK_1 = K^L$$
$$TK_2 = K^R$$
$$TK_3 = K^L \text{ XOR } K^R$$

For $i = 4$ **to** r **do** $TK_i = \text{Rotate}(TK_{i-3}, 1)$
For $i = 0$ **to** r **do** $TK_i = TK_i \text{ XOR } i$
$TK := \{TK_1, \ldots, TK_r\}$
For $i = 1$ **to** r **do**

$$C = (C^L \mid C^R) = \text{encrypt}(i, TK)$$
$$K_i = C^L \text{ XOR } C^R$$

The fifth key schedule simply uses independent round keys, that is, for the test cipher (an 8-bit Feistel cipher) the user-selected key is of a total of $4r$ bits.

For all the above key schedules an exhaustive search was implemented to find all differentials and linear hulls for all values of the user-selected key and for various number of rounds. For an r-round version of the cipher and for each key schedule the experiments were as follows:

For each value of the key all r-round differentials and all r-round linear hulls were computed. The hull and the differential with the highest probability taken over all inputs and all the keys were recorded. Also recorded was the deviation of the best differential/the best linear hull over all values of the keys and also the deviation of all differentials/all linear hulls over all values of the keys.

Clearly, for the fifth key schedule this experiment is very time-consuming for large numbers of rounds. However there is a more efficient implementation, here explained only for differential cryptanalysis. Compute a so-called transition matrix M for one round of the cipher, where an entry (i, j) contains the probability that a difference of i in the inputs to one round results in outputs of difference j. Thus M contains the probabilities of all one-round differentials. Then the probabilities all r-round differentials over the cipher can be found in M^r. A summary of the experiments are presented in the Tables 1, 2, 3 and 4.

3   Results

The tables containing the results for differential cryptanalysis are interpreted as follows: The column "Round" is the number of rounds used in the cipher and "KS" is the key schedule used. "Best diff" is the differential with the highest probability taken over all plaintexts and over all keys, and "probability" the corresponding probability p multiplied by 256 (number of inputs to the cipher).

Table 1. Best differentials on average for all keys and for one single key for 8-bit Feistel cipher with $F : \{10, 3, 11, 7, 5, 13, 2, 6, 8, 0, 4, 9, 12, 14, 1, 15\}$.

Round	KS	Best difference	Probability	Std. dev. best	Std. dev.
4	1	30→30	16.00	0.000	1.462
4	2	30→30	16.00	0.000	0.702
4	3	30→30	16.00	0.000	0.645
4	4	30→30	16.00	0.000	0.644
4	5	30→30	16.00	-	0.635
7	1	23→ac	10.00	0.000	1.411
7	2	50→50	3.62	2.853	0.366
7	3	30→30	3.12	3.432	0.149
7	4	30→30	2.41	2.615	0.120
7	5	30→30	2.20	-	0.051
10	1	58→cf	12.00	0.000	1.416
10	2	4b→f9	2.88	2.919	0.360
10	3	43→c3	1.56	1.603	0.140
10	4	24→14	1.44	1.707	0.108
10	5	30→30	1.07	-	0.006
16	1	0c→37	10.00	0.000	1.411
16	2	11→90	3.12	2.346	0.358
16	3	3e→5f	1.59	2.056	0.140
16	4	9f→10	1.45	1.649	0.109
16	5	30→30	1.00	-	0.004

Table 2. Best hulls on average for all keys and for one single key for 8-bit Feistel cipher with $F : \{10, 3, 11, 7, 5, 13, 2, 6, 8, 0, 4, 9, 12, 14, 1, 15\}$.

Round	KS	Best hull	Complexity	Std. dev. best	Std. dev.
4	1	ed→db	27.56	0.000	1.463
4	2	d4→ed	21.00	7.808	0.701
4	3	d4→ed	20.94	7.855	0.643
4	4	d7→ed	21.86	8.468	0.642
4	5	d4→ed	20.94	-	0.635
7	1	95→73	20.25	0.000	1.413
7	2	04→04	4.35	4.119	0.361
7	3	06→ed	2.15	2.429	0.135
7	4	0b→ed	2.20	2.264	0.103
7	5	06→ed	2.01	-	0.051
10	1	8b→90	18.06	0.000	1.417
10	2	7a→bd	3.53	5.108	0.355
10	3	93→ff	1.67	2.235	0.125
10	4	0d→1d	1.39	2.030	0.089
10	5	04→04	1.07	-	0.006
16	1	25→d2	18.06	0.000	1.413
16	2	8b→cb	3.31	6.525	0.353
16	3	51→5e	1.78	2.440	0.126
16	4	91→f0	1.40	1.896	0.089
16	5	08→ed	1.00	-	0.004

Table 3. Best differentials on average for all keys and for one single key for 8-bit Feistel cipher with $F : \{5, 11, 9, 4, 7, 13, 8, 1, 1, 15, 7, 14, 2, 7, 9, 9\}$.

Round	KS	Best difference	Probability	Std. dev. best	Std. dev.
4	1	e0→ce	16.00	0.000	1.457
4	2	c0→fc	9.50	2.403	0.627
4	3	c0→fc	9.50	2.403	0.562
4	4	fc→c0	9.81	2.309	0.559
4	5	c0→fc	9.50	-	0.550
7	1	d0→ec	12.00	0.000	1.414
7	2	50→50	3.50	3.782	0.369
7	3	10→10	2.59	3.142	0.150
7	4	c0→c0	2.87	3.623	0.122
7	5	c0→c0	2.79	-	0.055
10	1	ca→e2	12.00	0.000	1.429
10	2	0e→0c	2.62	2.209	0.359
10	3	44→81	1.55	1.647	0.140
10	4	0c→c0	1.45	1.630	0.109
10	5	c0→fc	1.15	-	0.008
16	1	19→9a	10.00	0.000	1.413
16	2	93→7c	2.88	1.870	0.358
16	3	7c→32	1.56	1.603	0.141
16	4	b6→dd	1.37	1.687	0.108
16	5	c0→f0	1.01	-	0.004

Table 4. Best hulls on average for all keys and for one single key for 8-bit Feistel cipher with $F : \{5, 11, 9, 4, 7, 13, 8, 1, 1, 15, 7, 14, 2, 7, 9, 9\}$.

Round	KS	Best hull	Complexity	Std. dev. best	Std. dev.
4	1	d6→cc	30.25	0.000	1.459
4	2	01→10	16.50	5.682	0.625
4	3	01→10	16.50	5.682	0.560
4	4	01→15	16.98	5.921	0.557
4	5	01→10	16.50	-	0.550
7	1	cc→a8	22.56	0.000	1.415
7	2	01→01	6.45	4.936	0.365
7	3	01→01	5.18	4.600	0.136
7	4	01→01	5.02	4.432	0.104
7	5	01→01	5.00	-	0.055
10	1	6d→6c	20.25	0.000	1.431
10	2	85→74	3.07	3.516	0.354
10	3	eb→fc	1.70	2.354	0.126
10	4	01→10	1.45	2.085	0.089
10	5	0c→0c	1.32	-	0.008
16	1	cb→4c	18.06	0.000	1.414
16	2	8a→a5	3.30	4.814	0.354
16	3	e2→bc	1.62	2.455	0.126
16	4	06→dc	1.41	2.060	0.089
16	5	0c→0c	1.01	-	0.004

The "Std. dev. best" is the standard deviation taken over all the keys for the best differential. The last column "Std. dev." is the standard deviation taken over all the keys and all the differentials. All the values are multiplied by 256 in order to get a mean equal to 1.0. Note that due to the way the experiments for key schedule five were implemented it is not possible to record the value of "Std. dev. best".

The results are calculated similarly in the linear case: "Best hull" is the linear hull with the highest bias ($|p - 1/2|$) taken over all plaintexts and all keys, and "complexity" the corresponding value $|p - 1/2|^2$. The deviations are calculated in the same way. All the values here are multiplied by $4 * 256$ in order to give a mean equal to 1.0. Also here it was not possible to record the value of "Std. dev. best" for key schedule five.

The computation for ciphers with independent round keys were carried out using transition matrices. Compute a matrix M with the probabilities of all one-round differentials. Then one can find the probabilities of all r-round differentials by calculation of the product M^r. Similar computations were done for linear hulls.

The results in Tables 1, 2, 3 and 4 suggest that a complex key schedule will add to the immunity against differential and linear attacks. By increasing the number of rounds it is seen that the probabilities of the best differential/linear hull converge the fastest to the uniform distribution with a complex key schedule. The standard deviation converges to zero as the probability distribution converges to the uniform distribution. It is also seen that the results for the most complex key schedule number four are closest to those using key schedule five, where independent keys are used.

Note that the standard deviations for four rounds in Table 1 are zero for the first four key schedules and in each case for the best four-round differential $30 \rightarrow 30$. A closer analysis reveals that this differential has equal inputs in the first and fourth rounds and uses the combination through F of $3 \rightarrow 3$ (which has probability $1/4$) in both the second and third rounds. So presumably for all keys this differential has probability $(1/4)^2$. The reason is that for any fixed key the inputs to two consecutive rounds in a Feistel cipher uniquely determine both plaintext and ciphertext. Hence, these two inputs take together all 2^n values exactly once. Thus, the probabilities of a differential for a fixed key in a Feistel cipher over two consecutive rounds can be found by computing the product of the individual one-round probabilities.

Also note that the standard deviation over all the keys for the best differential/linear hull for the first key schedule is always zero. This key schedule is reminiscent of that of LOKI[4] and it is well-known that it gives rise to a number of related-key properties [7, 1], see Figure 1. More precisely, if $c = e_K(p)$ is the encrypted value of p using the key $K^L \mid K^R$, then it holds that $e_{K \oplus \alpha}(p \oplus \alpha) = c \oplus \alpha$, where $\alpha = (K^L \mid K^R)$. However, it was not known until now (as far as these authors are informed) that if there is a differential of probability p for some particular value of the secret key (where the probability is taken over all plaintexts), then the same differential has probability p for any other value of the

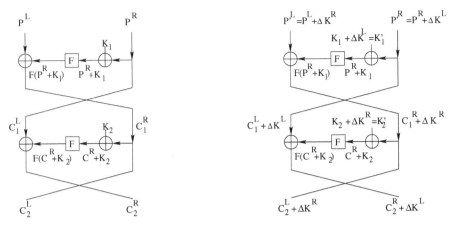

Fig. 1. Two rounds of a Feistel cipher where the keys in every second round are different by a constant. Two keys which differ by a value $\Delta K = (\Delta K^L, \Delta K^R)$ will have exactly the same dependency between the rounds for all keys during both differential and linear attacks. Notice that inputs and outputs of F are exactly the same in all rounds.

secret key. The reason is the following. Assume that there are s pairs of plaintexts $(p_{i,0}, p_{i,1})$ each of some difference β and which encrypted using the key value L yield $(c_{i,0}, c_{i,1})$ for $i = 1, \ldots s$, where the ciphertexts are of some difference γ. But then the s pairs of plaintexts $(p_{i,0} \oplus \alpha, p_{i,1} \oplus \alpha)$ which are of difference β encrypt to the pair $(c_{i,0} \oplus \alpha, c_{i,1} \oplus \alpha)$ of difference γ using the key value $L \oplus \alpha$. However this also means that for this cipher, the most likely differential for a fixed key is also the most likely differential for any other key. It is believed that this is the first reported example cipher in the literature with this property It is stressed however that this cipher is vulnerable to other attacks which are faster than exhaustive key search.

O'Connor [15] showed that for a randomly chosen n-bit permutation, the expected highest probability of a differential will be less than $2m/2^m$. In our tests, this bound is $16/256$. Empirical results indicate that the expected probability of the best differential for a randomly chosen eight-bit permutation is about $10/256$. This explains why for any number of rounds using the first key schedule the probability of the best differentials stay around $12/256$ and does not decrease with the number of rounds. Also, is explains exactly why the standard deviation over all keys for these differentials is zero. A similar phenomenon can be explained for the linear cryptanalysis case.

The second key schedule will also have some of these properties, but here only in the cases where $\Delta K^R = \Delta K^L$, which is only the case for one of $2^{n/2}$ keys.

It is anticipated that the results of our experiments will translate also to ciphers with bigger block size. However, exhaustive searches for differentials and linear hulls in a cipher for much higher values of n is very difficult. The complexities of these searches are $O(2^{3n})$ where n is the block size and the key size. Some further experiments in the reach of our computing capabilities were conducted.

- Feistel ciphers of size 10 and 12 bits were tested in the differential cryptanalysis case, where the nonlinear functions used were randomly chosen 5-
  bit respectively 6-bit bijective mappings, and where the key sizes are equal
  to the cipher size. The key schedules were chosen in a way similar to those
  reported in full detail above. The results of these tests are listed in Tables 5
  and 6.
- Feistel ciphers of size eight, where the nonlinear function is a 5 to 4 bit S-
  box. Here the four-bit input to the S-box is expanded to five bits, where after
  a 5-bit round key was added. The key size of this cipher was 10 bits. This
  cipher models DES-like ciphers where the nonlinear function varies with the
  keys.
- An SP-network of 8 bits was tested, where one round consists of two 4 to
  4 bit S-boxes together with a linear layer mixing the outputs of the boxes.
  The key size of this cipher is 8 bits.
- An SP-network of 9 bits was tested, where one round consists of three 3 to
  3 bit S-boxes together with a linear layer mixing the outputs of the boxes.
  The key size of this cipher is 9 bits.

The results show that the uniform distribution is reached faster for the 10-bit
and 12-bit block ciphers than for the 8-bit block ciphers reported on earlier.
However, the overall picture is the same as before. A cipher with a well-designed
key schedule reaches the uniform distribution of the probabilities of differentials
and linear hulls faster than with a badly designed key schedule. A good (complex)
key schedule therefore seems to help make a cipher more resistant to differential
and linear attacks.

Finally we note that there are many block ciphers which have key schedules which are very simple and reminiscent of the weak key schedules from our
experiments. A few examples are Skipjack[12], Noekeon[5], and MISTY[11].

4   Future Work

There is still open questions to try to explain from the experiments above. What
exactly is the influence of the different key schedules on the complexity of linear
and differential attacks. A few examples, why exactly is key schedule four better
than key schedule three? Could there be some weaker dependencies between the
round keys which also give high-probability differentials/hulls higher than the
ones assuming independent round keys? Could there be an approximation in one
round which when averaged over all inputs has a small probability but which
due to a round key dependency between the several rounds actually has a much
higher probability?

5   Concluding Remarks

There is a huge number of block ciphers proposed today, almost all of which has
an ad-hoc designed key schedule for which very little is known. In this paper it

Table 5. Best differentials on average for all keys and for one single key for a 10-bit Feistel cipher.

Round	KS	Best difference	Probability	Std. dev.
4	1	1c0→200	32.00	1.436
4	2	1c0→200	32.00	0.443
4	3	1c0→200	32.00	0.385
4	4	1c0→200	32.00	0.382
4	5	1c0→200	32.00	1.518
7	1	008→163	12.00	1.415
7	2	020→001	3.31	0.254
7	3	200→200	2.32	0.071
7	4	200→200	2.50	0.056
7	5	200→200	2.31	0.051
10	1	2d1→255	14.00	1.411
10	2	07a→250	2.38	0.252
10	3	253→3d4	1.31	0.070
10	4	1de→193	1.22	0.054
10	5	1c0→200	1.05	0.004

Table 6. Best differentials on average for all keys and for one single key for a 12-bit Feistel cipher.

Round	KS	Best difference	Probability	Std. dev.
4	1	040→300	16.00	1.418
4	2	040→300	16.00	0.236
4	3	040→300	16.00	0.194
4	4	040→300	16.00	0.168
4	5	040→700	16.00	2.673
7	1	0fb→df	16.00	1.414
7	2	040→001	3.34	0.178
7	3	3c3→229	1.25	0.047
7	4	240→240	1.16	0.027
7	5	ec0→ec0	1.15	0.029
10	1	2cd→3b9	16.00	1.414
10	2	0f6→315	2.03	0.178
10	3	11c→1e5	1.24	0.047
10	4	0ac→247	1.12	0.027
10	5	e80→e80	1.00	0.004

has been demonstrated by experiments that the key schedule of iterated ciphers influence the distribution of the probabilities of differentials and linear hulls. The more complex the key schedules, the better resistance against differential and linear attacks.

Due to the available computing resources these experiments were conducted on small toy ciphers, however the authors have found no indication why the results should not apply also to ciphers with larger blocks. In fact, the constructed toy ciphers with independent round keys (or with a well-designed key-schedule) are most likely strong ciphers relative to their sizes. Just imagine a scaled-up version with 64-bit blocks, that is, with a randomly chosen (bijective) 32-bit mapping in the round function. Such a cipher is likely to be stronger than e.g., DES used with the same number of rounds.

References

1. E. Biham. New types of cryptanalytic attacks using related keys. In T. Helleseth, editor, *Advances in Cryptology: EUROCRYPT'93, Lecture Notes in Computer Science 765*, pages 398–409. Springer Verlag, 1993.
2. E. Biham and A. Shamir. *Differential Cryptanalysis of the Data Encryption Standard*. Springer Verlag, 1993.
3. A. Biryukov and D. Wagner. Slide attacks. In L. R. Knudsen, editor, *Fast Software Encryption, Sixth International Workshop, Rome, Italy, March 1999, Lecture Notes in Computer Science 1636*, pages 245–259. Springer Verlag, 1999.
4. L. Brown, J. Pieprzyk, and J. Seberry. LOKI - a cryptographic primitive for authentication and secrecy applications. In J. Seberry and J. Pieprzyk, editors, *Advances in Cryptology: AusCrypt'90, Lecture Notes in Computer Science 453*, pages 229–236. Springer Verlag, 1990.
5. J. Daemen, M. Peeters, G. Van Assche, and V. Rijmen. Nessie proposal: NOEKEON. Submitted as an NESSIE Candidate Algorithm. Available from http://www.cryptonessie.org.
6. L.R. Knudsen. Cryptanalysis of LOKI'91. In J. Seberry and Y. Zheng, editors, *Advances in Cryptology, AusCrypt 92, Lecture Notes in Computer Science 718*, pages 196–208. Springer Verlag, 1993.
7. L.R. Knudsen. Cryptanalysis of LOKI. In H. Imai, R.L. Rivest, and T. Matsumoto, editors, *Advances in Cryptology: AsiaCrypt'91, Lecture Notes in Computer Science 453*, pages 22–35. Springer Verlag, 1993.
8. X. Lai, J.L. Massey, and S. Murphy. Markov ciphers and differential cryptanalysis. In D.W. Davies, editor, *Advances in Cryptology - EUROCRYPT'91, Lecture Notes in Computer Science 547*, pages 17–38. Springer Verlag, 1992.
9. M. Matsui. Linear cryptanalysis method for DES cipher. In T. Helleseth, editor, *Advances in Cryptology - EUROCRYPT'93, Lecture Notes in Computer Science 765*, pages 386–397. Springer Verlag, 1993.
10. M. Matsui. On correlation between the order of S-boxes and the strength of DES. In A. De Santis, editor, *Advances in Cryptology - EUROCRYPT'94, Lecture Notes in Computer Science 950*. Springer Verlag, 1995.
11. M. Matsui. New block encryption algorithm MISTY. In E. Biham, editor, *Fast Software Encryption, Fourth International Workshop, Haifa, Israel, January 1997, Lecture Notes in Computer Science 1267*, pages 54 68. Springer Verlag, 1997.
12. NSA. Skipjack and KEA algorithm specifications. http://csrc.ncsl.nist.gov/encryption/skipjack-1.pdf, May 1998.
13. K. Nyberg. Linear approximations of block ciphers. In A. De Santis, editor, *Advances in Cryptology - EUROCRYPT'94, Lecture Notes in Computer Science 950*, pages 439–444. Springer Verlag, 1995.
14. O'Connor and Golic. A unified Markov approach to differential and linear cryptanalysis. In Josef Pieprzyk and Reihaneh Safavi-Naini, editors, *Advances in Cryptology – ASIACRYPT '94, Lecture Notes in Computer Science 917*, pages 387–397. Springer-Verlag, 1994.
15. L.J. O'Connor. On the distribution of characteristics in bijective mappings. In T. Helleseth, editor, *Advances in Cryptology - EUROCRYPT'93, Lecture Notes in Computer Science 765*, pages 360–370. Springer Verlag, 1994.

16. National Bureau of Standards. Data encryption standard. Federal Information Processing Standard (FIPS), Publication 46, National Bureau of Standards, U.S. Department of Commerce, Washington D.C., January 1977.

17. Toshio Tokita, Tohru Sorimachi, and Mitsuru Matsui. Linear cryptanalysis of LOKI and s2-DES. In Josef Pieprzyk and Reihanah Safavi-Naini, editors, *Advances in Cryptology – ASIACRYPT '94, Lecture Notes in Computer Science 917*, pages 293–303. Springer Verlag, 1994.

A Public-Key Encryption Scheme
with Pseudo-random Ciphertexts

Bodo Möller*

University of California, Berkeley
bmoeller@eecs.berkeley.edu

Abstract. This work presents a practical public-key encryption scheme that offers security under adaptive chosen-ciphertext attack (CCA) and has pseudo-random ciphertexts, i.e. ciphertexts indistinguishable from random bit strings. Ciphertext pseudo-randomness has applications in steganography. The new scheme features short ciphertexts due to the use of elliptic curve cryptography, with ciphertext pseudo-randomness achieved through a new key encapsulation mechanism (KEM) based on elliptic curve Diffie-Hellman with a pair of elliptic curves where each curve is a twist of the other. The public-key encryption scheme resembles the hybrid DHIES construction; besides by using the new KEM, it differs from DHIES in that it uses an authenticate-then-encrypt (AtE) rather than encrypt-then-authenticate (EtA) approach for symmetric cryptography.

1 Introduction

Where *encryption* converts a message *(plaintext)* into a scrambled message *(ciphertext)* such that revealing the latter does not expose the former, *steganography* goes further and seeks to hide even the fact that secret communication is taking place. A cryptography-based approach is to encrypt the plaintext to be hidden, in this context also known as the *hiddentext,* and embed the resulting ciphertext in a seemingly innocuous message, the *covertext.* The recipient extracts the ciphertext from the covertext and then uses the appropriate cryptographic decryption key to recover the hiddentext. Formal treatments of public-key steganography based on this approach have recently appeared in [3] and [5].

Public-key encryption schemes usually do not output ciphertexts that are pseudo-random in the sense of being indistinguishable from uniformly random bit strings of the same length. Given just the public key, it is typically easy to tell that certain bit strings cannot have come up during proper encryption (e.g., a bit string interpreted as an integer would exceed the modulus that would have been used during encryption). Thus the prospects will often be good for an adversary who tries to distinguish actual ciphertexts from random bit strings: In random bit strings, if an invalid encoding appears, this will clearly reveal that the bit string in question is not an actual ciphertext. Conversely, depending on the

* Supported by a DAAD (German Academic Exchange Service) Postdoc fellowship.

P. Samarati et al. (Eds.): ESORICS 2004, LNCS 3193, pp. 335–351, 2004.
© Springer-Verlag Berlin Heidelberg 2004

probability that random data will give a valid encoding, seeing a valid encoding or repeatedly seeing valid encodings can provide possibly strong indication that these values are not random.

The present work provides a public-key encryption scheme with pseudo-random ciphertexts as required for public-key steganography constructions like those from [3] and [5]. Some previous schemes do exist (e.g. based on RSA encryption or Diffie-Hellman, see [3, Section 4]), but their downside is the length of ciphertexts; and the expense of having relatively long ciphertexts can be especially high in the context of steganography. (The number of bits available for embedded ciphertexts typically is a small fraction of the covertext length. To avoid detection of the steganographic communication, one would generally want to have to use as little cover channel communication as possible.)

Our scheme uses elliptic curve cryptography to obtain short ciphertexts. Ciphertext pseudo-randomness is not immediate with any single cryptographically secure elliptic curve. Our trick to achieve it is to use a pair of elliptic curves over a field $\mathbb{F}_{2^m}$ such that each curve is a twist of the other. (The idea to use elliptic curves with their twists has also come up in [21] and [22].)

The construction is hybrid and resembles DHIES [2] (also known as DHAES from the earlier version [1] of that publication): it involves a key encapsulation mechanism (KEM), a one-time message authentication code (MAC), and a stream cipher. While our elliptic curve KEM is novel and will be described in detail, a wide range of existing MACs and stream ciphers are available that can be plugged into the construction.

Like DHIES, our scheme achieves security in a strong sense, namely security under adaptive chosen-ciphertext attack (CCA). Besides by using a new KEM, it differs from DHIES in that it applies the symmetric cryptographic primitives in a different order: While DHIES uses an *encrypt-then-authenticate* (EtA) approach by computing the MAC on a symmetric ciphertext, our construction uses an *authenticate-then-encrypt* (AtE) approach by computing the MAC of the plaintext and then symmetrically encrypting the MAC and the plaintext. This modification is needed to prove ciphertext pseudo-randomness without requiring additional security assumptions. Just as for DHIES, the security assumptions are mostly standard with the exception of a less conventional oracle Diffie-Hellman assumption (which finds justification in the random-oracle model based on a more usual gap-Diffie-Hellman assumption [30], but is a concrete computational assumption that can be expressed without resorting to this idealized model).

We also provide an appropriate pair of elliptic curves over $\mathbb{F}_{2^{163}}$ to make the proposed scheme practical, thanks to Reynald Lercier who ran his point counting algorithms to find suitable curves for the requirements of the scheme. The curve pair is verifiably pseudo-random (like the well-known curves as in [13]) to allow for independent verification that it has been generated properly from a seed value using a standardized process.

Section 2 gives formalizations of public-key encryption and key encapsulation with the relevant notions of security, CCA security and ciphertext pseudo-randomness. Section 3 presents our elliptic curve KEM as the essential new cryptographic primitive. Subsequently, Section 4 looks at well-known symmetric primitives, namely MACs and pseudo-random bit string generators for use as stream ciphers. Section 5 puts the primitives together to build a public-key encryption scheme, giving quantitative security results for CCA security and ciphertext pseudo-randomness. Finally, Section 6 summarizes our conclusions.

2 Public-Key Cryptography with Pseudo-random Ciphertexts: Concepts

2.1 Public-Key Encryption

We formalize public-key encryption with two security notions, security under adaptive chosen-ciphertext attack and ciphertext pseudo-randomness. Section 5 will show how to build a public-key encryption scheme with these properties using appropriate primitives.

We start by describing the notion of public-key encryption in terms of its interface. Note that algorithms are in general probabilistic.

Definition 1. *A* public-key encryption scheme PKE *specifies a* key generation *algorithm* PKE.KeyGen *and algorithms* PKE.Encrypt *and* PKE.Decrypt. *Algorithm* PKE.KeyGen *takes no input; it outputs a key pair* (PK, SK) *consisting of a* public key PK *and a* secret key SK. *For a plaintext* m *(an arbitrary bit string, possibly subject to length limitations for the specific public-key encryption scheme),*

$$\mathsf{PKE.Encrypt}(PK, m)$$

returns a bit string c *as* ciphertext. *On arbitrary input* c',

$$\mathsf{PKE.Decrypt}(SK, c')$$

may either return some string m' *or fail and return the special value* $\bot$. *If the key pair* (PK, SK) *has been output by* PKE.KeyGen *and* c *has been output by* PKE.Encrypt(PK, m), *then evaluating* PKE.Decrypt(SK, c) *will return the original bit string* m.

To capture security notions quantitatively, we assume that an adversary interacts with the cryptographic scheme in question in a specific attack game and define the adversary's *advantage* in this game. An adversary is an interactive probabilistic algorithm with bounded running time. Saying that a cryptographic scheme is *secure* under some security notion means that the advantage will be very low for every practical adversary (i.e. every adversary from some limited class of admissable adversaries), with details left open on what adversaries would be considered practical and what advantage would be considered sufficiently low. (Cryptographic schemes are often described as parameterized by an integer security parameter determining features such as the length of keys. Then security can be formalized as a requirement that any polynomial-time adversary's advantage be negligible in the security parameter, i.e. asymptotically smaller than the reciprocal of any polynomial. We avoid explicit security parameters, which amounts to having a fixed security parameter built into algorithms such as PKE.KeyGen.) The security result for our public-key encryption scheme in Section 5 will relate the security of the public-key encryption scheme to the security of its underlying primitives: intuitively, if all primitives are secure under their respective security notions, then the complete scheme will be secure.

As the first security notion for public-key encryption, we describe security under *adaptive chosen-ciphertext attack* (CCA), *CCA security* for short. We use a well-known *find-then-guess* attack game that expresses security as *indistinguishability under CCA* (IND-CCA). The term *indistinguishability* refers to the idea that adversaries should not be able to tell apart encryptions of any two plaintexts, a notion due to [19]; the CCA scenario, which provides the adversary with a decryption oracle, is due to [31]. For equivalent formalizations of CCA security, see [8], [33], and [18, Chapter 5].

Definition 2. *In the* IND-CCA *attack game, an adversary interacts with a public-key encryption scheme* PKE *as follows.*

1. *The adversary queries a* key generation oracle, *which uses* PKE.KeyGen *to determine a key pair* (PK, SK) *and responds with* PK *(while secretly storing* SK*).*

2. *The adversary makes a sequence of queries to a* decryption oracle. *Each query is an arbitrary bit string* s, *and the oracle responds with* PKE.Decrypt (SK, s) *before the adversary proceeds.*

3. *The adversary chooses plaintexts* m_0 *and* m_1 *with* $|m_0| = |m_1|$ *(i.e., of the same length) and sends them to an* encryption oracle. *This oracle chooses* $b \in \{0, 1\}$ *uniformly at random and determines*

$$c = \mathsf{PKE.Encrypt}(PK, m_b),$$

which is returned to the adversary as the challenge ciphertext.

4. *The adversary again makes a sequence of queries to a* decryption oracle *as in stage 2, where this time the decryption oracle refuses being asked for the decryption of the challenge ciphertext* c *(responding* $\perp$ *for this case).*

5. *The adversary outputs a value* $\tilde{b} \in \{0, 1\}$.

If A is any adversary in the IND-CCA attack game, its CCA advantage *against the public key encryption scheme is*

$$\mathsf{Adv}^{\mathsf{IND\text{-}CCA}}_{\mathsf{PKE}, A} = \left| \Pr\left[\tilde{b} = 1 \mid b = 1\right] - \Pr\left[\tilde{b} = 1 \mid b = 0\right] \right|.$$

The value $\tilde{b}$ output by the adversary can be thought of as its guess for b.

The second (less usual) security notion for public-key encryption is *ciphertext pseudo-randomness*. We describe it through a *real-or-ideal* (ROI) attack game.

Definition 3. *In the* real-or-ideal attack game *for a public-key encryption scheme* PKE, *an adversary interacts with* PKE *as follows.*

1. *The adversary queries a* key generation oracle, *which uses* PKE.KeyGen *to determine a key pair* (PK, SK) *and responds with* PK.

2. *The adversary makes a query to a* real-or-ideal *encryption oracle, or* encryption oracle *for short. The query consists of a plaintext m of any length valid for* PKE. *The encryption oracle determines*

$$c_0 = \mathsf{PKE.Encrypt}(PK, m),$$

generates a uniformly random bit string c_1 with $|c_1| = |c_0|$, chooses $b \in \{0, 1\}$ uniformly at random, and responds with c_b.
3. *The adversary outputs a value $\widetilde{b} \in \{0, 1\}$.*

An adversary A in this attack game is also called a real-or-ideal *distinguisher or simply a* distinguisher. *Its* real-or-ideal *advantage against* PKE *is*

$$\mathsf{Adv}^{\mathsf{ROI}}_{\mathsf{PKE}, A} = \left| \Pr\left[\widetilde{b} = 1 \mid b = 1 \right] - \Pr\left[\widetilde{b} = 1 \mid b = 0 \right] \right|.$$

The real-or-ideal encryption oracle operates as a real encryption oracle if $b = 0$ and as an ideal encryption oracle if $b = 1$.

2.2 Key Encapsulation

Following Shoup [32], we use the term *key encapsulation mechanism* (KEM) for a scheme in public-key cryptography that is similar to public-key encryption except that plaintexts cannot be arbitrarily specified by the party that creates a ciphertext: instead, the randomized "encryption" algorithm, given some public key, outputs both a pseudo-random plaintext and a corresponding ciphertext such that the plaintext can be recovered from the ciphertext given the appropriate secret key. Such plaintexts can be used as keys for symmetric cryptography; hence the term *key encapsulation*.

Definition 4. *A* key encapsulation mechanism KEM *specifies a key generation algorithm* KEM.KeyGen *and algorithms* KEM.Encrypt *and* KEM.Decrypt. *Algorithm* KEM.KeyGen *takes no input; it outputs a key pair (PK, SK) consisting of a public key PK and a secret key SK. Algorithm*

$$\mathsf{KEM.Encrypt}(PK)$$

generates a bit string K of a fixed length KEM.OutLen *and a ciphertext $\mathfrak{K}$ of a fixed length* KEM.CipherLen, *and outputs the pair $(K, \mathfrak{K})$. Evaluating*

$$\mathsf{KEM.Decrypt}(SK, \mathfrak{K})$$

will return said bit string K if the key pair (PK, SK) has been generated by KEM.KeyGen. *On arbitrary input $\mathfrak{K}'$, the computation* KEM.Decrypt$(SK, \mathfrak{K}')$ *may either return some bit string K' or fail and return the special value $\bot$.*

Similarly to Section 2.1, we use attack games to express two security notions: security under adaptive chosen-ciphertext attack (CCA security) and ciphertext pseudo-randomness. Section 3 will describe a KEM based on elliptic curve Diffie-Hellman designed to meet these notions.

Definition 5. *In the* real-or-random CCA attack game, *an adversary interacts with a key encapsulation mechanism* KEM *as follows (cf. [14, Section 7.1.2]).*

1. *The adversary queries a* key generation oracle, *which uses* KEM.KeyGen *to compute a key pair* (PK, SK) *and responds with* PK.
2. *The adversary makes a sequence of queries to a* decryption oracle. *Each query is an arbitrary bit string* s *of length* KEM.CipherLen; *the oracle responds with* KEM.Decrypt(SK, s) *before the adversary proceeds.*
3. *The adversary queries a* real-or-random key encapsulation oracle, *or* key encapsulation oracle *for short. This oracle uses* KEM.Encrypt(PK) *to obtain a pair* $(K_0, \mathfrak{K}_{\mathsf{oracle}})$, *generates a uniformly random bit string* K_1 *with* $|K_1| = |K_0|$, *chooses* $b_{\mathsf{KEM}} \in \{0, 1\}$ *uniformly at random, and responds with*

$$(K_{b_{\mathsf{KEM}}}, \mathfrak{K}_{\mathsf{oracle}})$$

   as challenge.
4. *The adversary again makes a sequence of queries to a* decryption oracle *as in stage 2, where this time the oracle refuses the specific query* $\mathfrak{K}_{\mathsf{oracle}}$ *(responding* $\perp$ *for this case).*
5. *The adversary outputs a value* $\widetilde{b}_{\mathsf{KEM}} \in \{0, 1\}$.

If A is any adversary in the real-or-random CCA attack game, its CCA advantage *against the key encapsulation mechanism KEM is*

$$\mathsf{Adv}^{\mathsf{ROR\text{-}CCA}}_{\mathsf{KEM}, A} = \left| \Pr\left[\widetilde{b}_{\mathsf{KEM}} = 1 \mid b_{\mathsf{KEM}} = 1 \right] - \Pr\left[\widetilde{b}_{\mathsf{KEM}} = 1 \mid b_{\mathsf{KEM}} = 0 \right] \right|.$$

The real-or-random key encapsulation oracle operates as a real key encapsulation oracle if $b_{\mathsf{KEM}} = 0$ and as a random key encapsulation oracle if $b_{\mathsf{KEM}} = 1$.

Definition 6. *In the* real-or-ideal attack game *for a key encapsulation mechanism* KEM, *an adversary interacts with* KEM *as follows.*

1. *The adversary queries a* key generation oracle, *which uses* KEM.KeyGen *to determine a key pair* (PK, SK) *and responds with* PK.
2. *The adversary queries a* real-or-ideal key encapsulation oracle, *or* key encapsulation oracle *for short. The key encapsulation oracle uses* KEM.Encrypt(PK) *to determine a pair* $(K, \mathfrak{K}_0)$, *generates a uniformly random bit string* $\mathfrak{K}_1$ *of length* KEM.CipherLen, *chooses* $b_{\mathsf{KEM}} \in \{0, 1\}$ *uniformly at random, and responds with* $\mathfrak{K}_{b_{\mathsf{KEM}}}$.
3. *The adversary outputs a value* $\widetilde{b}_{\mathsf{KEM}} \in \{0, 1\}$.

An adversary A in this attack game is also called a real-or-ideal distinguisher *or simply a* distinguisher. *Its* real-or-ideal advantage *against* KEM *is*

$$\mathsf{Adv}^{\mathsf{ROI}}_{\mathsf{KEM}, A} = \left| \Pr\left[\widetilde{b}_{\mathsf{KEM}} = 1 \mid b_{\mathsf{KEM}} = 1 \right] - \Pr\left[\widetilde{b}_{\mathsf{KEM}} = 1 \mid b_{\mathsf{KEM}} = 0 \right] \right|.$$

The real-or-ideal key encapsulation oracle operates as a real key encapsulation oracle if $b_{\mathsf{KEM}} = 0$ and as an ideal key encapsulation oracle if $b_{\mathsf{KEM}} = 1$.

3   An Elliptic Curve KEM with Random Ciphertexts

We need a key encapsulation mechanism (KEM) that is CCA-secure and provides ciphertext pseudo-randomness.

First consider CCA security (Definition 5). The scheme DHIES from [2] uses *hash Diffie-Hellman* (HDH) as a CCA-secure KEM. The idea of HDH is to employ Diffie-Hellman [15] in some group followed by the application of a *key derivation function* (KDF) to obtain pseudo-random bit strings from group elements. We will use HDH with *elliptic curve Diffie-Hellman* (ECDH, due to [28] and [23]) following the idea originally proposed in [28] that it suffices to transfer just x-coordinates of points. The assumption that HDH schemes are CCA-secure key encapsulation mechanisms amounts to accepting an *oracle Diffie-Hellman assumption;* see [2]. (By appealing to the *random-oracle model* [9], this assumption can be justified based on a gap-Diffie-Hellman assumption [30], i.e. an assumption on the hardness of the computational Diffie-Hellman problem given a decisional Diffie-Hellman oracle; cf. [2] and [14, Theorem 9]. There are concerns about the use of the random-oracle model [11], but here this idealized model would be only a locally used tool to explain the plausibility of a specific security assumption on the KEM; the oracle Diffie-Hellman assumption can be expressed directly without employing the random-oracle model.)

Now consider ciphertext pseudo-randomness (Definition 6). Our KEM will be constructed to have ciphertexts that are uniformly random bit strings of length KEM.CipherLen, which implies $\mathsf{Adv}_{\mathsf{KEM},A}^{\mathsf{ROI}} = 0$ for any adversary.

We arrive at the KEM by first presenting some preliminaries on elliptic curves (Section 3.1), then discussing system parameters (Section 3.2 with specific values in Appendix A), and finally specifying the actual KEM (Section 3.3).

3.1   Preliminaries on Elliptic Curves

The KEM will use elliptic curves over some finite field $\mathbb{F}_{2^m}$ (refer to e.g. [10] for introductory material on elliptic curve cryptography). There are well-known requirements for cryptographically secure elliptic curves over such fields [20], which we will take into account (Section 3.2). We require that m be an odd prime as there are security concerns about $\mathbb{F}_{2^m}$ with m composite. Every non-supersingular curve over $\mathbb{F}_{2^m}$ is isomorphic to a curve described by a curve equation

$$E_{a,b}: \quad y^2 + xy = x^3 + ax^2 + b$$

where coefficients a and b are elements of $\mathbb{F}_{2^m}$, $b \neq 0$. The group $E_{a,b}(\mathbb{F}_{2^m})$ of rational points on such a curve consists of the set of solutions (x, y) of that equation with $x, y \in \mathbb{F}_{2^m}$, and an additional point $\mathcal{O}$. We have

$$\left| \#E_{a,b}(\mathbb{F}_{2^m}) - 2^m - 1 \right| < 2 \cdot 2^{m/2}$$

(Hasse's inequality). The group operation (see [10] or [20] for the definition) is commutative, and by convention is written as addition. $\mathcal{O}$, the *point at infinity,* is the neutral element; the inverse of any element (x, y) is $(x, x + y)$. The group

operation canonically gives rise to scalar multiplication kP of a point P by an integer k.

If $\mathrm{Tr}_{\mathbb{F}_{2^m}/\mathbb{F}_2}a = \mathrm{Tr}_{\mathbb{F}_{2^m}/\mathbb{F}_2}a'$, the curves

$$E_{a,b}: \quad y^2 + xy = x^3 + ax^2 + b,$$
$$E_{a',b}: \quad y^2 + xy = x^3 + a'x^2 + b$$

are isomorphic with a group isomorphism $E_{a,b}(\mathbb{F}_{2^m}) \to E_{a',b}(\mathbb{F}_{2^m})$ given by

$$(x,y) \mapsto (x, y + sx)$$

where $s \in \mathbb{F}_{2^m}$ satisfies $a' = a + s + s^2$ (such an s always exists in this case); otherwise $E_{a,b}$ and $E_{a',b}$ are called *twists* of each other.

If $E_{a,b}$ and $E_{a',b}$ are twists of each other, then for every $x \in \mathbb{F}_{2^m}$ there is a $y \in \mathbb{F}_{2^m}$ such that (x,y) is a point on one of the two curves. Specifically, each x occurs exactly twice: either there are two different points (x,y) and $(x, x+y)$ on the same curve; or $(x,y) = (0, \sqrt{b})$, which is a point on both curves. The total number of points (taking into account $\mathcal{O}$ for each curve) is

$$\#E_{a,b}(\mathbb{F}_{2^m}) + \#E_{a',b}(\mathbb{F}_{2^m}) = 2^{m+1} + 2.$$

Hasse's inequality implies $\#E_{a,b}(\mathbb{F}_{2^m}) \approx 2^m \approx \#E_{a',b}(\mathbb{F}_{2^m})$.

3.2   System Parameters

If in the situation of Section 3.1 we vary coefficient a for fixed b, we obtain curves in one of two equivalence classes depending on whether $\mathrm{Tr}_{\mathbb{F}_{2^m}/\mathbb{F}_2}a = 0$ or $\mathrm{Tr}_{\mathbb{F}_{2^m}/\mathbb{F}_2}a = 1$. All curves within a single class are isomorphic; the other class contains their twists. We have $\mathrm{Tr}_{\mathbb{F}_{2^m}/\mathbb{F}_2}0 = 0$ and $\mathrm{Tr}_{\mathbb{F}_{2^m}/\mathbb{F}_2}1 = 1$ as m is odd, so we can use $E_{0,b}$ and $E_{1,b}$ as a canonical pair of curves that are twists of each other. (The explicit isomorphism shown in Section 3.1 means that the specific choices for a affect only y-coordinates.) Coefficient b remains to be chosen such that the groups $E_{0,b}(\mathbb{F}_{2^m})$ and $E_{1,b}(\mathbb{F}_{2^m})$ are both cryptographically secure. Requirements for suitable curves are ([12, Section 3.1.2.1], [4, Annex A.3.2]):

- The group order $\#E_{a,b}(\mathbb{F}_{2^m})$ must be a product $h_{a,b}\, p_{a,b}$ with $1 \leq h_{a,b} \leq 4$ and $p_{a,b}$ prime.
- For said prime, it must hold that $2^{mB} \not\equiv 1 \pmod{p_{a,b}}$ for $1 \leq B \leq 20$ (the *MOV condition* [27]).

The curve $E_{0,b}$ has a point $\left(\sqrt[4]{b}, \sqrt{b}\right)$ of order 4, so we will use $h_{0,b} = 4$; note that the group $E_{0,b}(\mathbb{F}_{2^m})$ will then necessarily be cyclic. From $\#E_{0,b}(\mathbb{F}_{2^m}) + \#E_{1,b}(\mathbb{F}_{2^m}) \equiv 2 \pmod{4}$, it follows that $h_{1,b} = 2$; thus $E_{1,b}(\mathbb{F}_{2^m})$ will be cyclic too. Define t_b such that

$$\#E_{0,b}(\mathbb{F}_{2^m}) = 2^m + 1 - t_b = 4\,p_{0,b},$$
$$\#E_{1,b}(\mathbb{F}_{2^m}) = 2^m + 1 + t_b = 2\,p_{1,b};$$

a pair of suitable curves can be generated by choosing $b \in \mathbb{F}_{2^m} \setminus \{0\}$, determining t_b through *point counting* techniques (see [26] for fast algorithms), and verifying that

$$p_{0,b} = \frac{2^m + 1 - t_b}{4} \qquad \text{and} \qquad p_{1,b} = \frac{2^m + 1 + t_b}{2}$$

are indeed both prime and satisfy the MOV condition. Heuristically, for random b, the integer $p_{0,b}$ will be prime with probability about $1/m$ ([17] gives more precise estimates), and $p_{1,b}$ will be prime as well with probability about $1/m$; the MOV condition is not likely to cause problems if b is actually random. Thus, one has to expect to have to test approximately m^2 random choices for b before finding a suitable one.

It is common to use standardized pre-generated elliptic curves over appropriate fields instead of generating new curves as part of key generation. Parameters provided to others are usually expected to be *verifiably pseudo-random* with b derived from some *seed* value through a standardized process, typically with SHA-1 as specified in [4, Annex A.3.3.1] and [20, Annex A.12.6]. We provide a verifiably pseudo-random pair of curves over $\mathbb{F}_{2^{163}}$ in Appendix A.

Now let $b \in \mathbb{F}_{2^m} \setminus \{0\}$ be fixed such that the curves $E_0 = E_{0,b}$ and $E_1 = E_{1,b}$ are both cryptographically suitable with orders

$$\#E_0(\mathbb{F}_{2^m}) = 4\,p_0 = n_0 \qquad \text{and} \qquad \#E_1(\mathbb{F}_{2^m}) = 2\,p_1 = n_1$$

where p_0 and p_1 are prime. As additional parameters, for $a \in \{0, 1\}$, let G_a be a generator of $E_a(\mathbb{F}_{2^m})$, i.e. any element of order n_a. Note that $n_0 + n_1 = 2^{m+1} + 2$.

3.3   Specification

We assume that system parameters as discussed in Section 3.2 have been fixed, and that mappings

$$\text{encode}: \mathbb{F}_{2^m} \to \{0, 1\}^m \qquad \text{and} \qquad \text{decode}: \{0, 1\}^m \to \mathbb{F}_{2^m}$$

that are inverses of each other have been agreed upon (cf. FE2OSP and OS2FEP in [20] or FieldElement-to-OctetString and OctetString-to-FieldElement in [12] and [4]). We also assume that a key derivation function (KDF) that outputs bit strings of some length KEM.OutLen has been specified (for a practical example, see KDF1 in [20] or ANSI-X9.63-KDF in [12]). The KDF will be used only on input bit strings of length $2m$. We now show a key encapsulation mechanism KEM with KEM.CipherLen $= m$.

KEM.KeyGen: Choose integers s_0 and s_1 independently uniformly at random among those satisfying $0 < s_a < n_a$ with s_a and n_a relatively prime. Then compute the points $P_a = s_a G_a$ for $a \in \{0, 1\}$. Output the *public key PK* $= (P_0, P_1)$ and the *secret key SK* $= (s_0, s_1)$.

KEM.Encrypt(PK): Choose $a \in \{0,1\}$ with probability $\frac{n_0 - 1}{2^{m+1}}$ for $a = 0$, $\frac{n_1 - 1}{2^{m+1}}$ for $a = 1$. Then choose a uniformly random integer u with $0 < u < n_a$. Compute $Q = uG_a$ and $R = uP_a$ in the group $E_a(\mathbb{F}_{2^m})$; these points will never be $\mathcal{O}$ with valid system parameters and a valid public key, so they can be written as coordinate pairs (x_Q, y_Q) and (x_R, y_R). Finally, set

$$K = \mathrm{KDF}(\mathfrak{K} \,\|\, \mathrm{encode}(x_R)),$$
$$\mathfrak{K} = \mathrm{encode}(x_Q)$$

($\|$ denotes concatenation) and return the pair $(K, \mathfrak{K})$.

KEM.Decrypt($SK, \mathfrak{K}$): Set $x = \mathrm{decode}(\mathfrak{K})$. Then determine a $y \in \mathbb{F}_{2^m}$ such that (x, y) is a point on E_0 if there is such a y; if so, set $a = 0$. Otherwise, determine a $y \in \mathbb{F}_{2^m}$ such that (x, y) is a point on E_1 and set $a = 1$. In either case, set $Q = (x, y)$ and compute $R = s_a Q$ in the group $E_a(\mathbb{F}_{2^m})$. This point will never be $\mathcal{O}$ with valid system parameters and a valid secret key, so it can be written as a coordinate pair (x_R, y_R). Finally, set

$$K = \mathrm{KDF}(\mathfrak{K} \,\|\, \mathrm{encode}(x_R))$$

and return K.

Determining y given x in KEM.Decrypt amounts to performing *point decompression;* for algorithms, cf. [4, Section 4.22], [20, Annex A.12.9], or [12, Section 2.3.4].

In KEM.Encrypt, each element of $\mathbb{F}_{2^m}$ can come up as x_Q with probability 2^{-m} (any given x_Q appears exactly twice among the x-coordinates of the $n_0 - 1$ points of $E_{0,b}(\mathbb{F}_{2^m}) \setminus \{\mathcal{O}\}$ and the $n_1 - 1$ points of $E_{1,b}(\mathbb{F}_{2^m}) \setminus \{\mathcal{O}\}$). Thus, the distribution of $\mathfrak{K} \in \{0,1\}^m$ is uniform.

Assuming that a has been correctly recovered, the point Q computed in KEM.Decrypt will be either identical to or the inverse of the point Q originally used in KEM.Encrypt; the same relationship will apply to the respective points R (we have $\pm R = \pm u P_a = \pm u s_a G_a = \pm s_a Q$); so x_R will come out correctly as inversion affects only y-coordinates. KEM.Decrypt can unequivocally recover a in all cases except one, when $x = 0$ so that $Q = (0, \sqrt{b})$ is the point of order 2 on either $E_0(\mathbb{F}_{2^m})$ or $E_1(\mathbb{F}_{2^m})$; but in this case (of negligible probability) the same result would be obtained in either group.

As discussed earlier, it is reasonable to make an oracle Diffie-Hellman assumption implying that this KEM provides CCA security. Ciphertexts generated as described above are uniformly random. By Hasse's inequality (Section 3.1), a simplified variant of KEM.Encrypt that picks a uniformly random $a \in \{0,1\}$ would still achieve ciphertext pseudo-randomness.

4   Symmetric Primitives

4.1   Message Authentication Code

The usual notion of a message authentication code (MAC) allows using a single key for authenticating multiple messages. Like DHIES, we only need a one-time MAC.

Definition 7. *A* one-time message authentication code MAC *specifies a key length* MAC.KeyLen, *an output length* MAC.OutLen, *and a deterministic algorithm that, given a bit string K of length* MAC.KeyLen *(a key) and a bit string m, returns a bit string* $MAC(K, m)$ *of length* MAC.OutLen *(a tag).*

The security of a one-time MAC is expressed as follows.

Definition 8. *In the* forgery attack game, *an adversary interacts with a one-time MAC as follows.*

1. *The adversary submits a bit string m to a MAC oracle. This oracle generates a uniformly random bit string K of length* MAC.KeyLen *and responds with* $MAC(K, m)$.
2. *The adversary outputs a list $(m_1, t_1), (m_2, t_2), \ldots, (m_l, t_l)$ of pairs of bit strings.*

Let A be any adversary in the forgery attack game. (Its running time bound implies a bound on the length l of the list.) We say that adversary A has produced a forgery if there is some k such that $MAC(K, m_k) = t_k$ and $m_k \neq m$. The adversary's forgery advantage against MAC, *denoted* $\mathsf{Adv}^{\mathrm{Forge}}_{\mathrm{MAC}, A}$, *is the probability that it produces a forgery in the above game.*

A popular MAC construction is HMAC [6]; a specific variant with MAC.KeyLen = 160 and MAC.OutLen = 80 is HMAC-SHA1-80 [24].

4.2 Pseudo-random Bit String Generator

Our hybrid construction for public-key encryption uses a stream cipher to perform symmetric encryption. While other notions of stream ciphers are conceivable, for simplicity we assume a stream cipher based on the usual XOR paradigm: symmetric encryption and decryption are the same operation, namely XOR with a pseudo-random bit string generated from a key.

Definition 9. *A* pseudo-random bit string generator STREAM *specifies a key length* STREAM.KeyLen *and a deterministic algorithm that, given a bit string K of length* STREAM.KeyLen *(a key) and an integer n, generates an output bit string* $STREAM(K, n)$ *of length n.*

Security is described through a *real-or-ideal* attack game.

Definition 10. *In the* real-or-ideal attack game *for a pseudo-random bit string generator* STREAM, *an adversary interacts with* STREAM *as follows.*

1. *The adversary sends an integer n to a real-or-ideal bit string oracle. The oracle generates a uniformly random K with $|K| =$ STREAM.KeyLen, sets*

$$stream_0 = STREAM(K, n),$$

generates a uniformly random $stream_1$ with $|stream_1| = n$, chooses $b_{\mathsf{STR}} \in \{0, 1\}$ uniformly at random, and responds with $stream_b$ as challenge. (It is understood that the adversary's running time bound implies a bound on n.)

2. *The adversary outputs a value $\widetilde{b}_{STR} \in \{0, 1\}$.*

An adversary A in this attack game is also called a real-or-ideal distinguisher *or simply a* distinguisher. *Its* real-or-ideal advantage *against* STREAM *is*

$$\mathsf{Adv}^{\mathsf{ROI}}_{\mathsf{STREAM}, A} = \left| \Pr \left[\widetilde{b}_{\mathsf{STR}} = 1 \mid b_{\mathsf{STR}} = 1 \right] - \Pr \left[\widetilde{b}_{\mathsf{STR}} = 1 \mid b_{\mathsf{STR}} = 0 \right] \right|.$$

An example implementation is the *counter mode* (CTR) of a symmetric block cipher such as AES (see [7] and [29]). (For $n \leq$ STREAM.KeyLen, it is also be possible to define $\mathsf{STREAM}(K, n)$ as simply the n-bit prefix of K; then any distinguisher would have real-or-ideal advantage 0.)

5 Public-Key Encryption with Pseudo-random Ciphertexts: Hybrid Construction

Now we are ready to show how a public-key encryption scheme PKE as discussed in Section 2.1 can be built from primitives KEM (Section 2.2 and Section 3), MAC (Section 4.1), and STREAM (Section 4.2). Section 5.1 presents the hybrid construction, which follows DHIES except that it uses an *authenticate-then-encrypt* (AtE) rather than an *encrypt-then-authenticate* (EtA) approach. Section 5.2 gives security results for CCA security and ciphertext pseudo-randomness.

5.1 Specification

We require that KEM.OutLen $=$ MAC.KeyLen $+$ STREAM.KeyLen. The *key generation algorithm* PKE.KeyGen is the same as KEM.KeyGen. The *encryption algorithm* determines $\mathsf{PKE.Encrypt}(PK, m)$ as follows.

1. Use $\mathsf{KEM.Encrypt}(PK)$ to generate a pair $(K, \mathfrak{K})$.
2. Split K into bit strings K_{MAC} of length MAC.KeyLen and K_{STR} of length STREAM.KeyLen; i.e., $K = K_{\mathsf{MAC}} \parallel K_{\mathsf{STR}}$.
3. Compute $\mathfrak{M} = \mathsf{MAC}(K_{\mathsf{MAC}}, m)$.
4. Compute $\mathfrak{C} = (\mathfrak{M} \parallel m) \oplus \mathsf{STREAM}(K_{\mathsf{STR}}, \mathsf{MAC.OutLen} + |m|)$.
5. Return the ciphertext $\mathfrak{K} \parallel \mathfrak{C}$.

We depict the resulting ciphertext structure with concatenation horizontally and XOR vertically:

$\mathfrak{K}$	$\mathsf{MAC}(K_{\mathsf{MAC}}, m)$	m
	$\mathsf{STREAM}(K_{\mathsf{STR}})$	

The *decryption algorithm* computes $\mathsf{PKE.Decrypt}(PK, c)$ as follows.

1. Abort with an error (return $\bot$) if $|c| < \mathsf{KEM.CipherLen} + \mathsf{MAC.OutLen}$.
2. Split c into a part $\mathfrak{K}$ of length KEM.CipherLen and a part $\mathfrak{C}$ (i.e., $c = \mathfrak{K} \parallel \mathfrak{C}$).

3. Compute

$$K = \mathsf{KEM.Decrypt}(SK, \mathfrak{K}).$$

If this computation fails, abort with an error (return $\perp$).
4. Split K into bit strings K_{MAC} of length $\mathsf{MAC.KeyLen}$ and K_{STR} of length $\mathsf{STREAM.KeyLen}$ (i.e., $K = K_{\mathsf{MAC}} \parallel K_{\mathsf{STR}}$).
5. Compute

$$P = \mathfrak{C} \oplus \mathsf{STREAM}(K_{\mathsf{STR}}, |\mathfrak{C}|).$$

6. Split P into a part $\mathfrak{M}$ of length $\mathsf{MAC.OutLen}$ and a part m (i.e., $P = \mathfrak{M} \parallel m$).
7. Compute

$$\widetilde{\mathfrak{M}} = \mathsf{MAC}(K_{\mathsf{MAC}}, m).$$

If $\widetilde{\mathfrak{M}} \neq \mathfrak{M}$, abort with an error (return $\perp$).
8. Return m as decryption result.

Let c be a ciphertext generated as $\mathsf{PKE.Encrypt}(PK, m)$. It is straightforward to verify that $\mathsf{PKE.Decrypt}(SK, c)$ will indeed recover m if KEM is a key encapsulation mechanism according to Definition 4 and the key pair (PK, SK) has been generated properly. (Note that decryption step 3 cannot actually fail for the KEM from Section 3 with valid system parameters and a valid secret key.)

In practical use for steganography, the exact length of the ciphertext to be considered may not always be known in advance when some postfix has been added. In this case, multiple conceivable lengths can be tried during decryption. Observe that many such decryption attempts can easily be combined into a single algorithm such that KEM.Decrypt is used only once.

5.2 Security Results

We relate the security of the public-key encryption scheme PKE to the security of the underlying primitives KEM, MAC, and STREAM.

First consider CCA security. Let A be an adversary attacking PKE in the IND-CCA attack game (Definition 2). It can be shown that there are adversaries A_1 against KEM in a real-or-random CCA attack game, A_2 against MAC, and A_3 against STREAM, all having essentially the same running time as A, such that

$$\mathsf{Adv}_{\mathsf{PKE},A}^{\mathsf{IND\text{-}CCA}} \leq 2 \cdot \left(\mathsf{Adv}_{\mathsf{KEM},A_1}^{\mathsf{ROR\text{-}CCA}} + \mathsf{Adv}_{\mathsf{MAC},A_2}^{\mathsf{Forge}} + \mathsf{Adv}_{\mathsf{STREAM},A_3}^{\mathsf{ROI}} \right).$$

The proof uses standard techniques (see e.g. [14]) and requires essentially no changes for the hybrid AtE construction with a stream cipher compared with the conventional hybrid EtA construction. We omit the details for lack of space.

Now consider ciphertext pseudo-randomness. Let A be an adversary attacking PKE in the real-or-ideal attack game (Definition 3). It can be shown that there are adversaries A_1 against KEM in a real-or-random CCA attack game, A_2 against KEM in a real-or-ideal attack game, and A_3 against STREAM, all having essentially the same running time as A, such that

$$\mathsf{Adv}_{\mathsf{PKE},A}^{\mathsf{ROI}} \leq 2 \cdot \left(\mathsf{Adv}_{\mathsf{KEM},A_1}^{\mathsf{ROR\text{-}CCA}} + \mathsf{Adv}_{\mathsf{KEM},A_2}^{\mathsf{ROI}} + \mathsf{Adv}_{\mathsf{STREAM},A_3}^{\mathsf{ROI}} \right).$$

Details of the proof are given in Appendix B.

6 Conclusions

A new variant of elliptic curve Diffie-Hellman employing a pair of curves where each curve is a twist of the other provides a key encapsulation mechanism (KEM) with short random ciphertexts.

Such a KEM can be used for CCA-secure public-key encryption with pseudo-random ciphertexts, as needed for steganography. Our hybrid construction resembles DHIES, but uses an AtE rather than EtA approach in the interest of provable ciphertext pseudo-randomness. In practice, the ciphertext length can be as short as the length of the plaintext plus 243 bits (163 bits for the KEM with elliptic curves over $\mathbb{F}_{2^{163}}$, 80 bits for the MAC).

References

1. ABDALLA, M., BELLARE, M., AND ROGAWAY, P. DHAES: An encryption scheme based on the Diffie-Hellman problem. Submission to IEEE P1363a. http://grouper.ieee.org/groups/1363/P1363a/Encryption.html, 1998.
2. ABDALLA, M., BELLARE, M., AND ROGAWAY, P. The oracle Diffie-Hellman assumptions and an analysis of DHIES. In *Progress in Cryptology – CT-RSA 2001* (2001), D. Naccache, Ed., vol. 2020 of *LNCS*, pp. 143–158.
3. AHN, L. V., AND HOPPER, N. Public key steganography. In *Advances in Cryptology – EUROCRYPT 2004* (2004), C. Cachin and J. Camenisch, Eds., vol. 3027 of *LNCS*, pp. 323–341.
4. AMERICAN NATIONAL STANDARDS INSTITUTE (ANSI). Public key cryptography for the financial services industry: The elliptic curve digital signature algorithm (ECDSA). ANSI X9.62, 1998.
5. BACKES, M., AND CACHIN, C. Public-key steganography with active attacks. Cryptology ePrint Archive Report 2003/231 (revised 16 Feb 2004), 2004. Available from http://eprint.iacr.org/.
6. BELLARE, M., CANETTI, R., AND KRAWCZYK, H. Keying hash functions for message authentication. In *Advances in Cryptology – CRYPTO '96* (1996), N. Koblitz, Ed., vol. 1109 of *LNCS*, pp. 1–15.
7. BELLARE, M., DESAI, A., JOKIPII, E., AND ROGAWAY, P. A concrete security treatment of symmetric encryption. In *38th Annual Symposium on Foundations of Computer Science (FOCS '97)* (1997), IEEE Computer Society, pp. 394–403.
8. BELLARE, M., DESAI, A., POINTCHEVAL, D., AND ROGAWAY, P. Relations among notions of security for public-key encryption schemes. In *Advances in Cryptology – CRYPTO '98* (1998), H. Krawczyk, Ed., vol. 1462 of *LNCS*, pp. 26–46.
9. BELLARE, M., AND ROGAWAY, P. Random oracles are practical: A paradigm for designing efficient protocols. In *First Annual Conference on Computer and Communications Security* (1993), ACM, pp. 62–73.
10. BLAKE, I. F., SEROUSSI, G., AND SMART, N. P. *Elliptic Curves in Cryptography*, vol. 265 of *London Mathematical Society Lecture Note Series*. Cambridge University Press, 1999.
11. CANETTI, R., GOLDREICH, O., AND HALEVI, S. The random oracle methodology, revisited. E-print cs.CR/0010019, 2000. Available from http://arXiv.org/abs/cs/0010019.
12. CERTICOM RESEARCH. Standards for efficient cryptography – SEC 1: Elliptic curve cryptography. Version 1.0, 2000. Available from http://www.secg.org/.

13. CERTICOM RESEARCH. Standards for efficient cryptography – SEC 2: Recommended elliptic curve cryptography domain parameters. Version 1.0, 2000. Available from http://www.secg.org/.

14. CRAMER, R., AND SHOUP, V. Design and analysis of practical public-key encryption schemes secure against adaptive chosen ciphertext attack. *SIAM Journal on Computing*. To appear. Available from http://shoup.net/papers/ (2003).

15. DIFFIE, W., AND HELLMAN, M. E. New directions in cryptography. *IEEE Transactions on Information Theory 22*, 6 (1976), 644–654.

16. FOUQUET, M., GAUDRY, P., AND HARLEY, R. Finding secure curves with the Satoh-FGH algorithm and an early-abort strategy. In *Advances in Cryptology – EUROCRYPT 2001* (2001), B. Pfitzmann, Ed., vol. 2045 of *LNCS*, pp. 14–29.

17. GALBRAITH, S., AND MCKEE, J. The probability that the number of points on an elliptic curve over a finite field is prime. CACR Technical Report CORR 99-51, 1999. Available from http://www.cacr.math.uwaterloo.ca/techreports/1999/.

18. GOLDREICH, O. *Foundations of Cryptography – Vol. II: Basic Applications*. Cambridge University Press, 2004.

19. GOLDWASSER, S., AND MICALI, S. Probabilistic encryption. *Journal of Computer and System Sciences 28* (1984), 270–299.

20. INSTITUTE OF ELECTRICAL AND ELECTRONICS ENGINEERS (IEEE). IEEE standard specifications for public-key cryptography. IEEE Std 1363-2000, 2000.

21. KALISKI, JR., B. S. A pseudo-random bit generator based on elliptic logarithms. In *Advances in Cryptology – CRYPTO '86* (1987), A. M. Odlyzko, Ed., vol. 263 of *LNCS*, pp. 84–103.

22. KALISKI, JR., B. S. One-way permutations on elliptic curves. *Journal of Cryptology 3* (1991), 187–199.

23. KOBLITZ, N. Elliptic curve cryptosystems. *Mathematics of Computation 48* (1987), 203–209.

24. KRAWCZYK, H., BELLARE, M., AND CANETTI, R. HMAC: Keyed-hashing for message authentication. RFC 2104. Available from http://www.ietf.org/rfc/rfc2104.txt, 1997.

25. LERCIER, R. Finding good random elliptic curves for cryptosystems defined over $\mathbb{F}_{2^n}$. In *Advances in Cryptology – EUROCRYPT '97* (1997), W. Fumy, Ed., vol. 1233 of *LNCS*, pp. 379–392.

26. LERCIER, R., AND LUBICZ, D. Counting points on elliptic curves over finite fields of small characteristic in quasi quadratic time. In *Advances in Cryptology – EUROCRYPT 2003* (2003), E. Biham, Ed., vol. 2656 of *LNCS*, pp. 360–373.

27. MENEZES, A., OKAMOTO, T., AND VANSTONE, S. Reducing elliptic curve logarithms to logarithms in a finite field. *IEEE Transactions on Information Theory 39* (1993), 1639–1646.

28. MILLER, V. S. Use of elliptic curves in cryptography. In *Advances in Cryptology – CRYPTO '85* (1986), H. C. Williams, Ed., vol. 218 of *LNCS*, pp. 417–428.

29. NATIONAL INSTITUTE OF STANDARDS AND TECHNOLOGY. Recommendation for block cipher modes of operation – methods and techniques. NIST Special Publication SP 800-38A, 2001.

30. OKAMOTO, T., AND POINTCHEVAL, D. A new class of problems for the security of cryptographic schemes. In *Public Key Cryptography – PKC 2001* (2001), K. Kim, Ed., vol. 1992 of *LNCS*, pp. 104–118.

31. RACKOFF, C. W., AND SIMON, D. R. Non-interactive zero-knowledge proof of knowledge and chosen ciphertext attack. In *Advances in Cryptology – CRYPTO '91* (1992), J. Feigenbaum, Ed., vol. 576 of *LNCS*, pp. 433–444.

32. SHOUP, V. A proposal for an ISO standard for public key encryption. Version 2.1, December 20, 2001. http://shoup.net/papers/.
33. WATANABE, Y., SHIKATA, J., AND IMAI, H. Equivalence between semantic security and indistinguishability against chosen ciphertext attacks. In *Public Key Cryptography – PKC 2003* (2003), Y. G. Desmedt, Ed., vol. 2567 of *LNCS*, pp. 71–84.

A   Example Parameters

We use hexadecimal representations of octet strings and encode field elements of $\mathbb{F}_{2^{163}}$ as polynomials over $\mathbb{F}_2$ based on the reducing polynomial given as

$$080000000000000000000000000000000000000000C9;$$

see e.g. [12] for a detailed explanation. A suitable pair of elliptic curves for the KEM in Section 3 is given by

$$b = \mathtt{05846d0fda255361606711bf7a99b0722e2ec8f76b}.$$

This b has been generated verifiably pseudo-randomly with SHA-1 from the seed

$$\mathtt{f391f2426f9ca3af80bc4537dd7224d43c1639aa}.$$

following [4, Annex A.3.3.1] and [20, Annex A.12.6]. The curves $E_{0,b}$ and $E_{1,b}$ have

$$n_0 = 4\,p_0 = 4 \cdot 2923003274661805836407371179614143033958162426611,$$
$$n_1 = 2\,p_1 = 2 \cdot 5846006549323611672814736302501978089331135490587$$

rational points, respectively, with both p_0 and p_1 prime. The curves $E_{a,b}(\mathbb{F}_{2^{163}})$ have points $G_a = (x_a, y_a)$ of order n_a for example for $x_0 = 0000\ldots01$ and $x_1 = 0000\ldots02$.

The above coefficient b was provided by Reynald Lercier, who applied the point counting algorithms described in [25] and [16] to a list of verifiably pseudo-random b values and factored the curve orders to detect suitable curve pairs. Out of the 30 000 ($\approx 163^2$) choices for b examined, five had the desired properties.

B   Security Proof: Ciphertext Pseudo-randomness

Let $\mathbf{G}_0$ denote the real-or-ideal attack game from Definition 3 where a distinguisher A attacks PKE. The encryption oracle stage in $\mathbf{G}_0$ can be expressed as follows for PKE from Section 5.1: A submits m; the encryption oracle uses KEM.Encrypt(PK) to generate $(K_{\mathrm{oracle}}, \mathfrak{K}_{\mathrm{oracle}})$, splits $K_{\mathrm{oracle}} = K_{\mathsf{MAC}} \| K_{\mathsf{STR}}$, computes $\mathfrak{M} = \mathsf{MAC}(K_{\mathsf{MAC}}, m)$ and $stream = \mathsf{STREAM}(K_{\mathsf{STR}}, \mathsf{MAC.OutLen} + |m|)$, sets $c_0 = \mathfrak{K}_{\mathrm{oracle}} \| ((\mathfrak{M} \| m) \oplus stream)$, generates a uniformly random c_1 with $|c_1| = |c_0|$ and a uniformly random $b \in \{0, 1\}$, and finally responds with c_b.

Let $\mathbf{G}_1$ be like $\mathbf{G}_0$ but with K_{oracle} uniformly random (of appropriate length); $\mathbf{G}_2$ like $\mathbf{G}_1$ but with $\mathfrak{K}_{\text{oracle}}$ uniformly random; $\mathbf{G}_3$ like $\mathbf{G}_2$ but with *stream* uniformly random. We can expose A to these different games and look at $\Pr_{\mathbf{G}_i}[\widetilde{b} = b]$. We will build adversaries A_1 against KEM in a real-or-random CCA attack game, A_2 against KEM in a real-or-ideal attack game, and A_3 against STREAM. These adversaries run A and provide it with an encryption oracle by performing the encryption oracle stage as above, using pre-generated values K_{oracle}, $\mathfrak{K}_{\text{oracle}}$, and b.

A_1 attacks KEM in a real-or-random CCA attack game (Definition 5). First it picks a uniform random $b \in \{0, 1\}$ and queries its real-or-random key encapsulation oracle to obtain a pair $(K_{\text{oracle}}, \mathfrak{K}_{\text{oracle}})$. Then it runs A (relaying PK from its key generation oracle), playing the role of the encryption oracle. Finally, when A outputs $\widetilde{b}$, A_1 outputs 1 if $\widetilde{b} = b$ and 0 otherwise. Observe that

$$\left| \Pr_{\mathbf{G}_1}[\widetilde{b} = b] - \Pr_{\mathbf{G}_0}[\widetilde{b} = b] \right| = \mathsf{Adv}_{\mathsf{KEM}, A_1}^{\mathsf{ROR\text{-}CCA}}$$

($\mathbf{G}_1$ corresponds to $b_{\mathsf{KEM}} = 1$, $\mathbf{G}_0$ to $b_{\mathsf{KEM}} = 0$).

A_2 attacks KEM in a real-or-ideal attack game (Definition 6). First it generates $b \in \{0, 1\}$ and a bit string K_{oracle} of length KEM.OutLen uniformly at random and queries its real-or-ideal key encapsulation oracle to obtain a bit string $\mathfrak{K}_{\text{oracle}}$. Then it runs A (relaying PK from its key generation oracle), playing the role of the encryption oracle. Finally, when A outputs $\widetilde{b}$, A_2 outputs 1 if $\widetilde{b} = b$ and 0 otherwise. Observe that

$$\left| \Pr_{\mathbf{G}_2}[\widetilde{b} = b] - \Pr_{\mathbf{G}_1}[\widetilde{b} = b] \right| = \mathsf{Adv}_{\mathsf{KEM}, A_2}^{\mathsf{ROI}}$$

($\mathbf{G}_2$ corresponds to $b_{\mathsf{KEM}} = 1$, $\mathbf{G}_1$ to $b_{\mathsf{KEM}} = 0$).

A_3 attacks STREAM (Definition 10). First it generates $b \in \{0, 1\}$ and bit strings K_{oracle} of length KEM.OutLen and $\mathfrak{K}_{\text{oracle}}$ of length KEM.CipherLen uniformly at random. Then it runs A, playing the role of the key generation oracle (by using KEM.KeyGen) and the role of the encryption oracle. Finally, when A outputs $\widetilde{b}$, A_2 outputs 1 if $\widetilde{b} = b$ and 0 otherwise. Observe that

$$\left| \Pr_{\mathbf{G}_3}[\widetilde{b} = b] - \Pr_{\mathbf{G}_2}[\widetilde{b} = b] \right| = \mathsf{Adv}_{\mathsf{STREAM}, A_3}^{\mathsf{ROI}}$$

($\mathbf{G}_3$ corresponds to $b_{\mathsf{STR}} = 1$, $\mathbf{G}_2$ to $b_{\mathsf{STR}} = 0$) and clearly $\Pr_{\mathbf{G}_3}[\widetilde{b} = b] = \dfrac{1}{2}$.

Since b is uniformly random, by definition we have $\mathsf{Adv}_{\mathsf{PKE}, A}^{\mathsf{ROI}} = 2 \cdot \left| \frac{1}{2} - \Pr_{\mathbf{G}_0}[\widetilde{b} = b] \right|$; putting all together, we obtain

$$\mathsf{Adv}_{\mathsf{PKE}, A}^{\mathsf{ROI}} = 2 \cdot \left| \sum_{1 \leq i \leq 3} \left(\Pr_{\mathbf{G}_i}[\widetilde{b} = b] - \Pr_{\mathbf{G}_{i-1}}[\widetilde{b} = b] \right) \right|$$

$$\leq 2 \cdot \left(\mathsf{Adv}_{\mathsf{KEM}, A_1}^{\mathsf{ROR\text{-}CCA}} + \mathsf{Adv}_{\mathsf{KEM}, A_2}^{\mathsf{ROI}} + \mathsf{Adv}_{\mathsf{STREAM}, A_3}^{\mathsf{ROI}} \right).$$

A Host Intrusion Prevention System for Windows Operating Systems

Roberto Battistoni, Emanuele Gabrielli, and Luigi V. Mancini

Dipartimento di Informatica , Università di Roma "La Sapienza"
Via Salaria 113, 00198 Roma
r.battistoni@computer.org, {gabrielli,lv.mancini}@di.uniroma1.it

Abstract. We propose an intrusion prevention system called WHIPS that controls, entirely in kernel mode, the invocation of the critical system calls for the Windows OS security. WHIPS is implemented as a kernel driver, also called kernel module, by using kernel structures of the Windows OS. It is integrated without requiring changes to either the kernel data structures or to the kernel algorithms. WHIPS is also transparent to the application processes that continue to work correctly without source code changes or recompilation. A working prototype has been implemented as a kernel extension and it is applicable to all the Windows NT family OS, e.g. Windows 2000/XP/2003. The WHIPS first contribution is to apply the system call interposition technique to the Windows OS, which is not open source. It is not straightforward to apply this technique to Windows OS, also because Windows kernel structures are hidden from the developer, and furthermore, its kernel documentation is poor.

1 Introduction

Attacks on the security of network clients and servers are often based on the exploitation of flaws that are present in a specific application process. By means of well known techniques [Al96,Co00], a malicious user may corrupt one or more memory buffers so that while returning from a function call, a different piece of code, which is injected by the attacker, is executed by the flawed application process. Of course, the buggy application process maintains its special privileges (if any). As a consequence, if the attack is successful against a privileged process the attacker may gain full control of the entire system. For example, the malicious code could execute a shell in the privileged application context and allow the attacker to become a system administrator. An example of a recent exploit using buffer overflow is the slammer worm [MPSW03] that attacks the MS-SQL server for Windows 2000/XP to gain high privileges and then saturates the network bandwidth causing a denial of service attacks.

This paper presents the design and implementation of a Host Intrusion Prevention System (HIPS) for Windows OS that immediately detects security rules violations by monitoring the system calls made by the application processes. The proposed prototype, working entirely in kernel mode employs interposition at the

P. Samarati et al. (Eds.): ESORICS 2004, LNCS 3193, pp. 352–368, 2004.

system call interface to implement the access control functionality, and requires no change to the kernel code or to the syntax and semantics of existing system calls. Basically, the system call execution is only allowed when the invoking process and the value of the system call arguments comply with the rules kept in an Access Control Database (ACD) within the kernel. The task of the proposed HIPS is to protect the Windows OS against any technique that would allows an attacker to hijack the control of a privileged process. The REMUS system [BGM02] has shown that immediate detection of security rules violations can be achieved by monitoring the system calls made by processes in Linux. Here, we propose to apply a similar technique to the Windows 2000/XP/2003 family.

The HIPS being proposed here is called WHIPS, Windows-NT family Host Intrusion Prevention System. Indeed, Intrusion Prevention Systems (IPSs) strive to stop an intrusion attempt by using a preventive action on hosts to protect the systems under attack. Our WHIPS prototype runs under Windows 2000/XP and Windows 2003. Herein, by the term Windows we refer to Windows XP, but the consideration and the prototype design are applicable to all the Windows NT family OS. WHIPS' first contribution is to apply the system call interposition technique to the Windows OS. Though this technique is generally known, we could not find any related works that follow similar ideas as for Windows OS which is not open source. This is mainly because it is hard to design and to implement solutions in the Windows OS kernel structures which are hidden from the developer. On the contrary, there are many IPS that are implemented as wrapper executed in user mode such as [Ep00]. Moreover, many implementations of the system call interposition technique are well known on Linux OS. A related study for the Linux OS is the REMUS Project [BGM02] which implements a reference monitor for the system call invocations in a loadable Linux kernel module. In REMUS, root processes and setuid processes are privileged processes, and a dangerous system call is defined as a critical system call invoked by a privileged processes.

This paper is organized as follows. Section 2 characterizes the privileged and dangerous processes, and defines when a system call is critical and dangerous for a Windows system, showing how the Windows system calls are invoked by the user processes. Section 3 proposes the WHIPS prototype, showing the implementation, a brief example of its effectiveness, and the performance analyzes of the prototype.

2 Privileged Processes and Critical System Calls

In order to gain control of an OS, an attacker has to locate a target process that runs with high privileges in the system. For example, if the OS belongs to *Linux family*, the privileged processes include *daemons* and *setuid* processes that execute their code with the effective user *root* (EUID=0). In the following, first we introduce the Windows processes security context, then we characterize when a process is *privileged* or *dangerous* and when a system call is *critical* or *dangerous* in Windows.

2.1   Windows Processes Security Context and Privileges

This section examines the *Security Identity Descriptor* (SID), the *Access Token* (AT) and the impersonation technique, which are the components of a process structure that represents its security context. Then we examine the Windows privileges.

Security Identity Descriptor: SIDs identify the entities that execute operations in a Windows system and may represent users, groups, machines or domains. A SID contains a so-called *RID* (relative number) field that distinguishes two SIDs otherwise equal in a Windows system. Every Windows system has a lot of SIDs; some of them identify particular users or groups and are called Well-Known SIDs [Mi02a].

Access Token: The SRM (Security Reference Monitor) is a Windows kernel component that uses a structure called *Access Token* to identify a thread or a process security context [RuS01]. A *security context* is a set of privileges, users and groups associated to a process or a thread. During the log-on procedure, *Winlogon* builds an initial token that represents the user rights, and links this token to the users shell process. All the processes created by the user inherit a copy of the initial AT. We have two types of AT: *primary token* and *impersonation token*. Every process has an AT called *primary token*. Every process in Windows has associated a primary thread and a variable number of secondary threads that executes the process operations. The primary thread inherits a copy of the primary token, whereas a secondary thread may inherit a copy of the primary token, or may obtain a restricted copy of the primary token by the *impersonation* mechanism.

Impersonation: It is a mechanism that allows a security context of a process or a thread to migrate in another security context. For example, an impersonation occurs when a server accesses its resources on behalf of a client. In this case, the impersonation mechanism allows the server process to use the security context of the client that requested that particular operation [RuS01]. To avoid an improper use, Windows does not permit to a server to impersonate a client process without the client consensus. Some impersonation levels follow: *SecurityAnonymous, SecurityIdentification, SecurityImpersonation, SecurityDelegation*. If a client does not choose an impersonation level, *SecurityImpersonation* is the default.

Windows Privileges: A *privilege* in Windows is the right to operate on a particular aspect of the entire system, so a privilege acts on the entire system, whereas a *right* acts on an object of the system [Scm01]. A privilege may be assigned to a user or a group in Windows. When a user logs on a Windows system, a process will be created and assigned to the user, then the privileges assigned to the user or the group will be added in the AT privileges list of the user process. There are many privileges in Windows, each allowing a particular action on the system, but not every privilege is dangerous for the system security. Only a subset of the entire set of Windows privileges contains dangerous privileges that can be exploited by a malicious user.

Definition 1. *A dangerous privilege is a Windows privilege that can be used by a malicious user to compromise the availability, the confidentiality and the integrity of the system.*

Examples of some dangerous privileges reported in [HLB01] are: *SeBackupPrivilege*; *SeTcbPrivilege*; *SeDebugPrivilege*; *SeAssignPrimaryTokenPrivilege*; *SeIncreaseQuotaPrivilege*.

2.2 Privileged and Dangerous Processes

As discussed above, some privileges are dangerous in Windows OS and if we want to know if a process is dangerous, we can look to the process AT of the user that activates this process. A malicious user can attack a dangerous process executing malicious code in its security context and gaining all the process privileges. We can say that if a process privilege is dangerous, then the process is dangerous too. To identify a dangerous process we can look for dangerous privileges into the process AT. Now we introduce some definitions to summarize the concepts:

Definition 2. *A privileged process is a process with some Windows privilege.*

Definition 3. *A dangerous process is a privileged process that has some dangerous privilege.*

If in the AT privileges list there are one or more dangerous privileges, the process, owner of the AT, belongs to the set of dangerous process. In the following, we discuss a particular set of privileged processes: the *Windows Services.*

Services Identification. Almost every OS has a mechanism to start processes at system start up time that provide services not tied to an interactive user. In Windows, such processes are called *services*. Services are similar to UNIX daemon processes and often implement the server side of client/server applications. On Windows, many services log-on to the system with a predefined account: *System* account (called *LocalSystem*). This account belongs to group *Administrators* and it is very powerful because it has many dangerous privileges. This is a critical account for the Windows security.

Often a careful analysis of services by the administrator could restrict the services privileges. This could be done with a new account created for the specific service, where this account has less privileges then the *System* account. Following this idea, in Windows XP/2003 there are two new accounts for services: *local service* and *network service*. These new accounts have the minimum privileges necessary to the execution of some services, typically Internet and network services. So, an attack to these services is less powerful than an attack to a service that log-on with the *System* account [HLB01]. *LocalSystem* has almost all the Windows privileges whereas each of *LocalService* and *NetworkService* has a subset of the *LocalSystem* privileges. In general, the SIDs in the process AT identify the services, precisely the so-called *Well Known SIDs*. We have two possibilities:

if the service logs onto the system with *LocalSystem* account, the user account
SID in the AT is equal to string *S-1-5-18*, Local System SID. Otherwise, we must
look in the AT group SIDs; the process is a service if there is the *Well-Known
SID Service* represented by the string *S-1-5-6*. Summarizing, the following rules
help us to know exactly when a process is a service:

Proposition 1. *Process is a Service* ⇒ *Access Token User SID is equal to Local
System SID, or in the Access Token Group SIDs is present Service SID.*

Proposition 2. *Access Token Group SIDs contains Service SID* ⇒ *process is a
Service.*

Proposition 3. *Access Token User SID is equal to LocalSystem SID* ⇒ *process
is NOT necessarily a service.*

Note that if user SID is *LocalSystem* the process owner of the AT is not
necessarily a service, it could be a system process too. If we consider only the
first rule, we will find a set of processes that contains the set of services, but is
not necessarily equals to this set.

2.3   Critical and Dangerous System Calls

In this section, we introduce the definition of *system calls* in Windows and then
we characterize when a system call is *critical*.

Native APIs: Windows System Calls. APIs (Application Programming
Interfaces) are programming functions held in dynamic library, and run in user-
mode space and kernel-mode space. We call *native APIs* [Ne00] the APIs in
kernel-mode that represent the system call of Windows. We simply call APIs,
the APIs in user-mode space.

Four dynamic libraries export APIs of the Win32 subsystem: *user32.dll,
gdi32.dll, kernel32.dll, advapi32.dll*. The APIs in *user32.dll* and *gdi32.dll* invoke the APIs implemented in kernel mode by *win32k.sys* module, which is the
kernel module of the Win32 subsystem. The APIs exported by *kernel32.dll* (system APIs) use a particular library named *Ntdll.dll* that invokes native APIs in
the kernel. Native APIs invoked by ntdll.dll are the Windows system calls.

Figure 1 shows that, when an API of *kernel32.dll* is called by an application,
this API recalls one or more functions present in *ntdll.dll*. This library represents
a bridge between user-mode and kernel-mode space [Ne00,Osr03]. The user-mode
library *Ntdll.dll* is the front-end of the native APIs, which are implemented in
the Windows kernel *ntoskrnl.exe*. *Ntdll.dll* exports all the native APIs with two
type of function name prefix: *Nt* and *Zw*. True native APIs (in the kernel) have
the same name of APIs exported by *Ntdll.dll*.

Figure 2 shows an example of the native API *NtCreateFile*, obtained disassembling *ntdll.dll*. Function *NtCreateFile* loads registry EAX with the index
$0x1A$ of the native API in a particular table called *System Service Table* (KiServiceTable), then EDX registry points to the user-mode stack, *ESP+04*, where

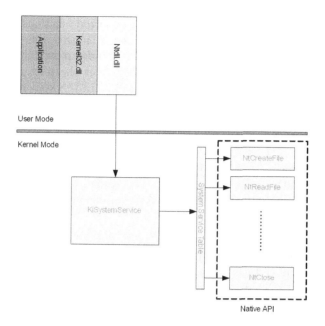

Fig. 1. System Service Table (SST)

```
NtCreateFile:
mov eax,0x0000001A
lea edx,[esp+04]
int 0x2E
ret 0x2C
```

Fig. 2. NTCreateFile assembly code

there are the parameters of native API, and finally raises interrupt $0x2E$ that executes the *System Service Dispatcher* of Windows. System Service Dispatcher is the kernel routine that invokes the true native API in the kernel. Not all the native API exported by *Ntdll.dll* are exported by *ntoskrnl.exe*. This seems to prevent the unauthorized use of particular and dangerous native APIs within any module implemented as a kernel driver. Disassembling the library *ntdll.dll*, we can observe that every *Nt* native API and its corresponding *Zw* native API have the same assembly code, fig. 2. If we disassemble *ntoskrnl.exe*, the true native APIs with the *Nt* prefix contain the true code of native API, and the native APIs with the *Zw* prefix have the representation in the example of figure 2, see also [Ne00,Osr03,Scr01] for details.

System Service Dispatcher. Dispatcher of interrupt $0x2E$ is the *System Service Dispatcher* routine. It is implemented in the executive layer of the Windows kernel, through the kernel function *KiSystemService*. APIs in *gdi32.dll* and *user32.dll* call directly the dispatcher *KiSystemService*, and after the dispatcher invokes functions in *win32k.sys* module. The APIs in *kernel32.dll* invoke the functions exported by *ntdll.dll* and then these exported functions call the native APIs in Windows kernel. When *KiSystemService* is invoked, the dispatcher runs a series of checks. First, it controls the validity of index passed in EAX register, then it controls if the argument space expected for the native API parameters is correct and finally executes the native API in the kernel. When *KiSystemService* invokes the native APIs, it uses a structure called *System Service Descriptor Table (SDT)*, represented by the *KeServiceDescriptorTable* structure [Scr01,HLB01]. *KeServiceDescriptorTable* has two table pointers: *KiServiceTable (System Service Table, SST)* and *KiArgumentTable*. The first table contains an index for every native API, used by native API code in *ntdll.dll*, to invoke the corresponding native API in the kernel. The second table contains, for every native API, the allocation space for this API parameters. This space is used for the kernel-stack memory allocation.

Critical and Dangerous Native APIs. A native API can be considered as a Windows system call. But when is a system call in Windows a critical system call? A native API is a generic kernel function; it has a function name, a series of parameters and a return value. If we consider a native API by itself, it is not critical, but it becomes critical when it has dangerous parameters. Consider a simple example: the native API *NtOpenFile*. Typically this native API opens a handle to a file on the File System. Its only parameter is a pointer to a string that represents the file name (with path) that will be opened. If the file name is *readme.txt*, this native API is not critical for the system. But, if the file to open is equal to *c:\winnt\cmd.exe*, the Windows shell, *NtOpenFile* with this particular parameter is critical because it could be used to open a system administrative session. So we introduce some definition:

Definition 4. *A parameter of a Native API is dangerous if it can be used by a malicious user to compromise the availability, the confidentiality and the integrity of the system.*

Definition 5. *A critical system call is a native API that could be invoked with dangerous parameters.*

Definition 6. *A dangerous system call is a critical system call invoked by a dangerous process.*

Note that a *critical system call* is dangerous for the system only if the invoking process is a *dangerous process*. A dangerous process that calls a native API with dangerous parameters may represents an attack of a malicious user.

Native API Classification. Native APIs in Windows 2000 and XP are about 250, and only 25 of them are documented by Microsoft within the Driver Development Kit (DDK). All others native APIs are not documented. A good support for native API documentation is *Windows NT/2000: Native API reference* [Ne00] which is not an official Microsoft documentation of Windows OS.

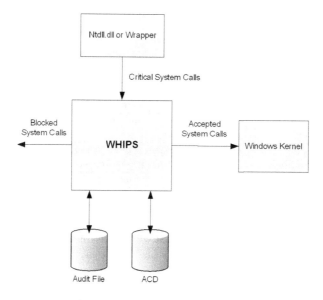

Fig. 3. WHIPS Reference Monitor

Table 1 represents a first classification of native APIs by category (21 categories) which is derived from [RuS01,Ru98], and shows that in Windows we have many system calls. Linux give us more information with its source code on its system calls, whereas Windows does not give us any information on its system call.

3   The WHIPS Prototype

WHIPS is a Reference Monitor (RM) for the detection and the prevention of Windows dangerous system calls invocation. This prototype is based on an initial idea related to the REMUS Project [BGM02]. REMUS is a RM for Linux OS and it is implemented with a dynamic loadable module of Linux kernel. WHIPS is implemented as a kernel driver, also called kernel module, using undocumented structure of Windows kernel and the routines typically employed for drivers development [BDP99]. The WHIPS prototype can be seen as a system call RM for Windows and the implementation technique utilized is the system calls interposition. As you can see in Figure 3, WHIPS is a module that filters every critical system call invoked by a Windows service and establishes if the critical system call is dangerous by checking its actual parameters. If the system call is not dangerous it will be passed to the kernel for the execution, otherwise it will be stopped and not executed. RM control policies are established by a small database called *Access Control Database* (ACD).

The ACD defines the allowed actions on the system by means of a set of rules. Every time a dangerous process invokes a critical system call through *ntdll.dll* or a *wrapper* (a code that rise *int 0x2E*), the call of the process is checked by WHIPS that matches the process name, the critical system call with its parameters, with

Table 1. Native API categories

Index	Category	Description
1	Special Files	These APIs are used to create files that have custom characteristics.
2	Drivers	These functions are used by NT to load and unload device driver images from system memory.
3	Processor and Bus	Processor registers and components can be controlled via these functions.
4	Debugging and Profiling	The profiling APIs provide a mechanism for sample-based profiling of kernel-mode execution.
5	Channels	Provide access to a communications mechanism.
6	Power	Native API for power management.
7	Plug-and-Play	Like the Power API.
8	Objects	Object manager namespace objects are created and manipulated with these routines.
9	Registry	Win32 Registry functions basically map directly to these APIs.
10	LPC	LPC is NT core interprocess communications mechanism.
11	Security	The Native security APIs are mapped almost directly by Win32 security APIs.
12	Processes and Threads	These functions control processes and threads. Many have direct Win32 equivalents.
13	Atoms	Atoms allow for the efficient storage and referencing of character strings.
14	Error Handling	Device drivers and debuggers rely on these error handling routines.
15	Execution Environment	These functions are related to general execution environment.
16	Timers and System Time	Virtually all these routines have functionality accessible via Win32 APIs.
17	Synchronization	Most synchronization objects have Win32 APIs, with the notable exception of event pairs. Event pairs are used for high-performance interprocess synchronization by the LPC facility.
18	Memory	Most of NT virtual memory APIs are accessible via Win32.
19	File and General I/O	File I/O is the best documented of the native APIs since many device drivers must make use of it.
20	Miscellaneous	These functions do not fall neatly into other categories.
21	Jobs	These functions are essentially a group of associated processes that can be controlled as a single unit and that share job-execution time restrictions.

the ACD rules. If a rule exists that satisfies this invocation, the native API is executed otherwise is not executed because the system call invoked is classified as dangerous.

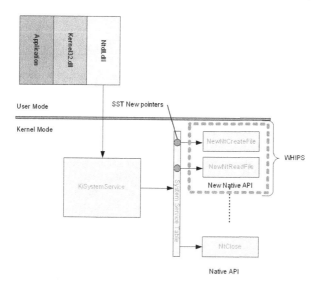

Fig. 4. WHIPS implementation architecture

The implementation technique used by WHIPS, suggested by [CRu97,BDP99], replaces the native APIs pointers in the System Service Table (fig. 4), with pointers to the new native APIs supplied by the prototype. The new native APIs are wrappers to original native APIs and implement the RM checks.

For every original critical native API we have introduced a new native API, which has the same function name with a prefix *New* (ex. *NewNtCreateFile*). This new API analyzes its invoking process and its parameters. If the invoking process is dangerous and the native API is critical, a check is performed on the actual parameters considering the rule in the ACD. If there is not a corresponding rule in the ACD the original native API is not invoked, since the native API may be dangerous. Otherwise it is invoked and executed.

3.1 Access Control Database

The ACD is implemented by a simple text file (protected by the system ACL and accessible only to the Administrator or Administrative groups). ACD is loaded at the driver start-up and it is allocated entirely in main memory; no other accesses are needed to the file and this avoid performance problem. A generic rule in the ACD is represented in table 2.

These ACD rules state that *Process* can execute the specific *Native API* with the specific *Param[1..N]*. The specification of the rules to insert into the ACD is possible in a manual or automatic manner. In the first case, the administrator of the system must specify all the Native APIs critical and allowed for the system. This can be done with approximation, step by step, but a period of control of the system is necessary. In fact some omissions could prevent the correct operation of some application.

Table 2. ACD Rule schema

Rule Type	Process name	Native API Name	ParamAPI [1..n]

- *Rule Type:* can be *debug* or *rule*; when the type is *rule*, this means that the rule filters the execution of system call. When the type is *debug*, the execution of a critical system call will be traced but not blocked.
- *Process Name:* is the name of the executable image that has activated the dangerous process; this name is a string that identifies only the name and not the complete path; WHIPS prototype works entirely in kernel-mode and it has not access to process block to retrieve the complete path of executable image because this information is accessible only in user-mode.
- *Native API:* is the name, with prefix *Nt*, of the critical native API invoked by *Process*.
- *Param [1..N]:* are the legal actual parameters of the critical system call.

The second case is to implement a robot that analyzes all the system calls invoked by the system in a trusted environment and create the correct rules for the ACD.

The performance of the system depends on the number of rules in the ACD and how the matching algorithm is implemented. In this first prototype the ACD is scanned sequentially with a computational cost of $O(n)$, where n is the number of rules in the ACD. In a preliminary study we have estimated that the number of these rules is not more than 1000, so the sequential search seems computational acceptable. Alternatively one could implement other more efficient algorithms to lower the computational cost of the rule search.

3.2   System Service Table Modified

WHIPS is a kernel module, also called a driver in Windows. Now we examine a C-like representation of the source code that implements the patch to the System Service Table (SST) of Windows. The main function of the WHIPS prototype is the common main function of all the drivers in Windows OS, called *DriverEntry*. In WHIPS,this function does not drive any peripheral of the system and the only work that it does is calling the *HookServices* function at driver start-up.

Figure 5 shows the C-like representation of the System Service Table (SST) patch. The first operation that it does is to load the ACD database in the kernel memory with *LoadDB*, and then it patches the SST. With macro *SYSTEMSER-VICE*, the *HookServices* function saves the old references to the native APIs in *OldNtApiName*, and then substitutes the old references in the SST with the new references to the new native APIs supplied by the prototype.

3.3   New Native API Implementation

To explain the implementation of the new native APIs, figure 6 shows the representation in C-like of the *NewNtOpenProcess*. When a process wants to call the

```
HookServices() {
  LoadDB("RmDB.rbt", &ruleArrayRM, &numruleRM);
  OldNtCreateFile=SYSTEMSERVICE(ZwCreateFile);
  .

  .
  OldNtClose=SYSTEMSERVICE(ZwClose);
  Disable_Interrupt;
  SYSTEMSERVICE(ZwCreateFile)=NewNtCreateFile;
  .

  .
  SYSTEMSERVICE(ZwClose)=NewNtClose;
  Enable_Interrupt;
  return;
}
```

Fig. 5. WHIPS Patch function

NtOpenProcess, it really calls the corresponding new native API *NewNtOpen-Process*. The new native API detects its invoking process name and its only parameter: the process name that will be opened by the native API. Then the *NewNtOpenProcess* stores this data in a temporary rule called *rule*. The format of this temporary rule is similar to the format of the rules in the ACD, this is to simplify the check of the rule.

Next the procedure evaluates if the invoking process is a dangerous process. The function *isProcessDangerous* analyzes the AT of the invoking process and return *true* if the process is dangerous, *false* otherwise. Remember that in this version of the prototype dangerous processes are Windows services or Windows system processes (refer to section 2.2). The function *VerifyDebugNativeAPI* analyzes if the native API must be traced in the debug environment, whereas *VerifyNativeApi* looks into the ACD database to find a rule that allows the execution of the invoked API. Only if this function return true, original native API is called with the invocation of *OldNtOpenProcess* saved in *HookServices*.

3.4 Prototype Effectiveness

The WHIPS prototype can be tested with the *Web Server File Request Parsing* vulnerability of *IIS* in Windows NT/2000 up to Service Pack 2. This vulnerability permits to execute shell command in a web browser with an URL not well-formed. If for example, we call the URL:

http://host/scripts/..%255c..%255cwinnt/system32/cmd.exe?/c+dir+c:

We obtain a shell that shows the list of files of the *C:* partition hard drive. But, this vulnerability may become very dangerous if a shell command is passed as an argument to delete or to modify some configuration files not protected by the ACLs. Now we explain how this vulnerability works.

The Web Server IIS, *inetinfo.exe*, executes in its thread the shell command for an incorrect interpretation of the URL format. This thread has *IUSR_HOST*

```
NewNtOpenProcess(phProcess,...,pClientId) {
  startTime0=KeQueryPerformanceCounter(&frequency);
  GetProcess(currProc);
  GetProcessByProcessID(pClient,pClientId);
  rule.processName=currProc;
  rule.api="ntopenprocess";
  rule.numparam=1;
  rule.api_param[0]=pClient;
  CurrentProcessIsDangerous=isProcessDangerous();
  if (VerifyDebugNativeAPI(rule,CurrentProcessIsDangerous))
    Print_Debug_Information;
  if (VerifyNativeAPI(rule,CurrentProcessIsDangerous)) {
    endTime0=KeQueryPerformanceCounter(&frequency);
    Show_Overhead_Information;
    OldNtOpenProcess(phProcess,...,pClientId);
  } else {
    endTime0=KeQueryPerformanceCounter(&frequency);
    Show_Overhead_Information;
  }
  return;
}
```

Fig. 6. WHIPS New Native API implementation

privileges (guest privileges). So the Web server erroneously executes code out of the web server directory. In other situations, the attacker could obtain administrator privileges if the threads owned by a process have the same privileges of the administrator.

If WHIPS prototype is running, the thread created by privileged process *inetinfo.exe* is analyzed. In the ACD database is not present a rule for the native API *NtOpenFile* with shell (*cmd.exe*) parameters, for IIS privileged process (and its threads), so the execution of the native API is stopped and also the attack to the Web server. This experiment shows that WHIPS permits only the allowed Native APIs to operate on the systems, and consequently stops every malicious actions of the dangerous processes.

3.5   Performance Evaluation

The actual impact of WHIPS on the global system performance is negligible for all practical purposes, mainly because the number of critical system call invocations is small with respect to the total number of instructions executed by a process. However, in order to evaluate even the minimal overhead introduced by the WHIPS prototype, we have devised further experiments based on micro benchmark. In particular, the kernel function *KeQueryPerformanceCounter* exported by the kernel is used. *KeQueryPerformanceCounter(PerformanceFrequency)* returns the clock ticks counter ($\#tick$) from system boot, whereas the clock tick counter per second ($\#tick/sec$) is expressed by *PerformanceFrequency*. A generic invocation time T_i of the kernel function $KeQueryPerformanceCounter$ is given in microseconds by:

$$T_i = \frac{\#tick_i}{PerformanceFrequency}. \tag{1}$$

Now assume that ΔT is the execution time of a generic code block between two invocations of $KeQueryPerformanceCounter$. These two invocations determine respectively T_1 and T_2, where T_1 is the first invocation time and T_2 is the second invocations time, and $\Delta T = T_2 - T_1$.

We must consider that the execution of the function $KeQueryPerformance-$ $Counter$ introduces an overhead too, we call this $\Delta T_{OverheadKeQuery}$. To estimate $\Delta T_{OverheadKeQuery}$, we have measured two consecutive invocations of $KeQueryPerformanceCounter$.

We define the *elaboration block* as the WHIPS code block that implements the control of the native API parameters and the control on the invoking process. The overhead introduced by a generic new native API is:

$$\Delta T_{OverheadNewNAPI}$$
$$= (T_{2,OverNewNAPI} - T_{1,OverNewNAPI}) - \Delta T_{OverheadKeQuery}, \tag{2}$$

whereas the execution time of the original native APIs in Windows is called $\Delta T_{NativeAPI}$ which is computed measuring a native API execution in a way similar to equation 2.

3.6   Measurements

The system utilized for the measurement is a PC with AMD Athlon CPU, with clock frequency of 1200 Mhz, 512 Mbytes of RAM and Windows 2000 OS. We have measured only four native API and specifically three critical native API: $NewNtOpenFile$, $NewNtCreateFile$ and $NewNtOpenProcess$, and one not critical, $NewNtClose$. For every native API, intercepted by the WHIPS prototype, we have done a significant number of measurements ($\sim$10.000), and we have elaborated these to obtain the average times without spiced values. We have determined $\overline{\Delta T}_{OverheadNewNativeAPI}$, the average overhead introduced by each new native API, and $\overline{\Delta T}_{NativeAPI}$, the average time of the original native API. The average overhead of function $KeQueryPerformanceCounter$, called $\overline{\Delta T}_{OverheadKeQuery}$, is $\sim$0,82 μsec on our test PC.

Table 3 compares the execution time of the original native API (A) with the overhead introduced by the corresponding new native API (O). This is to measure the impact of the WHIPS prototype implementation respect to the original system. As you can see, all the overheads (O) are almost the same in value, except for the $NtClose$ case, because $NewNtClose$ performs few operations in the *elaboration block*; in fact these new APIs determine the name of the process or the handle passed to them. The last column (I) shows the percentage incidence of the new native API overhead on the execution time of the original native API.

Table 3. Comparative table ApiTime and OverheadTime

API	Average Execution Time		API Incidence
	API Time (A) $\Delta T_{NativeAPI}$	Overhead Time (O) $\Delta T_{OverheadNewNativeAPI}$	% Overhead (I) I: O/A*100
NtClose	7,68 μsec	6,37 μsec	83%
NtCreateFile	246,74 μsec	21,52 μsec	9%
NtOpenFile	53,56 μsec	20,67 μsec	39%
NtOpenProcess	8,49 μsec	23,23 μsec	274%

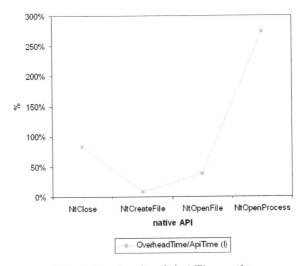

Fig. 7. Overhead and Api Time ratio

The figure 7 shows a line chart with percentage incidence (I) of every native API intercepted by the WHIPS prototype. As you can see the highest is the *NewNtOpenProcess* case that introduces an overhead of 274% respect to *NtOpenProcess* execution time. Lowest incidence is of *NewNtCreateFile* that introduces an overhead of 9% respect to *NtCreateFile* execution time. In figure 8 you can see a comparative line chart between the overhead introduced by new native APIs (O) and the execution time of the original native API (A). Higher is the difference from the overhead and the execution time and higher is the percentage incidence (I). If we consider the *NtClose*, we have a minimum difference, and this means that the overhead introduced by WHIPS is close to the execution time of the original native API. In the case of *NtCreateFile* the overhead is less than the execution time and the incidence is low. In *NtOpenProcess* the overhead is bigger than the original native API execution time and the incidence is high.

4   Concluding Remarks

Our work defines privileged processes in Windows OS and proposes a methodology to discover the processes that can be dangerous for the system. Identifying

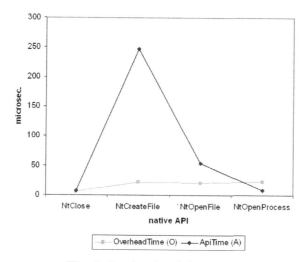

Fig. 8. Overhead and Api Time

dangerous processes is the first and most important step in the design of this type of HIPS. The *Access Token* (AT) privileges list of a process can be used to identify if a process is dangerous. In particular, if in the AT privileges list there are one or more dangerous privileges, the process, owner of the AT, belongs to the set of dangerous process. For simplicity in this paper we have focused on a subset of dangerous process: the *Windows Services*. The relation between the dangerous processes and the critical system calls leads to the concept of dangerous system calls (see section 2.3). The implementation of the WHIPS prototype is based on the above concepts. WHIPS stops common exploits that use the buffer overflow technique to carry out the privilege escalation on a system. If a malicious user wants to execute a shell in a context of the exploited service, WHIPS will prevent the attack by stopping the execution of the dangerous system call that invokes the shell.

Future research will include the inspection of the entire native API in Windows OS, for a full classification of the system calls. Another step could be to implement a Web-service like *Windows Update*, named *WHIPS Update* that allows the user to download new sets of rules in order to configure the ACD automatically. This simplifies the definition of the rule in the ACD database.

WHIPS could be even more efficient if it were implemented directly into the Windows kernel, instead of as a kernel driver, but in order to do so the source code of the Windows kernel must be accessed.

Acknowledgments

The authors gratefully acknowledge dr. R.Bianco for the helpful discussions and the anonymous reference for their helpful comments. This work is funded by the

Italian MIUR under the projects: FIRB WEB-MINDS and PRIN 2003 *WEB-based management and representation of spatial and geographic data.*

References

[Al96]   Aleph One, *Smashing the stack for fun and profit*, Phrack Magazine, vol 49, 1996.

[BGM02] Bernaschi, Gabrielli, Mancini, *REMUS: a security-enhanced operating system*, ACM Transactions on Information and System Security, Vol. 5, No. 1, pp. 36-61, Feb. 2002. http://remus.sourceforge.net/.

[BDP99] Borate, Dabak, Phadke, *Undocumented Windows NT*, M&T Books, 1999.

[CRu97] Cogswell, Russinovich, *Windows NT System-Call Hooking*, Dr. Dobb's Journal, p. 261, 1997.

[Co00] Cowan et al, *Buffer Overflows: attacks and defences for the vulnerability of the decade*, Proc. IEEE DARPA Information Survivability Conference and Expo, Hilton Head, South Carolina, 2000.

[Ep00] Epstein et al., *Using Operating System Wrappers to Increase the Resiliency of Commercial Firewalls* , Proc. ACM Annual Computer Security Applications Conference, Louisiana, USA, Dec. 2000.

[HLB01] Howard, LeBlanc, *Writing Secure Code*, Microsoft Press, 2001.

[MPSW03] Moore, Paxson, Savage, Shannon, Staniford, Weaver, *Inside the slammer worm*, IEEE Security&Privacy, pp.33-39, July-August 2003.

[Mi02a] Microsoft, *Well-Known Security Identifiers in Windows 2000*, Knowledge Base 243330, 2002, http://support.microsoft.com/default.aspx?scid=KB;EN-US;Q243330&.

[Ne00] Nebbet, *Windows NT/2000: Native API reference*, Macmillan Technical Publishing (MTP), 2000.

[Osr03] OSR Open System Resources Inc, *Nt vs. Zw - Clearing Confusion On The Native API*, The NT Insider, Vol 10, Issue 4, August 2003.

[RuS01] Russinovich, Solomon, *Inside Windows 2000: Third Edition*, Microsoft Press, 2001.

[Ru98] Russinovich, *Inside the Native API*, Systems Internals, 1998, http://www.sysinternals.com/ntdll.htm.

[Scm01] Schmidt, *Microsoft Windows 2000 Security Handbook*, Que Publishing, 2001.

[Scr01] Schreiber, *Undocumented Windows 2000 Secrets*, Addison Wesley, 2001.

Re-establishing Trust in Compromised Systems: Recovering from Rootkits That Trojan the System Call Table

Julian B. Grizzard, John G. Levine, and Henry L. Owen

School of Electrical and Computer Engineering
Georgia Institute of Technology
Atlanta, Georgia 30332–0250, USA
{grizzard,levine,owen}@ece.gatech.edu

Abstract. We introduce the notion of re-establishing trust in compromised systems, specifically looking at recovering from kernel-level rootkits. An attacker that has compromised a system will often install a set of tools, known as a *rootkit*, which will break trust in the system as well as serve the attacker with other functionalities. One type of rootkit is a kernel-level rootkit, which will patch running kernel code with *untrusted* kernel code. Specifically, current kernel-level rootkits replace trusted system calls with trojaned system calls. Our approach to recover from these type of rootkits is to extract the system call table from a *known-good* kernel image and reinstall the system call table into the running kernel. Building on our approach to current generation rootkits, we discuss future generation rootkits and address how to recover from them.

1 Introduction

Modern computer systems are vulnerable to a wide variety of attacks. As attackers develop methods to exploit these vulnerabilities, a large number of systems are compromised. Compromises are costly to individuals, companies, governments, and other organizations in terms of data breach, downtime, administration, and recovery. The number of new vulnerabilities discovered each year is growing, and as such we believe system compromises will continue to be a problem for the foreseeable future.

Much work has been done on preventing and detecting system compromises; however, system compromises continue to be a problem. To date we have seen little work done in terms of methods for recovering from system compromises. Conventional wisdom states that one should wipe the system clean, reinstall, and patch with the latest updates.

In this paper, we begin to explore alternatives to conventional wisdom in terms of recovering from system compromises. In certain cases, it may not be possible or desirable to shutdown the system to perform a fresh install. We study kernel-level rootkit modifications to compromised systems and present tools to recover from kernel-level rootkits. Our work focuses on the Linux kernel and Red

P. Samarati et al. (Eds.): ESORICS 2004, LNCS 3193, pp. 369–384, 2004.

Hat Linux distribution. The results of our work should be applicable to other operating systems, especially those on the *x86* architecture.

We specifically discuss one of the most common tactics of modern kernel-level rootkits: trojaning the system call table. When the system call table is trojaned, even known good system binaries will not report true information about the system. Our approach to recover from such attacks is to insert a trusted system call table from a known good kernel image into the running kernel. This approach gives control back to the system administrator and is the first step in recovering from a root compromise in which a kernel-level rootkit has been installed.

Future generation kernel-level rookits may trojan other types of kernel code instead of the system call table. We discuss possible directions for future root-kits and alternative kernel penetration techniques. Our recovery approach of bootstrapping trusted code into the kernel may be useful to recover from future generation rootkits.

1.1 Definition of Compromised System

When an attacker has gained some level of permissions on a computer system, the system is said to be *compromised*. If the attacker gains root access, the compromise is considered a root-level compromise. With root-level privileges, the attacker can change any state within the system. The attacker *owns* the system. The attacker can modify the system so that the original trusted reporting processes no longer report accurate information. Some level of trust must be restored to the system before all reporting information can be relied upon, depending on how trust is broken.

Compromised System – If a system is compromised, then the following conditions are true.

1. An attacker has gained some level of privileges on the system.
2. The attacker can read or modify some portion of the state within the system.

Root-level Compromised System – One specific class of compromised systems are *root-level* compromises. If a system is compromised with *root-level* access, then the following conditions are true.

1. An attacker has gained unlimited access to the system.
2. Any state within the system can be read or modified by the attacker.
3. Trust can be broken in the system.

1.2 Definition of Rootkit

A *rootkit* may be considered as a form of a *Trojan Horse* as discussed in [1]. Once an attacker has compromised a system, he or she often use a rootkit as a tool to covertly retain access to that system. A rootkit can contain utilities to allow the attacker to retain access, hide processes and activities, and break trust in the local system reporting and querying functions.

We classify rootkits into *user-level* and *kernel-level* rootkits. A user-level rootkit will alter operating system tools at the user level (which usually involves adding or modifying system binaries such as /bin/login). A kernel-level rootkit will alter or insert kernel-space executing code (e.g. system calls).

1.3 Definition of Trust

Trust can be defined as the level to which a user believes a computer system executes as specified and does nothing else. If a compromise occurs on that computer system and the user discovers it, the level at which the user trusts the system is significantly lessened. The lowered level of trust is understandable because, for example, a rootkit may be installed on the compromised system such that file listing commands hide certain files and thus not execute as specified.

1.4 Overview and Organization

The rest of our paper is outlined as follows. Section 2 discusses the problem of kernel-level rootkits and previous work. Section 3 discusses current generation rootkits that modify the system call table. Section 4 describes our approach for recovering from current generation rootkits. Section 5 shows results of applying our techniques to real-world rootkits. In Section 6 we look at future generation rootkits in terms of their penetration techniques and kernel targets to trojan. Further, we discuss a concept to strengthen our algorithm described in Section 4. Finally, we discuss our conclusions and future work in Section 7.

2 Motivation

With the proliferation of exploits targeted to today's computer systems, an attacker has the ability to compromise a number of systems. Once an attacker has compromised a system, he or she will want to retain access to that system even if the original security hole is patched. In order to retain access to a compromised system, the attacker will often install a rootkit onto the target system. The rootkit will add a backdoor onto the target system that the attacker can use to reenter the system at a later time. We set up a Red Hat 6.2 system on the Georgia Tech honeynet [2], and within a matter of days an attacker had compromised the box and installed a kernel-level rootkit, *r.tgz*, on the system.

If the system administrator notices that an attacker has compromised the system, the administrator will immediately take pervasive actions to block the attacker from reentering the system. However, the attacker may have installed a rootkit to hide the attacker's activities, files, and backdoor entry point. To accomplish this goal, the rootkit will break trust in system reporting facilities (e.g. */bin/ls, /usr/bin/top, /sbin/lsmod*).

With a user-level rootkit, the system administrator can restore trust in the system by using known good utilities (e.g. */mnt/cdrom/ls, /mnt/cdrom/top, /mnt/cdrom/lsmod*). A kernel-level rootkit does not replace binaries but rather replaces running kernel code. We are not aware of any current methodology for restoring trust in a running system in which a kernel-level rootkit has been installed except for a complete reinstallation.

2.1 Related Work

Thimbleby, Anderson, and Cairns developed a mathematical framework to model Trojans and viruses [3]. They discuss a virus that could infect a system querying program in such a way that the querying program itself would be unable to detect that it was infected. This recursive infection leads to the idea behind kernel-level rootkits. When a kernel-level rootkit is installed, tools that check to see if a rootkit is installed are relying on an infected program, the kernel.

Recent research has been conducted developing a methodology for characterizing rootkits [1, 4, 5]. The methodology to characterize rootkits involves determining the Δ between a baseline system and a system compromised with a kernel-level rootkit. The Δ is used to characterize rootkits based on checksums, number of files replaced, number of files added, user level verses kernel level, penetration into the kernel, and so forth.

Government organizations have begun to investigate rootkits. The National Infrastructure Security Co-ordination Centre for the United Kingdom has recently published a report on Trojans and rootkits that discusses detection, remediation, and prevention of rootkits [6]. Their report describes Trojans as Remote Access Tools (RATs) that provide the attacker with a backdoor into the compromised system. The report discusses some of the functionality of RATs, which includes: monitoring system activities (i.e. watch users keystrokes and monitor users), monitor network traffic, use system resources, modify files, relay email (i.e. *spam*).

Other work has been conducted towards detecting and preventing kernel-level rootkits. Kim and Spafford show how a file system integrity checker, *tripwire*, can be used to monitor files for corruption, change, addition, and deletion [7]. In addition to other uses, tripwire can notify system administrators that system binaries have changed. Tripwire must establish a *baseline* for a known good file system. To establish a baseline, tripwire takes a hash (e.g. MD5, CRC, Snefru) of the files at a known good point. The baseline can be used for comparison at later points in time. A binary-level rootkit will replace system binaries, which will set off the "trip wire" and alert the administrator. However, a rootkit designer can counteract tripwire by breaking trust in the reporting tools upon which tripwire relies.

The open source and hacker communities have developed various tools to detect and prevent rootkits, which include: *chkrootkit* [8], *kern_check* [9], *CheckIDT* [10], and *Saint Michael* [11]. The chkrootkit tool is a script that checks systems for signs of rootkits. The chkrootkit script can detect many rootkits including both user-level rootkits and kernel-level rootkits, however some rootkits may evade detection. The kern_check tool is used to detect kernel-level rootkits. The kern_check tool compares the addresses of system calls as defined in the *System.map* file, generated at kernel compile time, to the current addresses of system calls. The CheckIDT tool is a user-level program that can read and restore the interrupt descriptor table, of which the *0x80th* entry points to the system call handler. Saint Michael is a kernel module that monitors the ktext (kernel code in memory) for modifications and attempts to recover from any modification to running kernel code. Saint Michael, however, must be installed prior to a system compromise and is not always successful.

2.2   Broader Scope

Intrusion prevention and intrusion detection have not slowed the growth of computer compromises to an acceptable rate. Research is drifting towards intrusion tolerance, and one element of intrusion tolerance is repair and recovery. In this paper, we begin to explore recovering from system compromises. There may be certain circumstances where the traditional format and reinstall is undesirable such as military systems, enterprise servers, or large clusters of machines.

We are also motivated by the need to perform forensics analysis on compromised systems. When a system is compromised, it is important to gather evidence that can be used for legal purposes[1]. It is important to understand the attack in order to prevent future attacks. Much of the evidence in a compromised system might only be resident in memory, so the evidence must be recovered before powering off the machine. In order to retrieve accurate information in the system, trust must be restored.

Although our work focuses on methods to recover operating system structures from system compromises, in many cases the most damaging part of a compromise is the data on the system that was compromised. This data can include passwords, credit cards numbers, keys, or other sensitive information. Our work does not solve the problem of data compromise, but we think it is another step in that direction. We envision self-healing systems that automatically detect system compromises and halt all attacker activity as quickly as possible in order to minimize the damage done.

3   Analysis of Current Generation Kernel-Level Rootkits

Kernel-level rootkits are rootkits that modify or insert code that runs in kernel mode. These types of rootkits may include user-level components but must have some functionality that resides at the kernel level. From our experience of examining rootkits, we characterize kernel-level rootkits based on two additional characteristics: *Penetration* into the kernel and *Modification* of the system call table.

3.1   Penetration

In terms of *Penetration*, we classify current generation kernel-level rootkits into two types based on their technique used for modifying kernel code. The subclassifications of kernel-level rootkits are:

- *Module* – Kernel-level rootkit that enters malicious code into the kernel by way of a loadable kernel module (LKM). The LKM, once inserted, will usually hide itself from system reporting facilities (i.e. */sbin/lsmod*). We consider these type of rootkits generation I kernel-level rootkits.

---

[1] From discussions with Office of Information Technology personnel at Georgia Tech.

– *User* – Kernel-level rootkit that patches running kernel code with malicious code from a user-space process. Usually, this type of rootkit will access kernel memory through the */dev/kmem* file. The Linux kernel provides access to kernel memory to user-space processes through the */dev/kmem* file. We consider these type of rootkits generation II kernel-level rootkits.

3.2 Modification

In addition, to classifying kernel-level rootkits in terms of penetration, we also classify rootkits in terms of how they modify the system call table, denoted *Modification*. Below are the subclassifications of *Modification*:

– *Entry Redirection* – Redirects individual system calls within the system call table. Modifies original system call table.
– *Entry Overwrite* – Overwrites individual system call code. Does not modify original system call table.
– *Table Redirection* – Redirects the entire system call table. Does not modify original system call table.

Figure 1(a) shows how a kernel-level rootkit can redirect individual system calls within the system call table (SCT). The picture represents kernel memory after a kernel-level rootkit with *Entry Redirection* has been installed on the system. In Figure 1(a), the *sys_fork* system call is unmodified. Notice, however, that system calls number three and number four point to Trojan system calls. The trusted *sys_read* and *sys_write* are still resident in memory, but there are no references to them. The system call table now points to *trojan_read* and *trojan_write*. Any binary executable that relies upon the system calls *sys_read* and *sys_write* will receive untrusted information from the trojaned system calls.

Figure 1(c) represents kernel memory after a rootkit with *Entry Overwrite* has been installed. Again, the *sys_fork* system call is unaltered. Notice, however, that the two system calls *sys_read* and *sys_write* have been overwritten. The actual code for the system calls has been overwritten as opposed to the corresponding table entry that references the system calls. The system call table itself is unaltered with this type of rootkit. We have not seen this type of rootkit but speculate that one could be constructed. The advantage of this type of rootkit is that a program such as *kern_check* [9] would not be able to detect the presence of the rootkit as *kern_check* only checks the system call table, but that is only a short-lived advantage as new tools are developed.

Figure 1(b) represents kernel memory after a rootkit with *Table Redirection* has been installed. The picture depicts kernel memory for the i386 architecture and the Linux kernel. Within the Linux kernel code exists a table called the Interrupt Descriptor Table (IDT) that points to kernel handlers for each interrupt. The *0x80th* vector is a software interrupt that points to the system call table. All user processes invoke a software interrupt *0x80* in order to call a system call [12]. When software interrupt *0x80* is invoked, the interrupt handler for interrupt *0x80* is called, which is the system call handler. The system call handler

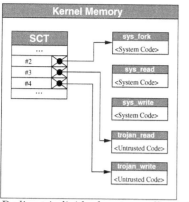

(a) Redirect individual system call pointers

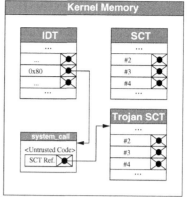

(b) Redirect pointer to entire system call table

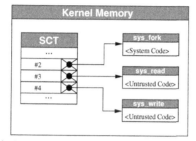

(c) Overwrite individual system call code

Fig. 1. Current rootkit methods to trojan system call table

takes arguments from a user-space process and invokes the requested system call. The system call handler contains a reference to the system call table, which is used to lookup requested system calls. This reference can be changed in order to redirect the entire system call table.

As Figure 1(b) shows, the entire system call table has been redirected to a *Trojan* system call table. The trojan system call table usually contains many of the same entries as the original system call table but with a few key system calls replaced with trojan system calls. We have not shown how the Trojan system call table points to system calls in Figure 1(b) as it is similar to Figure 1(a).

3.3 Sample Rootkits

Table 1 shows a sample listing of kernel-level rootkits that we have classified in terms of their characteristics. We show three rootkits that penetrate kernel space through a *Module* and use *Entry Redirection* to trojan the system call table. The *heroin* rootkit is one of the earliest known kernel-level rootkits and is simply a kernel module that redirects a few key system calls. The *knark* and

Table 1. Sample classification of kernel-level rootkits

Rootkit	Penetration	Modification
heroin	Module	Entry Redirection
knark	Module	Entry Redirection
adore	Module	Entry Redirection
sucKIT	User	Table Redirection
zk	User	Table Redirection
r.tgz	User	Table Redirection

adore rootkits are other module based rootkits that redirect system call table entries.

The second group of rootkits listed are *sucKIT*, *zk*, and *r.tgz*. These rootkits all use table redirection and access kernel memory through the */dev/kmem* file. The *sucKIT* rootkit appears to be one of the pioneering rootkits for *Table Redirection*. The *r.tgz* rootkit was captured on a honeynet [13].

We have not seen any kernel-level rootkits that use *Table Redirection* and are also kernel modules. Similarly, we have not seen any kernel-level rootkits that penetrate the kernel from user space and also use *Entry Redirection*. We speculate that different combinations of rootkit characteristics are possible but see no motivation to build them. In addition, we also speculate that future kernel-level rootkits may redirect the software interrupt handler or the entire interrupt descriptor table, but have not seen any rootkits to date that use this technique. Finally, we have not seen any rootkits that use *Entry Overwrite* to trojan system calls.

4   Recovery by Bootstrapping Trust into the Running Kernel

Since kernel-level rootkits modify the system call table, the system call table must be repaired in order to recover from a kernel-level rootkit. Kernel-level rootkits overwrite portions of the kernel memory, so some information is lost. However, all of the kernel code can be found elsewhere. In Linux based systems, all that is needed is a copy of the kernel image, *vmlinux*. The kernel image contains the system call table and system calls.

Our approach to bootstrap trust into the running kernel is to, essentially, build a whitehat kernel-level rootkit. Our techniques is similar to sucKIT derivative rootkits. We bootstrap a trusted system call table into the running kernel and redirect the entire system call table to our trusted system call table. We strip out a trusted system call table from a known good kernel image, which is on known good media. Below, we discuss our algorithm, implementation, and tools.

4.1   Algorithm

The algorithm has five steps. We use some of the techniques of the sucKIT rootkit.

1. For each system call, allocate kernel memory for the system call and copy a trusted version of the system call into the allocated space. The offset for x86 *call* instructions within each system call must be adjusted when copying the system call to a new location in memory.
2. Allocate kernel memory for the system call table and set the entries of the system call table to point to the trusted system calls from Step 1.
3. Allocate kernel memory for the system call handler and copy a trusted system call handler into the memory. Note that the system call handler should reference the newly allocated trusted system call.
4. Query the *idtr* register to locate the interrupt descriptor table.
5. Set the *0x80th* entry in the interrupt descriptor table to the newly allocated system call handler.

Note that the trusted system calls will come from a trusted image of the kernel. In addition to the sucKIT rootkit's redirection of the entire system call table, we also redirect the *0x80th* entry of the interrupt descriptor table, the system call handler. The reason for this redirection is that we speculate future rootkits may redirect the system call handler and our goal is to rely on as little trust in the system as possible.

It is interesting to note that machine code in the Linux kernel cannot simply be copied from one memory location to another byte by byte. Kernel code compiled with the gcc compiler has many x86 *call* instructions. One form of the *call* instruction specifies a relative offset to the target. When moving kernel code around in memory, these *call* instructions must be modified by adjusting the relative offset. This depends entirely on where the *call* instruction and target are located in memory. Additionally, a known good hash of the code being copied will no longer be valid after modifying the offset value.

4.2   Implementation

We have developed our tools for the i386 architecture. The target system for development is Red Hat 8.0 with the default Linux kernel 2.4.18-4. The installation includes the normal development tools and the Linux kernel sources. Our implementation is a whitehat kernel-level rootkit that can be classified as a *User rootkit that performs Table Redirection.* Below we describe a few aspects of the implementation.

In order to strip the system calls out of a Linux kernel image, we use code from the gdb debugger. The gdb debugger has the ability to parse binaries and strip out functions, which in our case are system calls. Our implementation strips all of the system calls from the given kernel image, vmlinux-2.4.18-14, and feeds them to our whitehat kernel-level rootkit, *recover_kkit.*

Our code uses *Table Redirection* in order to bootstrap trusted code into the running kernel. We use sucKIT's technique to locate the address of the system call handler. Once we have the address of the system call handler, we can parse the system call handler code and locate the reference to the system call table. By replacing the reference to the system call table so that it points to a trusted

```
struct idtr idtr;
struct idt idt80;
ulong old80;
/* Pop IDTR register from CPU */
asm("sidt %0" : "=m" (idtr));
/* Read kernel memory through /dev/kmem */
rkm(fd, &idt80, sizeof(idt80), idtr.base +
    0x80 * sizeof(idt80));
/* Compute absolute offset of
 * system call handler for kmem */
old80 = idt80.off1 | (idt80.off2 << 16);
```

Fig. 2. Source code to find address of system call handler

```
#define   rr(n, x) ,n ((ulong) x)
#define __NR_oldolduname   59
#define  OURSYS __NR_oldolduname
#define syscall2(__type, __name, __t1, __t2) \
    __type __name(__t1 __a1, __t2 __a2)       \
{                                             \
   ulong __res;                               \
   __asm__ volatile                           \
   ("int $0x80"                               \
   : "=a" (__res)                             \
   : "0" (__NR_##__name)                      \
     rr("b", __a1)                            \
     rr("c", __a2));                          \
   return (__type) __res;                     \
}
#define   __NR_KMALLOC OURSYS
static inline syscall2(ulong, KMALLOC, ulong, ulong);
```

Fig. 3. Source Code - Kmalloc as a System Call

system call table, trust can be re-established. The code for locating the system call table can be seen in Figure 2. The key line is the assembly instruction

{asm("sidt %0" : "=m" (idtr));}

This assembly instruction copies the contents of the idtr register into the *idtr* variable. The absolute offset of the interrupt descriptor table can be calculated to locate the interrupt descriptor table. The *0x80th* entry of the interrupt descriptor table points to the system call handler.

Since our implementation is a *User* type implementation, a tricky part of the implementation becomes allocating kernel memory. We use the same technique that the sucKIT rootkit uses. Figure 3 shows the source code used to wrap *kmalloc()*, the kernel memory allocator, into a system call. In the Figure, KMALLOC is the virtual address of the *kmalloc()* function within kernel space. Our code first locates the current system call table by reading the reference to the current table from the system call handler. Then an unused system call, *sys_olduname*, is taken over and replaced with a system call that we will call *sys_kmalloc*. Now a user-space program can allocate kernel memory simply by issuing the system call *sys_kmalloc*.

Using the techniques described above, we have implemented a whitehat rootkit called *recover_kkit*. Our implementation follows the algorithm described above. Below we discuss our tools.

4.3   Tools

Including our whitehat rootkit, we have implemented a suite of tools that can be used to check for and recover from kernel-level rootkits. Our tools can be found on our website [14]. The *read_sctp* tool reads the address of the current system call table and can be used to compare the actual system call addresses to the ones found in the *System.map* file. Our approach differs from *kern_check's* method in that our program looks up the actual system call table as referenced in the running system call handler. Another tool we created is called *ktext*. The *ktext* tool can be used to capture portions of kernel memory in the running kernel. We have used the *ktext* tool to determine a Δ for kernel-level rootkits [5]. Other tools provide the ability to dump system call table entries to a file and write individual system call table entries to kernel memory. Finally, the *recover_kkit* tool can be considered a whitehat kernel-level rootkit that can be used to recover from blackhat kernel-level rootkits.

5   Results on Current Generation Rootkits

In order to test our *whitehat* kernel-level rootkit, we have selected three *blackhat* kernel-level rootkits to recover from. We have chosen to test *knark*, *sucKIT*, and *r.tgz*. These three rootkits represent kernel-level rootkits that penetrate the kernel from both user space and from a kernel module. Also, our tools are tested against both *Entry Redirection* and *Table Redirection* type rootkits. Finally, we also test our tool against *r.tgz* because it represents a rootkit that was captured in the wild on the Georgia Tech Honeynet. Recovering from the *r.tgz* demonstrates how our research can be applied to real-world scenarios. Figure 4 shows the results of our testing.

5.1   Recovering from Knark

In our first scenario, we have installed *knark* on a Red Hat 8.0 system with a Linux 2.4.18 kernel. The results can be seen in Figure 4(a). The first step is to install *knark*. Since knark is loaded as a kernel module, we insert knark with the *insmod* command. The kernel prints a message warning that *knark.o* does not have an agreeable license. The second step is to hide a binary, which we have placed in the */bin* directory, called *rootme*. The *rootme* binary is part of the knark rootkit and is used to execute binaries with root-level permissions from a regular user account. The *hidef* utility is part of the knark rootkit and is used to hide utilities. In the third step, we list files in the */bin* directory that begin

```
[root@h1 cd]# insmod ./knark.o
Warning: loading knark.o will taint the
kernel: no license See
http://www.tux.org/lkml/#export-
tainted
for information about tainted modules
Module knark loaded, with warnings
[root@h1 cd]# ./hidef /bin/rootme
hidef.c by Creed @ #hack.se 1999 <creed
@sekure.net> Port to 2.4 by Cyberwinds
#Irc.openprojects.net 2001
[root@h1 cd]# ./ls /bin/root*
ls: /bin/root*:
No such file or directory
[root@h1 cd]# ./recover_kkit
Trust has been Re-established!
[root@h1 cd]# ./ls /bin/root*
/bin/rootme
```

(a) Recovering from knark

```
[root@h2 cd]# ./sk
/dev/null RK_Init: idt=0xc037d000,
sct[]=0xc0302c30,
kmalloc()=0xc0134fa0, gfp=0x0
Z_Init: Allocating kernel-code
memory... Done,
12747 bytes, base=0xc8090000
BD_Init: Starting backdoor daemon...
Done, pid=1435
[root@h2 cd]# ./ls /sbin/init*
/sbin/init
/sbin/initlog
[root@h2 cd]# ./recover_kkit
Trust has been Re-established!
[root@h2 cd]# ./ls /sbin/init*
/sbin/init
/sbin/initlog
/sbin/initsk12
```

(b) Recovering from sucKIT

```
[root@h3 cd]# ./all
[===== INKIT version 1.3a, Aug 20 2002 <http://www.usg.org.uk> =====]
[====== (c)oded by Inkubus inkubus@hushmail.com> Anno Domini, 2002 ======]
RK_Init: idt=0xc027a000, sct[]=0xc0248928, kmalloc()=0xc0121b88, gfp=0x15 Z_Init:
Allocating kernel-code memory...Done,
13147 bytes, base=0xc9498000 BD_Init: Starting backdoor daemon...Done, pid=1213
[root@h3 cd]# ./ps -p 1213
PID TTY TIME CMD
[root@h3 www]# ./recover_kkit
Trust has been Re-established!
[root@h3 cd]# ./ps -p 1213
PID TTY TIME CMD
1213 ? 00:00:00 all
```

(c) Recovering from r.tgz

Fig. 4. Testing recover_kkit Tool on Three Kernel-Level Rootkits

with *root*. No files are shown indicating that our system cannot be trusted. The fourth step is to install our trusted system call table with our tool *recover_kkit*. We use a read-only cdrom to run our tools. Now notice that upon listing files again, the file *rootme* is seen. Trust has been re-established in the compromised host.

5.2   Recovering from sucKIT

In our second scenario, we have installed *sucKIT* on a Red Hat 8.0 system. The results can be seen in Figure 4(b). The steps are similar to that of knark. We install the rootkit, show that some files are hidden when running the *ls* utility, restore trust, and finally show that the hidden files appear. The *sucKIT* rootkit hides files that have a certain extension, in our case "sk12". The initsk12 file is used in coordination with the init file to load sucKIT upon a reboot. Trust has been re-established in a system that has been compromised with a kernel-level rootkit that performs *Table Redirection*.

5.3   Recovering from r.tgz

In our third scenario, we have installed *r.tgz* on a Red Hat 6.2 system. The results can be seen in Figure 4(c). This rootkit is an example of a real-world scenario. In our scenario, an attacker has compromised the system and starts a Trojan process with the *all* utility. The *all* utility is part of the *r.tgz* rootkit. Initially, the process is hidden, as seen by the first *ps* execution. Then, we install our trusted system call table and issue the *ps* command again. You can see that this time the hidden process shows up. We have successfully re-established trust in a compromised host that was compromised in the wild.

6   Future Generation Rootkits and Recovery

6.1   Possible Penetration Techniques

We have discussed current generation rootkit kernel penetration techniques in Section 3.1. In this section, we discuss kernel penetration techniques that we have not seen in current rootkits while studying existing rootkits. Based on our experience, we speculate that future generation rootkits may use these techniques as more security features are added to kernels to prevent current generation rootkits (i.e. do not allow module loading or access via /dev/mem). Some of these techniques have been discussed in hacker communities; perhaps the techniques are already in use, but we have not seen any evidence to sustain such claims.

- *DMA* – These type of kernel-level rootkits could patch running kernel code with malicious code by programming an attached hardware device to use direct memory access (DMA) to modify kernel code. The concept was introduced in [15], but we have not seen any implementations.
- *Swapped-out Pages* – With root-level access, the attacker has raw access attached hard disks. Memory pages are swapped to the hard disk when memory becomes full. An attacker could use raw hard disk I/O to modify swapped out pages in order to penetrate the kernel. Normally the kernel code is never swapped to the disk, but an attacker could use indirect means to penetrate the kernel through swapped out pages.
- *Local Image* – The kernel image resides as a binary file on the file system. The attacker can modify the kernel image on disk and replace trusted code with trojaned code. The next time the system is rebooted, the trojaned kernel image will be loaded into memory, thus accomplishing the attacker's goal without modifying the running kernel.
- *Distributed Image* – The beginning of the chain of trust starts at the source code and binary distributors. An attacker could compromise a kernel image before it is ever installed on the system (i.e. replace code or binary files with trojans before the kernel is distributed). As Thompson points out, one must "trust the people who wrote the software," or in this case trust the people who distribute the kernel [16].

6.2   Kernel Targets for Kernel-Level Rootkits

The first kernel-level rootkits developed have focused on trojaning the system call table. The system call table is the gateway from user space to kernel space, and so is a natural target and easily trojaned. Tools are being developed to detect and counter these types of rootkits including our tools that allow recovery from a certain class of kernel-level rootkits. As such developments continue, the arms race is escalated. Attackers will continue to develop new means of trojaning the kernel. Below we outline such targets for kernel-level rootkits.

- *System Call Table and Interrupts* – Section 3 gives an extensive discussion of how the system call table is trojaned. Many widely examined rootkits use this means of trojan when targeting the kernel. The interrupt subsystem is a general target of the kernel as interrupts are often serviced on behalf of processes.
- *Redirecting Core Kernel Functionality* – Core kernel functionality is a target of kernel-level rootkits. Examples include the scheduler, process handler, authorization mechanisms, and the virtual file system mechanisms. The latest adore rootkit, adore-ng, targets the virtual file system [17].
- *Redirecting Extremity Functionality* – Extremity functionality includes subsystems of the kernel such as the network drivers, hard disk controllers, network stack, and so forth. For example, a rootkit may want to modify the network stack so that the kernel listens for incoming requests from the attacker, unbeknownst to the system administrator.
- *Modifying Kernel Data Structures* – Finally, the attacker may modify the kernel data structures in addition or instead of modifying the kernel code. For example, a kernel module can be hidden from the *lsmod* command by removing it from the linked list that contains currently loaded kernel modules. This specific technique is already in use today.

6.3   Using a Trusted Immutable Kernel Extension for Recovery

Our algorithm described in Section 4 works well for recovering from system call table modifications but relies on one assumption that must be addressed. The algorithm assumes that a core level of trust remains intact in the system that would allow our program to function as expected. As long as the rootkit installation is well understood and known to be in accordance with our assumption, the method is valid. However, we also address the case in which the full extent of the rootkit is unknown.

Our solution to this problem is a Trusted Immutable Kernel Extension (TIKE) as introduced in [18]. TIKE is an enabling extension that can be used to ensure a trusted path exists within the system even if a kernel-level rootkit is installed. One approach to building TIKE is through virtualization. The production guest system is isolated from the host operating system. The production system may be attacked, but we assume the host operating system is inaccessible from the guest operating system. Therefore, our recovery algorithm can be carried out on the host system, with some modifications, in order to incontestably re-establish trust in the compromised system.

Techniques similar to our recovery method for system call tables can be used for many classes of future generation kernel-level rootkits. Our approach is summarized as follows: For the given kernel function redirection, copy a known good function from a known good kernel image and redirect the running kernel function to the known good function. Furthermore, since the level of trust that is broken may be unknown, the recovery should take place through a mechanism such as TIKE. The technique must be applied to the entire chain of trust in order to be certain that trust has been restored. This technique does not cover all possibilities, but does work for a given class of compromises. For example, rootkits that modify kernel data structures are more difficult to recover from.

7 Conclusions and Future Work

We have studied how trust can be broken in a system, specifically when a kernel-level rootkit is installed. We have applied a methodology to characterize current generation kernel-level rootkits in order to determine how to recover from them. Kernel-level rootkits can be classified in terms of their *Penetration* method and in terms of their system call table *Modification* method. Modern kernel-level rootkits can *Penetrate* the kernel from user space and use *Table Redirection* in order to install a trojaned system call table.

After providing an understanding of kernel-level rootkits, we introduced tools that can be used to recover from kernel-level rootkits. Our tool strips a known good system call table from the provided kernel image and bootstraps the trusted system call table into the running kernel. We then looked at future generation rootkits, further strengthened our algorithm with TIKE, and introduced a methodology to recover from future generation rootkits.

We have begun to explore the notion of re-establishing trust in compromised systems. We have shown that trust can be restored to a system, even if a kernel-level rootkit has been installed. Continued work will include applying our algorithm to more real-world compromises on the Georgia Tech honeynet to help validate the approach. We will also extend our work to cover more than just the system call table towards the entire system in order to establish techniques for self-healing computer systems. Our current work has focused on the Linux operating system, but future work will look into how our methods can be applied to other widely used operating systems.

References

1. Levine, J., Culver, B., Owen, H.: A methodology for detecting new binary rootkit exploits. In: Proceedings IEEE SoutheastCon 2003, (Ocho Rios, Jamaica)
2. Georgia Tech honeynet research project. http://users.ece.gatech.edu/~owen/Research/HoneyNet/HoneyNet_home.htm (2004)
3. Thimbleby, H., Anderson, S., Cairns, P.: A framework for modelling trojans and computer virus infection. The Computer Journal **41** (1998) 445–458

4. Levine, J., Grizzard, J., Owen, H.: A methodology to detect and characterize kernel level rootkit exploits involving redirection of the system call table. In: Proceedings of Second IEEE International Information Assurance Workshop, IEEE (2004) 107–125

5. Levine, J.G., Grizzard, J.B., Owen, H.L.: A methodology to characterize kernel level rootkit exploits that overwrite the system call table. In: Proceedings of IEEE SoutheastCon, IEEE (2004) 25–31

6. Trojan horse programs and rootkits. Technical Report 08/03, National Infrastructure Security Co-Ordination Centre (2003)

7. Kim, G.H., Spafford, E.H.: The design and implementation of tripwire: A file system integrity checker. In: ACM Conference on Computer and Communications Security. (1994) 18–29

8. The chkrootkit website. http://www.chkrootkit.org/ (2004)

9. kern_check.c. http://la-samhna.de/library/kern_check.c (2003)

10. kad (pseudo): Handling interrupt descriptor table for fun and profit, issue 59, article 4. http://www.phrack.org (2002)

11. WWJH.NET. http://wwjh.net (2003)

12. Bovet, D., Cesati, M.: Understanding the Linux Kernel. O'Reilly&Associates, Sebastopol, CA (2003)

13. Levine, J.G., Grizzard, J.B., Owen, H.L.: Application of a methodology to characterize rootkits retrieved from honeynets. In: Proceedings of 5th IEEE Information Assurance Workshop. (2004) 15–21

14. Re-establishing trust tools. http://users.ece.gatech.edu/~owen/Research/trust_tools/trust_tools.htm (2003)

15. sd (pseudo), devik (pseudo): Linux on-the-fly kernel patching without lkm, issue 58, article 7. http://www.phrack.org (2001)

16. Thompson, K.: Reflections on trusting trust. Commun. ACM **27** (1984) 761–763

17. Labs, S.: Subverting the kernel. http://la-samhna.de/library/rootkits/basics.html (2004)

18. Grizzard, J.B., Levine, J.G., Owen, H.L.: Toward a trusted immutable kernel extension (TIKE) for self-healing systems: a virtual machine approach. In: Proceedings of 5th IEEE Information Assurance Workshop. (2004) 444–445

ARCHERR:
Runtime Environment Driven Program Safety

Ramkumar Chinchani, Anusha Iyer,
Bharat Jayaraman, and Shambhu Upadhyaya

University at Buffalo (SUNY), Buffalo, NY 14260
{rc27,aa44,bharat,shambhu}@cse.buffalo.edu

Abstract. Parameters of a program's runtime environment such as the machine architecture and operating system largely determine whether a vulnerability can be exploited. For example, the machine word size is an important factor in an integer overflow attack and likewise the memory layout of a process in a buffer or heap overflow attack. In this paper, we present an analysis of the effects of a runtime environment on a language's data types. Based on this analysis, we have developed Archerr, an automated one-pass source-to-source transformer that derives appropriate architecture dependent runtime safety error checks and inserts them in C source programs. Our approach achieves comprehensive vulnerability coverage against a wide array of program-level exploits including integer overflows/underflows. We demonstrate the efficacy of our technique on versions of C programs with known vulnerabilities such as Sendmail. We have benchmarked our technique and the results show that it is in general less expensive than other well-known runtime techniques, and at the same time requires no extensions to the C programming language. Additional benefits include the ability to gracefully handle arbitrary pointer usage, aliasing, and typecasting.

1 Introduction

Several research efforts have been invested in detecting and preventing vulnerabilities such as buffer overflows and heap corruption in programs. Static bounds checking approaches [1] attempt to detect overflows in arrays and strings. However, due to the undecidability of pointer aliasing [2, 3], some pointer approximations have to be used, which result in false positives. Other techniques like CCured [4] have augmented the C programming language type system to support safety properties, allowing programs to be statically checked based on this new stronger type system. While these techniques provide a systematic way to detect invalid memory accesses, the flexibility of the language is reduced. There is also an additional burden on the programmer to familiarize himself with the new dialect. Finally, runtime safety techniques [5] defer the actual process of checking till program execution. However, they are known to cause significant slowdown in program execution time.

In terms of coverage, while these approaches are able to detect and catch common vulnerabilities such as buffer overflows [6], there are other vulnerabilities in

P. Samarati et al. (Eds.): ESORICS 2004, LNCS 3193, pp. 385–406, 2004.

```
 1. char * alloc_mem(unsigned size) {
 2.   unsigned default_size = 4096;
 3.   unsigned max_size = 0;
 4.   char *retval = (char *)NULL;
 5.
 6.   size = size + 4; /* Add padding */
 7.   max_size = (default_size > size) ? default_size : size;
 8.   retval = (char *) malloc(sizeof(char) * max_size);
 9.   return retval;
10. }
```

Fig. 1. A strawman integer overflow vulnerability

software which manifest in most unexpected ways and have proven very difficult to catch. For example, innocuous-looking errors such as arithmetic overflows and integer misinterpretation have been successfully exploited in ssh [7] and apache [8] daemons. The code snippet in Figure 1 illustrates the possible repercussions of an integer overflow. The function alloc_mem allocates memory of a specified size. Now assume that another subroutine calls this function in order to copy a large string. On a 16-bit architecture, if an attacker is able to send a string whose length lies in the interval $[2^{16} - 4, 2^{16} - 1]$, then in line 6 when some padding is added, an arithmetic overflow will occur. This results in a smaller amount of memory being allocated in lines 7 and 8 than expected. On architectures with wider register words, strings of a much larger length will produce the same effect. Therefore, the same program behaves differently when compiled and executed on different architectures. Such overflow errors also occur in strongly typed languages like Java[1]. These kinds of errors do not speak well about portability and safety. The vulnerability in Figure 1 could have been prevented if an appropriate check was placed before line 6. But this is not a straightforward procedure since it requires the knowledge of the runtime architecture. A strong indication of the relationship between vulnerabilities and runtime architecture is seen in the information provided by CERT alerts which not only report the program which is vulnerable but also the relevant platforms.

1.1 Approach Overview

In this paper, we discuss a comprehensive, architecture-driven approach for statically analyzing and annotating C programs with runtime safety checks.

- **Runtime Environment Dependent Type Analysis**
  Our technique uses runtime environment information to define constraints on the domain of values corresponding to different data types and the operations defined on them. During the course of program execution, variables

---

[1] However, actual out of bound array accesses in Java do raise the java.lang.ArrayIndexOutOfBoundsException exception.

may assume different values, but from a program safety point of view, only a subset of them must be allowed. Pointer aliasing and dynamic binding prevents us from deriving all the constraints statically; for example, the set of valid addresses that can be accessed through pointer dereferencing changes dynamically with program execution. We achieve what compile-time type safety techniques like CCured can but without extending the programming language. Therefore, our technique is cleaner, but we pay a small price in terms of execution slowdown due to runtime checks.

- **Runtime Safety Checks for Data Types; Not Individual Variables**
  Our technique also differs from other runtime bounds checking approaches [5] in terms of the nature of the checks. Protection is achieved by deriving and asserting safety checks for each data type rather than enforcing separate bounds for individual data variables/objects. This allows us to perform the same check on all variables of a given data type. As a result, in spite of pointer aliasing and arbitrary typecasting, the runtime checks incur smaller overheads ($\sim$2-2.5X). We demonstrate that our technique performs comparably to CCured [4] ($\sim$1.5X) and significantly better than Jones and Kelly's bounds checking [9] ($>$ 30X) on the same suite of benchmarks. Moreover, the ability to detect vulnerabilities is not compromised as is evident from running Archerr on vulnerable versions of common C programs. We have been able to detect and preempt heap corruption attacks, buffer overflows, null pointer dereferences, and integer overflow attacks.

- **Checks Not Limited to Only Pointers**
  Pointers and integers are the primary data types of the C programming language. All other data types are either variations or some user-defined combination of these types. As shown in the earlier illustration, vulnerabilities can be directly attributed to not only pointers, but also integers. Therefore, we derive safety checks for both pointers as well as integer operations. To the best of our knowledge, this is the first technique to systematically handle integer-based attacks.

- **Ability to Handle Typecasting**
  A significant positive side-effect of our approach is the ability to handle arbitrary pointer usage, typecasting and complex array definitions. The coarse-grained data type checks on pointer variables implicitly assume that memory that they point to is not immutable. Therefore, typecasting is allowed as long as the variables satisfy the appropriate safety conditions. We explain this with examples in later sections.

1.2 ARCHERR Implementation

Archerr is implemented as a preprocessor for C source programs. Figure 2 gives an overview of the entire code transformation procedure. The original source program passes through a source transformation stage where annotations are inserted into the code. These annotations serve as hooks through which control can be transferred to safety checking routines (implemented as an external library) during runtime. The process of code transformation requires the runtime

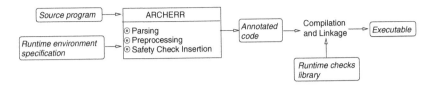

Fig. 2. Modifying the compilation process to integrate runtime specific safety properties

environment specification as a parameter, which is discussed further in the next section. The transformed source code when compiled and statically linked with the safety checking routines produces a safer version of the program. The entire process of code transformation is transparent to the programmer.

The rest of the paper is organized as follows. Section 2 presents the methodology that forms the core of our work. Section 3 enumerates a few optimizations to our main technique to reduce the runtime overhead. Section 4 reports the results that we have obtained through security and performance testing. Section 5 discusses the related efforts and puts our work in perspective, and Section 6 presents conclusions and gives suggestions for future work.

2   Runtime Environment Dependent Type Analysis

The environment we have chosen for our discussion and demonstration is 32-bit Intel architecture running Linux (kernel 2.4.19) and the object file format is *executable and linking format* (ELF) [10]. This is a popular and open development environment and we believe that our work would be most useful in these settings. We provide a brief background on some aspects of this runtime environment that are relevant to our technique as well as describe how they are specified in Archerr. Unless otherwise specified, any discussion will be in the context of only this runtime environment.

Machine Word Size. The ubiquitous Pentium belongs to a 32-bit processor family. The width of a register word is 32 bits and it can hold an absolute binary value in the interval $[0, 2^{32} - 1]$. This defines the domain for meaningful and consistent integer operations. The machine word size by default is 32-bit in the Runtime Environment Specification (REspec). It may also be specified as a command line argument to Archerr.

Memory Layout. When an ELF executable is produced using a compiler, it not only contains the machine code, but also directives to the operating system regarding the memory layout of the various parts of the binary. All this information is contained in the ELF executable header. We can think of the executable as two parts: 1) one containing code and data that directly pertains to the source program, and 2) the other containing control information for purposes like dynamic linking and loading (note: statically linked programs may not have this part). Memory violations can occur if information outside the first part is accessed or modified. Although the information in an ELF executable is created during link-time, it is still possible to create a memory map of the first part by inserting bookkeeping code at compile-time, which groups together variables of similar nature.

Various data types in a program are affected differently by a given runtime environment. We perform a runtime environment dependent type analysis to establish these relationships.

2.1   Analysis of Numerical Types

Let the entire set of signed integers be denoted by $\mathbb{I}$. Let $\mathbb{I}$ be represented by the interval $(-\infty, +\infty)$. For the sake of simplicity, we say that a variable is of type int if it assumes values in $\mathbb{I}$ and is closed under the successor ($succ$) and predecessor ($pred$) operations, that is,

$$x : \texttt{int} \Rightarrow x \in \mathbb{I} \tag{1}$$
$$succ(x : \texttt{int}) = x + 1 : \texttt{int} \tag{2}$$
$$pred(x : \texttt{int}) = x - 1 : \texttt{int} \tag{3}$$

The $succ$ and $pred$ primitives are defined at all points in $\mathbb{I}$. Moreover, the basic integer operations such as addition, subtraction, multiplication and division can all be expressed using these two primitives.

Taking into account the machine architecture, we denote the set of signed integers as $\mathbb{I}_n$ where the subscript n represents the size of a word. For example, the set of signed integers on a 16-bit architecture is $\mathbb{I}_{16}$. Similarly, we can define the machine architecture dependent integer type as $\texttt{int}_n$ where the subscript n denotes the size of a word.

$$x : \texttt{int}_n \Rightarrow x \in \mathbb{I}_n \tag{4}$$

Since the width of a machine word restricts the values that a signed integer can assume on a given architecture, the set $\mathbb{I}_n$ is represented by the interval $[-2^{(n-1)}, 2^{(n-1)} - 1]$. Now, the operations $succ$ and $pred$ can no longer be applied an arbitrary number of times on a given integer and still yield another valid integer. Therefore, the $succ$ and $pred$ operations are correctly defined only as:

$$succ(x : \texttt{int}_n) = \begin{cases} x + 1 & \text{for } x \in [-2^{(n-1)}, 2^{(n-1)} - 2] \\ undefined \text{ elsewhere} \end{cases} \tag{5}$$

$$pred(x : \texttt{int}_n) = \begin{cases} x - 1 & \text{for } x \in [-2^{(n-1)} + 1, 2^{(n-1)} - 1] \\ undefined \text{ elsewhere} \end{cases} \tag{6}$$

Given a program, performing classical type based analysis at the programming language level ensures that operations are correct only at a level described by equation (2) and (3). Clearly, this is not adequate as demonstrated by equations (5) and (6) where n becomes an important factor. We can present arguments on the similar lines for other numerical types such as unsigned int, long int, etc. Interpreting floating point types is a little more complicated. However, the IEEE standard [11] requires the width of a single precision value to be 32 bits and a double precision value to be 64 bits. This makes them relatively independent of the machine architecture.

Ensuring Safety Properties of Numerical Types

Safety properties of numerical types are ensured by asserting their correctness of operations in terms of set closure. For every operation over numerical types, it is important to assert that the properties (5) and (6) hold. The algorithm to generate assertions for some basic operations on the int type are given Table 1.

Table 1. Assertions for basic numerical operators

---

if $a \geq 0, b \geq 0$, then
$$a + b \Rightarrow assert : a \leq (\mathsf{MAXINT} - b)$$
if $a \geq 0, b < 0$, then
$$a - b \Rightarrow assert : a \leq (\mathsf{MAXINT} + b)$$
if $a < 0, b \geq 0$, then
$$a - b \Rightarrow assert : a \geq (\mathsf{MININT} + b)$$
if $a < 0, b < 0$, then
$$a + b \Rightarrow assert : a \geq (\mathsf{MININT} - b)$$

$\forall\, a,\, b,$

$a \times b \Rightarrow$ assert: $a \geq \lfloor \mathsf{MININT}/b \rfloor \,\wedge\, a \leq \lfloor (\mathsf{MAXINT}/b \rfloor$

$a \div b \Rightarrow$ assert: $b \neq 0$

$a \% b \Rightarrow$ assert: $b \neq 0$

Let $\diamond$ be an operator such that $\diamond \in \{+, -, \times, \div, \%\}$. Let a : int, b : int be the two operands of this operator. Let MAXINT be $2^{n-1} - 1$ and MININT be -2^{n-1}. Then, in order to ensure the safety of the operator $\diamond$, the assertions in Table 1 must be placed before the actual operation. For an insight into the validity of these assertions, consider the first assertion. When a, b are both nonnegative, there is no danger of an underflow under the operator $+$. All that remains is to check that $a + b \leq MAXINT$. This can be safely done by asserting $a \leq (MAXINT - b)$. Consider the bitwise operators $\{\&, |, \hat{}, <<, >>\}$. Among these, only the shift operators, $<<$ and $>>$ are unsafe. They are equivalent to multiplication and division by 2 respectively, and similar checks in Table 1 apply. The assignment operator $=$ does not cause any changes in values if it is applied to variables of identical types. Therefore, type correctness properties will ensure the right use of the assignment operator.

2.2 Analysis of Pointer Types

We now extend the architecture-dependent analysis to pointer types. A pointer variable has two aspects - a memory location and an association to a type. We will use the notation $p : q(\tau)$ to refer to a pointer variable p that points to a memory location q which holds a value of type τ. For example, a pointer of type char **p is represented as $p : q(\text{char } *)$ and it implies p is a pointer to a variable of type char *. The possible values for a pointer variable, like numerical types, are dependent on a given architecture and runtime environment. They are governed by the address format and the address space used. While a pointer variable may be assigned any arbitrary address, a *safe* assignment requires that the pointer variable be assigned a *valid* address. We evolve some theoretical machinery before any further discussion.

For the convenience of representation of sets, we use interval ranges. The set $\{a, a+1, a+2, \ldots, b\}$ is denoted as $[a, b]$. The insertion and deletion of ranges are defined in terms of set union and set difference as follows, where S is a given set and $[a, b]$ is a range that is inserted or deleted.

$$append(S, [a, b]) : S = S \cup [a, b] \tag{7}$$

$$remove(S, [a, b]) : S = S - [a, b] \tag{8}$$

Let $\mathbb{P}$ be the set of all valid addresses. The elements of $\mathbb{P}$ are represented as interval ranges $[a_i, b_i]$ and $\mathbb{P} = \bigcup_i [a_i, b_i]$. Then a pointer p is said to be *safe* if the following is true.

$$p : q(\tau) \Rightarrow \exists [a_i, b_i] \in \mathbb{P} \text{ s.t. } p \in [a_i, b_i] \ \wedge \ p + |\tau| \in [a_i, b_i] \tag{9}$$

where $|\tau|$ denotes the size allocated to data types of type τ and p used alone on the right hand side represents an address. Let us denote the function or primitive that enforces this property as *validate(p)*.

Pointer arithmetic is generally allowed in a language supporting pointers and we can define this arithmetic in terms of the successor and predecessor operations but unlike integer arithmetic these are interpreted slightly differently. An operation on a pointer variable containing an address yields another address. Note that these operations defined by (10) and (11) are safe only if they too obey (9).

$$succ(p : q(\tau)) \Rightarrow p + |\tau| \tag{10}$$

$$pred(p : q(\tau)) \Rightarrow p - |\tau| \tag{11}$$

Fig. 3 (a) and (b) show safe pointer assignments. The outer rectangle represents a valid address range and the shaded inner rectangle represents some variable or data object that pointer p points to. If the entire object lies completely inside a valid address range, then the assignment is safe. Fig. 3 (b) shows an object that straddles two valid address ranges but as these ranges are contiguous, they collapse into one and no part of the object lies in an invalid region.

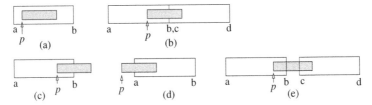

Fig. 3. (a), (b) Safe pointer assignments whereas (c), (d), (e) unsafe pointer assignments

However, when one of the address ranges becomes invalid, then any references to this object become invalid. In Fig. 3 (c), (d) and (e), the pointer p points to data objects or variables which are not completely inside a valid address range. This is possible because C language allows arbitrary type casting and memory referencing as illustrated by the example in Figure 4. In line 11, an unsafe pointer assignment allows a member of the structure to be accessed that actually lies outside the memory region allocated in line 7. This is an example of the scenario represented by Fig. 3 (c).

```
1. struct st { char ch; int i; };
2.
3. int main() {
4.   char *p;
5.   struct st *pst;
6.
7.   p = (char *) malloc(sizeof(char));
8.   pst = (struct st *) p;
9.   pst->i = 10;
10.
11.   return 0;
12. }
```

Fig. 4. An unsafe pointer assignment

The key to enforcing pointer safety within the Archerr framework involves bookkeeping of the various objects allocated/deallocated during the lifetime of a process' execution. This is accomplished through the premise that they must reside in one of the following regions and are accessible through the program itself.

Valid Address Map for Data Segment. The data segment holds all initialized and uninitialized global and static variables. The data segment is initialized based on the information present in the object file, which contains more than just these variables. Therefore, not all memory in the data segment should be accessible from the program. From a program's perspective, the memory that corresponds to only the global and static variables should be visible. However, virtual addresses and bounds for these sections are known only at link-time when all symbols and names have been resolved. But it is still possible to construct this address map at compile-time using a simple workaround. Let var_i be some variable declared in a C program as either a static, extern or a global variable. Then the address range which bounds this variable is given by $[\&var_i, \&var_i + |\tau_i|]$, where $\&$ represents the 'address-of' operator and $|\tau_i|$ is the size allocated for this ith variable which is of type τ_i. Some examples are the first three declarations and their corresponding ranges below:

```
int i;              [&i, &i + sizeof(i)];
char *str1;         [&str1, &str1 + sizeof(str1)];
char str2[10];      [&str2, &str2 + sizeof(str2)];
char *str = ''abc''; [&str, &str + sizeof(str)] ∪
                    [str, str + strlen(str)]
```

String literals which are used to initialize pointer variables of type char $*$ are allocated in the data segment. They, however, do not have an l-value and have to be handled differently as shown in the last declaration above. The accessible portion of the data segment, denoted by $\mathbb{D}$ is the union of all such memory ranges, i.e., $\mathbb{D} = \bigcup_i [\&var_i, \&var_i + |\tau_i|]$. Since the data segment persists unaltered until the termination of the program execution, $\mathbb{D}$ needs to be constructed only once and no further modifications are required. $\mathbb{D}$ is constructed at the program's entry point, typically the first executable statement of *main()*.

Valid Address Map for Heap Segment. Memory can also be allocated and deallocated dynamically during program execution via the *malloc()* and *free()* family of library calls. This memory resides in the heap segment, denoted by $\mathbb{H}$. Let *malloc()*, for example, allocate a chunk of memory, referenced by a pointer p, of type τ and size n. The corresponding address range is represented by $[p, p + n \times |\tau|]$. Then, $\mathbb{H} = \bigcup_i [p, p + n \times |\tau|]$. An additional level of verification is required for deallocation, i.e. the *free()* library function, to prevent heap corruption. The only addresses that can be passed as an argument to *free()* are those that were obtained as a return value of the *malloc()* family of calls.

Valid Address Map for Stack Segment. The stack segment contains memory allocated to not only the automatic and local variables, but also other information such as the caller's return address. This makes it one of the primary targets for an attacker since control flow can be diverted to a malicious payload by overflowing a buffer. We take advantage of the fact that variables on the stack are allocated within well-defined frames. Let $\mathbb{S}$ denote the set of valid addresses allocated on the stack. The stack frames on the Intel architecture are defined by the contents of the registers EBP and ESP at the function entry points. The address range corresponding to a stack frame is [ESP, EBP]. This range is added to $\mathbb{S}$ at a function's entry point and it is removed at each function exit point. Note even before the program begins execution, some information is already on the stack, i.e., *argc*, *argv* and *env* as described in [12]. The corresponding address ranges remain valid until the program terminates and they should be added only once to $\mathbb{S}$ at the program entry point. For our implementation, we used inline assembly to capture the values of the EBP and ESP registers. We observed that *gcc* (version 2.95.4) allocates all the memory required in increments of 16 bytes at function entry point whether there are nested blocks or not, hence making it relatively easy to obtain the bounds of a stack frame. Other compilers may implement this differently. For this reason, the above method gives a slightly coarse-grained bound on the stack frame. A tighter bound would be provided by the union of memory ranges occupied by variables on the stack just as in the case of the data segment. But this construction could cause significant computational overheads.

The bookkeeping operations that were described construct a map of valid address ranges, i.e., $\mathbb{P} = \mathbb{D} \cup \mathbb{H} \cup \mathbb{S}$. Figure 5 gives a simple example to show how $\mathbb{P}$ is constructed in a C program. More examples are provided in the appendix. Initially, $\mathbb{P}$ is an empty set and is populated and maintained as the program executes. In our implementation, address ranges belonging to the stack, data and heap are maintained in three separate linked lists. During address range search, these lists are indexed by the higher order bits of an address, for example, a stack address starts with 0xbfff –. Also, in order to exploit spatial and temporal locality of programs, we perform insertions and subsequent deletions at the head of the lists. We also maintain a LRU cache of range entries to speed up address range lookups. In spite of these careful optimizations, the worst case is still $O(n)$ in the number of address ranges. However, production level programs are rarely written in the manner which achieves this worst-case and our empirical observations have shown the common case to be $O(1)$. All the memory corresponding to the bookkeeping operations of Archerr have to be kept private and not be a part of $\mathbb{P}$ or else the set of valid addresses may reach an inconsistent or incorrect state defeating the very purpose of this technique. This is accomplished through the pointer checks which also assert that pointer dereferences never access this private memory.

Handling Function Aliasing Through Function Pointers

The stack segment is generally not marked non-executable[2] because some important operating system mechanisms (such as signal delivery) and software (such as xfree86 4.x) require that code be executed off of the stack. This makes it difficult to specify safety properties for function pointers since they need not point only to the text segment. Currently, Archerr handles function aliasing through function pointers by raising warnings during preprocessing if function names are encountered which are neither previously defined not already recognized by Archerr such as the malloc family of system calls. We extend this checking to runtime by maintaining a list of known function addresses and raising warnings when function pointers are assigned values not belonging to this list.

Handling String Library Functions

Most string functions operate on character pointers of type char * either through assignment or pointer increments. For example, *strlen()* function takes a variable

---

[2] Kernel patches are available that make the stack non-executable, but it breaks some applications and in any case, attacks exist that can bypass it.

Unannotated version	Annotated version
1. `struct st {`	1. `struct st {`
2. `  char ch;`	2. `  char ch;`
3. `  int i;`	3. `  int i;`
4. `};`	4. `};`
5.	5.
6. `struct st glbl;`	6. `struct st glbl;`
7.	7.
8. `int foo(int arg)`	8. `int foo (int arg)`
9. `{`	9. `{`
10. `static int sta;`	10. `static int sta;`
11. `...`	11. $append(\mathbb{P}, current\_stack\_frame)$
12.	12. $append(\mathbb{P}, [\&sta, \&sta + \texttt{sizeof(sta)}])$
13. `return 0;`	13. `...`
14. `}`	14. $remove(\mathbb{P}, current\_stack\_frame)$
15.	15. `return 0;`
16.	16. `}`
17.	17.
18. `int main(int argc, char *argv[])`	18. `int main(int argc, char *argv[])`
19. `{`	19. `{`
20. `char *buf;`	20. `char *buf;`
21.	21. $append(\mathbb{P}, \text{address ranges of argc, argv})$
22. `buf = (char *)` `malloc(sizeof(char)*32);`	22. $append(\mathbb{P}, current\_stack\_frame)$
23. `...`	23. $append(\mathbb{P}, [\&glbl, \&glbl + \texttt{sizeof(glbl)}])$
24. `foo(32);`	24.
25. `...`	25. `buf = (char *)malloc(sizeof(char)*32);`
26. `free(buf);`	26.
27. `return 0;`	27. `if (buf) {`
28. `}`	28. $append(\mathbb{P}, [buf, buf + \texttt{sizeof(char)*32}])$
29.	29. $\mathbb{H} = \mathbb{H} \cup buf$
30.	30. `}`
31.	31. `...`
32.	32. `foo(32);`
33.	33. `...`
34.	34. `if (buf` $\notin \mathbb{H}$`) then raise exception`
35.	35. $remove(\mathbb{P}, [buf, buf + \texttt{sizeof(char)*32}])$
36.	36. $\mathbb{H} = \mathbb{H} - buf$
37.	37. `free(buf);`
38.	38. $remove(\mathbb{P}, current\_stack\_frame)$
39.	39. `return 0;`
40.	40. `}`

Fig. 5. The construction of the map of valid address ranges $\mathbb{P}$ in a program

of type **char** * and increments it till it finds the end of string marker, i.e., the NULL character. We have specified earlier that if p is assigned a valid address, then the operations that increment or decrement are safe only when properties (10) and (11) hold. It is useful to define primitives that determine the amount by which p can be safely incremented or decremented. Since these primitives are essentially delta operators, they are denoted as Δ^+ and Δ^-. Let $p : q(\tau)$ be a pointer, then

$$\Delta^+(p) = \begin{cases} \lfloor (b-p)/|\tau| \rfloor & \text{if } \exists [a,\, b] \text{ and } a \leq p \leq b \\ 0 & \text{otherwise} \end{cases} \qquad (12)$$

$$\Delta^-(p) = \begin{cases} \lfloor (p-a)/|\tau| \rfloor & \text{if } \exists [a,\, b] \text{ and } a \leq p \leq b \\ 0 & \text{otherwise} \end{cases} \qquad (13)$$

Since *strlen()* merely attempts to find the end of string marker, i.e., the NULL character, we consider this function to be safe in terms of memory accesses. Other string functions potentially modify memory locations and the goal is to prevent any invalid accesses. Assertions are inserted before statements in the code to ensure safety properties. When an assertion fails, the program raises an exception and terminates gracefully. If the requirement is continued execution, then there is yet another approach. We can simply modify these statements to produce a safer version. Table 2 enumerates a few of such conversions. The min operator has its usual meaning of finding the argument with the smallest value. Note that all the arguments should first be valid addresses and hence, property (9) should be asserted before these annotated statements.

Table 2. Modified string library functions to support safety properties

Original statement	Safer annotated statement
strlen(str)	strlen(str)
strcpy(dest, src)	strncpy(dest, src, min(Δ^+(dest), Δ^+(src)))
strncpy(dest, src, n)	strncpy(dest, src, min(n, Δ^+(dest), Δ^+(src)))
gets(dest)	fgets(dest, Δ^+(dest), stdin)
fgets(dest, n, fp)	fgets(dest, min(n, Δ^+(dest)))
strcat(dest,src)	strncat(dest, src, min(Δ^+(dest + strlen(dest)), Δ^+(src)))
strncat(dest, src, n)	strncat(dest, src, min(n , Δ^+(dest + strlen(dest)), Δ^+(src), strlen(src))))

2.3   User Defined Types

User defined data types are constructed using the basic data types. The operations on these new data types can be translated to equivalent operations of the constituent basic data types and safety properties may be individually asserted on these members. For example, consider a user defined structure containing a pointer variable as in Figure 6. One can assign an instance of this structure to another and this implicitly results in the addresses contained by the pointer variables to be copied. As long as a member variable is validated before use, unsafe behavior will not occur. Similarly, union types are simply an instance of implicit typecasting. Since we validate data types and not objects, it is straightforward to handle union types.

```
1. typedef struct {
2.   char *str;
3.   int i;
4. } USERDEF;
5.
6. int main() {
7.   USERDEF a, b;
8.
9.   a.str = malloc(sizeof(char)*2);
10.  a.i = 0;
11.  b = a;
12.  strcpy(b.str, ''a''); /*safe*/
13.
14.  return 0;
15. }
```

Fig. 6. Handling user defined types

```
1. typedef struct { int a; int b; } LG;
2. typedef struct { int a; } SM;
3.
4. int main() {
5.   SM *a = (SM *) malloc(sizeof(SM));
6.   SM *b = (SM *) malloc(sizeof(SM));
7.   LG *a_alias;
8.
9.   a_alias = a;
10.  a_alias->a = b->a;
11.
12.  return 0;
13.}
```

Fig. 7. Undisciplined typecasting

2.4 Typecasting

void * is the generic pointer type in C and typecasting is done to retrieve the actual object. This type of conversion is commonly seen in C programs. In our approach, since the only enforced constraint is that a program's memory accesses remain confined to the map of valid addresses, it results in a minimal set of safety properties. Data within these confines can now be interpreted as required and therefore, there is no loss of flexibility even in the presence of pointer arithmetic and typecasting. However, there are instances where typecasting could introduce false positives in Archerr's framework. Consider the unannotated example in Figure 7. Before line 10, a_alias would be validated as of type LG * using rule (9). The code is valid, yet the check would signal a violation. This is due to the fact that our technique relies in small part on the static types of pointers at the preprocessing stage. This style of programming although not unsafe, is undisciplined. Archerr inadvertently discourages this style and therefore, false positives in such cases are acceptable.

3   Optimizations

An overly aggressive approach to code annotation introduces a large number of redundant checks causing an unnecessary overhead during execution. Fortunately, many aspects of our technique are amenable to optimization, reducing the slowdown significantly. Currently, some of these optimizations are done in an ad-hoc manner. Also, this is a partial list and research in this direction is a part of our ongoing and future work.

Arithmetic Operations. Our observation was that correctness of most of the arithmetic operations could be verified statically and therefore, checks do not have to be inserted for these operations. Typically, checks have to be inserted only for operations on integers whose values are determined at runtime and operations involving dereferenced integer pointers. Otherwise Archerr validates all statically resolvable operations during the preprocessing stage, significantly reducing the number of inserted runtime checks.

Pointer Dereferencing. Property (9) implies that when a pointer variable is encountered in a program either in simple assignment or dereference, it must be validated. This results in a large number of checks, many of which are redundant. Mere address assignments to pointer variables have no direct security implications. The only locations where checks are mandatory are those where pointer dereferencing occurs through the $*$ and $->$ operators. This reduces the number of checks and improves the execution performance without loss of safety. However, a downside to this optimization is that the point where an exception is raised due to an invalid memory access need not be the actual source of the problem; it could be several statements earlier.

Loops. When the primary purpose of a loop is to initialize or access data using an index, then the safety checks instead of being placed inside the loop can be placed outside. The following example shows an unoptimized piece of code followed by its optimized version. Note that Archerr currently does not implement this optimization, however it is on our list of future work.

Unoptimized version	Optimized version

```
1. char *buffer;              1. char *buffer;
2.                            2.
3. buffer = (char *)          3. buffer = (char *)
     malloc(sizeof(char)*100);    malloc(sizeof(char)*100);
4.                            4.
5. for (i = 0; i < 100; i++) { 5. validate(buffer) ∧
6.    validate(&buffer[i])         assert(Δ⁺(buffer) < 100)
7.    buffer[i] = (char)0;     6. for (i = 0; i < 100; i++) {
8. }                           7.    buffer[i] = (char)0;
                               8. }
```

4   Experiments and Results

We have evaluated Archerr both for vulnerability coverage and overheads due to runtime checks. Our test machine was a 2.2GHz Pentium 4 PC with 1024MB of RAM.

4.1   Security Testing

Our technique is a passive runtime checking approach that can detect vulnerabilities only when an exploit causes a safety violation in some execution path. Therefore, our security tests involve programs with known vulnerabilities and publicly available exploit code. The SecurityFocus website is an excellent repository of such vulnerabilities and corresponding exploit code.

sendmail-8.11.6. sendmail is a widely used mail server program. This particular version of sendmail shipped with RedHat Linux 7.1 has a buffer overflow vulnerability [13]. We installed this distribution and tested the exploit code, which successfully obtained a root shell. We rebuilt the sources after running it through Archerr and ran the same exploit. The attack was detected as soon as a pointer variable dereferenced an address outside the valid map.

GNU indent-2.2.9. indent is a C program beautifier. This particular version of indent has been reported to have a heap overflow vulnerability [14], which can be exploited using a malicious C program. Supposedly, it copies data from a file to a 1000 byte long buffer without sufficient boundary checking. The exploit code is able to construct this malicious file, which we used to launch the attack. At first, we caught a potential null pointer dereferencing bug. Once the corresponding check was disabled, we were able to catch the actual heap overflow.

man 1.5.1. This program is reported to have a format string vulnerability [15]. The exploit code is supposed to give an attacker a root shell through a format string argument to vsprintf(), which the attacker can control. However, when we tried to replicate the same conditions for the exploit code to work, we got a segmentation fault through the vsprintf() call. Nevertheless, this showed the existence of a format string bug. Archerr's annotations could not detect this attack mainly because vsprintf() is a part of an external library that has not been annotated. This attack could have been caught if Archerr annotations were applied to vsprintf() code. This is one of the limitations of Archerr that it cannot protect a source program if it has not been processed.

pine 4.56. pine is a popular mail client. Version 4.56 and earlier are susceptible to an integer overflow attack [16]. No exploit code was publicly available for this vulnerability. However, a mail posting [17] provided directions to construct an attack. The problem can be traced to addition operations on a user-controlled signed integer variable, which cause it to become negative. In the following code, it is used as an index into a buffer, resulting in this vulnerability. Compiling this version was very error-prone due to the non-standard build process. However, once it was setup and annotations were inserted, the attack was detected before an integer overflow could occur.

4.2   Performance Testing

We chose the Scimark 2 [18] benchmark for the purposes of evaluating the effect of Archerr's annotations on execution time. This benchmark uses the following kernels: 1) Fast Fourier Transform (FFT) - this kernel exercises complex arithmetic, shuffling, non-constant memory references and trigonometric functions, 2) Jacobi Successive Over-relaxation (SOR) - this algorithm exercises basic memory patterns, 3) Monte Carlo integration (MC) approximates the value of PI, by computing certain integrals, 4) Sparse Matrix Multiply (SMM) - this kernel exercises indirection addressing and non-regular memory references, 5) Dense LU

Matrix Factorization (LU) - this kernel exercises linear algebra kernels (BLAS) and dense matrix operations.

In order to understand the overheads imposed by Archerr, we ran the original benchmark without any source code annotations. Then we compiled only the pointer checks. Subsequently, we enabled the full functionality of Archerr. The overheads imposed are reported in Table 3. The overheads incurred by pointer checks alone are in the range of 1.2-3.8X. Additional checks on integer arithmetic causes an overall slowdown of 1.23-4.4X. The composite score of this benchmark suite gives an average slowdown of 2.3X with pointer checks and 2.5X with both pointer and integer checks. The overhead is noticeable but not excessive. We also ran the Scimark2 suite against two well-known language security techniques - CCured [4], a type-based approach, and Jones & Kelly's bounds-checking [9], a primarily runtime checking approach, for the purposes of comparison. CCuring the Scimark2 benchmarks caused them to run 1.5X slower on an average, and Jones and Kelly's technique incurs a composite performance hit of > 30X. The significant gains observed over Jones & Kelly's technique is mainly because our technique provides type-based coarse-grained safety as opposed to strict object-centric safety. Our technique is also only 1X more expensive than CCured. We noticed a peculiarity in our results that running the source code through some of these techniques seemed to improve the performance. Such anomalies have also been reported in [19] and are attributed to the compiler's internal optimizations.

Table 3. MFlops: original vs. only pointer checks vs. pointer and arithmetic checks, and comparison with CCured and Jones & Kelly's technique

Kernel	Original	Ptr Checks	Slow down	Ptr and Int Checks	Slow down	CCured	Slow down	J&K	Slow down
FFT	89.36	31.80	2.81X	24.42	3.66X	60.23	1.49X	5.22	17.12X
SOR	178.42	149.93	1.19X	145.07	1.23X	295.55	-1.66X	7.80	22.87X
MC	30.93	19.70	1.57X	16.72	1.85X	32.90	-1.06X	3.60	8.59X
SMM	271.93	70.27	3.87X	61.80	4.40X	103.70	2.62X	3.76	72.32X
LU	341.33	121.90	2.80X	116.10	2.94X	130.78	2.61X	6.86	49.76X
Composite score	182.39	78.28	2.33X	72.38	2.52X	124.63	1.46X	5.45	33.47X

4.3   Impact of Source Code Size and Runtime Image

The number of checks inserted is directly dependent on the number of pointer dereferences and integer operations that could not be resolved statically. We have seen a source code bloat in the order of 1.5-2.5X. Increase in the runtime image can be attributed to the statically linked library and the in-memory housekeeping information regarding address ranges. Our empirical results show that the overall impact on the runtime image is nomimal (1.2-1.4X). This is due to the following reasons. The Archerr library code is partly written in assembly and partly in C, and the resulting library image is small. Address ranges are implemented as very small data structures. Furthermore, our coarse-grained approach allows multiple address ranges to be collapsed to a single address range when memory on heap or new stack frames are allocated. Although addition or deletion of address ranges could potentially result in $O(n)$ behavior in the worst case, the memory consumption is not significant in the general case.

5   Comparison with Related Work

Several important research efforts have attempted to empower the programmer with techniques and tools to produce safe code. We briefly describe these approaches and compare them with the techniques proposed in this paper.

5.1   Bounds Checking

Several commercial and open-source tools [9, 20, 21] exist that perform memory access and bounds checking. Jones et al. [9] describe a technique that checks both pointer use and pointer arithmetic, and this work is the closest to our approach in this regard. Safety is addressed through source code annotations by ascertaining that pointer operations are only permitted to take place within an object and not across objects. However, there are some drawbacks that we improve upon. Most markedly, our technique is significantly more efficient than their technique. Also, their technique only addresses pointer usage, while we present a more holistic approach. By inserting dead space around each object, they can detect violations at runtime. This rigid check structure results in inability to handle complex data structures such as multi-dimensional arrays, arrays within arrays, arbitrary typecasting, and finally, excessive runtime overhead. We are able to address these aspects effectively in our approach, mainly due to the fact that we relax the strict object-centric view. Finally, they have implemented their technique as a GNU C compiler extension, while we make no modifications to the C compiler.

Purify [20] is a widely-used tool, which processes binary code to insert runtime memory access checks. However, Purify is used mainly for debugging purposes because of its inefficiency. Also, it will some times permit stack corruption by allowing a program to access past stack-allocated arrays. Archerr clearly guards against this misuse by maintaining maps of delimited stack frames. Wagner et al. [1] proposed a proactive static analysis technique that formulates the buffer overruns as a integer range analysis problem by specifying integer bounds on arrays and strings, and solving the constraint system. Since it is a compile-time technique that actively pursues violations, it can detect many of them even before compilation. In contrast, our technique is a runtime detection technique; hence, it is passive and violations are detected only when the corresponding execution path is active. However, [1] handles pointer typecasting and aliasing in an ad-hoc manner and this approximation raises several false positives.

5.2   Stack Protection

StackGuard [22], StackShield [23] and ProPolice [24] are effective runtime techniques that prevent stack overrun. StackGuard [22] is a compiler extension that adds a random padding called the *canary* around the return address on the stack. These bytes are checked at each function entry and exit. StackShield [23] moves the return address to a location that cannot be overflowed. Manipulating the stack frame affects compatibility and can break applications such as debuggers, which probe the stack frame for function call information. Protection in ProPolice [24] is accomplished by inserting checks during compilation and reordering variables to prevent pointer corruption. All these techniques use architecture-specific information about stack layout in a clever manner. Focussing mainly on stack protection, although very efficient, can allow attacks [25] to bypass these techniques.

5.3   Type Based Safety

Type theory provides a formal framework to express and verify certain correctness properties of programs. Statically analyzing programs based on type correctness can detect many common programmer errors. Some of these correctness notions have been extended to express safety properties. A few research efforts have targeted the C programming language's flexibility of pointers and have augmented the type system to produce safer dialects. Cyclone [26] introduces a notion of region based type theory into C. All variables apart from their type, have an additional attribute called a *region*, which is determined based on where the variable resides, i.e., stack or heap. Analysis with the help of this concept allows the detection of invalid region based memory accesses in programs. CCured [4] describes an augmented type system for C to prevent invalid memory accesses due to pointers. Based on their usage, pointers are segregated as safe and unsafe. Programs can be statically analyzed and while most pointer usage can be checked statically, some of them require runtime checks. There are cases where a program will stop even when it is safe and manual intervention is necessary. In the paper [4], they report a execution slowdown of up to 150% on their benchmarks. We have observed similar slowdown on our benchmarks and our technique is comparable to CCured in terms of overhead. The caveat to these approaches is that safety is not achieved transparently and the programmer is burdened by a possibly steep learning curve in both cases. Some of the concepts in this paper, such as static analysis of basic types, region and pointer-based analysis are similar. One advantage to our approach as well as to some of the other techniques described in Section 5.1 is that source code need not be rewritten or ported and programmers are minimally affected. Again, we cover pointers and more.

5.4   Other Relevant Techniques

From an attacker's point of view, chances of successfully overflowing a buffer are largely dependent on a good approximation of its address. Based on this premise, pointers and location of objects can be randomized in order to render attacks ineffective. Unlike the bounds-checking techniques, the following [19,27] incur much less overhead but possibly may be bypassable by attackers as discussed in [19]. The PAX project [28] incorporates the technique of ASLR (Address Space Layout Randomization). ASLR randomizes the location of key memory spaces, such as the stack and the heap. Sekar et al. [27] work to randomize the absolute locations of all code and data segments as well as the relative distance between memory objects. Cowan et al. in [19] describe the a similar, yet more fine-grained tool PointGuard that obfuscates all memory addresses via encryption using a key that is generated at run-time. Orchestrating a buffer-overflow attack in this scenario requires knowledge of the secret key. Similar to many of the above tools, these approaches are focused solely on ensuring safe pointer manipulation.

Libsafe [29] is a binary level technique that provides protection against buffer overflows by intercepting calls to "unsafe" string functions and performing a bounds check on the arguments. We address the problem of unsafe functions by inserting sanity checks on the arguments in the source code prior to compilation.

6   Conclusion and Future Work

In this paper, we have described a novel approach for statically analyzing and annotating code in order to ensure safe execution in a particular runtime environment. Access checks that are placed in the code ascertain that the code is performing numerical computations and accessing memory in a safe manner. Since there is no notion of well-defined and immutable objects per se, memory within the valid address ranges can be typecast arbitrarily. This largely retains the flexibility of the language. If code annotations are performed in an exhaustive way, then the slowdown is not negligible but very useful for debugging purposes. On the other hand, production systems require efficient execution and in such a scenario, optimizations can reduce the number of annotations. By making the runtime environment specification as a separate parameter, it is possible to generate annotated versions of the same source code that is safe for each instance of the specified runtime environment, subsequently, providing tighter security.

Although our technique provides coverage against a wide variety of vulnerabilities, the coverage is limited to the source code that our technique processes. Therefore, vulnerabilities in external libraries cannot be handled unless the libraries are also annotated. Like other code annotation techniques, there is little protection against runtime process image tampering and manipulation using programs such as *gdb*. This implies that protection against exploits is limited to those which do not require direct access to the process image. Although this technique is practical with small impacts on performance, it does not solve all the problems by itself. Therefore, our recommendation is to use this tool in tandem with more proactive approaches.

This paper lays the basic groundwork for a useful and efficient runtime detection technique to prevent exploits. We are investigating further improvements to the technique. In its present form, this technique is reactive and can only be used to prevent exploits. But there is scope to provide detection capabilities at the preprocessing stage itself. For example, pseudo interval ranges can be created even during compilation stage to represent the data segment and the stack frames, and then program execution can be simulated partially to detect possible violations. At this point, it is only a speculation and we are looking at issues regarding this possibility. The runtime environment specified in Section 2 has been the focus of this work. However, we are also looking at other combinations that can serve as a viable runtime environment. For example, a runtime specification for x86/win32/pe would certainly be very useful. As for the development of Archerr, our immediate goals are to implement further optimizations as well as mature the tool to handle large distributions without much manual interaction. We are planning on releasing an alpha version of Archerr very shortly. The long-term goal is to develop a robust, customizable tool that supports a myriad of runtime environments.

References

1. Wagner, D., Foster, J.S., Brewer, E.A., Aiken, A.: A First Step towards Automated Detection of Buffer Overrun Vulnerabilities. In: Network and Distributed System Security Symposium, San Diego, CA (2000) 3–17
2. Landi, W.: Undecidability of Static Analysis. ACM Letters on Programming Languages and Systems **1** (1992) 323–337
3. Ramalingam, G.: The Undecidability of Aliasing. ACM Transactions on Programming Languages and Systems **16** (1994) 1467–1471
4. Necula, G.C., McPeak, S., Weimer, W.: CCured: Type-safe Retrofitting of Legacy Code. In: Symposium on Principles of Programming Languages. (2002) 128–139
5. Jones, R.W.M., Kelly, P.H.J.: Backwards-Compatible Bounds Checking for Arrays and Pointers in C Programs. In: Automated and Algorithmic Debugging. (1997) 13–26
6. One, A.: Smashing the Stack for Fun and Profit. Phrack 49, Vol. 7, Issue 49 (1996)
7. Bianco, D.J.: An Integer Overflow Attack Against SSH Version 1 Attack Detectors. In: SANS Cyber Defense Initiatives. (2001)
8. Cohen, C.F.: CERT Advisory CA-2002-17 Apache Web Server Chunk Handling Vulnerability (2002)
9. Jones, R., Kelly, P.: (Bounds Checking for C)
   http://www-ala.doc.ic.ac.uk/~phjk/BoundsChecking.html.
10. TIS Committee: Tool Interface Standard (TIS), Executable and Linking Format (ELF) Specification, Version 1.2 (1995)
11. Standard for Binary Floating Point Arithmetic. ANSI/IEEE Standard 754-1985 (1985)
12. Boldyshev, K.: Startup State of a Linux/i386 ELF Binary. An article hosted on http://linuxassembly.org (2000) http://linuxassembly.org/articles/startup.html.
13. Bugtraq ID 7230: Sendmail Address Prescan Memory Corruption Vulnerability (2003) http://www.securityfocus.com/bid/7230.
14. Bugtaq ID 9297: GNU Indent Local Heap Overflow Vulnerability (2003) http://www.securityfocus.com/bid/9297/info/.
15. Bugtraq ID 7812: Man Catalog File Format String Vulnerability (2003) http://www.securityfocus.com/bid/7812.

16. Bugtraq ID 8589: Pine rfc2231_get_param() Remote Integer Overflow Vulnerability (2003) http://www.securityfocus.com/bid/8589.
17. Posting on Bugtraq Mailing List: (2003) http://archives.neohapsis.com/archives/bugtraq/2003-09/0181.html.
18. Scimark 2.0: (2003) http://math.nist.gov/scimark2/index.html.
19. Cowan, C., Beattie, S., Johansen, J., Wagle, P.: PointGuard: Protecting Pointers from Buffer Overflow Vulnerabilties. In: Proceedings of the 12th USENIX Security Symposium, Washington, D.C. (2003)
20. (Rational PurifyPlus) http://www-306.ibm.com/software/awdtools/purifyplus/.
21. (NuMega BoundsChecker) http://www.numega.com/products/aed/vc_more.shtml.
22. Cowan, C., Pu, C., Maier, D., Hinton, H., Bakke, P., Beattie, S., Grier, A., Wagle, P., Zhang, Q.: StackGuard: Automatic Adaptive Detection and Prevention of Buffer-Overflow Attacks. In: 7th USENIX Security Symposium, San Antonio, TX (1998)
23. Vendicator: (StackShield: A "Stack Smashing" Technique Protection Tool for Linux) http://www.angelfire.com/sk/stackshield/.
24. Etoh, H.: (GCC Extension for Protecting Applications from Stack-smashing Attacks) http://www.trl.ibm.co.jp/projects/security/ssp6.
25. Bulba, Kil3r: Bypassing StackGuard and StackShield. (Phrack Magazine, Volume 0xa Issue 0x38)
26. Jim, T., Morrisett, G., Grossman, D., Hicks, M., Cheney, J., Wang, Y.: Cyclone: A Safe Dialect of C. In: USENIX Annual Technical Conference, Monterey, CA (2002)
27. Bhatkar, S., DuVarney, D.C., Sekar, R.: Address Obfuscation: An Efficient Approach to Combat a Broad Range of Memory Error Exploits. In: Proceedings of the 12th USENIX Security Symposium, Washington, D.C. (2003)
28. PAX Project: (2003) "http://pax.grsecurity.net/docs/aslr.txt".
29. Bartaloo, A., Singh, N., Tsai, T.: Transparent Run-Time Defense Against Stack Smashing Attacks. In: 2000 USENIX Annual Technical Conference, San Diego, CA (2000)

Appendix

The following examples illustrate a few scenarios and how our technique handles them. Some of these examples are borrowed from [5, 26] for the purpose of comparison.

Dead Return Values

```
char * foo() {
    char buffer[32];
    return buffer;
}

int main() {
    char *p;
    p = foo();
    validate(p);
    strncpy(p, ''abc'',
        min(Δ⁺(p), strlen(''abc''), 3));
```

Multiple function exit points

```
int foo(void) {
    ℙ = ℙ ∪ current_stack_frame
    if (cond) {
        ℙ = ℙ - current_stack_frame
        return -1;
    }
    ℙ = ℙ - current_stack_frame
    return 0;
}
```

Nested blocks

```
int foo() {
    char *p = 0xBAD;
    append(ℙ, current_stack_frame)
    { char *p;
      validate(p);
      *p = 'a';
    }
    p = 0xBAD2;
    validate(p);
    *p = 'a';
```

Goto

```
int z;
{ int y = 0xBAD; goto L; }
{ int *y = &z;
L: validate(y); *y = 3;
}
```

Sets, Bags, and Rock and Roll[*]
Analyzing Large Data Sets of Network Data

John M[c]Hugh

CyLab and CERT Network Situational Awareness Center,
Carnegie Mellon University, Pittsburgh, PA 15313, USA
jmchugh@cert.org

Abstract. As network traffic increases, the problems associated with monitoring and analyzing the traffic on high speed networks become increasingly difficult. In this paper, we introduce a new conceptual framework based on sets of IP addresses, for coming to grips with this problem. The analytical techniques are described and illustrated with examples drawn from a dataset collected from a large operational network.

1 Introduction

It is not unusual for relatively modest networks today to exhibit trans border flows on the order of megabits per second. Monitoring even a small network with a few hundred hosts can generate many gigabytes of TCPDUMP data per day. Capturing only headers can reduce the volume somewhat, and more compact formats based on abstractions such as Cisco's NetFlow can reduce the volume further. Even so, the volume of data collected is sufficient to overwhelm many analysis tools and techniques. In general, the problem is one of grouping and classifying the data in such a way that uninteresting phenomena can be pushed aside, allowing the investigator to extract and further scrutinize data that is of interest. Recently, the CERT Network Situational Awareness Center has been involved in the analysis of large sets of NetFlow data. To support this effort, they have developed a set of tools, collectively known as the SiLKtools[1]. In the remainder of the paper, we begin by sketching our thesis and analysis

---

[*] The mantra "Sex, Drugs, and Rock and Roll" enjoyed currency in the 1960s. To the ears of an older generation, Rock and Roll was just a particularly unpleasant form of noise. Since the general theme of this paper is separating signal from noise in network data, the title is not too strained. This material is based upon work partially supported by the National Science Foundation under Grant No. 0326472. Any opinions, findings, and conclusions or recommendations expressed in this material are those of the author(s) and do not necessarily reflect the views of the National Science Foundation. This work is also supported by the Army Research Office through grant number DAAD19-02-1-0389 ("Perpetually Available and Secure Information Systems") to CyLab at Carnegie Mellon University

[1] The SLK are the initials of the late Suresh Konda who was instrumental in the initial development of the tool set

P. Samarati et al. (Eds.): ESORICS 2004, LNCS 3193, pp. 407–422, 2004.

approach. We then digress to describe the NetFlow data collected, noting that the analysis can be applied equally well to TCPDUMP or other data forms with a bit of preprocessing. The basic functionality of the SiLKtools suite and some of the extensions made in support of our analysis efforts are then described. The remainder of the paper will present examples of the analyses that we can perform using the tools supplemented by relatively simple programs to characterize and organize the reduced data. The paper concludes with a discussion of our plans for further extensions of the tools and additional analyses.

2   The Thesis and Approach

Sets and set theory are abstractions that facilitate reasoning about many classes of problems. We have been exploring the use of sets to provide a compact way of describing and reasoning about the Internet and about traffic observed at various points on it. For example, it is useful to consider such things as the set of hosts on a given network that are active during a given time interval. It might also be useful to consider the set of external hosts that are observed performing a questionable activity such as scanning during such an interval. Similarly, one might want to identify the set of users of some service provided by the local network to the outside world (e.g. web services) during the interval. In the case of the first set, the set of active machines, we could attempt to obtain the answer by asking the system administrators, by examining the state of the DHCP server responsible for leasing IP addresses to the network, by consulting the responsible DNS server, or we could approximate the result by observing those hosts within the network that either originate traffic or respond to connection requests. If we can observe the traffic passing in and out of the network at some transition point such as a border router, the observations may constitute a reasonable approximation of the active set[2] of hosts. The set of active hosts, can be used to partition incoming traffic into that addressed to active hosts (hits) and that which is not (misses). Arguably, the later partition consists of a mix of malicious traffic, indirect evidence of malicious traffic, and, possibly, some amount of benign, but misdirected traffic. This partition can be further processed to identify interesting classes of senders. For example, originators attempting TCP connections will send packets containing a SYN flag. If we select flows containing SYN flags and count the number of flows per source address using a "bag[3]", we can sort the bag and identify high volume scanners. It is not uncommon see a single host performing scans of an entire /16 network in the course of a relatively few minutes. Having identified such a scanner, it is trivial

---

[2] We assume that all traffic in and out of the monitored network passes through an observation point. Multiple border crossing points are possible. For the moment, we assume that hosts within the monitored network do not spoof addresses and that multiple responders such as honeypots are not deployed within the monitored network

[3] A bag is a counted set or multiset in which the number of occurrences of each member of the basis set is recorded

to find the flows from the scanner to the active or hit partition and create the set of active machines included in the flow. At that point, it is useful to determine if any of the targets responded to the scanner, and, if so to examine the traffic between the scanner and the target (and the subsequent behavior of the target) to determine if the target has changed its behavior in ways that might indicate that it has been compromised.

As can be seen from the example of the previous paragraph, the use of sets and bags, combined with simple filtering based on properties of the data records themselves allows the clustering of data with some particular security (or other) properties in common. Since we are dealing with many thousands of flows per minute on large networks, the constructions of sets and bags allows us to abstract from individual behaviors to clusters of activities. As the paper develops, we will elaborate on this thesis and develop the tools and techniques that we need in more detail, however, we have a number of utilities available including:

- An efficient set representation that allows us to represent IPv4 address sets directly in memory. There is also a compact disk representation that can be read and written efficiently
- An extension of the set representation, a bag, that allows a 32bit counter to be associated with each IP address. It too has an efficient disk representation.
- Routines that allow set unions and intersections to be computed, producing additional set files.
- Routines that allow sets and bags to be created from files containing network flow data.
- Routines that allow sets and bags to be created from ASCII lists of IP addresses in both "dotted" form (possibly containing wild cards), in CIDR block form, and in unsigned integer form.
- Routines to list the contents of sets and bags at various levels of detail, including the network structure (subnet relationships) of a set.

These are sufficient for our initial analysis, though we plan to add other programs to the suite as the need for them becomes clear.

3   NetFlow and Other Data Sources

NetFlow was developed by Cisco as a mechanism for gathering traffic statistics to support billing and network management. NetFlow operates on routers and switches to report traffic statistics on a per interface basis. Although it is not standardized, it is supported in more or less compatible ways by a number of other router and switch manufacturers. According to Cisco[4], the detailed traffic statistics collected by NetFlow include:

- Source and destination IP addresses
- Next hop address

---

[4] http://www.cisco.com/en/US/products/sw/netmgtsw/ps1964/products_user_
guide_chapter09186a00801ed569.html

- Input and output interface numbers
- Number of packets in the flow
- Total bytes (octets) in the flow
- First and last time stamps of packets that were switched as part of this flow
- Source and destination port numbers
- Protocol (and flags as appropriate)
- Type of service (ToS)
- Source and destination autonomous system (AS) numbers, either origin or peer (present in V5 and select V8 datagrams)
- Source and destination prefix mask bits (present in V5, V7, and V8 datagrams)

Note that NetFlow records include one or more packets, and represent unidirectional flows. As such, NetFlow lies somewhere in between TCPDUMP records which contain data about individual packets and connection records which would abstract an entire TCP session to a single record. Because NetFlow is resource intensive, there is a limit to the number of open flow records that the router can maintain at one time. New records are created whenever a new flow is seen. A flow is deemed to be new if it contains a (source/destination/protocol[5]) tuple that is not currently being monitored. A flow is closed if it has been inactive for a prescribed period of time(typically some seconds), if it has been explicitly closed (TCP FIN or RST), or if it has been open and active for a prescribed period of time (typically some minutes). Note that this has the effect of breaking up long, steady TCP sessions as well as intermittent TCP sessions with long pauses. It also creates pseudo sessions from sequences of UDP packets as might be associated with streaming media.

The individual flow records are aggregated and sent in batches encapsulated in a UDP packet to a central collection point for processing. In our case, the processing point stores the flow records in a compact format that can be sequentially searched and extracted based on times and a number of match criteria as discussed in the next section. Since our tools operate from this format, it is worth considering whether other forms of data might be stored in the same format and processed with the tools. The answer is a qualified yes. It would be trivial to extract most of the required data from packet based sources such as TCPDUMP or Argus records. Since packet data is typically captured on a link, router specific information such as interfaces, AS numbers, and next hop addresses are not available, but these seldom appear in our analysis. If we were to aggregate data from a number of collection points, these fields could be used to indicate the collection point and directionality of the packet.

We are currently investigating two approaches for obtaining flow data from packet data. There is a `libpcap` based flow accumulation program, `fprobe`[6] that will observe a link and create NetFlow records that can be sent to a collector. In addition one of our customers is building a high performance collector based

---

[5] In the case of TCP and UDP, ports are included

[6] Available from `http://sourceforge.net/projects/fprobe`

on a commercial TCPDump hardware capture board[7]. Both of these approaches would allow us additional flexibility in consolidating flows and would allow minor enhancements to the NetFlow format, e.g. recording whether the opening packet of a tcp flow was a SYN, SYN/ACK, or something else.

As far as we can determine, the first attempt to develop tools for security analysis from NetFlow data occurred at Ohio State University. These tools[1] are fairly special purpose and primitive compared to our approach.

4   The SiLKtools Suite and Its Extensions

According to the SiLK website[8]:

> SiLK, the System for Internet-Level Knowledge, is a collection of Net-Flow tools developed by the CERT/AC to facilitate security analysis in large networks. SiLK consists of a suite of tools which collect and examine NetFlow data, allowing analysts to rapidly query large sets of data. SiLK was explicitly designed with a trade off in mind: while traffic summaries do not provide packet-by-packet (in particular, payload) information, they are also considerably more compact and consequently can be used to acquire a wider view of network traffic problems.

> SiLK consists of two sets of tools: a packing system[9] and analysis suite[10]. The packing system receives NetFlow V5 PDU's and converts them into a more space efficient format, recording the packed records into service-specific binary flat files. The analysis suite consists of tools which can read these flat files and then perform various query operations, ranging from per-record filtering to statistical analysis of groups of records. The analysis tools inter operate using pipes, allowing a user to develop a relatively sophisticated query from a simple beginning.

> The vast majority of the current code-base is implemented in C, Perl, or Python. This code has been tested on Linux, Solaris, Free/OpenBSD, AIX and Mac OS X, but should be usable with little or no change on other Unix platforms.

> The SiLK software components are released under the GPL.

> The project is the fruits of work done at the CERT Coordination Center (CERT/CC) that is part of the Software Engineering Institute at Carnegie Mellon University.

---

[7] See http://www.endace.com/networkMCards.htm for additional information
[8] http://silktools.sourceforge.net/
[9] The SiLK Packing System is a server application that receives NetFlow V5 PDU's and converts them into a more space efficient format, recording the packed records into service-specific binary flat files. Files are organized in a time-based directory hierarchy with files cover an hour at the leaves
[10] The SiLK Analysis Suite is a collection of command-line tools for querying packed NetFlow data. The most important tool is **rwfilter**, an application for querying the central NetFlow data repository for NetFlow records that satisfy a set of filtering options

The analysis suite includes a number of applications and utility programs. We discuss in some detail only those that are used in the examples below, however, manual pages for the entire suite are available from the web site. For convenience, we refer to the packed data files used by some of the programs as "rwdata" files. In most cases, input can come from stdin or from a rwdata file and it is possible to associate an output of most programs with stdout, allowing chains of programs.

5 Examples and Sample Analyses

In this section, we illustrate our analysis techniques with two examples. One is a brief data sample from a large cross section of networks that have been aggregated together. the other represents a detailed view of a weeks activity on a /16. In all cases, no real IPs are contained in the analyses. We note that the analyses presented are exploratory in nature. At the present time, we are just beginning to come to grips with the issues of analyzing and understanding network traffic on this scale. Every time we look at a new sample of the data, we find previously unexpected behaviors. Our customer's analysts use scripts to invoke the tools to perform routine inspections for a variety of malicious activities. Our goal is to attempt to understand what we see in the hopes that it will lead to improved detection in the long run. For now, we are not attempting to produce turnkey procedures for system administrators and analysts but rather to aid networking experts in understanding their domain. The examples are offered as an enquiry, much in the spirit of Tukey[2]. Programs from the suite used in producing the examples are printed in **bold**. Details of these programs appear in Appendix A.

5.1 A Brief Examination of a Large Sample

Using the **rwfilter** program to extract data from the incoming (Internet to customer network) and outgoing (customer network to Internet) archives, we obtained files of data from a cross section of monitored networks for a small interval of time. Outgoing data was monitored for an interval began slightly before interval used for incoming data and extended slightly beyond it. This insures that the internal hosts that responded to traffic from the outside are included in the sample even in the incoming and outgoing clocks are not perfectly synchronized[11] or internal hosts respond only after a small delay. The set of active hosts in the internal network is approximated by by passing the outgoing data file to the **rwsuperset** program asking it to create a set file for the source addresses contained in it's input. The incoming data file is then passed to **rwfilter** along with the active host set file to partition the incoming file into hit and miss files, based on the destination address of the incoming flows.

About 2/3 (65.4%) of the flow records are directed at inactive (presumed nonexistent) targets, the remaining 1/3 (34.6%) are directed at active hosts.

---

[11] The data is aggregated from a number of routers. In some cases, separate routers handle incoming and outgoing traffic

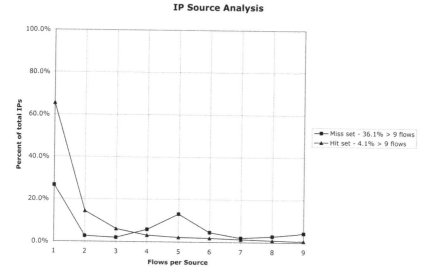

Fig. 1. Reduction in incoming IP Source Set Sizes as a Function of Number of Flows

Further partitioning by protocol, again using **rwfilter** simplifies subsequent analysis. As expected, the vast majority of the data is TCP. We further analyze the TCP data using **rwsuperset** to create bags for source and destination addresses for the hit and miss files. The fall off in set size is illustrated in Figures 1 and 2. Note that hit and miss set sizes follow similar, but distinct patterns. The big differences are between source and destination behaviors. About 36% of the source IPs in the miss partition generate ten or more flows while only 4% of those in the hit partition do so.

Using **readbag**, along with the system utilities `sort` and `head` we can identify the most commonly occurring addresses in the miss partition. Figure 3 shows some of the results of this analysis. A closer look at the top address is interesting. Using **rwfilter** to extract flows with this source address in the miss file extracts some 400K of records. The destination set for this contains 12994 hosts, all from XXX.YYY.0.0/16 The hit set also contains entries from this network, 7 in all. Using **rwcut** to extract the destination port, flag, and packet and byte count fields from the extracted files and clustering, using **cluster.sno** to determine and count the unique field combinations used, we find that all the flows sent to these addresses are 48 byte SYN packets addressed to port 4899 (listed as a "radmin" port by IANA, with other possible usages reported as ChiliASP and iMesh). An inspection of the outgoing traffic from this network indicates no responses to the connection attempts.

The second entry is somewhat different. The traffic from this address scans a different /16. looking for responses on port 7100[12] (X Font service according

---

[12] `http://www.cert.org/advisories/CA-2002-34.html` describes a vulnerability in the X font service on Solaris. It is likely that the scanner was looking for machines that could be attacked

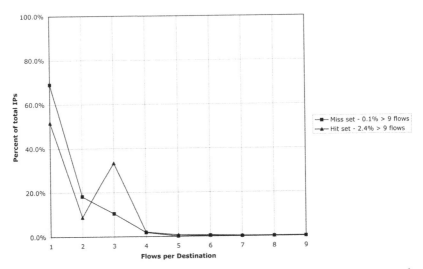

Fig. 2. Reduction in incoming IP Destination Set Sizes as a Function of Number of Flows

```
(39) lip $ readbag --count --print jcm-tcp-s-10+.bag| sort -r -n | head
     12994 AAA.BBB.068.218
      6598 CCC.DDD.209.215
      5944 EEE.FFF.125.117
      5465 GGG.HHH.114.052
      5303 III.JJJ.164.126
```

Fig. 3. The top five sources in the small sample

to IANA). Some 112 responses are seen from hosts SSS.RRR.QQQ.1-78,120-131,224-254. The contiguous ranges and the consistency of responses on a relatively obscure port may indicate the presence of a honey pot or a similar decoy. In all cases, the connection seems to have been broken after the probed host's SYN/ACK reply.

The third and fourth entries are scans of portions of other /16s, this time looking for service on port 20168. This appears to be associated with the "Lovegate" worm which binds a shell to this port on infected machines.

The fifth entry is a scan of a portion of yet another /16, this time looking for service on port 3127, listed by IANA as the CTX bridge port, but also in the range used by the ChiliASP module in Apache servers according to www.portsdb.org. This port is currently being used by the "MyDoom.C" worm on Linux[13].

---

[13] http://www.linuxworld.com/story/43628.htm

At the other end of the spectrum, there are 3335 external hosts that sent exactly one TCP flow into the monitored network during the analyzed time interval. Of these, only two port and flag combinations appear more than 100 times. SYN probes for port 8866[14] are seen 449 times. SYN probes for port 25 (SMTP - email) are seen 271 times. The vast majority of the remainder are SYNs to a variety of ports, mostly with high port numbers. There are a number of ACK/RST packets which are probably associated with responses to spoofed DDoS attacks.

5.2 A Week in the Life of a /16

We obtained hourly flow data from a /16 within the monitored network for the one week period from 11 - 17 January 2004. plus two additional days, 26 and 27 January. The data set consists of nearly 400Mb of data divided into hourly files for inside to outside traffic and for outside to inside traffic. The inside to outside traffic was analyzed and a set of IP addresses computed that represent all the hosts that were seen to be active during the initial week. The observed network structure is shown in Table 1. Note that only about 6% of the available /24 subnets are occupied at all and that the utilization of those that are ranges from less than 1% to about 25%. The information shown in Table 1 has been adapted from the output of **readset** using a specification that causes subnet summarization at the /24 level and for the internet as a whole.

Table 1. Network Structure for the selected /16

MMM.NNN.24.x	66 hosts	MMM.NNN.25.x	60 hosts
MMM.NNN.26.x	46 hosts	MMM.NNN.27.x	49 hosts
MMM.NNN.28.x	57 hosts	MMM.NNN.29.x	7 hosts
MMM.NNN.30.x	70 hosts	MMM.NNN.31.x	67 hosts
MMM.NNN.32.x	54 hosts	MMM.NNN.33.x	62 hosts
MMM.NNN.34.x	50 hosts	MMM.NNN.35.x	4 hosts
MMM.NNN.120.x	2 hosts	MMM.NNN.127.x	1 host
MMM.NNN.140.x	1 host	MMM.NNN.251.x	4 hosts

Network Summary
600 hosts ($1.4 * 10^{-5}$%) of 2^{32}
1 occupied class /8 (0.4%) of 256
1 occupied class /16 (0.002%) of 65536
16 occupied class /24s ($9.5 * 10^{-5}$%) of 2^{24}

The set of active addresses seen during the week is an optimistic estimate of the active host set for this network since activity on several subnets was not

---

[14] "W32.Beagle.B@mm is a mass-mailing worm that opens a back door on TCP port 8866. The worm uses its own SMTP engine for email propagation. It can also send to the attacker the port on which the back door listens, as well as a randomized ID number." according to http://securityresponse.symantec.com/avcenter/venc/data/w32.beagle.b@mm.html

observed until late in the week. The set includes all hosts seen to be active during the additional days, as well. This set was used to partition each outside to inside hourly data set into hit and miss portions as described earlier. Since these files consist of a small amount of header data and fixed length records, the file sizes are a good surrogate for the number of flows observed.

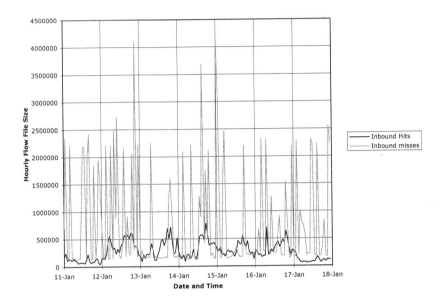

Fig. 4. Hourly flow file sizes for incoming hit and miss flows

Figure 4 shows the hit and miss file sizes for the base week of the data. It is interesting to note that many more flows miss than hit during most hours. We have looked at a few of the peaks in detail.

12 January 21:00 Two fairly complete scans of the entire /16, one for port 2000 TCP (61018 flows) and one for port 20168 TCP (60978 flows) with a total of 62616 unique IP addresses hit. Both scans came from a single IP address. As noted above, port 20168 is associated with the Lovegate worm. Port 2000 appears to be associated with a number of Windows remote administration tools (e.g. RemotelyAnywhere).

14 January 15:00 Two scans from different networks, each targeting port 80 TCP. One targets 58394 hosts, the other 53032.

15 January 00:00 Two fairly complete scans from two distinct source addresses, one for port 4000 TCP, the other for 5308 TCP, each from a separate source.

Port 4000 appears to be used by Remote-Anything from TWD Industries (http://www.twd-industries.com/en/index.htm).

Port 5308 is associated with CFengine, a configuration and administration mechanism[15].

Given the large numbers of peaks in the miss data, it was decided to run an IP frequency analysis on the entire week. This produced some interesting results both with respect to the the numbers of infrequent and frequent missers. The set of source IPs that attempt to contact hosts in the miss set contains 182632 distinct addresses. Of these, 145755 or almost 80% appear exactly once. 19751 or about 11% appear twice. 4382 (about 2%) appear 10 or more times, but these account for 3756029 of 4037208 or 93% of the total flows. The top scanners accounted for over 100000 probes each with 66 IP addresses registering more than 10000 flows (over 80/no obvious threshold or breakpoint in the distribution. In the 10000 flow range, adjacent entries in the table are separated by a few hundred flows. The set of the top 66 flow sources contains IP addresses from 65 distance /16 address ranges. In the one case where the addresses are in the same /16 they are also in the same /24 being only 16 addresses apart.

We extracted the miss data for the top 66 flow sources and clustered it based on TCP flags. All the flows are TCP (protocol 6) and the vast majority consist of flows having only a SYN flag. The presence of a substantial number of records containing other flags (especially ACK flags) is somewhat surprising.

Table 2. Flag clusters for the top 66 missed flow sources

Flags	Flows	Src IPs	Dst IPs	S	RA	SA	R	SRA	A
S	2955827	54	64936		22510	1734	8126	49	8
R A	197972	12	22510	1		843	2868	49	6
S A	66908	10	1734	0	9		193	49	6
R	33169	5	8212	1	5	4		9	2
SR A	725	8	49	0	7	8	4		6
A	8	3	8	1	2	2	1	2	

An analysis of the clustering is shown in Table 2. The numbers in the lower triangular section at the right hand side of the table represent counts of source addresses in common among the groups; the upper triangle represents the same analysis for destination addresses. We note that the sources of the SYN only flows are largely disjoint from the sources of the other flows. Since the source of the common RST/ACK and the RST flow are the same, only two IP addresses

---

[15] "CFengine, or the configuration engine is an autonomous agent and a middle to high level policy language for building expert systems which administrate and configure large computer networks. CFengine uses the idea of classes and a primitive intelligence to define and automate the configuration and maintenance of system state, for small to huge configurations. CFengine is designed to be a part of a computer immune system, and can be thought of as a gaming agent. It is ideal for cluster management and has been adopted for use all over the world in small and huge organizations alike." according to http://www.iu.hio.no/cfengine/

Table 3. Ports scanned by the top 54 SYNers

Rank	Count	Port	Service
1	1038778	80	HTTP
2	370404	4899	radmin
3	258538	4000	Remote-Anything
4	225665	21	ftp
5	191562	3389	Remote Desktop Protocol / ms-wbt-server
6	185400	20168	Lovegate worm
7	126142	5308	CFengine
8	64679	2277	
9	64679	554	Real time streaming protocol
10	64679	3410	NetworkLens SSL event
11	64675	1257	Shockwave 2
12	64312	1443	Integrated Engineering Software license manager
13	63166	5000	Cisco HIDS agent/console
14	63165	14232	ftp server as side effect of SMB exploit
15	61018	2000	RemotelyAnywhere / SCCP (Cisco phones)
16	31153	23	telnet

are in common with the SYN addresses. Based on this, we consider the SYN only case separately.

The remaining miss records contained some 25000 distinct ports, mostly high numbers. Analyzing the RST/ACK group separately, we find that the 12 IPs responsible for this behavior form a total of 69 groups when clustered by IP and source port. There is substantial overlap among the IPs in this group and the remaining groups leading us to conclude that it is highly likely that some or all of these hosts were undergoing denial of service attacks during the week of analyzed data. An examination of these flows indicates that it is likely that a number of distinct attacks were involved. One host emits single ACK/RST packets on a number of ports as well as from 1 to 20 or so RST packets on several thousand ports. For the other hosts, most of the activity is concentrated on a relatively few ports, but the patterns vary from host to host with port 80 being the most common. At this point, we do not know whether the activity is concentrated only in the monitored /16 or covers other monitored networks, as well.

Table 4. Clusters based on IP for significant flag combinations

Flags	Clusters	IPs
S	55	54
RA	6	12
SA	12	10
R	3816	5

Table 4 shows the number of unique port and IP combinations for the major flow types. The port used for the SYN flows was the destination port while source ports were used for the others. This is consistent with our view that flows other than the SYN flows are likely to be responses to abuses of the IP sources by spoofed traffic.

We also briefly examined the very low rate traffic. As noted earlier, the vast majority of the IPs responsible for the miss traffic generate a single flow during the week of observation. Four protocols are represented. There are 14 flows for protocol 0 (IPv6 Hop by Hop?). It is not clear whether these are legitimate, but they originate from 14 distinct /16s and target a single host within the monitored network.

There were a total of 864 ICMP messages. 2 were echo replys, 612 destination unreachable, 3 source quenches,1 host redirect, 242 TTL exceeded in transit, and 1 timestamp reply. Of the destination unreachable messages, 24 were network unreachable, 139 host unreachable, 1 protocol unreachable, 160 port unreachable, 46 communication with host administratively prohibited, and 242 communication administratively prohibited.

There are 13161 TCP flows of which 12541 have only the SYN flag set. 12242 of these target port 80 (http), with port 4662 (EDonkey, a peer to peer service) next with 28 flows. 11 flows target port 0 (possibly an error), and 10 target port 55592, and 8 target port 23 (telnet). The remainder of the flows have fewer that 5 flows per port with most being 1 flow per port. Of the non SYN only flows, there are 80 SYN/ACKs and 80 RST/ACKs to port 80. There are 14 RST/ACKs target port 1025 (network blackjack?) and 11 targeting port 21 (ftp) Ignoring ports in the analysis, there are 226 RST/ACK combinations, 177 RST, 82 SYN/RST, 46 ACK, and a handfull of other combinations.

The largest component of the low rate data is UDP. There are 131716 flows of which 131519 target destination port 53 (dns). The next highest counts are less than 30 flows to a single port and singleton flows appear at rank 25 (of 74). Clustering on source ports produces a different picture. 25228 ports appear in the list, again, most associated with a single flow. Port 53 is again the most common source port (89450 flows) followed by 1025 (1042 flows). Ports 10000, 1024, 1044, 1064, 10001, 1084, 60000, and 1026 round out the top 10 (tie for 10th place at 60 flows). Clustering on input and output port pairs shows that the combination (53,53) is most common with 89531 flows. Port 53 is the destination port in the 27 top flows and is either the source or destination port in the top 39 flows. (500,500) is the 40th most common combination with 14 flows and port 53 appears as the destination port for ranks from 41 through 197. Clustering by destination host and port is unproductive. The most frequent clusters all target a single host with 15 flows to port 6144, and 14 each to ports 53 and 16896 on the same host.

6   Enhancements and Extensions

The SiLKtools set has shown itself to be useful for a variety of analyses of large data sets of network flow data. For future work, there are a number of extensions that we would like to make. Extensions to the set and bag mechanism to allow adding of bags, conversion of a bag to its basis set, and to allow a set to be used to select portions of a bag would be particularly useful. While stand alone programs such as the ones we have used here are useful for exploratory work, we envision routine analyses that would benefit from being performed in an integrated program. To this end, we are proposing to the SiLKtools developers that they consider implementing the set and bag code as a subroutine library, along with a library of data structures and I/O routines that can be used to access and manipulate the raw data.

The underlying data representation also has some deficiencies that will be fixed in the near future. Time is currently represented only in whole seconds which makes it difficult to compare, for example flow start times. We are working on matching inbound and outbound flows for TCP sessions. Better timing information would help here, as would a flag that indicated that the first packet of the flow contained a SYN and not a SYN/ACK combination. As mentioned earlier, we are looking at creating flows from other data sources.

Extending the set and bag concept to other data types would be useful. We have need for efficient representations of active ports associated with individual IPs, for example. The bags currently provide 32 bit counters for the IPv4 space, but depend on the sparse non-zero counts to fit in memory. We have recently analyzed the several alternative representations and feel that we can build a set and bag framework that will allow much more compact representations than we have at present by taking advantage of observed address distributions. The current structures use one (sets) or 2 (bags) levels of indirection and then allocate blocks of storage at the /16 (sets) or /24 (bags) level. Because of the low occupancy of most of our customer's subnets combined with a tendency to allocate addresses at the low end of the subnets, it appears that /27 allocations of storage could reduce bag sizes by a factor of 4 to 8. Allocating 8 bit counters to the block initially and expanding to 16 bits or 32 bits as needed would reduce bag sizes by another factor of 2 or more.

We also have a need for set and bag like structures for things like connections (2 IP addresses and 2 port addresses, reversed for response) and connection attempts (Source IP, Destination IP and port). We have experimented with the use of Bloom filters[3] for determining connection sets and believe that these could play a major role in analyzing more complex behaviors such as determining the number of distinct connection attempts a given source IP makes over time. We are currently developing a plugin for **rwfilter** that will allow collection for continuation flows, i.e. groups of flows with the same IP, protocol, and port information, using a two stage Bloom filter. All flows will be entered into the first stage of the filter, but only flows that match the first stage are entered into the second filter which can then be used to separate singleton flows (the vast majority) from those that might be consolidated. Similarly, transposing source and destination inputs to a Bloom filter can simplify matching the two sides of a conversation.

And then there is the question of extending the concept to IPv6 ... .

7   Conclusions

We have introduced the concept of using sets and bags to facilitate the analysis of large sets of network flow data, provided some motivating examples and suggested further lines of inquiry. The tools we use are in a state of flux, but have already produced interesting and useful results in analyzing both aggregated data and data from single subnets.

Acknowledgments

Special thanks go to Mike Collins who has been the chief instigator of the SiLK-tools effort since the death of Suresh Konda. Carrie Gates and Damon Becknel have provided many useful contributions to the effort. Other members of the CERT analysis team have been most gracious in tolerating my code modifications.

References

1. Fullmer, M., Romig, S.: The OSU flow-tools package and Cisco NetFlow logs. In: LISA XIV, New Orleans (2000) 291–303
2. Tukey, J.W.: Exploratory Data Analysis. Addison-Wesley, Reading, MA. (1977)
3. Bloom, B.: Space/time trade-offs in hash coding with allowable errors. Communications of ACM **13** (1970) 422–426

A   Brief Descriptions of Selected SiLKtools Programs

rwfilter is the front end for the system. It extracts a subset of the centrally stored rwdata based on a number of aggregation and filtering criteria or applies filtering data to a previously extracted rwdata file. Although it is much more general than the usages we show, our typical use starts by selecting data based on some time interval and possibly some range of network addresses. This data will be stored in a single file and subsequently refiltered based on other criteria. The program can be used to partition data based on the filtering criteria. Thus, TCP data could be extracted to a file in one pass with other protocols going to different file (or piped to another invocation of rwfilter to extract UDP, etc. for as many levels as desired.) Since sets of IP addresses can be used as filter criteria, traffic whose source (and / or destination) addresses appear in given sets can be extracted or partitioned.

rwcut lists selected fields from an rwdata file, one line per flow, for subsequent analysis. A dynamic library facility allows derived quantities, e.g. bytes per packet, to be listed.

rwsuperset is my enhanced version of **rwset**. It can create multiple sets and bags from rwdata files based on source and / or destination addresses. An additional feature allows a diminished set of the input data (flows with IP addresses already in a set under construction) to be passed for source, destination or both. This allows us to cascade invocations using sets for the majority of flows with small counts and bags for the residue as seen in the following hack (to be obviated by a more efficient bag representation).

```
#!/bin/bash
# raw data file $1.rwf creates 9 levels of set files and a bag file.
# $2 is either s or d, for bagging on source or destination IPs
rwsuperset --p --$2-s=$1-$2-1+.set --$2-d=stdout $1.rwf |\
rwsuperset --p --$2-s=$1-$2-2+.set --$2-d=stdout |\
...
rwsuperset --p --$2-s=$1-$2-10+.set --$2-d=$1-$2-10+.rwf \
           --$2-i=10 --$2-b=$1-$2-10+.bag
```

readset reads in a set file and lists its contents in various ways including set size, a list of members, or an analysis of the network structure of the set.

readbag is similar to readset, but will only enumerate the bag,

buildset builds a set file from a list of IP addresses. Wildcards are permitted as are CIDR notations, useful in building sets for masking operations.

buildbag is like buildset except that it counts occurrences of each IP address.

setintersect performs intersection operations on set files or their complements.

rwsetunion performs the union of two or more set files.

rwcat concatenates multiple rwdata files into a single file or stdout stream.

rwsort provides the ability to sort rwdata files based on address, size or start time fields.

rwstats can provide a variety of statistics about the contents of an rwdata file.

cluster.sno is written in SNOBOL4[16] and counts the number of unique lines in its input. This is a simplistic view of clustering, but is adequate for now.

---

[16] Available at http://www.snobol4.org/

Redundancy and Diversity in Security*

Bev Littlewood and Lorenzo Strigini

Centre for Software Reliability, City University,
Northampton Square, London EC1V OHB, UK
{B.Littlewood,L.Strigini}@csr.city.ac.uk

Abstract. Redundancy and diversity are commonly applied principles for fault tolerance against accidental faults. Their use in security, which is attracting increasing interest, is less general and less of an accepted principle. In particular, redundancy without diversity is often argued to be useless against systematic attack, and diversity to be of dubious value. This paper discusses their roles and limits, and to what extent lessons from research on their use for reliability can be applied to security, in areas such as intrusion detection. We take a probabilistic approach to the problem, and argue its validity for security. We then discuss the various roles of redundancy and diversity for security, and show that some basic insights from probabilistic modelling in reliability and safety indeed apply to examples of design for security. We discuss the factors affecting the efficacy of redundancy and diversity, the role of "independence" between layers of defense, and some of the tra! de-offs facing designers.

1 Introduction

This paper is about the need for better understanding of how redundancy and diversity are applicable in security. This involves different issues:

- the extent of their useful applicability;
- the ways of evaluating their advantages so as to drive design.

Redundancy as a general approach is clearly understood to be a valid defense against physical faults. There is a rich set of understood design "tricks" that use redundancy against various forms of faults and failures, and knowledge about how to optimize them for different purposes, e.g. in terms of tradeoffs between cost of the redundancy during normal operation and the effectiveness and performance degradation in case of failure. When it comes to design faults, it is commonly accepted that some form of diversity may be necessary to tolerate them. However, whether fault tolerance itself is an appropriate approach is more controversial: many claim that for "systematic" failures the most effective

---

* This work was supported in part by the U.K. Engineering and Physical Sciences Research Council under projects DOTS (Diversity with Off-The-Shelf Component) and DIRC (Interdisciplinary Research Collaboration on Dependability of computer-based systems).

P. Samarati et al. (Eds.): ESORICS 2004, LNCS 3193, pp. 423–438, 2004.

and cost-effective procedure is simply to avoid them in the first place. We have argued elsewhere that these claims are the result of misunderstandings about terms like "systematic". When it comes to *intentional* faults, the value of fault tolerance in general is even les! s commonly accepted, although some authors have long argued its benefits [1, 2] and despite a recent increase of interest[1].

In part, the disagreements are an effect of the historical separation between the various technical sub-communities dealing with reliability/safety and with security, leading to different attitudes (not least to the use of probabilistic arguments), and some degree of reciprocal misunderstanding. A risk in cross-community discussion is over-generalization. "Redundancy" or "diversity" are just useful common names for generic design approaches, which have to be adapted to the needs of a specific design. All considerations of applicability and efficacy need to be referred to a specific situation, with its threats and dependability requirements. When we move from general discussions of applicability and intuitive desirability of these methods to deciding in which form (if any) they should be applied in a particular context, more formal, rigorous reasoning is needed. This has been provided, in reliability and safety, by probability models of diversity, giving some new, and s! ometimes surprising, insights (surveys of these results are in [3, 4]). We believe that these models are directly applicable to the use of diversity in security. This is the main topic of this paper. The recent resurgence of interest in diversity for security seems to include only limited interest in probabilistic study. In fact, some misunderstandings that arose early on about software fault tolerance seem to be occurring again, especially concerning notions of "independence". We will describe some aspects of the existing models that seem directly applicable to security. An area of security research in which there is interest in diversity and redundancy is intrusion tolerance, and we use this example in our discussion.

In the rest of this paper, we first deal with the preliminary issues. We argue the need for probabilistic reasoning about security (section 2). Then we discuss the concepts of redundancy and diversity and the ways of pursuing them (Sect. 3); and, in Sect. 4, we consider examples of these in recent work on security. We then proceed (section 5) to show how previous results about diversity can help in directing its application to improve security attributes of systems.

2   Probability, Redundancy and Security

Discussion of redundancy and diversity, whether it be for reliability, safety or security, must start from an understanding of uncertainty, and a recognition that probability is the appropriate formalism for dealing with uncertainty. This is accepted in the reliability area, because no redundant architecture deterministically prevents all system failures. One instead encounters frequent skepticism in the security community about the use of probabilities. This is reminiscent of

---

[1] Represented for instance by the U.S. DARPA sponsored OASIS project (http://www.tolerantsystems.org/) and the European MAFTIA project (e.g. http://www.newcastle.research.ec.org/maftia/). More references are in Sect. 4.

similar debates twenty years ago about the use of probabilities for software reliability. Then, it was said software failures were "systematic" and thus not open to probabilistic modelling. Now, it is said that security failures are deliberate and thus not open to probabilistic modelling. Both statements are, we believe, based upon mistaken views of the nature of the uncertainty in the two areas.

The term "systematic failure" arose to distinguish software failures (and other design fault-induced failures) from "random" hardware failures. The words "random" and "systematic" here are misleading: they seem to suggest that in the one case a probabilistic approach is inevitable, but that in the other we might be able to get away with completely deterministic reasoning. This is not so, and stochastic arguments seem inevitable in both cases.

When we use the word *systematic* here it refers to the fault mechanism, the mechanism whereby a fault reveals itself as a failure, and not to the failure *process*. In the case of software, the most widely recognized source of systematic failures, it is correct to say that if a program failed once on a particular input (and internal state), it would fail every time the same conditions occur again, until the offending program fault had been successfully removed. This contrasts with physical hardware failures, for which there is no such certainty. In this very limited sense, software failures are deterministic, and it is from this determinism that we obtain the terminology.

However, our interest really centers upon the failure *process*: what we see when the system under study is used in its operational environment. In a real-time system, for example, we would have a well-defined time variable (not necessarily real clock time) and our interest would center upon the process of failures embedded in time. We might wish to assure ourselves that the rate of occurrence of failures was sufficiently small, or that there was a sufficiently high probability of surviving some pre-assigned mission time. We would *not* instead be able to predict with certainty whether the next mission will end in failure: this depends on unknown details of the mission (the exact sequence of inputs to the system) and of the system (the possibility of unknown bugs). The important point is that this failure process is not deterministic for either "systematic" faults or for random faults.

Similar reasoning applies to security. One frequently hears objections to probabilistic measures of security because of the essentially unrepeatable nature of the key events. People are happy with estimates of the probability of failure of a hardware device because they can envisage testing a sufficient number of copies for long enough, and computing the estimate from the resulting data. For security - as for non-intentional software failures - the uncertainty often concerns one-off events. This requires a subjective, Bayesian interpretation of probability as "strength of belief".

Another objection to probabilistic reasoning about security stems from the deliberate nature of attacks. The attacker *knows* what he is doing, so where is the uncertainty? From the attacker viewpoint it lies, of course, in his uncertain knowledge about the *system*. The system owner, on the other hand, may have greater knowledge about the system, but is uncertain about the attackers' behavior. He knows that he is dealing with deliberately malign attackers, rather than merely randomly perverse nature, but this does not take away the intrinsic uncertainty about what he will see, e.g. when the next successful attack will occur.

So, like the notion of "systematic" failure, the notion of "deliberate" failure concerns the failure mechanism, not the failure process. To a system owner, observing the process of novel intrusions into his system, this will appear as a stochastic process. The nature of this random process characterizes the security of the system.

Of course, there are some ways in which the deliberate nature of (some) security events is important [5]. For example, in the previous paragraph we referred to *novel* intrusions: this is because once a security hole has been discovered, the subsequent process of intrusions will be different - the intruders may try to exploit the hole intensively - until the hole is fixed. Primary interest may be in the first process, e.g. in the random variable "time to first successful intrusion" - thus a simple example of a snapshot measure of security might be the mean of this random variable (*cf* mean time to failure). If holes are fixed as they are found, we may also be interested in the stochastic process of successive events: this is similar to the reliability growth processes for software *reliability*.

The important point here is that for security, as for reliability and safety, we must take account of *inherent* uncertainty. Eliminating the uncertainty completely is almost never an option: no system is completely secure, just as no system is completely safe, or completely reliable.

It follows that our discussion of the use of redundancy and diversity to increase security must be carried out in probabilistic terms. This need not mean that the probabilistic models will be the same as those used for reliability and safety, because the nature of the uncertainty may be different for security (although we believe that some models may carry across more-or-less unchanged).

By arguing for the *necessity* of a probabilistic approach, we do not intend to suggest that it presents no practical difficulties. Measurement and estimation are likely to be hard, and to depend upon a large element of expert judgement. But it is worth asking how judgements about system security are made *without* such a probabilistic formalism. What goes into the assertion "this system is sufficiently secure"? Indeed, what does "sufficiently" mean here?

The most-cited difficulty is that of estimating parameters, e.g. the probability of a specific kind of attack occurring over a certain period of time. From this viewpoint, security-relevant phenomena cover a range from recreational vandalism by large crowds, which allows extensive data collection and presumably some ability to extrapolate to the future (forecasts of mass human behavior are frequently successful in various areas, e.g. elections or buying preferences), to one-off attacks by hostile governments, for which statistical extrapolation will be close to impossible.

It is not necessary to have complete faith in the accuracy of numerical estimates of security for a probabilistic approach to have value. Even for hardware reliability, the numerical predictions obtained from "reliability models" are often just educated guesses: useful, but far from infallible. The strength of probabilistic methods is in allowing statements like: "with these components, design A will give better reliability than design B over short mission times", or "the crucial parameter for this system is the probability of errors being correctly detected in component C", which are true for wide ranges of the values of the model parameters. In more complex uses like safety cases, the main value of the use of probabilities is often in the way that formal reasoning allows an expert's argument to be laid out for scrutiny and critique. It enables third parties to question the contributions to the expert's decision of his various information, beliefs, assumptions and reasoning.

3 Redundancy, Diversity and Dependence

Redundancy and diversity are widely used to protect against mistakes and failures. Applications range from quite informal usage - e.g. having someone else check your arithmetic - to engineered fault tolerant systems.

If we look at the simple case of parallel redundant systems, the term "redundancy" usually indicates simple replication of a component in identical copies, as adopted against "random" hardware failures. The term "diversity" has come to be used especially for "multiple version software", in which redundant software "versions" are deliberately made to be different. This is because multiple copies of a program, with exactly the same fault, may provide little protection against software failures. With diverse versions, one hopes that any faults they contain will be sufficiently different for the versions to show different failure behaviour.

The distinction between redundancy and diversity is not a hard and fast one, but the notion of *deliberate difference* is the key to their use in computer systems to protect against design faults. This difference can be achieved in several ways, based on enforcing differences in the ways the versions are built. Thus different design teams may be used, different software engineering practices, etc.

It is here that the word "independent" has been over-used. In the early literature on software fault tolerance, it is possible to find people writing about "independent" teams building "independent" versions, in the hope that these would fail "independently". It is really only the last of these uses of the word that is formally defined and this statistical independence of version failures would indeed be a worthy goal. It would, for example, allow us to claim a probability of failure on demand (*pfd*) of 10^{-6} for a 1-out-of-2 system built from two versions each having *pfd* 10^{-3}. Claims for independence of failure are, unfortunately, hard to justify and rarely (if ever) correct. Indeed, experiments have shown that real software versions had failure processes that are quite strongly correlated, so that systems built from such versions would be much less reliable than an independence assumption would suggest. Nevertheless, there was benefit in the use of diversity: the multiple version systems were a lot more reliable on average than individual versions. The lesson here is that the gain from the use of diversity will depend on the degree of dependence between the failure processes of the versions, not only on their individual reliabilities.

We would stress that much of what we say applies more widely than to multi-version software. For example, work on diverse software fault-finding procedures [6] has shown (admittedly in an experimental context) that "better than independence" can actually be attained. In terms of system structure, there is no need for the complete similarity of functionality, implicit in parallel-redundant systems. One "version" may have a simple "get you home in an emergency" function, or a monitor/watchdog function, next to a "main" version of much greater complexity and functionality. But in all applications of diversity the key lies in *dependence* - we need to make this as low as we can to *achieve* dependability; we need to evaluate it in order to *assess* dependability.

Failure independence itself is clearly not the optimum result. The best effect of diversity would be a situation in which all the circumstances in which one version fails are ones where another succeeds, and vice-versa, so that the probability of common failure is 0. In fact, looking at designers' attitudes to seeking diversity between redundant subsystems, we can identify different categories, with different ideal best results (the names used below are tentative, just for use in our discussion):

1. "separation": designers simply seek to isolate redundant subsystems from as many as possible common potential causes of failure. To tolerate physical faults, this implies physical separation, separate power supplies, etc. In multiple-version software, one usually attempts to isolate the development teams so that biases and misunderstandings do not propagate between them. It is natural to see failure independence as the optimum that this approach can aim for, though one would not expect to achieve it. The models of Eckhardt and Lee and Hughes (see [3, 4]) show that any remaining common influence on the failure processes of two subsystems, *including the very fact of receiving the same input sequences*, will lead to positive correlation of failures;

2. "forced diversity": trying to diversify the way the unavoidable common influences affect the redundant subsystems. Using different, functionally equivalent components in redundant subsystems eliminates the certainty that any design faults will be identical among the subsystems. Forcing developers of "diverse" software versions to use different algorithms for the same function should reduce the risk that the common difficult areas in the requirements will lead to common mistakes in the implementations [7]. There is no clear guide to how much advantage this approach should produce, but the model of Littlewood and Miller (see [3, 4]) shows that, at least in some scenarios, everything else being equal, it can only be an improvement (i.e., reduce correlation between subsystem failures) and makes the goal of negative correlation between failures and even zero failure rate at least theoretically achievable;

3. "tailored diversity": if the designers know in some detail how their precautions affect susceptibility to causes of failure, this allows them to focus "forced diversity" for lower correlation between the effects of common influences on the redundant subsystems. For instance, redundant hardware subsystems could intentionally be selected so that they are most reliable in

different temperature ranges, within the range in which the redundant system is to operate. For multiple-version software, instead, there is rarely any attempt to "tailor" the versions to the particular kinds of faults that might be anticipated [7]. In any form of "defense in depth" (including computer security), this form of diversity demands that each successive layer of defense be especially strong against those threats most likely to penetrate the other layers. Again, the ideal system-level goal is 0 failure rate, though it may be unattainable due to the inevitable "leakage" of each level.

In the next sections, we look at various possible applications of diversity for security, and discuss them in light of these different possible approaches.

4   Redundancy and Diversity for Security

"Security" encompasses multiple attributes (confidentiality, availability, . . .) and defending against multiple threats. Just as in other areas of dependability, different security attributes may create conflicting demands on designers. Redundancy and diversity, in their turn, come in many forms.

Voted redundancy, often seen as the stereotypical form of redundancy against accidental faults, is comparatively rare in security. It may be used for decisions on trust, when there is low enough probability that a majority of the parties involved in voting has been compromised. A designer can adjust the degree of majority required for the desired trade-off between the needs for a low probability of the "bad guys" gaining a majority and determining the decision's outcome, and for a high enough probability of a decision being reached. The methods are the same as in design for reliability.

More common is the case of redundancy of resources, in an (ideally) 1-out-of-N configuration (i.e., in which the service can be provided, possibly in a degraded fashion, if at least 1 of the N redundant resources remains available). For instance, if a server (for any kind of service) can be disabled by an attack, having multiple servers is a defense. In general, whenever the goal of an attack is to cause effects similar to those of a physical fault, e.g. unavailability of a resource, it is natural for designers to consider the same defense. So, security benefits, in terms of ability to guarantee a service even after an attacker has inflicted some damage, are obtained from replication of communication lines, of messages, of stored data; and from data redundancy, watchdog and audit programs for detecting damage. Some security-oriented designs, like "secret sharing" [8, 9], combine resilience against part! ial damage with constraints on the loss of confidentiality that a successful attack on a subset of the servers can achieve.

It is in the forms of error propagation and common-mode failures that the analysis of a redundant scheme from a security viewpoint will differ from the analysis from a reliability viewpoint. The main objection to trusting redundancy for security is that if an attacker can defeat a certain system or defense, the same attacker will have no trouble defeating two copies of the same. This kind of objection cannot be discussed without reference to the multiplicity of security attributes, threats and design possibility mentioned before.

For instance, suppose we have multiple servers in an 1-out-of-N configuration. An example would be the Internet's root Domain Name Servers, which were repeatedly attacked recently [10]. They are meant to be a 1-out-of-13 parallel-redundant system. Against certain threats, this set-up is clearly effective:

– accidental local faults (hardware faults, flood, fire) at different sites, without a common cause, will be close to being independent events, giving vanishingly small probabilities of common failure of all 13: these events can reasonably be neglected in estimating the failure probability of the whole parallel system;
– physical attack to the premises of all the servers will require close to N times the effort required to attack one of them. How much this reduces the probability of system failure would be complex to assess, requiring assumptions about the attackers' resources and cost-benefit trade-offs, but still redundancy can be seen to be clearly effective.

Indeed [11] wrote before the attacks: "... root servers are extremely secure... The protocols that govern the 13 root servers call for complete diversity. The servers are geographically distributed, ... Those in the United States are almost evenly divided between the East and West coasts ....".

However, a common argument goes, attackers can easily steal resources around the Internet to use in massive attacks, making the cost of attacking all servers much lower. This makes it more likely that an attack that disabled one server could disable them all. Failures of the redundant channels will have high positive correlation, and the parallel-redundant nature of the system would no longer be a very useful defense. To continue the example, consider a different kind of attacker, one who would try to penetrate, undetected, the host computers to produce some subtler corruption of their data and software. How effective would redundant defenses then be?

– suppose that the attacker needs to guess a key or password for each server (and these have been chosen well to make the attack expensive). Then, the attacker's required effort is effectively multiplied by N;
– but if the attacker instead discovers a defect that creates a back door in all servers, the extra effort due to the multiple servers will be minimal. To avoid this risk, one would probably want some diversity of software among the servers (which in this example probably exists, although it did not seem important to the author of [11]), in addition to geographical separation;
– or the attacker could aim to penetrate just one server but to create local damage there that will subtly subvert the whole redundant set. The multiple servers become effectively a series system: compromising one will cause the whole system to fail.

These complexities are often quoted to caution against expecting too much help from redundancy. However, they are not specific to security. Designers in other areas of dependable design are familiar with similar complexities; one would not expect memory error-correcting codes to be a defense against application software bugs, or replicated CPUs to defend against power failures; or arrangements for safety to automatically benefit availability.

What can be generalized from these examples is perhaps obvious:

- different threats call for different kinds of redundancy, even in the same system;
- whether a certain kind of redundancy is a cost-effective defense depends on the detailed circumstances of the design problem;
- trade-offs may be required between various requirements, including security requirements. These inevitably require quantitative (albeit approximate) reasoning. Researchers have recently started publishing studies of security scenarios using tools originally developed for studying design compromises in fault-tolerant systems [12, 13].

A subtler point concerns "diversity". In which sense is the dispersion of servers over the world "diversity"? What does it add to simple "redundancy" (replication)?

This leads back to the various forms of "diversity" introduced in Sec. 3. Creating two copies of a server is, against accidental faults, simple "separation", which can be increased by further physical isolation between the two. Making the two servers use different software can be seen as further "separation", against accidental software faults. The different software for the two machines may be intentionally developed in different ways to reduce the chance of common faults: "forced diversity", through "separation" of the fault-producing processes; and the different ways may intentionally be chosen to have different known strengths and weaknesses [7]. Geographical distance, as a defense against physical causes of failure, is simply added "separation". Against software faults, it is not even that. Against physical attacks, it can be more than that: for an enemy with limited resources, it would make it unlikely that both servers can be attacked at once, and thus push towards negative correlation of attacks, and ! thus of the failures they may cause. Against distributed attacks with stolen resources, again it may not even confer "separation" [2].

This discussion shows again that the meanings of words like "redundancy" and "diversity" are somewhat ambiguous and ill-delimited. We do not advocate more stringent definitions, which would contrast with common usage; rather, in analyzing design solutions one needs to refer to the specific threats and mechanisms employed and how they affect the correlation among failures.

There is currently renewed interest in using diversity for security. Many recent papers invoke "diversity" as an aid for security. Without citing them all, we can identify a few basic categories. Economic factors, with the increasing common dependence on off-the-shelf products, naturally push towards greater application of fault tolerance for all aspects of dependability [14, 15]. A category of proposed designs for intrusion tolerance thus is meant to allow for diverse off-the-shelf applications or platforms to coexist in a system. Another category of proposals stems from the often repeated observation that lack of diversity in the computers on a network creates the potential for broad propagation of attacks,

---

[2] Similar reasoning applies to non-replication redundancy, e.g. error-detecting/correcting codes, redundant data structures, watchdog, monitor or audit processes.

as demonstrated by several Internet worm attacks. Authors have proposed e.g.: random diversification of compilations to defeat buffer overflow attacks [16]; generating "variants of many OS modul! es, so some of the variants will be resistant to new, previously unknown attacks" [17]; "randomizing" at installation time the choice of COTS components (among different, equivalent implementations) for forming a system [18]. HACQIT (Hierarchical Adaptive Control of Quality of service for Intrusion Tolerance) [19] uses diverse off-the-shelf applications. The Cactus architecture [20] and the SITAR architecture [21] are meant to support diversity among application modules to enhance survivability; similar ideas are proposed in [22]. Proposals for agent-based distributed intrusion detection [23] cite support of diversity as one of their goals. Last, discussion papers argue the general desirability of diversity; e.g., [24] proposes diversity among network elements, in along all possible dimensions of a design; [25] lists forms of diversity available at different system levels.

Most of these examples can be seen as degrees of the "separation" or "forced diversity" approaches: the hope is that "diversified" subsystems, though all having unknown vulnerabilities, will not succumb to the same attacks. There is no "tailoring" of diversity to threats. But, since general categories of attacks can be identified and the efficacy of defenses varies between them, there is also a role for "tailored diversity". We will return to this after looking at some weaknesses of the current debate about "diversity for security".

5   Applying Results from Diversity Research

The papers we cited demonstrate awareness, in the security community, of diversity as a potentially valuable tool. But, interestingly, none of these papers discusses how to choose among different diverse designs, that use e.g. different architectures or different selections of diverse components for the same architecture, or how to evaluate the effectiveness of the design once selected. The rare statements about these issues are somewhat simplistic, and limited to design factors that a designer can control directly, without consideration of how to evaluate their actual effect. For example:

- "The deployment environment is not susceptible to common-mode failures since ITDOS supports implementation diversity in both language and platform" [26]. This clearly refers to the intentions of the fault-tolerant design rather than its effectiveness;
- "An important factor ... is the *independence* of the methods used, where two methods A and B are independent if compromising A provides no information that makes it easier to compromise B, and vice versa. A simple example of non independence is when two encryption methods use the same key ... While the independence of encryption methods is difficult to argue rigorously, the risk of methods not being independent is likely to be minimized if the methods are substantially different or if they encrypt data in different size blocks" [27]. This emphasizes the need for *"separation"* against faults affecting both components or propagating between them, but does not address the other factors that may make common failures too likely.

Choosing among (diverse or non-diverse) solutions presents various difficulties. Practitioners are familiar with some of these, e.g. the difficulty of evaluating even a simple, non-redundant security system. We will discuss here some aspects specific to diversity, hoping that this will contribute to insight for practitioners and to selecting research directions.

An example of application of diversity is that of intrusion detection. Any criterion, and any implemented system, for recognizing hostile activity has incomplete coverage (less than 100% probability of recognizing such activity when it happens): it appears natural to combine multiple criteria, and one design solution is to deploy multiple intrusion detection systems (e.g., advertisements for intrusion detection products claim as self-evident that combining "anomaly-based" with "signature-based" intrusion detectors is desirable). The simplest model for their use would be a 1-out-of-N system: a threat is assessed to be present provided that at least one of the intrusion detection systems (IDSs) detects it. The problem would arise of deciding how effective the combined IDS would be, so as to choose them appropriately. In this simple form of combination, increasing the number of diverse IDSs in the system can only increase their combined coverage, but this may not be a fea! sible option: each added IDS increases cost (false alarms, ownership costs, run-time overhead).

To choose a single IDS from those available, one would try to rank them by performance, and choose the best one. Using the limited data known about commercial or research systems [28–30], plus one's opinions and anecdotal evidence, a designer will be able to choose the "best" system in view of his constraints.

Suppose now that one is to choose two IDSs to deploy together. Should one simply choose the two "best" IDSs from the previous ranking, supposing that they satisfy one's cost constraints? Not necessarily, since their combined effectiveness will depend on *both* their individual effectiveness *and* the correlation among their failures; any choice we make affects both.

Some help may come from a "tailored diversity" approach. Different IDSs will be effective against different attacks. It would then seem that the correct criterion for choosing is a deterministic coverage criterion: with the help of a comparison of the various IDSs' characteristics as in [31] and a knowledge of which characteristics help to detect which attacks, one would enumerate the attacks "covered" by each tool in isolation, and then by each pair of them in combination. Ranking the sets of attacks covered by each pair, one would then choose the "best" pair of IDSs, as proposed e.g. in [32]. This method, however, neglects the uncertainty on the actual detection of each specific attack. Again, we need to use probabilities. One clearly needs to combine the information about the classes of attacks covered and about how well they are covered.

It is here that some results from previous research on diversity may help (see [3, 4]). A first-cut description of the problem runs as follows. If we choose a *specific* attack x, a certain IDS, A, in the given operational conditions has a probability $\theta_A(x)$ of failing to detect it. Another IDS, B, will have a probability $\theta_B(x)$ of failing to detect it. As the attacks arrive unexpectedly, according to some probability distribution, the probabilities of A and B each missing the next, unknown attack will be weighted averages (over attacks) of the functions $\theta_A(x)$ and $\theta_B(x)$, say, Q_A and Q_B. A designer will try to protect the two IDSs from causes of common failure, e.g. if they monitor a network will try to run them on separate hosts, so that the activity of A will not affect the performance of B, and vice versa. There will be still some common influences on both: e.g., the amount of network traffi! c to be monitored. To take account of these common environmental conditions, we would include them in the description of the individual attacks. An idealized model, then, will assume that, for a *specific attack* x, the failures of the two IDSs are independent. But they will not be independent in general, for the next, random attack X. A well-known equation from the literature on diversity gives:

$$P\,(\text{A and B both fail to detect}\,X) = \sum_{x \in D} P(x)\theta_A(x)\theta_B(x) =$$

$$Q_A Q_B + cov_x\,(\theta_A(x), \theta_B(x)) \quad (1)$$

where $P(x)$ indicates the probability of the attack x in the environment of use, D is the set of all possible attacks, and *"cov"* designates the covariance of the two functions, roughly an indication of how similar the two "θ" functions are. When high, this indicates that attacks which are likely to be missed by A are also likely to be missed by B. Zero covariance indicates independence. Negative covariance is most desirable. Ideally, any attacks missed by A would be detected by B, and vice versa. While this is unlikely to be achieved, nothing in principle prevents the values of the covariance from being very low, especially if A and B were "tailored" for different methods of attack. The modelling confirms, though, that to evaluate the pair it is not sufficient to evaluate A and B separately. Somehow, one must evaluate either the left hand term of the equation (the effectiveness of the pair as a whole) or the separate terms of the right-hand side, which describe each IDS separately plus, through the covariance, the effect of combining them. In some experiments on software diversity against design faults, the covariance part dwarfed the product that precedes it. A difference when applying equation 1 to IDSs' failures to detect attacks is that "failure" encompasses not only the effects of software bugs, but also the natural limits of the! intrusion detection algorithms. Thus, we will expect the terms Q_A, Q_B to be greater than those observed in software diversity experiments; but also, on the other hand, a better chance for the designer of being able to rank the possible pairs of IDSs in terms of covariance, by looking at which cues individual IDSs use and thus which attacks they seem least able to detect. This possibility requires some more discussion.

The functions $\theta_A(x)$ and $\theta_B(x)$ are in practice unknowable: they describe the effectiveness of an IDS with respect to every possible attack episode, specified in minute detail. One can usually estimate (more or less accurately, by combining statistical measures and educated guesses) probabilities of missing attacks by *type* of attack. Given the attack types, $C_1, C_2, \ldots$, we would thus have variables $Q_{A|1}, Q_{A|2}, \ldots$ indicating the probability of e.g. IDS A failing to detect an attack of category 1, 2, etc. As shown in [33], equation 1 can be rewritten as:

$$P\left(\text{A and B both fail to detect}X\right) =$$

$$\sum_i P\left(X \in C_i\right) P\left(\text{A and B both fail to detect}X | X \in C_i\right) =$$

$$\sum_i P\left(X \in C_i\right) \left(Q_{A|i}Q_{B|i} + cov_{x \in C_i}\left(\theta_A(x), \theta_B(x)\right)\right) \tag{2}$$

This gives some practical improvements compared to (1). If we can choose our classification of attacks so that within each type at least one between A and B has practically constant value of its θ function for all the attacks of that type (a simple extreme case being that of deterministically detecting all, or none, of the attacks of one type), the covariance terms will be zero. If we can trust this *conditional independence* within each attack type, the problem is reduced to evaluating A and B separately, albeit in somewhat greater detail (i.e., for each attack type separately) than required if the covariance term were zero in (1). A designer will try to make the sum $\sum_i P(C_i)Q_{A|i}Q_{B|i}$ as small as possible, by choosing A and B so that their respective strengths and weaknesses are complementary (low covariance between the *average* probabilities of missing attacks of each type). One can also write this more ! modest inequality:

$$P\left(\text{A and B both fail to detect}X\right) =$$

$$\sum_i P\left(X \in C_i\right) P\left(\text{A and B both fail to detect}X | X \in C_i\right) \leq$$

$$\sum_i P\left(X \in C_i\right) min\left(Q_{A|i}, Q_{B|i}\right) \tag{3}$$

which, given the designer's preference for IDSs with "complementary" weaknesses, may give low enough upper bounds to demonstrate the advantage of the diverse system over either IDS alone. Of course, upper bounds are not sufficient for an *optimal* choice of a pair of IDSs: for this, it is inevitable to refer to some variation of equation 2, allowing for the large uncertainties on all its parameters.

Environmental conditions (e.g., network load) may influence the θ functions. It will then be advisable to use, in the categorization of attacks, not just qualities like the kind of security weakness they exploit, but also these environmental circumstances, e.g. the type "overflow exploit type X" would be divided into subtypes "..with heavy load" and "..with light load". In mathematical terms, this attempts to reduce the covariance term within each attack type simply by narrowing the range of variation of either θ function.

The important point here is that it is necessary to evaluate IDSs by types of attacks and of conditions of use. In practice, however, in the rare meritorious efforts to report the detection efficacy of IDSs [29, 28], only *average* measures of efficacy are often obtained. However, [30] classified test results by coarse categories of attack (8 categories); finer classifications may be needed. This greater attention in data collection to the variations in IDS efficacy would be useful in any case, irrespective of whether diversity is used, for system designers to gauge the range of effectiveness they can expect depending on variations in the attack population, which of course is under the control of attackers.

6   Conclusions

This is a very initial attempt to highlight important aspects of diversity for security and the need for more of a formal mathematical approach to estimating its effectiveness. Some immediate conclusions from applying earlier models are:

- the idea of "independence" must be treated with care, making sure not to confuse its various meanings;
- in choosing diverse subsystems from a given set, attention is needed to the trade-off between the goodness of the individual subsystems and their "diversity";
- it is important to measure the performance of IDSs by category of attack, rather than for some average mixture of attacks; to some extent, the equations help to combine one's assessments of specific aspects of IDSs into guidance for design.

We would be the first to admit that these results are rough and imprecise; for some readers, they will undoubtedly just confirm common sense. But we have seen in previous research that common sense about diversity is actually very different for different people, and often leads to conclusions that turn out to be demonstrably false. For example, the formal statement and proof of the elusiveness of failure independence has proven counterintuitive (and thus important) in reliability and safety, and will apply to many security scenarios as well.

Important directions for developing these ideas include:

- clarifying the roles of the various forms of uncertainties affecting any prediction, e.g. differentiating the effects of the unknown attack profiles from that of the unknown defects of the defender's system;
- analyzing the complex real-life systems, where redundancy/diversity are deployed in different guises, concurrently, against various threats.

We do not propose these approaches as a way for obtaining precise, demonstrably correct predictions of e.g. how many attacks will go undetected on a particular system. This is beyond the reach of probabilistic methods in most field of dependability, and the more so the fewer statistical data are available.

Much of the chance for security system designers to make well-guided choices depends on better empirical measurements of the actual effectiveness of their various defense methods and components. However, these will never be very accurate. Yet, design decisions should at least be consistent with the information that one does have. Explicit probabilistic modelling seems the only way for ensuring this consistency.

References

1. Randell, B., Dobson, J.E.: Reliability and Security Issues in Distributed Computing Systems. In Proc. 5th IEEE International Symposium Reliability in Distributed Software and Database Systems, Los Angeles (1986) 113-118.

2. Joseph, M.K., Avizienis, A.: A Fault-Tolerant Approach to Computer Viruses. In Proc. 1988 Symposium on Security and Privacy, Oakland, CA (1988).
3. Littlewood, B., Popov, P., Strigini, L.: Modelling software design diversity - a review. ACM Computing Surveys 33 (2001) 177-208.
4. Littlewood, B.: The impact of diversity upon common mode failures. Reliability Engineering and System Safety 51 (1996) 101-113.
5. Littlewood, B., Brocklehurst, S., Fenton, N.E., Mellor, P., Page, S., Wright, D., Dobson, J.E., McDermid, J.E., Gollmann, D.: Towards operational measures of computer security. Journal of Computer Security 2 (1994) 211-229.
6. Littlewood, B., Popov, P., Strigini, L., Shryane, N.: Modelling the effects of combining diverse software fault removal techniques. IEEE Transactions on Software Engineering SE-26 (2000) 1157-1167.
7. Popov, P., Strigini, L., Romanovsky, A.: Choosing effective methods for design diversity - how to progress from intuition to science. In Proc. SAFECOMP '99, 18th International Conference on Computer Safety, Reliability and Security, Toulouse, France (1999) 272-285.
8. Shamir, A.: How to share a secret. Comm. of the ACM 22 (1979) 612-613.
9. Deswarte, Y., Blain, L., Fabre, J.-C.: Intrusion tolerance in distributed systems. In Proc. IEEE Symp. on Research in Security and Privacy, Oakland, USA (1991) 110-121.
10. Cherry, S.M.: Took a Licking, Kept on Ticking. IEEE Spectrum December (2002).
11. Cherry, S.M.: Striking at the Internet's Heart. IEEE Spectrum December (2001).
12. Madan, B.B., Goseva-Popstojanova, et al: Modeling and Quantification of Security Attributes of Software Systems. In Proc. DSN 2002, International Conference on Dependable Systems and Networks - International Performance and Dependability Symposium, Washington, D.C., USA (2002).
13. Singh, S., Cukier, M., Sanders, W.H.: Probabilistic Validation of an Intrusion-Tolerant Replication System. In Proc. DSN 2003, International Conference on Dependable Systems and Networks - Dependable Computing and Communications Symposium, San Francisco, U.S.A. (2003) 615-624.
14. Popov, P., Strigini, L., Romanovsky, A.: Diversity for off-the-Shelf Components. In Proc. DSN 2000, International Conference on Dependable Systems and Networks - Fast Abstracts supplement, New York, NY, USA (2000) B60-B61.
15. Cowan, C., Pu, C.: Survivability From a Sow's Ear: The Retrofit Security Requirement. In Proc. Information Survivability Workshop - ISW '98, Orlando, USA (1998).
16. Forrest, S., Somayaji, et al: Building Diverse Computer Systems. In Proc. 6th Workshop on Hot Topics in Operating Systems (HotOS-VI), (1997) 67 -72.
17. Cowan, C., Pu, C.: Immunix: Survivability Through Specialization. In Proc. SEI Information Survivability Workshop, San Diego (1997).
18. Casassa Mont, M., Baldwin, A., Beres, Y., Harrison, K., Sadler, M., Shiu, S.: Towards Diversity of COTS Software Applications: Reducing Risks of Widespread Faults and Attacks. Trusted E-Services Laboratory, HP Laboratories Bristol, document HPL-2002-178, June 26 (2002).
19. Reynolds, J., Just, J., Lawson, E., Clough, L., Maglich, R., Levitt, K.: The Design and Implementation of an Intrusion Tolerant System. In Proc. DSN 2002, International Conference on Dependable Systems and Networks, Washington, D.C., USA (2002) 285-292.
20. Hiltunen, M.A., Schlichting, R.D., Ugarte, C.A., Wong, G.T.: Survivability through Customization and Adaptability: The Cactus Approach. In Proc. DARPA Information Survivability Conference and Exposition, (2000).

21. Wang, F., Gong, F., Sargor, C., Goseva-Popstojanova, K., Trivedi, K., Jou, F.: SITAR: A Scalable Intrusion-Tolerant Architecture for Distributed Services. In Proc. 2001 IEEE Workshop on Information Assurance and Security, West Point, New York, U.S.A (2001).

22. Ellison, R., Fisher, D., Linger, R., Lipson, H., Longstaff, T., Mead, N.: Survivability: Protecting your critical systems. IEEE Internet Computing 3 (1999) 55-63.

23. Dasgupta, D.: Immunity-Based Intrusion Detection System: A General Framework. In Proc. 22nd National Information Systems Security Conference, NISS, Arlington, USA (1999).

24. Zhang, Y., Vin, H., Alvisi, L., Lee, W., Dao, S.K.: Heterogeneous Networking: A New Survivability Paradigm. In Proc. NSPW'01, 2001 Workshop on new security paradigms, Cloudcroft, New Mexico, USA. (2001) 33-39.

25. Deswarte, Y., Kanoun, K., Laprie, J.-C.: Diversity against Accidental and Deliberate Faults. In Proc. Computer Security, Dependability and Assurance: From Needs to Solutions, York, England and Washington, D.C., USA (1998).

26. Sames, D., Matt et al: Developing a Heterogeneous Intrusion Tolerant CORBA System. In Proc. DSN 2002, International Conference on Dependable Systems and Networks, Washington, D.C., USA (2002).

27. Hiltunen, M.A., Schlichting, R.D., Ugarte, C.A.: Using Redundancy to Increase Survivability. In Proc. Third Information Survivability Workshop (ISW-2000), Boston, Massachusetts, USA (2000).

28. Durst, R., Champion, et al: Testing and Evaluating Computer Intrusion Detection Systems. Comm. of the ACM 42 (1999) 53-61.

29. Maxion, R.A., Tan, K.M.C.: Benchmarking Anomaly-Based Detection Systems. In Proc. DSN 2000, International Conference on Dependable Systems and Networks, New York, New York, USA (2000) 623-630.

30. Lippmann, R.P., Fried, D.J., Graf, I., Haines, J.W., Kendall, K.R., David McClung, Weber, D., Webster, S.E., Wyschogrod, D., Cunningham, R.K., Zissman, M.A.: Evaluating Intrusion Detection Systems: The 1998 DARPA Off-line Intrusion Detection Evaluation. In Proc. DARPA Information Survivability Conference and Exposition (DISCEX '00), Hilton Head, South Carolina, U.S.A. (1999) 12-26.

31. Jackson, K.A.: Intrusion detection system (IDS) product survey. Los Alamos National Laboratory, document LA-UR-99-3883, June (1999).

32. Alessandri, D.: Using Rule-Based Activity Descriptions to Evaluate Intrusion-Detection Systems. In Proc. 3rd International Workshop on Recent Advances in Intrusion Detection (RAID 2000), Toulouse, France (2000) 183-196.

33. Popov, P., Strigini, L. et al: Estimating Bounds on the Reliability of Diverse Systems. IEEE Transactions on Software Engineering SE-29 (2003) 345-359.

34. Kennedy, C.M., Sloman, A.: Closed Reflective Networks: a Conceptual Framework for Intrusion-Resistant Autonomous Systems. University of Birmingham, School of Computer Science, Technical Report CSR-02-3, February (2002).

Discovering Novel Attack Strategies
from INFOSEC Alerts

Xinzhou Qin and Wenke Lee

College of Computing
Georgia Institute of Technology
Atlanta, GA 30332, USA
{xinzhou,wenke}@cc.gatech.edu

Abstract. Correlating security alerts and discovering attack strategies are important and challenging tasks for security analysts. Recently, there have been several
proposed techniques to analyze attack scenarios from security alerts. However,
most of these approaches depend on *a priori* and hard-coded domain knowledge
that lead to their limited capabilities of detecting new attack strategies. In this
paper, we propose an approach to discover novel attack strategies. Our approach
includes two complementary correlation mechanisms based on two hypotheses
of attack step relationship. The first hypothesis is that attack steps are directly related because an earlier attack enables or positively affects the later one. For this
type of attack relationship, we develop a Bayesian-based correlation engine to
correlate attack steps based on security states of systems and networks. The second hypothesis is that for some related attack steps, even though they do not have
obvious and direct relationship in terms of security and performance measures,
they still have temporal and statistical patterns. For this category of relationship,
we apply time series and statistical analysis to correlate attack steps. The security
analysts are presented with aggregated information on attack strategies from these
two correlation engines. We evaluate our approach using DARPA's Grand Challenge Problem (GCP) data sets. The results show that our approach can discover
novel attack strategies and provide a quantitative analysis of attack scenarios.

1 Introduction

A large-scale deployment of information security (INFOSEC) mechanisms can provide
in depth protection for systems and networks. However, the sheer quantity of low level
or incomplete alerts output by INFORSEC devices can overwhelm and prevent security
analysts from making thorough analysis and rapid response. Therefore, it is important to
develop an advanced alert correlation system that can reduce the redundancy of alarms,
intelligently correlate security alerts, and detect attack strategies. Alert correlation is
therefore a core component in a security management system.

Recently, there have been several alert correlation proposals. With respect to correlation techniques, most of the proposed approaches (e.g., [5, 9, 12, 22]) rely on various
forms of prior knowledge of individual attacks such as attack pre-conditions and consequences. It is difficult for these approaches to recognize *new* attack strategies where
the attack or the relationship between attacks is new. It is obvious that the number of
possible correlations is very large, potentially a combinatorial of the number of (known

P. Samarati et al. (Eds.): ESORICS 2004, LNCS 3193, pp. 439–456, 2004.

and new) attacks. Therefore, it is infeasible to know *a priori* and encode all possible matching conditions between attacks. In fact, dangerous and intelligent adversaries will invent new attacks and novel attack strategies especially in information warfare.

We have two motivations in our work. First, we want to develop an alert correlation system that can discover *new* attack strategies without relying solely on domain knowledge. Second, we want to incorporate more evidence or indicators from other non-security monitoring systems to correlate alerts and detect attack strategies. For example, we can incorporate alerts from network management systems (NMS) into the security alert correlation. Although alerts from NMS may not directly tell us what attacks are present, they provide us information on the state of protected domains.

Our main contribution in this paper is the design of an integrated correlation system to discover novel attack strategies from INFOSEC alerts. The system includes two complementary correlation engines based on two hypotheses of relationships between attack steps. The first hypothesis is that attack steps are directly related because an earlier attack enables or positively affects the later one. For example, a port scan may be followed by a buffer overflow attack against a scanned service port. For this type of direct relationship, we develop a Bayesian-based correlation mechanism to reason and correlate attack steps based on security states of systems and networks. Our Bayesian-based correlation mechanism uses probabilistic reasoning technique and incorporates domain knowledge of individual attacks to reason and correlate alerts. Our approach does not rely on the strict pre-/post-condition matching and can also function on the partial correlation evidence. The second hypothesis is that some related attack steps still have temporal and statistical patterns even though they do not have an obvious or direct relationship in terms of security and performance measures. For this category of relationship, we apply statistical analysis to correlate attack steps. This correlation mechanism does not rely on prior knowledge of attacks. It correlates alerts by investigating and testing the temporal and statistical patterns of attack steps. Therefore, it is analogous to *anomaly detection*.

We evaluate our methods using DARPA's Grand Challenge Problem (GCP) data sets [8]. The results show that our approach can successfully discover new attack strategies and provide a quantitative analysis method to analyze attack strategies.

The remainder of this paper is organized as follows. Section 2 discusses the related work. We present our alert correlation approach in Section 3. In Section 4, we report the experiments and results on the GCP. We summarize the paper and point out some ongoing and future work in Section 5.

2   Related Work

Recently, there have been several proposed techniques of alert correlation and attack scenario analysis.

Valdes and Skinner [30] use probabilistic-based reasoning to correlate alerts by measuring and evaluating the similarities of alert attributes. Alert aggregation and scenario construction are conducted by enhancing or relaxing the similarity requirements in some attribute fields. Goldman et al. [12] build a correlation system based on Bayesian reasoning. The system predefines the relationship between mission goals and corresponding security events for further inference and correlation.

Porras et al. design a "mission-impact-based" correlation system with a focus on the attack impacts on the protected domains [26]. The system uses clustering algorithms to aggregate and correlate alerts. Security incidents are ranked based on the security interests and the relevance of attack to the protected networks and systems.

Debar and Wespi [9] apply backward and forward reasoning techniques to correlate alerts with *duplicate* and *consequence* relationship. They use clustering algorithms to detect attack scenarios and situations. This approach pre-defines consequences of attacks in a configuration file.

Morin and Debar [21] apply chronicle formalism to aggregate and correlate alerts. The approach performs attack scenario pattern recognition based on *known* malicious event sequences. Therefore, this approach is similar to *misuse detection* and cannot detect new attack sequences.

Ning et al. [22], Cuppens and Miège [7] and Cheung et al. [5] build alert correlation systems based on matching the pre-/post-conditions of individual alerts. The idea of this approach is that prior attack steps prepare for later ones. Therefore, the consequences of earlier attacks correspond to the prerequisites of later attacks. The correlation engine searches alert pairs that have a consequence and prerequisite matching. Further correlation graphs can be built with such alert pairs [22]. One challenge to this approach is that a new attack cannot be paired with any other attacks because its prerequisites and consequences are not defined. Recently, Ning et al. [24] have extended the pre-/post-condition-based correlation technique to correlate some isolated attack scenarios by hypothesizing missed attack steps.

Our approach aims to address the challenge of how to detect *novel* attack strategies. Our approach differs from other work in the following aspects. First, our approach integrates two complementary correlation engines to discover attack scenario patterns. We apply a Bayesian-based correlation engine to the attack steps that are directly related because prior attack enables the later one. Our Bayesian-based correlation engine differs from previous work in that we incorporate knowledge of attack step transitions as a constraint when conducting probabilistic inferences. The correlation engine makes the inference about the correlation based on broad indicators of attack impacts without using the strict hard-coded pre-/post-condition matching. We apply a statistical-based correlation engine to attack steps with temporal and statistical patterns. This approach differs from previous work in that it does not rely on prior knowledge of attack strategies or pre-/post-conditions of individual attacks. Therefore, this approach can be used to discover *new* attack strategies. In this respect, our approach is analogous to *anomaly detection* technique. To the best of our knowledge, this is the first approach to detecting new attack strategies. Our integrated approach also provides a quantitative analysis of the likelihood of various attack paths. With the aggregated correlation results, security analysts can perform further analysis and make inferences about high-level attack plans.

3   Alert Correlation

In this section, we introduce our two complementary correlation mechanisms based on probabilistic and statistical reasoning techniques respectively. In particular, we apply the Bayesian network to probabilistic inference and use *Granger Causality Test* (GCT) [13][1] for statistical analysis.

In our framework, we first *aggregate and cluster* raw alerts, then *prioritize* the aggregated alerts before conducting further alert correlation. The corresponding algorithms for alert aggregation and prioritization can be found in our prior work [27]. Briefly, alert aggregation and clustering reduces the redundancy of raw alerts while retaining important alert attributes, such as *time stamp, source IP, destination IP, port(s), attack class*. In this step, alerts corresponding to the same attacks from heterogeneous security sensors are aggregated. Aggregated alerts with the same attributes (except time stamps) are grouped into one cluster, called **hyper alert**. Alert prioritization is to rank each hyper alert based on its relevance to the configuration of protected networks and hosts, as well as the severity of the corresponding attack assessed by the security analyst. The relevance check downgrades the impacts of some alerts unrelated to the protected domains. For example, an attacker may blindly launch a buffer overflow attack against a host without knowing if the corresponding service exists or not. In practice, it is quite possible that a signature-based IDS will output an alert once the packet contents match the detection rules even though the service does not exist on the target host. This type of alert has a low priority.

3.1   Probabilistic Reasoning on Alert Correlation

Motivation. In practice, we observe that when a host is compromised by an attacker, it usually becomes the target of further attacks or a stepping-stone for launching attacks against other systems. Therefore, the consequences of an attack on a compromised host can be used to reason about a possible matching with the goals of another attack. It is possible to address this correlation by defining pre-/post-conditions of individual attacks and applying condition matching. However, it is infeasible to enumerate and precisely encode all possible attack consequences and goals into pre-/post-conditions. Therefore, we apply probabilistic reasoning to alert correlation by incorporating system indicators of attack consequences and prior knowledge of attack transitions. In this section, we discuss how to apply probabilistic reasoning to attack consequences and goals in order to discover the subtle relationships between attack steps in an attack scenario.

Model Description. Figure 1(a) shows the procedure of correlation inference. Given a stream of alerts, *evaluators* first analyze one or more features of alert pairs and output results as evidence to the *inference module*. The *inference module* combines the individual opinions expressed by the evaluators into a single assessment of the correlation by computing and propagating correlation beliefs within the inference network.

In our inference module, we use a Bayesian network [25] as our reasoning engine. Bayesian networks are usually used as a principle method to reason uncertainty and are capable of leveraging prior expert opinions with the learned information from data. A Bayesian network is usually represented as a directed acyclic graph (DAG) where

---

[1] In alert correlation, "causality" should be interpreted as correlation instead of conventional meaning of "causality". The term "cause" used between attack steps should be interpreted as attack step transition.

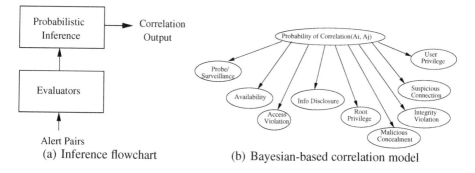

(a) Inference flowchart   (b) Bayesian-based correlation model

Fig. 1. Probabilistic reasoning model

each node represents a variable that has a certain set of states, and the directed edges represent the causal or dependent relationships among the variables. A Bayesian network consists of several parameters, i.e., prior probability of parent node's states (i.e., $P(parent\_state = i)$), and a set of conditional probability tables (CPT) associated with child nodes. CPT encodes the prior knowledge between child node and its parent node. Specifically, an entry of the CPT at a child node is defined by $CPT_{ij} = P(child\_state = j | parent\_state = i)$.

Figure 1(b) shows the structure of our Bayesian inference model for pair-wise correlation. Since we depend on domain knowledge to correlate directly related alert pairs, we design a one-level Bayesian network that is good enough to perform inference. In the inference model, the root node represents the *hypothesis* that two attacks are correlated. Specifically, the root node has two hypothesis states, i.e., "high correlation" and "low correlation". Each child node represents a type of attack consequences on the host. The evaluator on each child node detects the condition matching between the consequences and the necessary conditions of the two alerts being correlated. The evaluation result on each leaf node is mapped to a state of the child node. Each child node has three states: "matched", "not matched" and "unknown". The state "unknown" handles the case that there is no need of condition matching, e.g., some attacks do not necessarily have any pre-conditions in order to launch attacks. The output of the inference engine represents the probability or confidence of the correlation between two alerts being correlated, i.e., $P(correlation = high | evidence)$, based on the evidence (e.g., "matched" or "unmatched") provided by the leaf nodes. The inference is conducted by propagating belief messages among leaf nodes and the root node. Specifically, we denote e^k as the kth leaf node and H_i as the ith hypothesis of the root node. Given the evidence from the leaf nodes, assuming conditional independence with respect to each H_i, the belief in hypothesis at the root is: $P(H_i \mid e^1, e^2, \ldots, e^N) = \gamma P(H_i) \prod_{k=1}^{N} P(e^k | H_i)$, where $\gamma = [P(e^1, e^2, \ldots, e^N)]^{-1}$ and γ can be computed using the constraint $\sum_i P(H_i | e^1, e^2, \ldots, e^N) = 1$ [25]. Since the belief computation can be performed incrementally instead of being delayed until all the evidence is collected, the Bayesian inference engine can also function on partial evidence, and the lack of evidence input from an evaluator does not require special treatment.

As Figure 1(b) shows, each leaf node represents an attack consequence on the attack victim. We consider broad aspects of attack consequences when reasoning about the correlation between two alerts.

Probe/Surveillance: information on system or network has been gained by an attacker, e.g., a probing attack can get information on open ports. *Availability*: the system is out of service or the service is negatively affected by the attack, e.g., because of a DoS attack. *Access Violation*: an illegal access to a file or data of a system. *Information Disclosure*: the attacker exports (sensitive) data to external site. *Root Privilege* has been obtained by an attacker, for example, by a buffer overflow attack. *Malicious Concealment*: malicious binary codes have been installed on the system, e.g., a Trojan horse. *Integrity Violation*: the file on a system has been modified or deleted, violating the security policy. *Suspicious Connection*: a covert channel has been set up by the attack. *User Privilege* has been obtained by the attacker.

Table 1. Predicates used in impact evaluation

FailService	DegradeService	FailProcess
DegradeProcess	ModifyData	DeleteData
GainUserPrivilege	GainRootPrivilege	GainServiceInfo
GainOSInfo	InstallMaliciousDaemon	InstallTrojan
SetupCovertChannel	FailCovertChannel	ExportData
GainFile	AccessSystem	LeakInformation

Table 1 shows the set of predicates that we defined to assess the consequences of attack. Each attack impact shown in Figure 1(b) has been associated with a set of predicates defined in Table 1. For example, predicates "FailService" and "DegradeService" represent the attack impacts on the availability of the target's service. The definition of predicates is a broad template and each predicate can be instantiated to a specific consequence instance according to information provided by alerts. For example, when a port scan alert is output, its corresponding impact instance is *GainServiceInfo.TargetIP*. Each alert has also been defined a *pre-condition(s)* using the predicates shown in Table 1. Like the definition of impact of attack, *pre-condition(s)* of each alert can also be instantiated based on alert specific attributes. Each alert can provide the necessary information from its attributes, such as *source IP*, *target IP*, *attack class*.

Correlating two alerts includes the following steps. First, each alert first initializes its corresponding *pre-condition* and *impact* fields. Second, alert pairs are checked to see if they comply with certain constraints, e.g., an implicit temporal constraint between these two alerts is that alert A_i occurs before alert A_j. Third, evaluations are conducted by comparing the "*causal*" alert's impacts and *effected* alert's pre-conditions on each of the leaf nodes as shown in Figure 1. Fourth, results of evaluations are mapped to the states of leaf nodes, i.e., "matched", "unmatched" and "unknown". Finally, an overall probability computation is conducted based on the state evidence of each leaf node.

For example, alert *portscan* has a consequence defined as *GainServiceInfo.targetIP*. Alert *imap buffer overflow* has a pre-condition as *GainServiceInfo.targetIP*, where predicate "GainServiceInfo" is associated with attack consequence *Probe* shown in Figure 1(b). If *portscan* alert occurs before alert *imap buffer overflow* and they have the same target IP addresses, then their pre-/post-conditions are matched. The corresponding state of leaf node *Probe/Surveillance* in Figure 1(b) will be set as "matched". The Bayesian-model computes the evidence and outputs the probability or confidence of the correlation of these two alerts.

Parameters in Bayesian Model. When using a Bayesian model for inference, we need to set up two types of parameters, i.e., prior probability of root's states and CPT associated with each child node.

The prior probability of root states (e.g., $P(correlation = high)$) used in the inference engine is set based on the attack class of alerts being correlated. It indicates the *prior knowledge* estimation of the possibility that one attack class reasonably transits to another one. For example, it is reasonable for us to have a higher estimation of the possibility that an exploit attack follows a probe than the other way around. We use domain-specific knowledge based on prior experience and empirical studies to estimate appropriate probability values. Related work [30] also helps us on the probability estimation.

In alert correlation, the pair of alerts being evaluated in the correlation engine (as shown in Figure 1(b)) is only known at run-time. Therefore, we cannot use an inference engine with a fixed set of CPT parameters. Instead, we set up a set of CPTs based on each pair of attack classes (e.g., *Malicious Concealment* and *DoS*). At run-time, when correlating a pair of alerts A_i and A_j with respective corresponding attack classes $C(A_i)$ and $C(A_j)$ (e.g., alert *imap buffer overflow* with attack class *Super Privilege Violation* and alert *illegal file access* with attack class *Access Violation*), the inference engine selects the corresponding CPT parameters for the attack classes $C(A_i)$ and $C(A_j)$, and computes the overall probability that A_j is "caused" by A_i given the evidence from the evaluators, i.e., $P(correlation = high|e = evidence)$. An implicit temporal constraint between these two alerts is that alert A_i occurs before A_j. In this example, we can interpret the correlation as: the *imap buffer overflow* attack is followed by an illegal access to a file after the attacker gets root privileges on the target. Initial values of CPTs are pre-defined based on our experience and domain knowledge.

CPT values associated with each node adapt to new evidence and therefore can be updated accordingly. We apply an adaptive algorithm originally proposed by [1] and further developed by [6]. The motivation of using adaptive Bayesian network is that we want to fine-tune the parameters of the model and adapt the model to the evidence to fix the initial CPTs that may be pre-defined inappropriately. The intuition of the algorithms proposed by [1] is that we want to adapt the new model by updating CPT parameters to fit the new data cases while balancing movement away from the current model.

Specifically, we denote X as a node in a Bayesian network, and let U be the parent node of X. X has r states with values of x_k, where $k = 1, ..., r$ and U has q states with values of u_j, where $j = 1, ..., q$. An entry of CPT of the node X can be denoted as: $\theta_{jk} = P(X = x_k|U = u_j)$. Given a set of new data cases, denoted as D, $D = y_1, ..., y_n$, and assuming there is no missing data in evidence vector of y_t, where evidence vector y_t represents the evidence at the tth time, the CPT updating rules are:

$$\theta_{jk}^t = \eta + (1 - \eta)\theta_{jk}^{t-1}, \quad for \ P(u_j|y_t) = 1 \ and \ P(x_k|y_t) = 1. \tag{1}$$

$$\theta_{jk}^t = (1 - \eta)\theta_{jk}^{t-1}, \ for \ P(u_j|y_t) = 1 \ and \ P(x_k|y_t) = 0. \tag{2}$$

$$\theta_{jk}^t = \theta_{jk}^{t-1}, \ otherwise. \tag{3}$$

η is the learning rate. The intuition of the above updating rules is that, for an entry of CPT, e.g., θ_{mn}, we either increase or decrease its value (i.e., $P(X = x_n|U = u_m)$) based on the new evidence received. Specifically, given the evidence vector y_t, if the parent node U is observed in its mth state, i.e., $U = u_m$, and X is in its nth state, i.e., $X = x_n$, we regard the evidence as *supporting evidence* of the CPT entry θ_{mn}. We then increase its value (i.e., $P(X = x_n|U = u_m)$), which indicates the likelihood that X is in its nth state given the condition that parent node U is in its mth state, as shown in Eq. (1). By contrast, if node X is not in its nth state while its parent node U is in the mth state, we then regard the evidence as *un-supporting evidence* of θ_{mn} and decrease θ_{mn}'s value as shown in Eq. (2). We do not change the value of θ_{mn} if no corresponding evidence is received. The learning rate η controls the rate of convergence of θ. η equaling 1 yields the fastest convergence, but also yields a larger variance. When η is smaller, the convergence is slower but eventually yields a solution to the true CPT parameter [6]. We build our inference model based on above updating rules.

We also need to point out that the adaptive capability of the inference model does not mean that we can ignore the accuracy of initial CPT values. If the initial values are set with a large variance to an appropriate value, it will take time for the model to converge the CPT values to the appropriate points. Therefore, this mechanism works for fine-tuning instead of changing CPT values dramatically.

For an alert pair, (A_i, A_j), if its correlation value computed by the Bayesian-based model, denoted as P_{bayes}, is larger than a pre-defined threshold, e.g., 0.5, then we say Bayesian-based correlation engine identifies that alert A_j is "caused" by alert A_i.

Alert correlation with Bayesian networks has several advantages. First, it can incorporate prior knowledge and expertise by populating the CPTs. It is also convenient to introduce partial evidence and find the probability of unobserved variables. Second, it is capable of adapting to new evidence and knowledge by belief updates through network propagation. Third, the correlation output is probability rather than a binary result from a logical combination. We can adjust the correlation engine to have the maximum detection rate or a minimum false positive rate by simply adjusting the probability threshold. By contrast, it is not directly doable when using a logical combination of pre-/post-condition matching. Finally, Bayesian networks have been studied extensively and successfully applied to many applications such as causal reasoning, diagnosis analysis, event correlation in NMS, and anomaly detection in IDS. We have confidence that it can be very useful to INFOSEC alert correlation.

3.2   GCT-Based Alert Correlation

The motivation to develop another complementary correlation mechanism is that many existing correlation techniques depend on various forms of domain knowledge of attack scenario patterns. This is similar to *misuse detection*. In order to discover *new* attack strategies that are beyond the scope of *prior* knowledge on attack scenarios, we develop another correlation engine based on statistical analysis, in particular, the

Granger Causality Test (GCT) [13]. In this section, we briefly introduce our GCT-based correlation mechanism. Details can be found in [27].

Granger Causality Test (GCT) is a time series-based *statistical* analysis method that aims to test if a time series variable X correlates with another time series variable Y by performing a *statistical hypothesis test*. Although GCT was originally proposed and applied in econometrics, it has been widely applied in other areas, such as weather analysis (e.g., [18]), automatic control system (e.g., [4, 11]) and neurobiology (e.g., [17, 16]). In our prior work [3, 2], we have applied GCT-based analysis for pro-active detection of Distributed-Denial-of-Service (DDoS) attacks using MIB II [29] variables. The results have demonstrated the correlation strength of GCT in network security context.

In this work, we apply the GCT to alert streams for alert correlation and analysis. The hypothesis and intuition is that attack steps that do not have well-known patterns or obvious relationships may nonetheless have some *temporal and statistical* correlations in the alert data. For example, two attacks are associated when one or more alerts for one attack also occurs with one or more alerts for another attack. We can apply time series and statistical correlation analysis to correlate such alert pairs and describe the attack scenario.

Applying GCT to data analysis requires a series of statistical tests including testing if an individual data set is statistically stationary, if two time series variables are statistically independent of each other, and if they are co-integrated. Briefly, when applying the GCT to alert correlation, we test the statistical correlation of alert instances to determine the relationship between hyper alerts (i.e., aggregated alerts with same attributes except time stamp). Specifically, the correlation includes the following steps when identifying the "causal" alert with respect to hyper alert A. (1) For each pair of hyper alerts $(B_i, A), i = 1, 2, \ldots, l$, we compute the value of Granger Causality Index (GCI) g_i, which represents the strength of the "causal" relationship between B_i and A. (2) Given a significance level, we record the alerts whose GCI values have *passed* the F-test as the "causal" candidate alerts, and rank the candidate alerts according to their GCI values. (3) We then select the top m candidate alerts and regard them as being "causally" related to alert A. (4) These (candidate) "causal" relationships can be subject to more inspection by other analysis techniques.

The main advantage of GCT-based correlation engine is that it does not require *a priori* knowledge about attack behaviors and how the attacks can be related. This approach can identify the correlation between two attack steps if they have a statistical pattern, e.g., they repeatedly occur together. We believe that there are a large number of attacks, e.g., worms, with such attack steps. Thus, we believe that causality analysis is a very useful technique. As also discussed in [3, 2], when there is sufficient training data available, we can use GCT off-line to compute and validate very accurate "causal" relationships from alert data. We can then update the knowledge base with these "known" correlations for efficient pattern matching in run-time. When GCT is used in real-time and finds a new "causal" relationship, the top m candidates can be selected for further analysis by other techniques.

As a statistical data analysis tool, GCT also has its limitations because it studies the correlation between variables from a *statistical* point of view. Like any other statistical analysis techniques, the analysis result depends on the existence of statistical patterns

Fig. 2. An example of integration process. The bold line represents a new correlation found in the second step of integration process

in the data. GCT can also result in false causality if two unrelated alerts happen to have a strong statistical pattern. Lee et al. [19] empirically report the "pitfalls" of GCT when applying it to *co-integrated* time series variables. In our analysis, we test the co-integration of data sets before applying GCT to avoid the inaccuracy.

3.3   Integration of GCT-Based
and Probabilistic Reasoning Correlation Mechanisms

Integration Process of Two Correlation Engines.   Our two correlation engines are built on different techniques and focus on different correlation aspects. GCT-based correlation engine is similar to *anomaly detection*. Bayes-based correlation engine is analogous to an extension of pattern matching-based detection. We apply and integrate the two correlation mechanisms with the following steps:

(1) First, we apply Bayesian-based correlation engine on target hyper alerts. Target alerts are hyper alerts with high priorities computed by the *alert priority computation module* [27]. Thus, they should be the main interests in the correlation analysis to correlate with all the other hyper alerts. The result of this step can be a set of isolated correlation graphs.

(2) Second, for each target alert, we run GCT to correlate it with other hyper alerts that have not been identified as "causally" related to the target alert by Bayesian correlation engine. That is, GCT is used to attempt to discover more correlation between alerts and link the isolated graphs together.

For example, we have five hyper alerts, denoted as A_1, A_2, A_3, A_4, A_5. Alerts A_1, A_2 are target alerts. After applying Bayesian-based correlation engine, i.e., the first step of correlation, we get two isolated correlation graphs, as shown in Figure 2. The directed edge indicates the direction from "causal" alerts to the target alerts. Alert A_1 is correlated with alerts A_3 and A_4. Alert A_2 is correlated with alert A_5. In step 2, for alert A_1, we run GCT(A_2, A_1) and GCT(A_5, A_1) to check if they have any relationships. For alert A_2, we run GCT(A_1, A_2), GCT(A_3, A_2) and GCT(A_4, A_2) to test if there are any correlation. If we can find new relationship in step 2, then we can link these two isolated graphs. For example, the bold line in Figure 2 shows the new "causal" relationship from A_4 to A_2 identified in step 2.

The rationale of our integration process in alert correlation is analogous to intrusion detection where security analysts usually first apply *pattern-based detection*, then *anomaly detection* to cover the attack space that pattern-matching method cannot discover.

Probability/Confidence Integration.   In Section 3.1, we introduced our Bayesian-based correlation engine that outputs the correlation probability/confidence of two alerts, denoted as P_{bayes}. In practice, we have a threshold t, and when P_{bayes} is over the threshold t, we say the corresponding alert pair has a "causal" relationship identified by the Bayesian-based correlation engine. As discussed in Section 3.2, GCT Index (GCI) represents the strength of correlation between two alerts being correlated. It conforms to F-distribution with parameters of p and $N - 3p - 1$, where p is the number of history values of the time series variable used in the GCT computation, and N is the size of the time series variable. Therefore, for any two correlated alerts identified by GCT-based correlation engine, we can compute the corresponding F-distribution probability values, i.e., $P_{gct} = CDF_{F-distribution}(p, N - 3p - 1, GCI)$, where CDF represents the *cumulative distribution function*. P_{gct} represents the probability/confidence of correlation between two alerts.

When integrating the two correlation engines, we can normalize the confidence output from GCT-based engine as:

$$P_{gct\_normalized} = (P_{gct} - t) * \omega + t \tag{4}$$

In Eq. (4), t is the threshold defined in Bayesian-based correlation engine, and ω is a weight value that is determined based on prior experience and performance measurements of the two correlation engines. The normalized value of $P_{gct\_normalized}$ is in the range of $[0, t + \epsilon]$, where ϵ is a small positive number. The intuition of this normalization is that we want to downgrade the output of GCT-based correlation engine a little because it is based on statistical analysis that is less accurate than the domain-knowledge-based Bayesian correlation engine.

Therefore, for a correlated alert pair, e.g., (A_i, A_j), we can have a probability or confidence of its correlation (i.e., attack transition from A_i to A_j) computed by either Bayesian correlation engine or GCT-based correlation mechanism. We denote it as $correlation\_prob(A_i, A_j)$, which equals P_{bayes} when their "causal" relationship is identified by Bayesian engine or equals $P_{gct\_normalized}$ when GCT discovers its relationship.

We also note that two different approaches have been proposed to integrate isolated correlation graphs. Ning [23] et al. apply graph theory to measure and merge similar correlation graphs. In [24], Ning et al. link isolated correlation graphs based on attack pre-/post-conditions. Our approach is different from their work in that our integration method is based on the correlation probability evaluated by our two complementary correlation engines instead of graph or pre/post-condition-based merging algorithms.

Attack Strategy Analysis. A scenario/correlation graph can be constructed based on pairs of correlated alerts. A scenario graph is defined as a directed graph where each edge E_{ij} represents a "causal" relationship from alert A_i to A_j. Alerts with "causal" relationship compose the nodes in the scenario graph. We denote the node corresponding to the "causal" alert as *causal node*, and the node corresponding to the "effected" alert as *effected node*. A threshold t is pre-defined and alert A_j is considered to be "caused" by alert A_i only when $correlation\_prob(A_i, A_j) > t$. In constructing scenario graphs, we only include the correlated alert pairs whose $correlation\_prob$ values are over the threshold t.

Fig. 3. An example of correlation graph

In a correlation graph, each edge is associated with a correlation probability (i.e., *correlation_prob*) from *causal node* to *effected node*. Therefore, we can perform *quantitative* analysis on the attack strategies. Each path in the graph is potentially a subsequence of an attack scenario. Each path can be seen as a Markov chain [10, 28]. Therefore, based on the probability associated with each edge, for any two nodes in the graph that are connected by multiple paths, e.g., nodes A_1 and A_4 in the Figure 3, assuming the conditional independence of A_4 and A_1, we can compute the overall probability of each path, e.g., $P(A_1, A_2, A_4) = P(A_4|A_2)P(A_2|A_1)P(A_1) = p_1 * p_2 * p_{A1}$ [28], and then rank order and select the one with the highest overall correlation probability as the most likely sequence connecting the two alerts. Combining all the probability along each edge, an overall probability of two nodes connected with multiple paths can also be computed. For example, in the Figure 3, $P\{A_1 \text{ to } A_4\} = 1 - (1 - p_1 * p_2)(1 - p_3 * p_4)$.

4   Experiments

To evaluate the effectiveness and validity of our alert correlation mechanisms, we applied our algorithms to the data sets of the Grand Challenge Problem (GCP) version 3.1 provided by DARPA's Cyber Panel program [8, 15]. In this section, we describe our experiments with a focus on the analysis of GCP I.

4.1   The Grand Challenge Problem (GCP)

GCP version 3.1 includes two innovative worm attack scenarios to specifically evaluate alert correlation techniques. In addition to the complicated attack scenarios, the GCP data sets also include many background alerts that make alert correlation and attack strategy detection more challenging. In GCP, multiple heterogeneous security systems, e.g., network-based IDSs, host-based IDSs, firewalls, and network management systems, are deployed in several network enclaves. Therefore, GCP alerts are from both security systems and network management system. GCP alerts are in the Intrusion Detection Message Exchange Format (IDMEF) defined by IETF [14].

In order to compare the performance between our current integrated correlation system and the GCT-alone approach used in [27], we used the same data sets and preprocessed the raw alerts the same way as in [27]. According to the GCP documents that include detailed configurations of protected networks and systems, we established a configuration database. Information on mission goals enables us to identify the servers of interest and assign interest score to corresponding alerts targeting at the important hosts. The alert priority is computed based on our model described in [27].

For performance evaluation, we define two measures: *true positive correlation rate*, (i.e., (# *of correct correlated alerts*)/(*total # of correlated relationships*)) and *false positive correlation rate*, (i.e., (# *of incorrect correlated alerts*)/(*total # of correlated alerts*). Here, *correlated alerts* refer to the correlated alert pairs output by correlation engines. We refer to the documents with the ground truth to determine the *correlated relationships* among the alerts. Scenario graph is constructed based on alerts that have causal relationship identified by our correlation engines.

In formulating hyper alert time series, we set the unit time slot to 60 seconds. In the GCP, the entire time range is 5 days. Therefore, each hyper alert time series $x(k)$ has a size of 7,200 (units), i.e., k=0, 1, 2, ..., 7199.

GCP Scenario I. In the GCP Scenario I, there are multiple network enclaves in which attacks are conducted separately. The attack scenario in each network enclave is almost same. We select a network enclave as an example to show the correlation process.

The alert correlation processing is the following:

First, **alert aggregation**. We conduct raw alert aggregation and clustering in order to have aggregated hyper alerts. In scenario I, there are a little more than 25,000 low-level raw alerts output by heterogeneous security devices in all enclaves. After alert fusion and clustering, we have around 2,300 hyper alerts. In our example network enclave, there are 370 hyper alerts after low-level alert aggregation.

Second, **alert noise detection**. We apply the *Ljung-Box* statistical test [20] with significance level $\alpha = 0.05$ to all hyper alerts in order to identify background alerts. In scenario I, we identify 255 hyper alerts as background alerts using this mechanism. Most of background alerts are "HTTP_Cookie" and "HTTP_Posts". Therefore, we have 115 non-noise hyper alerts for further analysis.

Third, **alert prioritization**. The next step is to select the alerts with high priority values as the target alerts. The priority computation is described in [27]. In this step, we set the threshold $\beta = 0.6$. Alerts with priority scores above β are regarded as important alerts and are selected as target alerts. In this step, we identified 15 hyper alerts whose priority values are above the threshold.

Fourth, **alert correlation**. When applying correlation algorithms, we correlate each target alert with all other non-background alerts (i.e., the background alerts identified by the *Ljung-Box* test are excluded.). As described in Section 3.3, we have two steps in correlating alerts. First, we apply Bayesian-based correlation engine on each target hyper alert and discover its "causal" alerts. Figure 4 shows the resulting correlation graphs. Second, for each target hyper alert, we apply GCT-based correlation algorithm to correlate it with other hyper alerts, which are not its "causal" alerts after running Bayesian correlation mechanism in the first step. The resulting correlation graph is shown in Figure 5. The dotted line in Figure 4 and Figure 5 represent false positive "causal" relationship. The correlation probability or confidence of each alert-pair is associated with the edge in the correlation graph. In Eq. (4), ω equals 0.3 and t equals 0.6.

Fifth, **attack path analysis**. As discussed in Section 3.3, for any two nodes in the correlation graph that are connected on multiple paths, we can compute the probability of attack transition along each path, then rank and select the one with highest overall value. For example, from node *DB_FTP_Globbing_Attack* to node *DB_NewClient* in the graph shown in Figure 5, there are 6 paths that connect these two nodes. Based on the probability or confidence associated on the edge, we can compute the value of each path and rank the order.

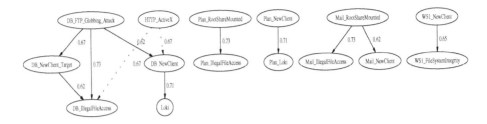

Fig. 4. The GCP scenario I: The correlation graph discovered by Bayesian-based approach

For example, the overall confidence for the attack path $DB\_FTP\_Globbing\_Attack\rightarrow$ $Loki\rightarrow DB\_NewClient$ is: $P(DB\_FTP\_Globbing\_Attack, Loki, DB\_NewClient) =$ $P(DB\_FTP\_Globbing\_Attack) * P(Loki|DB\_FTP\_Globbing\_Attack) * P(DB\_NewClient|Loki) = P(DB\_FTP\_Globbing\_Attack) * 0.7 * 0.72 = P(DB\_FTP\_Globbing\_Attack) * 0.5$. Table 2 shows the ordered multi-paths according to the corresponding path values. From the table, we can see that it is more confident to say that the attacker is more likely to launch *FTP Globbing Attack* against the Database Server, then *New Client* attack from the Database Server that denotes a suspicious connection to an external site (e.g., set up a covert channel).

Sixth, **attack strategy analysis**. In this phase, we perform attack strategy analysis by abstracting the scenario graphs. Instead of using hyper alerts representing each node, we use the corresponding attack class (e.g., *DoS* and *Access Violation*) to abstractly present attack strategies. While analyzing attack strategy, we focus on each target and abstract the attacks against the target. Figure 6(a) shows the high-level attack strategy on the Plan Server extracted from attack scenario graphs shown in Figure 5. From Figure 6(a), we can see that the attacker uses a covert channel (indicated by *Connection Violation*) to export data and import malicious code to root the Plan Server. The attacker accesses to the data stored on the Plan Server (indicated by *Access Violation*) to steal the data, then export the information. The activity of *Surveillance* has impacted the server on the performance (indicated by *Asset Distress*). Figure 6(b) shows the attack strategy on the Database Server. It is easy to see that the attacker launches an exploit attack against the Database Server in order to get root access. Then the attacker sets up a covert channel, accesses data and exports the data. The mutual loop pattern between attack class *Connection Violation, Access Violation* and *Exfiltration* indicates the attack continuously accesses file, exports data and downloads the malicious code.

4.2   Discussion

Applying our integrated correlation mechanism can discover more attack step relationships than using a single approach. Figure 4 shows that when we apply Bayesian-based approach alone, we can only discover partial attack step relationships. The reason is that the Bayesian-based correlation engine relies on domain knowledge to correlate alerts. Therefore, it is only capable of discovering the direct attack step transitions, e.g., attack *Mail_RootShareMounted* followed by attack *Mail_IllegalFileAccess*. When the alert relationship is new or has not been encoded into the correlation engine, such rela-

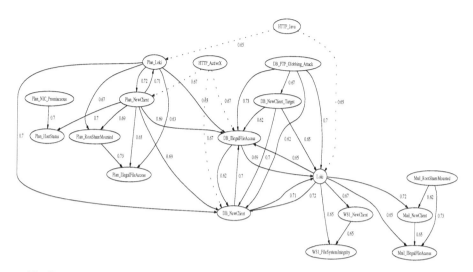

Fig. 5. The GCP scenario I: The correlation graph discovered by the integrated approach

Table 2. Ranking of paths from node *DB FTP Globbing Attack* to node *DB NewClient*. *P* denotes $P(DB\ FTP\ Globbing\ Attack)$

Order	Nodes Along the Path	Score
Path1	DB FTP Globbing Attack→DB NewClient	P*0.62
Path2	DB FTP Globbing Attack→Loki→DB NewClient	P*0.50
Path3	DB FTP Globbing Attack→DB NewClient Target→DB NewClient	P*0.47
Path4	DB FTP Globbing Attack→DB IllegalFileAccess→DB NewClient	P*0.45
Path5	DB FTP Globbing Attack→DB NewClient Target→Loki →DB NewClient	P*0.31
Path6	DB FTP Globbing Attack→DB NewClient Target→DB IllegalFileAccess →DB NewClient	P*0.23

tionship cannot be detected. Figure 5 shows that we can discover some more attack relationships using GCT-based correlation method so that we can link the isolated graphs output by Bayesian correlation engine. The reason is that GCT-based correlation mechanism correlates attack steps based on the temporal and statistical relationship between attack steps, e.g., the loop pattern of attack transitions among attack *DB_NewClient*, *DB_IllegalFileAccess* and *Loki*. This correlation engine does not rely on prior knowledge. On the other hand, given GCT-based correlation analysis does not use domain knowledge, it is less accurate than Bayesian-based correlation analysis for the direct attack step transitions. By incorporating the two correlation engines, in this experiment, we can improve the true positive correlation rate from 95.06% (when using GCT-based correlation engine alone) to 97.53%. False positive correlation rate is decreased from 12.6% (when using GCT-based correlation engine alone) to 6.89%.

Our correlation approach can also correlate non-security alerts, e.g., alerts from network management system (NMS), to detect attack strategy. Although NMS alerts

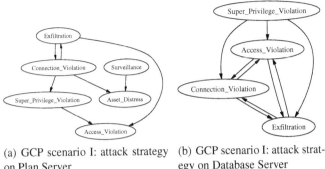

(a) GCP scenario I: attack strategy on Plan Server (b) GCP scenario I: attack strategy on Database Server

Fig. 6. GCP I: Attack strategy graph

cannot directly tell us what attacks are unfolding or what damages have occurred, they can provide us some useful information about the state of system and network health. So we can use them in detecting attack strategy. In this scenario, NMS outputs alert *Plan_Host_Status* indicating that the Plan Server's CPU is overloaded. Applying our GCT-based and Bayesian-based correlation algorithms, we can correlate the alert *Plan_HostStatus* with alert *Plan_NewClient* (i.e., suspicious connection) and *Plan_NIC_Promiscuous* (i.e., traffic surveillance).

We are aware of the limitations of using synthesized data only in our experiments although we believe that the simulation was integrated to be as realistic as possible. The real world will have more complicated and subtle attack strategies with more noisy attacks. We plan to apply our algorithms to real-life data so that we can further improve our work.

5   Conclusion and Future Work

In this paper, we presented an integrated correlation system to analyze INFOSEC alerts and detect novel attack strategies. We develop and integrate two complementary alert correlation mechanisms: (1) correlation based on Bayesian inference with a broad range of indicators of attack impacts, and (2) correlation based on the Granger Causality Test, a statistical-based correlation algorithm. Our Bayes-based correlation mechanism can discover alerts that have direct "causal" relationships according to domain knowledge. This correlation engine can also relax the strict hard-coded pre-/post-condition matching and handle the partial input evidence. GCT-based correlation engine can discover new attack relationships when attack steps have statistical relationship. Attack scenarios are analyzed by constructing correlation graphs based on the correlation results. A quantitative analysis of attack strategy is conducted using the outputs of our integrated correlation engines. Attack strategies are analyzed using correlation graphs. The results show that our approach can discover novel attack strategies with high accuracy.

We will continue to study alert correlation with a focus on attack plan recognition and prediction. We will also study situation assessment, e.g., damage assessment and situation analysis. We also note the limitation of the synthesized alerts in our experiments. Therefore, we will apply our algorithms to alert streams collected from live networks to improve our work.

Acknowledgments

This work is supported in part by NSF grants CCR-0133629 and CCR-0208655 and Army Research Office contract DAAD19-01-1-0610. The contents of this work are solely the responsibility of the authors and do not necessarily represent the official views of NSF and the U.S. Army.

References

1. E. Bauer, D. Koller, and Y. Singer. Update rules for parameter estimation in Bayesian networks. In *Proceedings of the Thirteenth Conference on Uncertainty in Artificial Intelligence (UAI)*, pages 3–13, Providence, RI, August 1997.
2. J. B. D. Cabrera, L. Lewis, X. Qin, W. Lee, and R. K. Mehra. Proactive intrusion detection and distributed denial of service attacks - a case study in security management. *Journal of Network and Systems Management*, vol. 10(no. 2), June 2002.
3. J. B. D. Cabrera, L. Lewis, X. Qin, W. Lee, R. K. Prasanth, B. Ravichandran, and R. K. Mehra. Proactive detection of distributed denial of service attacks using mib traffic variables - a feasibility study. In *Proceedings of IFIP/IEEE International Symposium on Integrated Network Management (IM 2001)*, May 2001.
4. P. E. Caines and C. W. Chan. Feedback between stationary stastic process. *IEEE Transactions on Automatic Control*, 20:495–508, 1975.
5. S. Cheung, U. Lindqvist, and M. W. Fong. Modeling multistep cyber attacks for scenario recognition. In *Proceedings of the Third DARPA Information Survivability Conference and Exposition (DISCEX III)*, Washington, D.C., April 2003.
6. I. Cohen, A. Bronstein, and F. G. Cozman. Online learning of bayesian network parameters. *Hewlett Packard Laboratories Technical Report, HPL-2001-55(R.1)*, June 2001.
7. F. Cuppens and A. Miège. Alert correlation in a cooperative intrusion detection framework. In *Proceedings of the 2002 IEEE Symposium on Security and Privacy*, pages 202–215, Oakland, CA, May 2002.
8. DAPRA Cyber Panel Program. DARPA cyber panel program grand challenge problem (GCP). http://www.grandchallengeproblem.net/, 2003.
9. H. Debar and A. Wespi. The intrusion-detection console correlation mechanism. In *4th International Symposium on Recent Advances in Intrusion Detection (RAID)*, October 2001.
10. C. W. Geib and R. P. Goldman. Plan recognition in intrusion detection system. In *DARPA Information Survivability Conference and Exposition (DISCEX II)*, June 2001.
11. M. R. Gevers and B. D. O. Anderson. Representations of jointly stationary stochastic feedback processes. *International Journal of Control*, 33:777–809, 1981.
12. R. P. Goldman, W. Heimerdinger, and S. A. Harp. Information modling for intrusion report aggregation. In *DARPA Information Survivability Conference and Exposition (DISCEX II)*, June 2001.
13. C. W. J. Granger. Investigating causal relations by econometric methods and cross-spectral methods. *Econometrica*, 34:424–428, 1969.
14. IETF Intrusion Detection Working Group. Intrusion detection message exchange format. http://www.ietf.org/internet-drafts/draft-ietf-idwg-idmef-xml-09.txt, 2002.

15. J. Haines, D. K. Ryder, L. Tinnel, and S. Taylor. Validation of sensor alert correlators. *IEEE Security & Privacy Magazine*, January/February, 2003.
16. W. Hesse, E. Moller, M. Arnold, H. Witte, and B. Schack. Investigation of time-variant causal interactions between two eeg signals by means of the adaptive granger causality. *Brain Topography*, 15:265–266, 2003.
17. M. Kaminski, M. Ding, W.A. Truccolo, and S. L. Bressler. Evaluating causal relations in neural systems: Granger causality, direct transfer function (dtf) and statistical assessment of significance. *Biological Cybernetics*, 85:145–157, 2001.
18. R. K. Kaufamnn and D. I. Stern. Evidence for human influence on climate from hemispheric temperature relations. *Nature*, 388:39–44, July 1997.
19. H. Lee, K. S. Lin, and J. Wu. Pitfalls in using granger causality tests to find an engine of growth. *Applied Economics Letters*, 9:411–414, May 2002.
20. G. M. Ljung and G. E. P. Box. On a measure of lack of fit in time series models. In *Biometrika 65*, pages 297–303, 1978.
21. B. Morin and H. Debar. Correlation of intrusion symptoms: an application of chronicles. In *Proceedings of the 6th International Symposium on Recent Advances in Intrusion Detection (RAID 2003)*, Pittsburgh, PA, September 2003.
22. P. Ning, Y. Cui, and D.S. Reeves. Constructing attack scenarios through correlation of intrusion alerts. In *9th ACM Conference on Computer and Communications Security*, November 2002.
23. P. Ning and D. Xu. Learnign attack strategies from intrusion alerts. In *Proceedings of 10th ACM Conference on Computer and Communications Security (CCS'03)*, October 2003.
24. P. Ning, D. Xu, C. G. Healey, and R. A. Amant. Building attack scenarios through integration of complementary alert correlation methods. In *Proceedings of the 11th Annual Network and Distributed System Security Symposium (NDSS'04)*, San Diego, CA, February 2004.
25. J. Pearl. *Probabilistic Reasoning in Intelligent Systems: Networks of Plausible Inference*. Morgan Kaufmann Publishers, Inc, 1988.
26. P. A. Porras, M. W. Fong, and A. Valdes. A Mission-Impact-Based approach to INFOSEC alarm correlation. In *Proceedings of the 5th International Symposium on Recent Advances in Intrusion Detection (RAID)*, October 2002.
27. X. Qin and W. Lee. Statistical causality analysis of infosec alert data. In *Proceedings of the 6th International Symposium on Recent Advances in Intrusion Detection (RAID 2003)*, Pittsburgh, PA, September 2003.
28. S. M. Ross. *Introduction to Probability Models*. Harcourt Academic Press, 7th edition, 2000.
29. W. Stallings. *SNMP, SNMPv2, SNMPv3, and RMON 1 and 2*. Addison-Wesley, 1999.
30. A. Valdes and K. Skinner. Probabilistic alert correlation. In *Proceedings of the 4th International Symposium on Recent Advances in Intrusion Detection (RAID)*, October 2001.

Author Index

Lecture Notes in Computer Science

For information about Vols. 1–3094

please contact your bookseller or Springer